Personal Tax Planning
Principles and Practice

Personal Tax Planning: Principles and Practice

Malcolm Finney

Bloomsbury Professional

Whilst every care has been taken to ensure the accuracy of the content of this work, no responsibility for loss occasioned to any person acting or refraining from action as a result of the material in this publication can be accepted by the author or by the publisher.

Bloomsbury Professional Ltd,
Maxwelton House,
41–43 Boltro Road,
Haywards Heath,
West Sussex,
RH16 1BJ

© Bloomsbury Professional Ltd 2010

All rights reserved. No part of this publication may be reproduced in any material form (including photocopying or storing it in any medium by electronic means and whether or not transiently or incidentally to some other use of this publication) without the written permission of the copyright owner except in accordance with the provisions of the Copyright, Designs and Patents Act 1988 or under the terms of a licence issued by the Copyright Licensing Agency Ltd, Saffron House, 6–10 Kirby Street, London EC1N 8TS. Applications for the copyright owner's written permission to reproduce any part of this publication should be addressed to the publisher.

Warning: The doing of an unauthorised act in relation to a copyright work may result in both a civil claim for damages and criminal prosecution.

Crown copyright material is reproduced with the permission of the Controller of HMSO and the Queen's Printer for Scotland. Any European material in this work which has been reproduced from EUR-lex, the official European Communities legislation website, is European Communities copyright.

A CIP Catalogue record for this book is available from the British Library.

ISBN: 978 1 84766 683 3

Typeset by Kerrypress Ltd, Luton, Bedfordshire

Printed and bound in Great Britain by Martins the Printers, Berwick-upon-Tweed, Northumberland

Preface

The aim of this book is to identify and explain the main principles and practice underlying personal tax planning. Thus, as might be expected, significant coverage is given to the two main capital taxes, namely, capital gains tax and inheritance tax.

The approach adopted is to first examine in some detail the critical components which underpin the rest of the book. Thus Part I, provides a brief overview of the UK tax system and its similarity or otherwise to other countries' tax systems and then examines in detail the issues of domicile and residence/ordinary residence. The importance of the concept of domicile cannot be underestimated, particularly in a world where mobility of the individual is at an all-time high. Part I also provides an explanation of two areas not often addressed in tax texts in any detail, namely, the issues of income source and asset situs and the legal principles underpinning property ownership.

Part II concentrates on the two major capital taxes, namely, capital gains tax and inheritance tax.

Part III concentrates on the major topic of trusts, both UK and non-UK resident.

Part IV is topic driven and looks at the tax treatment of some common types of investment and the tax issues in relation to an individual's main residence.

Part V is devoted exclusively to international tax issues including non-UK resident taxation; the non-UK domiciled individual and accessing offshore monies; the use and role of offshore financial centres; double tax agreements and the EU Savings Directive.

Part VI examines the important topic of wills and looks at the tax issues associated therewith including matters associated with post-death planning.

A particular feature of the book is the numerous examples throughout each chapter designed as an aid to the understanding of the points made in the accompanying text.

I would like to thank Sarah Blair of Bloomsbury Professional who agreed to take on the book and Paula Devine for her time and patience in correcting my manuscript.

Preface

Finally, without the help, support and valuable input of my partner Karen Donnelly, to whom I extend my grateful thanks, this book would never have seen the light of day.

Inevitably, and sadly, I anticipate that some errors have no doubt crept into the text despite the best intention of both publisher and author for which I alone am responsible. May I therefore apologise in advance for any such mistakes and trust these do not detract from your enjoyment of the book.

The text is intended to be current as at 31 July 2010, just after the Royal Assent of Finance Act (No 2) 2010.

Malcolm Finney

July 2010

About the author

Malcolm Finney, BSc MSc (Bus Admin) MSc (Org Psy) MCMI C Maths MIMA. Malcolm runs his own tax training firm, Pythagoras Training.

Malcolm was formerly an international tax consultant with the international finance and tax consultancy JF Chown & Company Ltd (now Chown Dewhurst LLP); partner and head of international tax at the international accountancy firm Grant Thornton LLP; and head of tax at the London-based law firm Nabarro Nathanson (now Nabarro).

Malcolm has written extensively on tax matters, has spoken at tax seminars both in the UK and abroad and has been a visiting lecturer at the University of Greenwich Business School.

Contents

Preface	*v*
About the author	*vii*
Table of Statutes	*xxiii*
Table of Statutory Instruments	*xxxiii*
Table of Cases	*xxxvii*
Table of Other Materials	*xli*
List of Abbreviations	*xliii*

Part I Basic issues	**1**
Chapter 1: Tax systems and their bases of taxation: an overview	**3**
Background	3
Categories of tax	4
Capital v income distinction	5
Worldwide v territorial tax systems	6
Income and capital gains taxes	6
Inheritance tax	8
Summary	10
Chapter 2: UK taxation: an overview	**11**
Background	11
Domicile, residence and ordinary residence	11
Domiciled individual	11
Non-domiciled individual	12
Persons other than individuals	14
UK taxes and the law	14
Capital v income	15
Income tax	16
FA 2008 (tax year 2008–2009)	16
FA 2009 (tax years 2009–2010 and 2010–2011)	19
FA 2010 and FA (No 2) 2010 (tax year 2010–2011)	20
Personal allowances	20
Capital gains tax	21
FA 2008 (tax year 2008–2009 and 2009–2010)	21
FA 2010 and FA (No 2) 2010 (tax year 2010–2011)	22
Inheritance tax	22
Tax returns	23
Income and capital gains tax	23

Contents

Inheritance tax	23
Timing of tax payments	24
Income and capital gains tax	24
Inheritance tax	24
Summary	24
Chapter 3: Domicile	**26**
Background	26
Domicile is a concept of common law not taxation	26
Meaning of the term domicile	28
England and Wales, Scotland and Northern Ireland	29
Importance of domicile for UK tax purposes	30
Categories of domicile	31
Domicile of origin	33
Domicile of dependence	39
Domicile of choice	46
Non-UK domiciled individuals spending significant time in the UK	67
UK domiciled individuals failing to acquire non-UK domiciles of choice	72
UK domiciled individuals who have successfully acquired non-UK domiciles of choice	76
Abandonment of a domicile of choice	85
Special categories of individual and domiciles of choice	88
Deemed UK domicile	89
Dealing with deemed UK domicile status	92
'Split' domicile	93
International dimension	94
Summary	94
Chapter 4: Residence and ordinary residence	**95**
Background	95
Residence and ordinary residence under HMRC6	98
The 183-day test	99
Temporary residence abroad	100
Non-temporary residence abroad	101
New arrivals in the UK	106
Permanent or more than three-year stays	106
Short- and long-term visitors	107
Working in the UK	107
True visitors	107
Short-term visitor	108
Longer-term visitor	110
Split tax years: income tax and capital gains tax implications	111
Income tax	112
Non-UK residence anti-avoidance provisions	116
Capital gains tax	116

Income tax	118
Summary	119

Chapter 5: Residence, ordinary residence and domicile: practice   **121**

Background	121
The tax return (and supplementary pages) 2009–2010	121
Supplementary pages: 'Residence, remittance basis etc' SA109/2010	122
Residence status	124
Domicile	125
Remittance basis	126
Any other information	126
Forms DOM1, P85 and P86 and domicile and residence rulings	127
Form DOM1	127
Form P86	127
Form P85	127
Current position	128
Inheritance tax	130
Summary	133

Chapter 6: Income source and asset situs   **134**

Background	134
UK domiciled individual	134
Non-UK domiciled individual	134
Non-resident individual	134
Foreign tax	135
Domestic law	135
Income source	135
Dividends	135
Interest	136
Trusts	137
Rental income	137
Asset situs	137
Inheritance tax	138
Capital gains tax	139
Implications: some comments	140
Nominees	140
Foreign currency and foreign currency bank accounts	142
Summary	147

Chapter 7: The principles and implications of property ownership: joint tenancy and tenancy in common   **149**

Background	149
Legal ownership	150
Beneficial ownership	150
Beneficial joint tenancy versus beneficial tenants in common	152
Land	152
Legal ownership	152

Contents

Beneficial ownership	152
Tax issues	153
Income tax	153
Capital gains tax	156
Inheritance tax	157
Non-tax issues	158
Non-UK domiciled individual	159
Summary	160
Part II Capital taxes	**161**
Chapter 8: Capital gains tax	**163**
Background	163
Persons liable to capital gains tax	165
Annual exempt amount	165
Rates of capital gains tax	167
Trustees	167
Personal representatives	167
Individuals	168
Capital gain computation	170
Gifts	171
Connected persons	172
Bargains not at 'arm's length'	173
Inter-spouse transfers	173
Payment of capital gains tax	175
Year of death	176
Gifts of assets (not inter-spouse)	178
Holdover relief	178
Immediate charge to inheritance tax (TCGA 1992 s 260)	181
Business assets (TCGA 1992 s 165)	185
Settlor-interested trusts	187
Non-UK situs assets, the non-UK domiciled individual and gifts	187
Entrepreneur relief	188
Disposal of the whole or part of a business	189
Disposal of one or more assets in use for the purposes of the business at the time at which the business ceases to be carried on	189
Disposal of one or more assets consisting of shares or securities of a company	189
Disposal qualifying as an 'associated' disposal	190
Relevant business assets	191
Claim for, and amount of, relief	192
Trusts	196
Offshore companies	196
Apportionment of non-UK resident company capital gains	197
De minimis limit	198

	Contents

Subsequent company distributions	198
Capital losses	198
Non-UK resident trusts	199
Offshore income gains	199
Non-UK domiciled but UK resident individuals	199
Departures and arrivals in the UK	200
Split tax years	201
Non-UK domiciled individuals	204
Summary	205

Chapter 9: Capital losses	**207**
Background	207
UK domiciled and UK resident individual	208
Connected person capital losses	210
Non-UK domiciled but UK resident individual	211
Pre-FA 2008 position	211
Post-FA 2008	212
Summary	221

Chapter 10: Inheritance tax: the basics	**223**
Background	223
Domicile	224
Deemed UK domicile	224
Rates of inheritance tax	225
Categories of lifetime transfer	227
Exempt transfer	227
Chargeable lifetime transfer	227
Potentially exempt transfers and chargeability	233
Seven-year cumulation period	236
Chargeable lifetime transfers and grossing-up	242
Potentially exempt transfers and grossing up	245
Death	245
Assets	245
Exemptions and reliefs	250
Rate on death and the nil rate band	251
Payment and the bearing of inheritance tax on death	253
Payment of inheritance tax on death	253
Bearing of the inheritance tax charge on death	255
Specific gifts bearing their own inheritance tax on death	258
Comprehensive example	260
Planning considerations: initial thoughts	264
Summary	265

Chapter 11: Inheritance tax: exemptions and reliefs	**267**
Background	267
Exempt transfers	267
Exempt transfers: lifetime only	268

Contents

Exempt transfers: death only	274
Exempt transfers: in lifetime and on death	274
Ordering of exemptions	281
Reliefs	282
Business property relief and agricultural property relief: general comments	283
Quick succession relief	300
Summary	303

Chapter 12: Inheritance tax: gifts with reservation — **304**

Background	304
The concept and implications	305
Gifts with reservation: non-application	307
Land and chattels 'let-out'	309
Tracing	310
Joint bank accounts	311
Trusts	311
Pre-owned assets	312
Land	313
Chattels	314
Intangible assets	315
Exemptions	315
Election	316
De minimis let-out	317
Summary	317

Chapter 13: Inheritance tax: excluded property — **318**

Background	318
Non-settled property	318
Settled property	319
Relevant property trust	319
'Qualifying' interest in possession trust	319
Excluded property and the non-UK domiciled individual	320
Loss of excluded property status for settled property	320
Deemed UK domicile risk	323
Minimum holding period	324
UK situs assets	325
Non-settled property	325
Settled property	328
Channel Islands and the Isle of Man	329
Mixing UK and non-UK situs settled assets	329
Excluded property and gifts with reservation	331
Excluded property trusts and *FA 2006*	332
The deed of variation and the mixed domiciled marriage	334
Summary	334

Chapter 14: Inheritance tax administration	**336**
Background	336
Lifetime transfers and trust property	336
Inheritance tax payable	338
Persons responsible for inheritance tax charge	339
Death estate	340
Excepted estate	341
Inheritance tax payable	344
Penalties	345
Interest on unpaid inheritance tax	345
Assessment and claims	346
Summary	346
Part III Trusts	**347**
Chapter 15: Trusts: an overview	**349**
Background	349
Trust definition	349
Equity	350
Trust creation	351
Trust classification	351
Express trust	351
Implied/resulting trust	352
Constructive trust	352
Bare trust	352
Trusts today	352
Protection of minors	353
Bankruptcy protection	353
Will substitute	353
The Perpetuities and Accumulations Act 2009	353
Tax aspects	354
Discretionary trust	354
Interest in possession trust	354
The Hague Convention	355
Summary	355
Chapter 16: Inheritance tax: trusts	**356**
Background	356
Relevant property trusts	357
Creation of the trust	357
Principles underlying the ten-yearly and exit charges	359
Computational principles of the exit and ten-yearly charges	360
Exit charge before the first ten-year charge	360
Nil rate band discretionary trust (*exit charge*)	363
First ten-year charge	365
Nil rate band discretionary trust (ten-year charge)	367

Contents

Exit charge arising between ten-year anniversaries	368
Charges after the first ten years	370
Addition of property after the trust commences	371
Additions of property and the ten-year charge	373
Additions of property and the exit charge	373
Life and death rates versus relevant property rates	375
Interest in possession trusts	375
Non-qualifying interest in possession	377
Lifetime termination of qualifying interests in possession	378
Transitional serial interest	381
Immediate post-death interest in possession	383
Accumulation and maintenance trusts	384
Relevant property versus qualifying interest in possession trusts	385
Pre-FA 2006	385
Post-FA 2006	385
Excluded property trusts	386
Summary	386

Chapter 17: UK resident trusts: income and capital gains taxation — **387**

Background	387
Trust residency	388
Pre-6 April 2007	388
Post-5 April 2007	388
Income tax	390
Discretionary (and accumulation and maintenance) trusts	391
Interest in possession trusts	401
Capital gains tax	405
Discretionary trusts and interest in possession trusts	405
Hold-over relief	407
Anti-avoidance provisions	407
Income tax	408
Capital gains tax	417
UK resident trusts: some concluding comments	418
Income tax	418
Capital gains tax	419
Inheritance tax	420
Summary	421

Chapter 18: Non-UK resident trusts: income and capital gains taxation — **422**

Background	422
Trust residency	423
Pre-6 April 2007	423
Post-5 April 2007	423
Income Tax	425
Discretionary (and accumulation and maintenance) trusts	426

Interest in possession trusts	435
Capital gains tax	439
Trustees	439
Beneficiaries	439
Anti-avoidance provisions	439
Income tax	440
Capital gains tax	454
Offshore income gains	470
UK resident trust	472
Non-UK resident trusts	472
Irish offshore funds	482
Trust income, offshore income gains and capital gains interaction	483
Non-UK resident trusts for UK domiciled and UK resident individuals: some general comments	484
Income tax	484
Capital gains tax	485
Inheritance tax	485
Non-UK resident trusts for non-UK domiciled but UK resident individuals; some general comments	486
Income tax	486
Capital gains tax	487
Inheritance tax	488
Summary	488
Part IV Investments and main residence	**491**
Chapter 19: Investments	**493**
Background	493
Deposit-based investments	494
Offshore deposits	495
Money market accounts	496
National savings income	496
SAYE interest	496
Ordinary shares	496
Alternative Investment Market shares	499
Individual Savings Accounts	499
Insurance-based investments	501
Term and whole of life assurance policies	501
Single premium bonds	502
Enterprise Investment Schemes and Venture Capital Trusts	511
Enterprise investment schemes	511
Venture Capital Trusts	513
Chargeable gain deferment possibilities (EIS only)	514
Collective investments	515
Offshore funds	515
Summary	515

Contents

Chapter 20: Main residence or home	**517**
Background	517
Capital gains tax	518
Overview	518
Two or more residences of the individual	519
Non-UK property	519
Married couple and cohabitees	520
Total v partial capital gains tax exemption	521
Profit motive	522
Residence	522
Two or more residences and the election	524
Married couples	527
Inter-spouse transfers	528
Deemed periods of residence	532
Lettings relief	535
Trusts and sole or main residence relief	537
Trusts, sole or main residence relief and hold-over relief claims	538
Death and sole or main residence relief	540
Divorce and separation	542
Inheritance tax	545
Overview	545
Downsizing	546
Shared home arrangements	547
Cash gift	548
Sale	549
Gift plus rent payable	549
General comments	550
Death and inheritance tax	550
Divorce	552
Summary	553
Chapter 21: Non-UK domiciliaries and UK homes	**555**
Background	555
Ownership structuring	556
Individual ownership	556
Company ownership	558
Trust ownership	559
Combination structure	561
General comments	562
Pre-owned asset provisions	563
Preliminary conclusions	563
Summary	563
Chapter 22: Stamp duty and stamp duty land tax	**565**
Background	565
Stamp duty and stamp duty reserve tax	565

Stamp duty land tax	566
Death	567
Trusts	567
Matrimonial home	568
Matrimonial breakdown	569
Arm's-length provisions	570
Linked transactions	571
Summary	571
Part V The international dimension	**573**
Chapter 23: Non-UK resident taxation	**575**
Background	575
Income tax	576
Individuals	576
Disregarded income	577
Trusts	580
Companies	581
Capital gains tax	582
Inheritance tax	582
General comments	583
Double taxation agreements	584
Income tax and capital gains tax	584
Inheritance tax	585
Summary	585
Chapter 24: The non-UK domiciled individual, foreign source income and foreign capital gains	**587**
Background	587
Remittance basis treatment: the claim	589
Consequences of the claim	593
Loss of allowances	593
The £30,000 tax charge	593
Nomination of foreign income and gains	594
Paying the £30,000 or not	607
Remittances to the UK	608
Alienation of foreign income and gains and asset purchase	611
Remittance conditions	611
Transitional provisions of *FA 2008*	620
Employment income	620
Relevant foreign income	621
Capital gains	625
Relevant debt and UK services	626
Exempt property	628
Clothing, etc and the 'personal use rule'	628
Property below £1,000 rule	629

Contents

Temporary importation rule	630
Repair rule	630
Property and public access rule	631
Exempt to non-exempt property	631
Mixed funds	632
(i) Arising basis and remittance basis mixed income	633
(ii) Income and capital gains taxable on remittance	633
(iii) Tax-free capital and remittance of taxable income	634
(iv) Tax-free capital and taxable capital gains	634
Offshore transfers	637
Segregation of 'income' and 'capital'	640
Gifts of non-UK assets	643
Source cessation	644
Offshore mortgages	645
Loans secured on property: inheritance tax impact	647
Loans secured on property: capital gains tax impact	647
Temporary non-UK residence	648
Summary	648
Chapter 25: The offshore dimension	**650**
Background	650
Offshore financial centres	651
Offshore financial centres: vehicles	655
Companies	655
Trusts	657
Offshore financial centres: uses	659
Tax planning	659
Probate mitigation/substitute will	660
Asset protection	660
Offshore financial centres: the choice	661
UK tax and information disclosure requirements	662
Relocation to an offshore financial centre	665
Summary	666
Chapter 26: International taxation	**668**
Background	668
Nature of a double tax agreement	669
Comprehensive double tax agreements	669
Administration	672
Inheritance tax agreements	673
Pre-1975 agreements	674
Post-1975 agreements	675
Tax Information Exchange Agreements	677
The European Union	678
The EU Savings Directive	678
Non-Member States and Tax Information Exchange Agreements	681

Implications of the Savings Directive	681
The Savings Directive and Directive 77/799/EEC	684
Human rights	684
Summary	685

Part VI Wills, probate and post-death issues — 687

Chapter 27: Wills and probate — 689

Background	689
Property not disposable by will	691
Joint tenancies	691
Pension scheme lump sum death benefits	691
Life insurance policies	692
Donatio mortis causa	692
Foreign situs assets	693
Types of will	693
Mutual wills	693
Joint will	694
International will	694
Capacity to make a will	694
Formalities of a will	694
Revocation	696
Types of gift	697
Legacies/devises	697
Failure of gifts	699
Lapse	699
Ademption	701
Disclaimer	701
Uncertainty	701
Capacity to inherit	702
Survivorship clauses	702
Foreign issues	707
Succession	707
Forced heirship	711
Community property	712
Probate	713
Assets not requiring probate	715
Executors	717
Intestacy	717
Summary	718

Chapter 28: Wills and taxation — 720

Background	720
Income tax	722
Pre-death	722
Administration period	723

Contents

Capital gains tax	724
Pre-death	724
Administration period	724
Inheritance tax	727
Married couples, cohabitees and single individuals	728
Married couples	728
Cohabitees	729
Single person	730
Charitable gifts	730
Post-death events	732
Disclaimers, deeds of variation and discretionary will trusts	732
Executor sales	743
Foreign aspects	747
Summary	748

Appendices	**751**
Appendix 1: Domicile	**753**
Categories of non-UK domiciled individual	753
Do I need to pay the £30,000 remittance basis charge?	754
Ascertaining when non-UK domiciled individual needs to make a claim for remittance basis treatment	755
Do I have an English domicile of origin?	756
Have I acquired a domicile of choice different from my English domicile of origin?	757
Appendix 2: Capital gains tax position on disposals pre-5 April 2008	**759**

Index	*769*

Table of Statutes

[All References are to Paragraph Numbers]

Administration of Estates
   Act 1925 .... 27.2, 27.116
     Pt IV 27.138
     s 25 .... 27.124
       28 .... 27.137
       36 .... 28.32
       41 .... 22.18
       42 .... 27.70
       46 .... 27.140, 27.141, 27.142
       47 .... 27.140, 27.142

Administration of Justice
   Act 1982
     ss 27, 28 .... 27.23

Adoption Act 1976 .... 3.49

Adoption and Children
   Act 2002 .... 3.49
     s 46 .... 3.49
       47 .... 3.50
       67 .... 3.51

Age of Legal Capacity
   (Scotland) Act 1991 .... 3.58
     s 7 .... 3.88

Births and Deaths Registration
   Act 1953 .... 27.114

Capital Transfer Act 1984 .... 10.4

Children Act 1989
     s 3 .... 27.70

Civil Evidence Act 1995 .... 3.120
     s 1 .... 3.118

Corporation Tax Act 2009 .... 2.20
     s 2 .... 8.98
       5 .... 23.20

Domicile and Matrimonial
   Proceedings Act 1973 .. 3.57, 3.62,
                     3.64, 3.66, 3.70,
                     3.113, 3.251,
                     27.101
     s 1 .... 3.67
       3 .... 3.57
       4 .... 3.62
       5 .... 3.100

Family Law Reform Act 1969 ..... 3.58
     s 3 .... 27.26

Family Law (Scotland)
   Act 2006 .... 3.37
     ss 21, 22 .... 3.37

Finance Act 1984 .... 19.48

Finance Act 1986 .... 2.21, 10.4
     s 102 ..... 10.61, 10.67, 11.21, 12.3,
                  12.5, 12.6, 12.9,
                  12.21, 13.43,
                  20.116, 21.28,
                  21.37
     102A 12.13
     102B 12.13, 20.109, 20.116
     102C 12.13
     102ZA 12.20
     104 .... 12.6, 12.11
     Sch 15 .... 20.119, 20.120
     Sch 20 .... 12.3, 12.9, 12.13, 12.18,
                        20.116

Finance Act 2000
     s 146 .... 26.42

Finance Act 2003 .... 22.3
     s 43 .... 22.10, 22.12
       48 .... 22.10
       53 .... 22.34
       76 .... 22.12
       108 .... 22.36
       119 .... 22.12
     Sch 3 .... 22.18, 22.19, 22.31
     Sch 4 .... 22.11, 22.16

Finance Act 2004
     s 84 .... 12.22
     ss 107–112 .... 26.55
         113, 114 .... 26.55, 26.60
     s 115 .... 26.55
     Sch 15 .. 12.22, 12.27, 12.33, 21.42

Table of Statutes

Finance Act 2006 ...... 2.20, 2.21, 2.54,
2.57, 2.70, 8.76,
10.105, 12.6, 12.20,
13.6, 13.45, 13.47,
16.2, 16.3, 16.5,
16.6, 16.8, 16.41,
16.44, 16.73, 16.90,
16.93, 16.94, 16.95,
16.97, 16.98,
16.101, 16.102,
17.6, 17.10, 17.18,
17.101, 18.6, 18.10,
18.18, 20.133,
28.34, 28.122
s 88 .... 8.74
89 .... 17.67
155 .... 2.52
Sch 12 .... 28.84

Finance Act 2007 .... 2.59
s 4 .... 2.53, 10.13, 28.38
92 .... 2.59
Sch 24 .... 14.33, 14.36

Finance Act 2008 ...... 1.10, 2.11, 2.12,
2.13, 2.20, 2.23,
2.24, 2.27, 2.46,
2.49, 2.52, 2.70,
4.72, 4.73, 4.77,
4.78, 4.82, 5.6, 5.9,
5.49, 6.53, 6.54,
6.61, 8.7, 8.8, 8.9,
8.15, 8.34, 8.77,
8.78, 8.79, 8.110,
8.114, 8.131, 8.132,
8.134, 8.135, 9.3,
9.4, 9.5, 9.6, 9.12,
9.13, 9.16, 9.17,
9.19, 9.29, 9.33,
9.37, 9.38, 9.39,
9.41, 10.113, 16.74,
17.20, 17.83, 17.99,
17.100, 17.101,
17.104, 17.125,
17.126, 18.24,
18.110, 18.114,
18.116, 18.131,
18.137, 18.138,
18.165, 18.166,
18.167, 18.181,

Finance Act 2008 – *contd*
.... 18.192, 19.23, 19.31, 19.33,
19.63, 19.64, 19.66,
19.102, 20.130,
21.12, 21.16, 21.39,
21.40, 23.7, 24.3,
24.4, 24.5, 24.6,
24.7, 24.36,
24.37 24.39, 24.40,
24.41, 24.42, 24.43,
24.44, 24.45, 24.50,
24.70, 24.72, 24.73,
24.74, 24.75, 24.77,
24.86, 24.92, 24.93,
24.101, 24.107,
24.109, 24.110,
24.116, 24.117,
24.119, 24.120,
24.122, 24.125,
24.126, 24.127,
24.129, 24.134,
24.135, 24.136,
24.145, 24.146,
24.147, 24.150,
26.69, App 2
s 1 .... 2.27
3 .... 2.29
4 .... 2.28
8 .... 2.46, 8.7, 8.23
9 .... 2.48, 8.19
10 .... 10.17, 11.44
24 .... 4.10, 4.11
25 .... 9.5
31 .... 19.71
34 .... 19.23
39 .... 14.40
ss 40A-42A ... 8.109, 17.45, 18.140
s 41 .... 2.20, 18.140
42 .... 18.140
118 .... 8.54
Sch 2 .... 2.46, 8.7
Sch 3 .... 2.48, 8.7, 8.19
Sch 5 .... 2.27
Sch 7. 9.5, 18.118, 18.122, 18.125,
18.126, 18.128,
18.130, 18.162,
24.36, 24.72, 24.81,
24.83, 24.132,
24.136, 24.137
Sch 39 .... 9.25, 24.8

Table of Statutes

Finance Act 2008 – *contd*
  Sch 40.................... 14.33, 14.36
Finance Act 2009 ...... 2.35, 2.37, 2.52,
                                  2.70, 24.92
  s 4.................................. 2.35
    5........................... 2.40, 23.7
    6.. 2.35
    10............................. 22.13
    40............................... 19.24
    58....................................... 2.35
    99............................... 14.40
    101.............................. 14.38
  Sch 1...................... 2.40, 23.7
  Sch 19........................... 19.24
  Sch 22........................... 18.140
  Sch 27............................ 24.92
  Sch 51................... 14.18, 14.40
  Sch 55................... 14.33, 14.34
  Sch 56................... 14.33, 14.35
Finance Act 2010 ...... 2.37, 2.50, 2.52,
                                2.70, 22.13
  s 4.................................. 2.51
  ss 6, 7............................. 22.13
  s 8................. 2.53, 10.13, 28.38
    30...................... 11.41, 28.56
Finance (No 2) Act 2010 .... 2.37, 2.70,
                                  8.10, 8.136
  s 2..... 2.50, 2.51, 4.74, 8.17, 8.20,
                      8.22, 8.24, 8.90,
                      8.91, 8.125, 17.54,
                      17.56, 17.100,
                  18.99, 19.52, 24.26,
                  24.117, 28.28,
                              28.99
    4..................................... 8.91
  Sch 1.. 2.50, 2.51, 4.74, 8.17, 8.20,
                      8.22, 8.24, 8.90,
                      8.91, 8.125, 17.54,
                      17.56, 17.100,
                  18.99, 19.52, 24.26,
                  24.117, 28.28,
                              28.99
Human Rights Act 1998 .. 26.44, 26.79
Immigration Act 1971 .... 3.100
Income and Corporation Taxes
  Act 1988 .... 2.20
  s 334.............................. 4.23
    336................................. 4.7
    416............................. 21.31
    700............................. 28.23

Income and Corporation Taxes Act
  1988 – *contd*
  s 704A.......................... 14.26
  ss 756A-763................... 18.140
  s 788...................... 26.7, 26.14
    806............................. 26.23
    808A............................. 26.9
    812............................... 26.9
    839............................. 22.11
  Sch 15........................... 19.47
Income Tax Act 2007 .... 2.20
  Pt 13 Ch 2....................... 18.60
  Pt 14 Ch A1.... 18.94, 18.121, 24.1
  s 6........................... 23.8, 23.9
    7.................................. 2.27
    8.................................. 2.27
    9................. 2.35, 17.17, 18.17
    11..................... 23.20, 23.25
    12............... 2.27, 17.17, 18.17
    14....................... 23.20, 23.23
    36................................. 2.29
    37................................. 2.29
    56........................ 2.41, 23.7
    58................................. 2.26
    131............................... 19.77
    133............................... 19.77
    157............................... 19.69
    158.... 19.70, 19.71, 19.73, 19.74
    163............................... 19.69
    166............................... 19.69
    209............................... 19.74
    260............................... 19.85
    262............................... 19.83
    263....................... 19.81, 23.8
    266............................... 19.84
    397............................... 23.13
    399............................... 23.13
    472............................... 28.84
    474........................ 17.3, 18.3
    475........................ 17.7, 18.7
    476........................ 17.7, 18.7
    479... 17.17, 17.21, 17.43, 17.45,
                  18.17, 18.19, 18.46,
                              18.48
    480.... 17.21, 17.43, 18.19, 14.86
    481............ 17.45, 17.71, 18.48
    482.. 17.45, 17.71, 18.48, 18.146
    486..................... 17.23, 18.26
    487............................... 18.26
    491...................... 17.20, 18.24

Table of Statutes

Income Tax Act 2007 – *contd*
- s 494.. 17.25, 17.77, 17.107, 18.28, 18.29, 18.30, 18.32
- 495............................. 17.77
- 496.... 17.26, 17.27, 17.31, 18.29
- 500............................. 17.44
- 503............................. 17.44
- 624............................. 18.68
- 686............................. 14.26
- 714............................. 18.69
- ss 714–751..................... 18.151
- s 716............................ 18.65
- 718............................. 18.66
- 720...... 4.1, 18.64, 18.69, 18.71, 18.73, 18.74, 18.82, 18.93, 19.60, 24.35
- 720 *et seq*..................... 12.36
- 721............................. 18.69
- 723............................. 18.70
- 724............................. 18.73
- 726........... 18.93, 18.94, 18.157
- 727...... 4.1, 18.64, 18.73, 18.75, 18.77, 18.79, 18.82
- 728............................. 18.75
- 729.................... 18.75, 18.76
- ss 731–735..................... 18.128
- s 731... 18.64, 18.65, 18.81, 18.83, 18.84, 19.60
- 732.............. 4.1, 18.82, 18.85
- 733............ 18.85, 18.87, 18.88
- 735............ 18.95, 18.96, 18.162
- 735A.................... 18.95, 18.97
- 737............................. 18.68
- 739............................. 18.68
- 743................... 18.74, 18.88
- 745............................. 18.72
- 746.................... 18.71, 18.72
- 809............................. 24.91
- 809A............................. 2.10
- 809B....... 2.10, 9.18, 9.19, 9.22, 9.23, 9.25, 9.26, 9.31, 9.40, 9.42, 18.93, 23.7, 24.7, 24.8, 24.11, 24.16, 24.19, 26.18
- 809C.......... 24.16, 24.19, 24.20
- 809D...... 9.19, 9.20, 9.26, 24.10, 24.11, 24.12, 24.14, 26.69

Income Tax Act 2007 – *contd*
- s 809E...... 9.19, 9.20, 9.26, 24.10, 24.11, 24.12, 26.69
- 809G....... 2.42, 2.44, 8.15, 9.32, 23.7, 24.15
- 809H................. 24.22, 24.25
- 809I.................... 24.23, 24.26
- 809J.. 24.17, 24.23, 24.26, 24.28, 24.29, 24.30
- 809K................. 24.37, 24.38
- 809L. 24.45, 24.46, 24.47, 24.48, 24.49, 24.62, 24.66, 24.85, 24.112, 24.135
- 809M.. 8.78, 8.112, 11.55, 17.51, 18.42, 18.53. 18.94, 21.2, 24.50
- 809N......................... 24.63
- 809O................. 24.66, 24.69
- 809P................. 24.55, 24.94
- 809Q............... 24.105, 24.109
- 809R................ 24.112, 24.114
- 809T.......................... 24.126
- 809V........................... 24.17
- 809W.......... 24.86, 24.87, 24.90
- 809X. 24.92, 24.93, 24.94, 24.96, 24.98, 24.100
- 809Y.......................... 24.102
- 809Z....... 24.92, 24.93, 24.100
- 809Z2.......................... 24.92
- 809Z3................. 24.92, 24.98
- 809Z4................. 24.92, 24.96
- 809Z5.......................... 24.94
- 809Z6.......................... 24.92
- 809Z7........................... 24.1
- 811.... 18.22, 23.11, 23.17, 23.18
- 812............ 18.20, 23.11, 23.19
- 813............ 17.37, 23.12, 23.18
- 815............................. 23.21
- 816............................. 23.21
- 825............ 18.22, 23.12, 23.22
- 826............ 17.37, 23.12, 23.22
- ss 828A-828D.................. 24.11
- s 829................ 4.15, 4.17, 4.23
- 830.............................. 4.32
- 831............... 4.2, 4.10, 4.41
- 832..................... 4.10, 4.41
- 834............................. 28.18
- 836.......... 7.25, 7.26, 7.31, 7.32
- 837..................... 7.27, 7.28

Table of Statutes

Income Tax Act 2007 – *contd*
s 850 .... 19.7
851 ..... 18.22, 19.7, 23.14, 23.24
856 .... 19.7, 23.24
858 ...... 18.22, 19.7, 19.8, 23.14, 23.16
861 .... 19.8
862 .... 19.9
866 .... 19.16
873 .... 19.7
874 .... 23.14
946 .... 9.20, 24.11
971 .... 23.9
972 .... 23.9
Sch 1 .... 2.27
Sch 2 .... 19.82
Income Tax (Earnings and Pensions) Act 2003 .... 2.20, 18.84
s 22 .... 24.1, 24.71, 24.72
25 .... 23.8
27 .... 23.8
97 .... 21.19
Income Tax (Trading and Other Income) Act 2005 .... 2.20
Pt 3 .... 20.1, 23.9
Pt 4 Ch 9 .... 19.49
Pt 5 Ch 5 ...... 17.21, 17.66, 18.19, 18.60, 18.147, 18.150
s 6 .... 23.8
69 .... 19.18
370 .... 19.6, 19.15
383 .... 19.22
397 .... 18.21, 18.22, 19.22
397A 17.71, 19.23, 19.24
399 .... 18.21, 18.22, 23.23
461 .... 17.45, 18.48, 18.67, 18.67
465A 19.49
ss 467, 468 .... 19.60
s 484 .... 19.53, 19.54, 19.63
491 .... 19.55
528 .... 19.65
ss 530, 531 .... 19.54
s 535 .... 19.54
619A 17.71
624 ... 12.34, 12.36, 17.66, 17.67, 17.71, 17.81, 17.86, 17.92, 17.93, 18.60, 18.63, 18.70, 24.35
625 .... 17.68, 17.69, 17.70

Income Tax (Trading and Other Income) Act 2005 – *contd*
s 629 ... 17.66, 17.84, 17.85, 17.86, 17.87, 17.88, 17.90, 17.93, 18.60, 18.63
631 .... 17.89
633 ... 17.66, 17.91, 17.92, 17.93, 17.95, 18.60, 18.63
634 .... 17.91, 17.98
640 .... 17.91, 17.94
646 .... 17.72, 17.74, 17.97
648 .... 17.82
653 .... 28.12
683 .... 17.30, 17.36, 17.37
685A 17.77
694 .... 19.32
702 .... 19.20
830 .... 2.11, 2.38, 17.84, 24.1
832 ..... 18.93, 24.1, 24.9, 24.129
832A 4.71, 4.78, 4.79, 19.66, 24.146
Inheritance (Provision for Family and Dependants) Act 1938 .... 27.106
Inheritance (Provision for Family and Dependants) Act 1975 .. 3.7, 3.8, 3.9, 3.10, 3.11, 3.163, 3.197, 3.198, 27.106, 27.107, 27.108, 27.109
s 1 .... 3.8
2 .... 3.165
Inheritance Tax Act 1984 ... 2.20, 2.21, 10.4
Pt II 10.21
Pt III 10.1
Pt IV 10.1
Pt VIII 14.1
Pt VI Chs III, IV 28.5, 28.29
s 1 .... 10.24
2. 2.58, 8.56, 10.21, 10.22, 10.23, 10.24
3 ...... 10.23, 10.24, 10.25, 12.17, 13.2
3A 2.58, 10.35, 10.36, 10.37
4 .... 10.60, 27.61, 27.62
5 ...... 3.248, 10.23, 10.60, 10.61, 10.66, 13.2, 21.12, 28.14

xxvii

Table of Statutes

Inheritance Tax Act 1984 – *contd*
s 6. 10.6, 13.2, 13.23, 13.36, 13.38,
16.23, 16.97, 19.95,
21.12, 21.25, 21.35
7........ 2.55, 10.13, 10.14, 10.19,
10.27, 10.28, 10.29
8................................. 28.38
ss 8A-8C........ 7.40, 11.44, 20.130
s 8A... 10.17, 11.55, 20.127, 28.36,
28.97
10..................... 10.2, 20.137
11............ 11.11, 12.38, 20.137
16..................... 11.57, 28.27
18........ 3.253, 7.46, 7.47, 10.21,
10.78, 11.10, 11.37,
11.40, 11.42, 12.12,
13.50, 14.29, 16.51,
16.77, 20.5, 20.137,
21.8, 21.9, 26.80,
28.115
19...... 10.20, 10.78, 11.2, 11.11,
12.38
20...... 10.78, 11.9, 11.11, 11.21,
12.12, 12.38
21.............. 11.10, 11.11, 12.12
22.............. 11.9, 11.11, 12.12
23, 24......... 11.41, 12.12, 14.29
s 25..................... 11.41, 12.12
41............................... 28.52
43....................... 13.4, 27.71
47............................... 13.11
48.............. 10.8, 13.11, 16.97
49....... 10.71, 16.8, 16.20, 16.49
49A..... 16.4, 16.47, 16.80, 16.81
49B............................. 16.59
49C.... 10.38, 16.4, 16.47, 16.59,
16.72
49D............ 10.38, 16.59, 16.77
49E............................. 16.59
51............................... 16.56
52............................... 16.65
58.. 13.9, 16.3, 16.4, 16.14, 16.47
59....................... 16.3, 16.20
61............................... 16.15
62........ 16.23, 28.6, 28.7, 28.30
64..................... 16.14, 16.26
ss 64–69............................ 2.57
s 65..................... 16.18, 16.33
66............................... 16.28
68..................... 16.23, 16.28

Inheritance Tax Act 1984 – *contd*
s 71............................... 16.87
80.............. 13.45, 13.52, 16.23
89....................... 16.5, 16.48
89B...................... 16.4, 16.47
92............................... 27.71
104............ 10.79, 11.60, 11.63
105..................... 11.64, 11.66
106............................. 11.73
108..................... 11.78, 11.79
110............................. 11.65
111..................... 11.66, 11.69
112..................... 11.70, 11.74
113A........................... 11.83
115............................. 11.97
116............ 10.79, 11.60, 11.97
131..................... 10.30, 10.31
141......... 11.60, 11.104, 11.105,
11.109, 27.81
142...... 20.80, 28.5, 28.8, 28.57,
28.58, 28.59, 28.67,
28.69, 28.74, 28.79,
28.80, 28.81, 28.86,
28.88, 28.91, 28.92,
28.95
143............................... 28.9
144... 20.132, 28.5, 28.57, 28.58,
28.59, 28.88, 28.89,
28.90, 28.91, 28.92,
28.93, 28.96, 28.97,
28.117
146............................... 3.10
157.............. 6.41, 11.39, 13.23
161......... 10.24, 11.107, 28.101,
28.114
176.................. 28.101, 28.114
ss 178–198..................... 28.101
ss 178, 179.................... 28.102
s 180........................... 28.105
187............................ 28.100
ss 190, 191.................... 28.107
s 199............ 10.27, 14.13, 14.14
200............ 10.27, 14.31, 27.136
201............................. 10.27
203............................. 14.13
211..................... 10.92, 10.96
216............................... 14.1
218..................... 14.4, 25.64
219, 219A..................... 14.2
s 223............................... 14.3

Inheritance Tax Act 1984 – *contd*
    s 226............... 14.3, 14.12, 14.30
    227................................. 14.3
    233............................. 14.39
    235............................. 14.39
    237............................. 14.17
    239............................. 14.32
    240............................. 14.18
    257............................... 14.1
    267. 2.14, 3.25, 3.232, 10.7, 10.9, 13.4, 13.21, 13.26, 13.27, 14.28, 21.9, 23.3, 23.42
    269............................. 11.76
    270............................. 11.70
    496............................. 16.75
    Sch 1.............. 2.55, 10.13, 10.80

Insolvency Act 1986
    s 264(1)(a), (b).................... 3.12
    265...................... 3.7, 3.12, 3.13
      (1)............................ 3.12

Interpretation Act 1978
    Sch 1...................... 3.19, 11.62

Law of Property Act 1925 . 7.12, 27.79
    s 1..................... 7.6, 7.16, 7.23
    21............................... 27.70
    36.......................... 7.6, 7.18
    46............................... 27.60
    184........... 27.59, 27.60, 27.61
    196.............................. 7.20

Law of Property (Miscellaneous Provisions) Act 1989 .. 6.28, 28.71

Legitimacy Act 1926.......... 3.27, 3.42

Legitimacy Act 1976................. 3.42
    s 2................................ 3.41
    9.................................. 3.42

Marriage Act 1949
    s 2................................ 3.57

Matrimonial Causes Act 1973
    Pt I.............................. 20.88
    Pt II............................. 20.88
    s 17.............................. 20.86
    18..................... 20.87, 27.38

Mental Capacity Act 2005 .... 27.25

Perpetuities and Accumulations Act 2009 .... 15.26, 15.28, 15.30, 15.31, 25.31
    s 5............................... 15.29

Perpetuities and Accumulations Act 2009 – *contd*
    ss 13, 14........................ 15.29

Recognition of Trusts Act 1987 .. 15.38

Senior Courts Act 1981
    s 109............................ 27.120

Stamp Act 1694 .... 22.3

Statutory Declarations Act 1835 .... 3.129

Taxation of Chargeable Gains Act 1992 .... 2.20
    Pt V Ch III........................ 8.80
    Pt VII............................. 20.9
    s 1................................ 2.43
    2....... 2.44, 8.12, 8.115, 9.7, 9.8, 9.29, 18.108
    3. 2.43, 2.44, 8.12, 9.7, 9.8, 9.21, 9.32, 17.58, 18.141, 20.3, 28.28
    4............................... 28.28
    9................................ 4.10
    10................ 8.2, 18.54, 23.26
    10A......... 4.71, 4.74, 4.76, 4.77, 8.124, 8.125, 8.127, 8.128, 8.130, 8.131, 8.132, 18.105, 18.143, 18.144, 19.66, 24.146
    12... 2.10, 8.1, 8.129, 24.1, 24.83
    13...... 8.99, 8.100, 8.104, 8.107, 8.110, 8.111, 8.125, 18.99, 18.127, 18.147, 18.150, 18.152, 21.16, 21.22, 21.31, 21.33, 21.39, 24.35
    14A.................... 8.111, 8.113
    15.................... 2.43, 8.3, 8.26
    16ZA. 9.5, 9.17, 9.22, 9.24, 9.25, 9.31
    16ZB............................. 9.5
    16ZC.. 9.5, 9.26, 9.27, 9.30, 9.36
    16ZD............................. 9.5
    17......... 8.28, 8.45, 12.6, 20.47, 24.125
    18......... 8.29, 8.30, 8.31, 20.63, 24.125
    22................................ 8.5
    28........................... 8.6, 20.8
    37............................... 8.26

Table of Statutes

Taxation of Chargeable Gains Act 1992 – *contd*
s 38.......................... 8.26, 8.27
39............................... 8.27
48..................... 8.26, 20.100
58. 3.253, 8.31, 8.33, 20.5, 20.43, 20.47, 20.91
ss 59A, 59B...................... 8.36
s 60..... 8.61, 8.62, 18.109, 18.142
62.. 8.40, 8.42, 9.8, 20.52, 28.25, 28.26, 28.67, 28.69, 28.74, 28.79, 28.80
68c............................. 28.84
69........... 17.3, 17.7, 18.3, 18.7
71.... 8.3, 8.64, 8.65, 8.66, 17.52, 20.97, 28.95, 28.96
72.................. 8.62, 8.63, 8.66
73................................ 8.66
74................................ 8.62
ss 77–79........................... 4.65
s 77..................... 17.101, 18.59
80..................... 17.11, 18.11
86...... 4.65, 8.108, 8.114, 8.125, 12.36, 18.99, 18.100, 18.102, 18.103, 18.104, 18.105, 18.108, 18.131, 18.150, 21.22, 21.40, 24.126
86A.................... 8.125, 18.105
87...... 8.108, 8.114, 9.30, 18.90, 18.108, 18.110, 18.117, 18.118, 18.119, 18.122, 18.128, 18.131, 18.132, 18.144, 18.151, 18.152, 18.156, 18.157, 18.159, 18.160, 18.161, 18.162, 18.164, 21.22, 21.24, 21.31, 21.33, 21.39, 24.38, 24.126
87A...... 18.110, 18.111, 18.114, 18.120, 18.137, 18.152
87B................. 18.118, 18.119

Taxation of Chargeable Gains Act 1992 – *contd*
s 91......... 18.132, 18.133, 18.135, 18.137, 18.144
97........... 18.89, 18.109, 18.152
100............................ 19.86
150A.......................... 19.76
150C........................... 19.87
165.. 8.37, 8.48, 8.49, 8.50, 8.54, 8.55, 8.58, 8.64, 8.67, 8.68, 8.69, 8.72, 8.73, 8.78, 17.62, 20.74
165A............................ 8.68
166............................. 8.49
167............................. 8.50
168............................. 8.51
169B.................. 8.74, 20.74
169C...................... 8.74, 8.75
ss 169D, 169E................... 8.74
s 169F........... 8.74, 17.101, 20.73
ss 169H, 169I.................... 8.82
s 169J............................ 8.95
169K............................ 8.82
169L............................ 8.88
169M.................... 8.89, 8.95
169N...................... 8.90, 8.91
169P............................ 8.86
169Q............................ 8.94
169S............................ 8.85
169N............................ 2.48
191........................... 28.110
222...... 20.1, 20.9, 20.10, 20.11, 20.14, 20.27, 20.37, 20.42, 20.44, 20.52, 20.61, 20.83, 21.6
223...... 20.1, 20.9, 20.11, 20.40, 20.41, 20.53, 20.63, 21.6, 21.17
224........................... 20.18
225... 20.11, 20.69, 20.70, 20.71, 20.76, 20.97, 21.17, 21.24, 21.32
225A.......... 20.11, 20.78, 20.82
226A.......................... 20.75
241............................. 8.68
ss 251, 252...................... 6.46

Table of Statutes

Taxation of Chargeable Gains Act 1992 – *contd*
s 260.. 8.37, 8.48, 8.49, 8.50, 8.54, 8.55, 8.56, 8.57, 8.59, 8.62, 8.63, 8.64, 8.66, 8.67, 8.68, 8.72, 8.73, 8.78, 17.62, 20.74, 20.76, 28.96
261.............................. 8.49
269.............................. 6.45
272............................. 28.26
274.................. 28.26, 28.100
ss 275, 275A..................... 6.31
s 280....................... 8.37, 8.38
281....................... 8.37, 8.39
286........ 8.29, 8.50, 8.104, 9.11, 20.91
288........ 8.29, 8.50, 8.99, 18.99
417............................. 8.100
Sch 1..... 8.12, 17.17, 17.58, 18.17
Sch 3............................. 2.48
Sch 5. 4.65, 18.99, 18.101, 18.106, 18.107
Sch 5A........................... 25.63
Sch 5B........................... 19.87
Sch 7....................... 8.52, 8.71
Sch 8A........................... 24.58
Taxes Management Act 1970 ...... 2.20
Pt VIII............................ 5.41
s 7................................. 2.3

Taxes Management Act 1970 – *contd*
s 8.... 2.59, 9.19, 9.25, 24.8, 24.11, 24.12
9A......................... 5.34, 5.41
42......................... 9.25, 24.8
43................. 8.54, 9.25, 24.8
59A............................. 2.64
74............................. 28.11
93............................. 2.61
Sch 1A........................... 5.34
Trustee Act 1925
ss 31, 32........................ 16.88
s 34............................. 7.16
Trustee Act 2000 .... 15.6, 15.12
Annex............................ 27.1
Trusts of Land and Appointments of Trustees Act 1996 .... 15.12
Variation of Trusts Act 1958 ..... 28.76
Wills Act 1837 .... 27.145
s 7............................... 27.26
9............... 27.27, 27.29, 27.32
15............................... 27.31
18............................... 27.35
18A.............................. 27.36
20............................... 27.33
33............................... 27.56
Wills Act 1963
s 1............................... 27.93
4............................... 27.97

Table of Statutory Instruments etc

[All References are to Paragraph Numbers]

Agent and HMRC Working Together June/July 2010 Issue 18 .... 5.32
Capital Gains Tax (Annual Exempt Amount) Order 2010, SI 2010/923 .... 2.44, 8.12
Double Taxation Relief (Estate Duty) (France) Order 1963, SI 1963/1319 ..... 26.24, 26.25, 26.27, 26.28, 26.29, 26.30, 26.31, 26.40
Double Taxation Relief (Estate Duty) (India) Order 1956, SI 1956/998 .... 26.24, 26.25, 26.26, 26.27, 26.28, 26.29, 26.30, 26.31
Double Taxation Relief (Estate Duty) (Italy) Order 1968, SI 1968/304 . 26.24, 26.25, 26.27, 26.28, 26.29, 26.30, 26.31
Double Taxation Relief (Estate Duty) (Pakistan) Order 1957, SI 1957/1522 ... 26.24, 26.25, 26.27, 26.28, 26.29, 26.30, 26.31
Double Taxation Relief (Taxes on Estates of Deceased Persons and Inheritances and on Gifts) (Netherlands) Order 1980, SI 1980/706 .... 26.24, 26.25, 26.26, 26.33, 26.34
Double Taxation Relief (Taxes on Estates of Deceased Persons and Inheritances and on Gifts) (Republic of Ireland) Order 1978, SI 1978/1107 .... 26.24, 26.25, 26.33, 26.34, 26.40
   art 5 .... 26.40
   art 8 .... 26.40
Double Taxation Relief (Taxes on Estates of Deceased Persons and on Gifts) (Republic of South Africa) Order 1979, SI 1979/576 .... 26.24, 26.25, 26.33, 26.34
Double Taxation Relief (Taxes on Estates of Deceased Persons and Inheritances and on Gifts) (Sweden) Order 1981, SI 1981/840 ..... 26.24, 26.25, 26.33, 26.34
Double Taxation Relief (Taxes on Estates of Deceased Persons and Inheritances) (Switzerland) Order 1994, SI 1994/3214 ...... 11.42, 26.24, 26.25, 26.33, 26.34, 26.39
   art 10 .... 3.256, 26.39
Double Taxation Relief (Taxes on Estates of Deceased Persons and on Gifts) (United States of America) Order 1979, SI 1979/1454 .... 3.72, 11.42, 26.24, 26.25, 26.33, 26.34
   art 8 .... 3.256, 26.39
Double Taxation Relief (Taxes On Income) (Cyprus) Order 1975, SI 1975/425
   art 24A 26.21
Double Taxation Relief (Taxes On Income) (Guernsey) Order 1952, SI 1952/1215 .... 26.21
Double Taxation Relief (Taxes On Income) (Isle of Man) Order 1955, SI 1955/1205 .... 26.21

Table of Statutory Instruments etc

Double Taxation Relief (Taxes on Income) (Japan) Order 2006, SI 2006/1924
    art 22 .... 26.20
Double Taxation Relief (Taxes On Income) (Jersey) Order 1952,
    SI 1952/1216 .... 26.21
Double Taxation Relief (Taxes on Income) (The United States of America)
    Order 2002, SI 2002/2848 .... 26.20, 3.71
    Sch
        Art 4(6) 3.71
        Art 10 .... 26.13, 26.20
        Art 23 .... 26.20
Enactment of Extra-Statutory Concessions Order 2009, SI 2009/730 .... 20.58, 20.59
'Extra-Statutory Concessions August 2009', HMRC 4.55
    ESC A11 .... 4.46, 4.54, 4.57, 4.58, 4.59, 4.60, 4.61, 4.62, 4.68, 4.83, 8.119,
                                                             17.14, 18.14, 24.14
    ESC A78 .... 4.35
    ESC B18 .... 17.35, 18.31, 18.32, 18.33, 18.34, 18.35, 18.39, 18.40, 25.62
    ESC D2 .... 4.46, 4.54, 4.65, 4.66, 4.67, 4.68, 4.76, 4.83, 8.119, 8.120, 8.121,
                                                        8.122, 8.123, 8.124, 8.126, 8.127, 17.14,
                                                                        18.14, 24.14
    ESC D3 .... 20.59
    ESC D4 .... 20.58
    ESC D6 .... 20.93, 20.94, 20.95, 20.97, 20.100
    ESC D21 .... 20.36
Family Provision (Intestate Succession) Order 2009, SI 2009/135 .... 27.140
Finance Act 2008, Schedule 39 (Appointed Day, Transitional Provision and
    Savings) Order 2009, SI 2009/403 .... 9.25, 24.8
HM Treasury Taxes (Interest Rate) Regulations 1989, SI 1989/1297 .... 14.38
HMRC 'IHT and Trusts Newsletter' (August 2007) 5.42
HMRC6 'Residence, domicile & the remittance basis' 3.77, 3.85, 3.95, 4.4, 4.5,
                                                                  4.8, 4.13, 4.14, 4.20, 4.21, 4.22, 4.25,
                                                                  4.27, 4.28, 4.30, 4.31, 4.35, 4.37, 4.38,
                                                                  4.41, 4.44, 4.45, 4.50, 4.52, 4.62, 4.63,
                                                                  4.64, 4.68, 4.80, 4.83, 5.1, 5.12, 8.119,
                                                                  8.123
HMRC Tax Bulletin 29 (June 1997) 5.31, 5.34
Income Tax (Benefits Received by Former Owner of Property) (Election for
    Inheritance Tax Treatment) Regulations 2007, SI 2007/3000 .... 12.39
Individual Savings Account Regulations 1998, SI 1998/1870 .... 19.32
Individual Savings Account (Amendment) Regulations 2009 .... 19.39
Inheritance Tax (Delivery of Accounts) (Excepted Transfers and Excepted
    Terminations) Regulations 2008, SI 2008/605 .... 14.1, 14.8, 14.9
Inheritance Tax (Delivery of Accounts) (Excepted Estates) Regulations 2004,
    SI 2004/2543 .... 14.25
Inheritance Tax (Delivery of Accounts) (Excepted Estates) (Amendment)
    Regulations 2006, SI 2006/2141 .... 14.25
Inheritance Tax (Delivery of Accounts) (Excepted Settlements)
    Regulations 2008 http://www.england-legislation.hmso.gov.uk/si/si200806
    – fn2, SI 2008/606 .... 14.1, 14.8, 14.11
Inheritance Tax (Double Charges Relief) Regulations 1987, SI 1987/1130 .... 12.6,
                                                                                12.9, 12.11

Table of Statutory Instruments etc

IR20	3.77, 3.85, 3.95, 3.111, 4.3, 4.4, 4.5, 4.23
IR Press Release 12 February 1976	16.4, 16.46
Offshore Funds (Tax) Regulations 2009, SI 2009/3001	2.20, 8.109, 18.140
reg 18	18.139, 18.147
reg 19	8.109, 18.145
reg 20	17.13, 18.13, 18.147, 18.150, 18.153
reg 21	18.67, 18.155
reg 23	18.143
reg 24	8.109, 18.147, 18.152
reg 34	18.142
regs 38, 39	18.141
reg 42	18.141
'Revenue & Customs Brief 17/09 Residence, Domicile and the Remittance Basis: Operational Changes'	5.30, 5.31, 5.41, 5.45
Revenue & Customs Brief 76/09	19.24
Revenue Interpretation	
RI 155	11.17
Statements of Practice	
SP10/79	16.4, 16.46
SP8/86	16.14
SP5/92	17.14, 18.14, 18.103
Taxation of Income from Land (Non-residents) Regulations 1995, SI 1995/2902	23.9
Taxes (Interest Rate) (Amendment) Regulations 2009, SI 2009/199	12.32
Taxes (Interest Rate) (Amendment) Regulations 2010, SI 2010/415	12.32, 21.19

Table of Cases

[All References are to Paragraph Numbers]

Agulian v Cyganik [2006] EWCA Civ 129, [2006] 1 FCR 406, [2006] All ER
   (D) 372 (Feb), CA 3.11, 3.75, 3.162–3.167, 3.197, 27.109
Aitchison v Dixon (1870) LR 10 Eq 589, 39 LJ Ch 705, 23 LT 97 .... 3.230
Al Fayed v Advocate General for Scotland (Representing The Inland Revenue
   Commissioners) [2002] STC 910 Ct of Sess (OH) 3.18, 3.77, 3.140
Allen and another (executors of Johnson, deceased) v Revenue and Customs
   Commissioners SpC 481; [2005] STC (SCD) 614, Commissioner . 3.206–3.207,
   3.209
Arnott v Groom (1846) 9 Court of Sess Cas (2nd Series) 142 .... 3.58
AG v Rowe (1862) 1 H&C 31, 31 LJ Ex 314 .... 3.189
AG v Yule and Mercantile Bank of India [1931] All ER Rep 400, (1931) 145
   LT 9, CA 3.130, 3.135
Baker v Archer-Shee [1927] AC 844, 96 LJKB 803, 137 LT 762, 43 TLR 758,
   71 Sol Jo 727, HL 17.25, 18.28
Barlow Clowes International Ltd v Henwood [2008] EWCA Civ 577, [2008]
   BPIR 778, [2008] All ER (D) 330 (May) 3.13, 3.75, 3.196
Bell v Kennedy (1868) LR 1 Sc & Div 307, HL 3.77, 3.86, 3.97, 3.98, 3.131
Bowie (or Ramsay) v Liverpool Royal Infirmary [1930] AC 588, 99 LJPC
   134, 143 LT 388, 46 TLR 465, HL (1930), HL, CA, HC 3.96
Bremer v Freeman (1857) 3 Moo PC 306 .... 3.139
Brownsville Holdings Ltd v Adamjee Insurance Co Ltd [2000] 2 Lloyd's Rep
   423 .... 3.120
Bryce v Bryce [1933] P 83, 102 LJP 1, 148 LT 351, 49 TLR 177, 77 Sol Jo
   49, [1932] All ER Rep 788, PDA 3.119
Bull v Bull [1955] 1 QB 234, [1955] 2 WLR 78, [1955] 1 All ER 253, 164
   EG 660, [1954] EGD 136, CA 7.11
Burden and Burden v United Kingdom [2008] STC 1305, ECHR Grand
   Chamber; (2006) 21 BHRC 640, [2007] STC 252, [2006] BHRC 640,
   [2007] 1 FCR 69, ECHR 26.80
Buswell v IRC [1974] 1 WLR 1631, [1974] 2 All ER 520, 118 SJ 864,
   [1974] STC 266, [1974] TR 97, 49 TC 334, CA; [1973] STC 267, [1973]
   TR 27, (1973) 117 SJ 488 .... 3.143, 3.148, 3.196
Casdagli v Casdagli [1919] AC 145; 88 LJP 49; 120 LT 52; 35 TLR 30; 63
   Sol Jo 39, HL 3.79, 3.127
Civil Engineer v IRC [2002] STC (SCD) 72, Commissioners 3.184
Clore (Deceased) (No 2), Re; Official Solicitor v Clore and Others
   [1984] STC 609, ChD 3.98, 3.116, 3.124, 3.173–3.178, 3.179
Cooper (Surveyor of Taxes) v Cadwalader (1904) 5 TC 101, Exch Ct 4.7
Craignish, Re; Craignish v Hewitt, [1892] 3 Ch 180, 67 LT 689, 8 TLR
   451, CA 3.131
Crookenden v Fuller (1859) (1859) 1 Sw & Tr 441 .... 3.132
Cyganik v Agulian. *See* Agulian v Cyganik

Table of Cases

Drevon v Drevon (1864) 34 LJ Ch 129, ChD 3.127
Douglas v Douglas (1871) LR 12 Eq 617, 41 LJ Ch 74, 25 LT 530, 20 WR
 55 .... 3.82
Dyer v Dyer (1788) 2 RR 14, 2 Cox Eq Cas 92, [1775–1802] All ER Rep
 205, 30 ER 42 .... 7.11
Executors of Robert Moore Deceased v CIR (2002), Commissioners. *See*
 Moore's executors v Inland Revenue Commissioners (Note)
F v IRC [2000] STC (SCD) 1, Commissioners 3.141
Fasbender v A-G, Kramer v A-G [1922] 2 Ch 850, 91 LJCh 791, 128 LT
 85, CA; [1922] 1 Ch 232, ChD 3.230
Frankland v IRC [1997] [1996] STC 735, ChD 16.20
Fuld's Estate (No 3), Re [1968] P 675, [1965] 3 All ER 776, PDA 3.76, 3.77,
 3.154, 3.155, 3.156, 3.192, 3.194, 3.195,
 3.196
Furse, Re [1980] 3 All ER 838, [1980] STC 596, ChD ... 3.147, 3.150, 3.151, 3.152,
 3.153, 3.157
Gaines-Cooper v RCC SpC 568; [2007] STC (SCD) 23, Commissioners 3.110,
 3.111, 3.117, 3.121, 3.122, 3.123, 3.185,
 3.202, 3.203, 4.23, 4.24
Gaines-Cooper v RCC [2007] EWHC 2617 (Ch), [2008] STC 1665, ChD 3.75,
 3.103, 3.111
Gaines-Cooper v RCC (2009), CA. *See* R (on the application of Davies and
 another) v Revenue and Customs Commissioners; R (on the application of
 Gaines-Cooper) v Revenue and Customs Commissioners
Goods of Raffenel, Re (1863) 3 Sw & TR 49 .... 3.220–3.221, 3.222
Grace v HMRC [2009] EWCA Civ 1082, 6 and 7 [2009] STC 2707, [2009]
 SWTI 2834 .... 4.6, 4.23
Grove, Re; Vaucher v Solicitor to the Treasury (1888) 40 Ch D 216,
 [1886–1890] All ER Rep Ext 1572, CA 3.139
Gubay v Kington [1984] 1 WLR 163, [1984] 1 All ER 513, [1984] STC 99,
 57 TC 601, HL; [1983] 1 WLR 709, [1983] 2 All ER 976, [1983] STC
 443, 57 TC 601, CA 4.53, 20.85
Gulbenkian v Gulbenkian [1937] 4 All ER 618, 54 TLR 241, PDA 3.64
Haji-Ioannou & others v Frangos [2010] 1 All ER (Comm) 303, [2009] All
 ER (D) 121 (Sep) 3.213, 3.215
Harrison v Harrison [1953] 1 WLR 865, 97 SJ 456 .... 3.64
Henderson v Henderson [1967] P 77, [1965] 2 WLR 218, [1965] 1 All ER
 179, 108 SJ 861 .... , PDA3.14, 3.36, 3.194, 3.195
Hodgson v De Beauchesne (1858) 12 Moo PC 286, 33 LTOS 36, 7 WR 397,
 14 ER 920, PC 3.133
Holland (Executor of Holland deceased) v IRC [2003] STC (SCD) 43,
 Commissioners 26.80
Holliday v Musa [2010] EWCA Civ 335, [2010] 2 FLR 702, [2010] All ER
 (D) 288 (Mar) 3.11, 3.162
Hoskins v Matthews (1856) 8 De GM & G 13, 25 LJ Ch 689, 26 LTOS 210,
 2 Jur NS 196, 4 WR 216, 44 ER 294 .... 3.211, 3.212
Ingram (Executors of the Estate of Lady Ingram) v IRC [1995] 4 All ER 334,
 [1995] STC 564, (1995) 92(23) LS Gaz 33, (1995) 139 SJLB 128, [1995]
 NPC 92, ChD 20.104
IRC v Brown (1926) 11 TC 292, KBD 4.7

Table of Cases

IRC v Bullock (Group Captain) [1976] 1 WLR 1178, [1976] 3 ALL ER 353,
  [1976] STC 409, 51 TC 522, CA; [1975] 1 WLR 1436, [1975] 3 ALL ER
  541, [1975] STC 512, 51 TC 522, 54 ATC 211, [1975] TR 179, ChD 3.18,
    3.28, 3.107, 3.147, 3.148, 3.149, 3.150,
    3.152, 3.153
IRC v Combe (1932) 17 TC 405, Ct of Sess (1 Div) 4.7, 4.23
IRC v Eversden [2002] EWHC 1360 (Ch), [2002] STC 1109, ChD 20.104
IRC v Duchess of Portland [1982] Ch 314, [1982] 2 WLR 367,
  [1982] 1 All ER 784, [1981] TR 475, (1984) 54 TC 648 .... 3.68, 3.93, 3.94,
    3.103, 3.104, 3.108, 3.112, 3.113, 3.185
IRC v Zorab v (1926) 11 TC 289, KBD 4.7
Jopp v Wood (1865) 4 De GJ & Sm 616, 5 New Rep 422, 34 LJ Ch 212, 12
  LT 41, 11 Jur NS 212, 13 WR 481, 46 ER 1057   ..... 3.170, 3.171, 3.172, 3.173,
    3.179
Lawton, Re [1958] TR 249, 37 ATC 216, ChD 3.134, 3.135, 3.217
Levene v IRC [1928] 1 AC 217, 13 TC 486, HL 4.7
Lysaght v IRC [1928] 1 AC 234, 13 TC 526, HL 4.7
Liddell-Grainger's Will Trusts, Re; Dormer v Liddell-Grainger
  [1936] 3 All ER 173 .... 3.136
Lord Advocate v Jaffrey [1921] 1 AC 146, 89 LJPC 209, 124 LT 129, 36 TLR
  820, 64 Sol Jo 713, HL 3.65
Mark v Mark [2005] UKHL 42, [2006] AC 98, [2005] 3 All ER 912,
  [2005] 2 FLR 1193, [2005] 2 FCR 467, HL 3.100
MacLaine Watson & Co Ltd v Department of Trade and Industry [1990] 2 AC
  418, [1989] 3 WLR 969, [1989] 3 All ER 523, [1990] BCLC 102, [1989]
  BCC 872, HL 26.7
Moore's executors v Inland Revenue Commissioners (Note) [2002] STC
  (SCD) 463, Commissioners 3.158, 3.159, 3.160, 3.161
Moorhouse v Lord (1863) 10 HL Cas 272, 1 New Rep 555, 32 LJ Ch 295, 8
  LT 212, 9 Jur NS 677, 11 WR 637, 11 ER 1030, HL 3.210, 3.211
Morgan v Cilento [2004] EWHC 188 (Ch), [2004] All ER (D) 122 (Feb),
  [2004] WTLR 457, ChD 3.11, 3.197–3.202, 3.203, 3.209
Pearson v IRC [1981] AC 753, [1980] 2 WLR 872, [1980] 2 All ER 479,
  [1980] STC 318, [1980] TR 177, (1980) 124 SJ 377, HL 16.4, 16.46
Plummer v IRC [1988] 1 WLR 292, [1988] 1 All ER 97, [1987] STC 698,
  (1988) 132 SJ 54, (1987) 84 LS Gaz 3415, ChD 3.107, 3.108, 3.179–3.183,
    3.224
Puttick v A-G and Puttick [1980] Fam 1, [1979] 3 WLR 542, [1979] 3 All ER
  463, (1979) 123 SJ 336, (1979) 10 Fam Law 51, FD 3.100
R v IRC, ex parte Fulford-Dobson [1987] QB 978, [1987] 3 WLR 277,
  [1987] STC 344, (1987) 131 SJ 975, (1987) 84 LS Gaz 2197, QBD 4.56
R v Secretary of State for Transport, ex parte Factortame Ltd (No 2)
  (C-213/89) [1991] 1 AC 603,   ... [1990] 3 WLR 818, [1991] 1 All ER 70, [1991]
    1 Lloyd's Rep 10, [1990] 3 CMLR 375,
    ECJ 26.45
R (on the application of Davies and another) v Revenue and Customs
  Commissioners R (on the application of Gaines-Cooper) v Revenue and
  Customs Commissioners [2010] EWCA Civ 83, [2010] STC 860, CA 3.111
Ramsay v Liverpool Royal Infirmary. *See* Bowie (or Ramsay) v Liverpool
  Royal Infirmary

Table of Cases

Reddington v MacInnes [2002] ScotCS 46, Ct of Sess (OH) 3.213–3.214
Reed (Inspector of Taxes) v Clark [1986] Ch 1, [1985] STC 323, 58 TC 528 ..... 4.7, 4.17, 4.23
RCC v Trustees of the Peter Clay Discretionary Trust [2008] EWCA Civ 1441, [2009] Ch 296, [2009] STC 469, CA; .. [2007] EWHC 2661 (Ch), [2008] Ch 291, [2008] STC 928. ChD 17.22, 18.25
Ross v Ellison (or Ross) [1930] AC 1, 96 LJPC 163, 141 LT 666, HL 3.137
Ross v Ross. *See* Ross v Ellison (or Ross)
Scullard, Re; Smith v Brock [1957] Ch 107, [1956] 3 WLR 1060, [1956] 3 All ER 898, 100 SJ 928, ChD 3.69, 3.70
Shaffer, Re; Morgan v Cilento. *See* Morgan v Cilento
Shepherd v HMRC Spc 484, [2005] STC (SCD) 644, Commissioner 4.7
Somerville v Somerville (1801) 5 Ves Jun 750, 787, 31 ER 839 .... 3.45, 3.77, 3.230
Spence deceased, Re; Spence v Dennis & Another [1990] Ch 197, [1989] 3 WLR 834, [1989] 2 All ER 679, [1990] 1 FLR 286, [1990] Fam Law 140, ChD 3.41
Stack v Dowden [2007] UKHL 17, [2007] 2 AC 432, [2007] 2 All ER 929, [2007] 1 FLR 1858, [2007] 2 FCR 280, [2007] NPC 47, [2007] BPIR 913, 71 Conv 352 .... 7.11
Steer, Re (1858) 3 H&N 594, 28 LJ Ex 22, 32 LTOS 130, 157 ER 606 ... 3.82, 3.83, 3.136, 3.217
Stone v Stone [1958] 1 WLR 1287, [1959] 1 All ER 194, 102 SJ 938 .... 3.97
Surveyor v IRC [2002] STC (SCD) 501, Commissioners 3.144, 3.203–3.205
Udny v Udny (1869) LR 1 Sc & Div 441, HL ... 3.26, 3.27, 3.36, 3.47, 3.107, 3.220, 3.225, 3.228
Wahl v A-G (1932) 147 LT 382, [1932] All ER Rep 922, HL 3.77, 3.142
Whicker v Hume (1858) 7 HL Cas 124, 28 LJ Ch 396, 31 LTOS 319, 22 JP 591, 4 Jur NS 933, 6 WR 813, 11 ER 50, [1843–1860] All ER Rep 450, HL 3.15
White v Tennant 31 W Va 790, 8 SE 596 (1888), West Virgina Sup Ct of Appeals 3.99
Winans v AG [1904] AC 287, [1904–1907] All ER Rep 410, 73 LJKB 613, 90 LT 721, HL; revsg SC (1901) 85 LT 508 ... 3.16, 3.29, 3.75, 3.91, 3.127, 3.191, 3.192
Young, Re (1875) 1 TC 57, Exch Ct (Scotland) 4.7
Zanelli v Zanelli (1948) 64 TLR 556, 92 SJ 646, [1948] WN 381, CA 3.222

Table of Other Materials

[All References are to Paragraph Numbers]

Bahamas Perpetuities (Amendment) Act 2004 .... 25.29
Bilateral Tax Information Exchange Agreements
    Bermuda/UK 25.21, 26.42
    British Virgin Islands/UK 25.21, 26.42
    Guernsey/UK 25.21, 26.42
    Isle of Man/UK 25.21, 26.42
    Jersey/UK 25.21, 26.42
Cayman Islands Special Trusts (Alternative Regime) Law 1997 .... 25.32
Convention Providing for a Uniform Law on the Form of an International
    Will 1973 .... 27.23
Double Tax Agreements
    Antigua 25.66
    Barbados 25.66
    Belize 25.66
    Cyprus 25.66
    Guernsey 25.66
    Isle of Man 25.66
    Jersey 25.66
    Malta 25.66
    Mauritius 25.66
European Convention for the Protection of Human Rights and
    Fundamental Freedoms 26.44, 26.79
EC Treaty 26.43
Non-Reciprocal Tax Information Exchange Agreements relating to the EU
    Savings Directive
    Anguilla/UK 25.21
    Cayman Islands/UK 25.21
    Turks and Caicos/UK 25.21
OECD Model Agreement 1966 .... 26.34
OECD Model Agreement 1982 .... 26.34, 26.35, 26.41
OECD Model Double Tax Agreement 1977 .... 26.12, 26.13, 26.19
    Art 4 .... 26.12, 26.15
    Art 6 .... 26.12
    Art 11 .... 26.12
    Art 13 .... 26.12
    Art 21 .... 26.12, 26.16, 26.17
    Arts 23A, 23B 26.14
    Arts 24–26 .... 26.12
Reciprocal Tax Information Exchange Agreements relating to the EU
    Savings Directive
    British Virgin Islands/UK 25.21, 26.42
    Guernsey/UK 25.21

Table of Other Materials

Reciprocal Tax Information Exchange Agreements relating to the EU Savings Directive – *contd*
Jersey/UK 25.21
Tax Information Exchange Agreements
  Antigua/UK 26.42
  Bahamas/UK 26.42
  Belize/UK 26.42
  Gibraltar/UK 26.42
  Grenada/UK 16.42
  Liechtenstein/UK 16.42
  SanMarino/UK 16.42
Directive 77/799/EEC of 19 December 1977 concerning mutual assistance by the competent authorities of the Member States in the field of direct taxation and taxation of insurance premiums. 26.78
Directive 2003/48/EC of 3 June 2003 on taxation of savings income in the form of interest payments (EU Savings Directive) [2003] OJ L157/38 .... 19.15, 25.14, 25.21, 26.46, 26.47, 26.48, 26.50, 26.51, 26.52, 26.53, 26.54, 26.55, 26.56, 26.60, 26.62, 26.63, 26.64, 26.66, 26.68, 26.69, 26.70, 26.71, 26.72, 26.73, 26.74, 26.75, 26.76, 26.77, 26.78, 26.85
French Civil Code
  Art 102 .... 3.2
Hague Convention on the Law Applicable to Trusts and on their Recognition of July 1st 1985 (Hague Trust Convention) signed 10.1.1986 .... 15.38
Trusts (Guernsey) Law 2007 .... 25.30
UK/Canada Double Tax Agreement
  Art 4 .... 26.17
  Art 20A 26.17
UK/US Double Taxation Agreement on Income Tax and CGT
  Art 4(6) 3.71
  Art 10 .... 26.13, 26.20
  Art 23 .... 26.20

List of Abbreviations

A&M trust	Accumulation and maintenance trust
AA 1976	Adoption Act 1976
ACA 1926	Adoption of Children Act 1926
ACA 2002	Adoption and Children Act 2002
AEA 1925	Administration of Estates Act 1925
AIM	Alternative Investment Market
AJA 1982	Administration of Justice Act 1982
ALCA 1991	Age of Legal Capacity (Scotland) Act 1991
APR	Agricultural Property Relief
APT	Asset protection trust
BDRA 1953	Births and Deaths Registration Act 1953
BPR	Business Property Relief
CA 1989	Children Act 1989
CAA 2006	Children and Adoption Act 2006
CEA 1995	Civil Evidence Act 1995
CLT	Chargeable lifetime transfer
DMPA 1973	Domicile and Matrimonial Proceedings Act 1973
DoV	Deed of variation
EC	European Community

List of Abbreviations

ECHR	European Court of Human Rights
ECJ	European Court of Justice
EEC	European Economic Community
ER	Entrepreneur relief
ESC	Extra Statutory Concession
FA	Finance Act
FIFO	First in first out
FLRA 1969	Family Law Reform Act 1969
FLS 2006	Family Law (Scotland) Act 2006
FSA	Financial Services Authority
GWR	Gift with reservation
HMRC	Her Majesty's Revenue and Customs
HRA 1998	Human Rights Act 1998
IA 1986	Insolvency Act 1986
IA 1978	Interpretation Act 1978
IBC	International Business Company
ICTA 1988	Income and Corporation Taxes Act 1988
IHT 1984	Inheritance Tax Act 1984
IMF	International Monetary Fund
IPDI	Immediate post-death interest in possession
IPFDA 1938	Inheritance (Provision for Family and Dependants) Act 1938
IPFDA 1975	Inheritance (Provision for Family and Dependants) Act 1975
ISA	Individual Savings Account
ITA 2007	Income Tax Act 2007

List of Abbreviations

ITEPA 2003	Income Tax (Earnings and Pensions) Act 2003
ITTOIA 2005	Income Tax (Trading and Other Income) Act 2005
LA 1926	Legitimacy Act 1926
LA 1976	Legitimacy Act 1976
LA 1972	Legitimation Act 1972
LDF	Liechtenstein Disclosure Facility
LIFO	Last in first out
LPA 1925	Law of Property Act 1925
LP(MP)A 1989	Law of Property (Miscellaneous Provisions) Act 1989
MA 1949	Marriage Act 1949
MCA 1973	Matrimonial Causes Act 1973
MCA 2005	Mental Capacity Act 2005
MWPA 1882	Married Women's Property Act 1882
NRB	Nil rate band
NCPR 1987	Non-Contentious Probate Rules 1987
OECD	Organisation of Economic Co-operation and Development
OEIC	Open-ended investment companies
OFC	Offshore financial centre
ODF	Offshore disclosure facility
OIG	Offshore income gains
PAA 2009	Perpetuities and Accumulations Act 2009
PCA 2002	Proceeds of Crime Act 2002
PET	Potentially exempt transfer
POA	Pre-owned asset

List of Abbreviations

PR	Personal representative
QSR	Quick succession relief
RCTA 1987	Recognition of Trust Act 1987
RFI	Relevant foreign income
RI	Revenue interpretation
RTI	Relevant tax increase
SCA 1981	Supreme Court Act 1981
SD	Stamp duty
SDA 1835	Statutory Declarations Act 1835
SDLT	Stamp duty land tax
SDRT	Stamp duty reserve tax
SP	Statement of Practice
TA 1925	Trustee Act 1925
TCGA 1992	Taxation of Chargeable Gains Act 1992
TIEA	Tax Information Exchange Agreement
TLATA 1996	Trusts of Land and Appointments of Trustees Act 1996
TMA 1970	Taxes Management Act 1970
TSI	Transitional serial interest
VAT	Value added tax
VTA 1958	Variation of Trusts Act 1958
WA 1837	Wills Act 1837
WA 1963	Wills Act 1963

Part I

Basic issues

Chapter 1

Tax systems and their bases of taxation: an overview

Background

1.1 Every country has its own rules which determine the extent of an individual's tax liabilities. Such liabilities may be those relating to an individual's income, capital gains and/or assets.

1.2 Typically, income is subject to some form of income tax; capital gains (often but not always) to some form of capital gains tax (CGT); and assets to some form of wealth and/or inheritance tax (IHT) on death and/or lifetime gifts.

1.3 Not all types of income are subject to income tax and not all gains are subject to some form of CGT. Some categories of asset are simply excluded from any IHT whether on death and/or lifetime gifts.

1.4 Rates of a particular tax will inevitably vary often depending upon the quantum of income/gains and upon the status of the individual taxpayer.

1.5 A taxable event (eg sale of an asset; death of an individual) may precipitate tax liabilities in more than one country; where this occurs double taxation is said to arise (ie tax is levied in more than one country on the same event).

As a consequence, in seeking to ascertain the tax implications of a particular transaction it is necessary to identify which countries' tax systems are in point, the status of the person concerned, the type of income/assets involved and the nature of the transaction.

Two simple examples may serve to illustrate the point.

Example 1

Henry Marlowe lives in England with his wife Mary and their two young children Joanne and James. All his assets are located within the UK.

1.6 *Tax systems and their bases of taxation: an overview*

Henry's father has died but his aged mother continues to live alone in her own home.

In this case as all the parties involved live within the UK; all assets are located, within the UK; and all income arises within the UK only the UK's tax regime is in point.

Example 2

Raymond Brown married Claudia Schmidt and they now both work in the UK where they have done so for 20 years. They own properties in the USA, the UK and Germany and have share investments in companies located in Hong Kong, Canada and South Africa. One of their two adult children, Samantha, now lives in Italy and the other, George, lives in Cyprus.

For Raymond the tax regimes of eight countries are in principle in point.

Optimal tax planning for Raymond in the event of his death is thus not, for example, necessarily achieved by simply mitigating any UK IHT liability if, in particular, in so doing the tax ramifications in the USA, for example, are made substantially worse.

A truly international approach is necessary.

Categories of tax

1.6 The main categories of tax (albeit not exhaustive) are those which apply to:

- income (income taxes);
- capital gains (CGT);
- inheritance (IHT);
- death (estate taxes); and
- wealth (wealth taxes).

1.7 Not all countries levy all these types of tax and sometimes the nomenclature adopted by a particular country may differ from that of another country when in fact the taxes being levied are basically the same. For example, in some countries (eg the UK) the term 'inheritance tax' is used to refer not only to the tax levied on an individual's death but also to the tax levied on any lifetime gifts

Tax systems and their bases of taxation: an overview **1.11**

made by such individual. In other countries the term 'inheritance tax' may be used to refer only to lifetime gifts (the term 'estate tax' being used to describe the tax levied on an individual's death).

Capital v income distinction

1.8 For some countries no distinction is made between income and capital gains (eg Belgium, Denmark, Italy, Japan, Spain and Sweden) with both being taxed at the same rates; in other countries income and capital gains are taxed at different rates (eg in the USA the marginal income tax rate is 35%; whereas capital gains are subject to tax at the marginal rate of 15%; indeed the UK, effective 6 April 2010, levies its marginal rate of income tax at 50% compared to a CGT rate of 18% and 28%); indeed, some countries not only tax income and capital gains at different rates but distinguish between short- and long-term gains (eg short-term gains refer to gains arising within two years in the case of France; three years in Italy; and 12 months in the USA); and in some countries (eg Barbados, Gibraltar, Guernsey and the Isle of Man) capital gains are simply not taxed at all.

1.9 The approach a country adopts is critical. Where a country's tax system distinguishes between income and capital gains (as does the UK) it is often the case that capital transactions are usually taxed more favourably. This usually arises either because the rates applicable to capital gains are lower than those applicable to income and/or the bases of computation are more favourable.

1.10 In the UK, for example, before the changes introduced in *FA 2008* although the marginal (ie highest) rates of income tax and CGT were the same (40%) the bases of computation were very different with the more favourable treatment being accorded to capital gains (primarily due to the application of taper relief which exempted a percentage of any indexed capital gain from CGT; taper relief did not apply in computing income tax liabilities; see Appendix 2). Following the changes introduced in *FA 2008*, however, the marginal rate of income tax remains at 40% for the tax years 2008–2009 and 2009–2010, but the rate of CGT is reduced to 18%; for the tax year 2010–2011 the marginal rate of income tax is 50% and CGT rates are 18% and 28%.

1.11 It is because of this difference in treatment that in some countries investment returns are often structured to provide the investor with capital gains, not income benefits, in order to produce an overall lower tax liability. To combat such approaches it is not unusual to find within the provisions of the relevant tax legislation so-called 'deeming type provisions' under which, quite simply, certain capital gain returns are re-characterised as income thus nullifying any tax advantage of structuring for capital as opposed to income treatment (eg the UK's tax treatment of gains arising on a disposal of an interest in a non-reporting offshore fund or gains arising on a disposal of an interest in an offshore single premium bond).

Worldwide v territorial tax systems

Income and capital gains taxes

1.12 The tax systems of most countries can be conveniently, albeit loosely, categorised as either a worldwide or a territorial-based system of taxation although some systems are a form of hybrid system neither exclusively worldwide nor exclusively territorial.

Worldwide basis

1.13 Under the worldwide system of taxation residents are taxed on their worldwide income and capital gains. In other words, irrespective of where any income or gains arise (whether within the country of residence or elsewhere) they will be subject to tax as appropriate by the country in which the individual entitled to the income or gains is resident. The UK has adopted a worldwide-based system as has, for example, Australia, Germany, Italy, Japan and the USA.

Territorial basis

1.14 Under the territorial system of taxation residents are taxed only on income and capital gains arising within the country of residence's borders; income and capital gains arising outside thereof are not subject to tax by that country. Countries adopting this approach include Bolivia, Ecuador, Ghana, Israel, Malaysia, Panama, Singapore, Venezuela and Zambia.

Hybrid basis

1.15 Some countries which adopt the territorial system, however, extend the tax base of residents to include overseas income and/or capital gains but only if such income or gains are remitted (ie brought back) to the country of residence. Countries adopting this approach include Ghana, Israel, Malaysia, Mauritius, Singapore and Thailand.

1.16 While there are, of course, variants on the above three tax systems, in principle, most countries' tax systems fall into one of the three categories.

Residency

1.17 Irrespective of the type of tax system adopted it is usual for liability to tax within a particular country to be based on the concept of residence which, broadly speaking, refers to the place where an individual lives. However, there are one or two notable exceptions which, while adopting a 'residence'-based tax system, also utilise additional criteria.

Citizenship test

1.18 The adoption of a citizenship criterion to determine an individual's tax exposure is unusual. The USA is the major exponent of the use of the citizenship test.

1.19 The USA adopts a worldwide basis of taxation, as does the UK, but unlike the UK and most other countries, the USA extends its tax system to tax the income and gains of its *citizens wherever they are resident.* Thus, while in many cases an individual can avoid a particular country's tax system by no longer residing in that country, a *citizen* of the USA does not escape US income and capital gains taxes simply by losing US residency (eg by moving to live in the UK or Bermuda).

Thus, a citizen of the USA who does not live in the USA (ie is not resident therein) but resides in, say, the UK is still in principle liable to US income tax and CGT on worldwide income and gains (as well as in this case being liable to UK income tax and CGT).

Other countries, which also levy tax on the basis of citizenship, include Ecuador, Liberia and South Korea.

1.20 Levying tax on the basis of citizenship is, however, very unusual. By far the most common system is for a country to simply levy its income tax and CGT only on the basis of residency (as applies in the UK).

Source basis

1.21 Whether a country's tax system is a worldwide-or territorial-based system typically a country will also levy its taxes on non-residents but only with respect to income and/or capital gains arising within the country's borders. In other words, if the source of the income arises within the country or the capital gain arises on an asset situated within the country then that country will tax the non-resident. For example, invariably any real estate income (eg rents) arising from real estate in any country will be subject to income tax in that country (ie where the real estate is located) even if the owner of the real estate is not a resident of the country.

Example 3

A German resident who owns UK real estate is subject to UK income tax on any rental income arising from the real estate even though the individual is not a resident of the UK (such individual may also be subject to German tax on the income as a resident of Germany).

Example 4

Henry Bone is a resident of the Cayman Islands and has invested in USA equities. Henry is liable to US taxation on any dividend income arising on his investments.

1.22 In the case of the UK, although UK source income of a non-UK resident is liable to UK income tax, certain types of UK source income are effectively treated as exempt. This approach is generally adopted in order to encourage foreign investment.

1.23 Although non-residents of a country are invariably subject to some form of tax in the country in which income arises the position with respect to capital gains may vary. Thus, some countries *do* levy their CGT on disposals of assets situated within their country by non-residents while other countries do not.

In the case of the UK, for example, a non-UK resident is not subject to CGT on the disposal of UK situs assets (unless the asset(s) form part of a UK-based trade or business).

Example 5

Joe America Junior, a US resident, has sold a number of his UK equity investments. Even though the assets sold are UK situs (ie located within the UK) no UK CGT charge arises on the sales.

Inheritance tax

1.24 Most countries levy some form of tax on the death of an individual. In addition, many countries levy some form of tax on gifts made by an individual during their lifetime.

Tax systems and their bases of taxation: an overview **1.31**

1.25 Terminology varies widely between countries as do the bases and underlying methodology upon which such taxes are levied. As to terminology, common terms include death tax, IHT, estate tax/duty and gift tax.

1.26 Unlike income tax and CGT which generally apply to residents of a country, taxes levied on death and/or lifetime gifts are often based upon an individual's domicile or nationality status. In addition, the form the tax may take also varies.

1.27 Sometimes (as in the UK) on death the amount of the individual's estate (assets owned at date of death less liabilities) is ascertained and tax is then levied on the estate (ie the tax payable on death is in fact paid out of the deceased's estate before any assets of the estate can be transferred to the beneficiaries under the deceased's will).

1.28 However, it is not unusual for some countries to levy their tax arising on death, not on the estate itself (as in the UK), but on those individuals who actually inherit a part of the deceased's estate (ie the heirs).

1.29 Some countries impose a tax on death and a different tax applies to lifetime gifts. The USA, for example, imposes two separate taxes: an estate tax, applying only on death and a gift tax, applying on lifetime gifts. In the UK the same tax – IHT – applies both on death and lifetime gifts.

1.30 Examples of differences amongst countries concerning death and related taxes include:

- *in the UK* the liability on death is that of the deceased's estate and the extent of the liability depends upon the *deceased's domicile status at the date of death*;
- *in Spain* the liability is that of the heirs with the liability depending upon the *principal residence* status of the *heirs*;
- *in South Africa* the liability is that of the deceased's estate and depends upon the *ordinary residence* status of the *deceased*; and
- *in Germany* liability is dependent upon the *domicile status* of the deceased and the heirs and is a liability of the heirs, the amount of liability depending upon the relationship of the heir to the deceased.

Trailing tax imposition

1.31 The term 'trailing tax' usually refers to the levying of a country's taxes on an individual even when, *prima facie*, the individual is no longer within that country's tax regime for tax purposes.

1.32 Tax systems and their bases of taxation: an overview

1.32 In the UK, for example, a UK-domiciled individual is liable to IHT on worldwide assets. However, even where such individual loses UK domicile status (eg by acquiring a non-UK domicile of choice) the individual still remains within the charge to UK IHT on worldwide assets for a further period of three years.

1.33 Similarly, a Dutch national is still within the Dutch death tax net for a further ten years after losing Dutch residency; a German national continues to be caught in the German death tax net for a further five years; and a US citizen or 'long-term' permanent resident who has renounced either status but is caught under the trailing income/CGT rules is automatically deemed to still be within the death/gift tax net for a ten-year period.

1.34 The concept of trailing taxes is often overlooked when considering an individual's tax affairs. It is most likely to apply where the individual has moved from one country to settle in another (possibly with the sole or main objective of mitigating taxes).

Summary

1.35 It is important to recognise that tax systems may vary significantly amongst different countries

1.36 The rules applicable in the UK are not necessarily adopted elsewhere.

1.37 Typically, the taxes levied by a country include some form of income tax on income; CGT on capital gains; and death tax and/or gift tax arising on death and/or lifetime gifts. Nomenclature adopted often varies amongst countries and the same term may be used in a different or the same sense in different countries.

1.38 Optimal tax planning may involve a consideration of the impact of different countries' tax systems on an individual's affairs and, in particular, their interaction if double taxation is to be avoided.

Chapter 2

UK taxation: an overview

Background

2.1   Since the mid-1990s the UK has adopted a self-assessment system of tax with respect to income tax and capital gains tax (CGT).

2.2   Thus, a taxpayer falling within the charge to UK income tax and/or CGT is required to complete a tax return (typically dispatched automatically to the taxpayer by HMRC) for the relevant tax year; to compute the associated tax liabilities for the tax year; and to ensure that both the tax return is lodged and any associated tax liabilities are paid on or before the statutory deadlines.

2.3   Any taxpayer who is chargeable to income tax or CGT in respect of income and/or capital gains for a tax year, but who has not received, for whatever reason, a tax return for completion, is under an obligation to notify HMRC within six months of the end of the tax year in which any such income and/or capital gains arise (*TMA 1970 s 7*). Failure to notify within the prescribed time limit results in a penalty.

2.4   The position with respect to inheritance tax (IHT) is slightly different from that applicable to income tax and CGT as there is no requirement to file annual returns.

Domicile, residence and ordinary residence

2.5   As discussed in Chapter 1, the tax exposure of an individual is typically determined according to that individual's residence (and possible ordinary residence) and domicile status.

Domiciled individual

2.6   A UK domiciled, *resident and ordinarily resident* individual is exposed to all forms of UK tax (income tax, CGT and IHT) on all income,

2.7 *UK taxation: an overview*

capital gains and assets wherever such income and gains arise and wherever such assets may be located (ie the worldwide basis of taxation). Such individual is subject to income tax and/or CGT on the so-called *arising* basis (ie as soon as any income/capital gains arise, wherever in the world, the individual is subject to tax thereon).

Example 1

An individual who is UK domiciled, resident and ordinarily resident is subject to UK income tax on any interest which arises on a Swiss bank account deposit even if the interest monies are retained in Switzerland; similarly, any capital gain arising on the sale of US equities is subject to UK CGT even if the sale proceeds are banked and kept in the USA.

2.7 With respect to IHT, a UK domiciled individual (whether resident or ordinarily resident in the UK or not) is liable to IHT on worldwide assets on death and on any lifetime gifts.

Example 2

A UK domiciled individual at the time of death owns UK equities, a Spanish villa and a bank account in the USA.

UK IHT arises on all the assets.

2.8 A UK domiciled individual who is resident but not ordinarily resident is subject to income and tax on the same basis as a non-UK domiciled individual (see paragraph 2.9). However, such individual is subject to CGT and IHT on worldwide assets.

Non-domiciled individual

2.9 For the *non-UK domiciled* individual, however, slightly different rules apply.

2.10 A non-UK *domiciled but resident and ordinarily resident* individual is subject to income tax and CGT on the *remittance* basis with respect to non-UK source income and non-UK source capital gains (assuming an appropriate claim is lodged with HMRC; *ITA 2007 ss 809A* and *809B*; *TGCA 1992 s 12*). UK source income and capital gains are, however, subject to UK income tax and

CGT in the same manner as applies to the UK domiciled individual (ie the arising basis; see paragraph 2.6).

Example 3

A non-UK domiciled but resident and ordinarily resident individual receives interest on a bank deposit in the UK; interest on a bank deposit in Luxembourg; rental income on a house in Spain; and dividends on UK equities.

The individual's non-UK domicile status means that a liability to income tax arises on the UK source bank interest and the dividends on the UK equities on the arising basis.

However, the interest on the Luxembourg bank deposit and the rental income from the Spanish property are subject to income tax only if and when the monies are remitted (ie brought to) the UK. Thus, should such monies remain outside of the UK no income tax liabilities arise thereon.

2.11 However, there was (ie pre-*FA 2008*) one exception to the remittance rule for non-UK domiciled but UK resident individuals which concerned the Republic of Ireland. Income (technically 'relevant foreign income'; *ITTOIA 2005 s 830*) which comprises dividend income, interest income, property income and trading income arising in the Republic of Ireland (and 'employment income' from employment with an employer resident in Ireland) was not subject to the remittance, but the arising, basis of tax. This treatment, however, was relatively recently (early 2007) found to be in breach of European Community rules. As a consequence, action was taken in *FA 2008* to correct what had been for many years an anomaly. Income arising on or after 6 April 2008 within the Republic of Ireland is now subject to remittance basis treatment for the non-UK domiciled but UK resident individual (subject to an appropriate claim; see paragraph 2.10).

2.12 Pre-*FA 2008*, investments (eg bank deposits) in the Republic of Ireland by a non-UK domiciled but UK resident and ordinarily resident individual, generally speaking, were thus not tax efficient, as income tax applied on the arising basis. This was particularly relevant with respect to Irish-based 'offshore mutual funds'. The *FA 2008* changes now mean that for such individuals investments in Irish-based mutual funds are no longer tax inefficient.

2.13 It is worth noting, however, that even pre-*FA 2008*, the remittance basis did apply to the non-UK domiciled but UK resident individual with respect to capital gains arising on the disposal of Republic of Ireland situs assets for UK CGT purposes. This continues to apply post-*FA 2008*.

2.14 *UK taxation: an overview*

2.14 With respect to IHT, the non-UK domiciled individual is liable to IHT on UK situs assets only; non-UK situs assets are not subject to IHT. The residence and ordinary residence status of an individual is in principle irrelevant to an individual's exposure to IHT (subject to the concept of 'deemed UK domicile'; *IHTA 1984 s 267*).

Example 4

An individual who is non-UK domiciled but UK resident and ordinarily resident at death owns a UK house; a house in Florida, USA; UK equities; Canadian equities; a bank deposit in Switzerland; a bank deposit in the UK; and a farm in South Africa.

The UK IHT liability arising on death applies to UK situs assets only, namely, the UK house, UK equities and UK bank deposits.

All the other assets fall outside any charge to UK IHT (although, of course, there may be liabilities arising due to death in the other countries).

2.15 In short, if a non-UK domiciled but resident and ordinary resident individual does not remit any non-UK source income or non-UK source capital gains to the UK any liability to income tax and CGT thereon is restricted to UK source income and UK source capital gains. On death, and with respect to lifetime gifts, IHT is also restricted to a charge on UK situs assets only.

Persons other than individuals

2.16 UK taxes are also applicable to:

- companies;
- trustees; and
- personal representatives (PRs).

2.17 Whilst trustees and PRs are in principle subject to the same taxes as individuals, companies which are UK resident are liable to corporation tax on their worldwide income.

UK taxes and the law

2.18 Her Majesty's Revenue and Customs (HMRC) is the body now responsible for tax assessment and collection. It was created in 2005, prior to

UK taxation: an overview **2.22**

which it was two separate bodies: the Inland Revenue and Her Majesty's Customs and Excise.

2.19 The UK taxes for which HMRC are responsible include:

- income tax;
- CGT;
- corporation tax;
- IHT;
- stamp duty (SD) and stamp duty land tax (SDLT); and
- value added tax (VAT).

2.20 The main legislation which deals with UK taxation is contained in various Acts of Parliament and includes:

- *Taxes Management Act 1970;*
- *Inheritance Tax Act 1984;*
- *Income and Corporation Taxes Act 1988;*
- *Taxation of Chargeable Gains Act 1992;*
- *Income Tax (Earnings and Pensions) Act 2003;*
- *Income Tax (Trading and Other Income) Act 2005;*
- *Income Tax Act 2007;*
- *Corporation Tax Act 2009;* and
- miscellaneous Finance Acts (eg *Finance Acts 2006* and *2008*).

In addition, much subordinate legislation now appears in Statutory Instruments (eg *SI 2009/3001* which contains regulations detailing the treatment of participants in offshore funds; *FA 2008 s 41*).

2.21 Unfortunately, no single Act contains all the legislation relating to a particular tax and therefore to determine tax liability at any point in time requires, typically, that a number of different Acts be examined (eg an IHT liability may require, *inter alia*, an examination of *IHTA 1984, FA 1986* and *FA 2006*).

Capital v income

2.22 The UK's tax system distinguishes between transactions which give rise to income and those which give rise to capital gains. The former is subject to income tax and the latter subject to CGT; two totally separate taxes.

2.23 *UK taxation: an overview*

2.23 As a very broad general rule capital rather than income treatment was, pre-*FA 2008*, more 'tax favourable' (primarily due to the availability of taper relief which only applied to capital gains and not income). Hence, many investments were structured to provide the individual investor with a capital gain on sale/maturity of the investment rather than an income return. Pre-*FA 2008*, for the higher rate income taxpayer any income arising on an investment would be charged at 40% whereas any capital gain, although subject to a nominal rate of 40%, would in many cases be subject to a much lower rate due to the effect of taper relief (eg a reduction to a possible effective rate of as low as 10% or 24% depending on the nature of the investment).

2.24 Post-*FA 2008*, the distinction between income and capital continues. However, for the tax years 2008–2009 and 2009–2010 while the marginal rate taxpayer continues to be exposed to income tax at 40% on income a new CGT rate of 18% has been introduced (possibly reduced further to 10% due to the newly introduced 'entrepreneur relief' (ER); taper relief and indexation have both been abolished effective 6 April 2008; see Appendix 2).

For the tax year 2010–2011 the marginal rate of income tax has been increased to 50% (the additional rate) and a two-tier CGT rate has been introduced with rates of 18% and 28% (the latter rate only applying to disposals on or after 23 June 2010). Despite the increase to 28% (where applicable) the attraction of a capital return over an income return continues.

Income tax

2.25 Income tax is levied on the income of an individual for a particular tax year. The 'tax year' or 'year of assessment' covers the period 6 April to the following 5 April inclusive. Thus, for example, the tax year 2010–2011 covers the period 6 April 2010 to 5 April 2011.

2.26 More specifically, income tax is levied on an individual's *taxable income* which is an individual's total income for a tax year from all sources (eg salary, bank interest, rental income etc) less certain allowances, reliefs and deductions (eg personal allowance; charitable payments, etc.). All resident individuals are entitled to a personal allowance and certain categories of non-UK resident individual also qualify (*ITA 2007 s 58*).

FA 2008 (tax year 2008–2009)

2.27 Prior to *FA 2008* the basic rate of income tax was 22% (applicable to non-savings income); a 20% rate applied to savings income; and a 'starting rate' of 10% applied to the first £2,150 of taxable income. Dividend income (which is not treated as savings or non-savings income) was subject to income tax at the 'dividend ordinary' rate of 10% and/or the 32.5% 'dividend upper rate'.

FA 2008 (for the tax year 2008–2009) reduced the basic rate of 22% to 20% (effective for income arising on or after 6 April 2008) and abolished both the 20% rate applicable to savings income and the 'starting rate' of 10%. In their place was introduced a single 10% 'starting rate for savings' which applied for the first £2,320 of savings income. The rates applicable to dividend income remained the same (*FA 2008 ss 1* and *Sch 5*; *ITA 2007 ss 7, 8* and *12* and *Sch 1*).

2.28 The basic rate of 20% applied to taxable income up to £34,800 and the 40% rate to taxable income above this limit (*FA 2008 s 4*).

2.29 Personal allowances were £6,035 for individuals under 65; £9,030 for individuals aged 65 to 74; and £9,180 for those individuals aged 75 and over (*FA 2008 s 3*). For those individuals aged 65 or over the personal allowance was reduced if the 'adjusted net income' of the individual for the tax year exceeded £21,800 (*ITA 2007 ss 36* and *37*). The reduction was equal to half the excess of the adjusted net income over £21,800 (but in any event the personal allowance could not be reduced below £6,035 (ie the personal allowance for those under 65 (*ITA 2007 ss 36* and *37*)).

2.30 However, as its name suggests, the new 10% 'starting rate for savings' (see paragraph 2.27) only applies to savings income (ie it does not apply to, *inter alia*, employment income; self-employed income; rental income or dividend income). The 10% 'starting rate for savings' should not be confused with the former 10% 'starting rate' applicable pre-2008–2009 (which applied to both savings and non-savings income (but not dividend income)).

2.31 It might appear that the abolition of the 10% 'starting rate' in favour of the 10% 'starting rate for savings' might be of limited impact. However, the effect for many taxpayers was that none of their taxable income fell to be taxed at the 10% 'starting rate for savings'.

The reason is that the legislation requires that non-savings income is subject to tax before savings income which is itself subject to tax before dividend income. As a consequence, if an individual's taxable non-savings income equalled or exceeded the 2008–2009 limit of £2,320 the 10% starting rate for savings was simply not applicable. In other words, if the individual's non-savings taxable income was, for example, £2,320 this would be subject to income tax at the new basic rate (ie 20%) and any savings income would also then be subject to income tax at the 20% basic rate.

Example 5

Joseph Turner for the tax year 2008–2009 anticipates receiving the following income:

Non-savings income (eg salary)	£8,355
Savings income (eg bank interest)	£5,320

For 2008–2009 the personal allowance was £6,035.

	Non-savings £	Savings £
Salary	8,355	
Bank interest		5,320
Less personal allowance	(6,035)	
Taxable income	2,320	5,320

Income tax liability = £2,320 × 20% + £5,320 × 20% = £1,528

Example 6

Joseph Turner's brother, Barry, for the tax year 2008–2009 anticipates receiving the following income:

Non-savings income (eg salary)	Nil
Savings income (eg bank interest)	£13,675

His personal allowance is £6,035.

	Non-savings £	Savings £
Salary	Nil	
Bank interest		13,675
Less personal allowance	—	(6,035)
Taxable income	Nil	7,640

Income tax liability = £2,320 × 10% + £5,320 × 20% = £1,296

2.32 In Examples 5 and 6 although the gross (ie pre-tax) income and 'taxable income" of each of Joseph and Barry are identical in amount, because Barry has no non-savings income he is able to utilise the newly introduced 10%

UK taxation: an overview **2.36**

'starting rate for savings'. However, as Joseph's non-savings taxable income exceeds £2,320 none of his savings income falls to be taxed at the 10% rate. Thus, Barry's tax liability is 10% of £2,320 (ie £232) less than Joseph's.

2.33 The 10% new starting rate for savings thus only applies to any savings income if the individual's non-savings taxable income is below £2,320 for 2008–2009.

2.34 Prior to 2008–2009 the 10% 'starting rate' applied to both non-savings and savings income and thus either an element of non-savings income and/or an element of savings income would always be taxed at the 10% rate.

FA 2009 (tax years 2009–2010 and 2010–2011)

2.35 *FA 2009* introduced changes some of which apply for 2009–2010 and some were not due to apply until 6 April 2010. The changes due to take effect only from 6 April 2010 (and not from 6 April 2009) are:

- introduction of an 'additional rate' of income tax applicable to individuals with taxable income in excess of £150,000 (*FA 2009 s 6*);

- introduction of a 'dividend additional rate' of 42.5% applicable to dividend income otherwise taxable at the new 50% rate (*FA 2009 s 6*);

- reduction of the personal allowance for those individuals under age 65 where their 'adjusted net income' exceeds £100,000; the reduction to equate to a reduction of £1 for every £2 the individual's adjusted net income exceeds £100,000 (*FA 2009 ss 4 and 58*); and

- increase in the 'trust rate' to 50% from 40% and an increase in the 'dividend trust rate' to 42.5% from 32.5% (*FA 2009 s 6; ITA 2007 s 9*).

For those individuals under 65 whose adjusted net income exceeds £100,000 by at least £12,950 the reduction in the personal allowance is £6,475 (ie to nil; see paragraph 2.36). For those individuals aged 65 or over it is also possible for their personal allowance to be reduced to nil.

2.36 The changes introduced to take effect for the tax year 2009–2010 include increases in the various personal allowances and the limit above which the higher rate of 40% applies:

- Personal allowance £6,475
- Personal allowance (age 65 to 74) £9,490
- Personal allowance (age 75 and over) £9,640

    (Reduction in over-65 allowance where adjusted net income exceeds £22,900)

2.37 *UK taxation: an overview*

- 40% higher rate applicable to taxable income in excess of £37,400 (£34,800 2008–2009).

FA 2010 and FA (No 2) 2010 (tax year 2010–2011)

2.37 Neither *FA 2010* nor *FA (No 2) 2010* made any changes to those introduced in *FA 2009* which are to apply on or after 6 April 2010 (see paragraph 2.35) and the personal allowances set for 2009–2010 continue to apply for 2010–2011.

2.38 An individual's taxable income can thus be seen to comprise three types of income, namely: 'non-savings' income, 'savings' income and 'dividend' income each of which are liable to income tax at different rates. For the tax year 2010–2011 these rates are:

Non-savings income (NSI) taxed at	20%/40%/50%
Savings income (SI) taxed at	10%/20%/40%/50%
Dividend income taxed at	10%/32.5%/42.5%

'Savings income' includes 'relevant foreign income' (RFI) (eg foreign interest and dividend income) and thus the above rates of income tax applicable to UK source savings income and dividend income are equally applicable to relevant foreign income (*ITTOIA 2005 s 830*).

2.39 For the non-UK domiciled but UK resident individual, however, RFI is subject to rates of 20%, 40% and 50% for 2010–2011 (ie the 10% 'starting rate for savings' does not apply to such individuals; neither do the 10%, 32.5% and 42.5% dividend rates).

Personal allowances

2.40 As a general rule individuals who are not resident in the UK are not entitled to any personal allowances. However, the terms of a number of double tax agreements (see Chapter 26) to which the UK is a party extend personal allowances to non-residents. Commonwealth citizens have also been entitled to claim personal allowances purely on the grounds of such citizenship. However, from 6 April 2010 personal allowances are no longer available to Commonwealth citizens purely on this ground alone (*FA 2009 s 5* and *Sch 1*). Those individuals primarily affected include citizens of the Bahamas, the Maldives, St Lucia, Tanzania, Tonga and Vanuatu.

2.41 Residents of the Channel Islands and Isle of Man and nationals of the EEA continue to be entitled to personal allowances (*ITA 2007 s 56*).

2.42 Certain non-UK domiciled but UK resident individuals who claim remittance basis treatment are denied entitlement to personal allowances (*ITA 2007 s 809G;* see paragraph 24.15).

Capital gains tax

2.43 Capital gains tax (CGT) is levied on, *inter alia*, the capital gains of individuals (*TCGA 1992 s 1*). Capital gains are gains which arise on the disposal (eg whether by sale or gift) of certain assets (eg shares; real estate). Basically, the capital gain arising on the disposal is the difference between sale proceeds and original cost less the relevant annual exempt amount (*TCGA 1992 ss 3* and *15*).

2.44 The annual exempt amount for 2010–2011 is £10,100 (*TCGA 1992 s 3; SI 2010/923*) which also applies for 2009–2010 (£9,600 for 2008–2009). The annual exempt amount is the amount of capital gains (after any offset for allowable capital losses; *TCGA 1992 s 2*) which an individual may make in a tax year which is exempt from CGT (see paragraph 8.12). Certain non-UK domiciled but UK resident individuals who claim remittance basis treatment are not entitled to claim this annual exempt amount (*ITA 2007 s 809G;* see paragraph 24.15).

2.45 For tax years prior to the tax year 2008–2009 such gains were treated as the highest part of an individual's income (ie the CGT liability of an individual was calculated assuming that the capital gains were taxed after non-savings income, savings income and dividend income had each been taxed). Thus, the rate of CGT applicable depended upon the individual's level of taxable income thus possibly precipitating a marginal CGT rate of 40%.

FA 2008 (tax year 2008–2009 and 2009–2010)

2.46 *FA 2008* fundamentally changed the basis of subjecting capital gains to CGT (including the abolition of the indexation allowance and taper relief; *FA 2008 s 8* and *Sch 2*).

2.47 For disposals effected on or after 6 April 2008 a flat rate of 18% applied to chargeable gains. The level of an individual's taxable income thus became irrelevant in determining the rate of CGT on or after 6 April 2008.

2.48 A new form of relief was also introduced (effectively to replace the former indexation allowance and taper relief) called ER (*FA 2008 s 9* and *Sch 3*) pursuant to which the rate of CGT is an effective rate of 10% (subject to satisfying the various conditions attached to the relief; *TCGA 1992 Sch 3*). The

2.49 *UK taxation: an overview*

ER rate of 10% applied up to a maximum lifetime allowance of £1 million (*FA 2008 Sch 3* and *TCGA 1992 s 169N*), (see paragraph 8.80)

2.49 The changes introduced by *FA 2008* continued to apply for the tax year 2009–2010.

FA 2010 and FA (No 2) 2010 (tax year 2010–2011)

2.50 *FA 2010* introduced a new rate of CGT of 28% applicable to disposals effected on or after 23 June 2010; the 18% rate continues to apply in effect producing a two-tier rate of CGT (*F (No 2) Act 2010 s 2* and *Sch 1*).

2.51 *FA 2010* increased the limit applicable to the 10% ER rate from £1 million to £2 million with respect to disposals on or after 6 April 2010 (*FA 2010 s 4*) but prior to 23 June 2010. *FA (No 2) 2010* increased the £2 million limit to £5 million with respect to disposals effected on or after 23 June 2010 (*F (No 2) Act 2010 s 2* and *Sch 1*).

Inheritance tax

2.52 *FA 2008*, *FA 2009* and *FA 2010* made virtually no changes to IHT except for an increase in the nil rate band (NRB). For the tax year 2008–2009 the NRB was fixed at £312,000 and for 2009–2010 it was fixed at £325,000 (*FA 2006 s 155*).

2.53 For 2010–2011 the NRB has remained at its 2009–2010 level (ie £325,000) and has been fixed at this level for tax years 2011–2012 through to 2014–2015 inclusive (*FA 2010 s 8*). There was a plan to increase the NRB to £350,000 for the tax year 2010–2011 (*FA 2007 s 4*); this increase has not taken place.

2.54 The provisions of *FA 2006* changed radically the manner in which IHT is to be levied on property within trusts, transfers into trust and transfers out of trusts (see Chapter 16). These changes continue to apply in 2010–2011.

2.55 Inheritance tax is levied on lifetime gifts made by an individual and on the estate of an individual on death. In lifetime, gifts are in principle subject to a 20% rate of IHT; whereas the estate of an individual on death is subject to a 40% rate (*IHTA 1984 s 7* and *Sch 1*).

2.56 As indicated in paragraph 2.53, the NRB for 2010–2011 is fixed at £325,000. Thus, a 0% rate applies to an individual's first £325,000 of lifetime and/or death transfers.

2.57 Property comprised within trusts may also be subject to IHT in particular following the *FA 2006* changes. Post-*FA 2006* most trust property comprised in trusts created in lifetime on or after 22 March 2006 is now subject to charges every ten years and when property leaves the trust (eg on appointment to a beneficiary; *IHTA 1984 ss 64* to *69*). The rate applicable to the ten-yearly charge is a maximum of 6% and where property leaves a trust the maximum rate is 5.85%. The classic trust to which these charges apply is the discretionary trust although technically the charges apply to 'relevant property trusts', (see Chapter 16).

2.58 Many lifetime gifts are categorised as potentially exempt transfers (PETs) (eg gifts between individuals) and if the donor survives seven years after making the gift no IHT charge arises on the gift. Gifts made on or after 22 March 2006 into most trusts, however, are not so categorised, falling to be treated as chargeable lifetime transfers (CLTs) in which case an IHT charge may arise on the making of the CLT (*IHTA 1984 ss 2* and *3A*; see Chapter 10).

Tax returns

Income and capital gains tax

2.59 Prior to the tax year 2007–2008 a tax return covering income tax and CGT was required to be filed on or before 31 January following the end of the relevant tax year (eg 31 January 2012 for tax year 2010–2011). However, for the tax year 2007–2008 and subsequent tax years (*FA 2007 s 92*) two separate filing dates were introduced (these amendments were introduced in *FA 2007*). For *paper* tax returns the new filing date is brought forward to 31 October after the end of the tax year concerned (eg 31 October 2011 for the tax year 2010–2011; *TMA 1970 s 8*). For tax returns filed *online* the filing date remains at 31 January following the end of the tax year concerned (eg 31 January 2012 for the tax year 2010–2011; *TMA 1970 s 8*).

2.60 Thus, for the tax year 2010–2011 the *online* filing date remains at 31 January 2012, but the *paper* filing date is brought forward to 31 October 2011.

2.61 Failure to file a tax return by the requisite deadline in principle precipitates an automatic penalty of £100; continuing failure to file attracts additional penalties (*TMA 1970 s 93*).

Inheritance tax

2.62 With respect to IHT there are no regular returns required. Unlike the tax return applicable for income tax and CGT which in principle requires filing

2.63   *UK taxation: an overview*

for every tax year, returns associated with IHT tend to be event driven (eg death or making of lifetime gift) rather than tax year/time driven.

Timing of tax payments

Income and capital gains tax

2.63   Income tax and CGT liabilities arising in respect of a tax year must be paid on or before the 31 January following the relevant tax year (eg for the tax year 2010–2011 these taxes need to be paid on or before 31 January 2012). Failure to pay the requisite tax by the deadline results in interest charges on late payment.

2.64   Payments on account (*TMA 1970 s 59A*) may need to be made during the tax year and before the 31 January deadline. Such payments are made on account of the ultimate tax liability for the tax year. They are based upon the income tax payable in the previous tax year and each payment on account is equal to 50% thereof. They are payable on 31 January within the tax year and on 31 July after the end of the tax year (eg on 31 January 2011 and 31 July 2011 in respect of the tax year 2010–2011). The need for such payments arises where the individual is in receipt of untaxed income; for example, a sole trader or a partner in a partnership. The 31 January payment after the end of the relevant tax year (ie 31 January 2012 in the above example) represents any balancing payment due for the tax year after taking into account the payments on account already made.

2.65   Payments on account are only made in respect of an individual's income tax liability for a tax year but not in respect of any CGT liability.

Inheritance tax

2.66   Unlike income and CGT payments, IHT payments are made, in general, six months after the end of the month in which any charge arises (be it a charge on a lifetime gift or on death) (ie IHT is payable according to the timing of a chargeable event rather than at set times as for income tax and CGT).

Summary

2.67   The main UK taxes affecting individuals are income tax, CGT and IHT.

UK taxation: an overview **2.71**

2.68 The extent of an individual's tax liabilities depends upon the domicile, residence and ordinary residence status of the individual and the source of the income/gains.

2.69 Each of the above three taxes are entirely separate and each have their own set of governing provisions.

2.70 *FA 2006* made material changes with respect to IHT; *FA 2008, FA 2009, FA 2010* and *FA (No 2) 2010* made significant changes with respect to income tax and CGT.

2.71 The tax treatment of UK domiciled and non-UK domiciled individuals is significantly different in the case of all three taxes.

Chapter 3

Domicile

Background

3.1 The domicile, residence and ordinary residence status of an individual are critical to a determination of the individual's potential exposure to income tax, capital gains tax (CGT) and inheritance tax (IHT). Any combination of these three attributes is possible, for example:

- domicile, resident and ordinary resident;
- domicile, resident but not ordinary resident;
- non-domicile, resident and ordinary resident; or
- non-domicile, non-resident and non-ordinary resident.

3.2 This chapter will examine in some detail the concept of domicile and Chapters 4 and 5 consider the concepts of residence and ordinary residence. It is important to appreciate that the term domicile is being used in this chapter (and indeed throughout the book) in the English sense of the word which may be very different from the domicile concept of other, generally speaking, civil law jurisdictions. For example, The French Civil Code (Article 102) states:

'... the domicile of any French person, as to the exercise of his/her civil rights, is the place where he/she is principally established ...'

This, however, is not the understanding of domicile in the English sense.

Domicile is a concept of common law not taxation

3.3 Despite the crucial importance of domicile in determining an individual's exposure to various UK taxes domicile is not defined in any of the UK's tax legislation. It is the common law which has developed the various rules and it is these rules which are applied for tax purposes. It is also these rules which are applicable in the area of the conflict of laws. Domicile is an artificial legal construct and has been imported for use in issues of taxation from the law of family relations and family property.

3.4 The general importance of the concept of domicile is that it is used to connect an individual to a particular jurisdiction and thus in turn permits the law governing that jurisdiction to apply to the individual. Thus, for example, an individual who possesses an English domicile has his personal relationships governed by English law including issues such as the validity of marriage; jurisdiction in divorce; legitimacy and adoption; wills and the devolution of movable property on an intestacy (ie the distribution of property on death where no will exists; see paragraph 27.2).

As a consequence, many of the cases heard by the courts on domicile are in fact nothing to do with tax but have direct implications for it.

3.5 Not all countries, however, adopt domicile as the relevant concept to determine which personal law is to apply to an individual. Many European countries with a civil law-based system (eg France, Germany) have tended to adopt the concept of nationality as the relevant personal law rather than that of domicile.

3.6 The English concept of domicile is adopted and followed in many other common law jurisdictions (eg Australia, the USA). However, a number of such jurisdictions (unlike England) have amended some of the common law rules by statute (eg in Australia and New Zealand the automatic resurrection of the domicile of origin has been abolished; see paragraph 3.46). It cannot therefore be assumed that the common law rules of domicile under English law at any point in time are reflected in identical form in other common law jurisdictions.

3.7 The importance of domicile (outside of the area of tax) can be seen in connection wth matrimonial proceedings, under *IPFDA 1975* and bankruptcy proceedings, under *IA 1986 s 265*.

3.8 Under *IPFDA 1975 s 1* certain classes of 'dependants' (eg surviving spouse; children; cohabitee) of the deceased are able to apply for an order from the court for maintenance out of the deceased's estate but only where the deceased dies domiciled in England and Wales. Thus, *IPDFA 1975, s 1* provides:

> '1 Application for financial provision from deceased's estate
>
> Where ... a person dies domiciled in England and Wales and is survived by any of the following persons ...'

3.9 *Domicile*

3.9 IPFDA 1975 came into force in respect of deaths occurring after 31 March 1976 but has no application to Scotland or Northern Ireland (Scotland has a system of fixed rights, referred to as legitim (forced share); and Northern Ireland has a statutory order similar to the *IPFDA 1975*).

3.10 Any orders made under *IPFDA 1975* may have tax consequences (including IHT implications (*IHTA 1984 s 146*).

3.11 Three recent examples where the courts had to consider domicile in the context of *IPFDA 1975* are *Holliday v Musa* (2010), *Cyganik v Agulian* (2006) and *Morgan v Cilento* (2005) (see paragraphs 3.162 and 3.197).

3.12 Domicile also is important in the area of bankruptcy proceedings. *Section 265* of *IA 1986* provides:

> '265. –(1) A bankruptcy petition shall not be presented to the court under section 264(1)(a) or (b) unless the debtor–
>
> (a) is domiciled in England and Wales ...'

3.13 In a very recent and important case decided by the Court of Appeal, *Barlow Clowes International Ltd v Henwood* (2008), the court specifically had to consider whether an individual (a Mr Peter Henwood) on whom a bankruptcy petition had been served was at that time (ie 19 December 2005) domiciled in England and Wales as required under *IA 1986 s 265*. The Court of Appeal (reversing the High Court) held that he had been so domiciled at the relevant time.

Meaning of the term domicile

3.14 In *Henderson v Henderson* (1965) it was said that:

> 'Domicile is that legal relationship between a person ... and a territory which invokes the system as [his] personal law ...'

3.15 Domicile is normally identified with an individual's permanent home. Lord Cranworth in *Whicker v Hume* (1858) said:

> 'By domicile we mean home, the permanent home.'

3.16 In *Winans v AG* (1904) it was said:

> 'A person may be said to have his home in a country if he resides in it without any intention of at present removing from it permanently or for an indefinite period'.

3.17 However, domicile cannot automatically be equated with home. An individual's domicile status may not in fact be related to the country of location of the individual's permanent home and indeed may be determined to be a country which the individual has never visited and in which no permanent home exists or has ever existed. Thus, an individual's domicile of origin may be such a country (see paragraph 3.33).

3.18 Domicile is not the same as nationality or citizenship. An individual may be a British citizen yet still possess a non-UK domicile. Similarly, the acquisition of British citizenship (ie the acquisition of a British passport) does not automatically result in the acquisition of a UK domicile. In *IRC v Bullock* (1976) it was stated:

> 'Domicile is distinct from citizenship ... and not to acquire UK citizenship would not be inconsistent with ... having acquired a domicile in the UK ...'

In the case of *Al Fayed v Advocate General* (2002) HMRC appears to accept that the acquisition of UK citizenship does not necessarily result in the acquisition of a UK domicile:

> 'The matter was taken further at the end of 1985 when the first petitioner's [Al Fayed] advisers raised the question of his acquiring United Kingdom citizenship. On 23 December 1985 Mr Sargent of PMM [Al Fayed's advisors] telephoned Mr Stribblehill [HMRC] to say that the brothers had it in mind to take out United Kingdom citizenship and that he had advised them that that was unlikely to affect their domicile status. Mr Stribblehill took the matter up with Mrs Winder of the Claims Branch [HMRC]. *She advised him that United Kingdom citizenship would have no effect on the first petitioner's domicile.* Mr Stribblehill then conveyed this advice to Mr Sargent and that particular matter came to an end'.

England and Wales, Scotland and Northern Ireland

3.19 When used in a statute, the term 'United Kingdom' has the meaning provided by the *IA 1978 Sch 1*, namely, Great Britain (ie including England, Scotland and Wales) and Northern Ireland. The term does not include the Republic of Ireland, the Channel Islands or the Isle of Man.

3.20 Domicile is, strictly speaking, linked to a particular system of law which may be that of a country, or it may be that of a subdivision thereof. Thus, while it is common practice to refer to an individual's 'UK domicile' status, strictly speaking, an individual cannot possess such a domicile. In this case the

3.21 *Domicile*

individual's domicile status is that of England and Wales (the same legal system applying to both) or Scotland or Northern Ireland.

3.21 Similarly, it is not possible for an individual to possess, for example, a Canadian, American or Australian domicile (ie a domicile in the federation). In such cases it is necessary to determine in which particular province or state the individual is domiciled (eg Alberta, British Columbia in Canada or California in the USA).

This may give rise to unexpected problems. For example, an individual possessing an English domicile of origin may move to Alberta in Canada, successfully acquiring a domicile of choice in Alberta. The individual, at a later date, decides to leave Alberta for good (ie has no intention of returning there) and moves to British Columbia but is not sure of his future intention at that time (ie he is not sure if he intends to remain indefinitely in British Columbia). The consequence of the move and the lack of clarity of intention is that the individual's English domicile of origin automatically resurrects even though the individual is simply moving from one province in Canada to another. Great care is thus needed when an individual moves from one province/state within a federation to another province/state within the same federation as there is a real risk of a resurrection of the individual's domicile of origin at that time (which may prove extremely problematic for UK tax purposes if that individual has a UK domicile of origin; see paragraph 3.46).

3.22 On the other hand, in the case of most other countries a single system of law applies throughout and an individual may then be said to possess that country's domicile (eg Norway, Sweden and Turkey).

For general legal purposes it is thus necessary to determine whether an individual is English/Welsh, Scottish or Northern Irish domiciled. However, for UK tax purposes this is not strictly necessary because the same tax laws apply to each of these countries (it is thus generally only necessary to identify whether an individual is UK domiciled or non-UK domiciled).

Accordingly, the term 'UK domicile' (and where appropriate, 'non-UK domicile') is adopted throughout this book whether, technically speaking, the actual domicile of the individual is English/Welsh, Scottish or Northern Irish.

Importance of domicile for UK tax purposes

3.23 The concept of domicile has been imported for UK tax purposes and its importance for an individual in the context of tax is that it is the primary determinant of an individual's exposure to IHT and also the determinant as to whether the 'remittance' as opposed to the 'arising' basis of tax applies to the non-UK source income and non-UK source capital gains of the individual (see paragraphs 2.6, 2.10, 10.5 and 10.6).

3.24 It is important to note that the term domicile is being used as it is used in its traditional sense in English law. In other countries the term may mean something different. Thus, it may be that English law determines that an individual is held to be domiciled in a country other than the UK (eg Italy) despite the fact that the laws of Italy (in this example) may treat the individual as domiciled outside of Italy. In other words, an individual's domicile status is determined under the UK's rules in this regard.

Categories of domicile

3.25 There are three primary categories of domicile under common law (although a fourth category, namely, that of 'deemed UK domicile', is created by *IHTA 1984 s 267* which is, however, only of application with respect to IHT; see paragraph 3.231). The three categories are thus:

- domicile of origin;
- domicile of dependence; and
- domicile of choice.

3.26 An individual can never be without a domicile (ie one of the above). Lord Westbury in *Udny v Udny* (1869) stated:

> 'It is a settled principle that no man shall be without a domicile, and to secure this result the law attributes to every individual as soon as he is born [a] domicile … This has been called the domicile of origin, and is involuntary …'

As a consequence, at birth, an individual automatically acquires a domicile of origin.

3.27 The case of *Udny v Udny* (1869) concerns the question of the legitimacy of a child born out of wedlock but whose parents subsequently married. Prior to the *LA 1926*, English law did not know the concept of legitimation, whereas Scottish law did. The case thus turned on the domicile status of Colonel Udny who had fathered a son out of wedlock (but subsequently married the mother). Legitimation of the child required the father to be domiciled in Scotland at both the date of birth and date of marriage. The court decided that Udny had possessed a Scottish domicile at the relevant times and thus the child was legitimated.

3.28 *Domicile*

3.28 At any point in time for any one purpose an individual may possess only one domicile status (*IRC v Bullock* (1976)) although this status may change through life. The change may be due to the operation of law (eg the imposition on a child of a domicile of dependence; see paragraph 3.59) or due to the individual's own choice (ie choosing a different domicile, a domicile of choice; see paragraph 3.74). Where an individual's domicile status changes at any point in time, for whatever reason, the individual's former domicile status is said to be *displaced* by the new domicile status.

3.29 There is, however, a presumption that an existing domicile status of an individual continues until it is proved that a new domicile has been acquired. The burden of proof of a change in domicile lies with the person who asserts it (*Winans v AG* (1904)).

Example 1

John Smith is born with a UK domicile of origin.

When John is 30 years old he decides to emigrate to Indonesia where he ultimately dies at 75 and is buried there.

It is likely that John has acquired an Indonesian domicile of choice subsequent to emigrating from the UK and, if so, this domicile of choice has displaced his original UK domicile of origin.

John therefore dies with a non-UK domicile (ie an Indonesian domicile of choice) for UK tax purposes (*inter alia*, as a consequence, any IHT liability on his estate arises only on UK situs assets; (see paragraph 10.6).

If, in Example 1, HMRC challenges John's change of domicile status (typically after he has died when the extent of any UK IHT liability needs to be ascertained) it is for John (or, strictly speaking, his executors in the event of his death) to prove the change from his UK domicile of origin to his Indonesian domicile of choice.

3.30 The domicile status of an individual may change more than once; for example, an original UK domicile of origin may be displaced by a subsequent domicile of choice which is itself at a later date then displaced with yet another domicile of choice.

3.31 Over the years many cases have come before the courts (a number of which are discussed later in this chapter) which have involved the courts having to rule as to whether or not an individual's domicile status has changed, due to

Domicile of origin

3.32 An individual's domicile is generally equated to the location of his permanent home (basically the place which the individual regards as his main home which usually means the country with which his ties are closest).

3.33 However, with respect to an individual's domicile of origin this is a concept of law and is determined at birth by law and may have no direct connection with the location of a permanent home. Accordingly, an individual's domicile of origin may be that of a country where the individual has never visited, never does visit and in which no permanent home has ever existed (this is one of the reasons that increasingly the use of the concept of domicile as a 'connecting factor' is subject to criticism; basically, it is now an outmoded concept).

3.34 It is vitally important to determine an individual's domicile of origin because even though an individual may subsequently acquire a domicile of choice circumstances at a later date may be such that the individual's domicile of origin resurrects (whether by design or by the operation of law); it is thus important to know precisely the jurisdiction of the domicile of origin which is being resurrected.

Domicile of origin: determination

3.35 The determination of a child's domicile of origin at birth depends upon the following circumstances existing at the date of birth:

- the legitimacy or otherwise of the child;
- the parental marital status;
- whether the father is alive; and
- legtimation.

Each of these is now considered in turn.

Legitimacy

3.36 The domicile of origin of a child is determined at birth by the domicile

3.36 *Domicile*

of the father if the child is legitimate or that of the mother if illegitimate (*Udny v Udny* (1869); *Henderson v Henderson* (1967)). Per Lord Westbury in *Udny v Udny* (1869):

> 'It is a settled principle that no man shall be without a domicile, and to secure this result the law attributes to every individual as soon as he is born the domicile of his father, if the child be legitimate, and the domicile of the mother if illegitimate'.

A child is legitimate if born in lawful wedlock (note that the English law concept of lawful wedlock may differ from that of the laws of other countries). In English law lawful wedlock refers to a marriage valid under English domestic law or the English conflict of laws. Thus, a child whose parents are lawfully married at the date of birth is legitimate; a child conceived before marriage but born thereafter is legitimate; a child conceived before the parent's divorce but born after a valid divorce is legitimate; however, a child conceived whilst a decree of judicial separation is in force is illegitimate.

Example 2

John and Mary Smith are *married*. They are each UK domiciled. Their son, Bob, at birth acquires a domicile of origin which is determined by his father and thus is UK.

Example 3

Henry Brown and Karen Smith are *cohabiting* as if they are a married couple but are not legally married. They are each UK domiciled. Their daughter Barbara at birth acquires a domicile of origin which is determined by her mother and thus is UK.

Example 4

Charles Johnston is *cohabiting* with Helga Schmidt as if they are a married couple but they are not legally married. Charles is UK domiciled and Helga is German domiciled. Their son Adolf at birth acquires a domicile of origin which is determined by his mother and thus is German.

Example 5

Charles Johnston is *married* to Helga Schmidt. Charles is UK domiciled and Helga is German domiciled. Their son Adolf at birth acquires a domicile of origin which is determined by his father and thus is UK (compare Example 4).

3.37 However, the position in Scotland has recently changed following the *FLS 2006*. Under this Act the status of illegitimacy is abolished and thus a child's domicile status is now determined in the same manner irrespective of whether the child is legitimate or not *(FLS s 21)*. In addition, rules are now provided (see *FLS s 22)* to determine the domicile status of a child under 16 (irrespective of whether the child is legitimate or illegitimate).

Parents married but separated

3.38 Where a child is legitimate but the parents are separated but not divorced at the date of birth (ie the child is conceived prior to a separation of the parents; see paragraph 3.36) the child acquires a domicile of *origin* which is that of his *father* but a domicile of *dependence* determined by that of his *mother*.

Father dead

3.39 If a child is legitimate but not born during the father's lifetime (ie the father is dead at the actual date of the child's birth) the child's domicile of origin is determined by the *mother's* domicile at the date of birth.

Legitimation

3.40 Strictly speaking, legitimation does not affect the determination of a child's domicile of origin status at birth. However, it does affect how a child's domicile status may change prior to attaining age 16 (ie legitimation affects a child's domicile of dependency; see paragraph 3.61).

3.41 Legitimation refers to a child acquiring legitimate status (having been born illegitimate) due to the subsequent marriage of the parents to each other *(LA 1976 s 2)*. As indicated in paragraph 3.36, an illegitimate child's domicile of origin is determined by that of the mother at the date of birth. However, on a subsequent legitimation (ie the marriage of the child's natural mother and father to each other) the child's domicile of origin is displaced by that of the father albeit as a domicile of dependency (*Re Spence deceased, Spence v Dennis & Another* (1990)). The child's domicile of origin status remains unchanged but, at the date of legitimation, is displaced (basically, overridden) by that of the father until further subsequent events change it; for example the death of the father before the child attains age 16 causes the child's domicile of dependency to revert to that of the mother.

Example 6

Using the facts of Example 4, Charles Johnston is cohabiting with Helga Schmidt. Charles is UK domiciled and Helga is German domiciled. Their son Adolf at birth acquires a domicile of origin which is determined by his mother (as Adolf is illegitimate) and thus is German.

3.42 *Domicile*

Subsequently, Charles and Helga get married to each other thus legitimating Adolf.

The effect of the legitimation is that Adolf's domicile of origin remains unchanged (ie German) but is now displaced by a domicile of dependence which is that of his father (ie the UK) which remains (assuming Charles does not die before Adolph attains 16) until Adolph attains 16 when his domicile of dependency becomes his domicile of choice (see paragraph 3.64).

3.42 Under the *LA 1976* an illegitimate individual is legitimated where the parents' marriage takes place on or after 1 January 1927 (see *LA 1976* and the *LA 1926* (which introduced the concept of legitimation)) and the father is English domiciled at the date of the marriage; the person's legitimacy is effective from the later of 1 January 1927 and the date of the marriage. Legitimation requires the parents to re-register the person's birth (*LA 1976 s 9*).

Domicile of origin: loss of

3.43 A domicile of origin is fixed for life and cannot be lost by mere abandonment (unlike a domicile of choice; see paragraph 3.218). It needs to be positively displaced. It is very cohesive in nature and its displacement is no easy matter but is certainly possible.

3.44 There are effectively two ways in which a domicile of origin can be displaced; first, if a child is under 16 a change of domicile status of the parent upon whom the child's domicile of dependence depends (typically by acquiring a domicile of choice) causes the child's domicile of origin to be displaced; and second, an individual's (age 16 or over) domicile of origin is displaced where the individual acquires a domicile of choice different from that of the domicile of origin.

Example 7

In Example 6 above Adolf's German domicile of origin is that of his mother's domicile at the date of his birth (as Adolf was illegitimate).

If Adolf's mother and father do not subsequently marry, Adolf's domicile of dependence depends upon the domicile status of his mother and thus changes if and when his mother's domicile status changes.

However, in the event of his subsequent legitimation (ie the marriage of his natural mother and father) his German domicile of origin is displaced by a UK domicile of dependence (namely, that of his father).

3.45 The mere abandonment of a domicile of origin is not possible; to displace it (as indicated in paragraph 3.43) requires the successful acquisition of a domicile of choice (*Somerville v Somerville* (1801)). This follows from the basic tenet that an individual must at all times possess a domicile; an individual's domicile status cannot at any point in time simply 'hang in the air' unknown.

Domicile of origin: resurrection of

3.46 Even where a domicile of choice displaces a domicile of origin (eg if the individual emigrates from the UK acquiring a domicile of choice in a new country) the individual's UK domicile of origin may be resurrected at any time in the future. A resurrection occurs if the individual's new domicile of choice is abandoned without, at the same time, a new domicile of choice being acquired at that time (ie contemporaneously).

Thus, the lack of abandonment of an acquired domicile of choice precludes the domicile of origin resurrecting.

Example 8

Susan Poole possesses a UK domicile of origin. She emigrates to Japan and in so doing acquires a Japanese domicile of choice which displaces her UK domicile of origin.

After 15 years in Japan she moves to Thailand having decided that she no longer wishes to remain permanently in Japan. However, she is not sure at the time of the move to Thailand that she intends to reside there indefinitely; she intends to live there for a period of time before taking any decisions.

Her UK domicile of origin automatically resurrects at the point she leaves Japan as she has abandoned her Japanese domicile of choice.

3.47 In essence, a domicile of origin may thus be displaced but it remains, as it were, in the background in abeyance waiting for resurrection if the facts support such resurrection.

Lord Westbury in *Udny v Udny* (1869) stated:

> 'As the domicile of origin is a creature of law, and independent of the will of the party, it would be inconsistent to suppose ... that it is capable of being by the mere act of the party, entirely obliterated and

3.48 *Domicile*

extinguished. It revives and exists whenever there is no other domicile ...'

3.48 However, in one circumstance only, a domicile of origin can actually be *replaced* and not just *displaced*. In this case the individual's domicile of origin (ie the domicile acquired at birth) is literally no longer deemed to exist having been totally replaced by a replacement domicile of origin status. This occurs where a child is adopted.

Domicile of origin: replacement by adoption

3.49 Adoption extinguishes the parental responsibility of the child's birth parents and vests it in the adopters (*ACA 2002 s 46*). Adoption is the complete legal transference of parental responsibility and makes the child a full legal member of the 'new family'. ACA 2002 came into force on 30 December 2005 replacing *AA 1976*.

3.50 A child must be under 18 to be adopted (*ACA 2002 s 47*).

3.51 An adopted person is treated in law as if the person is the legitimate child of the adopter(s) (ie the adopted child is treated in law as born to the adopter(s) in lawful wedlock; *ACA 2002 s 67*). The consequence of *ACA 2002 s 67* appears to be that an adopted child's 'original' domicile of origin (ie the domicile acquired at birth) is *replaced* by a 'new' replacement domicile of origin.

The adopted child's 'new' domicile of origin is generally accepted as being determined at the time of the child's birth, not at the date of adoption. This suggests that the 'new' domicile of origin is thus determined according to the domicile of the adopting father (as it is assumed that the adopted child is the legitimate child of the adopters) at the date of the child's birth (even if in fact at that time the adopting parents were not in fact married; in essence, a fiction is created).

3.52 The consequence of adoption is thus, *inter alia*, that the child's domicile of origin as originally determined by the child's natural parents (legitimate or not) is overridden by that of the adopting father.

3.53 Adoption is the only occasion when an individual's domicile of origin may literally be *replaced* (not just displaced) by a replacement domicile of origin.

Example 9

Henri Jacques and his wife Marie Jacques, both French domiciled, had a legitimate child François who thus acquires a French domicile of origin from his father. François was born in 2004.

In 2007 Francois is adopted by John and Mary Smith a married couple each UK domiciled.

François' original French domicile of origin is replaced by that which would have arisen if François had been born legitimately to John and Mary.

Assuming therefore François had been born legitimately in 2004 to John and Mary he would at that time have acquired a domicile of origin of his father (ie John), namely, the UK.

François' original French domicile of origin is replaced forever by a UK domicile of origin. It is this UK replacement domicile of origin that is capable of resurrection.

Example 10

Fred Gamble, who is UK domiciled, cohabits with Inga Sweden who is Swedish domiciled. Inga has a child, Jacob, who is illegitimate from a former relationship.

Fred and Inga decide to marry.

At birth Jacob acquires, as a domicile of origin, the domicile of his mother (as he is illegitimate), namely, Swedish.

However, no domicile consequences arise for any of the individuals on Fred and Inga's marriage (including that of Jacob as he is not legitimated on the marriage as Fred is not his natural father).

However, if following the marriage Fred decides to adopt Jacob, Jacob's original domicile of origin (Swedish) is replaced by that of Fred determined at the date of Jacob's birth (it being assumed that Jacob was born legitimately to Fred and Inga).

Jacob's domicile of origin is now that of the UK (ie that of Fred) which replaces forever his original Swedish domicile of origin.

Domicile of dependence

3.54 An individual's domicile of dependence, as the name suggests, is a domicile which is dependent upon, or determined by, the circumstances of someone else (usually that of the father or mother). The domicile of dependence

3.55 *Domicile* of an individual is the same as, and changes with, the domicile of the person on whom the individual is legally dependent.

3.55 A domicile of dependence is imposed.

3.56 The concept is potentially applicable in two circumstances:

- children; and
- married women.

Domicile of dependence: children

3.57 The *DMPA 1973* (which came into force on 1 January 1974) provides that a child can acquire an independent domicile (effectively a domicile of choice) from 16 onwards or, below 16, if validly married. Under English law a marriage is, however, void if one of the parties is under 16 (*MA 1949 s 2*). This part of *DPMA 1973* (namely s 3) only extends to England, Wales and Northern Ireland, not Scotland.

A child under 16 may be validly married under foreign law if each of the individual's governing law of domicile at that time permits it (thus, for example, a non-UK domiciled individual under 16 could possibly validly marry in Las Vegas, USA, an individual who is also non-UK domiciled if their respective laws of domicile permit).

3.58 Before 1 January 1974, at common law, a child ceased to be a dependent person on reaching the age of majority. Pre-1 January 1974 and post-1 January 1970 (when the *FLRA 1969* came into force) the age of majority was 18. Before 1 January 1970 the age of majority was 21.

In Scotland, prior to 25 September 1991, a child was able to acquire a domicile of choice on reaching 12, if a girl, or 14, if a boy (*Arnott v Groom* (1846)). However, *ALCA 1991* provides that the acquisition of a domicile of choice requires the individual to be at least 16 (thus bringing Scotland's age of majority in line with England, Wales and Northern Ireland).

Legitimate

3.59 The domicile of dependence of an unmarried legitimate child under 16 is determined by, and changes with, the domicile of the father during the father's lifetime. On the death of the father the child's domicile of dependence (assuming the child is still under 16) depends upon the mother's domicile.

Illegitimate

3.60 The domicile of dependence of an unmarried illegitimate child under 16 is determined by, and changes with, the domicile of the mother.

Legitimation

3.61 On legitimation (see paragraph 3.40) the domicile of dependence of the child is determined by, and changes with, that of the father at the date of the legitimation.

Parents live apart

3.62 Under common law (ie pre-*DMPA 1973*) the domicile of dependence of a legitimate child was determined by, and changed with, that of the father even though the child following a separation lived with the mother. Under *DMPA 1973 s 4* where a legitimate or legitimated child's parents live apart the child's domicile of dependence is that of the mother if the child has a home with her but not with the father (if the child, however, also has a home with the father the child's domicile of dependence is that of the father). In the event of the mother's death the child retains the dead mother's domicile as a domicile of dependence unless subsequently the child has a home with the father in which case the child's domicile of dependence is that of the father.

3.63 The domicile of a parent (whether that of origin or choice) may change through time. As a consequence, where the child's domicile of dependence is determined by such parent then the child's domicile also changes in line with that of the parent. The child's domicile of origin is thus displaced with the newly acquired domicile of dependence.

Where the child's domicile of origin changes to a domicile of dependency this latter domicile may itself subsequently change to another domicile of dependency should the parent's domicile, on whom the child's domicile depends, itself change.

Example 11

Tom and Susan Smith are married, each possessing a UK domicile of origin, and have a legitimate daughter Jane who possesses a UK domicile of origin.

Tom and Susan decide to emigrate and settle in Spain and in so doing each acquire a Spanish domicile of choice which now displaces their UK domicile of origin.

3.64 *Domicile*

The emigration occurs when Jane is five.

Jane acquires a Spanish domicile of dependence as her father's domicile, on whom Jane's domicile depends, has itself changed to Spanish.

Example 12

Using the facts of Example 11.

Tom and Susan after a number of years in Spain change their minds about residing in Spain indefinitely and decide to leave Spain and settle permanently in Italy, thus each acquiring Italian domiciles of choice.

Jane's Spanish domicile of dependence is now displaced with an Italian domicile of dependence (assuming that the move to Italy and the parents' change in domiciles occurred while Jane is under 16).

Domicile of dependence conversion to domicile of choice

3.64 A child's domicile of dependence remains as such until the child attains 16. The child's domicile of dependence on attaining 16 continues, albeit re-categorised as a domicile of choice (*DMPA 1973*, see also *Gulbenkian v Gulbenkian* (1937) and *Harrison v Harrison* (1953)).

Domicile of dependence: married women

Pre-1 January 1974 marriage

3.65 Prior to 1 January 1974, on marriage, a woman automatically acquired a domicile of dependence under common law which was the domicile of her husband at the date of marriage (*Lord Advocate v Jaffrey* (1921)). This displaces her domicile of origin and her domicile status thereafter changes with that of her husband's irrespective of her own wishes or intentions and irrespective of whether she lived with her husband or not.

3.66 The rule under which a woman *automatically* acquired her husband's domicile on marriage as a domicile of dependence was abolished effective 1 January 1974 by *DMPA 1973*. However, the Act is not retrospective and, thus, for marriages taking place before this date the 'old' rules continue to apply (ie on marriage the woman automatically acquired a domicile of dependence which would continue to be that of her husband post-1 January 1974 subject to an acquisition of a domicile of choice).

3.67   *Section 1* of the *DMPA 1973*, however, provides:

> 'Where immediately before [1 January 1974] a woman was married and then had her husband's domicile by dependence, she is treated as retaining that domicile (as a domicile of choice, if it is not also her domicile of origin) unless and until it is changed by acquisition or revival of another domicile on or after [1 January 1974]'.

Thus for a pre-1 January 1974 married woman, on 1 January 1974 her domicile of dependence is re-categorised as a domicile of choice. On or after this date she is then capable of acquiring a different domicile of choice (or she may cause her domicile of origin to resurrect) by doing whatever the law requires for a new domicile of choice to be acquired, or domicile of origin to be resurrected, whether she remains married or not. In practice, however, where the woman remains married and living with her husband this may prove extremely difficult.

3.68   Interestingly, only one case has come before the courts (post-1 January 1974) concerning the domicile status of a woman who married prior to 1 January 1974. This is the case of *IRC v Duchess of Portland* (1982) in which the Duchess of Portland failed to convince the courts that she had acquired a domicile of choice in Quebec (which in fact was her domicile of origin) after 1 January 1974 following her marriage (pre-1 January 1974) to a UK domiciled male.

Example 13

Christina Athens possesses a Greek domicile of origin.

In May 1970 she marries Herbert Spencer who possesses a UK domicile of origin.

On marriage, Christina acquires her husband's domicile (ie UK) as a domicile of dependence.

On 1 January 1974 her UK domicile of dependence is treated/re-characterised as a UK domicile of choice.

Example 14

Barbara Tree, a UK domiciled individual, marries Fergus O'Leary, a Republic of Ireland domiciled individual, on 30 May 1972.

On marriage Barbara acquires her husband's domicile (ie the Republic of Ireland) as a domicile of dependence.

3.69 *Domicile*

On 1 January 1974 her Republic of Ireland domicile of dependence is treated as a Republic of Ireland domicile of choice.

3.69 The case of *Re Scullard* (1956) concerned a woman who had married a UK-domiciled male in 1893 thus acquiring a UK domicile of dependence. Despite the marriage, she left her husband in 1908, never returned to him but remained married to him. In 1947 she went to live in Guernsey and expressed the intention of spending the rest of her days there.

She died in 1955 six weeks after her husband who died possessing a UK domicile, and between his and her death she had been too ill to evince any intention in respect of her domicile.

As she remained married she was unable in law to acquire a domicile different from that of her husband. The court, however, found that in her lifetime she had clearly expressed her intention to make her permanent home in Guernsey and there was no reason why this would not become effective in law once her husband had died; no overt act on her part was required after her husband's death.

3.70 As all relevant acts in *Re Scullard* were pre-1 January 1974 the *DMPA 1973* provisions were not in point. Had the marriage taken place pre-1 January 1974, but all other events had occurred post-31 December 1973 the same conclusion would no doubt be reached. The provisions of *DMPA 1973* permit a married woman to acquire a domicile independent of her husband after marriage (or retain her pre-marriage domicile) and, as a consequence, where the wife separates from the husband, as in *Re Scullard*, she is able to establish a different domicile from that of her husband if she satisfies the normal tests.

Exception to automatic domicile of dependence on marriage

3.71 Interestingly, there is, however, one exception to the automatic domicile of dependence arising on a pre-1 January 1974 marriage, namely, in the case of a female USA citizen. This exception does not arise under common law. It is specifically provided for in the terms of the bilateral double taxation agreement between the UK and the USA (*SI 2002/2848*; not the convention dealing with IHT but that dealing with income tax and CGT). Thus, Article 4(6) of the UK/US double taxation agreement on income tax and CGT provides:

'A marriage before 1st January 1974 between a woman who is a USA national and a man domiciled within the UK shall be deemed to have taken place on 1st January 1974 for the purpose of determining her domicile on or after 6th April 1976 for UK tax [*ie income tax and capital gains tax; not inheritance tax*] purposes'.

3.72 Thus, a female US citizen marrying a UK domiciled male before 1 January 1974 is *not* treated as automatically acquiring her husband's domicile (ie the UK) as a domicile of dependence. Her domicile status is determined under the normal rules. This position, however, applies only for UK income tax and CGT purposes (it does not apply for UK IHT purposes in which case the above domicile of dependence remains in point). This provision is unique amongst the UK's double tax agreements.

Example 15

Joan Texas, a US female citizen, marries Peter Joseph, a UK domiciled individual, prior to 1 January 1974.

In determining Joan's liabilities to UK income tax or CGT her domicile status will be determined on normal principles. She is thus not treated as having automatically acquired a UK domicile of dependence on her marriage to Peter.

Other things being equal, it is likely that she will retain her US domicile of origin and so be liable to UK income tax and CGT only on UK source income and UK source gains; non-UK situs income and non-UK source gains only falling to be taxed in the UK if remitted to the UK (see paragraph 2.10).

However, for IHT purposes she is deemed to have acquired a UK domicile of dependence on marriage (becoming re-characterised as a UK domicile of choice on 1 January 1974) and thus, in principle, is liable to UK IHT on her worldwide assets (the impact of the provisions of the UK/US double tax treaty on IHT (*SI 1979/1454*) may, however, affect in part her exposure to UK IHT in view of her continued US citizenship).

Post-31 December 1973 marriage

3.73 For marriages which take place on or after 1 January 1974, the woman's domicile is determined under the normal rules and no domicile of dependence is automatically assigned to her on marriage.

Thus a marriage on or after 1 January 1974 has, per se, no impact on the woman's domicile status at the time of marriage. However, if she lives with her husband in the country of his domicile (whether choice or origin) which will typically be the case, over time she may well acquire a domicile of choice which is the domicile of her husband at the time her domicile so changes.

3.74 *Domicile*

Domicile of choice

3.74 The acquisition of a domicile of choice is no easy matter. An individual's domicile of origin is extremely adhesive and can also automatically resurrect from time to time (see paragraph 3.46). Where a domicile of origin resurrects it does so at a particular point in time.

3.75 Similarly the acquisition of a domicile of choice occurs at a particular point in time but it is by no means easy to identify the precise moment at which an individual's domicile of origin changes to a domicile of choice as Mr Justice Lewison in *Gaines-Cooper v RCC* (2007) commented:

> '... It follows, therefore, that there will ... be a particular moment in time at which his [ie Mr Gaines-Cooper's] domicile changes if he acquires a domicile of choice which replaces his domicile of origin. Before that moment, his domicile will have been his domicile of origin. After that moment it will be his domicile of choice. Locating the moment may be a difficult question of fact'.

To ascertain this point requires a detailed consideration of all the relevant facts which in many cases will be substantial and will extend over many many years. An examination of the numerous cases on changes of domicile status shows that different courts arrive at different conclusions albeit on the exact same set of facts with often conflicting analyses to support their conclusions. Examples include the classic case of *Winans v AG* (1904) and, more recently, *Agulian v Cyganik* (2006) and *Barlow Clowes International Ltd (In liquidation) v Henwood* (2008).

3.76 An attempt appears to have been made to explain why such apparent contradictory conclusions and analyses arise by Scarman J in *Re Fuld's Estate (No 3)* (1968):

> '... that the difficulty of reconciling the numerous statements arises not from a lack of judicial thought, but from the nature of the subject. The cases involve a detailed examination of the facts and it is not surprising that different judicial minds concerned with different factual situations have chosen different language to describe the law'.

3.77 In determining whether a new domicile of choice has been acquired the courts have commented and/or found, *inter alia*, as follows:

- a special motive for residing in a country (father's dying wishes) does not preclude domicile of choice arising (*Somerville v Somerville* (1801));

Domicile **3.78**

- actual residence *and* an intention to reside in the new country must be present although the length of actual residence, per se, is not important (*Bell v Kennedy* (1868));
- proof of a change of domicile is 'on a balance of probabilities' basis (as opposed to a 'beyond all reasonable doubt' basis) (*Re Fuld's Estate (No 3)* (1968));
- acquisition of nationality and a passport in a new country is not conclusive evidence of the acquisition of a new domicile of choice in that country. Conversely, acquisition of British citizenship which includes the need to sign a declaration that the individual intends to reside in the UK does not, per se, mean that a UK domicile of choice arises (*Wahl v IRC* (1932); *Fayed v AG* (2002)); and
- registering on the electoral roll as an overseas elector is also ignored in determining UK domicile status (formerly IR20 now HMRC6; see para 4.2, page 22).

3.78 Some of the factors which have been considered in deciding whether changes of domicile have occurred include:

- membership of clubs;
- churches attended;
- naturalisation;
- lifestyle;
- wife and/or children accompaniment;
- burial arrangements;
- health;
- wills;
- bank accounts;
- statements made in autobiographies;
- statements made orally to relations and third parties;
- relationships with the local vicar;
- location of dwellings;
- length of time in country;
- business interests; and
- allocation of time.

3.79 Domicile

3.79 The requirement that all aspects of an individual's life needs to be considered when seeking to ascertain whether his domicile status has changed was addressed in the case of *Casdagli v Casdagli* (1919) as follows:

> 'Nothing must be neglected that can possibly indicate the bent of the resident's mind ... His aspirations, whims, amours, prejudices, health, religion, financial expectation – all are taken into account'.

Accordingly, it appears that no issue, however trivial, is to be ignored although inevitably the importance to be attached to the various different factors is likely to vary according to the particular circumstances under consideration.

Misleading nature of the word 'choice'

3.80 Arguably, the term 'choice' in the phrase 'domicile of choice' is perhaps a little misleading. In two situations domiciles of choice are provided by law and do not arise as a consequence of any choice made by the individual.

3.81 First, the law specifically provides for a domicile of choice to take effect on a child attaining 16 where the child's domicile of origin has been displaced by a domicile of dependence; similarly, the law also provides for a domicile of choice of a married woman to take effect on 1 January 1974 displacing her domicile of dependence on her husband arising on a pre-1 January 1974 marriage.

3.82 Second, a UK domicile of choice, may inadvertently be acquired by law. This situation might arise where the individual resides in the UK and where, on the facts, the courts conclude that it is the individual's intention to reside there permanently or indefinitely. This the court may conclude on the factual evidence before it even if the individual has not explicitly stated this is the case or where the individual challenges this assertion.

Thus, in *Douglas v Douglas* (1871) it was stated:

> 'If the [requisite] intention exists and if it is sufficiently carried into effect certain legal consequences follow from it, whether such consequences are intended or not and perhaps even though the person in question may have intended the exact opposite'.

This was, in fact, also the situation in *Re Steer (1858)* where Mr Steer was held to have died domiciled (a domicile of choice) in Germany despite an explicit declaration in his will that he had no intention of renouncing his English domicile of origin.

3.83 There are, of course, two significant reasons why HMRC may want to argue that an individual who possesses a non-UK domicile of origin has in fact acquired a UK domicile of choice (see *Re Steer* mentioned in paragraph 3.82), namely:

- the individual owns significant non-UK situs assets (in which case IHT is leviable thereon only if he is UK domiciled; see paragraphs 10.5 and 10.6); and/or
- the individual has significant non-UK source income and/or non-UK source capital gains (in which case income tax and CGT is leviable thereon on the 'arising' rather than the 'remittance' basis only if he is UK domiciled; see paragraphs 2.6 and 2.10)).

3.84 Nevertheless, a domicile of *choice* (as the name suggests) may be acquired *voluntarily* by an individual by personal choice. It is perfectly possible for an individual to explicitly acquire a domicile of choice (see paragraph 3.87) different from that individual's domicile of origin or indeed different from an already acquired domicile of choice. The newly acquired domicile of choice then displaces either the domicile of origin or the earlier acquired domicile of choice.

A domicile of choice arises if an individual effectively makes a permanent home in a country different from the country of his domicile of origin. For example, such individual may emigrate from the UK (the domicile of origin) to Canada thus acquiring a domicile of choice in Canada which displaces the individual's UK domicile of origin (technically, the domicile of choice needs to be within one of the Canadian Provinces not Canada, *per se*; see paragraphs 3.20 and 3.21). Such individual might then subsequently abandon his acquired Canadian domicile of choice and immediately acquire, for example, a domicile of choice in Sweden.

Domicile of choice: requirements

3.85 HMRC6 'Residence, domicile & the remittance basis' (see paragraph 4.4) provides in paragraph 4.3.2 page 23:

'You have a legal capacity to acquire a new domicile at the age of 16. Broadly, to acquire a domicile of choice you must leave your current country of domicile and settle in another country. You need to provide strong evidence that you intend to live there permanently or indefinitely. The following factors will be relevant, though this list is not exhaustive:

- your intentions;
- your permanent residence;

3.86 *Domicile*

- your business interests;
- your social and family interests;
- your ownership of property; and
- the form of any will you have made.'

This is almost a repeat of the same statement made originally in HMRC6's predecessor IR20 which provides:

> 'You have the capacity to acquire a new domicile (a domicile of choice) when you reach age 16. To do so, you must broadly leave your country of domicile and settle in another country. You need to provide strong evidence that you intend to live there permanently or indefinitely. Living in another country for a long time, although an important factor, is not enough in itself to prove you have acquired a new domicile.'

3.86 Lord Chelmsford in *Bell v Kennedy* (1868) stated:

> 'A new domicile is not acquired until there is not only a fixed intention of establishing a permanent residence in a new country, but until also this intention has been carried out by actual residence there.'

3.87 Thus, the acquisition of a domicile of choice requires positive action to be taken by the individual and he must satisfy the following three conditions:

- the individual is 16 or over;
- the individual must actually take up residence in another country; and
- the individual must have the fixed intention of residing permanently (or indefinitely) in the new country of residence.

Domicile of choice: age requirement

3.88 To acquire a domicile of choice an individual (whether of England and Wales, Northern Ireland or Scotland) must be 16 or over. However, prior to the introduction of *ALCA 1991* (*s* 7 of which introduced the minimum age of 16 requirement, effective 25 September 1991) a child (in Scotland) was able to acquire a domicile of choice at the end of pupillarity: 14 for a boy and 12 for a girl; see paragraph 3.58).

Domicile of choice: actual residence and intention

3.89 Satisfaction of one of the two legs is insufficient; actual residence *without* intention of permanent residency *or* intention of permanent residency *without* actual residence does not result in the acquisition of a domicile of choice. It does not matter which of the two aspects occurs first. An individual may thus form an intention to reside in a country followed by actual residence there or, alternatively, the individual may acquire actual residency with the requisite intention to reside there indefinitely arising thereafter.

Example 16

Michael Furlow possesses a UK domicile of origin.

He emigrates to Italy in 2005, age 25, where he has since resided. In 2010 he states that he has taken the conscious decision to continue to reside there indefinitely.

Michael has acquired an Italian domicile of choice in 2010 which displaces his UK domicile of origin.

Example 17

Tom Furlow, Michael's brother (see Example 16), also possesses a UK domicile of origin and also left the UK to live in Italy at the same time.

However, unlike his brother Michael, Tom isn't sure whether he wants to remain in Italy indefinitely.

Tom's UK domicile of origin continues to subsist and he, unlike his brother, has not acquired an Italian domicile of choice.

However, if in due course Tom does decide to remain in Italy indefinitely then at that point in time he acquires an Italian domicile of choice.

3.90 The issue of an individual's 'intention' is perhaps one of the most difficult and contentious areas of domicile. It is often made even more difficult by the fact that the death of an individual may be the trigger for a domicile determination to be made at which time, of course, the individual is no longer around to contribute to any determination.

3.91 *Domicile*

3.91 Perhaps a classic example which illustrates the difficulty of determining an individual's intention is illustrated by the different conclusions reached in the various courts which heard the case of *Winans v AG* (1904) just over a century ago.

The case concerned an eccentric American millionaire who was born in the USA in 1823 and lived there until 1850. He then moved to Russia, thereafter spending time in both Russia and the UK (in particular to avoid the Russian winters; Winans was paranoid about his health) between 1860 and 1893. From 1893 until his death four years later in 1897 he lived entirely in England. After leaving the USA he never returned.

He dreamed of one day returning to the USA and of building a fleet of cigar-shaped ships which he said would allow the USA to gain superiority over the British fleets. The ships were to be docked in Maryland, USA.

The case was heard in the UK by all three courts, namely, the High Court, the Court of Appeal and was finally decided by the House of Lords.

The House of Lords decided by a majority of two to one in favour of Winans, that he had retained his domicile of origin (which was either New Jersey or Maryland in the USA) and had not acquired a UK domicile of choice.

On the other hand, the High Court and Court of Appeal, comprising in total five judges, had unanimously found against Winans stating that he had acquired a UK domicile of choice.

Conflicting statements made in the House of Lords by each of the Lords included the following:

> 'When he came to this country [UK], he was a sojourner and a stranger, and he was I think a sojourner and a stranger in it [UK] when he died' (per Lord Macnaghten)

> 'He had one and only one home, and that was in this country [UK]' (per Lord Lindley)

The third Lord, Lord Halsbury, was simply unable to make up his mind and thus the presumption of continuance applied (ie no change in Winans' domicile status had been clearly shown to have occurred).

3.92 This case admirably illustrates the difficulties in domicile determinations and, in particular, the difficulties associated with ascertaining an individual's intentions in this regard.

Residence

Meaning

3.93 The term 'residence' when used in the context of domicile is not the same as when the term is used for general UK taxation purposes (see Chapter 4). For the purposes of the law of domicile the term *residence* in a country refers to:

> 'physical presence in that country as an inhabitant of it. In this regard, residence must be more than casual residence or residence as a visitor however often and however extensive those visits may be' (per Nourse J in *IRC v Duchess of Portland* (1982)).

3.94 It is possible for an individual to reside in more than one country at the same time. Nourse J in *Duchess of Portland* stated:

> '... a case where the domiciliary divides his physical presence between two countries at the same time ... it is necessary to look at all the facts in order to decide which of the two countries is the one he inhabits'.

Duration of residence

3.95 Length of residence in a particular country may be indicative of the acquisition of a domicile of choice therein but, per se, is not conclusive. IR20 states:

> 'Living in another country for a long time, although an important factor, is not enough in itself to prove you have acquired a new domicile'.

Whilst this statement continues to be correct it is not, for some reason, repeated in the comparable paragraph 4.3.2 page 23 of HMRC6 (see paragraph 3.85).

3.96 In *Ramsay v Liverpool Royal Infirmary* (1930) it was stated:

> '... mere length of residence by itself is insufficient evidence from which to infer the animus [intention]; but the quality of the residence may afford the necessary inference'.

Ramsay v Liverpool Royal Infirmary (1930) concerned a Mr George Bowie who was born in 1845 in Glasgow, with a Scottish domicile of origin, and who died in 1927 in England and was buried in England. The issue at stake was the validity of his will which would have been valid if he had died in Scotland, but invalid if he had died in England. In 1882, aged 37, he gave up working for a

3.97 *Domicile*

living and for the rest of his life lived off his mother, sisters and brothers. In 1892 he moved to Liverpool, again living with his family and after this time left England only twice, never returning to Scotland. He expressed to others that he never intended to return to Scotland (and stating his desire to be buried in Liverpool). His mother died while he was alive but he refused to attend her funeral which was held in Scotland. His will provided for the residue of his estate to be left equally between three Glasgow- and one Liverpool-based charities. The House of Lords on appeal from the decision of two lower Scottish courts held (confirming the earlier decisions) that he had died domiciled in Scotland.

3.97 Residence, for the purposes of the law of domicile, may only need to be for a few days or even for part of a day. Thus, an immigrant may acquire a domicile of choice immediately upon arrival in the country in which the immigrant intends to permanently settle. Ownership or the renting of a house/flat is not necessary for residence to arise; for example, a room in a hotel or a friend's house (*Stone v Stone* (1958)) is sufficient. Length of residence in effect is, per se, irrelevant. What is important is that residence must be residence in the pursuance of an intention to settle permanently or indefinitely. Thus, in *Bell v Kennedy (1868)* Lord Chelmsford stated:

> 'If the intention of permanently residing in a place exists then residence in pursuance of that intention, *however short*, will establish a domicile'.

3.98 *Bell v Kennedy* (1968) concerned a determination of the domicile status of Mr Bell whose wife had died and at the time of her death possessed a domicile of dependency upon him; thus a determination of her domicile status could be determined only once that of Mr Bell had been determined.

Mr Bell had a Jamaican domicile of origin having been born in Jamaica of Scottish parents. He had been educated in Scotland but then returned to Jamaica. He left Jamaica for good in 1837 arriving in Scotland with his wife to look for an estate to buy and to then settle in Scotland. While in Scotland he resided with his mother-in-law. In the event, for various reasons (including the weather), Mr Bell could not decide whether he wanted to settle in Scotland, England or the south of France. At this point in 1838 his wife died. The court held that:

> 'The question is, had he any settled fixed intention of being permanently resident in Scotland on 28th September 1938 [date of wife's death] … he was resident in Scotland [at the date of his wife's death], but without the *animus manendi* [the intention to remain], and therefore he still retained his [Jamaican] domicile of origin'.

The court so held despite very clear evidence that he was determined never to return to Jamaica. Nourse J. in *Re Clore (No 2)* (1982) in a similar vein stated:

'... if the evidence of intention is there, particularly where the motive is the avoidance of taxes, the necessary intention will not be held to be missing merely because the period of actual residence is a short one'.

3.99 The adequacy of even a very short period of residency to acquire a domicile of choice if intention of permanent residency is present is ably demonstrated in the American case of *White v Tennant* (1888) where it was held that residence in the new domicile (the State of Pennsylvania) of one afternoon (ie literally a few hours) was sufficient for Mr White to have acquired a new domicile of choice in the State of Pennsylvania.

Mr White had previously possessed a domicile of origin in West Virginia and had returned there after one afternoon at the new house in Pennsylvania, as Mrs White, due to the poor condition of the house, had refused to spend a night there until its state had been improved. Mr White died before he could return to Pennsylvania. The court (the Supreme Court of Appeals, West Virginia) held:

'He [Mr White] had taken the decision to move to Pennsylvania; arrived in Pennsylvania in order to become an inhabitant of it; and had the intention of residing there indefinitely. Mr White had simply returned to West Virginia on a temporary basis, with no intention of moving back their again permanently. This was sufficient to satisfy the requirements.'

Illegal residence

3.100 Until recently, an illegal presence in a country was perceived as precluding the possibility of the acquisition of a domicile of choice in that country (*Puttick v A-G* (1980)). However, it is now accepted that a domicile of choice may be acquired even if the individual is resident in a country illegally.

In *Mark v Mark* (2005) (a matrimonial case involving the jurisdiction of the court to entertain a divorce petition within *DMPA 1973 s 5*) the House of Lords decided that the legality of a wife's presence in the UK (illegal presence in the UK was a criminal offence under the *Immigration Act 1971*) was irrelevant to a determination of her domicile of choice (overriding *Puttick v A-G* (1980)).

3.101 Nevertheless, the illegality may (perhaps not surprisingly) cast doubt on the individual's intention to remain in the country indefinitely.

Dual residence

3.102 It seems unclear from the decided cases precisely what is meant by 'dual residence'. The term 'residence' when used in the context of domicile refers to physical presence as an inhabitant thereof (see paragraph 3.93). Thus,

3.103 *Domicile*

if an individual is dual resident this suggests that the individual is in fact an inhabitant of two countries.

3.103 The case of *IRC v Duchess of Portland* (1982) is often cited as involving dual residence. In Lewison J's judgment in *Gaines-Cooper v Revenue and Customs Commissioners* (2007) referring to Nourse J's judgment in *IRC v Duchess of Portland* he said:

> '... gives guidance [ie Nourse J's judgment] where a person is physically present in two countries as an inhabitant of both. ...'

However, Nourse J goes on to state:

> '... divides his physical presence between two countries at a time. In that kind of case it is necessary to look at all the facts in order to decide which of the two countries is the one he inhabits.'

However, Lewison J also continues:

> 'Thus, *Duchess of Portland* indicates that a person can be resident in two countries at the same time in which case, in deciding where he is resident for the purposes of the law of domicile, it is necessary to look at all the facts in order to decide which of the two countries is the one he inhabits.'

3.104 The comments of Lewison J seem to suggest that the individual concerned (ie the Duchess of Portland) was resident in two countries which suggests she is an inhabitant of both (by definition of the term 'residence') yet he then states it is as a consequence necessary to 'decide which of the two countries is the one she inhabits'.

3.105 There appears to be no outright suggestion that an individual cannot in fact be an inhabitant of more than one country although the requirements of being an inhabitant (ie more than being casually present) may in many cases mean that this is not readily achievable.

3.106 Nevertheless, the cases do appear to use the terms 'residence' and 'inhabitant' somewhat interchangeably.

3.107 In the earlier case of *IRC v Bullock* (1976) different terminology was used when discussing 'dual-residence'. Buckley LJ noted:

> 'A man may have homes in more than one country at one time. In such a case, for the purposes of determining his domicile, a further enquiry may have to be made to decide which, if any, should be regarded as his *principal home*.'

Similarly, in *Plummer v IRC (1987)* Hoffmann J stated that in cases of dual or multiple residence (as was the situation in *Plummer*) guidance can usefully be obtained from the comments of Lord Westbury in *Udny v Udny* (1869):

> 'Domicile of choice is a conclusion or inference which the law derives from the fact of a man fixing voluntarily his sole or *chief residence* in a particular place, with an intention of continuing to reside there for an unlimited time.'

Continuing, Hoffmann J stated:

> '... loss of a domicile of origin or choice is not inconsistent with retention of a place of residence in that country if the chief residence has been established elsewhere'.

3.108 The terms 'chief residence', 'principal home' and 'place of residence' are used without reference to the term 'inhabitant'. Indeed, Hoffmann J in *Plummer v IRC* criticised the test formulated in *Duchess of Portland* and commented:

> '... while I find the contrast between an inhabitant and a person casually present useful to describe the minimum quality of residence which must be taken up in a new country before domicile there can be acquired, the concept of being an inhabitant seems to me less illuminating in cases of dual or multiple residence such as the present'.

Hoffmann J continued:

> '... The commissioners ... asked themselves whether the taxpayer had made her grandmother's house in Guernsey 'her chief place of residence'. They regarded this question, in my judgment rightly, as being the same as whether 'in the sense in which the term is used in this context the taxpayer had become an inhabitant of Guernsey'.'

3.109 A determination as to which of an individual's residences takes precedence (ie which is the individual's chief residence) leads to satisfaction of the requirement of actual residence in that country for domicile purposes; nevertheless, intention to reside there permanently/indefinitely also needs to be demonstrated before a domicile of choice in that country can be said to have occurred (ie identifying an individual's chief residence is of itself insufficient to establish the acquisition of a domicile of choice in that country).

3.110 Unfortunately, neither of the phrases 'principal home' or 'chief residence' used in the above cases were explained or discussed. However, in the

3.111 *Domicile*

recent case of *Gaines-Cooper v RCC* (2006) the Commissioners, commenting upon these two phrases, stated:

> '... but a country which is of most importance to an individual, or the centre of his interest, is likely to be the place of his *chief or principal residence*'.

3.111 The case of *Gaines-Cooper v RCC* (2006) considers specifically the issue of dual residence.

Mr Gaines-Cooper, currently aged 69, possessed an English domicile of origin but had tried to argue that for the period 1992–1993 to 2003–2004 he had in fact acquired a domicile of choice in the Seychelles. The Commissioners disagreed holding that he had never abandoned his domicile of origin and thus remained for this period English domiciled (ie a Seychelles domicile of choice had never been acquired).

This decision was subsequently confirmed by the High Court in 2007. Mr Gaines-Cooper then applied for a judicial review which was initially refused by the Administrative Court, but was then granted by the Court of Appeal in mid-2009. The purpose of the judicial review is to examine whether HMRC was right to disapply its longstanding guidance (contained in IR20).

Prima facie, Mr Gaines-Cooper appeared to do 'all the right things'. He bought a house in the Seychelles; he expressed the wish that his ashes be scattered there; he married a Seychellois woman; and in his wills he stated that he lived there and his domicile status was that of the Seychelles.

Unfortunately, this, according to the Commissioners, was not enough to have resulted in a domicile of choice in the Seychelles having been acquired.

The strong connections which Mr Gaines-Cooper retained with the UK were perceived by the Commissioners as continuing and arguably fatal to his claim of the acquisition of a domicile of choice in the Seychelles. In particular, and of decisive impact was the acquisition and retention of significant properties in the UK in which he and his family lived, albeit that for certain periods the properties were rented out to third parties. In this regard the Commissioners said that:

> 'We regard as significant the fact that nearly all of the Appellant's connections with the UK were located in a comparatively small area of the contiguous counties of Berkshire and Oxfordshire ... born there ... went to school ... mother lived there ... married twice ... purchased two houses ... business offices ... attended Royal Ascot ... son went to school ... We also regard the 1999 will ... to be of significance. It was prepared by English solicitors; it is to be construed and take effect according to English law; and the ...

guardians of [the son] live in the UK ... retained his British citizenship and did not apply for citizenship in the Seychelles ...'

Mr Gaines-Cooper was resident (for the law of domicile purposes) in two places, namely, the UK and the Seychelles, and as a consequence it was necessary for the Commissioners to determine which of these two residences was in fact Mr Gaines-Cooper's chief or principal residence.

The Commissioners not only felt that Mr Gaines-Cooper's chief residence remained that of the UK and not the Seychelles but also were of the view that he lacked the 'intention' to reside in the Seychelles indefinitely. He thus failed to satisfy either of the two legs of the test used to ascertain whether a domicile of choice has been acquired.

3.112 The case of *IRC v Duchess of Portland* (1982) involved the issue, post-1 January 1974, of a pre-1 January 1974 marriage and a degree of dual residence. The court held that the Duchess of Portland, at the time of her death, had not lost her domicile of dependence acquired automatically on her marriage (pre-1 January 1974) to the Duke (her non-UK domicile of origin having been displaced). The Duchess had been dually resident in the UK and Canada.

Pre-1 January 1974 (ie in 1948), a lady with a domicile of origin in Quebec married the Duke of Portland (thus becoming the Duchess of Portland) who possessed a UK domicile of origin. The Duchess visited Quebec regularly; maintained a home there; stated that she intended to return there if her husband should pre-decease her and he had agreed to retire to Quebec. The Duchess argued that she had acquired a domicile of choice in Quebec during the summer of 1974, whereas HMRC argued that she had a UK domicile of choice.

The court held that she was UK domiciled. It stated that this domicile could only be abandoned by her ceasing to reside in the UK *and* also by intending to cease to reside there. The Duchess had not in fact ceased to reside in the UK and had been a visitor to Quebec *but had not become an inhabitant thereof.*

More specifically, Nourse J said:

'Her physical presence in Quebec has been for periods of limited duration ... to which [ie Quebec] it is her intention to ultimately return. That is not enough to have made her an inhabitant of Quebec'.

3.113 On marriage, the Duchess had acquired a UK domicile of dependence on her husband which, on 1 January 1974, was treated (under *DMPA 1973*) as a UK domicile of choice. Had she married the Duke *after* this date she would not have automatically acquired his domicile as a domicile of dependence. On marriage, *prima facie*, her domicile of origin in Quebec would have continued

3.114 *Domicile*

to subsist. As she always intended to return to Quebec then it is highly likely she would not have acquired a UK domicile of choice, remaining domiciled in Quebec throughout. This seems to suggest that, other things being equal, a woman married pre-January 1974 is treated less favourably than a woman married on or after this date.

Intention

Evidentiary issue

3.114 The establishment of a non-UK domicile of choice by an individual, originally possessing a UK domicile of origin or an earlier acquired domicile of choice, to the satisfaction of the courts (or HMRC) is basically an evidentiary issue.

3.115 Thus, the primary need is to be able to prove that not only has a residence in a foreign country been established as the sole (or principal/chief residence if more than one residence is maintained) residence but also that a clear intention to reside there indefinitely or permanently subsists.

3.116 It seems clear from a number of the decided cases (eg *Re Clore* (1984)) that statements an individual may make in lifetime, whether in writing (eg in an autobiography or memoir) and/or verbally to close friends and others, can often be crucial in the determination of domicile. This may be perhaps because the courts view such utterances as representing the 'real' truth and intentions of the individual. Not surprisingly the courts are perhaps sometimes a little sceptical of statements of intent made in 'official' communications to various authorities (eg HMRC in particular on Forms DOM1, P85 and P86; see Chapters 4 and 5) or by way of explicit statements of declaration, whether statutory or otherwise.

Hearsay evidence

3.117 An individual may, of course, testify as to his intentions (as did Mr Gaines-Cooper in the *Gaines-Cooper* case) but as is evident from a number of the cases discussed above and below, domicile determinations are quite often made after the individual has died, at which time, of course, the individual concerned cannot speak for himself.

3.118 Hearsay is defined in *CEA 1995 s 1* for civil proceedings as:

'a statement made otherwise than by a person while giving oral evidence in the proceedings which is tendered as evidence of the matters stated'.

At common law hearsay is defined as:

'an assertion other than one made by a person while giving oral evidence in the proceedings ... as evidence of any fact asserted'.

3.119 Hearsay evidence was in the past generally inadmissible but now in civil proceedings this is no longer the case; thus, declarations of intention by an individual to others made out of court may be given in evidence (*Bryce v Bryce* (1933)).

3.120 The *1995 Act* obliges a judge to take into account:

'any circumstances from which any inference can reasonably be drawn as to the reliability or otherwise of the evidence when estimating the weight (if any) to be attached to an item of hearsay evidence'.

Thus, *inter alia*, no doubt any judge would form a view as to the reliability of a witness and consequently the reliability of his/her hearsay evidence. An example, albeit not concerned with either taxation or domicile, is the case of *Brownsville Holdings v Adamjee Insurance* (2002). The case concerned the loss of a yacht.

A witness, called by the insurers, confirmed that the owner of the lost yacht had made an informal admission to the witness that he (the owner) had ordered the yacht to be scuttled so as to be able to recover the insurance proceeds. The court gave no weight to this testimony on account of the witness's evident motive not to tell the truth, her unreliability in other respects and the inherent probability that the owner of the yacht would have confessed to her in the circumstances existing at the time.

3.121 In the *Gaines-Cooper* case Mr Gaines-Cooper testified on his own behalf. Oral evidence was also given by various other individuals. With respect to Mr Gaines-Cooper's testimony the Commissioners commented as follows:

'Before finding the facts we comment on the evidence of [Gaines-Cooper] ... gave evidence for four and a half days of the ten day hearing. *As many of our findings depend upon his oral evidence* we have to say how we found him as a witness ... did his best to be truthful and honest but ... he made mistakes ... we looked for corroborating evidence ... but much of his oral evidence was digressive and discursive and unsupported by any documents. Some of the evidence related to events as far back as 1971 which is now thirty five years ago. [Gaines-Cooper] had an impressive memory but was not always certain about dates ...

... [Gaines-Cooper] ... sometimes appeared [confused] ... full supporting documentation was not produced ... we are not confident that all the dates and names given in oral evidence were accurate ...

3.122 *Domicile*

> ... For these reasons we approach the oral evidence of [Gaines-Cooper] with some caution. We bear in mind that the burden of proof in these appeals is on [Gaines-Cooper]'.

3.122 With respect to the oral evidence of a number of the third-party witnesses the Commissioners commented:

> '... we bear in mind that the witnesses admitted that they knew very little of the Appellant's life outside the Seychelles ... We regard the evidence of these witnesses, therefore, as of relevance to the Appellant's attachment to the Seychelles rather than establishing the place of his principal attachment'.

3.123 In the High Court, on appeal, Mr Justice Lewison commented:

> 'Clearly they [the Commissioners] did not accept his [Gaines-Cooper's] evidence ... In my judgment the Special Commissioners' evaluation of Mr Gaines-Cooper as a witness demonstrates no error of law.'

3.124 In *Re Clore* (1984) (see paragraph 3.173), however, it is patently clear that the judge in arriving at his decision placed great weight on the hearsay evidence of Clore's friends and family which, it would seem, outweighed the other factors considered in the case.

Declaration of intention

3.125 Declarations of intention may be made in writing and/or in testimony by the individual concerned and/or verbally to a third party who may testify in court under the hearsay rule exception.

3.126 When in the form of writing such declarations, typically, are either 'free-standing' documents or more likely are included as part of an individual's will.

3.127 In determining an individual's domicile status, in *Drevon v Drevon* (1864) Kindersley V-C stated:

> 'There is no act, no circumstances in a man's life, however, trivial it may be in itself, which ought to be left out of consideration in trying the question whether there was an intention to change domicile. A trivial act might possibly be of more weight with regard to determining this question than an act which was of more importance to a man in his lifetime'.

In *Casdagli v Casdagli* (1919) Lord Atkinson, referring to the case of *Winans v AG* (1904) said:

'... the tastes, habits, conduct, actions, ambitions, health, hopes, and projects of Mr Winans deceased were all considered as keys to his intention to make a home in England'.

3.128 Nevertheless, despite statements such as these the issue of 'declarations of intent' has been in virtually all decided cases at best noted and at worst completely ignored.

3.129 All forms of declarations of intention whether made informally (albeit in writing) or by way of a statutory declaration (ie a written statement of facts which the person making it (the declarant) signs and solemnly declares to be true before a commissioner for oaths; *SDA 1835*) or in testimony whether by the individual concerned or a third party have, perhaps, not surprisingly been viewed by the courts with extreme suspicion.

3.130 The courts have indicated that declarations of intention which specifically refer to the word 'domicile' are unlikely to be of any real value as the individual making the declaration is generally unlikely to fully appreciate or understand the significance or meaning of the word. Thus, Romer LJ in *AG v Yule and Mercantile Bank of India* (1931) stated:

'I am not prepared to attach any importance to a declaration by a man as to his domicile unless there is some evidence to show that the man knew what 'domicile" means ... Domicile is ... a legal concept on which the views of a layman are not of much assistance.'

3.131 However, even where the courts can be persuaded that the individual did demonstrate an understanding of the concept of domicile, the courts, in any event, view such declarations with, it seems, a high degree of scepticism. In *Bell v Kennedy* (1868) the Lord Chancellor stated:

'An Appellant [Bell, who had testified on his own behalf in the case] has, naturally, on an issue like the present [ie domicile] a very strong bias calculated to influence his mind, and he [ie Bell] is, moreover, speaking of what was his intention some twenty-five years ago [ie at the date of his wife's death in 1838].'

Similarly, in *Re Craignish (1892)* the court viewed with scepticism the husband's testimony that he and his wife (who had died) considered her to be domiciled in Scotland at her death, noting that the consequence was that he (the husband) became entitled to one-half of her property.

3.132 According to *Crookenden v Fuller* (1859):

'... [declarations as to domicile are] ... the lowest species of evidence ...'.

3.133 *Domicile*

3.133 With respect to testimony made by an individual to whom an oral statement as to intention has been made, the courts are particularly concerned with credibility of the witness giving the testimony. In *Hodgson v De Beauchesne* (1858) it was stated:

> '... the court must be satisfied not only of the veracity of the witness who depose to such declarations, but of the accuracy of their memory, and that the declarations contain a real expression of the intention of the deceased'.

3.134 It is not uncommon for declarations as to domicile status to be made by individuals in their wills along the following lines:

> 'Inasmuch as I am a British subject having my original domicile in England (which domicile I have never relinquished or abandoned) it is my wish and intention that this my will ... shall be construed and operate so far as the case admits as if I were now and remained until my death domiciled in England.'

(made by Frank Lawton in his will; see *Re Lawton* (1958))

3.135 In *Re Lawton* (1958), despite Lawton's declaration in his will, the courts held that he had in fact died domiciled in France where he had died having been living there for the best part of 63 years. Interestingly, the use of the phrase '... domicile I have never abandoned' by Mr Lawton in his will perhaps lends some support to the comments made by Romer LJ in *AG v Yule and Mercantile Bank of India* (1931) that typically an individual does not understand precisely the nature of the concept of domicile; technically, a domicile of origin cannot simply be abandoned (see paragraph 3.43) and thus Mr Lawton's reference thereto could perhaps be used to illustrate that he did not really understand what he was writing and therefore little credibility should be attached to it.

3.136 Similarly, in *Re Steer* (1858), Mr Steer was held to have died domiciled in Germany despite an explicit declaration in his will that he had no intention of renouncing his English domicile of origin. See also *Re Liddell-Grainger's Will Trusts* (1936) where, again, declarations in a will were basically disregarded.

3.137 Although apparently viewed with extreme suspicion and scepticism, irrespective of the form a declaration as to domicile status may take, the courts accept that in principle they are a factor to be considered. Thus, in *Ross v Ross* (1930) (a case concerning a choice of law rule (*Italy v UK*) applicable to a will of a female British citizen who had died domiciled in Italy and who had cut her son out of her will) the court stated:

'Declarations as to intention are rightly regarded in determining the question of a change of domicile, but they must be examined by considering the persons to whom, the purposes for which, and the circumstances in which they are made, *and they must be further fortified and carried into effect by conduct and action consistent with the declared intention.*'

3.138 Thus it seems that declarations of intention are in principle, per se, acceptable as evidence of intention but of very limited, if any, value in practice at least as far as the courts are concerned. It is the reality and true facts which ultimately decide issues of domicile status not mere statements of intent even if made with the best of intention.

3.139 The court will thus examine whether the individual's declarations of intention are carried through in practice. In this regard the conduct of the individual after the point in time at which a change of domicile may have occurred may also be taken into consideration. In *Re Grove* (1888) Lopes J said:

'... in order to determine a person's intention at a given time, you may regard not only conduct and acts before and at the time, but also conduct and acts after the time, assigning to such conduct and acts their relative and proper weight and cogency'.

See also *Bremer v Freeman* (1857).

Acquisition of citizenship

3.140 It is not decisive as a matter of law that the acquisition by an individual of citizenship of a particular country confirms an intention to remain in that country indefinitely or permanently (*Al Fayed v AG* (2002); see paragraph 3.18). Thus, it does not follow that the acquisition of citizenship means the automatic acquisition of a domicile of choice or indeed vice versa.

3.141 In *F v IRC* (2000) an Iranian exile who died in the UK in 1992 and had spent the bulk of his life in England, was held not to have acquired a UK domicile of choice.

At the time of the Iranian revolution F had sent his wife and children to live in the UK. He had been placed on an exit bar list in Iran due to alleged non-payment of certain tax liabilities which up to the date of his death he had attempted to have removed. He regarded Iran as his home. He owned a UK home and in 1980 obtained indefinite leave to remain in the UK. In 1982 he acquired British citizenship in order to obtain a British passport to ease his international travel in the course of his business. In applying for British citizenship he had falsely claimed that he had left Iran to escape religious persecution. Despite this lie the Commissioners held that he had always

3.142 *Domicile*

intended to return to Iran when it was safe to do so and thus he retained his Iranian domicile of origin. In effect the Commissioners were of the view that the statement made on the application for citizenship did not in fact represent F's true intentions. The Commissioners' comments included the following somewhat bizarre statement arguably containing references to factors somewhat irrelevant to a serious consideration of F's domicile status:

> 'He disliked the English weather, English fruit and the English class system and he thought that England and its economy were on a downward spiral ... his house adjoined the local church but his relationship with the local vicar was poor and he took no part in village life.'

3.142 In an earlier case (*Wahl v AG* (1932)), some 70 years earlier, a not dissimilar conclusion had also been reached on not dissimilar facts. In that case Wahl made statements in the course of applying for British citizenship which did not prejudice his non-UK domicile status. In the course of applying for British citizenship Wahl (a German citizen and possessing a German domicile of origin) had made a statutory declaration to the effect that he intended to continue to reside in the UK indefinitely and had no intention of leaving the UK. Despite the statement the courts held that it was not sufficient to outweigh the other evidence to the contrary.

3.143 Similar issues arose in the case of *Buswell v IRC* (1974). Buswell possessed a Transvaal domicile of origin, married an English woman, acquired South African nationality and acquired a property in South Africa visiting there on average three months per year. In 1952, however, he had completed Form P86 and in so doing had answered the question thereon 'Do you propose to remain permanently in the UK?' in the affirmative; answering the follow-up question 'If not, how long do you expect to remain in this country' by simply inserting a 'dash'.

The High Court agreed with the finding of the Commissioner that Buswell had acquired a UK domicile of choice; in so doing they attached great weight to the answers given on Form P86 (see paragraph 5.27).

However, the Court of Appeal disagreed. They found that Buswell had not acquired a UK domicile of origin stating:

> '... that in attributing a decisive importance to ... answers on the Form P86, given at a time when he had been back in this country less than five months after an absence of ten years and against the background to which I have referred, the Commissioners acted upon a view which could not reasonably be entertained'.

Domicile **3.149**

3.144 Thus, while statements/answers made/provided on Form P86 or indeed Form DOM1 (see paragraph 5.25) are extremely important (*Surveyor v IRC* (2002); see paragraph 3.203) and need to be made with great care, it appears that the courts do not necessarily take them at face value and may effectively discount them if all other facts point to a contradictory conclusion.

Non-UK domiciled individuals spending significant time in the UK

3.145 There are many cases where individuals, each possessing non-UK domiciles of origin, but who have spent significant amounts of time in the UK, have found themselves (or their executors) seeking to argue that despite the length of time spent in the UK and their lifestyles they have not, de facto, acquired UK domiciles of choice.

3.146 Such cases do not, in general, auger well *vis-à-vis* the UK domiciled individual seeking to assert non-UK domicile status on the grounds of having acquired a domicile of choice overseas. This is particularly so if one of the main arguments is premised upon length of residence in the overseas country concerned.

3.147 Typically, such cases have turned on the issue of 'intention'. Two leading cases, namely, *IRC v Group Captain Bullock* (1976) and *Re Furse* (1980), both involve individuals possessing non-UK domiciles of origin and each of whom spent significant time in the UK and indeed each of whom died in the UK. Despite apparent similarities between the two cases and the decision in *Re Furse* coming within four years of the *Bullock* case the courts reached different conclusions as to their respective domicile status.

3.148 In *IRC v Group Captain Bullock* (1976) the Court of Appeal (reversing the decision of the High Court) held that an individual who had lived in the UK for more than 40 years who had a domicile of origin in Nova Scotia, Canada, had not acquired a UK domicile of choice on the ground that he always intended to return to Canada after the death of his wife who was English. The court held that this contingency was of sufficient substance to represent a real determination to return home; it was not simply a vague hope or aspiration. This, however, had the perhaps unintended consequence that his wife (because of the marriage in 1946 to an English male before 1 January 1974) was also domiciled in Canada despite the fact that she apparently hated the place (see also *Buswell v IRC* (1974)).

3.149 Factors considered by the court in arriving at their conclusion included the following aspects of Captain Bullock's lifestyle:

- the fact that he retained his Canadian nationality and passport;

3.150 *Domicile*

- no British passport was ever acquired;
- he was an avid reader of the local Toronto newspaper;
- he never voted in any UK elections;
- his will was drawn up under Nova Scotia law and contained a statement of his intention to return to Nova Scotia should his wife predecease him.

Buckley LJ in the Court of Appeal commenting upon 'intention', said:

> 'I do not think it is necessary to show that the intention to make a home in a new country is irrevocable ... or that ... he will have no opportunity to change his mind. In my judgment the true test is whether he intends to make his home in the new country until the end of his days unless and until something happens to make him change his mind.'

As to the degree of seriousness of intention which is required Buckley LJ said:

> 'The question can perhaps be formulated in this way where the contingency is not itself of a doubtful or indefinite character: is there a sufficiently substantial possibility of the contingency happening to justify regarding the intention to return as a real determination to do so upon the contingency occurring rather than a vague hope or aspiration.'

3.150 In *Re Furse* (1980) a different conclusion to that in the *Bullock* case was reached, arguably, on not dissimilar facts.

3.151 *Re Furse* (1980), decided only four years later, involved an American (domiciled in Rhode Island, USA) who had spent the last 39 years of his life farming a farm which he and his wife had purchased in England. He was married with children, originally coming to England at the age of four.

He died aged 80 in England but had expressed an intention to return to the USA if he became unable to operate his wife's farm due to incapacity. The High Court held that his intention was too vague and indefinite and that on the balance of probabilities he really wanted to remain in the UK until his death and held that he died having acquired a domicile of choice in England.

3.152 Fox J commented upon the *Bullock* case as follows:

> 'In *IRC v Bullock* (1976) both the requirements referred to by Buckley LJ were satisfied [in that case]. The contingency was a

Domicile **3.156**

wholly clear and well-defined contingency, namely whether the propositus survived his wife; and there was a substantial possibility that the contingency might occur, having regard to the respective ages of the propositus and his wife.'

He then went on to contrast Bullock with his own case:

'The present case, it seems to me, is very different. The fundamental difference in outlook between Group Captain Bullock and the testator [Mr Furse] was that, while Group Captain Bullock had every wish to leave England, the testator was entirely happy here.'

3.153 It would appear that the different conclusions in the above two cases to a great extent centred around what constituted an 'acceptable' contingency (as defined by Buckley LJ in *Bullock*). In *Bullock* the contingency was 'acceptable' whereas in *Furse* it was not.

3.154 The case of *Re Fuld's Estate (No 3)* (1968) concerned the validity of a will and a number of subsequent codicils executed by Peter Fuld. Fuld had been born in 1921 in Germany with a German domicile of origin. He died in England in 1961 following serious illness. He spent his time between the UK and Germany and had married a German lady. The court held that he had died possessing his German domicile of origin as at no time had he indicated any intention of remaining in the UK permanently. As a result, his will and the first of its four codicils were held valid; the remaining three codicils were held invalid.

3.155 Scarman J commented upon intention as follows:

'If a man intends to return to the land of his birth upon a clearly foreseen and reasonably anticipated contingency ... the 'intention" required by law [ie the intention to reside in the new territory indefinitely] is lacking ... .but, if he has in mind only a vague possibility, ... such a state of mind is consistent with the intention required by law'.

He went on to say that the ultimate decision in each case is one of fact which would need to take into account:

'the weight to be attached to the various factors and future contingencies in the contemplation of the propositus, their importance to him, and the probability, in his assessment, of the contingencies he has in contemplation being transformed into actualities'.

3.156 By way of example, Scarman J in *Re Fuld's Estate (No 3)* (1968) stated that a clearly forseen and reasonably anticipated contingency upon which a

3.157 *Domicile*

return to the country of the individual's domicile of origin might be the end of a job but a return premised upon making a fortune (or some sentiment about dying in the land of his father's) would be unacceptable.

3.157 In *Re Furse* (1980) the court did not accept that returning to the USA if and when some ill-defined deterioration in health occurred was, in Scarman J's language, 'a clearly foreseen and reasonably anticipated contingency'.

3.158 The case of *The Executors of Robert Moore Deceased v CIR* (2002) involved ascertaining whether a US citizen who died in the UK had acquired a UK domicile of choice. Unlike the cases above, however, the time spent in the UK was not, relatively speaking, excessive.

3.159 Robert Moore had a domicile of origin in Missouri; was a US citizen; and travelled on a US passport. He died in March 1997 in London where his funeral took place but his ashes were scattered in Ireland. He had properties in both the UK and the USA. In 1991 Mr Moore was granted leave to enter the UK for the limited purposes of his employment as an artist and in answer to a question raised by the immigration officer said: 'I am planning to use the UK as a base to travel to the continent regularly'. The leave to enter the UK expired in March 1995 and although it was not renewed, he remained in the UK. He travelled on a US passport and filed US tax returns (but no UK tax returns were filed).

Two wills were made, one of which (the US-prepared will) dealt with his US assets and the other (the UK prepared will) dealt with all non-US assets. His New York connections remained including the fact that his investments were managed from New York.

3.160 Two witness statements stated that the witnesses regarded Mr Moore as an American and one of them stated that he did not wear British clothes or eat British food. One of them also stated that they thought he wanted to go to the USA for medical treatment but died before actually doing so.

3.161 The Commissioners held that Mr Moore had not acquired a UK domicile of choice at the date of his death as there was no clear evidence that he had intended to acquire a domicile of choice in the UK, but there was a lot of evidence that demonstrated that he had kept up his connections with New York. The Commissioners also referred to the statement to the immigration officer which they suggested did not indicate that Mr Moore wanted to make England his permanent home.

3.162 Two more recent cases involving a long-stay in the UK followed by death therein is that of *Holliday v Musa* (C/A 2010) and *Agulian & Anr v Cyganik* (C/A 2006); two cases decided by the Court of Appeal. The facts in each case were surprisingly very similar although the Court of Appeal's

Domicile **3.168**

findings were not the same; the Court of Appeal overturned the decision of the High Court in *Agulian* but confirmed the decision (albeit on a different approach to that adopted by the High Court) in *Holliday* (in view of the similarity only *Agulian* is considered below).

3.163 The case considered the domicile status of a Cypriot national, not in fact for tax purposes, but for the purposes of the *IPFDA 1975* (see paragraph 3.8).

3.164 Mr Andreas Nathanial died in the UK in 2003 aged 63, having been born in Cyprus in 1939. He had come to England aged 18 for safety reasons. He had lived in England for approximately 43 years although he had returned to Cyprus for a brief period in 1972; had a significant UK business (UK assets worth £6.5 million); and had made a will in 1995 under which his fiancée Renata Cyganik, with whom he had lived as man and wife (who was in fact in the UK illegally) and to whom he became engaged in 1999 and intended to marry in 2003, was to inherit £50 000.

3.165 Ms Cyganik brought a claim under *IPFDA 1975 s 2* against Agulian's estate for financial provision. In order for such a claim to be brought required that she was able to establish that the deceased had died domiciled in England (ie he had acquired a domicile of choice in England displacing his Cypriot domicile of origin).

3.166 The Court of Appeal, reversing the High Court (which had held that he had acquired a UK domicile of choice at some point between making his will in 1995 and his engagement in 1999), held that he had not acquired an English domicile of choice in the UK but his Cypriot domicile of origin had subsisted; this was based on the fact that he had maintained significant connections with Cyprus throughout his life (eg he had sent one of his daughters to be educated in Cyprus where she remained; watched Cypriot TV as well as speaking Greek while in the UK; sent significant sums of money to Cyprus; and had bought two flats in Cyprus). It was accepted that he had become deemed domiciled for IHT purposes (see paragraph 3.231).

3.167 The *Agulian v Cyganik* case is yet another example of an individual who, despite having spent a significant amount of his lifetime living in the UK, was held not to have acquired a UK domicile of choice; his original non-UK domicile of origin persisting.

3.168 The above cases tend to suggest that long-term UK residency whilst an indicator of the possible acquisition of a UK domicile of choice is not in fact of the utmost importance but just one, and not necessarily a powerful, indicator. It may be prima facie evidence of the acquisition of a UK domicile of choice but if other factors suggest otherwise the latter may be given greater weight. The cases also appear to support the fact that an individual's domicile of origin is

3.169 *Domicile*

extremely adhesive and acquiring a UK domicile of choice (or any domicile of choice) is no easy matter; this does not auger well for those individuals possessing UK domiciles of origin who seek to acquire domiciles of choice elsewhere.

UK domiciled individuals failing to acquire non-UK domiciles of choice

3.169 While there are cases where UK domiciled individuals have successfully acquired non-UK domiciles of choice (see paragraph 3.186), for many this has proved, not surprisingly, impossible.

3.170 In *Jopp v Wood* (1865) the courts held that an individual who had possessed a UK (in fact Scottish) domicile of origin had not subsequently acquired an Indian domicile of choice.

3.171 The case of *Jopp v Wood* concerned a John Smith who went to India in 1805, as a minor, acquiring his majority in 1807. His father died in 1814 and Smith wrote a letter to his mother indicating strongly his intention ultimately to return to Scotland. In 1819 he returned to Scotland taking an active part in the management of the family estate. He then returned to India but kept up constant correspondence with the agents of the estate. In this correspondence he constantly referred to his return to Scotland; directed that different parts of the estate be planted; and mentioned his intention of building upon it. He also purchased an adjoining property and sent money back to Scotland to discharge charges against the estate. At the date of his death John Smith had lived in India for some 25 years.

3.172 On these facts the court held that John Smith, far from having acquired a domicile of choice in India, had shown a desire at all times to retain his Scottish domicile of origin. This hardly seems a surprising decision as it did not appear that John Smith had, in any event, any intention of losing his Scottish domicile.

3.173 The case of *Re Clore* (1984) was very different from that of *Jopp v Wood* above although the conclusion was the same.

3.174 Sir Charles Clore, an extremely wealthy man, possessed a UK domicile of origin. He had emigrated to Monaco and had become a Monégasque resident. He had left the UK solely to avoid UK death tax by acquiring a Monégasque domicile of choice. On his death it was held that he had never acquired such a domicile and his English domicile of origin had subsisted.

3.175 This case admirably illustrates the importance and significance of utterances, whether in writing or by word of mouth, made by an individual to others in determining an individual's domicile status.

3.176 The court considered that there was evidence to support the acquisition of a domicile of choice in Monaco. This evidence included the fact that Sir Charles Clore had severed various important connections with the UK; had established connections with Monaco including residing there; and the fact that he had received professional advice as to the need to acquire a non-UK domicile if UK estate duty was to be avoided. With respect to this last point Nourse J stated:

> '... the professional advice which Sir Charles received was given not solely with the immediate object of his acquiring a non-resident status for income tax and CGT purposes, but with the long term objective of his acquiring a foreign domicile ...'.

With reference to Clore's motive for seeking to acquire a non-UK domicile status (ie UK estate duty avoidance) Nourse J had no problem commenting:

> '... if the evidence of intention is there, particularly perhaps where the motive is the avoidance of taxes, the necessary intention will not be held to be missing merely because the period of actual residence is a short one'.

However, the court decided that other factors overrode the above.

3.177 In particular, a number of his closest friends testified as to parol (anything done by word of mouth) declarations which had been made by Sir Charles late in his life which confirmed that: he had never been happy in Monaco; he continued to be interested in buying properties in Israel and/or France; and that, in his 'heart of hearts', he had never truly abandoned England – he often referred to England as 'home' and right up to his death in London certain of his actions were tentative in nature. Accordingly, Nourse J held that he had died domiciled in England.

3.178 What this case seems to show is that statements made, whether in writing or simply orally, whether to family and/or friends may be viewed by the courts as extremely important and indicative of an individual's true intentions (assuming that the court perceives those testifying as to such utterances as responsible, honourable and truthful in nature).

3.179 Four years later in *Plummer v IRC* (1988) yet another individual (female in this case) possessing a UK domicile of origin failed to convince the court of her acquisition of a domicile of choice in Guernsey. Unlike *Re Clore* (1984) and *Jopp v Wood* (1865), however, Elizabeth Plummer was alive at the

3.180 *Domicile*

court date and thus able to testify. The case involved issues of UK income tax (not death tax).

3.180 Plummer was born of UK-domiciled parents in 1965. In 1980 her mother and sister moved to Guernsey but her father only spent weekends and holidays there (he remained in the UK). Plummer continued to remain in the UK for her education but spent weekends and holidays in Guernsey at her mother's house. She had acquired, *inter alia*, a Guernsey passport, bank account and driving licence. She stated that her intention was to settle permanently in Guernsey once her education in the UK had finished.

3.181 The court considered that Plummer was in fact a resident of both the UK and Guernsey and thus the court needed to identify her chief residence. The court was of the view that Plummer had not in fact settled in Guernsey as an inhabitant of it and the reasons why she had not (namely, due to her need to finish her education in the UK) were, the court said, irrelevant. It was inappropriate to consider that her mother's house was Plummer's chief residence.

3.182 Interestingly, the court said:

> 'If the taxpayer had in 1980 broken altogether with England and settled in Guernsey like her mother and sister and then, even after a relatively short interval, returned to England for study, the quality of her presence here [UK] might have been such as to prevent a revival of her domicile of origin.'

3.183 What the court seems to be suggesting is that a severance of links with the UK in 1980 would have resulted in Plummer acquiring a Guernsey domicile of choice. Returns thereafter to the UK for educational purposes would not have been sufficient to cause her UK domicile of origin to have automatically resurrected.

3.184 In *Civil Engineer v IRC* (2002) an individual had spent 30 years living and working in Hong Kong. The Commissioners, however, found no evidence to support his argument that he had acquired a domicile of choice in Hong Kong (even if so held, his UK domicile of origin had resurrected as, following his return to the UK, he appeared to have no intention of a return to Hong Kong; in effect, holding that even if a domicile of choice had been acquired he no longer resided in Hong Kong and had by his actions demonstrated an intention no longer to reside there permanently).

3.185 Two other important cases (although very different) where a failure to acquire a non-UK domicile of choice occurred are *IRC v Duchess of Portland* (1982) (see paragraphs 3.68, 3.103 and 3.112) and the recent case of *Gaines-Cooper v RCC* (2007) (see paragraphs 3.110 and 3.121).

Domicile **3.185**

Example 18

Felipe Sanchez possesses a Spanish domicile of origin.

He meets and marries a UK domiciled woman in 1975. Since that time they have both lived in the UK.

In 1980 they had two children who are educated in the UK and continue to live in the UK (now adults).

Felipe owns no property in Spain and has visited Spain only once since 1975.

Felipe dies in 2009 and is buried in the UK having previously made a will governed by UK law and drawn up by a UK firm of solicitors.

On these facts it is highly likely, whether Felipe intended or not, that he has died possessing a UK domicile of choice which has displaced his Spanish domicile of origin.

Prima facie, Felipe appears to have behaved in a manner which suggests he intended to remain in the UK indefinitely and showed no indication of any serious intention to return to Spain.

Example 19

Manuel Sanchez, Felipe's brother (see Example 18), possesses a Spanish domicile of origin.

He met a UK-domiciled woman and marries her in 1975. Since that time they have both lived in the UK.

In 1980 they had two children who were educated in the UK and continue to live in the UK (now adults).

Here the resemblance to Felipe's life changes.

Manuel has maintained his villa in Spain and has, since arriving in the UK, returned to Spain for visits on a regular basis. He has always stated to everyone in his family that as soon as the children have finished full-time education in the UK he (with his wife) intends to return to live in Spain.

He has been advised to make two wills, one under Spanish law and one under UK law (to deal only with UK real estate), which he has done.

3.186 *Domicile*

Compared to his brother, Felipe, Manuel's Spanish domicile of origin is likely to have remained intact. It is highly unlikely that Manuel has acquired a UK domicile of choice as he has never confirmed, or behaved in a manner which is consistent with, an intention to remain indefinitely in the UK.

UK domiciled individuals who have successfully acquired non-UK domiciles of choice

3.186 It is important to appreciate that in most common law systems the concept of 'domicile' is central to many issues of law not just issues of taxation. A change in an individual's domicile status may thus have implications beyond taxation.

3.187 The general importance of the concept of domicile in such systems is that it is used to connect an individual to a place and thus in turn permits the laws governing that place to apply to the individual. Thus, for example, an individual who possesses an English domicile will find that it is English law which will govern his personal relationships including issues such as the validity of marriage; jurisdiction in divorce; legitimacy and adoption; wills and the devolution of movable property on an intestacy (ie the distribution of property on death where no will exists).

3.188 Those individuals driven by the need to mitigate or even avoid outright UK taxes by seeking to establish non-UK domiciles of choice are perhaps not mindful of the much wider consequences which inevitably follow from such action.

3.189 There is a presumption that an individual's domicile status at any point in time persists (*AG v Rowe* (1862)) until it can be shown that it has changed due to action taken by the individual concerned, whether intended or not.

3.190 For an individual to acquire a domicile of choice requires positive action and satisfaction of two conditions (see paragraph 3.87):

- the individual must actually take up residence in another country; and
- the individual must have the intention of residing permanently or indefinitely in the new country of residence.

This does, however, raise two questions, namely:

- on whom is the onus placed to demonstrate a change in an individual's domicile status?
- what is the standard of proof?

3.191 Irrespective of on whom the burden is placed and irrespective of the standard of proof required the burden is an extremely heavy one as is evidenced in the statement by Lord Macnaghten in *Winans v AG* (1904):

> 'How heavy is the burden cast upon those who seek to show that the domicile of origin has been superseded by a domicile of choice!'

3.192 It is clear that the onus of proving a change in domicile lies fairly and squarely with the person so asserting, as is clear from statements made in *Winans v AG* (1904) and in *Re Fuld's Estate (No 3)* (1968). In *Winans v AG* (1904) it was stated:

> 'The onus of proving that a domicile has been chosen in substitution for the domicile of origin lies upon those who assert that the domicile of origin has been lost.'

Similarly, in *Re Fuld's Estate (No 3)* (1968):

> 'It is beyond doubt that the burden of proving the abandonment of a domicile of origin and the acquisition of a domicile of choice is upon the party asserting the change.'

This is, of course, a double-edged sword.

3.193 For the UK domiciled individual wishing to argue the acquisition of a new non-UK domicile of choice the onus of proof clearly lies with the individual. On the other hand, where such an individual has been successful in so arguing, any attempt by HMRC at a subsequent date to argue that the individual's UK domicile of origin has resurrected lies with HMRC.

3.194 With respect to the standard of proof, two decided cases appear to differ. Both cases were heard in the Probate Division; one case concerned a petition for divorce (*Henderson v Henderson* (1965)) and the other, *Re Fuld's Estate (No 3)* (1968), concerned challenges to the validity of a will and codicils thereto.

3.195 In *Henderson v Henderson* (1965) Sir Jocelyn Simon stated:

> '... clear evidence is required to establish a change of domicile. In particular, to displace the domicile of origin in favour of a domicile of choice, *the standard of proof goes beyond a mere balance of probabilities*'.

3.196 *Domicile*

However, around the same time, Scarman J in *Re Fuld's Estate (No 3)* (1968) when considering the issue of changes in the domicile status of an individual commented:

> 'It is beyond doubt that the burden of proving the abandonment of a domicile of origin and the acquisition of a domicile of choice is upon the part asserting the change ... but ... is it to be proved beyond reasonable doubt or upon a balance of probabilities ...? ... but I see no reason to infer from these salutary warnings the necessity for formulating in a probate case a standard of proof in language appropriate to criminal proceedings. ...*The formula of proof beyond reasonable doubt is not frequently used in probate cases, and I do not propose to give it currency* ...Two things are clear; first, that unless the judicial conscience is satisfied by evidence of change, the domicile of origin persists; and secondly, the acquisition of a domicile of choice is a serious matter not to be lightly inferred from slight indications or casual words ...'.

3.196 In *Buswell v IRC* (1974) Orr LJ commenting upon Scarman J's comments in *Re Fuld's Estate (No 3)* (1968) stated:

> 'I am satisfied that Scarman J. was not recognising the existence of some general standard of proof intermediate between criminal and civil standards but was merely emphasising that in the application of the civil standard the degree of proof required will vary with the subject-matter of the case.'

Lady Justice Arden in *Barlow Clowes International Ltd v Henwood* (2008) in referring to the *Buswell* case stated:

> 'In ... *Buswell v. IRC* ... it was conceded before this court that Scarman J was correct to say that the standard of proof was always the civil standard and not the criminal standard ...'

It is thus now accepted that the proof required is the civil law's standard (ie on a balance of probabilities).

3.197 One of the most recent cases, where an individual possessing a UK domicile of origin successfully acquired a non-UK domicile of choice, is that of a Mr Anthony Shaffer in the case *Re Shaffer, Morgan v Cilento* (2004). The case, as in *Agulian v Cyganik* (CA 2006), concerns a claim under *IPFDA 1975*. More specifically, the court had to consider whether Mr Shaffer's original UK domicile of origin had resurrected at the time of his death.

3.198 The *Shaffer* case was decided by the High Court and revolved around a claim made by a Ms Minutolo who had had a relationship with Mr Shaffer during the latter part of his life (during which time Shaffer was still married to Diane Cilento) and sought to claim under *IPFDA 1975*. For the courts to entertain such a claim Mr Shaffer would have had to have died domiciled in England (or Wales).

3.199 Mr Anthony Shaffer, the playwright, possessed an English domicile of origin. He died aged 75 in late 2001 in England. However, he had spent a significant amount of time in Australia having acquired a visa in March 1985 entitling him to stay indefinitely; the visa was periodically renewed (last occasion 11 June 1999 valid until 23 October 2002). He never applied for Australian citizenship (due apparently, according to his wife Diane Cilento, to his dislike of 'pomp and circumstance').

3.200 The court held that he had acquired a domicile of choice in Queensland, Australia, and his UK domicile of origin had not revived before his death (despite returning to the UK and dying there) as he had not abandoned his non-UK domicile.

In concluding that Shaffer had acquired a domicile of choice in Queensland, Australia, the judge said:

'The particular factors to which I have given weight ... are:

... [marriage] in Queensland and ... matrimonial home there;

... most of his personal possessions were [shipped] to Queensland where they remain;

it was the place where he was most creative, and creation was perhaps the most important thing in [his] life;

by 1985 [left UK March 1985] he had sold almost all his assets in England and for the best part of a decade owned no home there either directly or indirectly;

he had deliberately acquired residence in Australia for tax purposes, and part of his desire to do so was the abolition of death duties in Queensland;

his bank account and credit card were Australian;

when the Studio [a flat in the UK] was acquired [1995] it was an Australian company which acquired it not Anthony;

in September 1997 he stated in an official form that he intended to live permanently or indefinitely in Australia;

3.201 *Domicile*

> he exercised the right to vote in Queensland;
>
> ...
>
> until the mid-1990s he spent the majority of his time in Australia;
>
> in 1999 he made a will in Queensland;
>
> ...
>
> he never stopped talking about Karnak as his home;
>
> on the day [fifth] before he died [6th November 2001], he stated that he lived in England for only half the year; and answered the questions applicable 'if you are from abroad" [these answers were given in a questionnaire for the purpose of registering with an NHS doctor]'.

3.201 With respect to whether Shaffer's UK domicile of origin had resurrected (ie if Shaffer had abandoned his domicile of choice) the judge said:

> 'I have not taken it [ie a memoir written by Shaffer in his last year of his life and published on the day of his death] as evidence of historical facts, but it has helped me in forming a view about Mr Shaffer's state of mind during its composition ... the memoir seems to me to show that Anthony still regarded Karnak as his home in the early summer of 2001 [the year of death] and that he was not contemplating a return to England full time ... may be [by the date of death] his return to Queensland was withering. But I do not consider it died before Anthony did'.

This was so held despite the fact that Shaffer had:

- retained his memberships of London clubs but he was an overseas member or absent member of each;
- he was registered on the electoral role at the studio;
- joined the Conservative party in his local constituency;
- subscribed to a residents' association;
- visited the UK; and
- died while in the UK.

His visits to the UK, according to the court, were motivated by:

'... his need for cultural stimulation over and above what Australia could give him. Part of it was also ... to see his two daughters ... [and] his mother ... But part of it was also his need for medical treatment ... Yet London also grated. Sir Peter [Shaffer's twin brother] told me that Anthony deplored the changes that had taken place in England during his lifetime and that he felt that London was 'no longer his place'.'

3.202 The contrast between the *Gaines-Cooper* and the *Shaffer* cases could not perhaps be much greater and the different conclusions reached by the courts seem hardly surprising.

3.203 In another relatively recent case, *Surveyor v IRC* (2002), an individual who possessed a UK domicile of origin was also held to have acquired a Hong Kong domicile of choice. To some degree this case seems, on its facts, to lie somewhere between *Gaines-Cooper* and *Shaffer*.

3.204 The individual in 1986 took up an employment opportunity in Hong Kong which had been offered by his UK employer. In 1990 he married a UK national who was living in Hong Kong but the marriage took place in the UK. All three children were born in Hong Kong. In 1997 the individual (plus wife) applied for permanent residence status in Hong Kong (which was granted) which enabled him to live and work in Hong Kong without the need for a work permit; to travel in and out of Hong Kong without requiring a passport or visa; and an entitlement to vote in elections. The individual rented accommodation due to the high cost of purchase but did purchase an apartment in 1994 which in the event was too small for a family home; it was sold and a move back into rented accommodation occurred.

In 2000 the individual was transferred to the employer's Singapore business where accommodation was provided by the employer. Regular visits were made back to Hong Kong and strong links were maintained there. Two years later the individual resigned and returned to Hong Kong purchasing an apartment as a family home.

In 1998 a 30-year lease of a plot of land was acquired in Thailand and in 1999 building commenced on what was to be a holiday home.

In February 1999 Form DOM1 (see paragraph 5.25) was completed and a ruling sought from HMRC as to the individual's domicile status. No immediate ruling was forthcoming and following a transfer of approximately £250,000 into a Jersey discretionary trust in August 1999 HMRC refused to accept that the individual had acquired a Hong Kong domicile of choice.

On Form DOM1 the individual stated that he had acquired a Hong Kong domicile of choice; that his general intention was to remain in the Far East (not

3.205 *Domicile*

explicitly Hong Kong) as was evidenced by the building of the home in Thailand.

3.205 The Commissioners found that in August 1999 (the date of the £250,000 transfer) the individual had the intention of residing permanently in Hong Kong until the end of his days unless something happened to make him change his mind. The individual had the intention of leaving the UK and not returning. The Commissioners also found no problem with the building of the house in Thailand or the statement on Form DOM1 (see paragraph 5.25). The Commissioners were of the view that the existence of the Thai house did not alter the intention to make Hong Kong a permanent home nor did it suggest the individual intended to reside in more than one country. The move to Singapore was held not to have affected the intention to reside permanently in Hong Kong or to have resulted in the resurrection of the UK domicile of origin.

Further, evidence concerning the individual's family, social, business and financial ties all supported the Hong Kong connection and there was no evidence in this regard to suggest the individual's residence in Hong Kong was purely for commercial reasons.

3.206 The case of *Allen v RCC* (2005) involved an elderly lady who had returned to the UK for medical reasons and had then died in the UK having lived with her family for the last six years of her life. She had possessed a UK domicile of origin but had subsequently acquired a Spanish domicile of choice.

She maintained a house in Spain and had said that she wanted to return there and would have done so if her family had agreed to have looked after her in Spain.

3.207 Despite her expressed intention to want to return to Spain she had not long before her death bought a house in the UK. Nevertheless, the Commissioners held that she had died domiciled in Spain (ie she had not abandoned her Spanish domicile of choice) appearing to have accepted that she would have returned to Spain if she could have done so. Weight also seems to have been attached to the fact that she had spent very little of her adult life in the UK.

In the light of the purchase of a UK property it is perhaps surprising that the lady in question was not held to have died with her UK domicile of origin resurrected; the purchase, *prima facie*, suggesting an intention to return and remain in the UK.

3.208 The impact of health issues on domicile status are complex.

3.209 In the cases of *Shaffer* and *Allen* despite returns to the UK, in part driven by illness and the fact of dying in the UK, it would seem that other factors were perceived by the courts to be overriding thus resulting in the foreign domiciles of choice in both cases subsisting.

3.210 In the case of *Moorhouse v Lord* (1863) Lord Kingsdown stated:

> 'Take the case of a man labouring under a mortal disease. He is informed by his physicians that his life may be prolonged for a few months by a change to a warmer climate and that at all events his sufferings may be mitigated by such a change. Is it to be said that if he goes to Madeira he cannot do so without losing his character as an English subject, without losing his right to the intervention of the English laws as to the transmission of property after his death, and the construction of his testamentary instruments. My Lords, I apprehend that such a proposition is revolting to common sense and common feelings of humanity.'

3.211 The above comments and inference from *Moorhouse v Lord* (1863), however, contrast with the earlier decision in *Hoskins v Matthews* (1856).

3.212 In *Hoskins v Matthews* (1856), a Mr Matthews, who possessed a UK domicile of origin, moved to Florence in Tuscany, at the age of 60. The move was motivated by a spinal injury which he thought would benefit from the warm climate. He died there 12 years later and was held to have acquired a domicile of choice in Tuscany. Turner LJ stated:

> '[Mr Matthews on moving to Tuscany was not at the time of the move] in any immediate danger or apprehension. He was, no doubt, out of health, and he went abroad for the purpose of trying to effect other remedies and other climates ... but I think he was not driven to settle in Italy by any cogent necessity. I think that in settling there he was exercising a preference, and not acting upon a necessity, and I cannot venture to hold that in such a case the domicile cannot be changed.'

3.213 Two more recent cases involving health issues, to a degree, are *Reddington v MacInnes* (2002) and *Haji-Ioannou & others v Frangos* (2009). *Reddington* was a case of testamentary succession.

A Mr John Grant Riach possessed a Scottish domicile of origin. He died in Bournemouth, England, age 95 in December 1999. The issue arose as to whether he died domiciled in England or Scotland.

Mr Riach had contracted emphysema during the latter part of his working life and on his retirement returned to Falkirk with his wife in 1966. His emphysema deteriorated and he experienced difficulty in breathing. He and his wife had spent holidays in Bournemouth in the past and he enjoyed the climate which he thought was good for his health. The family purchased a house in Bournemouth and moved there in 1976.

3.214 *Domicile*

It was said that on moving to Bournemouth he had on a number of occasions said 'I'm not making another move' and when asked 'Would you ever move back to Scotland?' he had always replied in the negative.

3.214 The judge commented as follows:

> '… the question of what the deceased's motive had been in moving to Bournemouth in 1976, I am not satisfied, that ultimately, in this case, much turns on that factor … I suspect that the choice of Bournemouth may well have been motivated by both considerations [to enable his wife to be closer to her family and his wish to live in a more temperate climate].
>
> I have reached the clear conclusion that, by the date of his death, the deceased had acquired a domicile of choice in England. The evidence:
>
> - his repeated remarks that his move to England was to be his last move;
> - the length of his residence in England;
> - the fact that he remained in England after his wife died; and
> - lastly and perhaps, most tellingly, his directions, in his will, that his remains should be buried in Bournemouth,
>
> taken together, in my judgment, establish that the deceased had made England his permanent home where he intended to end his days'.

3.215 The case of *Haji-Ioannou* concerned an attempt by Mr Haji-Ioannou to recover a substantial debt of $49 million from his son-in-law, a Mr Ioannis Frangos which, *inter alia*, involved a need to determine Mr Haji-Ioannou's domicile at the date of his death; in particular whether he had acquired a domicile of choice in Greece.

Mr Haji-Ioannou had British nationality and had been born in Cyprus, acquiring a domicile of choice in Monaco in the late 1980s/early 1990s. Due to serious illness he had spent the bulk of the last ten years of his life in Athens undergoing medical treatment, finally dying in Athens leaving a widow and children. Nevertheless, his widow and children claimed that his Monégasque domicile of choice subsisted at the date of his death (ie he had not acquired a Greek domicile of choice following abandonment of his Monégasque domicile).

Despite his time in Greece where he had substantial assets he fully maintained his home in Monaco including club memberships (eg of the local yacht club) and had renewed his residence permit every year.

It is not necessary in order to acquire a new domicile of choice that a prior domicile of choice is lost (see paragraph 3.219); all that is required is the abandonment of the former domicile of choice. Slade J decided that he had not abandoned his Monégasque domicile of choice which continued to subsist at the time of his death. She said:

> 'This was not a case of someone going to live in a country because the air and general living conditions are better there. When Mr Haji-Ioannou went to live in Athens he was already seriously ill. There is no evidence that but for his wish to receive medical treatment in Athens he would have ceased to live in Monaco. If he had recovered no doubt he would have returned to Monaco ...'.

3.216 It is arguable that the above four cases suggest that no change of domicile will occur where the move to the other country is to receive medical treatment or to alleviate suffering even where death is likely to occur in the country and the individual knows he will never return to the home country. Thus, even in the case of an individual with a UK domicile of origin who has subsequently acquired a non-UK domicile of choice, a return to the UK in these circumstances should not automatically cause the resurrection of the UK domicile of origin.

However, where although the move may be due to health reasons it is not perceived as a move motivated by one of necessity, but of preference, the individual may well be held to have either acquired a new domicile of choice or to have resurrected a domicile of origin.

3.217 On the other hand, the consequences for domicile status of a move motivated by, or involving, health considerations may be determined on factors perceived to be of more weight than *the issues associated with the individual's health (see also Re Steer* (1858) and *Re Lawton* (1958)).

Abandonment of a domicile of choice

3.218 A domicile of choice (unlike a domicile of origin) having been acquired (whether by design or otherwise) may subsequently be lost by abandonment. In practice, this requires:

- the ceasing of residence in the country; *and*
- the ceasing to intend to reside permanently in the country concerned.

3.219 It is not necessary for an individual to have acquired another domicile of choice; the act of giving up residence and the intention to remain permanently is sufficient; although one without the other is insufficient.

3.220 *Domicile*

3.220 Thus, in *Udny v Udny* Lord Westbury said:

> '... expressions are found ... that the first or existing domicile remains until another is acquired. This is true ... [for] the domicile of origin, but cannot be true ... [for a] domicile of choice ...'.

It is thus not necessary to acquire a new residence for a loss of a domicile of choice to occur; the act of ceasing to reside in a country (and ceasing to have the intention of residing there permanently) is sufficient. However, the need to cease actual residence is admirably demonstrated in the case of *In the Goods of Raffenel* (1863).

3.221 A woman (Madam Raffenel) with a domicile of origin in England had married a Frenchman pre-1 January 1974 thus acquiring a French domicile of dependence. They both lived in France. The husband died. The wife decided to leave France to return to live permanently in England which would mean the loss of her French domicile of dependence and the resurrection of her UK domicile of origin. She boarded the ship (a paddle steamer) in Calais but became seriously ill before it left and so she disembarked and returned to Dunkirk where she died.

The court held that she had not abandoned her French domicile of dependence because although her intention was to return and live permanently in England she had not in fact actually lost her French residency. It was stated:

> '... the French domicile was [not] abandoned so long as the deceased remained in the territory of France ... she never left France, and intention alone is not sufficient ...'.

3.222 Similarly, the case of *Zanelli v Zanelli* (1948) concerned a petition for divorce by an English woman from her Italian husband who had acquired an English domicile of choice but who had deserted her and had subsequently returned to Italy. The issue to be decided was whether the husband at the time of desertion was domiciled in England; if he was then the English courts could hear the petition and grant the divorce if appropriate (which they did in fact do). Lord Parq commented:

> '... he cannot be said to have lost his domicile of choice even at the moment when he stepped into the train with his ticket in his pocket. Having regard to what was decided ... *In the Goods of Raffenel* ... I do not think that, when he stepped on board the ship which was to carry him to the Continent, he had yet lost his domicile of choice ... although the husband may have given up an intention to reside here [UK at the time of desertion], he certainly had not given up residence here [UK] ...'.

3.223 In effect, residence will cease not when arrival elsewhere occurs, but when it is given up (ie when the individual has left that country's boundaries or legal jurisdiction).

3.224 However, it is now strongly arguable that, strictly speaking, it is not even necessary to cease to reside in the country of the domicile of choice if the individual's chief residence is in fact established elsewhere (*Plummer v IRC* (1988)). This might be the case where, for example, an individual possessing a UK domicile of origin successfully acquires a non-UK domicile of choice. Subsequent thereto, whether by design or otherwise, the individual acquires de facto a 'second' domicile of choice which is decided to be the individual's chief residence and thus new domicile of choice (even though residence in the country in which a domicile of choice was initially established has not ceased).

3.225 For the UK-domiciled individual who acquires a non-UK domicile of choice this latter domicile is thus lost if the individual ceases to reside in the country concerned and expresses the intention of no longer wishing to reside there indefinitely. The danger for such individual is that unless another domicile of choice is immediately acquired the original UK domicile of origin automatically resurrects (*Udny v Udny* (1869)).

3.226 In the case of the non-UK domiciled individual who acquires a UK domicile of choice this latter domicile is similarly lost if the individual ceases to reside in the UK and expresses the intention of no longer wishing to reside there indefinitely.

3.227 It is this aspect of the concept of domicile of origin (namely, its ability to automatically resurrect) that causes it to be regarded as extremely adhesive.

Example 20

Mario Milan and his wife arrive in the UK in the mid-1950s. Both possess Italian domiciles of origin.

In 1970 they both express an intention to remain in the UK indefinitely thus each acquiring UK domiciles of choice.

In 2007, however, on retirement they decide that as they no longer work in the UK and the fact that the majority of their family are in Italy they leave the UK for good and return to Italy.

The consequence of this decision in 2007 is that their previously acquired UK domiciles of choice are abandoned and their original Italian domiciles of origin automatically resurrect.

Example 21

Henry and Joyce Hodges, both possessing UK domiciles of origin, emigrate to France on retirement in 1990 and, in so doing, each acquire a French domicile of choice.

In 2005 they decide that perhaps, on reflection, Spain might have been a better choice and so move there with the immediate intention of remaining in Spain indefinitely.

Henry and Joyce, as a consequence, lose their French domiciles of choice on the move to Spain but immediately acquire domiciles of choice in Spain.

In this case their respective UK domiciles of origin are not resurrected following the abandonment of their French domiciles of choice as Spanish domiciles of choice are immediately acquired.

In practice, the Hodges may have found their Spanish domiciles of choice subject to attack by HMRC had one or both of them died within a short period of taking up residence in Spain; HMRC would no doubt have sought to argue that their UK domiciles of origin had resurrected at this point as the Hodges, whilst Spanish residents, had not formed the requisite intention to reside in Spain indefinitely. It would be for the executors of the deceased to argue and prove that a Spanish domicile of choice had been acquired.

Special categories of individual and domiciles of choice

3.228 Lord Westbury in *Udny v Udny* (1869) stated:

> 'Domicile of choice ... which the law derives from the fact of a man fixing voluntarily his sole or chief residence in a particular place ... There must be a residence freely chosen, and not prescribed or dictated by external necessity, such as the duties of office, the demand of creditors, or the relief from illness ...'.

3.229 What precisely constitutes 'freely chosen' in this context is debateable.

The issue as to whether a residence is freely chosen appears, *prima facie*, to be of particular relevance where residence in a country is partly or totally driven by issues of the individual's health; where the individual is required to work outside the UK by his employer; or where the individual is a member of the armed forces or in the diplomatic service.

3.230 Despite Lord Westbury's comments, in a number of cases domiciles of choice have been held to have arisen arguably in circumstances where the residence was not freely chosen. The cases include, for example, where an individual resided in a country in deference to his father's dying injunction (*Somerville v Somerville* (1801)); where an individual resided in a country in deference to his wife's wishes (*Aitchison v Dixon* (1870)); and, in order to marry (*Fasbender v AG* (1922)).

Deemed UK domicile

3.231 Domiciles of origin, dependence and choice discussed above are determined according to the UK's common law rules (not by statute).

3.232 The concept of *deemed UK domicile* is, however, a tax fiction created by tax statute and is of relevance only in the context of IHT (*IHTA 1984 s 267*; see paragraph 10.9) (ie it is of no relevance for income tax and/or CGT or indeed for any other non-tax purposes).

3.233 It is thus quite possible for an individual to possess a non-UK domicile for general law purposes (eg a non-UK domicile of origin) yet still be deemed UK domiciled for IHT purposes only.

3.234 The concept of deemed domicile was only introduced in 1974 when capital transfer tax (the forerunner to IHT) was introduced.

3.235 An individual may be deemed UK domiciled in one of two circumstances:

- a UK domiciled individual (determined under general law) is deemed UK domiciled for a further three-year period (note, not tax years but normal calendar years) following the acquisition of a new domicile of choice (the three year rule); and

- a non-UK domiciled individual (determined under general law) is deemed UK domiciled if the individual has been resident in the UK for at least 17 out of the 20 tax years ending in the relevant year (ie the tax year in which a determination needs to be made (note, unlike the three-year rule above it is tax years which are relevant to this rule)) (the 17/20 rule).

3.236 The three-year rule is of application to those individuals domiciled in the UK under common law; whereas the 17/20 rule is primarily of application to those individuals who are non-UK domiciled under common law it may also impact on those UK domiciled under common law. Under the three-year rule (see paragraph 3.235) an individual's UK domicile status subsists for three

3.237   *Domicile*

more years from the date of the acquisition of a non-UK domicile of choice (an example of a so-called trailing tax; see paragraph 1.31). For example, an individual who ceases to be UK domiciled on, say, 1 May 2002 (ie because of the acquisition of a non-UK domicile of choice on that date) will be deemed to continue to be UK domiciled until 30 April 2005 (ie for a further three-year period).

3.237   The commencement of the three-year period does not automatically commence on the date an individual leaves the UK but from the date when a new domicile of choice is operative.

3.238   The 17/20 rule is a straightforward mechanical test and applies in two situations.

3.239   The first situation is where, for example, a non-UK domiciled individual is continuously resident in the UK for the tax years 1993–1994 to 2009–2010 (ie 17 tax years); such individual is deemed UK domiciled effective 6 April 2009 (ie commencement of the seventeenth tax year).

3.240   Technically an individual may become deemed domiciled after 15 tax years plus two days of residence; for example, an individual arrives in the UK on 5 April 1991 with the intention of remaining in the UK for at least three years, thus becoming resident (and indeed ordinarily resident) from the day of arrival (see paragraph 4.38). He remains in the UK and on 6 April 2007 becomes deemed domiciled in the UK. He has been resident for 15 (complete) tax years (ie 1991–1992 to 2006–2007 inclusive) but also resident in each of the tax years 1990–1991 and 2007–2008 although only in fact residing in these two tax years for one day in each; a total of 17 tax years. Furthermore, even were the individual to leave the UK becoming non-UK resident on, say, 7 April 2007 he remains deemed domiciled until 5 April 2008 (as on 5 April 2008 he still has been resident for the last 17 tax years).

3.241   The second situation referred to in paragraph 3.235 is where an individual, UK domiciled under general law (and who has been resident for many, at least 17 tax years), acquires a non-UK domicile of choice. Both the three-year rule and the 17/20 rule are of application.

For example, if the individual leaves the UK on 6 April 2008 acquiring a new non-UK domicile of choice on 7 April 2008 he remains UK-deemed domicile until 6 April 2011 (under the three-year rule). However, on 6 April 2011 the individual has still been UK resident for 17 out of the last 20 tax years and will remain so until 5 April 2012. In short, deemed domicile status persists until 5 April 2012 (ie beyond simply the three years following the acquisition of a new non-UK domicile of choice).

3.242 However, an individual who is under general law non-UK domiciled but who is caught under the deemed UK domicile rule because of the satisfaction of the 17/20 rule does not continue to be deemed UK domiciled for a further three years after leaving the UK (ie the three-year rule only applies to those individuals UK domiciled under general law).

Example 22

Sarah Tobin possesses a UK domicile of origin but has not resided in the UK for the past 17 out of the last 20 tax years.

On 1 May 1998 she leaves for Italy but is unsure of her long-term intentions.

On 1 July 2005 she decides that she wishes to remain in Italy indefinitely.

From 1 July 2005 under the normal common law rules she acquires an Italian domicile of choice.

However, for IHT purposes only, she remains deemed UK domiciled for three more years (ie until 30 June 2008).

Example 23

Chuck Timber possesses a Canadian domicile of origin.

He arrives in the UK on 1 September 1980 intending to return to Canada when he retires.

However, he dies in the UK in August 1996 prior to retiring.

He thus died in the tax year 1996–1997. In that year Chuck has been resident in the UK for 17 tax years.

He thus dies deemed UK domiciled for IHT purposes even though he probably retains his Canadian domicile of origin for other UK tax (and non-tax) purposes.

3.243 As indicated in paragraph 3.54 a child's domicile of dependence follows that of the parent on whom the child's domicile legally depends. However, if the parent becomes deemed UK domiciled for UK IHT purposes the status of the parent has no effect on the child's domicile of dependence.

3.244 *Domicile*

Example 24

Johan and Magya Kupp each possess Danish domiciles of origin. They decide to spend some time in the UK but have no intention of remaining in the UK indefinitely. Their intention is always to return to Denmark.

They each become deemed UK domiciled for IHT purposes after having resided in the UK for 17 tax years.

Despite their deemed UK domicile status for IHT purposes their daughter, Ursula, aged 10 continues to possess her Danish domicile of origin (ie that of her father).

3.244 For those non-UK domiciled individuals whose stay in the UK is very much long term, deemed UK domicile status is a real threat. However, the UK is a party to a number of IHT conventions (see Chapter 26) and under some of these, namely, those with France, India, Italy and Pakistan (all pre-1975), the concept of deemed UK domicile is not recognised (ie for the purposes of the convention an individual can only be exposed to UK IHT on worldwide assets if UK domiciled under common law). However, the other conventions to which the UK is a party do not preclude the concept from applying.

Dealing with deemed UK domicile status

3.245 In principle, it is not difficult for an individual who is non-UK domiciled to ensure that this domicile status is retained. Primarily, the individual needs to be able to demonstrate that he has no intention of remaining in the UK indefinitely (and has thus not acquired a UK domicile of choice).

3.246 However, for IHT (and only IHT) purposes, it is possible for a non-UK domiciled individual to become deemed UK domiciled simply due to the passage of time (ie falling to be treated as UK resident for 17 out of the past 20 tax years). As a general rule, avoiding deemed UK domiciled status is probably the 'better' option but this may not always be feasible.

3.247 Avoidance requires not falling foul of the 17/20 rule. If just prior to becoming resident for the seventeenth tax year the individual leaves the UK becoming non-UK resident for at least four tax years (re-acquiring UK residency thereafter) the 17/20 'clock' is effectively restarted from scratch. This option may, however, not always be practical, in which case appropriate planning needs to be put in place.

3.248 The consequence (subject to any overriding IHT convention) of becoming deemed UK domiciled is an exposure to IHT on worldwide assets (a non-UK domiciled individual is exposed only in respect of UK situs assets). However, protection from an IHT charge on non-UK situs assets is achievable by settling such assets in a non-UK resident trust prior to becoming deemed domiciled. This property then falls to be treated as 'excluded property' (*IHTA 1984 s 5;* see Chapter 13) and falls outside any charge to IHT; such trusts are commonly referred to as 'excluded property trusts' (see paragraph 13.8).

3.249 Once an individual becomes deemed UK domiciled the option of utilising the excluded property trust concept disappears.

3.250 Even UK situs assets, if these are capable of relocation outside the UK, may also be settled as above, thus turning assets otherwise chargeable to IHT into excluded property (eg an antique painting hung on the walls of the individual's house in the UK could be removed to a location outside the UK and then settled).

'Split' domicile

3.251 Following the change in law contained in *DMPA 1973* (effective from 1 January 1974), *inter alia*, a woman who marries on or after this date does not automatically acquire the domicile status of her husband at the date of marriage (see paragraph 3.66). The woman simply retains her domicile status at the date of marriage and her future domicile status is determined under the normal rules.

3.252 One consequence of this change in law is that it is no longer unusual for a husband and wife to possess different domiciles, so-called 'split domiciles'. There are thus four possible permutations for a married couple:

1. both UK domiciled;
2. both non-UK domiciled;
3. UK-domiciled husband/non-UK domiciled wife; or
4. UK-domiciled wife/non-UK domiciled husband.

3.253 As a general rule, any transfer of assets between spouses can be effected without precipitating any CGT (*TCGA 1992 s 58*) or IHT (*IHTA 1984 s 18*) consequences (see paragraphs 8.31 and 11.42) However, with respect to IHT, only the first £55,000 of transfers (*IHTA 1984 s 18*) is actually exempt from IHT where the transfers are *from a UK* domiciled spouse *to a non-UK* domiciled spouse (see points 1, 3 and 4 above). Transfers in excess of this amount are treated as potentially exempt transfers (PETs) (see paragraph 11.42) and thus may be subject to IHT should the transferor spouse die within seven years thereof.

3.254 *Domicile*

This provision severely restricts the ability for the UK domiciled spouse (liable to IHT on worldwide assets) to transfer any non-UK situs assets to his/her non-UK domiciled spouse thus removing non-UK situs assets outside the charge to IHT.

3.254 In the case of all other inter-spouse transfers (ie other than UK to non-UK domiciled spouse) there is no £55,000 limit.

3.255 In the case of CGT there is no equivalent provision limiting inter-spouse transfers and thus, in principle, all inter-spouse transfers may be made without precipitating any CGT liability (see paragraph 8.31).

International dimension

3.256 It should be noted that the IHT convention between the UK and Switzerland (*SI 1994/3214*) and between the UK and USA (*SI 1979/1454*) each provide for the £55,000 limit to be increased albeit in somewhat convoluted language (see Articles 10 and 8 respectively; see paragraph 26.39).

Summary

3.257 Domicile is probably the most important characteristic of an individual which determines the individual's liabilities with respect to income tax, CGT and IHT.

3.258 The three main categories of domicile are domicile of origin, dependence and choice. Every individual must at all times possess a domicile and only one domicile can apply at any one point in time for any specific purpose.

3.259 A domicile of origin is acquired at birth but later in life a domicile of choice may be acquired which displaces the individual's domicile of origin.

3.260 Deemed UK domicile is a status applicable only for IHT purposes.

3.261 An individual may be deemed UK domiciled for UK IHT purposes while being non-UK domiciled under common law.

Chapter 4

Residence and ordinary residence

Background

4.1 The terms 'residence' and 'ordinary residence' are similar but not identical. The difference can be very important. Thus, whether an individual is UK resident and *ordinarily* resident or is UK resident but *not ordinarily* resident may be critical to the individual's tax liabilities. If an individual is UK domiciled, UK resident but not ordinarily resident in the UK the remittance basis of taxation applies to the individual's non-UK source income in the same manner as applies in the case of a non-UK domiciled but UK resident individual.

In addition, some of the anti-avoidance provisions contained in the tax legislation are inapplicable to those individuals who are not ordinarily resident (*ITA 2007 ss 720, 727* and *732;* see paragraph 18.65).

Example 1

John Smith is UK domiciled and UK resident but is *not* ordinarily resident in the UK.

John has a bank account in Belgium which earns interest; the interest is directly credited to the account. John also receives dividends on a holding of Hong Kong equities which are credited to his bank account in Jersey.

Although John is UK domiciled and UK resident because he is *not* ordinarily UK resident the interest and dividend income are not liable to UK income tax unless remitted to the UK.

4.2 Although reference is made in certain statutory provisions (eg *ITA 2007 s 831*) to the term 'residence' such references are for specific purposes only and there is in fact no general definition of the term for all purposes. However, an individual is, by law resident and/or ordinarily resident for a tax year; the law makes no provision for splitting a tax year into periods of

4.3 *Residence and ordinary residence*

residence and non-residence (although by HMRC concession such splitting is allowed; see paragraphs 4.3 and 4.4).

4.3 For many years a booklet produced by HMRC referred to as IR20 entitled 'Residents and non-residents: Liability to tax in the UK' contained HMRC's views and practice with respect to residence, ordinary residence and domicile; in effect this was regarded as the law for all practical purposes although from time to time the views expressed therein were subject to challenge in the courts.

The views expressed by HMRC were supposedly extrapolated from a large number of court decisions. HMRC also attempted to provide pragmatic solutions where the strict application of the law would produce inequitable consequences. Perhaps the classic example is that IR20 permitted, in certain restricted circumstances, the tax year to be split between a period of residency and a period of non-residency (or vice versa); under the law there is no provision for such a split.

4.4 However, as from 6 April 2009 booklet IR20 was withdrawn and replaced by HMRC6 'Residence, Domicile and the Remittance Basis'. Subsequently, this version of HMRC6 has been updated to February 2010; the later version contains 12 chapters and some 81 pages. The only difference between the two HMRC6 versions is in chapter 5 which deals with the remittance basis. In principle much of IR20 is repeated in HMRC6 although there are differences.

4.5 It is important to appreciate that HMRC6 is not the law, but effectively HMRC's view of the law. In practice (as with IR20) it is likely to continue to be followed by practitioners subject to challenge where appropriate. Confirmation of this appears on page 3:

> 'This guidance outlines our (the HMRC) view and interpretation of legislation and case law. The material is guidance only. It has no legal force, nor does it seek to set out regulation or practice. When it seeks to give practical examples of what the relevant law means, it contains no interpretation of that law'.

Lower down the page:

> 'Whether this guidance is appropriate in a particular case will depend on all the facts of that case'.

4.6 The difficulty in deciding an individual's residence and ordinary residence status is highlighted not only by the arguably contradictory conclusions often reached by the courts in different cases but also by different levels of court with respect to the same case. With respect to the latter, in *Grace v HMRC* (2008), the High Court found that Mr Grace was resident in the UK but the

Special Commissioner found differently (ie that Grace was not UK resident); in 2009 the Court of Appeal commented as follows:

> 'The issue in these proceedings is whether the appellant, Mr Grace, was resident in the UK for tax purposes during the tax years from 1997/8 to 2002/3. Whether he was ordinarily resident for those purposes is also in issue, but on the facts of this case it is common ground that if, and only if, he was resident, then he was ordinarily resident, so it is not necessary to consider that question separately. Dr Brice, the Special Commissioner, held that he was not resident; on appeal Lewison J held that he was resident. With permission granted by Jacob LJ Mr Grace appeals to this court, contending that the Special Commissioner was right, or alternatively that if there was any error of law in her ruling, the question should be remitted for a fresh decision.
>
> For that reason, although I agree with the judge that the Special Commissioner misdirected herself, and I consider that he was right to allow the appeal, in my judgment he ought to have remitted the issue for re-determination. That is the order that I would make, allowing the appellant's appeal though only to that extent. The remittal will be to the First Tier Tribunal (Tax Chamber). We have had the benefit of written submissions from the parties in the light of the draft version of this judgment. In the light of those the court's order will be that the appeal is allowed and the question of the appellant's residence (and, so far as necessary, ordinary residence) be remitted to the First-Tier Tribunal (Tax Chamber) for reconsideration (if practicable, by Dr Brice) in the light of our judgment. The parties are to apply to the Tribunal for directions as to that reconsideration'.

4.7 Perhaps the most recent illuminating statement concerning the meaning of the terms 'resident' and 'ordinary resident' is that provided by the Special Commissioner of Income Tax, Dr A N Brice, in *Shepherd v HMRC* (2005). After considering various previous decided cases she commented as follows:

> 'From these authorities I derive the following principles.
>
> - that the concept of residence and ordinary residence are not defined in the legislation; the words therefore should be given their natural and ordinary meanings (*Levene*);
> - that the word 'residence' and 'to reside' mean 'to dwell permanently or for a considerable time, to have one's settled or usual abode, to live in or at a particular place' (*Levene*);
> - that the concept of 'ordinary residence' requires more than mere residence; it connotes residence in a place with some degree of

4.8 *Residence and ordinary residence*

continuity (*Levene*); 'ordinary' means normal and part of everyday life (*Lysaght*) or a regular, habitual mode of life in a particular place which has persisted despite temporary absences and which is voluntary and has a degree of settled purpose (*Shah*);

- that the question whether a person is or is not resident in the United Kingdom is a question of fact for the Special Commissioners (*Zorab*);
- that no duration is prescribed by statute and it is necessary to take into account all the facts of the case; the duration of an individual's presence in the United Kingdom and the regularity and frequency of visits are facts to be taken into account; also, birth, family and business ties, the nature of visits and the connections with this country, may all be relevant (*Zorab*; *Brown*);
- that a reduced presence in the United Kingdom of a person whose absences are caused by his employment and so are temporary absences does not necessarily mean that the person is not residing in the United Kingdom (*Young*);
- that the availability of living accommodation in the United Kingdom is a factor to be borne in mind in deciding if a person is resident here (*Cooper*) (although that is subject to *s 336*);
- that the fact that an individual has a home elsewhere is of no consequence; a person may reside in two places but if one of those places is the United Kingdom he is chargeable to tax here (*Cooper* and *Levene*);
- that there is a difference between the case where a British subject has established a residence in the United Kingdom and then has absences from it (*Levene*) and the case where a person has never had a residence in the United Kingdom at all (*Zorab*; *Brown*);
- that if there is evidence that a move abroad is a distinct break that could be a relevant factor in treating an individual as non-resident (*Combe*); and
- that a person could become non-resident even if his intention was to mitigate tax (*Reed v Clark*)'.

Residence and ordinary residence under HMRC6

4.8 As indicated above, determining an individual's residence and ordinary residence status is complex and dependent upon a variety of factors. HMRC6 states that:

'... it is not simply a question of the number of days you are physically present in the UK during a tax year although this is an

Residence and ordinary residence 4.11

important consideration' (paragraph 2.2, page 16). The above applies with one exception – the so-called "183-day test".

The 183-day test

4.9 An individual who is physically present in the UK for 183 days or more in a tax year is automatically resident in the UK; there are no exceptions to this rule. However, an individual may be resident in the UK even where the number of days spent in the UK is less than 183 days.

Before 6 April 2008 there was no statutory definition of a 'day' for determining residence status for all tax purposes; broadly, any time spent in the UK was treated as a day although days of arrival and departure were generally ignored.

4.10 With effect from 6 April 2008, whilst in theory the position has been clarified (*FA 2008 s 24*) it is arguably not entirely clear. A statutory definition of a 'day' has now been provided (*FA 2008 s 24*) but this is only for certain tax purposes (eg *TCGA 1992 s 9* (capital gains tax (CGT)); *ITA 2007 ss 831* and *832* (foreign income and employment income)). However, it is understood that HMRC regard the definition in *FA 2008 s 24* to be generally applicable.

4.11 Thus, a day is counted only if the individual is in the UK at the end of the day (ie at midnight).

Example 2

Inga Johanson is contemplating visiting the UK sometime in the tax year 2008–2009. She indicates that on current plans she will make three separate visits as follows:

(I)   arrive 10 November 2008; leave 15 November 2008;

(ii) arrive 20 December 2008; leave 3 January 2009;

(iii) arrive 6 March 2009; leave 31 March 2009.

She calculates that she will be in the UK for 41 days in 2008–2009.

However, in the light of the FA 2008 changes she will in fact be spending 44 days in the UK.

However, where an individual arrives in the UK as a passenger ignore the day of arrival where the individual departs the UK on the next day and between arrival

4.12 *Residence and ordinary residence*

and departure the individual does not engage in activities that are to a substantial extent unrelated to the individual's passage through the UK (*FA 2008 s 24*). For the passenger neither the day of arrival nor the day of departure is thus counted.

4.12 The exception in paragraph 4.11 thus applies, for example, to an individual travelling from the USA to France who lands late in the day in the UK, spends the night in the UK, before picking up a connecting flight the next day to France.

4.13 HMRC regard activities as unrelated to a passage through the UK if, for example, the individual attends a business meeting; visits a property he owns; arranges to meet people socially or attends social activities; in such cases the day spent on such activities must be counted if the individual is in the UK at the end of the day (HMRC6 para 2.3, p 16).

4.14 For periods both pre-6 April 2008 and on or after 6 April 2008 any days spent in the UK due to exceptional circumstances beyond the individual's control are not ignored when ascertaining whether the 183-day test is satisfied although they are ignored when counting days in the UK for other tests (eg the 91-day test; see paragraph 4.27) (HMRC6 paras 2.2 and 8.9 on pp 16 and 54 respectively).

The only provided example in HMRC6 of such circumstances is illness although no clarification is provided as to whether this has to be an illness of the individual or whether it might apply to an illness of an accompanying spouse.

Temporary residence abroad

4.15 If an individual has left the UK for the purpose of occasional residence abroad and at the time of leaving the individual was both resident and ordinarily resident in the UK he is treated as UK resident for the purposes of determining any liability to income tax for any tax year in which the individual remains outside the UK for occasional residence abroad (*ITA 2007 s 829*). The section does not apply for CGT purposes.

4.16 The effect of the section is simply to continue to levy income tax on the individual as if he had never left the UK.

4.17 As to what constitutes occasional residence abroad is left to the courts to decide. In the case of the 1960s pop star Dave Clark namely, *Reed v Clark* (1985), Clark who was outside the UK for just over one year was found not to have been abroad only for the purpose of occasional residence abroad and thus fell outside the provisions of *ITA 2007 s 829*, thus escaping a charge to income tax for his period of absence.

Non-temporary residence abroad

4.18 Where an individual leaves the UK (other than for occasional residence abroad) residency and ordinary residency may be lost. This depends upon the reasons for leaving the UK.

4.19 Loss of residence and ordinary residency occurs where the individual:

- leaves the UK permanently or indefinitely; or
- leaves the UK to work abroad (either as an employee or self-employed).

Leaving the UK permanently/indefinitely

4.20 Leaving the UK permanently or indefinitely results in an individual becoming not resident and not ordinarily resident in the UK from the day following the day of departure (HMRC6 para 8.2, p 51).

4.21 HMRC distinguishes between permanently and indefinitely. An individual leaves the UK *permanently* where the individual leaves the UK to live abroad and will not return to the UK to live; effectively emigration (HMRC6 para 8.1, p 50).

An individual leaves the UK *indefinitely* where the individual leaves to live abroad for a long time (ie at least three years) but the individual recognises he may return to live in the UK at sometime in the future (HMRC6 para 8.1, p 50).

4.22 Whether, de facto, having left the UK non-UK residency and ordinary residency occurs involves a consideration of all the surrounding factors; such factors include the extent to which ties with the UK remain; the extent of return visits to the UK; the nature of such return visits; the existence of a permanent home abroad; etc. (HMRC6 paras 8.1 and 8.2, pp 50 and 51).

4.23 Central to the issue of permanent or indefinite residence abroad is the concept of a distinct break from previous ties within the UK. In the Court of Appeal decision in *Gaines-Cooper v HMRC* (2010) Moses LJ commented as follows:

> 'The adhesive quality of residence is reflected in the reference in s 334 ICTA [now s 829 ITA 2007] to 'occasional residence abroad'. The notion of a distinct break from previously held ties provides a clear test as to whether previously held residence, for example in the UK, has ceased permanently or indefinitely ...

4.24 *Residence and ordinary residence*

The notion of a distinct break appears in *IRC v Combe* [1932] 17 TC 405, in which a full time apprenticeship was served in New York. Lord Sands (411) attached importance to the distinct break in residence in the UK (referred to in *Grace* at [6] (xiii) and see also the application of that concept in *Reed v Clark* [1985] STC 323 at 346h). Whilst IR20 is designed to guide and simplify, I cannot accept that it provides a warrant for ignoring so obvious a factor for determining whether a taxpayer hitherto resident and ordinarily resident in the UK has ceased to be so and has left permanently or indefinitely. IR20 itself, at 1.4, requires a value judgement to be made as to whether a taxpayer, claiming to come within 2.7–2.9, has ceased to be resident in the UK. There can be no sensible reason why one of the most telling features of such a cessation, a distinct break from family and social ties in this country, should be ignored. It would not create clarity or simplicity; it would merely remove from consideration an obvious test of permanent or indefinite absence abroad.'

4.24 As the case of *Gaines-Cooper v RCC* (2010) illustrates, retaining significant ties with the UK, after purportedly leaving the country in order to lose UK residency and ordinary residency, is simply likely to lead to a finding that a distinct break with the UK has not occurred. In this case, Mr Gaines-Cooper retained significant personal and business interests in the UK.

4.25 As is evident from HMRC6 (see para 4.19) where an individual leaves the UK permanently or indefinitely part way through a tax year HMRC are prepared to accept that the tax year of departure may be split between a period of residency and a period of non-residency.

Return visits to the UK

4.26 Assuming non-UK residency and non-ordinary residency is achieved, visits back to the UK may cause a re-acquisition of both residency and non-residency.

4.27 Visits back to the UK precipitate a re-acquisition of residency and ordinary residency where they average 91 days or more per tax year (HMRC6 para 8.2, p 51). To calculate annual average visits:

[Total days visiting the UK/Total days since leaving] x 365

The calculation is a rolling calculation carried out over a maximum period of four tax years. Days spent in the UK before departure are ignored for this purpose (this formula is different from that used for 'new arrivals'; see paragraph 4.47).

Example 3

Giles Farmer left the UK permanently on 5 October 2006.

Visits to the UK have been:

30 days between 6 October 2006 and 5 April 2007.

50 days between 6 April 2007 and 5 April 2008 (note: a leap year and thus contains 366 days).

The first review is carried out as at 5 April 2008 (ie after one complete tax year of absence):

[[30 + 50]/[182 + 366]] x 365 = 53.28 days.

Assume further visits of 70 days between 6 April 2008 and 5 April 2009.

The second review is carried out as at 5 April 2009:

[[30 + 50 + 70]/[182 + 366 + 365]] x 365 = 59.97 days.

The third review is carried out as at 5 April 2010 and the fourth review as at 5 April 2011.

The review as at 5 April 2011 only now takes in the period 6 April 2007 to 5 April 2011 as the period 6 October 2006 to 5 April 2007 drops out of account.

Thereafter as one tax year is added to the review one tax year is removed.

4.28 The effect of the above calculation is that residence and ordinary residence occurs once the average of visits is 91 days or more. The calculation is carried out over a maximum period of four tax years (the tax year of leaving counting as the first tax year). However, the calculation is performed not just over a fixed four tax year period but after the end of each tax year of absence; the first calculation occurring after the end of the tax year 12 months after the end of the tax year of leaving the UK (see Example 3).

Thus, if after any calculation (within the first four tax years of absence) the average number of days is 91 days or more, residence and ordinary residence arises. HMRC6 appears to be silent as to the precise date from which such residence and ordinary residence arises. However, *prima facie*, where the average number of days is 91 days or more in the first four tax years of absence residence and ordinary residence appears not to have been lost (as if no departure from the UK has occurred).

4.29 *Residence and ordinary residence*

In Example 3, if the review carried out at the end of the tax year, say, 5 April 2009 produced an average number of days of, say, 93 days (not the 59.97 days) residence and ordinary residence would appear to never have been lost and the individual (Giles Farmer in Example 3) simply continues to remain resident and ordinary resident.

4.29 Where the 91 days or more average is breached only over a period of four tax years where the tax year of leaving the UK does not form part of the calculation residence and ordinary residence, *prima facie*, resumes from the 6 April of the first tax year forming part of the calculation.

In Example 3, if the review carried out at the end of the tax year, say, 5 April 2011 (ie the period 6 October 2006 to 5 April 2007 no longer forms part of the calculation) produced an average number of days of, say, 95 days residence and ordinary residence would appear to have resumed from 6 April 2007 (in which case at least in theory the period 6 October 2006 to 5 April 2007 is a period of non-residence and non-ordinary residence; in practice this would be very unlikely as no doubt HMRC would adopt the argument that no distinct break with the UK had occurred; see paragraph 4.23).

Once residence and ordinary residence is re-acquired presumably the rolling four-tax-year calculation ceases; residency and ordinary residency having been re-acquired can then only be lost again by leaving the UK permanently or indefinitely involving a distinct break from the UK (and so effectively the whole process starts over again).

This approach to the four tax year calculation, if correct, is different from that which is applicable to 'new arrivals' where the determination of the 91 days or more is always made over a four tax year period (see paragraph 4.45).

Working abroad

4.30 Where the following conditions are satisfied an individual becomes neither UK resident nor ordinarily resident from the day following the day of departure. The conditions are:

- the individual leaves the UK to work abroad full time under a contract of employment for at least a whole tax year;
- absence from the UK must be for at least a whole tax year;
- leaving the UK must be to begin the employment and not for other purposes (eg to have a holiday prior to starting the employment); and
- return visits to the UK after having left to start the employment must total less than 183 days in any tax year and average less than 91 days (averaged over a maximum four-tax-year period).

(HMRC6 para 8.5, p 53; but note the short list of exceptions at para 8.4, p 52).

4.31 On returning to the UK, on cessation of the employment, UK residency and ordinary residency recommences (from the day of arrival in the UK) unless the return is for a short period of time between two periods of full-time employment abroad (HMRC6 para 8.6, p 53).

4.32 Any living accommodation in the UK is ignored when determining an individual's residence whilst working abroad (*ITA 2007 s 830*).

Example 4

Brian Brown has managed to secure for himself a contract of employment with a company based in Bahrain.

The contract is for the period 1 March 2009 to 30 June 2010 (and thus spans a complete tax year, namely, 2009–2010) and the contract also requires him to work full time.

Brian leaves the UK to take up his contract on 25 February 2009 and returns to the UK on 7 July 2010. He makes only one return visit to the UK during his period of absence to see his parents at Christmas; the visit lasts for seven days.

Brian will be treated as neither resident nor ordinarily resident from 26 February (ie the day after his departure from the UK) to 6 July (the day before his return to the UK) inclusive.

Had Brian's contract of employment run from 1 March 2009 to, say, 31 January 2010 then Brian would be treated as remaining resident and ordinarily resident in the UK throughout this period as the contract of employment does not span a complete tax year.

4.33 Full-time employment is typically an employment whose standard pattern of hours is not dissimilar to a typical UK working week or, where appropriate, a comparison to local working practices can be made.

4.34 Any changes in the employment whilst the individual is abroad may cause the original loss of UK residency and ordinary residency to become invalid; this will depend upon the nature of the change but if, for example, the employment were to cease prior to completing one complete tax year this may well invalidate the loss of residency and ordinary residency. Thus, simply remaining abroad after the employment has ceased does not guarantee non-residency and non-ordinary residency.

4.35 *Residence and ordinary residence*

4.35 Accompanying spouses in principle receive the same treatment as the working spouse under ESC A78 (HMRC6 para 8.9, p 54).

Example 5

In Example 4 if Brian is accompanied by his wife, Mary, even though Mary is not working abroad she is similarly treated as neither resident nor ordinarily resident during her period of absence.

4.36 Individuals who are to work abroad, not as employees, but self-employed, are accorded the same treatment as employees.

New arrivals in the UK

4.37 The residency and non-residency of 'new' arrivals depends upon the reasons for coming to the UK (HMRC6 para 7.1, p 44). This leads to a classification of new arrivals into one of a number of categories. These categories are, however, creations of HMRC with little case law support. Nevertheless, practitioners tend to operate within these guidelines.

4.38 New arrivals are therefore treated as falling into one of the two following categories:

- intention is to live in the UK permanently or to live or work in the UK for three years or more; or
- intention is to visit the UK for less than three years.

Visitors to the UK for less than three years are sub-divided into 'short term' and 'long term visitors' (HMRC6 para 7.4, p 45).

Permanent or more than three-year stays

4.39 An individual who comes to the UK with the intention of living in the UK permanently is treated as resident and ordinarily resident from the day of arrival. Similarly, an individual who does not come to live in the UK permanently but who comes to the UK to live or work for at least three years is also treated as resident and ordinary resident from the day of arrival.

4.40 The tax year of arrival is thus split into a period of non-residency prior to the date of arrival and a period of residency from the date of arrival.

Short- and long-term visitors

4.41 This classification refers to 'visitors'. For this purposes a visitor is an individual who is in the UK for a temporary purpose (HMRC6 para 7.4, p 45). The concept of temporary purpose is not defined in HMRC6 otherwise than by way of exception.

Case law has from time to time considered the matter as *ITA 2007 ss 831* and 832 use the term; where the individual is in the UK for a temporary purpose relevant foreign income (RFI) (*ITA 2007 s 831*) and employment income (*ITA 2007 s 832*) of the individual are subject to income tax as if the individual is not resident.

4.42 Individuals spending 183 days or more in the UK are automatically resident irrespective of all other factors (see paragraph 4.9).

Working in the UK

4.43 Individuals who come to the UK for a specific purpose (eg to work) who will as a consequence remain in the UK for at least two years are not regarded as visitors (ie are not in the UK for a temporary purpose) and thus become resident (but not ordinary resident) from the day of arrival.

This infers that an individual who thus comes to the UK for a specific purpose which does require him to be here for at least two years does not fall to be treated as resident under this classification; but, *prima facie*, falls to be treated as a visitor (see paragraph 4.44).

True visitors

4.44 An individual who is not in the UK for at least 183 days; does not come to the UK permanently or for at least three years; and who is not in the UK for a specific purpose pursuant to which he will be in the UK for at least two years results in the individual being classified as a 'visitor'. It is then necessary to sub-classify the individual as a 'short-term' or 'longer-term' visitor. Once so classified the rules for that category can then be applied to determine residence and ordinary residence.

A short-term visitor is where the individual is not going to remain in the UK for an extended period but anticipates visits to the UK over one or more tax years albeit limited in nature (HMRC6 para 7.4, p 46).

4.45 *Residence and ordinary residence*

A longer-term visitor is where the individual has come to the UK indefinitely (but not permanently) or for an extended period which might cover several tax years (HMRC6 para 7.4, p 46).

The distinction here appears somewhat arbitrary resting on vague and undefined terms (eg 'extended term'). The minimum three-year test (see paragraph 4.38) appears to conflict with visitors who intend to visit the UK 'indefinitely'. However, the distinction rests on the fact that an individual who comes to the UK satisfies the minimum three year test if he effectively resides in the UK (ie he remains in the UK) for the tax years (ie is not simply visiting). On the other hand, an individual who intends to visit the UK for many years without residing (ie remaining in the UK) in the UK is classified as a longer-term visitor.

Short-term visitor

4.45 An individual visiting the UK (assuming the 183-day test is not breached) is regarded as resident and ordinarily resident after averaging 91 days or more per tax year calculated over a four tax year period. If on the first visit the individual is unclear as to over what period he is likely to be visiting the UK but breaches the 91 days average per tax year over his first four tax years of visits he is treated as resident and ordinary resident from the start of the fifth tax year (HMRC6 para 7.5, p 46). Thus, despite the earlier tax year visits neither residency nor ordinary residency arises for each of those tax years.

If, however, on the first visit the individual knows that his visits are going to be an average of 91 days or more per tax year the individual is treated as resident and ordinary resident from the 6 April of the tax year of his first visit (HMRC6 para 7.5, p 46).

Example 6

Inga Johanson arrives in the UK for the first time on 1 October 1999. At that time she is uncertain of her likely future intentions.

In the event, her visits to the UK over the first four tax years (ie 1999–2000 to 2002–2003) averaged 103 days per tax year (the 183-day test not breached in any of the tax years).

As a consequence of breaching the 91-day per tax year average over her first four tax years of visits Inga is classified as resident and ordinarily resident from 6 April 2003 (ie commencement of the fifth tax year after arrival).

Thus, despite spending time in the UK in the previous four tax years Inga is treated as neither resident nor ordinarily resident in any of them.

Example 7

Inga Johanson's sister, Ulrica, also arrives in the UK for the first time on 1 October 1999. At that time she knows that she will be averaging at least 91 days per tax year in the first four tax years of her visit.

Unlike her sister, Inga, Ulrica is treated as resident and ordinary resident from 6 April 1999.

4.46 It is to be noted that effectively a degree of backdating occurs where the individual's intentions are known at the commencement of any visit to the UK (ie in Ulrica's situation in Example 7 she is treated as resident and ordinary resident for a period, namely, 6 April 1999 to 30 September 1999 when in fact she was not in the UK). For income tax and CGT purposes relief is, however, available for this period (ESC A11 and ESC D2; see paragraph 4.54).

4.47 The calculation used to determine the average number of days per tax year spent in the UK is slightly different from that used for individuals who have left the UK but thereafter make return visits (see paragraph 4.26). The formula is:

[Total days visiting the UK/Tax years you have visited the UK (in days)] x 365

Example 8

Henrique visits the UK as follows:

70 days in 2007–2008

110 days in 2008–2009

75 days in 2009–2010

115 days in 2010–2011.

Henrique's average days per tax year in the UK is:

[[70 + 110 + 75 + 115]/[366 + 365 + 365 + 365]] x 365 = 92.44 days.

4.48 *Residence and ordinary residence*

4.48 Where on arrival the individual's future intentions are unclear but at some time before the commencement of the fifth tax year it becomes clear that visits over the first four tax years of visits are to equal or exceed 91 days per tax year, residence and ordinary residence is treated as commencing from the 6 April in which this realisation occurs.

Example 9

Henri Jacques arrives in the UK on 10 December 2007 with unclear intentions as to his future visits.

He is in fact in the UK for 80 days in the first tax year 2007–2008. In the tax year 2008–2009 he is in the UK for 120 days.

In the third tax year 2009–2010 his intentions become clear such that over the first four tax years his visits will average at least 91 days in each tax year (ie on average over the four tax years 2007–2008, 2008–2009, 2009–2010 and 2010–2011).

He is, as a consequence, treated as resident and ordinarily resident from 6 April 2009 (ie the commencement of the tax year in which his intentions become clear).

4.49 If at the date of the first visit it is expected that the 91 days per tax year will be breached, but in the event after the first four tax years of visits this does not happen (ie average days per tax year are below the 91 days), the individual no longer falls to be treated as resident and ordinarily resident from the 6 April of the tax year of arrival.

Longer-term visitor

4.50 An individual visiting the UK (assuming the 183-day test is not breached) is regarded as resident and ordinarily resident after averaging 91 days or more per tax year. If on the first visit the individual is unclear as to over what period he is likely to be visiting the UK but breaches the 91 days average per tax year over his first four tax years of visits he is treated as resident and ordinarily resident from the start of the fifth tax year (HMRC6 para 7.7, p 47). Thus, despite the earlier tax year visits neither residency nor ordinary residency arises for each of those tax years.

If, however, on the first visit the individual knows that his visits are going to be an average of 91 days or more per tax year the individual is treated as resident and ordinarily resident from the 6 April of the tax year of his first visit (HMRC6 para 7.7, p 47).

4.51 Where on arrival the individual's future intentions are unclear but at some time before the commencement of the fifth tax year it becomes clear that visits are to exceed 91 days per tax year, residence and ordinary residence is treated as commencing from the 6 April in which this realisation occurs.

4.52 An individual coming to the UK for at least two years (but less than three years) is treated as resident from the day of arrival (HMRC6 para 7.7.1, p 47).

Split tax years: income tax and capital gains tax implications

4.53 An individual is resident and/or ordinarily resident for a complete tax year; as a matter of law a tax year cannot be split for this purpose and an individual by law cannot thus be resident for part of a tax year but non-resident for the other part of the tax year (*Gubay v Kington* (1984)).

However, by concession HMRC accept that in certain circumstances a tax year can be split into such periods; the issue then arises as to how the individual's income tax and CGT liabilities are to be ascertained for the tax year of arrival/departure.

4.54 Two specific statutory concessions, namely, ESC A11 and ESC D2, detail how the individual's income and CGT liabilities are to be calculated in such circumstances.

4.55 HMRC's booklet 'Extra-Statutory Concessions August 2009', which details all concessions then in force, in its introduction makes the following comment:

> **'Introduction**
>
> This guide details the Extra-Statutory Concessions previously operated by Inland Revenue in use at 10 August 2009. ...
>
> An Extra-Statutory Concession is a relaxation which gives taxpayers a reduction in tax liability to which they would not be entitled under the strict letter of the law. Most concessions are made to deal with what are, on the whole, minor or transitory anomalies under the legislation and to meet cases of hardship at the margins of the code where a statutory remedy would be difficult to devise or would run to a length out of proportion to the intrinsic importance of the matter.

4.56 *Residence and ordinary residence*

The concessions described within are of general application, but it must be borne in mind that in a particular case there may be special circumstances which will need to be taken into account in considering the application of the concession. A concession will not be given in any case where an attempt is made to use it for tax avoidance'.

4.56 An example of the refusal to apply a concession concerning split tax years is the case of *R v IRC, ex parte Fulford-Dobson* (1987). In this case a wife gave her husband an asset just prior to his taking up full-time employment abroad which he then sold, albeit before the following 6 April. HMRC refused to apply any concessional treatment (ie refused to accept that from the day following Mr Fulford-Dobson leaving the UK he had lost his UK residency) and, as a consequence of denying Mr Fulford-Dobson non-UK residence status, levied CGT on the gain he had made from the sale. The court upheld HMRC's treatment and a subsequent judicial review of HMRC's approach by the taxpayer was also unsuccessful. Mr Fulford-Dobson's attempt to thus split his tax year of his departure from the UK was thus unsuccessful.

Income tax

4.57 As indicated in paragraph 4.53, ESC A11 makes provision for split tax years of residence/non-residence.

ESC A11 states:

'The Income and Corporation Taxes Acts make no provision for splitting a tax year in relation to residence and an individual who is resident in the United Kingdom for any year of assessment is chargeable on the basis that he is resident for the whole year.

But where an individual

(a) comes to the United Kingdom to take up permanent residence or to stay for at least two years; or

(b) ceases to reside in the United Kingdom if he has left for permanent residence abroad;

liability to United Kingdom tax which is affected by residence is computed by reference to the period of his residence here during the year. It is a condition that the individual should satisfy the Board of Inland Revenue that prior to his arrival he was, or on his departure is, not ordinarily resident in the United Kingdom. The concession would not apply, for example, where an individual who had been ordinarily resident in the United Kingdom left for intended permanent residence abroad but returned to reside here before the end of the tax year following the tax year of departure.

This concession is extended to the years of departure and return where, subject to certain conditions, an individual goes abroad for full time service under a contract of employment'.

4.58 ESC A11 thus does not apply to those new arrivals who do not intend to take up permanent residence or to stay for at least two years; in essence therefore the concession requires a new arrival to stay for at least two years. In addition, the individual must not have been ordinarily resident in the UK prior to arrival (for new arrivals this is unlikely to be problematic).

4.59 ESC A11 does not apply where the individual leaves the UK for any period of time other than a permanent departure unless the departure is to work full time abroad under a contract of employment spanning at least one complete tax year.

Thus, an individual leaving the UK for, say, a period of, say, five or seven years cannot take advantage of the concession.

4.60 There appears to be no rationale as to the precise terms of ESC A11 and why it does not appear to apply to certain bona fide circumstances.

4.61 When ESC A11 does apply the individual's income tax liability is computed by reference to periods of residency (ie from the date of arrival to the end of the tax year of arrival or from the previous 6 April to the day of departure).

4.62 It is HMRC6, not ESC A11, which provides for more detail as to the precise exposure to income tax in tax years of arrival and departure.

Employment income

4.63 Employment earnings are not subject to income tax up to the day before the date of arrival if the earnings are from the duties of an employment carried on outside the UK (HMRC6 para 10.7, p 63).

Employment earnings up to and including the day of departure are subject to income tax but thereafter are not subject to income tax assuming that the earnings are from an employment which is carried out wholly abroad (HMRC6 para 10.7, p 64).

Investment income

4.64 Investment income includes bank interest; dividends on shares; rental income (unless part of a trading business (eg furnished holiday lettings)).

4.65 *Residence and ordinary residence*

Foreign investment income arising before the date of arrival is not subject to income tax (HMRC6 para 10.14.1, p 71). Foreign investment income arising up to and including the day of departure is subject to income tax but not thereafter (HMRC6 para 10.14.2, p 72).

Capital gains tax

4.65 As indicated in paragraph 4.54, ESC D2 provides for split tax year treatment in tax years of arrival and departure and the extent of any CGT liability in those tax years. ESC D2 states:

'1. An individual who comes to live in the United Kingdom and is treated as resident here for any year of assessment from the date of arrival is charged to capital gains tax only in respect of chargeable gains from disposals made after arrival, provided that the individual has not been resident or ordinarily resident in the United Kingdom at any time during the five years of assessment immediately preceding the year of assessment in which he or she arrived in the United Kingdom.

2. An individual who leaves the United Kingdom and is treated on departure as not resident and not ordinarily resident here is not charged to capital gains tax on gains from disposals made after the date of departure, provided that the individual was not resident and not ordinarily resident in the United Kingdom for the whole of at least four out of the seven years of assessment immediately preceding the year of assessment in which he or she left the United Kingdom.

...

4. This concession does not apply to the trustees of a settlement who commence or cease residence in the United Kingdom or to a settlor of a settlement in relation to gains in respect of which the settlor is chargeable under Sections 77–79 TCGA 1992 [Note: These sections have been repealed from 6 April 2008], or Section 86 and Schedule 5 TCGA 1992.

5. This revised concession applies to any individual who ceases to be resident or ordinarily resident in the United Kingdom on or after 17 March 1998, or becomes resident or ordinarily resident in the United Kingdom on or after 6 April 1998.'

4.66 Thus, ESC D2 does not apply to those individuals arriving in the UK if such individuals have been resident or ordinarily resident in any of the five tax years preceding the tax year of arrival.

ESC D2 does not apply to those individuals who leave the UK but who were either resident or ordinarily resident or both for at least four out of the seven tax years prior to the tax year of departure.

4.67 Where ESC D2 does apply any CGT liability is restricted to disposals made on or after the date of arrival for individuals arriving in the UK or, for those individuals leaving the UK, disposals made after the day of departure.

Failure to satisfy ESC A11 or ESC D2

4.68 Both ESC A11 and ESC D2 relate to charges to income tax and CGT. They do not, per se, split the tax year into periods of residence and non-residence; this is granted under HMRC6.

4.69 Both concessions are therefore only in point once a tax year has been split for residence and ordinary residence purposes.

4.70 A failure to satisfy the relevant concession does not therefore deny the individual split residence treatment for the tax year of arrival or departure. The consequence of a failure to satisfy the relevant concession is that the individual's income tax or CGT liability is calculated based on his income/capital gains for the whole of the tax year of arrival or departure not just the residence period.

Example 10

An individual arrives in the UK on 4 August 2010 and is treated as resident and ordinarily resident from that date. He has not been resident or ordinarily resident in the UK during the five prior tax years.

In May 2007 he had sold his holding of UK equities in XYZ Ltd making a capital gain of £200,000 and in October 2007 sold his holding of UK equities in ABC Ltd making a capital gain of £150,000.

Under ESC D2 he will not be liable to CGT on the sale of the XYZ Ltd shares but will be subject to CGT on the sale of the ABC Ltd shares.

However, if the individual prior to arriving in the UK on 4 August 2007 (ie in the tax year 2010–2011) had been, say, resident in the UK in the tax year 2005–2006 (ie within the five previous tax years (prior to tax year 2010–2011) CGT would have been levied on both of the above share sales (even though one of the sales had in fact occurred prior to the acquisition of residency in the UK).

4.71 *Residence and ordinary residence*

Non-UK residence anti-avoidance provisions

4.71 Individuals who leave the UK for a period of non-UK residency would normally expect to fall outside the charge to UK income tax (other than on UK source income) and CGT once non-resident.

However, anti-avoidance provisions may apply to deny such exemptions thus continuing to levy tax even though the individual has acquired non-UK residency unless certain conditions are satisfied (*ITTOIA 2005 s 832A; TCGA 1992 s 10A*).

4.72 Pre-*FA 2008*, subject to satisfying certain conditions CGT continued to be charged on non-UK resident individuals on disposals made after leaving the UK whether the individual was UK domiciled or not (albeit that non-UK domiciled individuals were able to circumnavigate the section as it did not apply in a number of cases; *FA 2008,* however, extended the ambit of the section with respect to non-UK domiciled individuals).

4.73 Pre-*FA 2008*, there was no equivalent anti-avoidance provision which applied for income tax purposes. However, *FA 2008*, introduced a new anti-avoidance provision applicable for income tax purposes, but which, however, only applies to non-UK domiciled individuals.

Capital gains tax

4.74 Where the individual has been resident in the UK for at least four of the immediately preceding seven tax years prior to the tax year of departure and becomes non-UK resident for less than five complete tax years, any capital gains arising on disposals of assets (during the complete tax years of absence) owned prior to departure are subject to CGT (and any capital losses are allowable; *TCGA 1992 s 10A;* see paragraph 8.125).

The CGT charge, however, arises in the tax year of return not the tax years of the actual disposals (where *TCGA 1992 s 10A* applies, any capital gains subject to charge on resumption of residence during the tax year 2010–2011 are treated as arising before 23 June 2010 (*F(No 2) 2010 s 2* and *Sch 1*) and thus are charged at the 18% (not 28%) rate).

4.75 If the five-tax-year period of absence condition is satisfied any capital gains (or capital losses) arising in any of these five tax years (in respect of assets owned at the time of departure) are not subject to CGT (or allowable).

Similarly, if the individual is not resident for at least four out of the seven tax-year periods prior to the tax year of departure, non-UK residence for a period of five tax years is not required in order to dispose of assets owned on departure without a CGT charge.

4.76 Assets acquired during the balance of the tax year of departure following departure or during the five complete tax-year period of absence but sold during the five complete tax years of absence are not subject to CGT under the above rule; thus, neither gains nor losses arising on the disposal of such assets are chargeable/allowable.

Example 11

An individual, Dick, leaves the UK on 6 November 2009 for five subsequent complete tax years. Dick has been resident and ordinarily resident in the UK for at least four out of the seven tax years prior to the tax year of departure (ie prior to 2009–2010).

In February 2010 (having left the UK) Dick sells a piece of UK real estate (owned prior to departure) making a capital gain and also sells UK equities (owned prior to departure) making a capital gain in June 2010.

At both dates of sale Dick has left the UK, and indeed lost his UK residency and ordinary residence status.

TCGA 1992 s 10A is not in point as Dick is absent for five complete tax years.

However, the terms of ESC D2 are not satisfied and thus the capital gain arising on the sale of the UK real estate in the tax year of absence (ie 2009–2010) is subject to CGT in that tax year.

The capital gain arising on the sale of the UK equities in the tax year following the tax year of departure is not be subject to a CGT charge.

4.77 Where *TCGA 1992 s 10A* applies and the non-UK domiciled individual claims remittance basis treatment in the tax year of return the capital gains subject to CGT in the tax year of return comprise those gains made during the period of absence on UK situs assets; those gains on non-UK situs assets which are remitted during the period of absence; and those gains made before departure but remitted during the period of absence.

The capital gains made during the period of absence on non-UK situs assets but not remitted during the period of absence are subject to CGT only on subsequent remittance.

4.78 *Residence and ordinary residence*

Capital gains arising on disposals of non-UK situs assets owned and disposed of pre-6 April 2008 but remitted on or after 6 April 2008 are also subject to *TCGA 1992 s 10A* in its post-*FA 2008* form.

Income tax

4.78 Under the new rules contained in *FA 2008* RFI (broadly, interest and dividends arising outside the UK) of a non-UK domiciled individual remitted to the UK while the individual is non-UK resident may fall subject to income tax in the tax year of the individual's return to the UK (*ITTOIA 2005 s 832A*).

4.79 *ITTOIA 2005 s 832A* applies where the individual has been resident in the UK or ordinarily resident therein for at least four tax years out of the immediately preceding seven tax years prior to the tax year of departure and the individual is non-UK resident less than five full tax years between the tax year of departure and the tax year of return. In this case any RFI which is remitted to the UK after the tax year of departure and before the tax year of return is treated as remitted in the tax year of return and subject to income tax in that tax year of return.

The RFI to which this applies is that which has arisen in the tax year of departure or an earlier tax year (including such income which arose before the tax year 2008–2009 (ie there is no transitional relief for pre-2008–2009 relevant foreign income when *ITTOIA 2005 s 832A* was not in point).

Thus, any RFI which arises during the complete tax years of absence may be remitted without income tax charge whether remitted whilst the individual is non-resident (as *ITTOIA 2005 s 832A* does not apply to such income) or after his return to the UK (because as the income arose whilst the individual is non-resident it is not within the charge in any event).

Example 12

Billy Florida Snr, a non-UK domiciled but UK resident individual, has been UK resident for the last ten tax years prior to the tax year 2008–2009.

During this period he generates RFI of £175,000 which is credited to his bank account in Dubai.

He leaves the UK on 6 June 2008, losing his UK residency, intending to return to the UK on 6 April 2014. In the tax year 2010–2011 he remits the whole £175,000 to his bank account in the UK so as to enjoy the monies in the UK on his return.

Assuming that he fulfills his plans no income tax arises on the remittance as he will have remained non-UK resident for at least five complete tax years, namely, 2009–2010, 2010–2011, 2011–2012, 2012–2013 and 2013–2014.

Example 13

A non-UK domiciled individual, Enrique, leaves the UK on 6 November 2006 returning on 15 April 2010 (ie within five complete tax years). Enrique was resident and ordinarily resident in the UK for at least four out of the seven tax years prior to the tax year of departure (ie prior to 2006–2007).

In October 2009 (having left the UK) the individual remits relevant foreign income to the UK which he had received in the tax years prior to the tax year of departure.

This relevant foreign income is subject to income tax in the tax year 2010–2011 (ie the tax year of return).

Summary

4.80 Determination of the individual's residence and ordinary residence status for a tax year is important. While the law is to a degree somewhat vague in this regard, HMRC6 adopts a pragmatic approach and provides reasonable guidelines.

4.81 Any individual spending at least 183 days in the UK in any tax year will automatically be resident irrespective of all surrounding circumstances. However, other tests may also cause the individual to become resident and ordinarily resident even if the 183-day test is not breached.

4.82 *FA 2008* has introduced a statutory definition of when an individual is regarded as spending a day in the UK. If the individual is in the UK at midnight, then that day counts as a day in the UK. This new statutory rule applies from 6 April 2008. Pre-6 April 2008, days of arrival and departure were normally ignored.

4.83 The strict application of the law which fails to recognise split tax years

4.84 *Residence and ordinary residence*

for residence and ordinary residence purposes is ameliorated by HMRC6, ESC A11 and ESC D2.

4.84 Anti-avoidance provisions exist which continue to levy income tax and CGT on individuals whilst non-resident if certain conditions are not satisfied.

Chapter 5

Residence, ordinary residence and domicile: practice

Background

5.1 Chapter 4 examines the statutory provisions, case law and HMRC pronouncements (primarily those contained in HMRC6) relating to residence, ordinary residence and domicile.

5.2 The present chapter examines some of the practical issues associated with these three concepts including an examination of the 2009–2010 Tax Return and Supplementary Pages applicable to the individual resident in the UK (whether UK domiciled or not); the demise of Form DOM1; the proposed withdrawal and re-issue of Form P86 and the issue of residence and domicile rulings.

The tax return (and supplementary pages) 2009–2010

5.3 The tax return is probably the main source of information for HMRC in relation to an individual's income and capital gains for a tax year. Typically, an individual is required to file a tax return for each tax year (for guidance as to whether a Tax Return needs to be filed or not see www.hmrc.gov.uk/sa/need-tax-return.htm). The tax return comprises a small number (TR1 to TR6) of core pages (SA100 2010) plus various Supplementary Pages (see paragraph 5.5).

The core pages require disclosure of the individual's personal details and information in relation to certain types of income (eg bank interest; dividends; pensions) and also the disclosure of, inter alia, any charitable donations and contributions to employer registered pension schemes. The bulk of disclosure, however, arises from the requirement for many individuals to complete one or more sets of the Supplementary Pages.

For both the tax return and for each set of Supplementary Pages detailed notes are provided by HMRC with respect to their completion. For example, with

5.4 *Residence, ordinary residence and domicile: practice*

respect to the Supplementary Pages 'Capital gains summary SA108/2010' information as to their completion is provided on 'Capital gains summary notes SA108 notes 2010' comprising some 20 pages.

5.4 The UK's tax system is now one of self-assessment which means that an individual is responsible for filing a tax return (where necessary), computing his tax liability for the relevant tax year and discharging (ie paying) the liability so calculated; all this needs to be effected within statutory time limits any failure to so do resulting in interest charges and possible penalties.

Supplementary pages: 'Residence, remittance basis etc' SA109/2010

5.5 The ascertainment of an individual's tax liability for a tax year requires a determination by the individual as to his residence, ordinary residence and domicile status. Such determinations form part of the tax return (specifically the Supplementary Pages 'Residence, remittance basis etc' SA109/2010).

5.6 The *Finance Act 2008* dramatically affects the manner in which non-UK domiciled individuals are subject to income tax and to accommodate the changes the tax return (in particular the Supplementary Pages 'Residence, remittance basis etc' SA109/2009) for the tax year 2008–2009 was amended from the version applicable to the tax year 2007–2008.

5.7 For present purposes the section 'What makes up your Tax Return' on page TR2 of the tax return is of relevance and the starting point in the completion of any tax return.

It is therefore of the utmost importance that before any advice and/or wealth management planning is commenced the status of the individual with respect to each of these three attributes is clarified. The page is designed to ascertain whether any of the Supplementary Pages (of which there are eight separate categories, namely, Employment; Self-employment; Partnership; UK property; Foreign; Trusts etc; Capital gains summary; and Residence, remittance basis etc) require completion. An 'X' is inserted in the 'Yes' or 'No' boxes as appropriate. In some cases so-called 'Additional information' pages need to be completed as mentioned on page TR2 (these pages relate to less common kinds of income and disclosure of tax avoidance schemes).

5.8 Category 8 'Residence, remittance basis etc' on page TR2 asks:

> 'Were you, for all or part of the year to 5 April 2010, one or more of the following – not resident, not ordinarily resident or not domiciled in the UK and claiming the remittance basis; or dual resident in the UK and another country?'

A tick in the 'Yes' box requires the individual to then complete the Supplementary Pages: 'Residence, remittance basis etc'.

If the individual is UK resident, ordinary resident in the UK but non-UK domiciled but remittance basis treatment is not to be claimed for 2009–2010 then completion of these pages is not required; if remittance basis treatment is to be claimed then completion of these pages is required.

These pages also need completion by the non-UK resident individual (in receipt of UK source income) irrespective of his domicile status. This individual would not of course claim remittance basis treatment as non-UK source income/capital gains as they are not in any event within the charge to UK tax (thus, certain parts of the Supplementary Pages are superfluous and need not be completed: Boxes 22 to 26 concerning 'Domicile' and Boxes 27 to 34 concerning remittance basis treatment).

5.9 The tax return for 2007–2008, Category 8 'Non-resident', was slightly different and read as follows:

> 'Were you, for all or part of the year to 5 April 2008, one or more of the following – not resident, not ordinarily resident, not domiciled, in the UK or were you dual resident in the UK and another country?'

No reference was made here to the remittance basis. This is because *FA 2008*, of course, had no application to the tax year 2007–2008 and the procedure for claiming remittance basis treatment for 2007–2008 was different. Category 5 'Foreign' on page TR2 of the main part of the tax return 2007–2008 specifically asked:

> 'Did you receive any foreign income or income gains (other than from employment or self employment)?
>
> Do you want to claim relief for foreign tax paid?
>
> You may not need the Foreign Pages if ... you are claiming the remittance basis ... '

Box 1 of page F1 of the Supplementary Pages headed 'Foreign' asked:

> 'If you are making a claim for the remittance basis, put 'X' in the box'.

The 'Notes' to page F1 state:

> 'If you did not bring in or transfer any overseas income to the UK during the year you do not have to complete the "Foreign" pages just

5.10 *Residence, ordinary residence and domicile: practice*

to claim the remittance basis. Put a note in the "Any other information" box on your Tax Return to say you are claiming the remittance basis, but had no remittances during the year.'

In short, the procedure for claiming the remittance basis for the tax year 2007–2008 was different from that applicable for the tax year 2009–2010 (or 2008–2009).

5.10 For the tax year 2009–2010 the Supplementary Pages 'Residence, remittance basis etc' are divided into seven sections headed:

- Residence status
- Time spent in the UK
- Personal allowances
- Residence in other countries and Double Tax Relief
- Domicile
- Remittance basis
- Any other information.

Some of these sections are discussed in more detail below.

Residence status

5.11 Boxes 1 to 9 are designed to ascertain the individual's residence and ordinary residence status for the tax year 2009–2010. Boxes 1 to 5 are simple statements of fact (as understood by the individual). Boxes 6 to 9, however, are designed to elicit information which may cause HMRC to challenge (or at least enquire further) the residence/ordinary residence status claimed by the individual.

5.12 For example, Box 9 asks:

'If you have come to the UK to live or to remain here for a period of 2 years or more, put 'X' in the box'.

If the individual 'has come to the UK to live' they will be characterised as resident and ordinary resident from the date of arrival (see paragraph 4.38; see also Chapter 7 of HMRC6); the individual may, however, have answered Box 1 ('If you were not resident in the UK for 2009–2010 put 'X' in the box') and/or Box 2 ('If you were not ordinarily resident in the UK for 2009–2010 put 'X' in the box') by inserting an "X" in the boxes. Thus, the information gathering under Boxes 6 to 9 (and the answers provided in Boxes 1 to 5) effectively allows

Residence, ordinary residence and domicile: practice **5.15**

HMRC to quickly form a view as to whether *prima facie* evidence exists of incorrect status being assumed/claimed by the individual.

Boxes 10 to 14 represent further information gathering by HMRC.

Domicile

5.13 Boxes 22 to 26 are designed to ascertain the individual's domicile status for the tax year 2009–2010. They are as follows:

- Box 22. If you are domiciled outside the UK and it is relevant to your Income Tax or Capital Gains Tax liability, put 'X' in the box;
- Box 23. If 2009–2010 is the first tax year that you have told us that your domicile is outside the UK, put 'X' in the box;
- Box 24. If you have put 'X' in Box 22 and have a domicile of origin within the UK, enter the date on which your domicile changed;
- Box 25. If you were born in the UK but have never been domiciled here, put 'X' in the box; and
- Box 26. If you have put 'X' in Box 22 and you were born outside the UK, enter the date you came to live in the UK.

5.14 As with respect to the above discussion on residence/ordinary residence (see paragraphs 5.11 and 5.12) HMRC have effectively placed 'cross-checks' in this section. For example, if the individual places an 'X' in Box 22 but also places an 'X' in Box 24 this is likely to alert HMRC to the need for further investigation (on the *prima facie* ground that it is very difficult for an individual to lose a UK domicile of origin and acquire a non-UK domicile of choice; see paragraph 3.43)).

5.15 It will be noted that Box 24 asks for the date on which the individual's UK domicile status changed; a most difficult question (if not impossible) to answer. The Notes (SA109/2010 page RRN10) comment as follows:

> 'When completing box 24, if you do not have a specific date on which your domicile changed, please use 5 April at the end of the tax year in which the change took place. If the tax year is an approximation, please make a note of this in the "Any other information" box, box 35'.

An alternative answer, and perhaps the better option, with respect to Box 24 is to insert the precise date of arrival in the new country of domicile as the date when the new domicile was acquired. Certainly, if a UK domiciled (of origin) individual emigrates from the UK to country 'X' with the firm intention of

5.16 *Residence, ordinary residence and domicile: practice*

remaining indefinitely in country 'X' then the date of arrival is the date of the acquisition of the new domicile of (in this case) choice in country 'X'. If this approach is adopted it is then advisable to enter into Box 35 a statement to this effect as justification for the date entered in Box 24.

5.16 It should be noted, however, that according to the Notes (SA109/2010 page RRN16) Boxes 22 to 26 should not be completed if the remittance basis of taxation is not being used (ie claimed). In other words, if the remittance basis is not being claimed then the individual's domicile status is irrelevant to his income tax and CGT liabilities (see wording of Box 22).

Remittance basis

5.17 Boxes 27 to 34 are designed to elicit information which is necessary following the introduction of the new rules for non-UK domiciled individuals in *FA 2008*; rules which introduced a more formal approach. They are, however, only relevant and thus only need be completed if remittance basis treatment is to be claimed.

5.18 Box 27 is a very important box and placing an 'X' in the box indicates the lodgement of a claim for remittance basis treatment for the tax year 2009–2010; in this regard, it is to be noted that such a claim is an annual claim (ie not a once-and-for-all claim).

5.19 Box 28 provides for remittance basis treatment without the need for a formal claim. This is possible where for 2009–2010 the amount of unremitted foreign income and capital gains is less than £2,000. Placing an 'X' in Box 28 means that Box 27 should also be completed and Boxes 29 and 30 should also be completed if they apply.

5.20 Box 29 identifies the non-UK domiciled individual who needs to pay the £30,000 remittance basis charge. This applies where the individual has been resident in the UK for at least seven of the nine tax years immediately preceding the tax year 2009–2010; accordingly an 'X' must be placed in the box.

5.21 Box 30 requires an 'X' to be placed in the box if the individual is under age 18 on 5 April 2009. In this case it may be that no claim needs to be lodged to obtain remittance basis treatment.

5.22 The remaining four boxes (31 to 34) are relevant only if Boxes 27 and 29 apply.

Any other information

5.23 Box 35 (a clear white space) must be used to supply additional information where Boxes 31 or 32 and 33 have been completed. These three boxes require completion only where Boxes 27 and 29 have been completed; otherwise they have no relevance.

5.24 Box 35 might also usefully be used to disclose further information which, for example, may clarify earlier responses (see paragraph 5.15 for example).

Forms DOM1, P85 and P86 and domicile and residence rulings

5.25 Historically, Forms DOM1, P85 and P86 were used by HMRC to obtain information about the individual in order to then provide rulings as to the individual's residence, ordinary residence and domicile status.

Form DOM1

5.26 Form DOM1 is headed 'Income and Chargeable Gains – Domicile'. The purpose of the form is to gather information to enable HMRC to form a view as to an individual's domicile status.

Form P86

5.27 Form P86 is headed 'Arrival in the United Kingdom'. The purpose of the form is to gather information on an individual on arriving in the UK for the first time to enable HMRC to form a view as to the individual's residence, ordinary residence and indeed domicile status.

Form P85

5.28 Form P85 is headed 'Leaving the UK'. The purpose of the form is to gather information on an individual leaving the UK to enable HMRC to form a view as to the individual's residence, ordinary residence and indeed domicile status.

5.29 None of these three forms are statutory forms in the sense that an individual is not required by law to complete any of them (unlike the position re completion of a tax return). In practice many individuals (or their advisors) do complete them.

5.30 *Residence, ordinary residence and domicile: practice*

It would, however, be perfectly legitimate to supply all relevant information instead by way of letter. One advantage of this latter approach is that only directly pertinent information needs to be disclosed. Arguably, some of the information requested on the forms does not have a direct bearing on a determination as to an individual's residence or domicile status.

For example, if an individual has never been UK resident in the past prior to his arrival in the UK the question on Form P86 asking 'Where and for whom did you work during the five years before your arrival in the UK?' (Question 7a) is arguably of no relevance to a determination of the individual's residence (and indeed domicile) status (similarly the follow-up, Question 7b (relating to employment dates) is also of no relevance). This is certainly the position if none of the duties under the employment were performed in the UK (Question 7c).

Current position

5.30   'Revenue & Customs Brief 17/09 Residence, Domicile and the Remittance Basis: Operational Changes' (available at www.hmrc.gov.uk/briefs/income-tax/brief1709.htm) which was issued on 25 March 2009 provided an update with respect to Form DOM1 and P86.

5.31   The following is an extract therefrom which succinctly stated the position as at March 2009 with respect to Form DOM1, P86 and also with respect to domicile and residence rulings:

> 'Tax Bulletin 29 [available at ...], published in June 1997, announced that following the introduction of self assessment HMRC would no longer provide a residence rulings service. However, we continued to accept initial non-domicile claims on forms DOM1 and P86 ...
>
> The publication of our new guidance on domicile, plus the fact that from 2008/09 onwards a claim to the remittance basis is no longer mandatory, and must be made on a year by year basis where an individual has unremitted foreign income or gains of £2,000 or more arising in the tax year, mean that HMRC will no longer accept initial non-domicile claims on form DOM1 or form P86. Form DOM1 is being withdrawn completely. It will be replaced by the new comprehensive domicile guidance mentioned above that will allow the vast majority of people to self assess their own domicile status. Form P86 will also be withdrawn soon and replaced by a new form. Until such time as the new form is issued individuals do not need to fill in boxes 12 to 17 on the P86 when submitting it. If they choose to fill in those boxes HMRC will ignore the content when processing the form.

Any DOM1 forms received by HMRC by close of business 25 March 2009 will still be processed but any received after that date will be returned unexamined ...

Where an individual has already submitted a form DOM1 or P86 and obtained an initial view from HMRC about their domicile status it will be unusual for us to open an enquiry into domicile status in the few years after that, unless new information becomes available that indicates our initial view was incorrect or there has been a change in circumstances. However, with passage of time, circumstances and intentions change and so that initial view from HMRC can become less and less useful as an indicator of domicile status ...'

5.32 Form P86 was subsequently withdrawn on 1 June 2010 (see 'Agent and HMRC Working Together June/July 2010 Issue 18').

5.33 Form P85 remains unscathed and continues to be utilised by HMRC in its unchanged form.

5.34 For completeness, the historic position with respect to domicile and residence rulings is set out below based upon extracts from HMRC publications.

Historically (ie before the introduction of self-assessment in the mid-1990s) it was not necessary to make annual claims with respect to either residence or domicile status. It was possible to obtain from HMRC a ruling as to an individual's residence and domicile status. This ruling would then apply for the foreseeable future (not just for one tax year) subject, of course, to any material change of circumstance on the part of the individual concerned.

Below is an extract from HMRC's Tax Bulletin 29 (June 1997):

'Domicile Ruling

Initial non-domicile claims may be made on form DOM 1, form P86 or in the SA tax return. We will continue to deal with initial non-domicile claims which are made before we have received the return for the year in which the claim is made. And we will let claimants know how their claim to be non-domiciled in the UK has been treated. But we may ask questions to check the validity of the claim as part of a formal Schedule 1A TMA 1970 enquiry into the claim or as part of a Section 9A TMA 1970 enquiry into the SA tax return ...

But where, for example, an individual:

- has a domicile of origin outside the UK; and

5.35 Residence, ordinary residence and domicile: practice

- has come to the UK only for the purpose of employment; and
- intends to resume residence abroad when the employment ceases; and
- has given such information on a Form P86
- we are unlikely to issue an enquiry into the domicile position'.

A similar statement was made re residence:

'Residence Ruling

Because individuals will, in appropriate cases, self-certify their residence status on their SA return, there is no need for the Inland Revenue to give a prior 'ruling' on an individual's residence status. And so we have changed our procedures regarding such residence 'rulings'. We will continue to ask individuals for information about their residence or ordinary residence status. But neither tax offices nor Financial Intermediaries and Claims Office (FICO) intend to provide residence 'rulings' as we have done in the past.

Given that individuals will decide what they regard their residence status to be, we propose to end our existing practice of advising an individual in the fourth year of the consequences of continuing to make regular visits to the UK exceeding an average of 90 days per year'.

5.35 In short, the introduction of the self-assessment system of tax in the mid-1990s followed by the major changes to the tax position of the non-UK domiciled individual has finally led to an individual having to ascertain his own domicile and residence status and file his tax return accordingly. The onus is fairly and squarely on the individual, not HMRC.

Inheritance tax

5.36 Inheritance tax (IHT) may arise on the death of an individual or on such individual making lifetime gifts.

5.37 The individual's domicile (but not resident status except in limited circumstances) status at the relevant time is critical in a determination of the extent of any such liability.

5.38 Where there is any IHT to pay on the death of an individual Form IHT400 (and a number of various Schedules) needs to be completed. Form IHT400 and accompanying schedules were introduced relatively recently, on

17 November 2008. Form IHT400 plus schedules replaced Form IHT200 and the 'D' supplementary pages (which continued to be usable until 9 June 2009; however, from that date the new Form IHT400 and schedules must be used).

5.39 One of the new schedules is Form IHT401 'Domicile outside the United Kingdom' which has to be completed where, on death, it is claimed that the individual is non-UK domiciled. *Inter alia*, information requested on the form which presumably according to HMRC is relevant in this regard includes:

- nationality of the deceased;
- where the deceased was born;
- outline of educational and employment history;
- date of leaving UK to set up their main residence abroad;
- dates of return to the UK;
- length of stay in the UK; and
- purpose of stay in the UK.

5.40 It is to be appreciated that while such information is requested on the individual's death for IHT purposes HMRC may already have on file information concerning the individual's domicile status (eg following an earlier ruling as to the individual's domicile status; or, simply general information provided by the individual on Form DOM1 and/or Form P86). Indeed, Box 2 on Form IHT401 specifically asks:

> 'Has the deceased's domicile status been agreed for other HM Revenue & Customs purposes?'

5.41 It is not unusual for HMRC to enquire into an individual's domicile status whether for income tax, CGT or IHT. Where following such an enquiry HMRC express a view as to the individual's domicile status for that particular tax the view expressed will also apply for the other taxes. In this regard HMRC in their HM Revenue & Customs Brief 17/09 (see paragraph 5.30) commented:

> 'Where HMRC has expressed a view on an individual's domicile status for income tax or capital gains tax, as a result of an enquiry [under section 9A TMA 1970], then that view will also apply for inheritance tax purposes at that time. Likewise a HMRC view expressed for inheritance tax purposes, following a Part VIII IHTA [1984] enquiry, will also apply for income tax and capital gains tax purposes at that time'.

HMRC also state:

> 'Where a claim to remittance basis treatment is not challenged for that year it does not mean HMRC necessarily accepts the

5.42 *Residence, ordinary residence and domicile: practice*

individual's domicile is outside the UK and does not prevent HMRC from later opening an enquiry to consider the domicile status of the individual in relation to that, or any earlier year'.

5.42 In an earlier pronouncement in 'IHT and Trusts Newsletter' (August 2007) HMRC commented as follows:

> 'Domicile is an important factor for Inheritance Tax; on death, the deceased's domicile determines the succession to personal property, so it may affect the amount of spouse or civil partner exemption available. For both the transfer on death and for lifetime transfers, the deceased/transferor's domicile determines the territorial scope of IHT. And for transfers between spouses or civil partners the amount of exemption is limited to £55,000 if the deceased/transferor is domiciled in the UK but the spouse or civil partner is not.
>
> We sometimes receive calls to our Helpline asking for assistance to establish the deceased/transferor's domicile. Our agents can help with filling in form D2/D31 and can talk in general terms about the impact of domicile for IHT. But they are not able to provide a definitive answer about a taxpayer's domicile over the phone. That decision can only be made once an account for the chargeable event concerned has been delivered. When delivering the account, please make sure that you complete form D2/D31 as fully as practicable, as this allows us to resolve the question of domicile as efficiently as possible.
>
> Naturally, we are unable to comment about a person's domicile unless an event which gives rise to an IHT charge occurs'.

5.43 For those individuals where a domicile ruling has not been obtained carrying out any form of tax planning is inevitably less certain. Thus, for example, those individuals arriving in the UK and remaining here for some years may not know whether, de facto, they have acquired a UK domicile of choice. Similarly, those individuals leaving the UK (who at the date of departure are UK domiciled) may never be too sure as to whether a new non-UK domicile of choice has subsequently been acquired.

5.44 It is often suggested that an individual in such circumstances may 'force' HMRC into expressing a view by undertaking a transaction the tax consequences of which are unclear until the individual's domicile status is clarified.

5.45 HMRC in Revenue & Customs Brief 17/09 in this regard comment as follows:

> 'An individual setting up a non-resident trust ... considers they are non-UK domiciled is not obliged to submit an inheritance tax

account to HMRC. But if an inheritance tax account is submitted in these circumstances, HMRC will continue its existing practice and only open an enquiry into that return if the amounts of inheritance tax at stake make such an enquiry cost effective to carry out. At present [ie March 2009] that limit is £10,000'.

The reference to the figure of £10,000 has thus been withdrawn.

However, *Revenue and Customs Brief 34/10* (24 August 2010) has superseded the above comments. It provides as follows:

> 'In future HMRC will consider opening an enquiry where domicile could be an issue, or making a determination of inheritance tax. ... HMRC does not consider it appropriate to state an amount of tax that would be considered as significant. ... HMRC will take into account the potential costs in pursing an enquiry.'

Summary

5.46 Under self-assessment the individual is required to determine his residence, ordinary residence and domicile status for each tax year. HMRC may choose to investigate whether the individual's determinations are, in its view, correct.

5.47 Rulings from HMRC as to an individual's domicile or residence status can no longer be obtained. It may be possible to cause HMRC to examine a particular transaction so as to 'force' HMRC to form a view of the individual's domicile status. This may or may not be desirable.

5.48 The tax return and Supplementary Pages thereto are the major source of information for HMRC.

5.49 Following *FA 2008*, a non-UK domiciled individual must formally claim remittance basis treatment (by completing Supplementary Pages 'Residence, remittance basis etc') each tax year.

Chapter 6

Income source and asset situs

Background

6.1 The need to identify the source of a particular category of income and/or the situs of a particular category of asset is necessary to determine if, and the extent to which, a liability to tax (whether income, capital gains or inheritance) arises.

UK domiciled individual

6.2 A UK domiciled individual is subject to inheritance tax (IHT) on UK and non-UK situs assets. Such an individual, if UK resident, is subject to capital gains tax (CGT) on capital gains arising from disposals of UK and non-UK situs assets; income tax arises on UK and non-UK source income.

Non-UK domiciled individual

6.3 A non-UK domiciled individual is subject to IHT on UK situs assets only. Such individual, if UK resident, is subject to CGT on capital gains arising from disposals of UK situs assets, but is subject to CGT on non-UK situs assets only if the gains in respect thereof are remitted to the UK; income tax arises on UK source income, but only arises on non-UK source income if this is remitted to the UK.

Non-resident individual

6.4 An individual who is not resident in the UK is subject to IHT according to their domicile status (see paragraphs 6.2 and 6.3). A non-UK resident individual is not subject to CGT even on UK situs assets (unless these assets are related to a trade carried on in the UK) but is subject to income tax, albeit only on UK source income.

Foreign tax

6.5 A UK resident individual in receipt of non-UK source income and/or non-UK situs capital gains, either of which has been exposed to a charge to overseas tax, is in principle eligible for foreign tax credits (ie the foreign tax is offset against any UK tax on the same income/gains).

6.6 It is important, however, that the income and/or capital gains are in fact non-UK source/situs.

Domestic law

6.7 The rules set out in this chapter are those applicable under UK domestic law. In certain cases these rules may be modified by the terms of a double taxation agreement to which the UK is a party (see Chapter 26).

6.8 Identifying the source of income and/or the situs of an asset is complex and the rules are not always clear, particularly where it is case law (rather than statute) which provides guidance. The following should thus be treated with caution as the approach adopted is to make generalised comments to provide guidance rather than to get embroiled in detailed and complex analysis on each issue.

Income source

6.9 UK common law applies to determine the source of income for income tax purposes (ie income tax legislation does not have its own set of rules to determine source).

6.10 The location of a source of income is, perhaps surprisingly, not always the same as the location of the asset from which the income arises (eg dividend income arising on registered shares may have a source location different from the situs of the shares) although often the two will be the same.

6.11 The source identification rules for the main types of income are set out below.

Dividends

6.12 The source of dividend income arising on shares in a company is the location of the company's residence which will usually (but not always) be the place of incorporation/registration of the company.

6.13 *Income source and asset situs*

Under UK tax law a company is UK resident if it is incorporated in the UK or its 'central management and control' is exercised from within the UK (broadly applicable if the company's board of directors meet and take key strategic decisions in the UK). Thus, a UK-incorporated company is automatically UK resident and any dividends arising from its shares are UK source income.

6.13 Where a foreign incorporated/registered company is UK resident, due to its central management and control being exercised from within the UK, any dividends arising on its shares are UK source.

6.14 Open-ended investment companies (commonly referred to as OEICs) are companies and the rule in paragraph 6.13 applies to them in the same way (ie any dividends arising on the shares in an OEIC will possess a UK source if the OEIC is UK resident).

Typically, many offshore (ie non-UK resident and indeed non-UK registered) mutual funds are structured as OEICs; and dividends arising on an investment in such an OEIC (which is a shareholding interest therein) constitute non-UK source income.

Interest

6.15 There appears to be no single factor which determines the source of interest income. Factors which are important include:

- the debtor's residence status (not 'tax' residence, but residence in the sense of identifying the location where the creditor has the right to sue);
- the place where the debt is enforceable; and
- the place at which payment of the interest on the debt is made.

6.16 All things being equal, it is likely that interest credited on a deposit account with either a UK incorporated bank/building society or the UK branch of an overseas incorporated bank/building society will possess a UK source as the debt is likely to be enforceable, and any interest is likely to be credited, in the UK.

The corollary of the above is that interest credited on a deposit account with a foreign incorporated bank or the overseas branch of a UK incorporated bank possesses a non-UK source.

The above applies whether the deposit is in sterling or foreign currency.

Income source and asset situs **6.23**

Trusts

6.17 The source of a payment made by trustees of a discretionary trust to one of the beneficiaries is probably the location where the beneficiary may enforce his rights against the trustees (ie where the trustees reside (not determined as for tax purposes but determined as the location where the creditor has the right to sue)). This follows from the analysis that the source of income for the beneficiary is not the underlying income of the trust but the trust itself, (see paragraph 17.25).

6.18 Paragraph 6.17 contrasts with the position of an interest in possession trust. In this case, the source of the income of the beneficiary with the interest in possession (eg the life tenant) is the source of the trust's underlying income (ie not the trust itself). However, this may not be the case where the governing law of the trust is not English common law.

6.19 As indicated in paragraph 6.14, many offshore mutual funds are structured as OEICs. However, it is also true that many such funds are structured in the form of trusts.

Where the trust structure is used the source of any dividends arising on the investment in the fund is the location of the trustees' residence (not determined as for tax purposes but determined as the location where the investor has the right to sue); however, this assumes that the trust is to be regarded as a separate 'non see-through' entity; otherwise (ie where the trust is a 'see through' entity), the source of the dividend income is the trust's underlying income.

Rental income

6.20 The source of rental income is the location of the real estate giving rise to the income.

Asset situs

6.21 The situs of assets is primarily relevant for CGT and IHT purposes. However, perhaps surprisingly, different rules apply for each of these two taxes.

6.22 The IHT legislation provides no provisions to determine asset situs. It is thus the common law which applies.

6.23 The CGT legislation does, however, contain provisions which govern asset situs but these provisions are not exhaustive. Thus, where the CGT legislation makes no provision it is necessary to fall back on common law.

6.24 *Income source and asset situs*

6.24 Despite this difference in approach between the two taxes in many cases (but not always) the situs of an asset is in fact found to be the same for both CGT and IHT purposes.

Inheritance tax

Registered shares

6.25 The registered shares of a company are situated where the principal share register of the company is maintained (ie not where the company is resident which applies re dividend income source identification; see paragraph 6.12).

Bearer shares

6.26 Bearer shares are located where the bearer share certificates are physically situate at the relevant time (treated basically the same as tangible property; see paragraph 6.27). Thus, their location is not dependent upon any share register (as applies for registered shares).

Tangible property

6.27 Tangible property (eg real estate; paintings; antique furniture; jewellery) is located where the asset is physically situate at the relevant time.

Intangible property

6.28 Choses in action are generally situate in the country where they are recoverable and/or can be enforced. Debts, bank accounts (a form of debt) and life insurance policies all constitute choses in action.

The situs of an *ordinary* debt is basically where the debtor resides (ie where the debt is normally recoverable). Whether the debt is secured or not makes no difference.

The situs of a *speciality* debt (ie an obligation under seal securing the debt; a deed is a written document which must be signed, witnessed and delivered and it must be made clear that it is intended to be a deed, although sealing is now no longer required; *LP(MP)A 1989* post-1 August 1990) is where the deed is physically located (similar to the situs of bearer shares; see paragraph 6.26).

A *bank account* is, generally speaking, an ordinary debt and is thus situate at the place of residence of the debtor (ie the location of the branch of the bank where the account is kept).

A *life insurance policy* is treated as a debt and thus the residence of the debtor rule applies. Thus, a policy under hand as opposed to a policy under seal (ie a deed) is situate where the debtor company (ie life insurance company) is resident. Where the policy terms specifically provide for payment elsewhere the location is the place of payment so provided. A policy under seal (ie a speciality debt) is located where the instrument (ie policy) is located.

Nominees

6.29 The location of assets held by nominees is determined according to the rules applicable to the category of the asset held by the nominee not where the nominee itself may be situated (ie nomineeship is effectively transparent for asset situs location purposes).

Land

6.30 Land is located where the land is physically situate.

Capital gains tax

6.31 As indicated above, the CGT legislation has its own rules which determine the situs of a number of assets for CGT purposes (*TCGA 1992 ss 275 and 275A*). Where these rules do not determine a particular asset's situs the normal common law rules will apply.

Registered shares

6.32 Registered shares are generally situate where the principal share register of the company concerned is located; usually, the company's place of incorporation/registration.

Bearer shares

6.33 No provisions are provided in the CGT legislation and thus the normal common law rule applies (ie the situs is wherever the bearer share certificates are physically situate at the relevant time).

6.34 *Income source and asset situs*

Intangible property

6.34 Unlike the common law rule applicable to *debts* (see paragraph 6.28), for CGT purposes the location of an ordinary debt is that of the residence of the creditor (not debtor).

Thus, any creditor who is resident in the UK and holds monies in a foreign *bank account* causes that bank account to possess a UK situs. However, where the foreign bank account is in foreign currency a currency other than sterling) *and* held by a non-UK domiciled individual it is treated as non-UK situs (ie the creditor rule is superseded).

A *life insurance policy* is not regarded as a debt and thus not subject to the above 'creditor' rule. A life insurance policy subject to UK law has its situs in the UK.

Tangible property

6.35 No provisions are provided in the CGT legislation and thus the normal common law rule applies (ie tangible property (eg real estate; paintings; antique furniture; jewellery) is located where the asset is physically situate at the relevant time).

Nominees

6.36 The location of assets held by nominees is determined according to the rules applicable to the category of the asset held by the nominee not where the nominee itself may be situated (ie nomineeship is effectively transparent for asset situs location purposes).

Land

6.37 No provisions are provided in the CGT legislation and thus the normal common law rule applies. Land is located where it is physically situate.

Implications: some comments

Nominees

6.38 A common misconception is that the utilisation of a nominee (eg a nominee company) can change the underlying situs of a particular asset and is thus a useful tool to mitigate both CGT and particularly IHT. Thus, it is often suggested, for example, that the use of an overseas situs nominee is effective to remove an otherwise UK situs asset from the UK. It is not.

Example 1

Michelle Paris is a non-UK domiciled individual who owns a 25% shareholding in a listed UK incorporated company. Her investment in the shares is thus UK situs both for CGT and IHT.

The shareholding is extremely valuable and in the event of her death will be subject to IHT.

Her advisor has suggested that she should have the shares held not directly in her name but in the name of a Swiss-based corporate nominee which, it is suggested, would cause the shares to be no longer UK (but non-UK) situs.

Unfortunately, this is not the case and the shares would remain UK situs and within the charge to IHT on death.

6.39 There is thus no UK IHT advantage to be gained by a non-UK domiciled individual holding any UK situs asset via an offshore nominee. However, if the offshore vehicle utilised is a non-UK registered company owned by the individual which is the beneficial owner (ie is not a nominee) of the UK situs asset, then the situs of the asset now held by the individual is non-UK (ie the shares of the non-UK registered company).

6.40 The corollary of the above is that the use of a UK based corporate nominee to hold non-UK situs assets for a non-UK domiciled individual will not cause the otherwise non-UK situs assets to become UK situs (ie the underlying asset situs remains offshore).

Hence, the use by a non-UK domiciled individual of the nominee services of, for example, a UK based stockbroker (or bank) to hold non-UK situs shares and securities will not create UK situs assets for IHT purposes. This is particularly important for the non-UK domiciled individual because the ownership by such individual of non-UK situs property constitutes 'excluded property' for IHT purposes (and does not fall within the charge thereto; see Chapter 13).

Example 2

Friedrich Berlin, a non-UK domiciled individual, owns significant USA and UK equities.

6.41 *Income source and asset situs*

His UK stockbroker has suggested that, for convenience, all Friedrich's share portfolio should be held by the stockbroker's UK nominee company.

This does not cause Friedrich's holding of USA equities to become UK situs.

Foreign currency and foreign currency bank accounts

6.41 For IHT purposes the location of a bank account (sterling or otherwise) is the location of the residence of the debtor (ie the bank/branch; see paragraph 6.28). However, for the non-UK domiciled individual who is also neither UK resident nor ordinary resident, a foreign currency bank account with a UK bank (ie UK situs) may be left out of account when ascertaining any IHT liability arising on death (*IHTA 1984 s 157*; see paragraph 13.28).

Thus, although such foreign currency bank accounts with UK banks do not generally present problems *vis à vis* IHT on death, they may precipitate IHT charges with respect to lifetime transfers.

6.42 For CGT purposes, although the creditor rule applies to bank accounts this is not so for foreign currency bank accounts held outside the UK by non-UK domiciled individuals (see paragraph 6.34). This exception to the creditor rule is helpful to the non-UK domiciled individual resident in the UK as it allows any CGT liabilities arising with respect to the utilisation of a foreign currency non-UK bank account to be subject to remittance basis treatment (ie as the account is regarded as non-UK situs).

Foreign currency

6.43 Foreign currency is itself a chargeable asset for the purpose of CGT. Thus, the conversion of any foreign currency into, say, sterling (or indeed any other foreign currency) constitutes a disposal for CGT purposes and a possible CGT charge arises. A capital gain arises if sterling has depreciated against the foreign currency between acquiring the currency and its conversion.

Example 3

Ingrid Berg, a Norwegian-domiciled individual, resident in the UK is given $10,000 by her uncle at a time when the rate of exchange is $2 to the £ (ie $-worth £5,000).

Income source and asset situs **6.47**

After six months whilst in the UK she converts the $ into £ at a rate of $1 to the £ (ie $-worth £10,000).

Ingrid precipitates a capital gain of [£10,000 – £5,000] (ie £5,000).

6.44 A disposal of foreign currency may also arise without the need for actual conversion. For example, the act of depositing foreign currency into a bank account is a disposal of the foreign currency for CGT purposes as is the simple spending of the foreign currency.

6.45 However, where foreign currency has been acquired for an individual's (or his family's or his dependant's) personal expenditure outside the UK it is an exempt asset for CGT purposes (*TCGA 1992 s 269*).

This let-out will not, generally speaking, apply to the non-UK domiciled individual (but will often be of relevance to a UK domiciled individual) who will typically have acquired the foreign currency not specifically for personal expenditure outside the UK, but simply as a consequence of personal activities (eg foreign currency generated from overseas earnings or investments; gifts of foreign currency from family members; asset sales; etc).

Foreign currency bank accounts

6.46 A foreign currency bank account is simply a debt due to the depositor by the bank. As a consequence, a disposal arises where a withdrawal of, or transfer out of, the foreign currency therein occurs. The withdrawal/transfer of the currency is a satisfaction by the bank of its debt obligation to the depositor and the depositor is thus deemed to have made a disposal of a chargeable asset (ie a disposal of the debt due from the bank (which is a chargeable asset; *TCGA 1992 ss 251* and *252*)).

As indicated above, the 'withdrawal' may be effected either by literally withdrawing the funds in person or having the monies moved inter-bank from one account to another.

It is not necessary for a CGT charge to arise for the foreign currency to be converted into sterling at any point; all that is required is that a chargeable disposal is made.

6.47 The quantum of any CGT liability is based upon the difference between the sterling value of the amount of the withdrawal at the date of the withdrawal and the sterling value of that foreign currency amount at the date it was deposited. A capital *gain* thus arises where sterling has *depreciated* against the particular currency over the relevant time period and a capital *loss* arises where sterling has *appreciated* against the particular currency.

6.48 *Income source and asset situs*

Example 4

Tom Bellinger Jnr, a non-UK domiciled but UK resident individual, opens a dollar denominated bank account in the UK. A transfer into the account of $100,000 is made by his father as a gift; the sterling equivalent is £75,000.

Three years later Tom withdraws the whole amount which at the date of withdrawal has a sterling equivalent of £85,000 due to the depreciation of the sterling/dollar rate.

Tom Bellinger Jnr has thus made a taxable chargeable gain of £10,000.

If, on the other hand, sterling had appreciated against the dollar (ie at the date of withdrawal the sterling equivalent was, say, £70,000) a sterling loss (£5,000) would arise which would be available for relief.

6.48 The withdrawal by Tom in Example 4 could have been made either literally by making a cash withdrawal or, alternatively, by arranging for the dollars to be transferred to, say, his dollar account back in the USA. Irrespective of which of these two routes is adopted a disposal of the debt due from the bank in the UK has arisen (ie the UK bank has satisfied its debt due to him).

6.49 On 28 January 2010 HMRC issued Guidance Note 'Residence and Domicile – foreign currency bank accounts' which provides for an extension of SP10/84 'Foreign Bank Accounts' to non-UK domiciled individuals (prior to the extension only UK domiciled individuals were able to disregard transfers between non-UK bank accounts denominated in the same foreign currency thus precipitating no CGT charge on such transfers). Under the extension, transfers by non-UK domiciled individuals between non-UK bank accounts denominated in the same foreign currency are disregarded (ie neither capital gains nor capital losses arise on such transfers). Previously, such transfers precipitated capital gains (albeit not allowable capital losses) unless the transfers were between UK bank accounts denominated in the same foreign currency. The new practice applies to transfers effected on or after 6 April 2008 (ie is back-dated).

6.50 Transfers between UK and non-UK foreign currency bank accounts denominated in the same foreign currency continue to precipitate potential capital gains/losses as do transfers between bank accounts denominated in different foreign currencies.

6.51 For transfers effected before 6 April 2008 (other than between UK foreign currency bank accounts denominated in the same foreign currency) capital gains may have arisen which, if remitted to the UK, will precipitate a CGT charge (pre-6 April 2008 capital losses on non-UK situs assets are not allowable capital losses for non-UK domiciled individuals; see paragraph 9.4).

Example 5

Bob Wind, a non-UK domiciled but UK resident individual, has three dollar bank accounts. Two, OB1 and OB2, are with banks in the USA and one, UKB, is with a UK based bank in the UK.

On Bob's birthday, Bob's father gives him a present of $700,000 by transferring the monies into Bob's account, OB1. At that time the rate of exchange is $2/£1.

For UK CGT purposes no taxable event has occurred other than the fact that Bob has now acquired a chargeable asset (ie a debt due from OB1) worth in sterling £350,000.

A couple of months later (pre-6 April 2008) Bob transfers the whole amount to OB2. At that time the exchange rate is $1.75/£1. The sterling equivalent of the withdrawal from OB1 is thus £400,000.

For CGT purposes at that time Bob has made a chargeable gain of £50,000. It is not immediately subject to CGT as Bob has not remitted the monies to the UK (as a non-UK domiciled but UK resident individual the remittance basis applies to non-UK source chargeable gains).

Three months later (pre-6 April 2008) Bob transfers the monies to his UK bank account, UKB. At that time the exchange rate is $1/£1. The sterling equivalent of the withdrawal from OB2 is thus £700,000.

The remittance of the $700,000 from OB2 to UKB has unfortunate tax consequences for Bob.

First, the £50,000 gain arising on the transfer from OB1 to OB2 is now subject to CGT as the monies (ie the $700,000) have now been remitted to the UK.

Second, the £300,000 gain arising on the transfer from OB2 to UKB is subject to CGT as the monies (ie the $700,000) have now been remitted to the UK.

Bob thus faces a CGT charge on two chargeable gains (ie the £50,000 and the £300,000) even though all that has happened is that he has transferred the monies (namely, $700,000) from bank account to bank account.

Had Bob effected the two transfers on or after 6 April 2008, no CGT consequences would have arisen on the OB1 to OB2 transfer, but the OB2 to UKB transfer would have precipitated the £300,000 capital gain as above.

6.52 *Income source and asset situs*

6.52 If Bob in Example 5 subsequently transfers the monies from UKB (ie $) to another account overseas, a potential CGT charge (or allowable capital loss) arises depending upon the movement in the $/£ rate of exchange.

6.53 Capital losses may also arise on a foreign currency transaction and it might be expected that perhaps on balance over time any sterling movements will tend to be both up and down against a particular foreign currency, thus over time, any gains which might arise are simply offset by any losses which might arise. While this may be the case 'in the real world', pre-*FA 2008* any such loss which arose was *not* an allowable loss for CGT purposes if the loss arose on a non-UK bank account and therefore could not be offset against any capital gains. For the non-UK domiciled but UK resident individual, inequity of treatment with respect to non-UK foreign currency bank account gains and losses thus arose (ie gains were taxable but losses could not be offset).

6.54 *FA 2008* has, however, modified the above treatment. Any capital loss arising on a disposal of a non-UK situs asset (eg a non-UK situs foreign currency bank account) on or after 6 April 2008 is now in principle an allowable loss (ie the loss may be offset against capital gains). This is a much improved position compared to that pre-6 April 2008, (see Chapter 9).

However, *FA 2008* also details specific rules as to when and how any such capital losses may in fact be so utilised – not perhaps as advantageous as might be thought at first sight.

Example 6

Kalari Sahara, a non-UK domiciled but UK resident individual, has opened dollar accounts with banks OB1 and OB2 and euro accounts with OB3 and OB4 all situated outside the UK. In OB1 she has deposited $500,000, a gift from her father. In OB3 she has deposited $400,000, a gift from her mother. OB2 and OB4 have a nil balance.

In the tax year 2008–2009 she transfers the $500,000 dollars from OB1 to OB4 precipitating a capital gain of £100,000. Later in the tax year she transfers $400,000 dollars from OB3 to OB2 precipitating a loss of £75,000.

No remittances to the UK are made in the tax year 2008–2009.

As no remittances are made to the UK, under the new *FA 2008* rules the capital loss is first offset against any non-remitted capital gains. Thus, Kalari is able to offset the capital loss against the capital gain giving rise to a net gain of £25,000.

Should Kalari decide to remit any of the euros to the UK from OB4 she triggers a CGT charge on the net capital gain of £25,000. However, should she remit the $ from OB2, no CGT charge arises as the transfer of this amount is that in respect of which a capital loss arose. This amount can therefore be remitted without tax charge.

6.55 Inevitably, the typical non-UK domiciled but UK resident individual may often be involved in transactions which involve more than one foreign currency and where deposits and withdrawals frequently occur.

The ability to keep track of such withdrawals and deposits and the consequent potential capital gains and/or capital losses, in practice, may be somewhat difficult, if not impossible. Nevertheless, these difficulties do not remove the tax charge and, in practice, it may be necessary to carry out some sort of averaging over time to arrive at the overall CGT position.

6.56 The following points are perhaps worth noting:

- *first,* non-UK domiciled but UK resident individuals should not maintain foreign currency bank accounts with banks in the UK;
- *second,* transfers effected pre-6 April 2008, even between overseas foreign currency bank accounts, may precipitate chargeable gains which will be subject to a CGT charge if the monies are ever remitted to the UK;
- *third,* conversion into sterling is not a prerequisite to a CGT charge arising;
- *fourth,* capital losses arising on movements on foreign currency bank accounts located outside the UK can only be offset with respect to losses precipitated on disposals made on or after 6 April 2008; and
- *fifth,* UK-based foreign currency bank accounts are also in principle within the charge to UK IHT.

6.57 For the non-UK domiciled and non-UK resident individual, however, none of the above issues arise with respect to CGT. CGT only applies if an individual is either UK resident or UK ordinarily resident.

Summary

6.58 The rules relating to the determination of the source of income or the situs of assets tend to be taken for granted and are thus often overlooked.

6.59 The two issues are extremely important and go to the heart of the taxability of both the UK and non-UK domiciled individual.

6.60 *Income source and asset situs*

6.60 Unless specific provision is made in the tax legislation with respect to income source or asset situs the common law rules apply.

6.61 CGT issues arising out of foreign currency bank accounts are primarily restricted to the non-UK domiciled but UK resident individual. *FA 2008* has to some degree ameliorated the adverse consequences which existed pre *FA 2008* with respect to non-UK source capital losses.

Chapter 7

The principles and implications of property ownership: joint tenancy and tenancy in common

Background

7.1 Tax planning often involves transfers of property (of all types) amongst family members and/or trusts. It is thus important to appreciate the basic nature of property ownership.

7.2 English law recognises two forms of property ownership: legal ownership and beneficial ownership. Thus, it is possible for the legal ownership of property to be divorced from the beneficial ownership and, of course, it is perfectly possible for the legal *and* beneficial ownership to be held by the same person.

This possible split of ownership is a concept well understood in common law jurisdictions (eg the UK; Australia; Canada; the USA) and most commonly arises where property is held under a trust; in this case the trustees are the legal owners of the property and the beneficiaries are the beneficial owners, (see Chapter 15).

7.3 However, the trust is not a concept readily understood in civil law jurisdictions (eg Belgium; France; Germany (although under the 'CLATAR 1986' the signatories (including the UK) thereto agree to recognise the concept when applying their domestic laws). Nevertheless a similar concept, the usufruct, does exist in civil law jurisdictions. Under the usufruct a temporary split of ownership occurs (whether by contract, will, or by the operation of law); the usufructor has effective beneficial ownership of the property with the bare-proprietor owning the legal title. Typically, on the death of the usufructor (or after the passage of a certain period of time) the usufruct terminates and the bare-proprietor regains both legal and beneficial ownership of the property subject to the usufruct.

7.4 For UK tax purposes it is the beneficial ownership of property which is

7.5 *The principles and implications of property ownership*

important. Thus, if an individual 'X' is shown as the registered owner of shares in company 'C' (ie in the share register of company 'C'), *prima facie*, dividends paid on those shares belong to 'X'. However if, for example, 'X' has executed a formal declaration of trust in favour of individual 'Y' (or has simply orally agreed to the hold the shares for 'Y') then for tax purposes it is 'Y' who is the beneficial owner of the shares and any dividends paid belong to 'Y' not 'X', and the income tax liability thereon is that of 'Y' not 'X'.

'X', in this example, is said to be the *legal* owner of the shares while 'Y' is the *beneficial* owner. Although in this example the legal and beneficial ownership is split between 'X' and 'Y' in many cases the legal and beneficial ownership resides with the same person; this would be the case in the current example were 'Y' to be shown as the registered owner of the shares in company 'C'.

7.5 Beneficial ownership refers to the right of enjoyment of the property. Legal ownership, without beneficial ownership, grants no rights of enjoyment to the legal owner who is required to deal with the property only as the beneficial owner dictates.

Legal ownership

7.6 Where property (*excluding* land) is owned by two or more individuals (ie co-ownership) legal ownership may be in the form of *joint tenants* or *tenants in common*. In the case of land, however, legal ownership can only take the form of a joint tenancy (*LPA 1925 ss 1* and *36*).

7.7 A key feature of a joint tenancy (whether with respect to land or other forms of property) is that each co-owner is not treated as owning a share in the land although in aggregate all the co-owners own the whole land. Thus, it is not possible for a joint tenant to leave his interest in the property by will (as in effect he does not own an identifiable share therein) and on his death his interest therein ceases and accrues automatically to the remaining (ie surviving) joint tenant(s) by survivorship (which is not the case with respect to tenants in common; see paragraph 7.9); this has important implications for structuring property ownership not only for tax purposes but also for succession purposes.

Beneficial ownership

7.8 Where property (*including* land) is owned by two or more individuals (ie co-ownership) beneficial ownership may be in the form of joint tenants or tenants in common.

7.9 A tenancy in common, unlike a joint tenancy, confers on a co-owner a notional share of the property which is capable of being left by will (failing which the laws of intestacy will apply); thus, the other co-owners do not take his interest on death by survivorship as is applicable to a joint tenancy; as indicated above, this has important implications for structuring property ownership not only for tax purposes but also for succession purposes.

The notional share owned by a tenant in common in the property is an undivided share and, as a consequence, each co-owner is in fact entitled to possession of the whole of the property not just his share.

7.10 Ideally, on the acquisition of property by two or more persons, agreement should be reached as to how the respective beneficial interests in the property are to be held (ie joint tenants or tenants in common) and documented accordingly (see paragraph 7.12 re documenting interests in land). However, such agreement is not always resolved on the acquisition of property (often, simply by default) and problems surface typically when, for example, one owner wishes to sell or transfer their interest or dies, or in the case of married couples, divorce. At such times it is then necessary to examine all the facts to determine whether the property is held beneficially as joint tenants or tenants in common and in what proportions.

7.11 In making such a determination equity has developed various rules/maxims. In broad terms, the general rule for all property is that 'equity follows the law' and thus if the legal title is held as joint tenants (as is required re land) then the beneficial interest is also so held (*Dyer v Dyer* (1788)). If the legal title is held as tenants in common (only possible re property other than land) the beneficial interest is also so held. This general rule is not, however, always followed. For example, there is an equitable presumption of a tenancy in common where the co-owners purchasing the property contribute unequal purchase monies (*Bull v Bull* (1955)); although this maxim no longer applies where the property concerned is the family home, following the decision of the House of Lords in *Stack v Dowden* (2007), or where the property concerned is of a commercial nature.

7.12 As indicated in paragraph 7.6, in the case of land (post-*LPA 1925*) the legal title is always held as joint tenants. However, on the purchase of land by two or more persons, the Land Registry Form TR1 ('Transfer of whole of registered title(s)') in Box 11 ('Declaration of trust') specifically provides for the purchasers to state how the beneficial interests in the land are to be held (eg as joint tenants; as tenants in common 60/40, 70/30, or 50/50 etc). However, Box 11 is not always completed (strictly speaking this is not necessary although it is desirable); this does not preclude registration of the purchased interests in the land with Land Registry but leaves the beneficial ownership unresolved (in the absence of any other external documentation (eg an explicit declaration of trust) detailing the requisite ownership percentages).

7.13 *The principles and implications of property ownership*

Beneficial joint tenancy versus beneficial tenants in common

7.13 From a tax and/or succession planning perspective beneficial ownership as tenants in common is generally to be preferred over beneficial ownership as joint tenants because of the greater flexibility offered by the former over the latter, (although in some cases a joint tenancy may offer some advantage).

7.14 In practice it is probably with respect to land (as opposed to other forms of property eg bank accounts; life insurance etc) that the decision as to the 'better' form of beneficial ownership is particularly important. Before considering the comparative advantages/disadvantages of each form of ownership a brief look at one or two issues relating to land will be examined.

Land

Legal ownership

7.15 The acquisition of the legal title to land is effectively a three-stage process. The first stage is the conclusion of a legally binding contract between vendor and purchaser (commonly referred to as 'exchange'); the second stage is the conveyance/transfer of the legal title to the property to the purchaser (commonly referred to as 'completion'); and the third stage is the registration of the legal title of the purchaser with the Land Registry (until this registration the vendor remains the legal owner of the property). Where more than one purchaser effects the purchase, the legal title is registered in their respective names as co-owners in the form of a joint tenancy. It is not possible for the legal title to be held as tenants in common (see paragraph 7.6).

7.16 The law also dictates that no more than four persons can hold the legal title to land (ie only four joint tenants can hold the legal title; *TA 1925 s 34*) and to hold legal title requires that the individual be of full age (ie age 18 or over; *LPA 1925 s 1*).

Beneficial ownership

7.17 Co-owners of equitable (ie beneficial) interests in land may hold their interests in the form of a joint tenancy or tenancy in common.

7.18 A conversion from joint tenants to tenants in common may be achieved by the simple act of 'severance' (*LPA 1925 s 36*); note severance may also be effected with respect to any form of property joint ownership, not just land.

The principles and implications of property ownership **7.24**

If land is held, for example, beneficially by two joint tenants either tenant can sever the joint tenancy by simply writing to the other joint tenant notifying him of the intention to sever. The consequence of severance is that the land is then held by the two tenants as tenants in common in equal shares. *Inter alia*, the principle of survivorship will then no longer apply to their respective interests.

7.19 If the land is held by a number of joint tenants (ie more than two) any one joint tenant can sever their joint tenancy by writing, as above, to all the other joint tenants. The consequence in this case is that the individual effecting the severance owns as tenant in common but the others continue to hold their respective interests as joint tenants. Thus, *inter alia*, the individual who then owns as tenant in common is free to dispose of his interest by will whilst the remaining individuals are subject to the survivorship rule (see paragraph 7.7) unless and or until one or more also choose to sever their interest.

7.20 Perhaps, surprisingly, severance by any joint tenant does not require the consent of the other joint tenants, merely notification to them in writing of the act of severance (*LPA 1925 s 196*).

7.21 Whilst severance in lifetime is possible, severance by will is not. Nevertheless, for IHT purposes, a fictional world is in fact created under which a beneficial joint tenancy may be deemed to have been severed, immediately before the deceased's death by the surviving joint tenant(s) enabling a redirection by the surviving joint tenant(s) of the deceased's interest in the property. Such redirection may be to any other person(s) whether such person(s) are, or are not, beneficiaries under the deceased's will. This IHT fiction involves the use of an 'instrument of variation' more commonly referred to as a 'deed of variation (see paragraph 28.71) whose purpose is typically (but not always) to reduce any IHT charge on the deceased's estate.

7.22 The act of severance, per se, precipitates no tax consequences for any of the parties.

7.23 Severance of *legal* ownership of land is not possible; legal ownership of land only being possible by way of a joint tenancy (*LPA 1925 s 1*).

Tax issues

Income tax

Spouse joint ownership

7.24 Special rules apply to the income tax treatment of income arising from property of any type (ie land, bank accounts or otherwise) held by spouses who live together (ie are not separated) in their joint names.

7.25 The principles and implications of property ownership

7.25 Any income arising from the property held by spouses in joint names (ie the legal title is held jointly and not only in the name of one spouse) is treated as income to which the husband and wife are entitled equally (*ITA 2007 s 836*). They are thus treated as each being entitled to 50% of the income arising from the property. This rule applies irrespective of the beneficial ownership percentages held by the spouses and/or the respective contributions with respect to the property.

For example, if a husband and wife purchase a 'buy to let' property in joint names with the husband contributing £100,000 cash to the purchase price and the wife contributing £50,000, for income tax purposes each spouse will be treated as entitled to one half of any rents receivable (despite their unequal contributions).

7.26 The above rule does not, however, apply with respect to all types of income arising from jointly held property (eg it does not apply to partnership income and income arising from furnished holiday lettings; *ITA 2007 s 836*) although it does apply to monies held jointly in bank/building society accounts.

However, where the rule does apply it is possible for it to be displaced.

7.27 Thus, in the example in paragraph 7.25, the spouses are able to make a declaration of their respective beneficial interests in the property and in the rental income arising therefrom (*ITA 2007 s 837*). Each spouse is then subject to income tax on the income arising on their respective interests. In the above example, the declaration would be made in line with their respective capital contributions (ie the husband would own two-thirds of the property beneficially and the wife one-third and any rental income is then treated as arising to each spouse in line with their beneficial interest).

However, the spouses could agree despite their respective capital contributions to own the property in different proportions (eg 60/40; 80/20). Implicit in such an agreement is that one of the spouses has made a gift of part of their interest to the other. If a declaration is to be made the income entitlement must reflect the underlying beneficial interests.

It is thus not possible for the interests in the underlying property to be owned in a different proportion to that in respect of which the rental income is treated as arising for tax purposes (eg the declaration cannot specify a property split of, say, 67/33 with an income split of, say, 60/40; the income split must be in line with the underlying property split (ie 67/33)).

7.28 HMRC provide for such a declaration to be made on Form 17 'Joint property and income'. To be effective for income tax purposes notice of the declaration must be given to HMRC within a period of 60 days from the date of the declaration and must be in the prescribed form, namely, 'Form 17, Joint

The principles and implications of property ownership **7.30**

property and income'. The declaration has effect for income arising on or after the date of the declaration and continues until there is any change in the beneficial interests of the spouses in either the income or the property from which the income arises (*ITA 2007 s 837*). A declaration on Form 17 requires the husband and wife to be living together.

HMRC do not, however, accept that such a declaration is possible with respect to jointly held bank/building society accounts (see notes on Form 17) on the grounds that each owner of the account is entitled equally to the whole account and any income (ie interest thereon) arising on the account is paid to both parties jointly (ie 50/50 applies). However, if the true position is that the joint legal owners are not equally entitled to the underlying capital and interest credited thereon, there appears to be reason why an appropriate declaration cannot be made.

7.29 From a tax planning perspective the assumption of equal entitlement to income may be used to advantage. For example, if a husband and wife open a bank account in joint names where the husband contributes £10,000 cash to the account and the wife contributes £5,000 cash to the account any interest arising on the account (say £1,500) is allocated for income tax purposes as to £750 to the husband and £750 to the wife. If the husband is subject to income tax at a marginal rate of 50% for the tax year 2010–2011, whereas the wife is a basic rate taxpayer (20% for 2010–2011), there is an income tax saving on the 'extra' £250 interest allocated to the wife even though, strictly speaking, her entitlement should only be one third of the £1,500 interest income.

7.30 Another example might be where the husband owns a valuable piece of income producing real estate (eg a buy to let). As, say, a 40% taxpayer he is exposed to this rate of income tax on all the rental income. His wife may have no taxable income in which case, *inter alia*, her personal allowance is wasted. The husband may not wish to transfer any significant beneficial interest in the real estate to his wife but would like to reduce his income tax liability on the rental income.

He could therefore transfer his 100% legal ownership into the joint legal ownership of himself and his wife (as indicated above, the legal ownership would then be held as joint tenants). On the Land Registry form TR1 (which effects the transfer of legal ownership to him and his wife) the respective beneficial interests (shown in Box 11 of the form) may be shown as tenants in common under which he retains 99% of the property and his wife acquires a 1% beneficial interest. However, no declaration is made on Form 17. As a consequence, under the above assumed 50/50 rule, each spouse is subject to income tax on 50% of the aggregate rental income despite the husband's actual entitlement to 99% of the rental income. The husband has effectively reduced his income tax liability on 50% of the aggregate rental income (as 50% is deemed allocated to his wife) whilst still retaining beneficial ownership of the bulk (ie 99%) of the property.

7.31 *The principles and implications of property ownership*

7.31 It is important for the 50/50 rule to apply so that each spouse possesses a beneficial interest in the property, however small (otherwise the settlement provisions apply; *ITA 2007, s 836*).

Non-spouse joint ownership

7.32 In the case of property ownership in joint names where the individuals concerned are not spouses, the rules are slightly different. There is no rule (as applies to property held jointly by spouses) under which income from property in joint names is automatically split 50/50 (ie *ITA 2007 s 836* does not apply).

7.33 The beneficial entitlements to both the underlying property and any income therefrom are determined according to the facts and agreement between the parties. Thus, it is quite feasible for property to be owned beneficially in proportions which do not reflect the respective beneficial entitlements to income (a scenario not possible for spouses).

For example, two brothers purchase a buy to let property in their joint names. Brother 1 contributes £75,000 to the purchase price and Brother 2 £25,000. Despite their respective contributions the brothers agree that Brother 1 is to be beneficially entitled to, say, 80% of the property, but is only beneficially entitled to, say, 40% of the rental income arising on the property.

Such an agreement could not be made by a husband and wife living together; for a husband and wife the ownership of the underlying asset must be in line with the income therefrom if a Form 17 election is to be lodged with HMRC (see paragraph 7.27).

Capital gains tax

Spouse joint ownership

7.34 Property in the joint names of husband and wife is assumed for capital gains tax (CGT) purposes to be held equally beneficially. Any gain arising on a disposal of the property (eg gift or sale) is thus apportioned equally. This applies where there is no explicit evidence confirming how beneficial ownership is to be held (eg a declaration of trust confirming beneficial ownership is to be held as tenants in common in the ratio 60/40).

Thus, where husband and wife purchase property and the property is simply registered jointly, with no indication of how beneficial ownership is split, for CGT purposes any capital gain on a future disposal will be assumed to be divided equally. However, if the contributions to the purchase price are in fact unequal (but there is no definitive statement as to how the beneficial ownership

The principles and implications of property ownership **7.39**

is to be held) any capital gain on disposal is in principle split in accordance with the respective purchase price contributions (ie treating the beneficial ownership as held as tenants in common – note, however, that recent case law has caused this approach to be changed where the property concerned is a 'family home'; in such cases the assumption is that ownership is joint, even if contributions to the purchase price are unequal unless it can be demonstrated that this was not the intention of the parties).

7.35 Where there is explicit evidence as to beneficial ownership split this determines the CGT position and any capital gain is split accordingly. Hence, if a declaration of trust confirms beneficial ownership as joint tenants any capital gain on disposal will be divided equally (irrespective of whether the respective contributions are equal or not). On the other hand, if a declaration of trust confirms beneficial ownership as tenants in common and identifies the relative percentage ownership (eg 60/40) any capital gain on disposal will be divided accordingly (irrespective of whether the respective contributions are 60/40 or not).

7.36 In all cases, in the absence of a completed Form 17, for income tax purposes any income arising from the property is split equally.

Non-spouse joint ownership

7.37 There is no equivalent assumption (see paragraph 7.34) with respect to non-spouse joint ownership for CGT purposes. Each case is thus to be determined according to the particular facts. Where there is no explicit evidence confirming how beneficial ownership is to be held the above discussion also applies to such situations.

Inheritance tax

7.38 Prior to 9 October 2007 (ie the date of the Chancellor's 2007 Pre-Budget Report), for inheritance purposes, ownership of property by way of beneficial tenants in common (as opposed to beneficial joint tenants) was often preferred, particularly in connection with the matrimonial home.

7.39 The prime reason for the preference for the tenants in common structure is that this enables the first spouse to die to leave their (typically 50%) share in the home to, for example, a discretionary trust (set up under their will) for the benefit of their surviving spouse and/or children. This has the effect of ensuring that the first spouse to die does not waste their nil rate band (NRB) (see paragraph 11.44).

7.40 *The principles and implications of property ownership*

If the matrimonial home had been owned as beneficial joint tenants then the respective interest of the first spouse to die passes on death by survivorship to the surviving spouse (ie could not be left by will). The effect for inheritance tax (IHT) is that the inter-spouse exemption applies to the share of the deceased spouse on passing to the surviving spouse but with the attendant possibility that the deceased's NRB remains unutilised, either in whole or in part; this is very inefficient for IHT purposes.

7.40 However, the 2007 Pre-Budget Report introduced the concept of the transferable NRB between spouses ((*IHTA 1984 ss 8A–8C*); not cohabitees). This has, to a degree, removed the need for the use of the discretionary will trust and, in turn, the need for ownership as beneficial tenants in common. Nevertheless, there may still be other reasons why ownership of the matrimonial home as beneficial tenants in common is preferable to ownership as beneficial joint tenants (see paragraph 11.54).

7.41 The valuation of an interest in property (eg matrimonial home) for IHT purposes is exactly the same irrespective as to how the property is held (ie joint tenants or tenants in common). However, where a house is jointly held the valuation of the interest held by one of the joint owners is likely to be subject to some form of discount (eg 10% to 15%) due to the fact that any person acquiring that interest does not have sole occupation rights.

It is understood, however, that HMRC do not accept no such discount applies to joint ownership by spouses.

Non-tax issues

7.42 Whilst tax issues are in most cases very important it may be that other factors also need to be considered. For example, irrespective of the form of the asset, a particular attraction of assets being held as beneficial joint tenants is the application of the survivorship rule and the consequent lack of the need for a grant of representation (ie probate on the death of one of the joint tenants; see paragraphs 27.125 and 27.126).

7.43 The lack of the need for probate in such circumstances arises because the joint tenant's interest in the property is not regarded as part of the individual's estate on death *for probate purposes* (although, of course, it is included as part of the deceased's estate for IHT purposes). As a consequence, the surviving beneficial joint tenant simply has immediate access to the whole of the property. This may be particularly important with respect to cash held in joint bank accounts.

7.44 A bank account held jointly by husband and wife as beneficial joint tenants may continue to be accessed by the surviving spouse following the death of the other spouse; no probate is required and no 'freezing' of the account occurs; in effect the operation of the account continues in the same way as before the death of the deceased spouse (technically, a bank account may be held as tenants in common although for all practical purposes this is not often feasible).

Non-UK domiciled individual

7.45 Particular care is required when considering the form of property ownership where one spouse is UK domiciled and the other is non-UK domiciled. The issue is primarily one of IHT.

7.46 Inter-spouse transfers are exempt for IHT purposes and thus no charge arises thereon. This exemption applies in three out of four possible spouse combinations. Thus, transfers between two UK domiciled spouses, two non-UK domiciled spouses and transfers from a non-UK domiciled to a UK domiciled spouse are all exempt transfers (*IHTA 1984 s 18*). However, transfers from a UK domiciled to a non-UK domiciled spouse may precipitate IHT liabilities.

7.47 More specifically, transfers of property from the UK to the non-UK domiciled spouse are exempt for IHT purposes (*IHTA 1984 s 18*; see paragraph 11.42) but only in respect of the first £55,000. Aggregate transfers in excess of £55,000 (assuming lifetime transfers) are treated as PETs (see paragraph 11.42); the effect of which is that if the transferor dies within seven years of the date of the transfer an IHT charge arises subject to the NRB.

If the transfers are on death, any excess over £55,000 is chargeable to IHT at 40% subject to the NRB.

7.48 It is important therefore that transfers from a UK to a non-UK domiciled spouse do not arise by accident. This may arise where an asset is held as beneficial joint tenants and the UK domiciled spouse dies first (the surviving non-UK domiciled spouse inheriting automatically by survivorship).

By way of example, if the matrimonial home is owned as beneficial joint tenants and worth, say, £2 million if the UK domiciled spouse dies first (in 2010–2011), £1 million less £380,000 (ie the NRB of £325,000 plus £55,000 – £620,000) falls subject to IHT at 40% (ie a charge of £248,000) on passing to the surviving non-UK domiciled spouse. Although the same inheritance consequence arises even if the property ownership is structured as beneficial tenants in common, the latter form of structure permits the option of, for example, leaving the interest in the property to a discretionary trust (with the children and surviving spouse as beneficiaries) or to the children directly which may result in a lower overall IHT charge for the whole family following the death of the surviving spouse.

7.49 *The principles and implications of property ownership*

For example, using the above figures, if the UK domiciled spouse by way of will left an interest worth £325,000 to the children and the balancing £675,000 to the surviving spouse and the surviving non-UK domiciled spouse left her interest including the £675,000 from the husband on death to the children, the IHT on the aggregate £2 million estate would be reduced (ie it would be [40% of £620,000 + 40% of £1,350,000 compared to [40% of £620,000 + 40% of £1,675,000]; these figures assume a NRB of £325,000.

7.49 The problem also arises with respect to other jointly held property, in particular, jointly held bank accounts. However, as indicated above, bank accounts cannot usually in practice be held as beneficial tenants in common; the answer is for each spouse to hold monies in separate accounts each in their own name only (preferably with the non-UK domiciled spouse's primary bank account located outside the UK constituting excluded property; see Chapter 13). This then enables the cash in the account to be left by way of will allowing IHT to be minimised.

7.50 Thus property held as beneficial tenants in common permits a degree of flexibility re tax planning (and succession) not available to property held as beneficial joint tenants (unless lifetime severance occurs). Nevertheless, beneficial joint tenancies whilst not permitting the same flexibility can from a probate perspective prove preferable, (see paragraph 7.42).

Summary

7.51 Ownership of property under English law may take the form of legal and beneficial ownership. The latter is important for all UK tax purposes.

7.52 The two forms of beneficial ownership are joint tenancy and tenancy in common. Under the former, interests in the property on death pass automatically to the survivor. Under the latter, the interests may be left by will.

7.53 Whilst there are pros and cons for each form of beneficial ownership, probably on balance, tenants in common offers the greater flexibility from the tax planning perspective although may have drawbacks *vis à vis* probate matters.

Part II

Capital taxes

Chapter 8

Capital gains tax

Background

8.1 UK domiciled individuals who are either UK resident or ordinarily resident are subject to capital gains tax (CGT) on disposals of worldwide assets. Non-UK domiciled individuals who are UK resident or ordinarily resident are subject to CGT only on disposals of UK situs assets unless any gains arising on non-UK assets are remitted to the UK in which case CGT is levied thereon (*TCGA 1992 s 12*; assuming remittance basis treatment is claimed; see paragraph 24.7).

8.2 Capital gains tax is thus not levied on UK situs assets of those who are neither UK resident nor UK ordinarily resident (unless such non-residents are trading in the UK; *TCGA 1992 s 10*).

8.3 Any capital gain arising on the disposal of an asset is a chargeable gain (ie subject to CGT) unless expressly provided otherwise (*TCGA 1992 s 15*). Thus, for example, the disposal of paintings; jewellery; shares; options; etc. all precipitate chargeable gains (chargeable gains may thus arise on both tangible and intangible assets). The disposal of an asset may be an actual disposal or a deemed disposal; both may precipitate tax charges.

An actual disposal generally refers to a disposal pursuant to which an actual transfer of ownership from one person to another of the asset occurs at the time of the disposal whereas this is not necessarily the case with a deemed disposal. An example of an actual disposal is the sale of an asset by one individual to another or the sale by trustees of assets during the administration of a trust.

A deemed disposal arises where no actual disposal takes place but is deemed to take place, for example, where a beneficiary becomes absolutely entitled to settled assets as against the trustees which might occur where a beneficiary attains a certain age (eg age 18 or 21) or where trustees exercise a power of advancement/appointment (in this case the trustees are deemed to have sold the asset for market value and reacquired the asset then holding it as bare trustee for the beneficiary; *TCGA 1992 s 71*).

8.4 Capital gains tax

8.4 Some assets are, however, exempt from CGT including:

- an individual's main residence;
- national savings certificates and premium bonds;
- motor vehicles suitable for private use;
- most government securities (ie gilts);
- life assurance policies when held by the original beneficial owner;
- investments held within Individual Savings Accounts (ie ISAs);
- foreign currency for an individual's private use;
- pension rights; and
- prizes and betting winnings.

8.5 A disposal of an asset typically takes the form of a sale or gift although it may also include, for example, the loss or destruction of an asset (eg the burning down of a property) or the creation of one asset out of another (eg the grant of a lease out of a freehold) (*TCGA 1992 s 22*).

8.6 A disposal is regarded as having occurred at the date of execution of an unconditional contract (eg the date of disposal of land is typically the date of the 'exchange' of contracts not 'completion') or the date when the condition is satisfied if the contract is conditional (*TCGA 1992 s 28*).

8.7 *FA 2008* (*s 8* and *Schs 2* and *3*) made significant amendments to the rules applicable to CGT. The new rules introduced by *FA 2008* apply to any disposal on or after 6 April 2008 irrespective of the date of acquisition of the asset.

8.8 The changes affect both UK and non-UK domiciled individuals albeit in different ways and in different degrees.

The key changes introduced by *FA 2008* are:

(1) introduction of a single rate of CGT (ie 18% but see paragraphs 8.17, 8.20 and 8.22);

(2) introduction of a new form of relief, 'entrepreneur relief' (ER);

(3) amendments to the offshore 'settlor-interested' trust provisions;

(4) amendments to the offshore 'capital payments' trust regime;

(5) amendments to the rules with respect to 'remittances' of offshore capital gains;

(6) amendments to the rules with respect to offshore capital losses;

(7) abolition of the indexation allowance;

(8) abolition of taper relief; and

(9) abolition of the UK resident 'settlor-interested' trust provisions.

All these changes became effective with respect to any form of disposal effected on or after 6 April 2008 irrespective of the date of acquisition of the asset.

8.9 Of the above nine key changes those that affect the UK domiciled individual are, in particular, (1), (2), (7), (8) and (9).

Of the above nine key changes those that affect the non-UK domiciled individual are, in particular, (3), (4), (5) and (6).

Nevertheless, any consideration of the CGT position of either UK or non-UK domiciled individuals, post-*FA 2008*, should take account of all of the above changes (and, of course, those introduced by subsequent Finance Acts).

8.10 In particular, *F (No 2) 2010* introduced changes which are effective from 23 June 2010 (ie unusually, part way through the tax year 2010–2011). Thus, disposals effected between 6 April 2010 and 22 June 2010 inclusive are subject to different provisions from those applicable to disposals effected on or after 23 June 2010.

Transitional provisions are included to resolve issues which may arise from this difference in treatment in the same tax year.

Persons liable to capital gains tax

8.11 Individuals, trustees and personal representatives (PRs) are in principle liable to CGT (but not companies).

Annual exempt amount

8.12 The annual exempt amount is the element of the 'taxable amount' for a tax year which is exempt from a charge to CGT (*TCGA 1992 s 3*).

The 'taxable amount' for a tax year is the aggregate of the individual's capital gains for the tax year less capital losses of that tax year and less any unused capital losses brought forward from earlier tax years (albeit subject to possible restriction; see paragraphs 9.7 and 9.9)(*TCGA 1992 s 2*).

8.13 *Capital gains tax*

For *individuals* the annual exempt amount for the tax year 2010–2011 is £10,100 (*SI 2010/923 'The Capital Gains Tax (Annual Exempt Amount) Order 2010'*); *PRs* are entitled to an annual exempt amount for the tax year of death of the individual and the immediately following two tax years only (*TCGA 1992 s 3*); and *trustees* are entitled to one-half of the annual exempt amount available to individuals (ie £5,050 for the tax year 2010–2011 (*TCGA 1992 Sch 1*).

8.13 Pre-6 April 2010 (ie for tax years prior to 2010–2011), the annual exempt amount is simply deducted from the net capital gains for the tax year to arrive at the quantum of capital gains subject to CGT. However, for the tax year 2010–2011 the rate of CGT is 18% for capital gains arising between 6 April 2010 and 22 June 2010 inclusive, but for capital gains arising on or after 23 June 2010 the rate of CGT is either 18% or 28% (see paragraph 8.22).

For 2010–2011 the annual exempt amount can be deducted from those capital gains which mitigate the CGT charge for that tax year and thus are not simply deducted from the aggregate net capital gains for that tax year (see paragraph 8.24).

Example 1

Alistair Ash has taxable income for the tax year 2010–2011 of £20,000.

He has capital gains of £7,000 made in May 2010; £8,000 made on the 20 June 2010; £16,400 made in July 2010 and £6,000 made in November 2010.

None of the gains qualify for entrepreneur relief.

The £7,000 and £8,000 are subject to CGT at the 18% rate (pre-23 June 2010).

Alistair's unused basic rate band is £17,400 (ie £37,400 less £20,000).

The capital gains of £16,400 and £6,000 (ie £22,400) exceed the £17,400 by £5,000.

Thus, £17,400 is subject to CGT at the 18% rate with the balancing £5,000 subject to CGT at the 28% rate.

The annual exempt amount (£10,100 for 2010–2011) is used against the capital gains subject to the 28% rate with any unused balance being deducted from those capital gains subject to the 18% rate.

Thus, Alistair's CGT liability is:

Capital gains tax **8.20**

28% × [£5,000 – £5,000 (of the annual exempt amount)]

+ 18% × [[£7,000 + £8,000 + £17,400] – £5,100 (the unused balance of the annual exempt amount)]

ie [£nil + £4,914] = £4,914.

(see paragraph 8.22).

8.14 Any unused element of the annual exempt amount for a tax year cannot be carried forward (or back) for future (or earlier) use and is thus lost.

8.15 Following changes introduced in FA 2008 certain non-UK domiciled but UK resident individuals who claim remittance basis treatment for a tax year are denied the annual exempt amount (and, in addition, any entitlement to any of the personal allowances) (*ITA 2007 s 809G; see* paragraph 24.15).

8.16 Personal allowances (ie allowances available to reduce income subject to income tax) are not deductible in arriving at the amount of capital gains subject to CGT in a tax year.

Rates of capital gains tax

Trustees

8.17 Disposals effected on or after 23 June 2010 are subject to a flat rate of CGT of 28% (*F (No 2) Act 2010 s 2* and *Sch 1*).

Disposals effected prior to 23 June 2010 but on or after 6 April 2010 are subject to a flat rate of 18% rate. This rate also applies to disposals effected on or after 6 April 2008 to 5 April 2010.

8.18 Disposals effected prior to 6 April 2008 (and from 6 April 2004) are subject to CGT at a flat rate of 40% (34% prior to 6 April 2004 and post-6 April 1998).

8.19 For disposals effected on or after 6 April 2008 a rate of 10% may apply where ER applies (see paragraph 8.79; *FA 2008 s 9* and *Sch 3*).

Personal representatives

8.20 Disposals effected on or after 23 June 2010 are subject to a flat rate of CGT of 28% (*F (No 2) Act 2010 s 2* and *Sch 1*).

8.21 *Capital gains tax*

Disposals effected prior to 23 June 2010 and on or after 6 April 2010 are subject to a flat rate of 18% rate. This rate also applies to disposals effected on or after 6 April 2008.

8.21 Disposals effected prior to 6 April 2008 (and from 6 April 2004) are subject to CGT at a flat rate of 40% (34% prior to 6 April 2004 and post-6 April 1998).

Individuals

8.22 For disposals effected on or after 23 June 2010 the rate of CGT applicable to individuals is 18% where the individual's total taxable income and chargeable capital gains (after all allowable deductions including losses, the personal allowance and the annual exempt amount) are less than the upper limit of the basic rate band (ie £37,400 for the tax year 2010–2011) (*F (No 2) Act 2010 s 2* and *Sch 1*).

A rate of 28% applies to chargeable capital gains (or parts thereof) above this limit.

Capital gains qualifying for ER (see paragraph 8.79) on or after 23 January 2010 are set against any element of the unused basic rate band before any capital gains made on or after 23 June 2010 which do not so qualify.

Capital gains which arise on or after 6 April 2010, but before 23 June 2010, are ignored when ascertaining rates of CGT applicable to capital gains arising on or after 23 June 2010.

Example 2

Charlie Chin realises capital gains of £27,000 in May 2010; £15,000 in August 2010; and £12,000 in October 2010.

Charlie's taxable income for 2010–2011 is £15,000.

Charlie has not used any of his lifetime allowance for ER purposes.

The capital gain in October (£12,000) qualifies for ER (at a rate of 10%).

Charlie's unused basic rate band is £22,400 (ie £37,400 less £15,000). To ascertain the rate of CGT applying to the August capital gain involves the £12,000 of capital gain qualifying for ER utilising £12,000 of the £22,400 leaving £10,400 available to the August capital gain of £15,000.

Capital gains tax **8.25**

Thus, £10,400 of the £15,000 is subject to CGT at the 18% rate with the balance (ie £4,600) falling subject to CGT at the 28% rate (the annual exempt amount is deductible from the £4,600 with any unused balance then being deducted from capital gains subject to CGT at the 18% rate).

The capital gain of £27,000 which arose before 23 June 2010 is ignored when ascertaining the rates of CGT applicable to capital gains arising on or after 23 June 2010.

For the non-UK domiciled but UK resident individual non-UK source capital gains are treated as arising when remitted. Thus, the applicable rate of CGT is determined at the date of remittance. For the tax year 2010–2011 non-UK source capital gains are thus subject to the 18% rate where the remittance occurs pre-23 June 2010; where the remittance occurs on or after 23 June 2010 the rate is either 18% or 28% (see paragraph 24.117).

8.23 For disposals effected prior to 23 June 2010 and on or after 6 April 2010 the rate of CGT is 18% irrespective of the level of the individual's taxable income (*FA 2008 s 8*).

The 18% rate also applies to disposals effected on or after 6 April 2008.

8.24 Provisions are made under which the annual exempt amount (see paragraph 8.12) may be deducted in the manner which is most beneficial (*F (No 2) 2010 s 2 Sch 1*).

This is likely to mean that the annual exempt amount is deducted:

- *first,* from capital gains (other than gains qualifying for ER) arising on or after 23 June 2010 that are chargeable at the 28% or 18% rate;
- *second,* from capital gains arising between 6 April 2010 and 22 June 2010 (including gains qualifying for ER that have been reduced by 4/9ths) that are chargeable at the single 18% rate; and
- *third,* from capital gains arising on or after 23 June 2010 that qualify for ER and are chargeable at the new 10% rate.

8.25 Capital gains made prior to 23 June 2010 (and on or after 6 April 2010) are not taken into account in calculating an individual's rate of CGT for the balancing period 23 June 2010 to 5 April 2011.

Example 3

Brutus Brown sold various assets in the tax year 2010–2011.

8.26 *Capital gains tax*

Between 6 April 2010 and 22 June 2010 his capital gains amount to £15,000.

Between 23 June 2010 and 5 April 2011 his capital gains amount to £20,000.

None of the gains qualify for entrepreneur relief.

Brutus' taxable income is £30,000 for 2010–2011.

Brutus' taxable income is [£37,400 – £30,000] ie £7,400 less than the basic rate band limit (£37,400). Thus, of the £20,000 capital gains part (ie £7,400) is subject to 18% and the balance (ie £20,000 less £7,400) at 28%.

It therefore makes sense to deduct the £10,100 annual exempt amount from the £12,600 subject to the 28% rate giving £2,500.

The CGT liability on the £20,000 is thus:

28% x £2,500 + 18% x £7,400 = £2,032.

The £15,000 of capital gains are subject to CGT at the 18% rate (no annual exempt amount available to reduce this £15,000) ie [18% x £15,000], namely, £2,700.

Brutus' aggregate CGT liability for 2010 is [£2,032 + £2,700] (ie £4,732).

Capital gain computation

8.26 A chargeable gain arising on an asset disposal is in principle the difference between the disposal proceeds and the asset's original cost (*TCGA 1992 ss 15, 37* and *38*). Any consideration which is taken into account in the computation of a charge to income tax is excluded (ie income tax takes priority over CGT (*TCGA 1992 s 37*); see also paragraph 8.27).

The 'costs' that are deductible comprise:

- the consideration (whether in money or money's worth) together with incidental costs incurred in acquiring the asset;
- expenditure incurred enhancing the value of the asset being expenditure reflected in the state or nature of the asset at the time of disposal;
- expenditure wholly and exclusively incurred in establishing, preserving or defending title to the asset; and

- the incidental costs of making the disposal.

(TCGA 1992 s 38)

No allowance in the computation is made for the fact that any consideration arising on the disposal may be deferred *(TCGA 1992 s 48)*.

8.27 Incidental costs include, for example, fees, commission or remuneration paid for the professional services of a surveyor, accountant and/or legal advisor together with any stamp duty/stamp duty land tax (SD/SDLT). Costs of advertising to find a buyer or seller are also included *(TCGA 1992 s 38)*. However, such costs are not deductible if they are eligible for deduction for income tax purposes (eg in computing the profits of a trade, profession or vocation (eg furnished holiday lettings) or in computing any other income/profit for income tax purposes; *TCGA 1992 s 39*).

Example 4

Gordon Green purchases a buy to let property for £450,000 selling the property five years later for £750,000.

SDLT of £1,350 (ie 3%) and legal fees of £1,500 are incurred on the purchase and £1,500 of estate agent fees are incurred on the sale together with legal fees of £2,000.

Gordon's chargeable gain is:

[£750,000 − £3,500] − [£450,000 + £2,850] = £293,650.

Gifts

8.28

A disposal may take the form of a gift. For CGT purposes a gift is deemed to be made at market value *(TCGA 1992 s 17;* see paragraph 8.31 with reference to inter-spouse gifts). A gift may, for example, be from one individual to another individual or may arise on a transfer into trust.

Example 5

Gordon Green purchases some shares for £15,000 and two years later gifts them to an old friend. At the time of the gift the shares are worth £50,000.

8.29 *Capital gains tax*

Gordon's chargeable gain is £35,000 as it is based on the market value of the shares at the date of the gift precipitating the CGT charge (even though Gordon receives no monies from the gift).

Connected persons

8.29 Where a transaction occurs between 'connected persons' it is assumed that the transaction is effected at market value irrespective of the actual price (if any) paid (*TCGA 1992 s 18*). For this purpose a person is connected with:

- his spouse;
- his relatives (ie brothers, sisters, ancestors and lineal descendants);
- the relatives of his spouse; and
- the spouses of his and his spouse's relatives.

(*TCGA 1992 s 286*)

A person who is a trustee of a trust is 'connected' with, *inter alia*:

- the settlor; and
- any person 'connected' with the settlor.

(*TCGA 1992 s 286*)

A person is 'connected' with another person if that person has 'control' (*TCGA 1992 s 288*) of it or if that person and persons 'connected' with him together have control of it (*TCGA 1992 s 286*).

Example 6

Gordon Green purchases some shares for £15,000 and two years later his sister purchases the shares from Gordon for £20,000 at a time when the shares are worth £50,000.

Gordon's chargeable gain is £35,000 as Gordon's disposal is to a connected person (ie his sister) and is thus based on the market value of the shares. If Gordon had gifted the shares to his sister his CGT position would have been the same.

Any capital loss which arises on a disposal to a particular connected person may only be offset against capital gains arising on disposals to the same particular connected person (*TCGA 1992 s 18*).

Bargains not at 'arm's length'

8.30 Market value imputation also applies to a disposal between two persons where it is a transaction 'otherwise than by way of a bargain made at arm's length' (*TCGA 1992 s 18*). This suggests that a disposal between persons who are not 'connected' persons may still be treated as occurring at market value. Prima facie, this is unlikely to apply in practice as it is difficult to imagine where two persons who are not connected persons would transact at other than market value. Nevertheless, it seems likely that a disposal between persons who are not connected, if at less than market value, will be deemed by HMRC to be a bargain not at arm's length and market values imputed.

Example 7

Mary purchases a buy to let flat for £200,000 cash.

A few years later her boyfriend, Dick, agrees to purchase half of the flat for £185,000 when the flat is valued at £400,000.

HMRC are likely to deem Mary's disposal of half of her interest to have been effected for market value ie £200,000, not the £185,000.

Inter-spouse transfers

8.31 Although spouses are connected persons and thus, *prima facie*, the market value rule in *TCGA 1992 s 18* applies (see paragraph 8.29), it is displaced by a rule specifically applicable to spouses (*TCGA 1992 s 58*).

8.32 A disposal between spouses is treated as if the disposal gives rise to neither a capital gain nor a capital loss for the transferor spouse. In effect this means that the transferee spouse acquires the asset at the original cost to the transferor spouse subject to any enhancement expenditure and associated acquisition fees etc (see paragraphs 8.26 and 8.27).

Example 8

Jon Smith purchases shares worth £55,000 in 2003 and in 2010 transfers the shares to his wife, Barbara, when the shares are worth £100,000. Jon incurs costs at the date of his original purchase of £2,000.

8.33 *Capital gains tax*

Jon is assumed to transfer the shares for £57,000 irrespective of their market value at the date of transfer. A transfer for £57,000 produces neither capital gain nor capital loss for Jon (ie £57,000 less [£55,000 + £2,000]).

Barbara is assumed to have acquired the shares for £57,000 (irrespective of what she may or may not have in fact paid).

If Barbara sells the shares when they are worth £165,000 she makes a capital gain of £108,000.

8.33 The above inter-spouse transfer rule applies where the spouses are both married and living together (*TCGA 1992 s 58*) (contrast the inter-spouse rule for IHT purposes; see paragraph 11.42). It is therefore inapplicable to transfers following a divorce or to transfers after the end of the tax year in which separation occurs (but does apply to the balance of the tax year of separation; ie the period from the date of separation to the end of the tax year in which separation occurs).

The rule applies irrespective of the domicile status (see Chapter 3) of the spouses.

8.34 For inter-spouse transfers effected on or before 5 April 2008 account also had to be taken of any indexation allowance (see Appendix 3). *FA 2008* abolished both indexation allowance and taper relief for disposals effected on or after 6 April 2008.

In order to prevent any loss of any 'accrued' indexation allowance typically inter-spouse transfers were effected before 6 April 2008 to 'lock in' such allowance for the future.

Example 9

Jon Smith had purchased shares worth £25,000 in 1995 and in February 2008 (ie pre-*FA 2008*) transfers the shares to his wife, Barbara, when the shares were worth £100,000.

The indexation allowance available to Jon amounts to, say, £35,000.

Jon would be treated as having transferred the shares for £60,000 (ie original cost of £25,000 plus the indexation allowance of £35,000) irrespective of their market value at the date of transfer. This would then give rise, on Jon's part, to neither a capital loss nor a capital gain.

Barbara is assumed to have acquired the shares for £60,000 (irrespective of what she may or may not have in fact paid).

If Barbara sells the shares when they are worth £165,000 she makes a capital gain of £105,000.

If Jon had transferred his shares on 6 April 2008 no indexation allowance would have been available. Thus, he would have been treated as if he had disposed of the shares for £25,000 and Barbara as having acquired them for £25,000. On the sale by Barbara for £165,000 her capital gain would then have been £140,000 (compared to £105,000 above) thus producing a greater CGT liability for Barbara.

8.35 The inter-spouse transfer rule applies irrespective of the domicile status of the spouses. Accordingly this can present planning opportunities.

For example, a UK domiciled and resident spouse gifts (or sells thus avoiding any potential IHT liability) a non-UK situs asset to his non-UK domiciled but resident spouse. As an inter-spouse transfer no CGT liability arises on the gift.

The non-UK domiciled but UK resident spouse is then able to sell the asset without precipitating a CGT charge if none of the sale proceeds are remitted to the UK. Alternatively, the recipient spouse could settle the asset on a non-UK resident trust, which would not at that time precipitate a CGT charge (assuming he has claimed remittance basis treatment) nor in fact any IHT charge (as the property is excluded property; see Chapter 13).

Payment of capital gains tax

8.36 CGT for a tax year is payable on or before the 31 January following the tax year in which the chargeable gains arise (*TCGA 1992 s 59B*). It is not subject to the requirement to effect payments on account as is the case for income tax (*TCGA 1992 s 59A*).

Example 10

Herbert Jones sells a number of his personal chattels (antique paintings; jewellery; and shares) on 20 April 2010 realising aggregate chargeable gains of £55,000 (pre-annual exempt amount of £10,100).

The CGT liability arising on £44,900 (ie 18% thereof) is payable on or before 31 January 2012.

8.37 *Capital gains tax*

8.37 There are, however, provisions providing for a CGT liability for a tax year to be discharged by instalments as opposed to one lump sum. Instalment payments may be used where:

(a) the consideration received from the disposal is itself payable in instalments over a period exceeding 18 months from the date of the disposal;
(b) the gift is of assets comprising unquoted shares;
(c) the gift is of quoted shares where the donor has 'control' (broadly, owns at least 51% of the voting capital); or
(d) the gift is of land.

(TCGA 1992 ss 280 and 281)

However, payment by instalments under (b), (c) or (d) is not possible if a hold-over election could be made (whether it is made, *de facto* or not, is irrelevant) under *TCGA 1992 ss 165* or *260* (see paragraph 8.45).

8.38 Under (a) in paragraph 8.37 the instalments of tax payable may be spread over a maximum period of eight years (although the last tax instalment may not be made later than the date of the last instalment of the consideration arising from the disposal) if an election is made by the vendor. Agreement of HMRC is required to the instalment proposal of the vendor. No interest is charged under this option unless any of the tax instalment payments are made after the due dates *(TCGA 1992 s 280)*.

8.39 Under (b), (c) or (d) in paragraph 8.37 the tax instalments may be made over a period of 10 years by 10 equal annual instalments if an election is made by the donor. The first instalment is to be paid on the date on which the CGT liability would normally have been payable in the absence of payment by instalments (ie the 31 January following the tax year in which the disposal is made). Unlike the position under (a), interest is charged on the outstanding instalments and should the asset be subsequently sold (after the initial gifting) any outstanding tax payments (plus interest) become payable in full unless the initial gift is made to a donee who is not connected (see paragraph 8.29) with the donor *(TCGA 1992 s 281)*.

Year of death

8.40 On the death of an individual there is no assumed deemed disposal of the deceased's assets *(TCGA 1992 s 62)*. Thus, no CGT liability arises on an individual's death.

All assets beneficially owned by the deceased at death are revalued to their market values at the date of death (ie probate value). There is thus an automatic uplift in the values of the assets owned at death without a concurrent CGT arising; any latent gains on the assets owned at death are thus 'wiped out'.

8.41 Beneficiaries under the deceased's will (or intestacy) are thus deemed to inherit the deceased's assets at their market values at the date of death (ie their probate value).

Example 11

George Kay dies on 6 July 2010. At the date of his death his estate comprises:

- cash at bank £300,000;
- quoted shares with a market value at death £400,000; and
- an antique painting with a market value at death £150,000.

George had originally purchased the shares for £50,000 and the painting for £110,000.

No CGT liability arises on George's death.

All his estate is left to his daughter, Georgina. Georgina thus inherits the assets at their value at the date of George's death.

If a week later Georgina sells the shares for £410,000 her chargeable gain is £10,000 (ie £410,000 less £400,000) not £360,000 (ie £410,000 less £50,000).

8.42 In the tax year of death any capital losses arising on disposals prior to death may be utilised not only against capital gains made prior to death in the tax year of death but may also be carried back to the three immediately preceding tax years and offset against capital gains assessable in those tax years on a last in first out (LIFO) basis (at no other time can capital losses be carried back to prior tax years) (*TCGA 1992 s 62*).

Any capital losses of the deceased in the tax year of death, but prior thereto, must be first offset against capital gains of that tax year (prior to death) even if for that tax year part or all of the annual exempt amount is lost/wasted before any surplus unused capital losses can be carried back to prior tax years (*TCGA 1992 s 62*). However, losses carried back need to be offset against capital gains of those earlier tax years only to the extent that the annual exempt amount is not lost. This may lead to a refund of CGT for those tax years.

Example 12

Albert Brown dies on 17 June 2010. His capital gains and capital losses for 2010–2011 are £17,000 and £25,000 respectively; capital gains are £11,000 for 2009–2010 and £30,000 for 2008–2009.

The £25,000 is offset against the £17,000 even though the annual exempt amount for 2010–2011 is thus wasted. The balancing unused capital losses of £8,000 are carried back for offset against the capital gains of £11,000 for 2009–2010. The annual exempt amount for 2009–2010 is £10,100. Thus, only £900 of the £8,000 losses are offset against the £11,000 of gains. The remaining £7,100 of losses are offset against the gains of £30,000 for 2008–2009.

Gifts of assets (not inter-spouse)

8.43 Inter-spouse transfers (where living together) do not precipitate a CGT liability (see paragraph 8.31). They are assumed to have taken place at no gain/no loss. With one exception (ie transfers from a UK to a non-UK domiciled spouse) all inter-spouse transfers do not precipitate a liability to inheritance tax (IHT) (see paragraph 11.42).

The position with respect to non-inter-spouse transfers is different, typically giving rise to a charge to CGT (see paragraphs 8.28, 8.29 and 8.30).

8.44 Tax planning for families often involves the transfer of assets between family members. It is not unusual to effect such transfers in the form of gifts whether the gifts are from one individual to another or are gifts into trust or are gifts out of trust.

The gift of an asset (or indeed sale at undervalue) potentially precipitates both CGT and IHT consequences. An outright sale at market value, however, only precipitates a CGT liability.

Holdover relief

8.45 The gift of an asset for CGT purposes is deemed to have given rise to a disposal at market value (*TCGA 1992 s 17*); a liability to CGT may thus arise even though no cash or other form of consideration is given for the asset

The donor may thus be faced with a CGT liability even though having received no consideration from which to discharge such liability. In such circumstances 'hold-over relief' may be available to the person (ie individual or trust) effecting the disposal as a consequence of which any CGT arising is in fact deferred (ie no CGT is immediately payable on the gift).

8.46 In some cases this deferral may in fact turn out to be complete avoidance; this occurs where the donee (ie recipient) of the gift dies whilst still owning the asset, due to the 'uplift' on death (see paragraph 8.40).

8.47 The relief operates by reducing both the capital gain which otherwise arises (ie in the absence of hold-over relief) on the gift by the amount of the held-over capital gain and the base cost to the donee. In computing the capital gain no deduction of the annual exempt amount is permitted.

Where consideration is given for the disposal, albeit less than market value, hold-over relief is still available but subject to adjustment.

Example 13

Kate Bowen acquires an asset for £13,000 and gifts it into trust at a time when the asset is worth £38,000.

If hold-over relief is available (and claimed) Kate is assumed to have made a capital gain of nil (ie the deemed capital gain of £25,000 (£38,000 less £13,000) is reduced nil by hold-over relief equal to the deemed capital gain of £25,000).

The trust is correspondingly deemed to acquire the asset at a base cost equal to the deemed disposal proceeds less the hold-over gain (ie [£38,000 less £25,000] (ie £13,000)).

Example 14

Kate Bowen acquires an asset for £13,000 and sells it to a trust for £18,000 at a time when the asset is worth £38,000.

Her capital gain is £25,000 (as the asset is assumed to have been disposed of at its market value).

However, Kate receives consideration for the disposal and this has to be taken into account; in essence, it reduces the amount of the capital gain eligible for holdover relief.

If hold-over relief is available (and claimed) Kate is assumed to have made a capital gain of £25,000 (ie £38,000 less £13,000) but reduced by

8.48 *Capital gains tax*

hold-over relief equal to the deemed capital gain (ie £25,000) less actual gain (ie £18,000 – £13,000). Thus, hold-over relief equals £20,000. The balancing £5,000 of capital gain is then subject to CGT.

The trust is correspondingly deemed to acquire the asset at a base cost equal to the deemed disposal proceeds less the hold-over gain [£38,000 less £20,000] (ie £18,000).

8.48 Hold-over relief is available in two sets of circumstances under *TCGA 1992 ss 165* and *260*.

8.49 Whether relief under *TCGA 1992 ss 165* or *260* is in point such relief must be claimed (*TCGA 1992 ss165* and *260*).

Section 260 requires that the recipient (ie donee/transferee) of the gift must be either a UK resident or UK ordinarily resident *individual or trustee* and the donor must be either an *individual or trustee* (*TCGA 1992 ss 260* and *261*).

Section 165 requires that the recipient (ie donee/transferee) of the gift must be either a UK resident or UK ordinarily resident *person* (ie an individual, trust or company) and the donor must be either an *individual or trustee* (*TCGA 1992 ss 165* and *166*).

In addition, the gift must either be of a 'business asset' (*TCGA 1992 s 165*) *or* it must precipitate an immediate charge to IHT (*TCGA 1992 s 260*).

8.50 Thus, *inter alia*, gifts to non-UK resident individuals, non-UK resident trusts and non-UK resident companies do not qualify for hold-over relief under either *TGCA 1992 ss 165* or *260*.

Even if the company recipient is UK resident, no hold-over relief under *s 165* is available if the company is controlled (*TCGA 1992 s 288*) by person(s) who are neither UK resident nor UK ordinarily resident and connected (*TCGA 1992 s 286*) with the donor (*TCGA 1992 s 167*).

8.51 Where the recipient donee emigrates (ie becomes neither UK resident nor UK ordinarily resident) within six years of the end of the tax year in which the disposal occurs, any held-over gain is clawed back (assuming at the time of emigration the donee still owns the asset) (*TCGA 1992 s 168*). A capital gain is deemed to have arisen to the donee equal to the held over gain immediately before the emigration.

Thus, emigration after the six-year period does not precipitate any clawback of the held-over gain.

No clawback occurs where the donee's reason for becoming neither UK resident nor UK ordinarily resident is due to working full time outside the UK under a contract of employment if the donee reacquires UK residency or ordinary residency within three years of the date of becoming non-UK resident and non-UK ordinarily resident (still owning the asset) (*TCGA 1992 s 168*).

8.52 Hold-over relief may need to be adjusted (ie reduced):

- where the asset concerned has not been used throughout its period of ownership as a business asset (*TCGA 1992 Sch 7*); or

- where the gift is of shares in a company which owns assets which are not business assets and the company is the personal company of the individual donor at some time during the 12 months prior to the gift (*TCGA 1992 Sch 7*).

8.53 There is no restriction as to how many times capital gains may be 'held-over' by way of gift relief. Thus, for example, a father could give his shares to his son, both claiming gift relief. The son may subsequently gift the same shares to his brother, again both claiming gift relief, etc. It is, of course, important that all the gift relief conditions are satisfied at the dates of the various gifts.

In the event that after a number of such gifts the ultimate donee dies, not having disposed of the shares, all gains of all the parties are simply wiped out as, on death, the shares are simply revalued at their then market values (death does not give rise to disposals for CGT purposes; see paragraph 8.40).

8.54 The relief, whether under *TCGA 1992 ss 165* or *260*, is not given automatically and an election is required (the claim should be made on Help Sheet 295). The election must be made by both the donor and donee unless the gift is into trust in which case only the donor/settlor is required to lodge the election.

Effective 1 April 2010 the time limit for lodging the election is four (previously five) years from the end of the tax year in which the gift is made (*TMA 1970 s 43*; *FA 2008 s 118*).

Immediate charge to inheritance tax (TCGA 1992 s 260)

8.55 It is possible for a gift to qualify under both *TCGA 1992 ss 165* and *260*. Where this occurs, *s 260* operates in priority (*TCGA 1992 s 260*). A gift may fail to qualify under one section, but qualifies under the other (eg a gift from one individual to another individual cannot qualify under *s 260* (as it is a potentially exempt transfer (PET) and precipitates no IHT charge) but if it is a business asset may qualify under *s 165*).

8.56 Capital gains tax

8.56 A gift is within *TCGA 1992 s 260* if it is a chargeable lifetime transfer (CLT) for IHT purposes (*IHTA 1984 s 2*) ie a transfer that precipitates an immediate IHT charge (see paragraph 10.22). Thus, PETs cannot qualify for hold-over relief under s 260 as they do not precipitate an immediate charge to IHT.

Gifts made pre-22 March 2006 into most types of trust were PETs (see paragraph 10.37) and thus hold-over relief under *s 260* was generally not available; gifts between individuals, which both pre-and post-22 March 2006 constitute PETs (see paragraph 10.35) are equally unable to qualify for hold-over relief.

Gifts pre-22 March 2006 into relevant property trusts, typically discretionary trusts, qualify as CLTs and thus also qualify for hold-over relief under *s 260*.

Gifts made on or after 22 March 2006 into most forms of trust now qualify as CLTs (*IHTA 1984 s 2*) and are eligible for hold-over relief under *s 260*. Thus, gifts into relevant property trusts (as pre-22 March 2006) continue to qualify for hold-over relief under *s 260*; relevant property trusts, post-22 March 2006, now include not only discretionary trusts (as pre-22 March 2006) but most interest in possession trusts created on or after 22 March 2006.

Transfers of trust property out of a relevant property trust (eg an appointment to a beneficiary) qualify for hold-over relief under *s 260*.

8.57 Gifts to companies are not eligible for hold-over relief and neither are gifts by companies; this is because only individuals and trustees are able to take advantage of hold-over relief under *s 260*.

8.58 Appointments out of non-UK resident trusts to UK resident beneficiaries also qualify for hold-over relief unless the assets are non-UK situs and the trust was created by a non-UK domiciled settlor (in which case the property appointed out is excluded property precipitating no IHT charge; however, hold-over applies if *s 165* is satisfied).

8.59 Gifts from one individual to another individual (whether pre- or post-22 March 2006), however, do not precipitate an immediate IHT charge as such gifts constitute PETs and thus hold-over relief is not available on such gifts under *s 260*.

8.60 It should be noted that no IHT on the gift actually needs to be payable for 'an immediate inheritance tax charge to occur'. For example, a lifetime gift by an individual into a discretionary trust is a CLT and an immediate IHT charge arises. However, if the amount of the gift falls within the nil rate band (NRB) of the donor/settlor, no IHT is, de facto, payable as the liability thereon is at the nil rate; nevertheless, gift relief is available to the donor.

Similarly gifts to which 100% business property relief (BPR) for example, applies, are also eligible for hold-over relief.

Qualifying interest in possession trust: termination due to death of beneficiary

8.61 The termination of a qualifying interest in possession (see paragraph 16.4) may arise on the death of the interest in possession beneficiary or in lifetime. Following termination of the interest the trust may come to an end or it may continue.

Example 15

Trustees of the Barbara Burt trust hold trust property on trust to pay Henry, a beneficiary, the trust income for life (ie Henry is an interest in possession beneficiary, in this case commonly referred to as the life tenant) remainder to Tom.

On Henry's death the trust property becomes that of the remainderman, Tom (ie Tom becomes absolutely entitled to the trust property on Henry's death) and the trust terminates.

A beneficiary is absolutely entitled to trust property as against the trustees where he has the exclusive right to direct how the trust property is to be dealt with or would have such right subject only to his minority (*TCGA 1992 s 60*).

8.62 Where the qualifying interest in possession terminates due to the death of the beneficiary and the trust then terminates the trustees are deemed to have disposed of, and re-acquired, the trust assets for market value. However, no CGT charge is deemed to arise (*TCGA 1992 s 72*). The trustees effectively then hold the trust assets as bare trustees for the beneficiary(ies) entitled thereto, (*TGCA 1992 s 60*).

Where the trust assets which are deemed to have been disposed of and re-acquired were subject to an earlier hold-over relief claim (ie when the assets were first transferred into the trust) any such held-over capital gain falls subject to CGT on the part of the trustees (*TCGA 1992 s 74*). However, it is possible for this held-over capital gain to itself then be subject to a further hold-over relief claim under *s 260*.

Example 16

Terry Black creates an interest in possession trust for his brother, Gordon, in July 2004 settling shares then worth £30,000 precipitating a capital gain of £12,000 which is held-over. On Gordon's death his sister, Teresa, becomes entitled to the shares.

In August 2010 Gordon dies and the shares at that time are worth £45,000.

8.63 *Capital gains tax*

On Gordon's death the trustees are deemed to have disposed of the shares for £45,000 giving rise to a capital gain of [£12,000 + £15,000] (ie £27,000).

No CGT is chargeable on the capital gain of £15,000 (ie the growth in value whilst the shares are held in trust) but a CGT charge arises on the held-over gain of £12,000 (subject to any hold-over relief; *TCGA 1992 s 260* is satisfied due to an exit IHT charge arising on the shares leaving the trust and thus a hold-over claim is feasible).

8.63 Where the qualifying interest in possession terminates due to the death of the beneficiary but the trust does not then terminate basically the same consequences arise as set out in paragraph 8.62 (*TCGA 1992 s 72*). The trustees are deemed to have sold and re-acquired the assets for their market value but without precipitating a CGT charge (and as the trust continues the trustees will not, as above, hold the assets as bare trustees).

As above, any previously held-over capital gain falls chargeable to CGT on the part of the trustees subject to a claim for this held-over gain to itself be held over again under *s 260*.

Qualifying interest in possession trust: termination in lifetime of beneficiary

8.64 Where the qualifying interest in possession terminates in the lifetime of the beneficiary (ie not on death) and the trust then terminates (ie an individual becomes absolutely entitled as against the trustees) the trustees are deemed to have sold the assets and re-acquired them albeit in this case CGT is charged on any capital gain (*TCGA 1992 s 71*). Thus, unlike the positions outlined above in paragraphs 8.62 and 8.63, an actual charge to CGT arises on the part of the trustees. This charge extends to including any previously held-over capital gain. However, the whole of the deemed capital gain (including any earlier hold-over gain) cannot be held over under *s 260* as no IHT is precipitated as the termination of the interest in possession is a PET, (however, holdover relief under *s 165* may be available (see paragraph 8.72)).

8.65 Where on the lifetime termination of the qualifying interest in possession the trust does not terminate (ie the trust assets remain in the trust as no individual becomes absolutely entitled as against the trustees) no CGT consequences occur as no deemed disposal arises (ie the trust assets simply remain in the trust at their original costs) (*TCGA 1992 s 71*).

Non-qualifying interest in possession trust

8.66 With respect to terminations of non-qualifying interests in possession (eg an interest in possession which arises on or after 22 March 2006 but is not a transitional serial interest (TSI) or an immediate post-death interest (IPDI), whether on death or in lifetime, no CGT consequences arise unless on termination a beneficiary becomes absolutely entitled to the trust assets (*TCGA 1992 ss 72* and *73* are inapplicable to non-qualifying interests in possession; *TCGA 1992 s 71* is applicable to non-qualifying interests in possession, but only where an individual becomes absolutely entitled to trust assets on the termination).

Where an absolute entitlement occurs on the termination a charge to CGT arises on the deemed disposal and re-acquisition of the assets by the trustees although hold-over relief may be available on the whole capital gain (including any earlier held over gain) under *s 260 (TCGA 1992 s 71)*.

Example 17

Terry Black creates an interest in possession trust for his brother, Gordon, in July 2006 settling shares then worth £30,000 precipitating a capital gain of £12,000 which is held-over. On Gordon's death the shares are to be held on discretionary trust for Gordon's nieces and nephews.

In August 2010 Gordon dies and the shares at that time are worth £45,000.

As Gordon's interest in possession is not qualifying and as the trust does not terminate no CGT consequences arise on his death.

If on the other hand, on Gordon's death the trust terminates (for example where his sister, Teresa, becomes entitled to the shares) a CGT charge arises albeit subject to hold-over relief (under *TCGA 1992 s 260*).

Appointments made by the trustees out of relevant property trusts precipitate a charge to CGT on the trustees as the recipient beneficiary becomes absolutely entitled as against the trustees (*TCGA 1992 s 71*). However, hold-over relief is available under *s 260* as the appointment precipitates an IHT exit charge (see paragraph 16.18).

Business assets (TCGA 1992 s 165)

8.67 As stated in paragraph 8.55 if a claim to hold-over relief may be made under both *ss 165* and *260*, the latter takes precedence. *Section 260* cannot apply to gifts which constitute PETs (eg gifts between individuals) and thus in such cases only *s 165* is potentially available.

8.68 Hold-over relief under *s 165* requires that the gift is made by an

8.69 *Capital gains tax*

individual (*TCGA 1992 s 165*) to a UK resident recipient person (eg an individual, trust or company) and qualifies as a 'business asset' (see paragraph 8.71 for business assets held by trustees).

Business assets are defined as:

(a) any asset used by the donor for the purposes of a trade, profession or vocation carried on by the donor or his/her personal company;

(b) shares or securities held in the donor's *personal trading company*; or

(c) shares or securities of a trading company which are not listed on a recognised stock exchange.

(*TCGA 1992 s 165*)

A *personal company* is one in which the donor controls at least 5% of the voting rights and can be either quoted or unquoted.

A *trading company* is a company whose activities do not include, to a substantial extent, activities other than trading activities (*TCGA 1992 s 165A*) and includes the commercial letting of furnished holiday accommodation (*TCGA 1992 s 241*).

8.69 No hold-over relief, however, is available on a gift of shares/securities *to a company* (although transfers of land, for example to a company, would qualify for gift relief; *TCGA 1992, s 165*).

8.70 Hold-over relief applies to pure business asset transfers (ie there is no requirement for the transfer to be a business or part of a business).

8.71 *TCGA 1992 Schedule 7* effectively extends hold-over relief to trustees where the trustees of a trust make a disposal (otherwise than at arm's length) of business assets. For this purpose business assets are defined as:

(a) any asset used for the purposes of a trade, profession or vocation carried on by the trustees making the disposal or a beneficiary who has an interest in possession (whether 'qualifying' or not) in the settled property immediately before the disposal;

(b) shares or securities of a trading company which are not listed on a recognised stock exchange; or

(c) shares or securities of a trading company where not less than 25% of the voting rights are exercisable by the trustees at the time of the disposal.

(*TCGA 1992 Sch 7*)

8.72 Where transfers of property out of trusts do not precipitate an immediate charge to IHT (ie *s 260* does not apply) hold-over relief is available under *s 165* if the asset so transferred qualifies as a business asset.

For example, where a qualifying interest in possession terminates during the lifetime of the beneficiary and another beneficiary becomes absolutely entitled to the trust property in which the interest subsisted termination of the interest is a PET. Relief under *s 165* (but not *s 260*) is available where the trust property qualifies as a business asset (see paragraph 8.64).

Settlor-interested trusts

8.73 Care is required where a trust is 'settlor-interested'. Gifts made on or after 10 December 2003 into a settlor-interested trust do not qualify for hold-over relief either under *TCGA 1992 s 260* or *s 165*. However, transfers out of such trusts may still qualify for hold-over relief.

8.74 A trust is 'settlor-interested' for this purpose if any trust property is or may be used for the benefit of the settlor or his spouse. On or after 6 April 2006 a trust is also settlor-interested if any minor unmarried child of the settlor may benefit. The extension to include such children applies to trusts whether created before or after 6 April 2006 (*TCGA 1992 ss 169B* to *169F*; and *FA 2006 s 88*).

8.75 Gifts into trusts which are not at that time settlor-interested (and thus qualify for hold-over relief) but subsequently become such within six years of the end of the tax year in which the gift is made causes any hold-over relief to be withdrawn (*TCGA 1992 s 169C*).

8.76 The effect of the extension of the definition of a settlor-interested trust together with the other IHT changes to trusts introduced by *FA 2006* is to increase the probability that a trust is settlor interested and that a transfer into such a trust by the settlor will precipitate both a charge to CGT (as no gift relief is available as the trust is settlor-interested) and a charge to IHT (as the transfer is, post-21 March 2006, a CLT). No relief for any IHT charged on the transfer is available for offset against any CGT charged thereon.

Non-UK situs assets, the non-UK domiciled individual and gifts

8.77 Pre-*FA 2008* the gift of a non-UK situs asset by a non-UK domiciled but UK resident individual did not precipitate a CGT liability. Thus, for example, no CGT liability arose where such an individual transferred a non-UK situs asset into a non-UK resident trust or made a gift of the non-UK situs asset to another individual. The reason why no CGT liability arose was that the remittance basis applied to such an individual, and as no consideration was actually received, a remittance of the non-UK situs capital gain was not possible.

Nevertheless, the gift still constituted a disposal for CGT purposes and the donee, whether a trust or an individual, was deemed to have acquired the asset at its then market value (ie any capital gain on a future disposal by the recipient trust or individual would be calculated using this market value as the base cost).

The lack of any CGT charge on the donor meant that hold-over relief in such circumstances was not necessary.

8.78 Post-*FA 2008*, a gift effected on or after 6 April 2008 by a non-UK domiciled but UK resident individual of a non-UK situs asset to a non-UK resident trust or individual may result in a CGT charge on such individual if a remittance occurs; under the *FA 2008* rules such a remittance is deemed to occur if the asset gifted is brought to the UK (the remittance would need to be by or for the benefit of a 'relevant person') (see paragraph 24.50).

The CGT charge arising on any such remittance on the part of the original donor is not, however, eligible for holdover relief under either *s 165* or *s 260* where the gift is made to a non-UK resident (whether individual, trust or company).

However, a gift of a non-UK situs business asset to a UK resident individual (who qualifies as a relevant person; *ITA 2007 s 809M* and paragraph 24.36 and 24.50) which the recipient donee brings to the UK precipitates a CGT charge on the donor at that time but hold-over relief under *s 165* should be available. However, the gift of a non-UK situs, non-business or business asset to a non-UK resident trust constitutes a gift of excluded property for IHT in respect of which no charge to IHT thus arises; in which case *s 260* relief is unavailable but, in any event, hold-over relief requires the donee to be UK resident (*s 165* cannot apply as the recipient donee is non-UK resident).

Entrepreneur relief

8.79 Entrepreneur relief (ER) was introduced in *FA 2008* as a replacement for indexation and, in particular, taper relief both of which were abolished by *FA 2008* (see Appendix 2). However, it is much more akin to the former retirement relief (which was phased out between 1998 and 2003). However, unlike the former retirement relief, where the individual concerned needed to be at least 50 years old, there is no age requirement for ER.

8.80 In principle, ER applies to gains arising on disposals of businesses on or after 6 April 2008 (*TCGA 1992 Chapter III Part V*). It also extends to certain disposals effected before this date (see paragraph 8.94).

8.81 ER is available to individuals, trusts and PRs.

8.82 ER provides relief from CGT in respect of 'qualifying business disposals' (*TCGA 1992 s 169H*). Qualifying business disposals comprise material disposals made by an individual which comprise:

(a) a disposal of the whole or part of a business;

(b) a disposal of one or more assets in use for the purposes of the business at the time at which the business ceases to be carried on;

(c) a disposal of one or more assets consisting of shares or securities of a company; or

(d) a disposal qualifying as an 'associated' disposal.

(*TCGA 1992 ss169H, 169I* and *169K*)

However, the conditions attached to each of the above categories which need to be satisfied are different.

Disposal of the whole or part of a business

8.83 The business disposed of must have been owned by the individual throughout the period of one year ending with the date of the disposal.

Disposal of one or more assets in use for the purposes of the business at the time at which the business ceases to be carried on

8.84 The business must have been owned by the individual throughout the period of one year ending on the date on which the business ceases to be carried on and that date (ie the date of cessation) must be within three years of the date of the asset disposals.

Disposal of one or more assets consisting of shares or securities of a company

8.85 Throughout the period of one year ending with the date of disposal of the shares or securities the following conditions must have been satisfied:

- the company concerned must have been a trading company;

8.86 *Capital gains tax*

- the individual must have owned at least 5% of the ordinary share capital and 5% of the voting rights; and
- the individual must have been an officer or employee of the company.

Alternatively, all of the above conditions are satisfied throughout the period of one year ending with the date on which the company ceases to be a trading company and that date (ie the date the company ceases to be a trading company) is within the period of three years ending with the date of the disposal.

The term 'trading company' means a company which carries on a trade and whose non-trading activities and/or non-trading assets are not substantial (ie comprise not more than 20% of the company's business). There is no pro-rating of the ER where the company's activities comprise minor non-trading activities/non-trading assets; the ER is basically all or nothing. A letting business does not qualify as a trade other than furnished holiday lettings (*TCGA 1992 s 169S*).

Example 18

High Technology Ltd is a family trading company and its shares from inception of the company have been owned as follows:

	Nos of shares	holding
Ted	2,750	55
Bert	1,500	30
Anita	250	5
Sarah	250	5
Toby	250	5

Ted is the Managing Director and Chairman; Bert is a director; Anita is an employee; Sarah and Toby are the children of Ted but are not employees.

Shortly, the company is to be sold.

ER is available to Ted, Bert and Anita who each own at least 5% of the company and are also officers/employees.

Whilst Sarah and Toby own the requisite minimum 5% shareholding they are not officers/employees and thus on sale no ER is available to them.

Disposal qualifying as an 'associated' disposal

8.86 An 'associated' disposal does not stand alone but is reliant on an attachment to one of the above three categories of material disposal (*TCGA 1992 s 169P*).

Capital gains tax **8.88**

Three conditions need to be satisfied:

- *first,* a material disposal of business assets is made by the individual which consists of either the disposal of the whole or part of the individual's interest in the assets of a partnership or is the disposal of shares or securities of a company;
- *second,* is that the disposal by the individual is made as part of the individual's withdrawal from participation in the business carried on by the partnership or by the company; and
- *third,* is that throughout the period of one year ending with the earlier of the date of disposal of the material disposal of business assets and the cessation of the business of the partnership or the company the assets disposed of are in use for the purposes of the business.

It is the individual's withdrawal from participation in the business carried on by the partnership or by the company (the second condition above) which constitutes the disposal associated with a relevant material disposal.

Example 19

Tommy Tucker has always been a keen inventor and owns the intellectual property rights to a process used in the manufacture of plastics.

Some years ago he set up his own trading company to manufacture the plastics but he personally retained the rights to the process.

Tommy has just sold the shares in the company and the rights.

ER is available to Tommy on both the shares and rights; the latter because the sale of the rights constitutes an associated disposal.

Relevant business assets

8.87 Not all business assets necessarily qualify for ER.

8.88 Where the qualifying disposal does not consist of a disposal of shares or securities in a company (ie the disposal must fall within (a), (b) or (d) of paragraph 8.82) ER only applies to disposals of relevant business assets comprised in the qualifying disposal (including goodwill) which are:

- assets used for the purposes of a business carried on by the individual or a partnership of which the individual is a member (for (a) or (b) of paragraph 8.82);

8.89 *Capital gains tax*

- assets used for the purposes of a business carried on by the partnership or company.

(TCGA 1992 s 169L)

However, assets that do not qualify (ie excluded assets) are shares and securities and any other assets that are held as investments.

As the above only applies where the qualifying disposal does not consist of a disposal of shares or securities in a company there is no need to distinguish assets owned within the company on a sale of shares or securities in a company.

Claim for, and amount of, relief

8.89 Unlike the position with respect to business asset taper relief and the former retirement relief, where no formal claim to these reliefs was necessary, ER must be formally claimed *(TCGA 1992 s 169M)*.

The claim must be made by the individual on or before the first anniversary of the 31 January following the tax year in which the qualifying disposal is made (broadly, 22 months after the end of the relevant tax year) *(TCGA 1992 s 169M)*.

8.90 A claim may only be made, however, where the result of the qualifying disposal is a 'net gain'. The 'net gain' is the amount of capital gains arising on the disposals of any relevant business assets less any capital losses arising thereon.

For disposals before 23 June 2010 the net gain is then reduced by 4/9ths giving rise to a net amount of 5/9ths of the net gain which is then subject to CGT after deduction of the annual exempt amount. The rate of CGT is 18%. This produces an effective rate of CGT of 10% (ie 5/9ths of 18%) *(TCGA 1992 s 169N)*.

For disposals on or after 23 June 2010 ER applies to the net gain after deduction of the annual exempt amount at a rate of 10% (ie the 4/9 reduction ceases to apply) *(F (No) 2010 s 2 Sch 1)*.

Example 20

Stuart Book sells his shareholding in his unquoted trading company for £90,000 making a capital gain of £72,000.

Assume the sale is effected:

(a) pre-23 June 2010;

(b) on or after 23 June 2010.

Under (a) Stuart's capital gain subject to CGT is:

[[£72,000 − 4/9 x £72,000] − £10,100] x 0.18 = [£40,000 − £10,100] x 0.81 = £5,382

Under (b) Stuart's capital gain subject to CGT is:

[£72,000 − £10,100] x 0.10 = £62,000 x 0.10 = £6,200

The difference between the computations is always £808. For capital gains of £18,180 or less no CGT arises pre 23 June 2010 but on or after 23 June 2010 the CGT charge is £808 or less until the capital gains are £10,100 or less when the CGT charge is also nil.

Any other capital losses of the individual for the tax year in which the qualifying disposal is made and any other capital losses brought forward are offset only after ER has been applied for pre-23 June 2010 disposals.

Example 21

Graham Pub makes a capital gain of £54,000 on 18th May 2010 which qualifies for ER.

He has capital losses brought forward of £19,000.

Graham's CGT position is:

Capital gain subject to ER	£54,000
Less: ER of [4/9 x £54,000]	£24,000
	£30,000
Less; capital losses b/f	£19,000
	£11,000
Less: annual exempt amount	£10,100
Net capital gain subject to CGT	£900

8.91 However, account also needs to be taken of the possible restriction of the lifetime allowance of £5 million for disposals effected on or after 23 June 2010 (*F (No 2) 2010 s 2 Sch 1* and *TCGA 1992 s 169N*).

8.92 *Capital gains tax*

For disposals before 23 June 2010 but on or after 6 April 2010, the lifetime allowance is £2 million (*FA 2010 s 4* and *TCGA 1992 s 169N*).

For disposals effected before 6 April 2010 but on or after 6 April 2008 the lifetime allowance is £1million (*TCGA 1992 s 169N*).

If the net gain figure arising from a qualifying disposal in a tax year when added to the aggregate net gains from earlier qualifying disposals exceeds the relevant lifetime allowance at that time, only that amount of net gain which causes the aggregate of net gains to fall within the lifetime allowance qualifies for ER. The excess is subject to CGT at the rate of 18% (or, where appropriate, the 28% rate; applicable for disposals on or after 23 June 2010).

The £2 and £1 million lifetime allowances refer to aggregate net gains before the 4/9ths reduction is applied.

8.92 Where on a qualifying disposal the net figure is a net loss, no claim to ER on such a disposal can be made and such loss cannot be offset against any net capital gains.

Any gain or loss taken into account in arriving at a net gain figure on a qualifying disposal is not treated as a chargeable gain or an allowable loss for CGT purposes.

Example 22

Tommy Tinder prior to 6 April 2010 has utilised £1 million of his ER lifetime allowance.

He sells two of his businesses in 2010–2011, one in May 2010 realising net capital gains of £3 million and one in January 2011 realising net capital gains of £7 million.

Tommy's taxable income for 2010–2011 is £17,400.

Of the £2 million of lifetime allowance, as at the May 2010 disposal, £1 million has already been used leaving £1 million of the £3 million disposal gain subject to ER reduction by 4/9ths subject to CGT at 18% with the balancing £2 million of gain fully subject to CGT at 18% (with no reduction).

As at the date of the January 2011 disposal the lifetime allowance is £5 million of which £2 million has been used. Thus, £3 million of the £7 million disposal is subject to ER at 10%. The balancing £4 million is not entitled to ER. Tommy's taxable income is £17,400 leaving £20,000 of

Capital gains tax **8.94**

unused basic rate band (which is £37,400 for 2010–2011). Unfortunately the £3 million capital gain (although subject to the 10% ER rate) absorbs the £20,000 (see Note 2 below) which leaves the £4 million subject to CGT at 28% (albeit less the annual exempt amount).

Notes:

1. The annual exempt amount can be used in the most tax efficient manner; in this case is thus set against the capital gain of £4 million subject to the 28% rate.

2. In ascertaining what capital gains (if any) are subject to the 18% rate (ie on or after 23 June 2010) any capital gains subject to ER (on or after this date) are required to be offset against the unused part of the basic rate band before any capital gains which do not qualify for ER (thus the £3 million absorbs the unused part of the basic rate band of £20,000 leaving the £4 million less annual exempt amount subject to the 28% rate).

8.93 In the case of a disposal associated with a relevant material disposal (but only in such cases) special provisions exist. These provisions provide that only a proportion of any gain or loss may be eligible for inclusion in the calculation of the net gain/loss figure.

The extent of such inclusion depends upon, *inter alia*, whether the asset disposed of was in use for the purposes of the business throughout the period of ownership by the individual; whether the whole or only a part of the asset was used in the business; whether the individual is concerned in carrying on the business for only a part of the period during which the asset is used for the purposes of the business; and/or whether any rent was paid by the business for their use.

The balance of any amount which does not fall to be eligible for ER is, however, treated as a chargeable gain (and thus subject to 18% and/or 28% without any ER) for CGT purposes (thus, for example, other capital losses of the individual brought forward may be offset against such gains).

8.94 Although ER applies to disposals on or after 6 April 2008 certain pre-6 April 2008 disposals may still qualify for the relief (*TCGA 1992 s 169Q*).

For example, an individual may have sold shares in a company in exchange for shares in an acquiring company or a mixture of cash and loan notes. Where such transactions occur it may be that the capital gain on the transaction is not deemed to arise until the new shares acquired are sold or the loan notes are redeemed. If the sale or redemption takes place on or after 6 April 2008 the original gain (in whole or in part) is attributable to the post-6 April 2008

8.95 *Capital gains tax*

disposal. If the individual at the time of the original pre-6 April 2008 disposal would have been entitled to ER (ie at that time would have satisfied the relevant conditions on the assumption ER was in point on that date) then such relief is available to reduce the extent of any capital gains deemed to have arisen post-6 April 2008. Thus, advantage of the 10% effective rate can be taken.

It needs to be noted, however, that the post-6 April 2008 deemed gain does utilise part of the relevant lifetime allowance.

Trusts

8.95 In order for capital gains of trustees to qualify for ER on the sale of trust business assets the following conditions need to be satisfied:

- at the date of the relevant disposal the beneficiary has an interest in possession in the trust business assets which is not for a fixed term;
- the interest in possession beneficiary is carrying on the business as a sole trader, or as a partner or as an employee of the company in which he owns at least 5% of the shares;
- throughout the period of one year ending not earlier than three years before the disposal the business assets were used by the beneficiary in his sole trader business or by a partnership of which the beneficiary is a partner or the company was the beneficiary's personal company (and of which he was an employee) and the beneficiary ceased to carry on the business or ceased to be a partner in the partnership either on the date of the disposal or within three years before this latter date; and
- the claim for ER must be made jointly by the trustees and the beneficiary.

(TCGA 1992 ss169J and 169M)

8.96 Trustees of trusts without an interest in possession beneficiary (eg discretionary trusts) cannot qualify for ER.

8.97 The lifetime allowance (see paragraph 8.91) is not directly available to trusts. It is thus necessary for the interest in possession beneficiary to effectively transfer his own lifetime allowance (or part thereof) to the trustees.

Offshore companies

8.98 CGT does not apply to companies whether they are UK resident or not. UK resident companies are subject to corporation tax on their profits (*CTA 2009* *s 2*); non-UK resident companies are subject to corporation tax only in respect of profits of a trade carried on within the UK (otherwise such a company is liable to income tax on UK source income at the basic rate).

Apportionment of non-UK resident company capital gains

8.99 However, any capital gains which are made by non-UK resident companies may fall subject to CGT by way of an apportionment of the capital gains of the companies' to their shareholders (*TCGA 1992 s 13*). Such apportionment only applies if the company (were it to in fact be UK resident) qualifies as a close company (*TCGA 1992 ss 13* and *288*); thus capital gains of non-close companies are not subject to *TCGA 1992 s 13* apportionment.

A close company is broadly defined as a company which is under the control of five or fewer shareholders (*TCGA 1992 s 288*; basically, more than 50% of the voting power of the company).

8.100 Strictly speaking, the capital gains of the company are apportionable to 'participators' (*TCGA 1992 ss 13* and *417*; a term broader than the term 'shareholder') of the company; for ease of reading the term 'shareholder' is used here.

A 'participator' is any person having an interest in the capital or income of the non-UK resident company which, of course, includes shareholders.

8.101 Thus, every person (ie individual, company or trust) who at the time a capital gain accrues to a non-UK resident deemed close company is UK resident or ordinarily resident and is a shareholder therein is treated as if the capital gain had accrued to him in proportion to his shareholding in the company at that time (the apportionment is made at the time the capital gain accrues to the company and to shareholders in the company at that time; there is no aggregation of the company's capital gains for a tax year which are then apportioned.).

Non-UK resident trusts who are shareholders at the time any capital gains accrue to such a company are also subject to apportionment of the company's capital gains (although no other non-UK residents are subject to apportionment).

8.102 UK resident shareholders are subject to CGT (or, if a company, corporation tax) on their apportioned gain. The capital gains apportioned are calculated as if the non-UK resident company was UK resident (ie *inter alia*, the indexation allowance applies – this was abolished with effect from 6 April 2008, but only for individuals, not companies).

8.103 *Capital gains tax*

8.103   In practice any non-UK tax paid by the company on the capital gains is eligible for credit against the CGT charge on the part of the shareholder.

De minimis limit

8.104   There is a *de minimis* limit pursuant to which no CGT is charged on the shareholder where the shareholder's apportioned gains are less than 10% of the company's gains. Any capital gains apportioned to connected persons are taken into account for this purpose (*TCGA 1992 ss 13* and *286*). Thus, for example, if one spouse owned, say, 5% of the non-UK resident company and the other spouse also owned 5%, then each is charged to CGT on their respective apportioned gains; as connected persons the total gains apportioned equals 10% of the company's gains.

Subsequent company distributions

8.105   The non-UK resident company may subsequently effect dividend distributions to its shareholders (or may be liquidated precipitating capital distributions) causing its shareholders to be subject to tax twice on the same gain. Relief (albeit not complete relief) is available in one of two ways.

The original CGT payable on the apportioned gains is deductible from any subsequent CGT charge (eg if the company is liquidated) or is deductible from any subsequent income tax charge (eg on a dividend distribution by the company). For such relief to apply, the distributions must be made within three years of the end of the period of accounts of the company in which the capital gain accrued or, if earlier, within three years of the date on which the capital gain accrued.

Alternatively, the original CGT payable on the apportioned gains is deductible from any subsequent capital gain (not a deduction from the subsequent CGT charge itself) arising on a disposal of the shares by the shareholder; in this case there is no three-year time period restriction.

8.106   Both forms of relief are subject to various conditions which for the non-UK resident trust shareholder may be difficult if not impossible to achieve.

Capital losses

8.107   Capital losses made by non-UK resident companies are also apportioned in the same manner as capital gains. However, these apportioned losses can only be utilised by the shareholder against capital gains apportioned to him in the same tax year under *TCGA 1992 s 13* (including apportioned gains of other non-UK resident deemed close companies in which shares of at least 10% are held). Any excess unused capital losses cannot be utilised (ie are wasted).

If a surplus of apportioned capital gains subsists after apportioned capital loss, any capital losses of the shareholder may then be offset against the surplus apportioned capital gains in the normal manner.

Non-UK resident trusts

8.108 Non-UK resident trust shareholders in non-UK resident-companies are also subject to apportionment as indicated above (see paragraph 8.101) although no CGT charge arises on such apportioned gains as the trusts are non-UK resident. Nevertheless, the apportioned capital gains do fall within the potential charges under *TCGA 1992 ss 86* and/or *87* (see Chapter 18). The above rules relating to capital losses also apply to trustees.

Broadly, the capital gains of the non-UK resident company apportioned to its non-UK resident trust shareholder may be subject to CGT on the UK domiciled and UK resident settlor of the trust under *TCGA 1992 s 86* (the section does not apply to non-UK domiciled settlors) or on UK domiciled and UK resident beneficiaries who receive capital payments from the trust (or non-UK domiciled but UK resident beneficiaries who receive capital payments in the UK) under *TCGA 1992 s 87*.

Offshore income gains

8.109 The above discussion with respect to capital gains made by non-UK resident companies also applies to offshore income gains (OIGs) (*FA 2008 ss 40A–42A*; *OFTR 2009 (SI 2009/3001) reg 24* made by such companies. However, such apportioned gains are subject to income tax not CGT (see paragraph 18.99).

The remittance basis applies to non-UK domiciled individuals; however, in this case the OIG is treated as 'relevant foreign income' (RFI) not 'foreign chargeable gains' (*OFTR reg 19*).

Non-UK domiciled but UK resident individuals

8.110 Pre-*FA 2008*, shareholders subject to an apportionment were, *inter alia*, those shareholders who were UK domiciled and UK resident or ordinarily

8.111 *Capital gains tax*

resident individuals. Non-UK domiciled but UK resident individual shareholders were exempt from a *TCGA 1992 s 13* charge.

8.111 However, with respect to capital gains made on or after 6 April 2008, such individuals are no longer exempt from a *TCGA 1992 s 13* charge (*TCGA 1992 s 14A*). Nevertheless, the remittance basis is applicable to the apportioned capital gain where the asset disposed of by the non-UK resident company is non-UK situs and the individual has (where necessary) claimed remittance basis treatment (see paragraph 24.7). The capital gain apportioned is treated as a 'foreign chargeable gain' (*TCGA 1992 s 14A*).

The remittance basis does not apply to apportioned capital gains of the company which arise on disposals of UK situs assets.

8.112 A remittance may arise, for example, where the non-UK resident company effects a remittance of the sale proceeds (in whole or in part) arising on the disposal (the company qualifying as a relevant person; *ITA 2007 s 809M*; see paragraphs 24.36 and 24.50). The remittance of any sale proceeds is, in the first instance, a remittance of the capital gain element.

8.113 For the non-UK domiciled but UK resident individual, an apportioned capital loss is first set against apportioned capital gains (as is the case for the UK domiciled individual; see paragraph 8.107). However, for such offset, the apportioned capital gains (on non-UK situs assets) against which apportioned capital losses are offset must be remitted to the UK in the tax year in which gains arise; otherwise no such offset is possible (*TCGA 1992 s 14A*).

8.114 Post-*FA 2008*, capital gains apportioned to non-UK resident trust shareholders in non-UK resident deemed close companies on or after 6 April 2008 are subject to CGT on the part of non-UK domiciled but UK resident beneficiaries who receive capital payments in the UK from the trust; this applies whether the apportioned capital gains arise on UK or non-UK situs assets (*TCGA 1992 s 87*). Capital payments made by the trust outside the UK precipitate CGT charges on the part of the recipient non-UK domicile but UK resident beneficiary on any apportioned capital gains only when the capital payments are remitted to the UK.

The settlor interested provisions with respect to non-UK resident trusts are still, post-*FA 2008*, inapplicable to non-UK domiciled settlors (*TCGA 1992 s 86*).

Departures and arrivals in the UK

8.115 An individual is liable to CGT in a tax year if such individual is either resident *or* ordinarily resident in any part of the tax year (*TCGA 1992 s 2*). Thus,

CGT is leviable even if the individual is only resident and/or ordinarily resident for part of the tax year.

8.116 It is thus in principle possible for an individual to leave the UK, become neither resident nor ordinarily resident, dispose of assets then owned (including UK situs assets) and return to the UK without precipitating a CGT liability.

8.117 The rules applicable to UK residency and ordinary residency are discussed in detail in Chapter 4. Broadly, an individual may become not resident and not ordinarily resident in the UK by emigrating from the UK; leaving the UK for at least three years; and/or working full time abroad under a contract of employment (or self employment) for at least one complete tax year.

Recent cases confirm that under the first two of the above three options the individual must also have severed any ties with the UK (previously it was thought that, for example, leaving the UK for three years automatically resulted in the loss of UK residency and ordinary residency (subject to not spending 183 days etc back in the UK) and the severing of ties with the UK was not strictly necessary.

8.118 For CGT purposes it will be noted that a loss of UK residency (perhaps easier to achieve) is not sufficient for a charge to CGT to be avoided; loss of ordinary residence is also necessary. It is perfectly possible for an individual to lose UK residency but still remain ordinarily resident.

Split tax years

8.119 Tax law makes no provision for splitting a tax year for an individual into periods of residency and periods of non-residency. However, by concession, this is permitted. HMRC6, ESC A11 and ESC D2 each confirm such treatment (see paragraph 4.53).

8.120 Concession ESC D2 allows the tax year to be split so that the individual who arrives in the UK part way through a tax year, acquiring residency at that point, is subject to CGT only on disposals made on or after the date of arrival (ie the date of acquisition of residency (and possible ordinary residency)).

Similarly, ESC D2 provides that the individual who departs from the UK part way through a tax year will be subject to CGT only on disposals made up to and including the date of departure.

8.121 However, in the former case (ie arrival in the UK) ESC D2 only applies

8.122 *Capital gains tax*

where the individual has not been UK resident or ordinarily resident in any of the five tax years immediately prior to the tax year of arrival.

In the latter case (ie departure from the UK) ESC D2 only applies where the individual has not been UK resident or ordinarily resident for at least four out of the seven tax years immediately preceding the tax year of departure.

8.122 Where ESC D2 does not apply, the individual will be liable to CGT for the complete tax year of arrival or departure.

8.123 ESC D2, however, makes no reference to the CGT position in the tax year of arrival/departure with respect to capital losses (HMRC6 similarly makes no comments in this regard).

8.124 Where individuals departing the UK have been UK resident or ordinarily resident for at least four tax years out of the seven tax years preceding the tax year of departure ESC D2 does not apply and thus CGT continues to be charged for the balance of the tax year following departure.

Disposals of assets (held prior to departure) in any tax year following the tax year of departure (assuming residency or ordinary residency for at least four of the tax years out of the seven tax years prior to departure) are also within the charge to CGT unless the individual is neither UK resident not ordinarily resident for at least five complete tax years (*TCGA 1992 s 10A*; see paragraph 4.73).

8.125 Where *TCGA 1992 s 10A* applies, disposals of assets held prior to departure during the period of less than five complete tax years are treated as accruing in the tax year of return; thus, the rates, exempt amount etc applicable to such gains are those for the tax year of return not the tax year of the actual disposals (where *TCGA 1992 s 10A* applies, any capital gains subject to charge on resumption of residence during the tax year 2010–2011 are treated as arising before 23 June 2010 *(F(No 2) 2010 s 2 and Sch 1)* and thus are charged at the 18% (not 28%) rate).

In addition, any capital losses arising on the disposal of such assets are also treated as arising in the tax year of return.

Included in the quantum of capital gains are those apportioned under *TCGA 1992 ss 13* and *86* or *TCGA 1992 s 86A* (see paragraph 18.105).

8.126 Assets acquired and sold during any period of non-residence and non-ordinary residence absence (irrespective of the length of the period of absence) are not subject to CGT (unless acquired and sold within the balance of the tax year of departure where ESC D2 does not apply); capital losses arising thereon are similarly not allowable.

Capital gains tax **8.128**

8.127 Thus, where an individual has been UK resident and ordinarily resident in the UK for less than four tax years out of the seven tax years prior to the tax year of departure, any capital gains made after the day of departure are not subject to CGT (ie ESC D2 applies and *TCGA 1992 s 10A* is inapplicable (thus no five tax year minimum period of absence is necessary)).

However, in this scenario, capital gains made in the tax year of arrival back in the UK, but prior to arrival, are subject to CGT if the individual's period of absence is for less than five complete tax years (as required by ESC D2).

Example 23

Shelly Desk has been UK resident and ordinarily resident for three tax years prior to the tax year 2007–2008. She leaves the UK on 1 July 2007 becoming non-resident and non-ordinarily resident from 2 July 2007.

She returns to the UK on 1 October 2010.

She disposes of an asset, which she owned prior to departure, on 1 August 2010 making a significant capital gain.

TCGA 1992 s 10A is inapplicable as Shelly was not resident for four out of the seven tax years prior to her departure on 1 July 2007. There is thus no requirement for her to become non-resident and ordinarily resident for at least five complete tax years to avoid any CGT charge on disposals during her period of non-residency and non-ordinary residency.

However, ESC D2 is inapplicable to the tax year of her return (ie 2010–2011) as she has been UK resident within the five tax years prior to her tax year of return (ie she was resident in the tax year 2006–2007).

As a consequence, her significant capital gain of 1 August 2010, which is made in the tax year of her return, is subject to CGT (in 2010–2011).

If Shelly had remained outside the UK for at least five complete tax years (ie for the tax years 2008–2009; 2009–2010; 2010–2011; 2011–2012 and 2012–2013) and sold the asset on, say, 1 August 2013, prior to her arrival on say, 1 October 2013 (ie in the tax year 2013/14), no CGT charge arises as ESC D2 applies.

8.128 Effective 16 March 2005 it is specifically provided that the terms of any double taxation agreement to which the UK is a party do not override *TCGA 1992 s 10A*; previously, the section was overridden by some double tax agreements.

8.129 *Capital gains tax*

Non-UK domiciled individuals

8.129 As stated in paragraph 8.1 non-UK domiciled but UK resident individuals are subject to CGT on capital gains arising on UK situs assets, but only on capital gains arising on non-UK situs assets to the extent such gains are remitted to the UK assuming remittance basis treatment is claimed (*TCGA 1992 s 12*).

8.130 Capital gains arising on non-UK situs assets to non-UK domiciled but UK resident individuals are treated as accruing to the individual in the tax year in which a remittance of the gain occurs; thus, remittance of such capital gains in a tax year when the individual is non-UK resident precludes a CGT charge arising (subject to *TCGA 1992 s 10A*).

8.131 Prior to *FA 2008*, *TCGA 1992 s 10A* applied to non-UK domiciled individuals but not to the same extent as it now applies, post-*FA 2008*.

Non-UK domiciled individuals were within the ambit of the section where the disposal was of UK situs assets owned prior to departure from the UK. However, the section did not apply where non-UK assets were sold prior to departure but the proceeds were remitted during the period of absence; where the assets were disposed of during the absence from the UK but the proceeds were not remitted to the UK or where the proceeds were remitted after the tax year of return or were remitted during the period of absence.

FA 2008 has, however, broadened the scope of *TCGA 1992 s 10A*.

8.132 If the remittance basis is claimed in the tax year of return the capital gains subject to CGT in the tax year of return comprise those gains made during the period of absence on UK situs assets and those on non-UK situs assets which are remitted during the period of absence or those made before departure but remitted during the period of absence.

The capital gains made during the period of absence on non-UK situs assets but not remitted during the period of absence are subject to CGT only on subsequent remittance.

Capital gains arising on disposals of non-UK situs assets owned and disposed of pre 6 April 2008 but remitted on or after 6 April 2008 are also subject to *TCGA 1992 s 10A* in its post-*FA 2008* form.

Example 24

Billy Florida Snr, a non-UK domiciled but UK resident individual, has been UK resident for the last ten tax years prior to the tax year 2008–2009. During this period he generates foreign chargeable gains of £175,000 which are credited to his bank account in Dubai.

Capital gains tax **8.136**

He leaves the UK on 6 June 2008, losing his UK residency status, intending to return to the UK on 6 April 2014. In the tax year 2010–2011 he remits the whole £175,000 to his bank account in the UK so as to enjoy the monies in the UK on his return.

Assuming that he fulfils his plans no CGT arises on the remittance as he remains non-UK resident for at least five complete tax years: namely, 2009–2010, 2010–2011, 2011–2012, 2012–2013 and 2013–2014.

Example 25

Billy Florida Snr's son, Billy Florida Jnr, is in exactly the same position and leaves with his dad on 6 June 2008.

On 6 April 2013 Billy Florida Jnr reacquires UK residency as he is unable to remain outside the UK any longer due to family issues.

In the tax year 2010–2011 he remits his £175,000 to his UK bank account whilst he is non-UK resident. However, as he is not non-resident for five complete tax years, a CGT liability arises in the tax year of return (ie 2013–2014).

In addition, as Billy Jnr is not non-UK resident for five complete tax years any capital gains remitted to the UK arising on the disposal of non-UK assets (owned prior to departure) whilst non-UK resident are also subject to CGT in the tax year of return (ie 2013–2014).

However, remittances of capital gains which arise on disposal of assets acquired on or after 6 June 2008 (ie when non-UK resident) are not subject to CGT.

Summary

8.133 CGT applies to individuals, trustees and PRs but not companies.

8.134 *FA 2008* had a dramatic impact upon the CGT rules.

8.135 Notable changes introduced by *FA 2008* are the abolition of the indexation allowance and taper relief; a single rate for CGT of 18%; a new effective 10% ER rate; and new rules for non-UK domiciled individuals.

8.136 *F (No 2) 2010* has introduced a two-tier rate of CGT for individuals

8.137 *Capital gains tax*

applicable to disposals on or after 23 June 2010; thereafter the rates applicable are 18% and 28%. For trusts and PRs the rate is 28%.

8.137 CGT applies only where the person is either UK resident or UK ordinarily resident; non-UK residents are in general not subject to CGT, even on UK situs assets. However, capital gains of non-UK resident companies and/or trusts may fall subject to CGT on the part of shareholders, settlors or beneficiaries.

8.138 Various reliefs are available which remove and/or mitigate CGT charges; for example, hold-over relief allows for deferral of CGT on disposals by way of gift or below market value.

8.139 CGT does not arise on the death of an individual.

8.140 Capital losses can be offset against capital gains, but cannot be carried back for offset against capital gains of prior tax years (except on death).

8.141 Non-UK domiciled but UK resident individuals are subject to CGT on non-UK situs assets on the remittance basis (where claimed).

Chapter 9

Capital losses

Background

9.1 The disposal of assets may precipitate both capital gains and capital losses.

9.2 In principle capital losses can be offset against capital gains.

However, capital losses are not transferable and therefore cannot, for example, be transferred from one spouse to the other (and thus the capital gains of one spouse cannot be offset against the capital losses of the other).

9.3 The rules for UK domiciled and UK resident individuals are different from those for non-UK domiciled but UK resident individuals. Whilst *FA 2008* had no impact on the pre-*FA 2008* rules applicable to UK domiciled and UK resident individuals, the *FA 2008* changes had a significant impact on the non-UK domiciled but UK resident individual.

9.4 The key difference for the non-UK domiciled but UK resident individual, pre- and post-*FA 2008*, is that following *FA 2008*, such individual may now utilise capital losses arising on the disposal of non-UK situs assets; prior to *FA 2008*, capital losses arising on the disposal of non-UK situs assets by such an individual could not under any circumstances be utilised to offset the capital gains of such individuals, (although capital losses on UK situs assets could be offset against capital gains).

The changes apply to disposals on or after 6 April 2008 and thus any capital losses on non-UK situs assets which arose prior to this date fall under the 'old' rules and thus are not eligible for offset against capital gains.

9.5 Although the non-UK domiciled but UK resident individual may now, post-*FA 2008*, utilise non-UK situs capital losses, the manner in which they may be used is restricted and specifically laid down in *TCGA 1992 ss 16ZA* to *16ZD* (introduced by *FA 2008 s 25* and *Sch 7*).

9.6 *Capital losses*

Furthermore, the manner in which such individuals may use UK situs asset capital losses has also been changed post-*FA 2008*.

UK domiciled and UK resident individual

9.6 As indicated in paragraph 9.3, the pre-and post-*FA 2008* position with respect to the utilisation of capital losses, whether in respect of UK or non-UK losses, has not changed for such individuals.

9.7 Any capital losses which arise in a tax year must be offset against any capital gains for that tax year; this is compulsory (*TCGA 1992 s 2*). As a consequence, this may mean that an individual's annual exempt amount (*TCGA 1992 s 3*) for that tax year may be lost.

9.8 Capital losses of previous tax years which are un-utilised may be carried forward indefinitely for offset against subsequent tax year capital gains subject to possible limit (*TCGA 1992 ss 2* and *3*; see paragraph 9.9).

Current tax year capital losses are offset before any capital losses brought forward from earlier tax years may be used (*TCGA 1992 s 2*).

Capital losses cannot be carried back to earlier tax years except with respect to capital losses arising in the year of death of the individual (*TCGA 1992 ss 2* and *62;* see paragraph 8.42).

9.9 Any capital losses carried forward can be offset against any net capital gains for the tax year concerned (ie net capital gains are capital gains less capital losses of the tax year). However, any such losses brought forward are only offset against the net gains of the tax year so as to reduce the net gains to no less than the annual exempt amount for that tax year (thus preventing the loss of the annual exempt amount unnecessarily for that tax year). Any remaining unused capital losses may then be carried forward to the next and succeeding tax years until fully utilised. It should be noted that any unused part of the annual exempt amount is lost (ie it cannot be carried forward for future use). The same approach is adopted with respect to the carry back of capital losses following death.

9.10 There is no differentiation between capital losses arising on UK and non-UK situs assets. There is therefore no requirement to keep the amounts of each separate.

Capital losses **9.10**

Example 1

Henrietta Tree makes the following capital gains and capital losses:

	2008–2009	2009–2010	2010–2011
Capital gains	£20,000	nil	£35,000
Capital losses	nil	£7,000	£5,000
Annual exempt amount	£9,600	£10,100	£10,100

2008–2009

Capital gains chargeable to CGT:

£20,000 less £9,600 ie £10,400

2009–2010

Capital losses available for carry forward £7,000

2010–2011

Capital gains chargeable to CGT:

[[£35,000 – £5,000] – [£7,000]] – £10,100 = £12,900

Example 2

Henry Tree makes the following capital gains and capital losses:

	2008–2009	2009–2010	2010–2011
Capital gains	£20,000	nil	£17,000
Capital losses	£16,000	£7,000	£5,000
Annual exempt amount	£9,600	£10,100	£10,100

2008–2009

Capital gains chargeable to CGT:

[[£20,000 – £16,000] – £4,000*]] (ie £nil)

209

9.11 *Capital losses*

* the annual exempt amount is restricted to £4,000. The balance of £5,600 is lost.

2009–2010

Capital losses available for carry forward £7,000

2010–2011

Capital gains chargeable to CGT:

[[£17,000 – £5,000] – [£1,900*]] – £10,100 = £nil

The capital losses brought forward of £7,000 are restricted in their offset to £1,900 so as to ensure none of the annual exempt amount is wasted. Thus, the unutilised £5,100 (ie £7,000 less £1,900) of the £7,000 of capital losses brought forward are eligible for carry forward to 2011–2012 and future tax years.

Connected person capital losses

9.11 Where a capital loss arises on a disposal between connected persons (*TCGA 1992 s 286*; (eg disposals between brother and sister; settlor and trust)) the loss can only be relieved against any capital gains arising in the same or future tax years on disposals to the same connected person (ie any capital loss arising in such circumstances cannot be used in general to offset other capital gains).

Example 3

In 2010–2011 Bob sells an antique vase to his sister, Katrina, for its market value of £8,000 (which originally cost Bob £9,000) and a painting to his brother Tony for £2,000 (which originally cost Bob £5,500).

In 2010–2011 Bob also sold some shares to third parties making capital gains of £7,000 and a capital loss of £1,200.

The capital losses arising on the sales to Katrina and Tony of £1,000 and £3,500 respectively cannot be used to offset Bob's capital gains of £7,000. However, the capital loss of £1,200 can be offset against the £7,000.

Non-UK domiciled but UK resident individual

Pre-FA 2008 position

9.12 The pre-*FA 2008* position refers to disposals effected on or before 5 April 2008.

9.13 For the non-UK domiciled but UK resident individual the position, pre-*FA 2008*, was different with respect to the usage of capital losses compared to that for the UK domiciled and UK resident individual.

While capital gains arising on the disposal of non-UK situs assets were (and post-*FA 2008* continue to be) within the charge to CGT if and when such gains were/are remitted to the UK, capital losses arising on such disposals (ie disposals of non-UK situs assets) could not be used for offset against any gains (whether arising on UK or non-UK situs assets) of the individual.

Capital losses arising on disposals of UK situs assets were (and post-*FA 2008* continue to be) available for offset against capital gains arising on UK situs assets and on non-UK situs assets when remitted.

9.14 As capital losses arising on non-UK situs assets could not be offset against the individual's capital gains two basic options were open to the individual.

The simplest solution was for the individual to effect a gift of the asset outside the UK (to avoid any possible income tax remittance issues) to, say, his UK domiciled spouse (assuming, of course, the spouse was UK domiciled). As the gift was an inter-spouse gift it was regarded as taking place such that neither gain nor loss arose to the donor spouse. The recipient UK domiciled spouse could then effect the sale precipitating a capital loss which such spouse could then use to offset against his current or future capital gains.

Example 4

Henry Blue is married to Frida. Henry is UK domiciled but his wife is Swedish domiciled.

In 2007 Frida purchased some Swedish quoted shares for £100,000. The shares are now worth £20,000.

Should Frida sell the shares (pre-6 April 2008) the capital loss of £80,000 could not be used by Frida.

9.15 *Capital losses*

Frida therefore decides to gift the shares to Henry. The gift is assumed to have taken place at no gain and no loss to Frida (ie Henry is assumed to have acquired the shares for £100,000 (the original purchase price paid by Frida)).

Henry subsequently sells the shares for £20,000 realising a capital loss of £80,000 which he can use to offset against any capital gains he may make in the same tax year (or he can carry any surplus unused part of the loss forward to future tax years).

9.15 An alternative option, which allows the non-UK domiciled to retain the right to the capital loss, was to import the asset to the UK prior to disposal (although this may give rise to income tax remittance issues). The asset on importation becomes a UK situs asset and any capital loss arising thereon would be allowable (ie it can be offset).

Example 5

Agneta Schmidt, a non-UK domiciled but UK resident individual, bought an item of jewellery for £15,000 at an auction in Switzerland. She has kept the jewellery at her villa in Switzerland.

She discovers that the jewellery is in fact now only worth £11,000 and so she decides to sell it (pre-6 April 2008).

In order for the capital loss to be utilised against any of her capital gains, the situs of the asset must be UK. She accordingly brings the jewellery into the UK and then sells it producing a capital loss of £4,000 which she can then utilise against current and future capital gains.

Of course not all assets with a non-UK situs can readily be imported into the UK (eg real estate).

Post-FA 2008

9.16 The post-*FA 2008* position refers to disposals effected on or after 6 April 2008.

9.17 Whilst for the non-UK domiciled but UK resident individual the two options just discussed are still viable (post-*FA 2008*), capital losses arising on the disposal of non-UK situs assets (now referred to as 'foreign losses'; *TCGA*

Capital losses **9.20**

1992 s 16ZA) on or after 6 April 2008 can now be used to offset such individual's capital gains (whether such gains arise on UK or non-UK situs assets).

Capital losses arising on UK situs assets continue, as pre-*FA 2008,* to be available for offset (although in a different manner).

9.18 The manner in which capital losses (whether on UK or non-UK situs assets) are to be offset depends upon whether or not a formal remittance basis claim is lodged for a particular tax year under *ITA 2007 s 809B* (see paragraph 24.7).

9.19 The non-UK domiciled but UK resident individual, post-*FA 2008,* for any tax year falls into one of three categories:

(1) a formal claim is required to be made for remittance treatment (under *ITA 2007 s 809B*);

(2) no formal claim is required as remittance treatment applies automatically (under *ITA 2007 ss 809D* or *809E*); or

(3) no formal claim under *ITA 2007 s 809B* is required and notice is given (under *TMA 1970 s 8*) that *ITA 2007 s 809D* or *s 809E,* as appropriate, is not to apply (ie the remittance basis is not to apply).

Capital losses of individuals falling within either points 2 or 3 above are offset in the same manner as is applicable to the UK domiciled and UK resident individual (although see paragraph 9.26). Thus, in such cases, there is no distinction between UK capital losses and foreign losses in such cases.

Where no formal claim for remittance treatment is necessary

9.20 Individuals falling within point 2 of paragraph 9.19 comprise the following:

(a) those individuals whose 'unremitted foreign income and gains' (basically foreign income and capital gains arising in the relevant tax year less the amount of such income and/or gains which are remitted to the UK in that tax year) for the relevant tax year is less than £2,000 (*ITA 2007 s 809D*); or

(b) those individuals who have no UK source income or gains other than taxed investment income (income or gains within *ITA 2007 s 946* which have been taxed at source) of less than £100 arising in the relevant tax year, who have been UK resident in not more than six out of the nine tax years immediately preceding the relevant tax year and who have remitted no income or gains to the UK in the relevant tax year (*ITA 2007 s 809E*); or

9.21 *Capital losses*

(c) those individuals who have no UK source income or gains other than taxed investment income of less than £100 arising in the relevant tax year, who are under age eighteen throughout the relevant tax year and who have remitted no income or gains to the UK in the relevant tax year (*ITA 2007 s 809E*).

Example 6

Lorida Melbourne, a non-UK domiciled but UK resident individual, remits £10,000 (ie all) of her non-UK situs capital gains for 2010–2011 to the UK. She has also made non-UK situs capital losses of £17,000 in 2010–2011.

Her UK situs asset capital gains are £11,000.

She has not remitted £1,750 of interest which has arisen on her Isle of Man bank account in 2010–2011.

Lorida falls into point 2 of paragraph 9.19 and the remittance basis applies automatically for 2010–2011 (ie a formal claim for remittance basis treatment is not necessary).

£17,000 of capital losses may be offset against the £21,000 of capital gains.

9.21 For those individuals falling within points (a), (b) and (c) in paragraph 9.20, the annual exempt amount is available to use against net capital gains for a tax year (*TCGA 1992 s 3*).

Where formal claim for remittance treatment is necessary

9.22 The first tax year in respect of which the individual lodges a formal claim for remittance treatment under *ITA 2007 s 809B* requires the individual to also make an election under *TCGA 1992 s 16ZA* for that tax year if foreign losses for that tax year and subsequent tax years are to be capable of offset against capital gains.

A failure to make the election precludes forever the utilisation of foreign losses under any circumstances whatsoever (*TCGA 1992 s 16ZA*).

9.23 The first tax year in respect of which a claim for remittance basis treatment under *ITA 2007* s 809B can be made is 2008–2009.

9.24 The election is a 'one-off' irrevocable election and applies for the tax year in respect of which it is made and all future tax years (*TCGA 1992 s 16ZA*).

9.25 Where the non-UK domiciled but UK resident individual does not claim remittance basis treatment for the tax year 2008–2009 there is no requirement for the election (under *TCGA 1992 s 16ZA*) to be made in respect of that tax year. If, for example, such individual first makes a claim for remittance treatment in respect of, say, the tax year 2011–2012 then the election must also be made in respect thereof.

The election needs to be lodged within four years of the 31 January following the end of the tax year in respect of which the claim for remittance treatment is first lodged (*ITA 2007 s 809B* and *TMA 1970 s 43*); the limit of four years applies for tax year 2010–2011 and thereafter (*FA 2008 Sch 39* and *SI 2009/403*); for tax years prior to the tax year 2010–2011 the limit was five years.

However, where HMRC have served notice on the individual requiring completion of a tax return (under *TMA 1970 s 8*) *TMA 1970 s 42* requires that any claims for relief (including the election) must be included in the tax return itself (*TMA 1970 ss 42* and *43*).

9.26 The effect of the election is twofold:

- *first*, specific ordering rules apply with respect to the offsetting of both UK and foreign losses (*TCGA 1992 s 16ZC*; see paragraph 9.30); and
- *second*, the specific ordering rules continue to apply for all tax years thereafter even if in subsequent tax years no formal claim is necessary as the individual falls within (a), (b) or (c) of paragraph 9.20 (ie those individuals who fall within *ss 809D* or *809E* and thus are automatically entitled to remittance treatment without the need for a formal claim to be made under *ITA 2007 s 809B*).

However, where the individual (after having made the election) neither makes a formal claim for remittance treatment (which is otherwise necessary) nor gives the requisite notice (see paragraph 9.19) for a particular tax year the offset of capital losses for such tax year is not subject to the specific ordering rules; in which case the offset for that year of any capital losses available for offset is the same as applies to the UK domiciled and UK resident individual.

9.27 'Relevant allowable losses' (*TCGA 1992 s 16ZC*) refers to capital losses eligible for offset against capital gains and thus may comprise losses of the current tax year and unutilised losses brought forward.

9.28 Relevant allowable losses include:

- those arising on UK situs assets in the tax year;

9.29 *Capital losses*

- those arising on non-UK situs assets in the tax year (on or after 6 April 2008); and
- losses not previously utilised which have been brought forward including all losses brought forward on UK situs assets but only those arising on non-UK situs assets arising on or after 6 April 2008

In effect, a 'pool' of losses is created with no distinction between those arising on UK versus non-UK situs assets (ie UK losses and foreign losses are indistinguishable).

9.29 Capital losses of the tax year (ie UK and foreign losses) in which capital gains also arise are to be offset against such capital gains before any capital losses brought forward from prior tax years may be utilised. This merely continues the principle of capital offset which applies pre-*FA 2008* (*TCGA 1992 s 2*).

9.30 The mandatory order of offset of the relevant allowable losses for the tax year is as follows (*TCGA 1992 s16ZC*):

- current tax year losses are offset against gains arising on non-UK situs asset disposals which are remitted to the UK in the same tax year in which the disposals occur;
- any surplus of current tax year losses still remaining must be offset against gains arising on the disposals of non-UK situs assets arising in the tax year but not remitted to the UK;
- to the extent that any surplus of current tax year losses still remains, such surplus must be offset against any other chargeable gains arising in that tax year (other than gains arising on non-UK situs assets arising in earlier tax years but then subsequently remitted in the tax year concerned; and *TCGA 1992 s 87* gains (ie those gains apportioned to UK resident but non-UK domiciled individuals from non-UK resident trusts)). In essence, this category comprises gains arising on UK situs asset disposals; and
- any unutilised capital losses brought forward are then offset adopting the above ordering.

9.31 Where capital gains arising from the disposal of non-UK situs assets are not remitted until a later tax year, following the tax year of disposal, such remitted gains in that tax year of remittance are not eligible for reduction by any relevant allowable losses. It may be, however, that such gains have already been reduced in the tax year of the disposal by an offset of relevant allowable losses available for that tax year.

Example 7

Mate Sydney is a non-UK domiciled but UK resident individual.

Capital losses **9.33**

He makes an election under *TCGA 1992 s 16ZA* in respect of the tax year 2008–2009 as he claims remittance basis treatment for the tax year under *ITA 2007 s 809B*.

In the tax year 2008–2009 capital gains of £12,000 arose on non-UK situs assets.

In the tax year 2009–2010 he had the following capital gains and capital losses:

UK situs asset capital gains	£5,000
UK situs asset capital losses	£15,000

The non-UK situs asset capital gains of £12,000 which arose in the tax year 2008–2009 are remitted to the UK in 2009–2010.

Applying the ordering rules of paragraph 9.30 the capital loss of £15,00 is set against the £5,000 capital gain; leaving un-utilised capital losses of £10,000.

However, the £10,000 cannot be utilised against the non-UK situs asset capital gains of £12,000 arising in the tax year 2008–2009 but remitted and subject to CGT in the tax year of remittance (ie 2009–2010).

The £10,000 is available for carry forward.

9.32 Non-UK domiciled individuals who claim remittance basis treatment are denied the annual exempt amount (*TCGA 1992 s 3*; £10,100 for tax year 2010–2011) or indeed any form of personal allowance (for income tax purposes) (*ITA 2007 s 809G;* see paragraph 24.15).

9.33 A simple example illustrates the difference for the non-UK domiciled individual pre-and post-*FA 2008*.

Example 8

Heinz Berlin is a non-UK domiciled but UK resident individual who in the tax year 2007/08 has the following capital gains and capital losses:

UK situs asset capital gains	£25,000
UK situs asset capital losses	£5,000
Non-UK situs asset capital losses	£20,000
Non-UK situs asset capital gains (unremitted)	£8,000

9.34 *Capital losses*

Heinz's capital gains subject to CGT are:

[£25,000 – £5,000] = £20,000.

The unremitted capital gains of £8,000 are not subject to tax and the £20,000 of non-UK situs assets capital losses is not eligible for offset.

If the above figures arose in 2008–2009 the position is as follows (assuming a claim for remittance basis treatment is lodged):

Under the ordering rules of paragraph 9.30 the aggregate capital losses of the tax year of £25,000 are offset first against the unremitted capital gains of £8,000 leaving the balance of £17,000 for offset against the £25,000 of UK situs capital gains producing a charge to CGT on £8,000.

9.34

A slightly more complex example follows.

Example 9

Benito Italy, a non-UK domiciled but UK resident individual, has the following capital gains and capital losses. Any gains remitted are remitted in the same tax year as the gains arose. Appropriate claims and election are lodged.

Tax years:	2008–2009	2009–2010	2010–2011
	£	£	£
Capital gains (UK assets)	(1) 10,000	4,000	15,000
Capital losses (UK assets)	(2) 7,000	15,000	15,000
Capital gains (non-UK assets): unremitted	(3) 25,000	nil	9,000
Capital gains (non-UK assets): remitted	(4) 5,000	10,000	7,000
Capital losses (non-UK assets)	(5) 9,000	8,000	6,000
Offset as follows:			
Capital loss pool	16,000	23,000	[21,000 & 9,000]
Offset against (4)	(5,000)	(10,000)	(7,000)

	2008–2009	2009–2010	2010–2011
Offset against (3)	(11,000)	nil	(9,000)
Offset against (1)	nil	(4,000)	[5,000 & 9,000]
Capital loss pool c/f	nil	9,000	nil
Net taxable position:			
Tax years:	*2008–2009*	*2009–2010*	*2010–2011*
Capital gains (UK assets)	(1) 10,000	nil	1,000
Capital gains (non-UK assets) unremitted	(3) 14,000	nil	nil
Capital gains (non-UK assets) remitted	(4) nil	nil	nil
Taxable capital gains	10,000	nil	1,000
Potentially taxable when remitted	14,000	nil	nil

Notes

1. For the tax year 2008–2009 the aggregate capital losses are £16,000 and the aggregate chargeable gains are £15,000 (£10,000 plus £5,000). Nevertheless, a CGT charge still arises for this tax year as some £11,000 of the capital losses are absorbed by unremitted non-UK asset capital gains leaving none of the capital losses available to reduce the UK asset capital gains of £10,000.

2. The current year capital losses of £21,000 for 2010–2011 are first offset against capital gains of £21,000 with the capital losses brought forward of £9,000 being offset against the £9,000 of £10,000 remaining UK capital gains.

9.35 Where allowable capital losses have been offset against capital gains the quantum of allowable losses is correspondingly reduced. Thus, *inter alia,* the offset of relevant allowable losses against non-UK source gains which are not remitted in the tax year in which the disposal is made still effects a reduction in those gains and it is thus the net gains which, if remitted in a future tax year, are then subject to CGT (albeit that no capital losses can be offset against such remitted capital gains in the tax year of remittance; see paragraphs 9.30 and 9.31).

9.36 Where capital losses are offset against capital gains which have arisen in the tax year on the disposal of non-UK situs assets, but have not been remitted to the UK in that tax year and where such losses are insufficient to reduce such

9.37 *Capital losses*

gains to zero, a specific order of offset is provided (*TCGA 1992 s 16ZC*). The order of offset is as follows:

- *first*, capital losses are offset against the gains on the non-UK situs assets in the order in which the gains accrued but offsetting the losses against the later accrued gains first (effectively, a LIFO basis); and
- *second*, to the extent that certain gains accrued on the same day and the losses are insufficient to reduce such gains to zero, the losses are offset on a pro rata basis against each gain.

9.37 As no distinction is made between UK and foreign losses for offset purposes the new rules are advantageous to the extent that foreign losses are, post-*FA 2008*, allowable; however, UK losses can now, post-*FA 2008*, be offset against UK capital gains but only after they have been first offset against foreign capital gains (whether remitted or not) whereas, pre-*FA 2008*, UK losses could be offset against UK capital gains immediately (ie without having to be first offset against any foreign losses as is the case post-*FA 2008*).

This may mean that in the short term, the individual's CGT liabilities are higher than they would have been pre-*FA 2008* due to the absorption of losses against unremitted foreign gains; although in the long run aggregate CGT charges should fall.

Example 10

Norris Manilla, a non-UK domiciled but UK resident individual, anticipates making the same quantum of capital gains and capital losses for the tax year 2008–2009 as he had in the prior tax year 2007–2008. He assumed that because of the FA 2008 changes under which non-UK asset capital losses could be used to offset capital gains that his net capital gains (after capital loss offset) would be less for the tax year 2008–2009 and thus his CGT liability would be correspondingly smaller.

He does not remit the capital gains arising on non-UK assets.

His capital gains and capital losses are:

Tax year	2007–2008	2008–2009
	£	£
Capital gains (UK assets)	35,000	35,000
Capital losses (UK assets)	5,000	5,000
Capital gains (non-UK assets)	17,000	17,000
Capital losses (non-UK assets)	10,000	10,000

Capital losses **9.39**

	2007–2008	2008–2009
	£	£
Norris' net taxable capital gains are	30,000	35,000

As is clear, Norris' assumption is incorrect. This is because although the capital losses on the non-UK assets for tax year 2008–2009 are usable (whereas this is not the case for tax year 2007–2008) they are required to be first offset against the unremitted capital gains of £17,000 arising on the non-UK assets; thus not impacting on Norris's CGT liability for 2008–2009.

Strictly, the difference in his CGT liability is in fact greater than £5,000 due to the availability of the annual exempt amount of £9,200 for the tax year 2007–2008 (which is not available in 2008–2009 due to the remittance treatment claim).

If, however, Norris remits the capital gains arising on the non-UK situs assets in each tax year the position is:

	2007–2008	2008–2009
	£	£
Net chargeable gains	47,000	37,000

Taking the annual exempt amount into consideration for 2007–2008, the £47,000 2007–2008 figure is reduced by the then annual exemption of £9,200 giving a net figure of £37,800.

For 2008–2009 the figure of £37,000 remains as Norris is not entitled to the annual exempt amount for 2008–2009 (due to the remittance treatment claim).

9.38 The provisions of *FA 2008* have improved the CGT position of the non-UK domiciled but UK resident individual albeit at the cost of some complexity.

It does, however, mean that the CGT charge on the remittance of foreign capital gains to the UK is likely to be reduced to the extent that foreign losses are now available for offset. Indeed, with appropriate planning, it is possible to make use of foreign losses to reduce foreign capital gains yet only remit from the sale proceeds of assets in respect of which capital losses arose (see paragraphs 24.120 and 24.121).

Summary

9.39 FA 2008 introduces provisions under which foreign losses can now be offset against capital gains of non-UK domiciled but UK resident individuals.

9.40 *Capital losses*

9.40 An irrevocable election is required for such individuals in the first tax year a claim is made for remittance basis treatment (under *ITA 2007 s 809B*) to be able utilise the new rules; failure to make the election precludes forever the ability to utilise foreign losses against capital gains.

9.41 The position for UK domiciled and UK resident individuals remains the same both pre- and post-*FA 2008*.

9.42 The annual exempt amount is unavailable where a claim under *ITA 2007 s 809B* is made by the non-UK domiciled individual.

Chapter 10

Inheritance tax: the basics

Background

10.1 Inheritance tax (IHT) is a tax which is designed to tax an individual's wealth on death and, in order to preclude such an individual divesting himself of his wealth prior to death, IHT also applies to 'gifts' made during the individual's lifetime.

However, IHT not only applies to 'gifts' by individuals but also applies to 'settled property' (*IHTA 1984 Part III*), broadly, property held in trust. It also applies to 'close companies' which make 'gifts' (*IHTA 1984 Part IV*).

10.2 IHT does not, however, apply to transactions effected at market value. Thus, any sales made by an individual of assets owned for their fair market value (ie no gratuitous intent or element of bounty is involved) does not precipitate an IHT charge. This is because the quantum of the individual's estate remains the same both before and after the sale (ie disposition) and thus no transfer of value occurs (all that happens is that the individual exchanges one of his assets (eg an antique painting) for another (eg cash)).

A transaction effected by an individual which it transpires is a 'bad' deal (eg a book is sold for £2,000 when its true worth is £6,000 as it was not known that it was a first edition) does not precipitate an IHT charge where the individual can demonstrate that no donative intent or gratuitous benefit was intended (*IHTA 1984 s 10*).

10.3 It is to be appreciated that whilst a 'gift' may be subject to IHT this does not preclude a capital gains tax (CGT) charge also arising on the same transfer (see paragraph 8.28).

10.4 IHT replaced capital transfer tax for events occurring after 17 March 1986. Technically, the change of name only occurred from 25 July 1986 when the *Finance Act 1986* (which introduced IHT) received the Royal Assent.

Most of the capital transfer tax legislation was retained and the *Capital Transfer Tax Act 1984* was renamed the *Inheritance Tax Act 1984*.

10.5 *Inheritance tax: the basics*

On the introduction of IHT opportunity was taken to make some changes of principle to those which had applied with respect to capital transfer tax. For example, the so-called 'gifts with reservation' (GWRs) (see Chapter 12) provisions, previously contained in the estate duty provisions, were reintroduced; IHT was no longer to be charged on 'gifts' made in the seven years or more before death; and the cumulation period applicable to chargeable lifetime transfers (CLTs) was reduced from ten to seven years (see paragraph 10.45).

Domicile

10.5 IHT is levied on the worldwide assets of an individual who is UK domiciled. An individual's domicile status is, very broadly, the country which the individual regards as 'home' (see Chapter 3).

10.6 A non-UK domiciled individual (ie broadly, someone who does not regard the UK as 'home') is subject to IHT only on UK situs assets (*IHTA 1984 s 6*). The non-UK situs assets (and limited UK situs assets) of such individual are referred to as 'excluded property' (*IHTA 1984 s 6;* see Chapter 13).

10.7 The concept of 'deemed UK domiciled' (*IHTA 1984 s 267*) exists purely for IHT purposes; it has no application whatsoever for income tax and/or CGT.

10.8 Once an individual is deemed UK domiciled property which prior thereto was excluded property may no longer be so classified although non-UK situs property which is settled (whether in a UK or non-UK resident trust; see paragraphs 13.7 and 13.8) prior to the acquisition of deemed UK domicile status remains excluded property; *IHTA 1984 s 48*); hence the attraction of non-UK resident trusts in particular for the non-UK domiciled individual (see Chapter 18).

Deemed UK domicile

10.9 An individual who is non-UK domiciled at common law (ie as determined by the common law rules applicable to domicile; see Chapter 3) may nevertheless be categorised as 'deemed UK' domiciled for IHT purposes. This is the case if one or both of the following conditions are satisfied (*IHTA 1984 s 267; see* paragraph 3.231):

(1) the individual has been resident in the UK for at least 17 tax years out of 20 ending with the year of assessment in which relevant time falls; or

(2) the individual was UK domiciled within the three years preceding the relevant time.

10.10 The following points should be noted:

- the 17-out-of-20-year condition refers to 'tax years' whereas the prior three-year condition refers to 'calendar years';
- residency is determined according to the normal rules applicable for income tax (see Chapter 4);
- the conditions are inapplicable with respect to certain transactions pre-9 December 1974; and
- some IHT conventions to which the UK is a party may override the 'deemed UK' domicile concept.

10.11 Condition (1) in paragraph 10.9 is designed to bring the non-UK domiciled individual within the IHT charge on his worldwide estate where he has resided in the UK for a considerable time.

Condition (2) is designed to retain within the IHT charge, at least for three extra years, a UK domiciled individual who has managed to acquire a non-UK domicile of choice (see paragraph 3.74).

10.12 For a detailed discussion concerning a deemed UK domiciled individual see paragraph 3.231

Rates of inheritance tax

10.13 The relevant rates of IHT apply for a particular tax year and are contained in *IHTA 1984 Sch 1* (*IHTA 1984 s 7*). Although the rates applicable for the tax year 2009–2010 were due to increase for the tax year 2010–2011 (*FA 2007 s 4*) the new rates for 2010–2011 have not come into effect (*FA 2010 s 8*). The rates applicable for 2009–2010 are thus also applicable for 2010–2011.

10.14 For 2010–2011 the rate of tax applicable to CLTs is 20% (in the legislation expressed as one-half of the rate applicable on death (*IHTA 1984 s 7*); presumably should the rate applicable on death change the rate applicable on CLTs would correspondingly change); the rate applicable on death is 40%.

10.15 However, the first £325,000 of 'gifts' (as is discussed below, technically IHT applies to 'chargeable transfers', not just 'gifts' which, as will be seen later in the chapter, may not be the same; a 'chargeable transfer' is broader than a 'gift') is subject to a rate of 0% with only the excess subject to the 20% or 40% rate. The figure of £325,000 is referred to as the nil rate band (NRB) which

10.16 *Inheritance tax: the basics*

broadly changes (to date increases) each tax year. £325,000 applies to the tax year 2010–2011 and indeed, unusually, also to the previous tax year 2009–2010.

10.16 The NRB can effectively be replenished (ie it is not a 'once and for all' amount) due to the seven-year cumulation concept (see paragraph 10.45) applicable in determining the amount of the NRB at any point in time. It is thus quite possible for an individual during his lifetime to make gifts/chargeable transfers in aggregate in excess of £325,000 yet still precipitate no actual IHT charge on such transfers (all such transfers being subject at the 0% rate). This would be the situation if, for example, the individual makes a single CLT of £325,000 every seven years.

10.17 Furthermore, the NRB (either in whole or in part) is also capable of being transferred to the surviving spouse on the latter's death following the earlier death of the other spouse (*IHTA 1984 s 8A*). This 'transferability' concept was introduced relatively recently by *FA 2008 s 10* (see paragraph 11.44).

10.18 It is important to note that although the applicable rate may be 0% this does not mean the chargeable transfer is exempt from IHT; an exempt transfer (see paragraph 10.21) is simply outside the scope of any charge to IHT whereas a transfer subject to IHT, albeit at rate of 0%, is a chargeable, not an exempt, transfer.

Example 1

Bernard Coke dies in the tax year 2010–2011 with an estate valued at £550,000.

He has made no lifetime gifts.

The IHT liability arising on his death is:

0% × £325,000 + 40% × [£550,000 – £325,000] = £90,000.

Example 2

Henry Coke makes a CLT in the tax year 2010–2011 of £550,000.

He has made no lifetime gifts prior to this transfer.

The IHT liability arising on the transfer is:

0% × £325,000 + 20% × [£550,000 – £325,000] = £45,000

Inheritance tax: the basics **10.22**

10.19 In order to work out the IHT liability on a lifetime gift or on death involves a consideration of, *inter alia*, any CLTs which have been made in the immediately preceding seven years (*IHTA 1984 s 7*). Where such transfers have been made they will impact upon the availability of the NRB for utilisation against the current chargeable transfer. In Examples 1 and 2 none had in fact been made.

Categories of lifetime transfer

10.20 For the individual there are three types of lifetime transfer which can be made:

- exempt transfers;
- CLTs; and
- potentially exempt transfers (PETs).

One of the categories of exempt transfer is the annual exemption *(IHTA 1984 s 19;* see paragraph 11.12); the exemption is £3,000 per annum. In calculating the amount of any CLT or PET falling within the charge to IHT the annual exemption reduces the amount (eg CLT of £100,000 is reduced to £97,000 if the annual exemption for the tax year of the CLT has not been used). *However, throughout this chapter, and in particular in the examples, for ease of explanation and calculation the £3,000 deduction is ignored.*

Exempt transfer

10.21 A transfer of value may qualify as an exempt transfer of value (*IHTA 1984 Part II*); in which case, no IHT charge arises thereon as it is not a CLT (*IHTA 1984 s 2*). A number of transfers may so qualify (eg an inter-spouse transfer between two UK or two non-UK domiciled spouses are exempt transfers; *IHTA 1984 s 18*). Exempt transfers are considered in more detail in Chapter 11.

Chargeable lifetime transfer

10.22 A CLT is a transfer of value made by an individual which is not an exempt transfer (*IHTA 1984 s 2*). Transfers between individuals are not CLTs (but PETs; see paragraph 10.36) but transfers into most (but not all) trusts are CLTs (note that the position with respect to transfers into trusts may be different depending upon whether the transfer is effected on or after 22 March 2006 or prior thereto; see paragraphs 16.7 and 16.8).

10.23 Inheritance tax: the basics

10.23 IHT is a tax which is levied where an individual makes a chargeable transfer. A chargeable transfer (*IHTA 1984 s 2*) is a transfer of value (*IHTA 1984 s 3*). A transfer of value is a disposition (other than an exempt transfer) pursuant to which the individual's estate (broadly, the individual's assets less liabilities; *IHTA 1984 s 5*) is less after the disposition than it would otherwise be.

Example 3

Terry Block settles £10,000 cash and his antique desk (worth £40,000) on discretionary trust.

Each of these transfers constitutes a CLT and each when given diminishes Terry's estate.

In total, Terry's estate diminishes by £50,000.

10.24 IHT is levied on the quantum by which the individual's estate is diminished as a consequence of the transfer, not on the value of the transfer (ie the difference in the individual's estate before and after the transfer; *IHTA 1984 ss 1* to *3*). In most instances, however, the value of the transfer will be the same as the diminution in the donor's estate.

Example 4

Henry Tomb settles £385,000 cash on discretionary trust.

The gift is a CLT.

The quantum of the gift is £385,000 which is in fact also the quantum of the diminution in Henry's estate.

Henry's IHT liability is thus based on a transfer of £385,000.

However, this may not always be so. Consider the following Example 5:

Example 5

Henry Tomb owns 51% of the ordinary share of company XYZ Ltd.

He gifts 2% of his shareholding to his discretionary trust worth £10,000.

The gift is a CLT.

After the gift his shareholding is, of course, 49%.

Inheritance tax: the basics **10.26**

The consequence of making the gift, however, is that Henry's estate has diminished to a greater extent than the £10,000 (ie the value of the 2% gifted). This is because the value of a 49% shareholding is much less than a 51% shareholding (which gives Henry 'control' of the company).

Thus, for example, a 51% shareholding may be worth £300,000 whereas a 49% shareholding is worth £225,000 as a consequence of which Henry's estate diminishes by £75,000.

The transfer of value for IHT purposes is measured by the diminution of the donor's estate due to the gift (not the amount of the gift).

For Henry, his IHT charge will thus be based on £75,000 not £10,000.

The diminution in value of the individual's estate is also affected where the related property rules apply (*IHTA 1984 s 161*; see also paragraph 28.114).

Property of the spouse constitutes related property. Where the related property values apply the value of property of one spouse is a proportion of the aggregate value of that property and the related property assuming that this produces a higher value than the unrelated value. Thus if three antique chairs (value £30,000) are owned by the husband and one chair is owned by the wife (value £2,000) but as a set of four the chairs are valued at £40,000 the husband's chairs are valued at the higher value of £30,000 and [[£30,000/£32,000] x £40,000] (ie £37,500). Where the related property comprises shares it is the number of shares (not their values as applies to other assets) which form the numerator and denominator of the fraction (ie that shown in the square brackets).

10.25 The references to, *inter alia*, 'chargeable transfers' and 'transfers of value', are more commonly referred to as 'gifts'. The term 'gifts' is, however, not used in the legislation as certain transactions which are not gifts would not then be subject to IHT when nevertheless the individual has still caused his estate to dissipate (eg if an individual fails to exercise a right, say, to purchase a property at below its market value this may result in the individual having made a CLT or PET (*IHTA 1984 s 3*) even though in common parlance it might be argued that no actual 'gift' has been made). The use of these broader terms ensures that transactions such as these do not escape a charge to IHT.

For ease and to avoid constant repetition the terms 'gift', 'chargeable transfer' and 'transfer of value' will generally be used interchangeably throughout the text.

Chargeable lifetime transfer and chargeability

10.26 The consequence of an individual making a CLT is that it is subject to an IHT charge at the date it is made (either 0% and/or 20%), albeit payable at a

10.27 Inheritance tax: the basics

later date (see paragraph 14.12), and based on its value at the date it is made (although as is noted in paragraph 10.24, technically, the IHT charge is based upon the diminution of the individual's estate).

'Additional' liability

10.27 If the individual dies within seven years of making the CLT an *additional* charge to IHT also arises (*IHTA 1984 s 7*). The amount of this additional liability is based upon the quantum of the transfer of value *when originally effected* and on the time span between the date of the transfer and the death of the donor. The applicable rate is 40% (ie that applicable on death).

Note that the IHT charged on the CLT is the liability of the *donor* (ie the individual making the transfer; unless the donee agrees to pay it) whereas the *additional* IHT liability is that of the *donee* (ie the person receiving the transfer; typically, trustees) (*IHTA 1984 ss 199 to 201; see* paragraphs 14.12 and 14.13).

10.28 The effect of the time span between the date of the transfer and the date of death is to reduce the 40% rate according to a form of taper relief. In essence, the longer the individual survives the greater the percentage relief available. The relevant percentages are (*IHTA 1984 s 7*):

- transfer made more than three but not more than four years before death: 80%
- transfer made more than four but not more than five years before death: 60%
- transfer made more than five but not more than six years before death: 40%
- transfer made more than six but not more than seven years before death: 20%

Thus, where an individual survives for, say, just over four years (but not more than five years) the taper rate applicable is 60%; thus the 40% rate is reduced to 60% of 40% (ie 24%). Survival for three years or less causes no reduction in the 40% rate. It should be noted that the effect of the taper relief is to reduce the quantum of IHT charged (as the 40% rate is effectively reduced), not the value of the actual transfer.

This therefore means that where the original transfer by the individual is less than the NRB applicable on death taper relief has no application (as no IHT charge arises in any event due to the quantum of the transfer falling within the NRB).

10.29 IHT is thus charged twice on the same transfer assuming death within seven years of the date of the gift. However, the legislation provides for a credit (ie offset) for the IHT originally charged on the lifetime transfer against the subsequent additional IHT charge (this applies irrespective of who discharges the liability on the CLT; see paragraph 10.27). Any taper relief is applied in computing the additional tax charge before any offset for the inheritance already paid in lifetime. Should the additional IHT be less than that charged in lifetime no refund is available (*IHTA 1984 s 7*); thus, the IHT charge in such cases is the greater of the two charges.

Example 6

Brian Harris settles cash of £725,000 on his discretionary trust on 10 April 2010.

No earlier lifetime gifts have been made.

This gift is a CLT and an IHT liability thus arises at the date of the gift.

The quantum of the charge is:

$0\% \times £325,000 + 20\% \times [£725,000 - £325,000] = £80,000$

Example 7

Using the facts of Example 6, Brian subsequently dies on 15 October 2010.

An additional IHT charge now arises on the CLT based on the value at the date of the gift but applying the rate and NRB applicable on the death for the tax year in which death occurs ie 40% for 2010–2011.

The additional IHT charge is:

$[0\% \times £325,000 + 40\% \times [£725,000 - £325,000]] - £80,000 =$

$£160,000 - £80,000 = £80,000$

The additional IHT of £160,000 due to death within seven years is reduced by the £80,000 charged on the lifetime transfer.

No taper relief is available as death occurs not more than three years after the date of the lifetime gift.

10.30 *Inheritance tax: the basics*

Had Brian died on, say, 23 June 2014 (assume rates applicable in 2014–2015 are the same as for 2010–2011) the additional IHT would be:

[0% × £325,000 + 60% × 40% × [£725,000 − £325,000]] − £80,000 =

£96,000 − £80,000 = £16,000.

Reduction in value

10.30 It may be that between the date of the CLT and the date of death the market value of the transfer has fallen. In such a case the additional tax is computed on the lower of the two applicable market values (*IHTA 1984 s 131*). If, however, the value of the transfer has increased over this period the additional tax remains calculated based upon the value at the date of the lifetime transfer (ie the increase in value is ignored). Where the individual in receipt of the transfer has in fact sold the asset prior to the death of the transferor for a value lower than that at the time of the lifetime transfer, the lower value may be substituted (assuming a sale at arm's length).

Example 8

Mary Tree makes a CLT of shares in XYZ Plc on 13 May 2010 worth £525,000.

She dies on 15 October 2010; the shares are then worth £350,000.

The charge to IHT on the lifetime gift is:

0% × £325,000 + 20% × [£525,000 − £325,000] = £40,000.

The additional IHT due to death is:

[0% × £325,000 + 40% × [£350,000 − £325,000]] − £40,000 = £nil

As the additional IHT is lower than that charged on the lifetime gift, due to the fall in value of the gift, no additional IHT arises (equally no refund of any surplus paid in lifetime applies).

The value of such CLTs (or indeed PETs; see paragraph 10.41) used in the aggregation process in the seven-year cumulation period (see paragraph 10.45) is the original value of the CLT (or PET) not the reduced value.

10.31 In order for the lower value of the CLT at death to be substituted requires the donee of the transfer to make an appropriate claim (*IHTA 1984 s 131*).

10.32 Where either business or agricultural property relief (BPR or APR) is in point (see Chapter 11), the particular applicable market values at the relevant dates are reduced by the appropriate percentage relief.

10.33 As stated in paragraphs 10.24 and 10.27, the charge to IHT is calculated on the diminution of the donor's estate due to the transfer and the person liable for any such IHT due is that of the donor. The diminution of the donor's estate is thus in fact the aggregation of the amount of the transfer *plus* the amount of any IHT charge thereon. This requires the transfer to be 'grossed-up' (see paragraph 10.54). Where the donor and donee agree that the donee will accept responsibility for the liability arising on the transfer no grossing-up is necessary (as the donor's estate is diminished only by the transfer, not the IHT).

The extent of the grossing up depends upon how much of the NRB is available for offset against the transfer (which is in turn affected by the quantum of CLTs made by the donor in the immediately preceding seven years). If in fact having taken into account such CLTs the transfer (pre grossing-up) falls within the NRB no actual grossing-up is necessary.

10.34 Before considering the concept of grossing-up it is necessary to first discuss the workings of the ' seven year cumulation period' and the taxability of PETs.

Potentially exempt transfers and chargeability

10.35 Unlike a CLT, a PET is a transfer of value which remains exempt pending the extent to which the individual making the transfer survives thereafter.

Where the individual survives for seven years or more the PET becomes completely exempt. However, should the individual die within (ie less than) seven years the PET at that time becomes chargeable (*IHTA 1984 s 3A*).

10.36 A gift from one individual to another qualifies as a PET but only if the property transferred becomes comprised in the donee's (ie recipient's) estate or the donee's estate is increased in consequence of the transfer (*IHTA 1984 s 3A*).

Example 9

Stanley Knife gifts a cash sum of £12,000 to his daughter, Sandra.

10.37 *Inheritance tax: the basics*

This constitutes a PET (not CLT) as it is a transfer between individuals and Sandra's estate is increased in consequence of the transfer (as the cash becomes comprised in Sandra's estate).

Example 10

Henrietta Blow purchases a foreign holiday for her mother, Eileen, as a birthday surprise.

Although this is a gift between individuals, Eileen's estate is neither increased as a consequence of the gift nor has any property become comprised in her estate.

The transfer by Henrietta is thus a CLT (not a PET).

This conclusion could have been avoided if Henrietta had given Eileen the money to purchase the holiday; in this case the transfer is a PET (although perhaps less of a surprise!).

10.37 Gifts made on or after 22 March 2006 by individuals into trust are now CLTs although a transfer into a disabled trust qualifies as a PET (*IHTA 1984 s 3A*).

Pre-22 March 2006 gifts into interest in possession trusts or accumulation and maintenance trusts (but not discretionary trusts) qualify as PETs (although gifts into such trusts set up on or after 22 March 2006 now qualify as CLTs).

10.38 The lifetime termination of an interest in possession on or after 22 March 2006, which subsists pre-22 March 2006 qualifies as a PET if the trust then terminates or if a transitional serial interest (TSI) then arises (generally speaking, to qualify as a TSI the interest in possession subsisting on 22 March 2006 must have terminated before 6 October 2008 with the TSI immediately arising at that time; *IHTA 1984 s 49C*; although see *IHTA 1984 s 49D* where a TSI may arise post-6 October 2008 in the case of spouses).

10.39 With limited exceptions, a transfer on or after 22 March 2006 made by an individual is thus more likely to be a CLT unless the transfer is to another individual, in which case it is a PET.

Potentially exempt transfers and chargeability

10.40 Where the donor of the PET dies within seven years thereof the amount of IHT chargeable is based upon the value of the PET at the date of its transfer; the rate is that applicable on death (ie 40%).

10.41 As in the case of a CLT the same amount of taper relief is available (see paragraph 10.28) and relief may also be claimed where between the date of the PET and the date of death the value of the PET has fallen (see paragraph 10.30).

However, only one charge to IHT can arise on a PET (ie that which occurs due to the death of the donor within seven years); two charges, which may arise on a CLT, cannot arise with respect to a PET.

10.42 The donee (ie the recipient) of the gift is the person responsible for any IHT which may arise.

Example 11

Brian Harris makes a cash gift of £712,000 to his son, Herbert, on 6 February 2003 and a cash gift of £400,000 to his daughter, Samantha, on 14 August 2008.

Brian has made no other gifts.

Each of these gifts is made between individuals and each therefore qualifies as a PET and no IHT charge arises at the dates the gifts are made.

Example 12

Using the facts of Example 11, Brian subsequently dies on 15 December 2010.

The gift to his son made on 6 February 2003 is made more than seven years prior to Brian's death. No IHT charge thus arises and the gift becomes totally exempt.

However, the gift to his daughter on 14 August 2008 is made within seven years of Brian's death and as a consequence becomes liable to IHT.

The amount of the liability is:

$0\% \times £325,000 + 40\% \times [£400,000 - £325,000] = £30,000$.

(no taper relief applies as the death occurs within three years of the gift).

Example 13

Tom Smith dies on 18 September 2010 after he makes a gift to his daughter on 5 July 2005 of £825,000 (ie a PET).

Tom has made no other lifetime gifts.

10.43 *Inheritance tax: the basics*

Tom's death causes an IHT liability to arise on the gift as he has died within seven years of the date of the gift (more than five years but less than six years).

The rate of IHT is that applying on death (ie 40%) and the taper relief percentage is 40%.

The IHT charged is thus:

0% × £325,000 + 40% × 40% × [£825,000 − £325,000] = £80,000

Without taper relief the charge on death would have been:

[40% × £500,000] (ie £200,000).

10.43 As applies with respect to a CLT, the amount of the transfer of value when a PET is made normally equals the value of the transfer although IHT is actually charged on the amount of diminution in the individual's estate which arises due to the transfer; this, in turn, is the difference between the value of the estate before and after the transfer has been effected. As was illustrated in Example 5 there are circumstances when the value of the transfer will in fact be different from the amount of the estate's diminution due to the transfer. Another example is where an individual owns four valuable antique chairs which form a set. If one chair only is gifted this would destroy the set. The difference between the value of the set of four chairs and that of just three chairs (after a gift of just one chair) is likely to be much greater than the value of the single chair gifted (see paragraph 10.24).

10.44 The concept of grossing up referred to in paragraph 10.33 and discussed in paragraph 10.54 in connection with CLTs is inapplicable to PETs; this is because, the liability for any IHT charge arising on a PET is that of the donee and not that of the donor (see paragraph 10.42).

Seven-year cumulation period

10.45 CLTs are subject to IHT (and possibly additional IHT). PETs are subject to IHT only if the donor dies within seven years of making the transfer. No actual IHT arises where the transfers fall within the NRB.

10.46 However, it is necessary in calculating any IHT (or additional IHT) charge on such transfers to ascertain how much of the NRB is available for utilisation against the particular transfer.

10.47 This involves analysing transfers made by the individual within the

Inheritance tax: the basics **10.49**

seven years prior to the transfer under review; this enables a determination to be made as to how much of the NRB has been absorbed by such earlier transfers. As a PET is not chargeable unless death within seven years thereafter occurs, PETs within seven years of a CLT are ignored (as they do not absorb any part of the NRB as they are not chargeable). However, in calculating any additional IHT (which means that the individual has died) PETs then need to be taken into account as they fall chargeable.

10.48 In ascertaining the IHT charge on a CLT the applicable NRB is that applicable for the tax year in which the CLT is made. In ascertaining the additional IHT charge on the CLT (or the IHT charge arising on any PET which falls chargeable) the applicable NRB is that of the tax year of death.

The necessity of reviewing the prior seven-year period occurs every time a CLT is made.

It may also be necessary to take into account any grossing-up (see paragraph 10.54).

10.49 The following Examples 14, 15 and 16 illustrate the points made in paragraphs 10.45 to 10.48 (the effect of grossing-up is considered in paragraph 10.54). It is assumed in the examples that the person responsible for any IHT is that of the donee (ie the recipient) not the donor; grossing up can then be ignored.

Example 14

CLTs only made by the individual

Sharon Michaels has been advised to give away as much of her estate as she can during her lifetime in order to mitigate any IHT charge which arises on her estate should she die prematurely. She decides that the best way to do this is to set up a discretionary trust for various family members and to make regular transfers to it.

Accordingly, she makes transfers to the discretionary trust as follows:

1 June 1999	£92,000 CLT1
5 August 2000	£200,000 CLT2
10 December 2003	£100,000 CLT3
23 October 2008	£250,000 CLT4

All the gifts are CLTs.

10.50 *Inheritance tax: the basics*

The relevant NRBs are as follows:

1999–2000	£231,000
2000–2001	£234,000
2003–2004	£255,000
2008–2009	£312,000

1 June 1999: CLT1

In the previous seven years no CLTs have been made and thus the whole of the NRB of 1999–2000 is available.

IHT charge is thus: £92,000 @ 0% = £nil

(ie the whole of the gift falls within the NRB).

5 August 2000: CLT2

In the previous seven years CLT1 has been made and thus £92,000 of the NRB of £234,000 (the applicable NRB for 2000–2001) has been utilised leaving £142,000 unutilised.

IHT charge is thus: £142,000 x 0% + £58,000 x 20% = £11,600

10 December 2003: CLT3

In the previous seven years CLT1 and CLT2 have been made and thus £292,000 of the NRB of £255,000 (the applicable NRB for 2003–2004) has been utilised leaving no part of the NRB unutilised.

IHT charge is thus: £100,000 x 20% = £20,000

23 October 2008: CLT4

In the previous seven years only CLT3 has been made.

CLT1 and CLT2 were each made more than seven years before CLT4 and accordingly are ignored (ie they fall out of account).

Thus of the applicable NRB of £312,000 (the applicable NRB for 2008–2009) only £100,000 has been utilised (by CLT3).

IHT charge is thus: £212,000 x 0% + £38,000 x 20% = £7,600

10.50 The following points are worth noting on Example 14:
- the applicable NRB under consideration is that applicable to the tax year in which the CLT is made (and may thus vary as CLTs are made in different tax years);

Inheritance tax: the basics **10.51**

- if more than one CLT is made within a seven year period those CLTs made later in the period are likely to suffer an IHT charge due to the dissipation of the NRB; and
- over time the NRB is capable of being replenished as CLTs fall out of account (as applied to CLT1 and CLT2 above when computing the IHT charge on CLT4).

10.51 The effect of the individual dying and thus possibly precipitating additional IHT charges is now considered using the facts of Example 14:

Example 15

Additional IHT charge on CLTs due to death

The facts of Example 14 are assumed but Sharon Michaels dies on 3 June 2009.

As a consequence of her death any CLTs made within seven years thereof are now subject to additional IHT; thus only CLT3 and CLT4 are subject to this charge.

In ascertaining the quantum of the additional charge the applicable NRB is now that applicable in the tax year of death (ie £325,000).

10 December 2003: CLT3

In the previous seven years CLT1 and CLT2 have been made and thus £292,000 of the NRB of £325,000 (the applicable NRB for 2009–2010) has been utilised leaving £33,000 of the NRB unutilised.

Additional IHT charge is thus:

[£33,000 x 0% + £67,000 x 40% x 40%*] – £20,000** = £nil

(40%* refers to taper relief; £20,000** refers to the lifetime credit)

Note: in calculating the additional IHT charge on CLT3 it is necessary to take into account any CLTs made within the seven years prior to the date of CLT3 in order to ascertain the amount of the unutilised NRB.

23 October 2008: CLT4

In the previous seven years only CLT3 has been made.

CLT1 and CLT2 were each made more than seven years before CLT4 and accordingly are ignored (ie they fall out of account).

10.52 *Inheritance tax: the basics*

Thus of the applicable NRB of £325,000 only £100,000 has been utilised (by CLT3).

Additional IHT charge is thus:

[£225,000 x 0% + £25,000 x 40%] – £7,600* = £2,400

(£7,600* refers to the lifetime credit).

10.52 The impact of PETs is now examined and again the above facts of Examples 14 and 15 are used.

Example 16

It is now also assumed that in addition to making CLT1 to CLT4 two PETs are also made as follows:

1 March 1999	£30,000
17 June 2003	£125,000

Sharon's history of gifts is thus now:

1 March 1999	£30,000 PET1
1 June 1999	£92,000 CLT1
5 August 2000	£200,000 CLT2
17 June 2003	£125,000 PET2
10 December 2003	£100,000 CLT3
23 October 2008	£250,000 CLT4

Prior to Sharon's death the IHT charges in lifetime are exactly those computed in Example 14. This is because at the date of each PET (ie PET1 and PET2) no IHT charge arises and thus neither of the PETs absorb any of the relevant NRBs.

However, on Sharon's death matters change.

As a consequence of her death any CLTs made within seven years thereof are now subject to additional IHT but, in addition, any PETs made within this period now also fall subject to charge. Thus CLT3 and CLT4 are subject to this charge (as before; see Example 15) but in addition so is PET2 (PET1 is made more than seven years before death and thus is now an exempt, not merely potentially exempt, transfer).

Inheritance tax: the basics **10.53**

In ascertaining the quantum of the additional charge on CLT3 and CLT4 and the IHT charge on PET2 the applicable NRB is that applicable in the tax year of death (ie £325,000 (as was the case in Example 15)).

17 June 2003: PET2

In the previous seven years CLT1 and CLT2 have been made and thus £292,000 of the NRB of £325,000 (the applicable NRB for 2009–2010, the year of death) has been utilized leaving £33,000 of the NRB unutilised.

IHT charge is thus:

[£33,000 x 0% + £92,000 x 40% x 40%*] = £14,720

(40%* refers to taper relief)

10 December 2003: CLT3

In the previous seven years PET1, CLT1, CLT2 AND PET2 have been made. However, PET1 is not chargeable and thus does not absorb any of the NRB. Each of the remaining gifts do absorb some part of the NRB, in fact £417,000 in total and thus none of the £325,000 NRB remains unutilised.

Additional IHT charge is thus:

[£100,000 x 40% x 40%*] – £20,000** = £nil

(40%* refers to taper relief; £20,000** refers to the lifetime credit)

23 October 2008: CLT4

In the previous seven years only PET2 and CLT3 have been made.

PET1, CLT1 and CLT2 were each made more than seven years before CLT4 and accordingly are ignored (ie they fall out of account).

Thus of the applicable NRB of £325,000 only £225,000 has been utilised.

Additional IHT charge is thus:

[£100,000 x 0% + £150,000 x 40%] – £7,600* = £52,400

(£7,600* refers to the lifetime credit).

10.53 Comparing the additional IHT charges on the CLTs (and the IHT on

10.54 *Inheritance tax: the basics*

the PETs) illustrated in Examples 15 and 16 following Sharon's death shows the following:

	NO PETs MADE (Example 15)	PETs MADE (Example 16)
PET1	n/a	nil
PET2	n/a	£14,720
CLT1	£nil	£nil
CLT2	£nil	£nil
CLT3	£nil	£nil
CLT4	£2,400	£52,400

Even though one of Sharon's PETs (ie PET1) has had no impact whatsoever on the resultant additional IHT charges, PET2 has had a dramatic effect increasing the overall aggregate charge to £67,120 compared to £2,400. For the recipient of CLT4, the making by Sharon of PET2 has a dramatic increase in his additional IHT liability (a liability over which he has no control).

Chargeable lifetime transfers and grossing-up

10.54 The IHT liability (not the additional IHT liability) arising on a CLT is primarily that of the donor.

The effect of this liability falling on the part of the donor is to increase the actual amount of the transfer of value made by the donor. The donor is no longer simply transferring, say, £50,000 cash but is also having to discharge any IHT charge thereon with the consequence that the donor's estate in fact diminishes by the size of the transfer plus the IHT payable. In essence, the transfer is a net transfer; the gross transfer equalling the net transfer plus the accompanying IHT charge.

Example 17

Edward Comings transfers £400,000 into his discretionary trust on 1st June 2010.

This is a CLT.

As the donor, Edward has the primary liability to discharge the IHT arising on the transfer.

Assuming that Edward has exhausted his NRB (ie £325,000 for the tax year 2010–2011) due to having made other CLTs in the immediate seven prior years the grossed up amount of his £400,000 transfer is:

[£400,000/0.8] = £500,000

Inheritance tax: the basics **10.54**

This £500,000 is referred to as the gross transfer and the £400,000 the net transfer.

As there is no available NRB to set against the £500,000 the IHT liability is

20% × £500,000 = £100,000.

Thus, the split of the £500,000 is as follows:

- the discretionary trust receives £400,000; and
- the IHT charge is £100,000.

Edward's estate diminishes by £500,000 (albeit that £100,000 of it is to pay the IHT charge).

Example 18

Using the facts from Example 17, but assume that the whole of the NRB is available against the transfer into the discretionary trust which occurs, for example, if Edward has not made any earlier CLTs in the previous seven years. Of the £400,000 transfer the first £325,000 is charged at the nil rate giving an IHT liability of nil with the balance of £75,000 chargeable at 20%.

However, as Edward is liable for the IHT charge this amount subject at the 20% rate needs to be grossed up:

The amount which is chargeable at 20% is thus:

[£75,000/0.8] = £93,750

The IHT liability is [0% × £325,000 + 20% × £93,750] = £18,750.

The gross transfer of value is thus £418,750 (ie £400,000 + £18,750).

Thus:

- the discretionary trust receives £400,000; and
- the IHT charge is £18,7500.

Edward's estate is diminished by £418,750 (albeit that £18,750 of it is to pay the IHT charge).

Example 19

Toby Brewin transfers £250,000 in November 2010 into his discretionary trust.

He has made no earlier lifetime transfers. The whole of the NRB for 2010–2011 of £325,000 is thus available for offset against the transfer.

The IHT liability on the transfer is nil and no grossing up is necessary.

In this case the *gross* and *net* transfers are the same (ie £250,000).

10.55 A comparison of Examples 17, 18 and 19 shows the, perhaps not unsurprising, result that the greater the availability of the NRB the smaller the extent of the grossing up and a consequent smaller overall gross transfer. This, in turn, lowers the cost to the donor of effecting the CLT.

10.56 In the case of CLTs the parties to the transfer (the individual donor and the trustee donees) may agree that the donee (ie the trustees) pays the IHT liability, if any, which arises on the transfer. In this case the donor's estate will diminish only by the value of the gift and thus no grossing up is necessary. This produces a lesser cost for the donor but, on the other hand, the donees (eg the trustees) are left with less than the amount transferred due to the need for them to discharge the IHT liability out of the transfer.

Example 20

Using the facts in Example 17, if the trustees agree to discharge any IHT charge on the transfer the IHT liability arising is simply:

$20\% \times £400,000 = £80,000$

The donor, Edward, gifts £400,000 to the trust out of which the trust discharges £80,000 of IHT leaving the trust with net £320,000.

10.57 The decision as to who should pay the IHT on a transfer into trust will usually be dependent upon the outcome of discussions between the donor and the donee (ie trustees).

10.58 When reviewing CLTs made in the seven year cumulation period (see paragraph 10.45) to ascertain the availability of any NRB it is the *gross* (not net) transfer figures which are used.

Potentially exempt transfers and grossing up

10.59 The concept of grossing up has no relevance to the calculation of an IHT liability on PETs. This is because an IHT liability only arises on a PET if the donor dies within seven years of making the transfer and in such cases the primary liability is that of the donee.

Death

10.60 IHT is levied on the death of an individual (*IHTA 1984 s 4*). For this purpose it is assumed that the individual makes a transfer of value (ie a disposition) immediately prior to his death. The quantum of the 'deemed' disposition is the value of the individual's estate immediately before his death (*IHTA 1984 s 4*); this is a different measure than that applicable to a lifetime disposition (see paragraph 10.24). Nevertheless, the related property rules still apply (see paragraph 10.24)

In arriving at the value of the deceased's estate any liabilities of the deceased are deductible (*IHTA 1984 s 5*).

Assets

10.61 The estate of the deceased comprises (*IHTA 1984 s 5*) the following key categories:

- assets to which the deceased is beneficially entitled at death (including accrued income thereon up to the date of death);
- assets in respect of which the deceased had a general power of appointment; and
- 'qualifying' interests in possession in settled property.

The estate also includes gifts made by the deceased in lifetime in respect of which at death the deceased has reserved a benefit (so-called GWRs; *FA 1986 s 102; see* Chapter 12).

The estate does not, however, include excluded property (*IHTA 1984 s 5*; see Chapter 13).

10.62 The individual's 'free estate' excludes GWRs and qualifying interests in possession.

10.63 *Inheritance tax: the basics*

Assets beneficially owned

10.63 Typically, the main part of a deceased's estate comprises assets to which the individual is beneficially entitled (ie owns personally). Such assets may include, for example, cash at bank; shareholdings whether in listed or unquoted companies; premium bonds; chattels including paintings, jewellery, antique furniture; etc.

As a general rule such assets typically pass under the deceased's will (or under the intestacy rules if the deceased left no will).

Income which has accrued on such assets up to the date of death is also included. For example, interest may have accrued on the deceased's bank accounts or rental income may have accrued on land owned. The accrual is the appropriate time apportioned amount and is included "gross" unless the income has been subject to the deduction of income tax at source (eg interest credited on bank deposits; see paragraph 19.7). The income accrual is not only subject to IHT as part of the deceased's estate but is also subject to income tax on the part of the executors as the income falls to be treated as part of the income of the administration period and hence an element of double tax arises which is relieved in only limited circumstances (see paragraph 28.16).

10.64 The matrimonial home is also included in the deceased's estate. The extent of the inclusion depends upon the extent of the deceased's interest in the property. If the property is owned as to 100% by the deceased the full value of the property is included as part of the estate.

If, on the other hand, the individual owns the property as beneficial joint tenant with his/her spouse only 50% of the property's value is included as part of the deceased's estate. If the property is owned with the spouse as beneficial tenants in common the appropriate proportion is included. Thus, for example, the husband and wife may own the property 70/30 respectively. On death, the deceased spouse includes the relevant proportion which, in this example, is the 70% or 30% as appropriate.

10.65 Assets (including the matrimonial home) owned as beneficial joint tenants pass on death by survivorship not under the deceased's will (see paragraph 7.7) and probate is not required (see paragraph 27.126).

However, irrespective of the manner of ownership of the asset, the inheritance consequences are the same (ie the appropriate percentage ownership is valued and included as part of the deceased's estate).

General power of appointment

10.66 Where the deceased has a general power of appointment which enables him to dispose of any property (other than settled property) he is treated as if he is beneficially entitled to the property (*IHTA 1984 s 5*).

A classic example where the deceased may be treated as having a power of appointment over property is where he is a party to a joint bank account. Where this is the case the whole of the account is treated as forming part of the deceased's estate (not just a part, typically 50%, thereof); indeed the whole of the account is also treated as forming part of the other joint holder's estate where he is also regarded as possessing a power of appointment over the account. Whether such a power exists depends upon, *inter alia*, the conditions, if any, attached to the funds provided; the understanding and intentions of the parties; the terms of the bank mandate; etc (see paragraph 12.17).

Gifts with reservation

10.67 Although the deceased may during lifetime make a gift of property, to the extent that the deceased continues to derive some benefit from it (or is entitled to do so) the value of the gift at the date of death is included as part of the deceased's estate. Such gifts are referred to as GWRs (*FA 1986 s 102; see* Chapter 12).

10.68 A typical example is where a parent gifts the family home to one of the children but continues to live in it. Another example is where the deceased in lifetime settles property on a discretionary trust whilst also falling in the class of beneficiaries. Whether in fact the deceased benefits from the trust is irrelevant; the mere possibility is enough to cause the settled assets to fall within the estate on death as GWRs. If the deceased is not able to benefit from the trust, but his spouse can, this does not cause the gift to be treated as a GWR in which case it does not form part of the deceased's estate.

10.69 The value of the GWR, included as part of the estate, is the value of the gift at the date of death (not when made as applies to a CLT or PET).

'Qualifying' interests in possession

10.70 An interest in possession trust is a trust under which one (or possibly more) individual is entitled to the whole (or part) of the income which arises to the trust. Such an individual is commonly referred to as the life tenant.

10.71 For IHT purposes the life tenant is treated as owning the trust assets in respect of which the individual is entitled to the income which are then included as part of the individual's estate on death (*IHTA 1984 s 49*). This is in fact a tax 'fiction' as the individual, whilst being entitled to the income from such assets, does not in fact own the assets (they are property of the trustees held for the benefit of the trust beneficiaries).

This treatment only applies, however, if the interest in possession is a 'qualifying' interest (see paragraph 16.4).

10.72 *Inheritance tax: the basics*

'Qualifying' interests in possession include:

- interests in possession trusts created in lifetime before 22 March 2006; and
- interests in possession trusts created by will whether before, on or after 22 March 2006.

10.72 Thus, interest in possession trusts created in lifetime on or after 22 March 2006 do not qualify as qualifying interests in possession (and, as a consequence, the assets of the trust are not included as part of the estate of the interest in possession beneficiary on death).

10.73 The value of the assets comprised in the trust in which a qualifying interest in possession subsists is the value at the date of death not the value when the assets are first settled on trust.

Example 21

Albert Brown dies on 5 June 2010. At his death he owns a house worth £600,000; cash at bank of £25,000; and quoted equities worth £75,000.

He is the life tenant of an interest in possession trust set up in 2005 by his brother Ted whose assets in which his interest subsists are worth £225,000 on death. He is also the life tenant of a second interest in possession trust which had been set up in lifetime by Albert's uncle in November 2006.

He is also one of the beneficiaries of a discretionary trust which he had set up a few years ago (at death the trust assets are worth £150,000).

On his death the proceeds of a life assurance policy which he had taken out some years ago on his own life are paid out to the executors of his will, a sum assured of £750,000.

Albert's estate comprises:

Assets to which deceased was beneficially entitled
House	£600,000
Cash at bank	£25,000
Quoted equities	£75,000
Life policy	£750,000
	£1,450,000

Gift with reservation	£150,000
Settled property:	
Interest in possession	£225,000
Total estate	£1,825,000

Notes

1. Although Albert is the beneficiary of an interest in possession trust set up by his uncle, as the trust is set up in lifetime after 21 March 2006 Albert's interest is not classified as a 'qualifying' interest in possession and thus the trust assets do not form part of Albert's estate. Albert's interest in the trust set up by his brother Ted is a 'qualifying' interest.

2. The proceeds of the life policy fall subject to IHT on Albert's death as on his death the policy proceeds are paid to his executors and form part of his estate. Typically, this is not usually the case. An individual often takes out a life policy on his/her own life but then settles the policy in trust for, say, the spouse and children with the consequence that on the individual's death the policy proceeds are paid to the trustees of the trust and do not thus form part of the deceased's estate thus saving an IHT charge of 40% of the sum assured (see paragraph 19.40).

Liabilities

10.74 Liabilities of the deceased, subsisting at the date of death, are deductible in arriving at the deceased's *net* chargeable estate.

10.75 The deductible liabilities comprise those which have been incurred for a consideration in money or money's worth (eg a simple borrowing of money; a credit card debt) *or* are liabilities imposed by law (eg any outstanding income or CGT liabilities of the individual; also included are any IHT liabilities arising from a previous lifetime transfer if the liability thereon is that of the deceased; fines). The debt must be enforceable.

Other deductible liabilities include reasonable funeral expenses; the term 'reasonable' reflecting the deceased's standard of living and thus varies from one individual to another. Such expenses also include a reasonable amount for the mourning of the family and the cost of a gravestone.

The legal costs of administering the will are not, however, deductible.

10.76 Generally, where a liability is secured on property (eg a residential

10.77 *Inheritance tax: the basics*

mortgage) it is deductible from the value of that property. Any excess unrelieved part of the borrowing is then deductible against the balance of the individual's estate (note that such excess is not, however, deductible from any settled property in which the individual has a qualifying interest in possession).

Example 22

Using the facts in Example 21, Albert at his death has also incurred the following liabilities:

- a credit card unpaid bill of £3,000;
- an outstanding income tax liability of £14,000; and
- a mortgage on his house of £200,000.

Albert's death estate is as follows:

Assets to which deceased was beneficially entitled:		
House	£600,000	
Less: mortgage	(£200,000)	
		£400,000
Cash at bank of	£25,000	
Quoted equities worth	£75,000	
Life policy	£750,000	
		£850,000
Less liabilities:		
Income tax liability	(£14,000)	
Credit card bill	(£3,000)	
		(£17,000)
		£1,233,000
Gift with reservation		£150,000
Settled property:		
Interest in possession		£225,000
Total net chargeable estate on death:		£1,608,000

Exemptions and reliefs

10.77 Lifetime gifts and gifts made by will on death may fall to be treated as exempt or may be subject to some form of relief. Some transfers may be exempt transfers only if made in lifetime whereas others may be exempt whether made in lifetime or on death; similarly with respect to any reliefs granted (see Chapter 11).

10.78 Exempt transfers include inter-spouse transfers (applicable in lifetime and on death; *IHTA 1984 s 18*); lifetime annual transfers of £3,000 or less (*IHTA 1984 s 19*); and small lifetime annual transfers of £250 or less (*IHTA 1984 s 20*).

10.79 Two major forms of relief are business property relief (BPR) and agricultural property relief (APR) both available with respect to lifetime gifts and on death (*IHTA 1984 ss 104* and *116*; see Chapter 11).

Depending upon the type of property, BPR is either 50% or 100% of the value of the relevant property. Effectively, therefore, if 100% BPR applies the relevant property is included in the deceased's estate albeit at a 'nil' value.

BPR applies to the *net* value of the business qualifying for BPR; thus any liabilities incurred for the purposes of the business are deductible from the relevant asset values to arrive at the net value of the business. Unfortunately, this has the effect of wasting any 100% BPR. Ideally, therefore, if possible, liabilities of the business should be charged against other property of the individual concerned in respect of which neither BPR nor any other similar relief is available. The effect is thus to maximise any BPR and, at the same time, maximises the use of any liabilities of the deceased when calculating the death estate (see paragraph 11.65).

Rate on death and the nil rate band

10.80 The rate of IHT applying to the death estate is 40% (twice the lifetime rate of 20%). This applies to the excess of the value of the estate over any available NRB; £325,000 for 2010–2011 (*IHTA 1984 Sch 1*).

10.81 It is thus necessary to ascertain whether any of the NRB is available at the date of death. This requires consideration of any lifetime gifts (whether PETs or CLTs) made by the deceased within the seven years prior to death as such gifts will almost inevitably have utilised a part, or all, of the NRB available on death.

10.82 PETs as well as CLTs need to be considered in this seven year period. Although at the date of making a PET no IHT liability arises and thus no part of the NRB is in fact utilised at that time, any PET made within seven years of death then falls to be chargeable and at that time a part, or all, of the NRB is utilised by the PET.

10.82 *Inheritance tax: the basics*

Example 23

Tom Collins makes the following lifetime gifts:

1 January 2008	PET	£150,000
5 February 2009	CLT	£180,000

Assume Tom has made no earlier gifts.

Tom dies on 13 July 2010 with an estate of £600,000.

Assume that the trustees agree to bear any IHT charge on the CLT (this avoids the need to consider grossing up thus simplifying the example).

As Tom dies within seven years of each of the lifetime gifts the PET becomes chargeable and additional IHT arises on the CLT.

On Tom's death the position is as follows:

PET (£150,000)

The whole of the NRB (of £325,000 for 2010–2011) is available as no earlier gifts have been made.

Thus the IHT charge on the PET due to Tom's death is nil.

CLT (£180,000)

In the seven years prior to the CLT Tom has made the PET of £150,000.

Thus only £175,000 [£325,000 less £150,000] of the NRB remains.

The additional IHT charge on the CLT is:

£175,000 × 0% + £5,000 × 40% = £2,000

(subject to any taper relief, if any, and offset of any lifetime IHT paid on the CLT; for ease these are ignored for present purposes; see Example 7).

Estate on death

In the previous seven years a PET and a CLT have been made.

Together the two gifts have utilised, in full, the £325,000 NRB.

The IHT charge on the estate on death is therefore:

40% × £600,000 = £240,000

Payment and the bearing of inheritance tax on death

10.83 On death, IHT is charged on the deceased's estate. Two issues arise.

- *first*, who is responsible for the actual *payment* of any such liability; and
- *second*, who ultimately bears the tax so charged.

10.84 The person who discharges the IHT liability arising on death may not be the same person(s) who ultimately bears the liability.

Payment of inheritance tax on death

10.85 On death, the following IHT charges may arise on:

- PETs made within seven years of death;
- CLTs made within seven years of death; and
- the estate on death.

10.86 The person primarily responsible for the discharge of any IHT charge arising on death in the case of any PETs and/or CLTs made within the seven-year period prior to death is/are the donee(s). Not only are they responsible for discharging any IHT due but they are also the persons who bear (ie suffer) the liability.

10.87 The estate on death comprises assets to which the deceased is beneficially entitled at the date of his death; gifts made by the deceased in lifetime which comprise GWR; and certain categories of settled property (ie such property in which the deceased possesses a 'qualifying' interest in possession).

The responsibility for discharging the IHT liability arising on the estate is divided between three categories of person:

- the *personal representatives* (PRs) of the deceased are responsible for the IHT liability in relation to the assets to which the deceased is beneficially entitled;
- the *person in whom the property is vested (with respect to the GWR)* is responsible for the IHT liability in relation to the gift; and
- the *trustees* of the trust, in which the deceased at death has a qualifying interest in possession, are responsible for the IHT liability in relation to the trust assets.

10.87 *Inheritance tax: the basics*

Example 24

Using the facts in Example 22, Albert's estate is as follows:

Assets to which deceased was beneficially entitled:

House	£600,000	
Less: mortgage	(£200,000)	
		£400,000
Cash at bank of	25,000	
Quoted equities worth	£75,000	
Life policy	£750,000	
		£850,000
Less liabilities:		
Income tax liability	(£14,000)	
Credit card bill	(£3,000)	
		(£17,000)
		£1,233,000
Gift with reservation		£150,000
Settled property:		
Interest in possession		£225,000
Total net chargeable estate on death		£1,608,000

The IHT liability on the net chargeable estate is equal to:

$0\% \times £325,000 + 40\% \times £1,283,000 = £513,200$.

To determine the liabilities of the various persons the aggregate IHT liability (£513,200) arising on the estate (£1,608,000) is simply pro-rated according to the amounts comprised in the three categories.

Thus, the persons responsible for discharging this aggregate liability and the associated amounts are as follows:

Personal representatives:

[£1,233,000/£1,608,000] × £513,200 = £391,085.

Person possessing the gift which is subject to the GWR rules:

[£150,000/£1,608,000] × £513,200 = £47,873.

Trustees of settled property in which the donor at death has a qualifying interest in possession:

[£225,000/£1,608,000] × £513,200 = £71,809.

An alternative way of calculating these respective liabilities is to ascertain the average rate of IHT applicable on death and apply this rate to the respective figures. Thus:

Average rate = [£513,200/£1,608,000] × 100% = 31.915%.

Personal representatives:

31.915% × £1,633,000 = £393,511.

Person possessing the gift which was subject to the gift with reservation rules:

31.915% × £150,000 = £47,872.

Trustees of settled property in which the donor at death had an interest in possession:

31.915% × £225,000 = £71,808.

(The slightly different figures are due to rounding error re the % figure.)

Bearing of the inheritance tax charge on death

10.88 Example 24 illustrates the mechanics of calculation of the IHT charge arising on the estate on death and its division among those persons responsible for its discharge. It does not, per se, identify who ultimately bears the burden of the liability.

Gifts with reservation

10.89 With respect to any gifts with reservation effected by the deceased in lifetime, the person in possession of the property comprised in the gift not only has the responsibility of discharging the IHT applicable to the property but also bears the liability (ie the tax is paid out of the assets of the recipient).

Qualifying interests in possession

10.90 With respect to any qualifying interests in possession of the deceased at the date of death the trustees thereof not only have the responsibility of

10.91 Inheritance tax: the basics

discharging the IHT applicable to the interests but also bear the liability (ie the tax is paid out of trust assets).

Beneficial asset entitlement

10.91 The discharge of the IHT liability attributable to the assets (less liabilities) beneficially owned by the deceased at death is the responsibility of the PRs (eg the executors of the will) of the deceased. However, the PRs personally, of course, do not bear this liability. It is the beneficiaries of the will who ultimately bear the liability. It is thus necessary to identify the proportion of the IHT due which each beneficiary is to bear.

10.92 The *general rule* (ie where the deceased's will makes no references to the discharge of any IHT charges arising on death) is that the IHT liability attributable to the free estate is regarded as part of the general testamentary and administrative expenses of the deceased's estate (*IHTA 1984 s 211*). Thus, the IHT liability is paid out of, and thus borne by, the residue of the estate (ie that part of the estate which is left over after the various specific legacies, etc. have been made and all expenses/liabilities of the estate have been discharged).

It is thus the beneficiary(ies) entitled to the residue (the so-called residuary beneficiary(ies)) who in this case bear the liability (and thus to this extent are worse off).

10.93 Where the IHT liability is to be treated as a testamentary expense of the estate the quantum of IHT charged on the estate may vary according to how the testator's will is worded *vis-à-vis* which heirs are to receive (eg specific gifts) and which are to take the residue.

Example 25

Sally Holmes dies having made no lifetime gifts.

Her death estate comprises £925,000 cash.

In her will she leaves cash of £500,000 to her husband with the residue being left to her two children to be split equally between them. Her will makes no reference to IHT.

As the will makes no reference to IHT the liability on her death is paid out of residue.

Gifts to spouses are exempt from IHT. The £500,000 left to Sally's husband is thus not subject to IHT on her death.

The balancing £425,000 left to her two children is subject to IHT but part of this is covered by the £325,000 NRB as no part of this has been used within the seven years prior to Sally's death.

IHT liability = £325,000 × 0% + £100,000 × 40% = £40,000

This £40,000 is paid out of the residue (ie the children's inheritance). The children thus receive

[£425,000 − £40,000]/2, (ie £192,500 each)

Her husband receives the full £500,000.

The children's gifts are received out of residue and thus after the IHT liability arising on the whole of the estate.

Example 26

This is similar to Example 25 but in this case Sally's will is worded differently.

Sally Holmes dies having made no lifetime gifts.

Her estate comprises £925,000 cash.

In her will she leaves £425,000 to be split equally between her two children and the residue (ie in principle £500,000) is left to her husband. As in Example 25 her will makes no reference to IHT.

As the will makes no reference to IHT then the liability on her death estate is paid out of residue.

However, in this case (unlike Example 25) the specific gifts to the children are treated as gifts net of IHT and it thus becomes necessary to 'gross up' these gifts to ascertain the IHT liability on the estate taking into account any available NRB.

Thus:

Grossed up gifts = [[£425,000 − £325,000]/0.6] = £166,667

IHT liability = [£166,667] × 40% = £66,667

The children receive [£425,000]/2 = £212,500 each

The husband receives [£500,000 − £66,667] = £433,333

10.94 *Inheritance tax: the basics*

The children's gifts are received by them IHT free as far as they are concerned.

The husband is anticipating receiving £500,000 but as this is the residue of his wife's estate this has to bear the IHT charge on her estate; he accordingly receives the £500,000 less the charge of £66,667.

10.94 A comparison of Examples 25 and 26 shows the difference in the amount of IHT payable on death and the differences in the net inheritances by the beneficiaries depending upon how the will is drafted. The actual difference in the amount of inheritance payable is £66,667 less £40,000 (ie £26,667 a not insignificant amount).

In Example 26 the wording of the will is such that the gifts to the children are 'grossed up' which inflates the IHT chargeable and thus reduces the net amount received by the residuary beneficiary as it is the residue that bears the IHT chargeable.

The lesser amount of IHT on Sally's estate is payable where Sally's husband inherits £500,000 as a specific gift (Example 25). However, each of Sally's two children then inherit only £192,500 each. If Sally in fact wants her two children each to receive £212,500 (as in Example 26) there is be nothing to stop her husband (under Example 25), having inherited £500,000, then gifting (albeit as a PET) the shortfall (ie £20,000) to each of the two children.

The children then receive £212,500 (as Sally wants) and her husband is left with £460,000 (£500,000 less £40,000 gift to children), still £26,667 more (ie £460,000 less £433,333) than under Example 26.

Specific gifts bearing their own inheritance tax on death

10.95 Examples 25 and 26 highlight the different IHT liabilities and thus net inheritances by the beneficiaries which arise as a consequence of the different manner in which specific gifts and the residue are left to the various beneficiaries. Despite the different wordings, however, the IHT charge on the death estate is borne by the residue of the estate as a general testamentary expense of the estate.

10.96 The provision under which the IHT due on the deceased's estate is a testamentary expense (*IHTA 1984 s 211*) is subject to any contrary intention in the deceased's will (*IHTA 1984 s 211*). For example, the will may provide for some (not necessarily all) specific gifts to 'bear their own tax'. In such cases the IHT liability arising on the deceased's estate is allocated as appropriate and is borne in part by one or more specific beneficiaries (in relation to their specific inheritance) and in part by the residue.

Irrespective of any provisions in the deceased's will any assets located outside the UK bear their own tax and any property owned as beneficial joint tenants (under which the survivor automatically inherits) also bears its own tax.

Example 27

Using the facts from Example 26 above, Sally this time provides for the specific gifts to the two children each to bear their own tax.

Sally dies having made no lifetime gifts.

Her death estate comprises £925,000 cash.

In her will she leaves £425,000 to be split equally between her two children each gift to bear its own tax and the residue (ie £500,000) is left to her husband.

The IHT on the death estate is:

0% × £325,000 + 40% × [£425,000 − £325,000] = £40,000

Thus:

IHT liability = £40,000

The children receive [[£425,000 − £40,000]/2] = £192,500 each

The husband receives £500,000.

10.97 Comparing the consequences in Examples 26 and 27 shows that less IHT is payable if the specific gifts bear their own tax; this is because in such cases no grossing up is necessary (as applies in Example 26).

10.98 From the above examples it is clear that the IHT charge arising on the deceased's estate depends upon the quantum of lifetime gifts which may have been made within the immediately preceding seven years (as this will impact upon the amount of NRB available to offset against the estate); whether the will is silent as to who is to bear the IHT charge arising on the estate or whether it specifically provides for some or all of the specific gifts to bear their own IHT

10.99 *Inheritance tax: the basics*

charge; and the manner in which the will provides for the beneficiaries to inherit (eg specific gifts versus residue).

A further discussion on this aspect (ie wills) is found in Chapters 27 and 28.

Comprehensive example

10.99 The following example seeks to pull together the various issues discussed in this chapter. It considers:

- the IHT liability arising on lifetime transfers (PETS and CLTs);
- the IHT liability arising on lifetime transfers due to death; and
- the IHT liability on the estate on death.

Example 28

David Dough makes the following lifetime transfers:

1.1.02	CLT1	£80,000
5.6.03	PET1	£120,000
2.7.04	CLT2	£240,000
4.10.09	PET2	£300,000

David dies on 2 May 2010 with an estate of £800,000.

At the date of his death David also has a qualifying interest in possession in a trust which has been set up by his uncle in July 1991. At the date of David's death the assets of the trust in which his interest subsists are worth £125,000.

David has agreed to pay any IHT charge arising on the CLTs (thus, grossing up may be necessary).

In order to calculate the IHT liabilities it is necessary to:

- *first*, calculate the liabilities on the lifetime transfers at the dates they are made;
- *second*, calculate the liabilities on the lifetime transfers due to death; and

- *third*, calculate the liabilities on the estate on death.

Taking each of these in turn:

IHT liabilities on the lifetime transfers:

1.1.02   CLT1   £80,000

No transfers have been made in the previous seven years and thus the whole of the £242,000 NRB (for tax year 2001–2002) is available.

IHT liability = 0% × £80,000 = nil.

5.6.03   PET1   £120,000

As this transfer is a PET no IHT charge arises at this date.

2.7.04   CLT2   £240,000

In the previous seven years the only transfer is CLT1 (PETs are ignored as they utilise no part of the NRB). CLT1 used £80,000 of the £263,000 NRB (for tax year 2004–2005).

Thus, £183,000 of CLT2 is subject to IHT at the nil rate (ie 0%) but the balancing element of £57,000 is subject to tax. As David agrees to pay any IHT on the CLTs this amount (ie £57,000) is grossed up.

IHT liability = 0% × £183,000 + [£57,000/0.8] × 20% = £14,250.

The gross transfer is thus £254,250 (ie the net transfer of £240,000 plus the IHT liability £14,250 thereon).

4.10.09   PET2   £300,000

As this transfer is a PET no IHT charge arises at this date.

IHT liabilities on the lifetime transfers due to death:

Any PET or CLT made within seven years of death (ie on or after 3 May 2003) is subject to an IHT charge due to the death (in the case of a CLT the IHT is technically an 'additional IHT' charge).

1.1.02   CLT1   £80,000

CLT1 was made more than seven years before death.

Thus no additional IHT charge arises on CLT1.

5.6.03   PET1   £120,000

10.99 *Inheritance tax: the basics*

Although this transfer is a PET, death occurs within seven years of the date it is made and thus an IHT charge arises due to the death.

To ascertain the amount of the charge it is necessary to identify any transfers within the previous seven years which may have used some of the NRB.

CLT1 was made within this seven year period. CLT1 uses £80,000 of the £325,000 NRB (for tax year 2010–2011) leaving £245,000 unused.

Thus the IHT charge on PET1 is:

$0\% \times £120\,000 = $ nil.

2.7.04   CLT2   £254,250 (note it is the gross figure used here not the net figure).

As CLT2 is made within seven years of death an additional IHT charge arises on CLT2 due to the death.

To ascertain the amount of the charge it is necessary to identify any transfers within the previous seven years which will have used some of the NRB.

CLT1 and PET1 were each made within this seven year period. CLT1 used £80,000 and PET1 used £120,000 of the £325,000 NRB (for tax year 2010–2011).

This leaves £125,000 of the NRB unused.

Thus the IHT charge on CLT2 is:

$0\% \times £125,000 + 40\% \times £129,250 = £51,700$

However, taper relief is available and credit is also available for any lifetime IHT paid. Taper relief (40%) reduces the £51,700 to £20,680 and the lifetime credit of £14,250 reduces the £20,680 to £6,430.

4.10.09   PET2   £300,000

As this transfer was made within seven years of death an IHT liability arises due to death.

To ascertain the amount of the charge it is necessary to identify any transfers within the previous seven years which will have used some of the NRB.

PET1 and CLT2 were each made within this seven-year period. CLT1 was made more than seven years before PET2 and thus is now completely ignored in calculating the amount of the NRB available to PET2 (it is as if CLT1 never took place as far as ascertaining the NRB available is concerned).

In this case PET1 and CLT2 each used £120,000 and £254,250 respectively of the £325,000 NRB (for tax year 2010–2011).

There is thus no part of the NRB available for utilisation by PET2.

The IHT charge on PET2 is thus:

40% × £300,000 = £120,000

Estate on death

David dies on 2 May 2010 with an estate of £800,000 and a qualifying interest in possession worth £125,000.

To ascertain the NRB available it is necessary to look at any gifts which were made within the seven years preceding death (ie gifts made on or after 3 May 2003).

These gifts included PET1 of £120,000; CLT2 of £254,250; and PET2 of £300,000. Thus, all the £325,000 NRB (for tax year 2010–2011) has been used by these three gifts.

The IHT liability on death is thus:

40% × [£800,000 + £125,000] = £370,000.

Of this amount:

[£800,000/£925,000] × £370,000 = £320,000 is payable by David's personal representatives.

[£125,000/£925,000] × £370000 = £50,000 is payable by the trustees of the trust in which David has his qualifying interest in possession.

10.100 A number of comments on some of the principles contained in Example 28 may be useful:

- to work out any IHT liability on a transfer of value involves ascertaining the amount of NRB available for use by that transfer. To do this always requires a consideration of the immediately preceding seven years;

10.101 *Inheritance tax: the basics*

- in lifetime, PETs do not utilise any part of the NRB. However, on death any PET made within seven years of death then utilises some part of the NRB;
- as time moves forward certain transfers of value 'fall out of account' and thus are treated as no longer utilising any part of the NRB; in effect the NRB replenishes itself through time;
- transfers made within seven years of death utilise the NRB thus reducing the amount of the NRB available for utilisation by the 'estate on death';
- in the case of CLTs the amount of the CLT which is used in ascertaining the amount of NRB available for use by later CLTs (and/or PETs) is the gross not net amount; and
- the relevant NRB in calculating IHT on lifetime CLTs is that of the tax year of the CLT; however, in calculating the IHT charge on lifetime CLTs and PETs due to death the applicable NRB is that applicable in the tax year of death.

Planning considerations: initial thoughts

10.101 Theoretically, optimal IHT mitigation occurs where assets are given away in lifetime directly to, for example, members of the donor's family with the donor subsequently surviving for seven years and dying without any (or minimal) estate on death. The gifts constitute PETs and no IHT liabilities arise in such circumstances.

For many, however, such a simple strategy is not feasible as, typically, any assets owned are needed during lifetime and are not available for gifting.

10.102 The major asset is usually the home. In the past, schemes were developed which allowed the giving away of the family home yet still permitting the donors to continue living there but removing the home from their estate on death. Such schemes, generally speaking, are no longer IHT effective although some options are available (see Chapter 20).

10.103 Nevertheless, to the extent possible, gifts should be made as soon as practicable and some gifts are completely exempt from IHT and thus can be given away without even the requirement to survive seven years thereafter. Use of such exemptions should be maximised.

10.104 If the gift is a PET it may be possible to insure against the risk of an IHT liability arising due to the death of the donor within the seven-year period (see paragraph 19.41). Typically, cost effective term assurance policies are utilised; use of a seven-year decreasing term policy reduces premium levels. Writing such polices in trust for the beneficiaries makes the arrangements IHT effective.

10.105 Where an individual is in a position to make lifetime gifts to family members it may be preferable, for a variety of reasons (eg recipients are minor children), for use to be made of trusts rather than making the gifts directly to the individual(s) concerned. Pre-22 March 2006 gifts into certain trusts (eg interest in possession and accumulation and maintenance trusts; not discretionary trusts) are PETs and if the settlor survives seven years no IHT charge arises on the gifts. In many cases the NRB has not been utilised and thus even where death of the donor occurs within seven years of setting up the trust(s) the resultant IHT charge is nil (NRB discretionary trusts were, and continue to be, set up often by will rather than in lifetime; see paragraphs 16.24 and 28.88).

However, for gifts into trusts on or after 22 March 2006 in most cases such gifts qualify as CLTs thus potentially precipitating immediate IHT charges at 20% of the value of the gift (with the possibility of an additional IHT charge if death occurs within seven years) albeit subject to the availability of the NRB.

To this extent, the changes introduced in *FA 2006* (effective 22 March 2006) have made trusts less IHT effective.

Nevertheless, trusts continue to have a major role in tax planning (see Chapters 16, 17 and 18).

10.106 Effective drafting of wills is also an important element in any IHT planning. In particular, careful thought should be given as to who should bear any IHT charge which arises on the deceased's estate (see Chapters 27 and 28).

Summary

10.107 IHT is levied on gratuitous transfers made in lifetime and on death.

10.108 Both individuals and trust property are liable to IHT.

10.109 IHT is levied according to the domicile status of the individual. A UK domiciled individual is liable on worldwide assets whereas a non-UK domiciled individual is liable only on UK situs assets. However, in certain cases, an individual non-UK domiciled under UK common law may be 'deemed' UK domiciled for IHT purposes. An individual is 'deemed' UK domiciled for a period of time following the acquisition of a non-UK domicile.

10.110 Lifetime gifts comprise exempt transfers, potentially exempt transfers (PETs) or chargeable lifetime transfers (CLTs). PETs fall subject to IHT but

10.111 *Inheritance tax: the basics*

only if the donor of the transfer dies within seven years, whereas the latter are in principle subject to IHT at the date of the transfer.

10.111 The lifetime rate of IHT is 20% and the rate applicable on death is 40% (these rates applying for the tax year 2010–2011).

10.112 The NRB is £325,000 (for the tax year 2010–2011). Transfers falling within the NRB are subject to IHT at the nil (ie 0%) rate.

10.113 *FA 2008* has introduced, for the first time, the concept of the transferable NRB. Transferability applies where one or both spouses die on or after 9 October 2007. It does not apply where both deaths occurred prior to this date. The concept only applies to spouses.

10.114 The responsibility for discharging an IHT liability may vary as between donor and donee; sometimes the primary liability is that of the donor whereas on other occasions it is that of the donee. However, irrespective of where the primary liability may fall, provisions exist under which HMRC may seek to collect any inheritance due from others.

Chapter 11

Inheritance tax: exemptions and reliefs

Background

11.1 Lifetime transfers of value made by an individual may qualify as exempt, potentially exempt or chargeable and may be subject to some form of relief. A transfer that is exempt is simply not within the ambit of any charge to inheritance tax (IHT). A transfer which is subject to some form of relief in principle falls within the charge to IHT although the value of the transfer falling within the charge is relieved to the extent of the relevant relief (which may in fact equal 100%; see paragraph 11.60 re business property relief (BPR)).

11.2 Transfers arising on death may similarly be subject to exemption or relief; however, not all exemptions or reliefs available on lifetime transfers are available on transfers on death (eg the annual exemption; *IHTA 1984 s 19*; see paragraph 11.12).

11.3 Transfers which fall within an individual's nil rate band (NRB) are not exempt. Such transfers are liable to IHT albeit at a rate of 0% (this does not mean, however, that they are exempt; see paragraph 10.18).

11.4 Chapter 10 provides an overview of the various elements of IHT.

11.5 This chapter examines reliefs and exemptions applicable to lifetime and death transfers in more detail.

Exempt transfers

11.6 A lifetime transfer of value which is an exempt transfer is exempt from IHT whether or not the transferor survives for seven years thereafter or not.

11.7 A transfer of value may fall to be treated as exempt under more than one exemption category and thus it is possible for part of a transfer of value to be partially exempt under one category and part of it to be partially exempt under another.

11.8 *Inheritance tax: exemptions and reliefs*

11.8 Lifetime exempt transfers are a highly IHT-efficient manner of transferring wealth. Such transfers are exempt and utilise no part of the individual's NRB.

11.9 Some of the exemptions are event specific (eg gifts in contemplation of marriage, *IHTA 1984 s 22*; see paragraph 11.29) and thus are 'one-off' in nature; others are recurrent (eg the small gifts exemption; *IHTA 1984 s 20*; see paragraph 11.21) although if not used in a particular tax year cannot, in general, be carried back or forward for use in other tax years.

11.10 Perhaps the most underutilised, yet most IHT efficient, exempt transfer for the affluent individual is the 'normal expenditure out of income' exemption (*IHTA 1984 s 21*; see paragraph 11.23) and perhaps the most common and highly effective exemption is the inter-spouse exemption (available in lifetime and on death; *IHTA 1984 s 18*; see paragraph 11.42).

Exempt transfers: lifetime only

11.11 The main exempt transfers that apply only to lifetime transfers are as follows:

- annual exemption (*IHTA 1984 s 19*);
- small gifts exemption (*IHTA 1984 s 20*);
- normal expenditure out of income exemption (*IHTA 1984 s 21*);
- gifts in contemplation of marriage exemption (*IHTA 1984 s 22*); and
- dispositions for family maintenance exemption (*IHTA 1984 s 11*).

Each of these exempt gifts are now considered in turn.

Annual exemption

11.12 An individual may make transfers each tax year up to £3,000 without precipitating an IHT liability. If any part of the £3,000 remains unused at the end of the tax year the unused part may be carried forward one tax year only for use in the next tax year.

Thus, in the very first tax year in which an individual makes a lifetime transfer the annual exemption will be £3,000 (for the tax year in which the gift is made) plus £3,000 carried forward from the previous tax year in which the annual exemption remained unused (ie £6,000 in total).

11.13 The exemption applies irrespective of the status of the donee (ie the

Inheritance tax: exemptions and reliefs **11.18**

person receiving the gift) and thus applies to transfers into trust as well as to other individuals.

11.14 The £3,000 exemption may be offset against a larger transfer (ie the first £3,000 of a larger transfer is exempt under this exemption).

11.15 Where more than one transfer is made in any tax year by an individual the annual exemption is applied in time order; thus, the earlier transfer(s) absorb the whole or part of the exemption prior to later transfers in that tax year (ie no pro-rating of the exemption across all transfers made by an individual in a tax year applies). However, where in the tax year any potentially exempt transfers (PETs) are made the annual exemption is not set against such PETs even if the PETs are made prior to any chargeable lifetime transfers (CLTs) of that tax year.

Where (if at all) the PETs become chargeable (ie due to the death of the donor within seven years) the PETs are treated as made after the other CLTs of the tax year in which the PETs were made (but only for the purpose of allocation of the annual exemption).

However, where more than one transfer is effected on the same day, pro rating applies across the same-day transfers.

11.16 The lifetime termination of a 'qualifying interest in possession' may constitute a PET or CLT (see paragraphs 16.66 and 16.70) against which the annual exemption (if not already utilised) may be offset.

11.17 Where the reservation in connection with an earlier gift with reservation (GWR) is released such release constitutes a deemed PET (see paragraph 12.9). However, the quantum of the deemed PET so made is not eligible for reduction by the annual exemption (*RI 155*).

11.18 The annual exemption is available in addition to any of the other lifetime exemptions and is usually applied to any transfer after all other exemptions have been applied.

Example 1

Eric Beetle settles £53,000 cash on a discretionary trust on 3 June 2011. He has made no other gifts in the tax year or indeed in any prior tax year.

The gift is a CLT (irrespective of whether the gift is made on or after 22 March 2006 or before).

The first £6,000 (ie £3,000 represents the annual exemption for 2010–2011 and £3,000 is carried forward from 2009–2010) of the £53,000 is exempt (ie £47,000 is the amount of the CLT).

11.19 *Inheritance tax: exemptions and reliefs*

Example 2

Alison makes a PET of £3,000 in June 2010 and a CLT of £6,000 in October 2010 (having made no other lifetime gifts). The annual exemption of 2009–2010 and 2010–2011 are offset against the CLT.

Alison subsequently dies within seven years of the PET (which thus becomes chargeable). However, the PET is assumed to have been made after the CLT and thus the annual exemption remains offset against the CLT.

Alison makes a PET of £3,000 in 2009–2010 and a CLT, of £6,000, in 2010–2011.

The annual exemption for 2009–2010 and 2010–2011 is set against the CLT of £6,000 (reducing it to nil).

Alison dies within seven years of making the PET which thus becomes chargeable.

The annual exemption of £3,000 for 2009–2010 is now set against the PET reducing it to nil; the CLT of 2010–2011 is correspondingly increased to £3,000.

11.19 To avoid the possible complications referred to in paragraph 11.15 it is preferable to make CLTs before the PETs. This is to ensure that the £3,000 (or possibly £6,000) annual exemption applies against the earlier CLTs and not the later PETs. This ensures that the exemption is used most effectively.

11.20 Chapter 10 explains the method of calculating the amount of the NRB available to offset against a particular transfer. *Inter alia*, this involves identifying transfers (ie CLTs and failed PETs) made in the immediately preceding seven years. For simplicity, no account is taken in that chapter of any exemptions (and/or reliefs) which might apply (see paragraph 10.20). However, account of such exemptions (and/or reliefs) does need to be taken when ascertaining any charge to IHT on such transfers.

Example 3

Tom Sock makes lifetime transfers of £500,000 to his discretionary trust in the tax year 2009–2010 and £400,000 in the tax year 2010–2011.

Tom has made no earlier lifetime gifts.

Inheritance tax: exemptions and reliefs **11.24**

The CLT in 2009–2010 is £494,000 (ie £500,000 –£6,000) and in 2010–2011 £397,000 (ie £400,000 –£3,000).

The IHT liability on the 2009–2010 CLT (NRB of £325,000) is:

0% × £325,000 + 20% × (£494,000 –£325,000) = £33,800

The NRB available for the CLT in 2010–2011 is zero as the CLT in 2009–2010 utilises all of it.

The IHT liability is therefore:

20% × £397,000 = £79 400.

(It is assumed that the trustees agree to pay the IHT charges on the transfers ie no grossing up necessary).

Small gifts exemption

11.21 A transfer made by an individual of no more than £250 per donee (ie recipient) per tax year is exempt irrespective of how many such transfers are effected in a tax year (so long as the donees are not the same; *IHTA 1984 s 20*). The transfer must be an outright transfer (ie not a transfer into trust; *IHTA 1984 s 20*) and not a GWR (*FA 1986 s 102*).

11.22 Unlike the annual exemption (see paragraph 11.14 above) the small gifts exemption cannot form part of a larger transfer.

Normal expenditure out of income exemption

11.23 This exemption is probably one of the most underutilised yet highly effective exemptions. It applies if three conditions are satisfied:

- it is made as part of the normal (ie habitual) expenditure of the donor;
- it is made out of income taking one year with another; and
- after allowing for such transfers the donor is left with sufficient income to maintain his usual standard of living.

11.24 There is no monetary ceiling to the exemption and the amount of any transfer which may qualify under this exemption varies from individual to individual as its application depends upon the facts relating to the specific individual (ie what may be 'normal' expenditure for one individual may not be

11.25 *Inheritance tax: exemptions and reliefs*

so for another). In essence, the greater the level of annual income of an individual the greater the potential, other things being equal, for larger annual gifts to be made which would fall under this exemption.

11.25 'One-off' payments do not qualify; a pattern of giving needs to be established although the exact amount given need not be fixed (eg could be arrived at by formula such as x% of net income). The exemption does not require that the recipient be the same.

11.26 The term 'income' in the phrase 'normal expenditure out of income' refers to income arrived at using normal accountancy principles (not the tax rules) although is income after the deduction of, *inter alia*, any income tax liabilities. In practice it appears that transfers amounting to no more than one third of net income are generally acceptable as falling within the exemption.

For the purpose of this exemption (ie where calculating an individual's income) the 5% pa withdrawals under the single premium bond form of investment (see paragraph 19.61) are not regarded as income; the 5% withdrawals are partial surrenders representing a return of capital (ie a partial return of the original single premium). Similarly, the capital element of a purchased life annuity is not accepted as income for the purposes of the exemption.

11.27 A typical example of the use of the exemption is its application to payments of insurance premiums on a policy effected by the individual on his own life; such policy of insurance may be settled on trust (so as to ensure that on the death of the settlor the policy proceeds do not from part of his estate for IHT purposes) with the policy proceeds being used to discharge any IHT liability arising on the settlor's death.

In any event the annual exemption (see paragraph 11.12) applies to the premium payments should the normal expenditure out of income exemption prove inapplicable.

11.28 So long as the three conditions listed in paragraph 11.23 are satisfied this exemption offers the wealthy individual an excellent IHT-free route to reduce their estate by gifting significantly large sums of cash each year. However, an individual who possesses large tracts of real estate but with limited income is unlikely to find this exemption of much use as the exemption only applies to expenditure out of *income* not capital.

The exemption applies not only to gifts to other individuals but also to gifts into trust.

Gifts in contemplation of marriage exemption

11.29 Transfers made by one individual in respect of any one marriage are exempt if given in contemplation of marriage. This generally means that the gift needs to be made ideally before the marriage or, possibly, contemporaneously with it. The gift should also ideally be evidenced in some form; an accompanying letter confirming the fact that it is being made conditional on marriage is sufficient.

11.30 If the marriage does not in fact proceed the donor should recover the transfer but any unrecovered transfer constitutes a PET.

11.31 The quantum of any permitted transfer varies according to the relationship between donor and donee. The limits are as follows:

- the first £5,000 of any transfer by a parent of either party to the marriage;
- the first £2,500 by one party to the marriage to the other or by a grandparent or remoter ancestor; and
- the first £1,000 in any other case (eg a gift by a sibling or friend).

11.32 The above limits are per marriage not per donor/donee. Thus, for example, a parent of one of the parties to the marriage may give their son (or daughter) up to £5,000 which qualifies as exempt.

If more than one gift is made by the same individual in respect of the same marriage the exemption is applied pro rata to each gift according to their respective values.

11.33 The exemption applies not only to outright gifts from one individual to another individual (who is a party to the marriage) but also to gifts into trust where the trust is primarily for the parties to the marriage and their issue (and the spouses of their issue).

Dispositions for family maintenance exemption

11.34 Strictly speaking, this 'exemption' is not an exemption; dispositions for family maintenance are not treated as transfers of value (in which case no IHT charge arises in any event). Such dispositions are primarily made to the donor's family. Thus a disposition is not a transfer of value if it is made:

- by one party to a marriage in favour of the other party to the marriage (including a former spouse) for maintenance purposes;
- by one party to the marriage in favour of a child (includes adopted child, step-child and illegitimate child) of either party for the maintenance, education or training of the child and made up to the later of the child attaining age eighteen or ceasing full-time education; or

11.35 *Inheritance tax: exemptions and reliefs*

- in favour of a dependent relative (ie a relative of the donor or donor's spouse who is incapacitated by old age or infirmity from maintaining himself/herself) which constitutes reasonable provision for care or maintenance.

11.35 This exemption is particularly important as it permits, for example, the parent of a child to educate the child by way of exempt expenditure. Note that the exemption does not cover transfers for the maintenance of other persons' children.

11.36 Transfers effected on the occasion of the dissolution or annulment of a marriage (ie following a decree absolute) fall within this exemption.

11.37 Transfers between spouses, one of whom is UK domiciled and the other who is non-UK domiciled, are also protected under this 'exemption'; such inter-spouse transfers are subject to a £55,000 exemption limit (ie the general inter-spouse exemption is inapplicable; *IHTA 1984 s 18*; see paragraph 11.42).

11.38 In principle, transfers into trust do not appear to be precluded under this 'exemption' but transfers on death are not accepted by HMRC as falling to be treated as dispositions for family maintenance.

Exempt transfers: death only

11.39 Transfers exempt only on death are limited to foreign currency bank accounts of individuals who on death are non-UK domiciled, non-UK resident and non-UK ordinarily resident and payments following death on active service against an enemy (*IHTA 1984 s 157*).

Exempt transfers: in lifetime and on death

11.40 The exemption of most importance available in lifetime and on death is the inter-spouse exemption (*IHTA 1984 s 18*).

11.41 Other such exemptions include:

- gifts to UK registered charities (ie foreign charities are excluded) (*IHTA 1984 s 23*); but gifts made on or after 6 April 2010 to EU organisations equivalent to a UK charity are also exempt (*FA 2010 s 30*; see paragraph 28.56);

- gifts to 'qualifying' political parties (*IHTA 1984 s 24*); and

- gifts for national purposes (eg gifts made to The National Gallery; British Museum; English Nature) (*IHTA 1984 s 25*)

Inter-spouse transfers

11.42 All (subject to one exception; see below) inter-spouse transfers are exempt irrespective of timing and/or amount if at the date of transfer the spouses are married (ie no decree absolute issued). It is not necessary (as is required for exempt inter-spouse transfers for CGT purposes; see paragraph 8.33) for the spouses to be living together (ie they could thus be separated albeit not divorced).

The one exception to the exemption above is where a *UK domiciled* spouse effects transfers to a *non-UK domiciled* spouse. In this case there is a £55,000 cumulative exemption limit (*IHTA 1984 s 18*; although note that this amount is increased under the UK/Switzerland (*SI 1994/3214*) and UK/USA (*SI 1979/1454*) IHT conventions (see paragraph 26.39). Thus, only the first £55,000 of transfers is exempt and any lifetime transfers in excess of this amount constitute PETs. For the tax year 2010–2011 transfers up to £380,000 (ie £55,000 exempt plus £325,000 at the nil rate) in aggregate are transferable without IHT charge.

11.43 Inter-spouse transfers between two UK *or* two non-UK domiciled spouses *or* from one non-UK domiciled spouse to the UK domiciled spouse are not subject to the £55,000 limit.

Inter-spouse transferable NRB

11.44 The Pre-Budget Report of 9 October 2007 contained proposals (introduced in *FA 2008 s 10*; now contained in *IHTA 1984 ss 8A to 8C*) under which in principle the unutilised part of the NRB on the death of the first spouse was to be transferable to the surviving spouse. As a consequence, where one or both spouse deaths occur on or after 9 October 2007 transferability of the NRB is now possible. However, no such transfer is possible where both spouse deaths occur prior to 9 October 2007.

11.45 One of the main consequences of the introduction of the transferable NRB is the removal of the need for spouses to 'equalise' their respective estates; 'equalisation' in this context means to ensure that the estate of each spouse is at least equal to the NRB. Unless each spouse's estate is at least equal to the NRB the aggregate IHT charge arising on both estates following death is greater than it otherwise would be due to a wastage of a proportion of the NRB (on the part of the spouse whose estate falls below it).

Example 4

Bob and Jackie Fraser are married with three children. Bob and Jackie are each UK domiciled.

11.45 *Inheritance tax: exemptions and reliefs*

Bob's estate is worth £600,000. Jackie's estate is worth £50,000. They want their children to benefit from their joint estates.

Option 1 (no equalisation of estates)

Bob and Jackie's wills leave their respective estates to each other failing which to their children.

Assuming Bob dies first, his £600,000 estate passes to Jackie under his will inheritance free due to the inter-spouse exemption (which applies in lifetime and on death).

On Jackie's death (in tax year 2010–2011) her £650,000 estate passes to the children subject to an IHT charge of:

0% x £325,000 + 40% x [£650,000 – £325,000] = £130,000

Even if Jackie is the first to die the IHT consequences are the same.

If in their respective wills each gift their estate to the children the IHT position is as follows:

On Bob's death IHT is:

0% x £325,000 + 40% x [£600,000 – £325,000]

ie £110,000.

On Jackie's death no IHT arises.

Option 2 (equalisation of estates)

Due to the imbalance of the respective estates Bob transfers in lifetime by way of exempt inter-spouse transfer £275,000. Bob and Jackie's estates are now each worth £325,000 (ie the estates have been literally equalised).

Under their respective wills they each leave their estate to the children.

On Bob's death the IHT liability is 0% on £325,000 (ie nil).

On Jackie's death the IHT liability is 0% on £325,000 (ie nil).

Compare Options 1 and 2

A comparison of the two options shows that under Option 2 there is a saving of either £130,000 or £110,000 of IHT depending upon the precise nature of the wills.

Inheritance tax: exemptions and reliefs **11.49**

In effect Option 2 ensures that each of Bob and Jackie take advantage of their respective NRBs. Under Option 1, either Jackie or Bob fail to utilise their NRB.

11.46 On the death of the first spouse it is not necessary, in order to utilise their NRB, that their estate should be left absolutely to the children. The same objective (ie utilisation of the NRB) is also achieved if, for example, the estate is left on discretionary trust for the children and surviving spouse. This option may be particularly attractive where the children are young and/or the surviving spouse may require further financial support at some point in the future.

11.47 Equalisation of estates not only minimises the risk of a loss of a NRB it also enables each spouse to maximise their use of the various lifetime exemptions and reliefs. Thus, for example, it enables each spouse to gift £3,000 as annual exempt transfers; £5,000 in the event of a son or daughter getting married; etc.

Post-8 October 2007

11.48 The transferable NRB operates by permitting the percentage of the NRB unused on the death of the first spouse to be applied to the NRB applicable on the death of the second spouse which is then added to the surviving spouse's own NRB. It is not a transfer of an absolute amount but a percentage of the NRB which is unutilised; the transfer is thus between 0% and 100%.

11.49 The transfer is not automatic. It is necessary for a claim to be lodged by the executors of the will of the surviving spouse on his/her death. The claim must be lodged within two years of the end of month in which the surviving spouse dies and must be accompanied by various documentation (eg death certificate of the first spouse to die; marriage certificate; etc). The claim itself is made on Form IHT 402 (formerly Form IHT 216) and is typically lodged at the same time the Form IHT 400 is lodged with HMRC (see Chapter 14).

Example 5

Using the facts of Example 4 assuming each spouse leaves their respective estate to their surviving spouse failing which to the children. Assume Bob dies in June 2008 and Jackie dies in July 2010.

On Bob's death his £600,000 estate passes to Jackie under his will IHT free due to the inter-spouse exemption (which applies in lifetime and on

11.50 *Inheritance tax: exemptions and reliefs*

death). Thus, none of Bob's NRB is utilised (ie 100% of Bob's NRB is unutilised).

On Jackie's death the £650,000 estate passes to the children.

However, at the date of Jackie's death she is entitled to her own NRB (£325,000 for tax year 2010–2011) plus the percentage of Bob's NRB which is unutilised but applied to the NRB applicable on her (ie not his) death.

Jackie's NRB is thus equal to:

£325,000 + 100% x £325,000 = £650,000

(in essence Jackie becomes entitled to twice her own NRB; the fact that the NRB on Bob's death was £312,000 is irrelevant).

On leaving the £650,000 estate to her children under her will no IHT charge arises despite the fact that there was no equalisation of estates; the transferability of the NRB overcomes this problem.

Example 6

Mary dies on 15 May 2007 and her husband, Dick, dies on 9 August 2011.

The NRB in the tax year Mary dies is £300,000 and in the tax year Dick dies the NRB is £325,000.

On Mary's death 25% of her estate went to her children and 75% to Dick. Thus, 75% of her NRB is not utilised.

On Dick's death his NRB is equal to:

75% x £325,000 + £325,000 = £568,750.

11.50 As historically NRBs have increased tax year on tax year (or at least not reduced) the introduction of the transferable NRB is an extremely attractive and useful change, at least for married couples.

11.51 Although the unused percentage of the NRB of the first spouse to die can be transferred to the surviving spouse on the latter's death the calculation must take into account any gifts made by the first spouse to die within seven years before death. This is because such gifts 'eat' into the NRB on death (see paragraph 10.81) thus reducing the percentage otherwise unused.

Example 7

Mary dies on 15 May 2007 and her husband, Dick, dies on 9 May 2011. Mary leaves everything by will to Dick.

On her death Mary's estate amounts to £250,000 and within the seven years prior to her death Mary makes a PET of £80,000 and a CLT of £100,000. Both of these gifts utilise £180,000 of the £300,000 NRB available on Mary's death.

Thus, £120,000 of the £300,000 NRB remains unutilised on her death (ie 40%).

On Dick's death his NRB will equal:

40% x £325,000 + £325,000 = £455,000.

11.52 The maximum NRB for any surviving spouse is twice that applicable on the second death. This limit is necessary to prevent those individuals who, for example, survive two marriages claiming two NRBs (one from each deceased spouse) in addition to their own NRB.

Example 8

Cindy Purple is married to Jack Purple.

Jack Purple dies on 4 December 2008 leaving his whole estate to Cindy (ie utilising none of his NRB).

Cindy subsequently marries Nicholas Green on 7 July 2009.

Nicholas dies on 10 April 2010 leaving his whole estate to Cindy (ie utilising none of his NRB).

Cindy dies on 11 October 2010.

On Cindy's death a transfer of 100% of Jack's NRB plus 100% of Nicholas's NRB is in principle available to Cindy on her death in addition to her own NRB.

However, this gives Cindy three times the NRB (ie her own NRB plus that of each of Jack and Nicholas).

In such cases Cindy's aggregate NRB is restricted to twice that available on her death ie [2 x £325,000].

11.53 *Inheritance tax: exemptions and reliefs*

If Cindy marries Harry Blue on 8 September 2010 Cindy should ensure that she only leaves that part of her estate to Harry which exceeds two NRBs (as this is the amount of NRB to which she is entitled following her two earlier marriages).

Harry, on the other hand, should ensure that he utilises his NRB and thus should only leave Cindy that part of his estate in excess of the NRB.

11.53 It will be noted in Example 8 that despite three deaths (ie Jack Nicholas and Cindy only two NRBs are actually utilised ie one NRB appears to be wasted). There is a possible solution to this.

Example 9

Cindy Purple is married to Jack Purple.

Jack Purple dies on 4 December 2008. Instead of leaving his whole estate to Cindy (ie utilising none of his NRB) he leaves the amount of the NRB applicable on his death (ie £312,000) to a discretionary trust set up under his will thus utilising his NRB in full; Cindy is included as one of the beneficiaries of the trust and thus can benefit therefrom.

Cindy marries Nicholas Green on 7 July 2009.

Nicholas dies on 10 April 2010 leaving his whole estate to Cindy (ie utilising none of his NRB).

Cindy dies on 11 October 2010.

Cindy's NRB is increased by 100% due to the unutilised NRB of Nicholas.

Thus, in total three NRBs have in fact been utilised.

11.54 The introduction of the transferable NRB is likely to bring about a reduction in the use of NRB discretionary trusts in the wills of spouses which were, pre-9 October 2007, utilised to ensure that on the death of each spouse their respective NRB is fully utilised. Nevertheless the NRB discretionary trust is still a useful planning device. For example, where an individual marries for the second time he/she may wish that following their death any children from the first marriage inherit some (or all) of their estate; however, at the same time adequate provision needs to be made for the surviving spouse of the second marriage. The discretionary trust achieves these twin objectives whereas

Inheritance tax: exemptions and reliefs **11.58**

leaving the estate absolutely to the surviving spouse of the second marriage may not (eg the surviving spouse leaves the estate to her brother or new husband but not the children from the deceased spouse's first marriage).

11.55 Despite the attractiveness of the transferable NRB it is not available to all; it is only available to married couples (whether living together or not; *IHTA 1984 s 8A*) and then only where one or both spouses die on or after 9 October 2007. It is, as a consequence, of no application to:

- cohabitees, even if living as husband and wife (contrast the applicability of the new 'remittance' rules which do apply to such cohabitees; *ITA 2007 s 809M* ; see paragraphs 24.50 and 24.51);
- former spouses or divorcees (although it does apply to married but separated spouses); and
- single individuals.

11.56 Prior to the introduction of IHT, effective 18 March 1986, between 13 March 1975 and 18 March 1986 capital transfer tax applied under whose provisions exempt inter-spouse transfers was also possible. Before 13 March 1975 (when estate duty applied) exempt inter-spouse transfers could not be made until 21 March 1972 (but limited to transfers up to £15,000).

Thus, where the death of the first spouse to die occurs between 21 March 1972 and 13 March 1975 a claim to transfer the NRB to the surviving spouse is based on the amount of the tax-free band which is unused (ie which will occur if the £15,000 is exhausted). For deaths pre-21 March 1972 the transfer of the NRB is also based on the amount of the tax-free band which is unused (although for this period exempt inter-spouse transfers were not possible).

11.57 For the UK and non-UK domiciled spouse, if the former dies first the £55,000 restriction (*IHTA 1984 s 16*) means that, other things being equal, it is less likely that any NRB remains unutilised (because over £55,000 inter-spouse transfers on death (or in lifetime) are subject to IHT at the 0% rate thus eating into the deceased's NRB).

Ordering of exemptions

11.58 More than one exemption may apply to a particular transfer. There appear to be no rules as to the priority given to each exemption. Perhaps the 'best' approach is, where possible, to seek to ensure that a general transfer (ie a transfer not falling within an obviously specific exemption eg transfers on marriage) falls within the 'normal expenditure out of income' exemption, failing which the annual exemption.

11.59 Where more than one transfer is made in a tax year the relevant exemption is applied to the earlier transfers first. If more than one transfer has been made on the same day then the relevant exemption(s) are pro-rated.

Example 10

Charles Royal makes CLTs on 5 July, 10 September and 17 December in the tax year 2010–2011 of £2,000, £8,000 and £9,000, respectively. No transfers have previously been made by Charles.

Assuming the only applicable exemption is the annual exemption; £3,000 is carried forward from 2009–2010 to add to the £3,000 2010–2011 annual exemption making £6,000.

Applying the £6,000 against the earliest transfer first, ie the £2,000 of 5 July reduces this to nil; the unused balance of £4,000 is offset against the £8,000 of 10 September reducing it to £4,000.

Example 11

Betty Noon has a high net annual income and has for a number of tax years made transfers each tax year, amounting to £15,000 per tax year to one of her discretionary trusts.

In the tax year 2010–2011 HMRC accept that only £12,000 of the £15,000 for that tax year qualifies under the 'normal expenditure out of income' exemption.

Betty is able to utilise her £3,000 annual exemption for 2010–2011 to offset against the balancing £3,000 of the £15,000 thus reducing the chargeable amount to nil.

Reliefs

11.60 Each of three forms of relief are now considered. Two are of particular importance, namely:

- BPR (*IHTA 1984 s 104*); and
- APR (*IHTA 1984 s 116*).

Both reliefs apply to lifetime transfers and on death.

Inheritance tax: exemptions and reliefs **11.64**

The third form of relief is quick succession relief (QSR) (*IHTA 1984 s 141*) which applies only on death.

Business property relief and agricultural property relief: general comments

11.61 The importance of BPR and APR lies in the extent of the reliefs. In the case of BPR the relief is either 50% or 100% *of the value of the business property* transferred; similarly in the case of APR, the relief is either 50% or 100% *of the agricultural value of the agricultural property* transferred.

Clearly, if 100% BPR applies to a transfer of business property effectively the transfer is not subject to IHT. However, where 100% APR applies it is only applicable to the 'agricultural value' of the transfer, not the total value of the transfer and thus even in such cases an IHT charge may still arise; however, BPR may then apply to the excess value transferred not covered by APR.

11.62 Prior to 22 April 2009 APR (unlike BPR) only extended to property located in the UK, Channel Islands or the Isle of Man. With respect to transfers where IHT would have been payable on or after 22 April 2009 APR extends to property located in any EEA state (*IA 1978 Sch 1*). The extension also has effect for earlier transfers where IHT in respect of that transfer was due or paid on or after 23 April 2003 (*FA 2009 s 122*).

BPR, on the other hand, is not restricted in this manner.

Business property relief

11.63 Despite BPR applying to transfers of 'relevant business property' (*IHTA 1984 s 104*) the term 'business' is not explicitly defined in the legislation although certain businesses are explicitly excluded from qualifying for BPR.

11.64 Relevant business property is defined exhaustively as follows and qualifies for relief at the percentage shown (*IHTA 1984 s 105*):

- property consisting of a business or interest in a business (eg sole trader, share in a partnership): 100%;
- any unquoted shares in a company which are not listed on a recognised stock exchange (shares dealt in on the Alternative Investment Market (AIM), USM or OFFEX are all regarded as unquoted): 100%;
- unquoted securities in a company owned by the transferor which together with other such securities and/or unquoted shares so owned give the transferor 'control' of the company immediately before the transfer ('control', broadly, meaning voting control):100%

11.65 *Inheritance tax: exemptions and reliefs*

- shares (or securities) giving 'control' of a quoted company immediately before the transfer: 50%;
- land, buildings, machinery or plant used wholly or mainly for the purposes of a business carried on by a company controlled by the transferor or by a partnership of which the transferor is a partner: 50%; and
- land, buildings, machinery or plant used wholly or mainly for the purposes of a business carried on by the transferor which is settled property and in which the transferor had an interest in possession (it is *not* necessary for the 'interest in possession' to be a '*qualifying* interest in possession'): 50%

11.65 In the case of property consisting of a business or an interest in a business it is the *net* value of the business which is important (*IHTA 1984 s 110*). The net value is the total value of assets used in the business (including goodwill) less the aggregate amount of any liabilities incurred for the purposes of the business.

Liabilities are deductible only if they have been *incurred for the purposes of the business* which does not necessarily require that any such liabilities are secured against the business assets (however, a liability incurred to acquire a business is not deductible).

Example 12

Gerry Tincan owns all the shares in the unquoted family trading company.

The net value of the business is £1 million which is arrived at after deducting liabilities of £500,000 as they have been incurred for the purposes of the business.

It is irrelevant to the deductibility issue whether the liabilities are secured or not and whether, where secured, they are secured against assets of the business. Thus, even if the company's liabilities are secured against Gerry's home (ie not the company's assets) the debt is still deductible in arriving at the company's net value for BPR purposes.

Example 13

Katie Small decides that she would like to run a business selling women's clothes.

She is told of a sole trader business which is for sale and decides to buy it.

Her own funds are insufficient to effect the purchase so she borrows the balance from her local bank and secures the borrowing against her home.

The borrowing from the bank is not a deductible liability for ascertaining the net value of Katie's sole trader business for BPR purposes.

The borrowing is used to acquire the business and thus has not been incurred for the purposes of the business.

Example 14

Simon Grass died and at the date of his death he owns beneficially:

Cash at bank	£100,000
Listed UK equities in ABC Plc	£50,000
Unquoted shares in XYZ Ltd	£75,000
House	£600,000

He does not 'control' ABC Plc and thus the shares in the company do not qualify for BPR. The shares in XYZ Ltd, however, do qualify for BPR.

Simon's estate on death is thus:

Cash at bank		£100,000
Listed UK equities in ABC Plc		£50,000
Unquoted shares in XYZ Ltd	£75,000	
less: BPR (100%)	(£75,000)	
		Nil
House		£600,000
Estate on death		£750,000

If instead of the shareholding in XYZ Ltd, Simon had owned a factory worth £75,000 which had been used wholly for business purposes by a company over which Simon had control then on his death BPR would be available on the factory but at the rate of 50% and thus £37,500 would have been included in his estate on death.

11.66 BPR does not apply to certain businesses (or interests therein) or shares in a company if the business or the company's business consists *wholly or mainly* of one or more of the following (*IHTA 1984 s 105*):

11.67 *Inheritance tax: exemptions and reliefs*

- dealing in securities, stocks or shares, land or buildings; or
- making or holding investments.

Note, however, that shares in a 'holding' company are not so treated if the business of the holding company consists wholly or mainly in being a holding company of one or more companies whose business does not fall within the above (ie dealing in securities etc or making or holding investments). If any of the companies so held by the holding company do fall within the above, in ascertaining the value of the holding company shares subject to transfer qualifying for BPR the value of the relevant company(ies) are excluded in the holding company share valuation (*IHTA 1984 s 111*).

11.67 With respect to the phrase 'wholly or mainly', HMRC have indicated that 'mainly' means more than 50% and that any determination involves examining the business or the company's activities in totality and over a reasonable period of time prior to the transfer. Factors to consider include:

- the overall context of the business;
- the capital employed ie the value of the assets employed in the trading and investment sides of the business;
- the time spent by the directors and employees;
- how turnover is split between trading and investment elements; and
- the amount of profit derived from the investment and non-investment sides of the business.

11.68 Thus, even where a company is a trading company the shares therein may fail to qualify for BPR if at the same time the company is active in, say, property dealing with the latter activity being the dominant activity. If, however, the property dealing is, for example, a much smaller undertaking in the overall context of the company's trading activities BPR will be available without reduction.

It is perhaps worth noting that although property dealing and property investment are unacceptable businesses (ie cannot, per se, constitute relevant business property) property development would not seem to be 'caught'. The latter activity normally involves the acquisition of land and some form of building thereon prior to sale whereas property dealing is simply the buying and selling of land and property investment the acquisition of land whose sole or main purposes is the generation of passive income (eg rents) therefrom.

Individuals involved in the 'buy to let' business are unlikely to obtain any BPR. However, a furnished holiday letting business qualifies for BPR.

11.69 Corporate group structures may fall foul of the 'wholly or mainly' requirement (see paragraph 11.66). For example, where a company undertakes a trading activity but is also involved in a minor way of letting out properties BPR is available on the company's shares as the company is not wholly or mainly involved in any of the restricted activities (see paragraph 11.66). If, on the other hand, the company carries on the same trading activity but sets up a wholly-owned subsidiary to carry on the letting activity BPR on the shares in the former company is restricted (ie the value of the shares in the former company qualifying for BPR is the value ignoring the latter company; *IHTA 1984 s 111*).

Excepted assets

11.70 The value of relevant business property excludes any value attributable to 'excepted assets' (*IHTA 1984 s 112*). An excepted asset is an asset which has neither been used wholly or mainly for the purposes of the business throughout the whole of the last two years of the period immediately preceding the transfer nor is required at the time of the transfer for future use in the business. It is specifically provided (*IHTA 1984 s 112*) that an asset is regarded as not satisfying the above wholly or mainly condition if it has been used wholly or mainly for the personal benefit of the transferor (or a person 'connected' with him; *IHTA 1984 s 270*).

11.71 A classic example of an excepted asset is that of 'surplus' cash held by a trading company. If the cash has been held for sometime with little likelihood of it being required for use within the company in the foreseeable future excepted asset treatment is likely; as a broad brush, if the cash amounts to 25% or more of the company's turnover this may be unacceptable.

11.72 Where the relevant business property is shares, the proportion of the value of the shares which qualifies for BPR, where excepted assets subsist within the company, is determined as follows:

$$\text{Value of shares} \times \frac{\text{Company's eligible business property}}{\text{Company's total assets (before deducting liabilities)}}$$

Example 15

Natalie Shoe dies leaving an estate of £500,000. Comprised in the estate is a shareholding of 100% in an unquoted trading company, DEF Ltd, worth £150,000.

All the conditions for BPR are satisfied with respect to the shareholding in DEF Ltd.

11.73 *Inheritance tax: exemptions and reliefs*

However, the assets of DEF Ltd totalling £360,000 include a cash deposit of £120,000 which cannot be said to have been used in, or needed for, the company's business (ie it is an excepted asset).

The BPR available on her death with respect to the shareholding in DEF Ltd is:

BPR = [£150,000 x [£240,000/£360,000]] x 100% = £100,000

Thus, £50,000 (ie £150,000 – £100,000) of the value of Natalie's shareholding in DEF Ltd is included as part of her estate and thus subject to IHT.

Ownership condition

11.73 For BPR to apply requires not only that the property is relevant business property but that at the date of the transfer the property has been owned for a minimum period of two years (IHTA 1984 s 106). There is no taper relief-type adjustment to BPR for periods of ownership of less than two years; it is thus in this sense an all or nothing relief.

The two-year ownership requirement does not mean, however, that a particular asset has to itself have qualified as relevant business property for a minimum period of two years where the transfer is of a business, interest in a business or shares in a company (although, of course, the property must constitute relevant business property). This may permit, for example, shares held for at least two years in an unquoted investment company (which do not qualify as relevant business property) to qualify as relevant business property shortly after conversion of the company's activities from that of an investment activity to that of a qualifying trade. This may enable an individual who, for example, has been diagnosed with a terminal illness to relatively quickly convert non-relevant business property shares into relevant business property shares.

Example 16

At her death, Helen Brass has owned 50% of the shares in the family unquoted trading company for one year and eleven months exactly.

No BPR is available to reduce the value of the shares on her death.

Example 17

At her death Sheila Brass, Helen's sister (from Example 16), owns the other 50% of the family unquoted trading company which she has owned for just a little over two years.

BPR is available to reduce the value of the shares on her death.

Inheritance tax: exemptions and reliefs **11.75**

Example 18

Bert Blue has owned a shop for many years and has during this period carried on his sole tradership as a confectioner from the shop. Due to growth in his business Bert purchases a larger shop from which to carry on the business and moves into it.

Bert dies one year later.

BPR is available with respect to Bert's sole tradership business (including the shop) which is the relevant business property. Although the shop has not itself been held for two years this is not necessary; all that is required is that at the date of transfer (ie Bert's death) the sole tradership business qualified as relevant business property and has been owned (which it has) for at least two years.

11.74 In the case of land or buildings, machinery or plant used wholly or mainly for the purposes of a business carried on by a company of which the transferor has control or by a partnership of which he is a partner it is necessary for such assets to have been owned for at least two years immediately preceding the transfer as in this case BPR applies to that particular asset which comprises the relevant business property (*IHTA 1984 s 112*).

11.75 Where property has been replaced with other property and the original property and the replacement property together have been held for a period(s) which in aggregate total at least two years out of the last five years then the minimum two-year condition (see paragraph 11.73) is regarded as having been satisfied.

Example 19

Trevor Thatch is a cobbler and has been in practice as a sole trader for ten years.

Following advice from his accountant he incorporates his business (ie transfers his sole trader business to the company in exchange for an issue of shares) and now owns all the shares in his trading company (which is unquoted).

Unfortunately, one year later Tom dies thus having held the shares (ie the relevant business property) for only one year.

In ascertaining if BPR is available on the shares the period of ownership of the shares may take into account the period of ownership of the sole

11.76 *Inheritance tax: exemptions and reliefs*

tradership as the shares in the company constitute replacement property of the sole tradership.

As Tom has held the shares and the sole tradership business for at least two out of the previous five years prior to the transfer (ie on his death) BPR is available on his death.

11.76 With respect to relevant business property which comprises a shareholding in a listed company BPR applies only if the transferor has 'control' (broadly, more than 50% of the voting capital) of the company. However, while the ownership requirement demands that the transferor has owned the relevant business property being transferred for a minimum period of two years it is not necessary for the transferor to have had 'control' (*IHTA 1984 s 269*) for this two-year period. 'Control' at the date of transfer is sufficient.

Example 20

Jane Smythe has owned 48% of the shares in ABC Ltd, a listed trading company, for six years.

She has just died but six months before she died she managed to acquire an additional 5% of the shares in ABC Ltd, making her total shareholding at death 53% (ie control).

BPR (at 50%) is available on her death on the 48% shareholding (which has been owned for at least two years) because she has 'control' of ABC Ltd at the date of her death.

The balancing 5%, which has not been owned at her death for the two-year minimum period, will not be subject to any BPR.

Example 21

Tom and Dick each own 40% of a listed trading company XYZ Plc. They have each owned their shares for in excess of ten years.

The balancing 20% is owned by members of the public.

Following a buy-back of shares eighteen months ago (which results in the cancellation of shares bought back and the consequence that the issued share capital of the company is accordingly reduced) Tom finds that he owns 55% of the company's reduced issued share capital.

On Tom's death (even if within the two years since Tom acquired control of XYZ Plc) BPR is available on his whole shareholding as he possesses control of the company at the date of his death and he has owned his shares for more than two years (the buy-back did not affect Dick's shareholding).

Inter-spouse and family transfers

11.77 Usually inter-spouse transfers are treated the same for IHT purposes whether the transfers are effected in lifetime or on death; and usually no adverse tax consequences arise due to inter-spouse relief.

With respect to BPR this is not always the case.

11.78 The transfer on *death* of relevant business property from one spouse to the other permits the surviving spouse to aggregate the period of ownership of the deceased with that of the surviving spouse with respect to future transfers by the latter (*IHTA 1984 s 108*).

However, other things being equal, it is arguably inappropriate for relevant business property to be left by will to a surviving spouse. Inter-spouse transfers on death are in any event exempt and thus any BPR (whether 50% or 100%) is thus effectively wasted; relevant business property eligible for BPR should ideally be left to chargeable beneficiaries on death (eg the children or on trust).

Example 22

On Susan Billings' death her estate comprises £500,000 of which £300,000 relates to her shareholding in an unlisted trading company which qualifies for BPR.

In her will she leaves the shares to her husband.

The shares are thus not subject to IHT as they have been left to her husband which is an exempt inter-spouse transfer; thus the 100% BPR is effectively wasted.

If instead Susan leaves the shares to her son, BPR is not wasted (ie no IHT is charged on the shares due to the 100% BPR) and the balance of her estate, if left to her husband, is exempt from IHT.

It is therefore important, where possible, for business property qualifying for BPR to be left by will (or gifted in lifetime) to chargeable beneficiaries

11.79 *Inheritance tax: exemptions and reliefs*

(ie where an IHT charge arises) and not to be the subject of an inter-spouse transfer.

11.79 The aggregation of periods of ownership is *not*, however, applicable in the case of *lifetime* inter-spouse transfers of relevant business property (*IHTA 1984 s 108*). Thus, where relevant business property is transferred inter-spouse during their lifetime, the recipient spouse is required to satisfy the two-year condition if the relevant business property treatment is required on any subsequent transfer by the recipient spouse (whether in lifetime or on death).

11.80 The aggregation of periods of ownership only applies to *inter-spouse* transfers on death; transfers effected on death (or indeed in lifetime) between other family members do not qualify (eg from father to son or brother to brother). This 'danger' is often overlooked.

Example 23

Hector Revenue and his wife, Abigail, have been married for many years and have a son, Harold, aged 32.

After leaving the service of HMRC, Hector decides to set himself up as a sole trader manufacturing and selling curtains. Due to growth in the business, after five years Hector introduces his wife into the business as a full partner; henceforth, the business operates as a partnership.

Fifteen months later Abigail dies leaving her interest in the partnership to their son, Harold.

No BPR is available on Abigail's death as she has owned her interest in the partnership (albeit relevant business property) for less than two years; she is not able to include as part of her ownership period that of her husband Hector.

Example 24

In Example 23 assume instead that Hector operates as a sole trader for five years until his death and by will leaves the whole of the business to Abigail.

Abigail dies 15 months after Hector's death leaving the business to their son Harold.

BPR is available on Abigail's death as she is deemed to have owned the business for the actual period of ownership (ie 15 months) plus the five-year period of ownership by Hector.

11.81 A not uncommon situation in this regard is that of a father who owns 100% of the shares in the family company (an unquoted trading company) which he has built up over many years. In an attempt to 'enfranchise" his son and daughter, who both work full time in the business, their father transfers 40% of his shares to the two children (20% to each). Although perhaps unlikely, should either of the children die within two years of receiving their shares, BPR is not available with respect to their respective shareholding (the two-year minimum ownership condition not having been satisfied); 100% BPR is thus lost.

However, if the father simply retains ownership of 100% of the company and leaves his shareholding (or a percentage thereof) to the children on his death by will, BPR at 100% applies to the whole shareholding on his death (in addition, for capital gains tax (CGT) purposes the tax-free uplift on death applies; see paragraph 8.40).

There is thus, in such circumstances, a possible conflict between tax efficiency and the intangible benefit of 'enfranchisement'.

BPR and death within seven years of a lifetime transfer

11.82 A lifetime transfer of relevant business property is either a PET or a CLT. If the former (ie a PET), and the transferor survives for seven years, no IHT liability arises and whether BPR applies or not to the transfer is academic (albeit, effectively the BPR is wasted).

If the latter (ie a CLT), an immediate IHT liability arises at 20% of the value transferred (subject to the NRB). If BPR applies to the transfer at that time the value transferred is reduced either to nil (if BPR is 100%) or by 50% (if BPR at 50% applies).

11.83 Should the transferor die within seven years of the transfer, be it a PET or CLT, the availability of BPR has to be re-examined. This because in such circumstances *additional* conditions to those discussed earlier in the chapter need to be satisfied (recall that a PET becomes chargeable for the first time if the transferor dies within seven years of making it and a CLT becomes subject to *additional* IHT in these circumstances having already been charged in lifetime; see paragraphs 10.27 and 10.35).

The additional conditions which need to be satisfied on the death of the transferor are twofold (*IHTA 1984 s 113A*):

- the original property must be owned by the transferee throughout the period commencing with the transfer and ending upon the transferor's death; and

11.84 *Inheritance tax: exemptions and reliefs*

- immediately before the death of the transferor the property transferred must qualify as relevant business property on the part of the transferee (ignoring the minimum two-year ownership requirement).

Where the transferee dies before the transferor the above must be satisfied at the date of the transferee's death.

11.84 If both of the above conditions are satisfied at the date of death of the transferor (or transferee if earlier), where the original lifetime transfer is a PET the value of the PET is reduced by the BPR in calculating any IHT charge arising on the PET due to the transferor's death.

If both of the above conditions are satisfied at the date of death of the transferor (or transferee if earlier), where the original lifetime transfer is a CLT the value of the CLT is reduced by the BPR in calculating any *additional* IHT charge arising on the CLT due to the transferor's death.

11.85 Where, however, either or both of the above conditions are not satisfied, if the original lifetime transfer is a PET the IHT charge thereon (if any) is simply computed ignoring any BPR.

Where, however, either or both of the above conditions are not satisfied, if the original lifetime transfer is a CLT the IHT charge which arose at the date of the lifetime transfer (calculated including BPR) remains unchanged but the *additional* IHT charge arising due to death is calculated without the benefit of any BPR.

11.86 It is thus not correct to suggest that BPR on the original CLT is withdrawn if either or both of the conditions stated in paragraph 11.83 are not satisfied. As stated in paragraph 11.85, no change is made to the IHT charge already levied on the lifetime CLT (ie it has been correctly computed on the basis that at that time BPR was applicable) but the *additional* IHT charge arising due to the transferor's death is simply calculated without BPR applying to the lifetime transfer.

11.87 Where the transferee, prior to the transferor's death, replaces all or part of the property transferred with other relevant business property within three years of the date of disposal of the original transferred property utilising all of the sale proceeds from the disposal of the original property transferred the above two conditions are regarded as also being satisfied.

Example 25

Terry Ramsay owns all the ordinary shares in his unquoted trading company, Hardcore Steels Ltd, and has done so since he formed the company ten years ago.

On 2 January 2008 he transfers 10% of the shares to his son valued at £100,000.

On 5 March 2008 Terry settles a further 30% of the shares on a discretionary trust, the beneficiaries of which are his son, daughter and brother valued at £350,000.

On 16 July 2010 Terry dies.

Assume Terry's NRB has been utilised.

Lifetime IHT charges

The gift on 2 January 2008 is a PET and thus no IHT charge arises at that time.

The gift on 5 March 2008 is a CLT and in principle an IHT charge arises at that time. However, BPR of 100% applies and thus the CLT in fact equals [£350,000 – £350,000 (BPR)] (ie nil) and thus no IHT arises.

IHT on lifetime transfers due to Terry's death

Terry's death causes the PET to become chargeable and the CLT to become subject to the additional tax charge.

The IHT charge on the PET is:

Chargeable amount = £100,000 – £100,000 (BPR 100%) (ie nil)

The additional IHT charge on the CLT is:

Chargeable amount = £350,000 – £350,000 (BPR 100%) (ie nil)

Thus, on the assumption that on Terry's death all the requisite conditions are satisfied no additional IHT charges arise.

Suppose, however, that at the date of Terry's death both his son and the trust had each sold their shares without purchasing replacement relevant business property.

As a consequence no BPR is available on Terry's death on either transfer. The IHT due to Terry's death is then as follows:

PET

Chargeable amount = £100,000

IHT charge = £100,000 × 40% = £40,000

(no taper relief applies as death occurs within three years of the PET).

CLT

Chargeable amount = £350,000

Additional IHT charge = [£350,000 × 40% – nil] = £140,000

11.88 *Inheritance tax: exemptions and reliefs*

There is thus now an additional IHT charge on the CLT due to Terry's death with no offsetting lifetime tax credit (as no IHT is paid in lifetime due to BPR). However, the nil IHT charge in lifetime on the CLT remains unchanged.

The £140,000 is the liability of the trustees.

11.88 It is therefore important to ensure that where lifetime transfers of relevant business property occur, which at that time qualify for BPR, that the transferees are made aware of the conditions which need to be satisfied if BPR is to continue to be available thereafter, in particular should the transferor die within seven years of making the transfer. In particular, should any sale of the property be undertaken by the transferee (without replacement qualifying property being purchased), BPR is not available should the transferor die within the seven-year period (or if the property has been sold at the date of the transferee's death if earlier).

Any IHT liability which arises, whether on a PET or CLT due to the death of the transferor (within the seven-year period), is the liability of the *transferee* not the transferor (see paragraphs 10.27 and 10.44).

Ownership splitting problem

11.89 It is not unusual for land and buildings, in particular, to be held beneficially by a major shareholder of an unquoted family trading company which is let to the company for use in its trade. This approach avoids a possible double CGT charge arising on a liquidation of the company or where a sale by the company of its underlying business occurs.

From the perspective of BPR, *prima facie*, no problems arise. The shares in principle qualify for 100% BPR and the land and buildings qualify for 50% BPR.

11.90 Suppose, however, that the father who owns, say, 100% of the company's shares decides to transfer his shareholding as a lifetime transfer to his daughter and son (50/50). He, however, feels that he would like to retain the land and buildings but is happy to continue to let the company use them for its trade as in the past.

Six months later the father unexpectedly dies.

11.91 The share transfers to his son and daughter are PETs which now fall chargeable to IHT due to the father's death within seven years of the date of the transfers. At the date of making the PETs no IHT charge arises. On the father's death the two conditions of paragraph 11.83 need to be satisfied if BPR is to be available against the PETs (now chargeable) and in fact are satisfied and thus 100% BPR is applicable; as a consequence, no IHT charge arises on the PETs due to the father's death.

The land and buildings form part of the father's estate (they were not gifted). Under his will the father leaves the land and buildings equally to his daughter and son. Unfortunately, BPR is not applicable on his death.

BPR on the father's death requires that the property (ie land and buildings) has been owned by the father for a two-year minimum period (which is satisfied) *and* the property must at the time of death also have been used for the purposes of a business carried on by a company (which it was) *which the transferor (ie the father) 'controlled'* (which he does not). At the date of death the father owns no shares in the company (having given them away in lifetime).

The land and buildings are thus subject to IHT on the father's death at 40% of their then value (subject to the NRB).

This charge could, however, have been easily avoided by ensuring that the father simply left both the shares *and* the land and buildings in his will at death or transferred the land and buildings in lifetime to his son and daughter at the same time the shares are transferred.

Business property relief and settled business property

11.92 BPR (and APR) is still in principle available if the relevant business property is settled property (ie comprised in a trust). The type of trust determines the application of BPR (and APR).

11.93 The level of BPR available to settled property is the same as that applicable to individuals (see paragraph 11.64).

Relevant property trusts

11.94 The trustees of a relevant property trust (see Chapter 16) must satisfy the various conditions applicable to BPR if BPR is to apply to the trust property with respect to the exit or ten yearly charges. Thus, for example, the trustees must satisfy the minimum two-year ownership period.

11.95 Note, however, that with respect to any exit charge arising within the first ten years of the trust's creation the charge is calculated on the value of the trust property immediately after the trust commences ignoring any BPR (or APR) then available (see paragraph 16.23).

11.96 *Inheritance tax: exemptions and reliefs*

As BPR is available in calculating any ten-yearly charges any subsequent exit charge (which is based on the rate charged at the preceding ten-year anniversary) may thus be nil (if BPR at 100% applies at the preceding ten-year anniversary) (see paragraph 16.23).

Qualifying interest in possession trusts

11.96 In the case of qualifying interest in possession trusts it is the beneficiary, not trustees, thereof who must satisfy the conditions attaching to BPR. This is because it is the interest in possession beneficiary who is treated as owning the underlying property and thus it is the beneficiary (not trustees) who is regarded as effecting any transfer.

Thus, for non-qualifying interest in possession transfers it is paragraphs 11.94 and 11.95 which are in point, not paragraph 11.96.

Agricultural property relief

11.97 APR is available on transfers of agricultural property (*IHTA 1984 s 116*).

Agricultural property comprises agricultural land or pasture and any farm buildings, farmhouses and cottages that are occupied with the agricultural land as are of a character appropriate to the property (*IHTA 1984 s 115*). Effectively, occupation of such buildings must be ancillary to the agricultural land.

11.98 APR may also be available on transfers of shares in a farming company. This applies where the transferor has 'control' of the company immediately prior to the transfer and the agricultural property forms part of the assets of the company. However, APR only applies to the value of the shares which reflects the agricultural value of the property in the company; nevertheless BPR may also be available on that part of the value of the shares which reflects any non-agricultural value.

11.99 As with BPR, the form of the relief is a reduction in the transfer value of the agricultural land qualifying for the relief. The amount of the relief is either 100% or 50%.

APR applies where the transferor has the right to vacant possession immediately before the transfer or the right to obtain such possession within the next 12 months (possibly 24 months) or where the agricultural property is let on a tenancy granted on or after 1 September 1995; the rate of APR in either case is 100%.

11.100 BPR also applies in addition to APR. APR applies to the agricultural value of the property which is the value on the assumption that the property is subject to a perpetual covenant prohibiting its use otherwise than as agricultural property. It is highly likely that the market value of the property is greater than its value on this 'agricultural' basis and, if so, BPR may be available on this excess amount (assuming the conditions applicable to BPR are satisfied).

Ownership requirements

11.101 At the time of the transfer of the agricultural property the property must have been occupied by the transferor for the purposes of agriculture throughout the period of two years ending on the date of the transfer or have replaced agricultural property which together with the replacement property was occupied for agricultural purposes for at least two years out of the last five years ending with the date of transfer.

Alternatively, the agricultural property must have been owned by the transferor throughout the period of seven years ending with the date of the transfer and occupied for the purposes of agriculture by the transferor or another throughout the period.

Agricultural property acquired on the death of a spouse permits aggregation of periods of ownership.

Example 26

Farmer Giles began farming as a sole trader in August 2007 but dies just over three years later in December 2010.

As he occupies the property for the purposes of agriculture for at least two years ending on his death APR is available at 100%.

Example 27

Farmer Gumshoe owns agricultural land which has been occupied by his brother, Bill, as a tenant, for ten years when Farmer Gumshoe dies. APR is available at 100%.

APR and death within seven years of a transfer

11.102 APR is available on death and on lifetime transfers (ie whether PETs or CLTs).

11.103 *Inheritance tax: exemptions and reliefs*

11.103 For APR to apply on a failed PET (ie where the donor dies within seven years of the date of the gift) or where additional IHT arises on a CLT due to death within seven years of the date of the lifetime CLT the following conditions need to be satisfied:

- the original property must have been owned by the transferee throughout the period from the date of the lifetime transfer until the death of the donor; and
- immediately before the death of the donor the original property must qualify for APR on the part of the transferee.

Replacement property may not invalidate the above.

Quick succession relief

11.104 QSR is designed to offer relief from a double charge to IHT on the same property but only applies on death (unlike BPR and APR which apply to both lifetime and death transfers) (*IHTA 1984 s 141*).

Non-settled property

11.105 Where a person dies within five years of receiving a chargeable transfer (whether made on death or in lifetime) QSR is available with respect to the increase in IHT arising on death attributable to the transfer (*IHTA 1984 s 141*)

11.106 The extent of the relief is a function of the length of the time between the date of the transfer and the date of death. Where death occurs not more than one year of the transfer QSR of 100% is applicable. Thereafter the percentage relief is as follows:

- 80% if previous transfer more than one year but not more than two years before death;
- 60% if the transfer is more than two years but not more than three years before death;
- 40% if the transfer is more than three years but not more than four years before death; and
- 20% if the transfer is more than four years but not more than five years before death.

The percentage is applied to the IHT paid on the transfer reduced by the fraction 'net value transferred/gross chargeable transfer'.

Example 28

Elisabeth Terry dies in June 2010, having utilised her NRB, but with an estate on death of £625,000. The IHT liability is payable out of residue.

In her will she left her daughter, Samantha, £312,500.

Unfortunately, Samantha dies three and a half years later with an estate on death of £725,000 (and thus QSR is in principle available).

As Samantha dies within five years of her mother from whom she had received a chargeable transfer, on Samantha's death a measure of QSR is available. If no such relief is available in such circumstances then effectively IHT on the £312,500 is charged twice (once on Elisabeth's death and a second time on the death of Samantha).

Elisabeth's death

IHT liability = [£625,000 – £325,000] × 40% = £120,000.

The IHT rate on the estate is:

[£120,000/£625,000] = 19.2%.

The IHT applicable to the £312,500 left to Samantha is [19.2% x [£312,500/0.808]] ie £74,257 which is paid out of residue. The net and gross transfer are thus £312,500 and £386,757.

QSR = [£312,500/£386,757] x £74,257 x 40% = £24,000

(40% is the QSR from paragraph 11.106).

Samantha's death

IHT liability =[£725,000 – £325,000] × 40% = £160,000

Less: QSR of £24,000

Net IHT payable on Elisabeth's death:

£136,000.

Example 29

Tom Car has exhausted his NRB when he makes a PET of £16,000 to his sister Barbara.

11.107 *Inheritance tax: exemptions and reliefs*

Barbara dies two years after the date of the gift and Tom dies just under five years after the date of the gift.

Tom's death within seven years causes the PET to become chargeable with the IHT charge that of Barbara, or more technically, Barbara's executors.

The IHT charge on the PET is:

40% x £16,000 x 60% = £3,840

(the 60% representing taper relief applicable to the PET).

As Barbara dies within five years of the gift from Tom QSR is available.

QSR = [£12,160/£16,000] x £3,840 x 80% = £2,335.

QSR applies to the IHT charge attributable to the increase in the estate of the deceased. In this Example, Barbara's estate increases by the gift of £16,000 less the IHT payable by her estate on the gift of £3,840 ie £12,160. Thus, the IHT charge attributable thereto (ie to the £12,160) is [£12,160/£16,000] of £3,840. QSR of 80% then applies thereto.

11.107 It is not necessary for the property transferred to have been retained by the donee for QSR to apply. In addition, QSR also applies even where the earlier transfer is not to the individual who subsequently dies but to a person to which the related property rules (*IHTA 1984 s 161*) apply and thus which results in the deceased's estate increasing in value due to the earlier transfer.

11.108 The earlier transfer must, however, have been a chargeable transfer made on death. Thus, for example, inter-spouse transfers do not qualify (as such transfers are exempt).

Settled property

11.109 QSR applies to settled property albeit only where a qualifying interest in possession subsists (*IHTA 1984 s 141*). Thus, QSR may apply where such an interest terminates whether in lifetime or on death.

11.110 The earlier transfer in respect of which QSR may apply is either that made on creation of the trust or the termination of an earlier qualifying interest in possession.

Summary

11.111 Transfers whether in lifetime or on death may qualify as exempt transfers or, alternatively, may be subject to some form of relief.

11.112 Most (but not all) exempt transfers apply only on lifetime transfers. However, the inter-spouse exemption (perhaps one of the most important of the exemptions) applies to transfers whether in lifetime or on death.

11.113 For the particularly wealthy individual the 'normal expenditure out of income' exemption should not be overlooked.

11.114 One of the most important reliefs, available on lifetime transfers and on death, is BPR. Its importance lies in the extent of the relief which in a number of cases is 100%. However, it is important in order not to lose the relief that the donees of any transfers in lifetime are made aware of the conditions which need to be satisfied up to the date of death of the donor (or death of the donee if earlier).

11.115 APR is also an important and similar, although not identical, relief to BPR.

11.116 QSR is a useful relief which seeks to prevent a double IHT charge arising on the same property. It applies to both non-settled and settled property.

Chapter 12

Inheritance tax: gifts with reservation

Background

12.1 The concept of 'gifts with reservation' (GWR) is a tax fiction and of relevance only for inheritance tax (IHT) purposes. The concept thus has no implications for income or capital gains tax (CGT).

12.2 The GWR provisions are broadly intended to prevent an individual giving away property yet still thereafter continuing to enjoy the benefit of it whilst at the same time seeking to avoid an IHT charge on death on the basis that the property no longer forms part of his estate. The provisions apply to both settled and non-settled property.

Example 1

Henry Fosset has a number of valuable antique paintings hanging in his house.

He transfers the ownership of the paintings to his daughter but continues to leave the paintings in his house.

The gifts to his daughter are treated as GWR and, as a consequence, on Henry's death the value of the paintings at the date of death form part of Henry's estate for IHT purposes.

Example 2

Sharon and Keith Smith own an un-mortgaged and valuable home.

They transfer ownership of their home to their son and daughter but Sharon and Keith continue to live in the home as before.

The gifts to the son and daughter are treated as GWRs and, as a consequence, on the death of Sharon and Keith the value of the home forms part of their estates for IHT purposes.

12.3 The GWR provisions apply to lifetime gifts made on or after 18 March 1986 (*FA 1986 s 102* and *Sch 20*).

12.4 It is not possible for a gift made by will to constitute a GWR; this is because the testator, following his death, cannot of course continue to enjoy, or benefit from, property given away in his will.

The concept and implications

12.5 A GWR is defined in *FA 1986 s 102* as follows:

'... an individual disposes of any property by way of gift and either–

(a) possession and enjoyment of the property is not bona fide assumed by the donee at or before the beginning of the relevant period; or

(b) at any time in the relevant period the property is not enjoyed to the entire exclusion, or virtually to the entire exclusion, of the donor and of any benefit to him by contract or otherwise ...'

The 'relevant period' means a period ending on the date of the donor's death and beginning seven years before that date or, if it is later, on the date of the gift.

12.6 It is important to appreciate that a gift of property, treated as a GWR, is treated as forming part of the estate of the donor only at the date of death (*FA 1986 s 102*). From the date of the gift the property is, de facto, that of the donee. Should the donee die the property forms part of his estate as he is beneficially entitled to it.

If the recipient of the gift is an individual the gift qualifies as a potentially exempt transfer (PET) otherwise it is likely (post-*FA 2006*) to qualify as a chargeable lifetime transfer (CLT). In either case a liability (or additional liability) to IHT arises if the donor dies within seven years of making the gift.

A double IHT charge may thus arise on the death of the donor (ie because the GWR is included at death as part of the donor's estate but at the same time it also qualifies as a PET/CLT); relief is available to prevent this double charge (*FA 1986 s 104*; *SI 1987/1130*).

For CGT purposes the donee acquires the property gifted at the date of the gift and at its then market value (*TCGA 1992 s 17*; see paragraph 8.28).

12.7 *Inheritance tax: gifts with reservation*

12.7 On the death of the donor the value of the GWR is that at the date of death not the date the property forming the GWR is gifted; the property gifted may qualify for BPR (or APR) on the donor's death.

Example 3

Nelly Foot owns £150,000 worth of UK listed equities which on 15 July 2002 she gifts to her daughter, Karen, on condition that she (ie Nelly) retains all rights to future dividends on the shares until death.

The gift of the shares by Nelly is a GWR.

On Nelly's death on 13 June 2010, the value of the equities is £200,000 and it is this value (ie not the £150,000) which is included as part of her estate for IHT purposes.

Example 4

Tom purchases listed shares in XYZ Plc for £100,000.

He transfers the legal ownership of the shares to his brother, Sam, when the shares are worth £300,000 but Tom retains the rights to all dividends arising on the shares until his death.

The gift by Tom is a GWR.

Tom dies in June 2010 and the shares at that time are worth £650,000. For IHT purposes the shares are included as part of Tom's estate at £650,000 (not the £300,000 value).

Sam sells the shares in October 2010, after his brother's death, for £700,000.

For CGT purposes Sam makes a capital gain of £400,000 (ie £700,000 less £300,000) not £50,000 (ie £700,000 less £650,000).

12.8 Although the GWR forms part of the donor's estate on death any IHT liability arising in respect thereof is that of the donee not that of the donor's estate (see paragraph 10.87). Thus, although the IHT liability is that of the donee its quantum is determined by the circumstances of the donor.

Example 5

Geoff gifts his vintage car (worth £250,000) to his son, John, but keeps the car in his own garage and continues to use the car as if it still belongs to him. Geoff has utilised his NRB.

The gift by Geoff is a GWR.

Geoff dies in September 2010 with a chargeable estate of £625,000; of this, £265,000 represents the value of the car at the date of his death.

Geoff leaves his estate (which of course does not include the car) by will to his daughter, Isabella.

The IHT liability on Geoff's estate is:

40% × (£625,000 − £325,000) = £120,000.

The average rate of IHT on death is thus:

[£120,000/£625,000] × 100 = 19.2%

Thus, John is liable for IHT of 19.2% of £265,000 (not £250,000) (ie £50,880).

The executors of Geoff's will are responsible for IHT of £69,120 (ie £120,000 less £50,880).

Gifts with reservation: non-application

12.9 The GWR provisions do not apply if the donor is excluded (or virtually excluded) from all benefit during the whole of the relevant period *and* the donee has full possession and enjoyment of the property either at or before the beginning of the relevant period (*FA 1986 s 102* and *Sch 20*). The relevant period is the period beginning seven years before death of the donor or, the date of the gift if later, ending on the donor's death (*FA 1986 s 102* and *Sch 20*).

Following a gift which constitutes a GWR the donor may subsequently release the reservation; at the date the reservation is released (ie ceases) the donor is treated as having made a PET (*FA 1986 s 102*).

12.10 *Inheritance tax: gifts with reservation*

Example 6

Samantha Uptight has a piece of valuable jewellery which she gifts to her daughter, Cynthia, in March 1997 (a PET).

However, Samantha continues to retain the jewellery in her own home and continues to wear it as and when she chooses. In June 2000 Samantha hands over the jewellery to Cynthia and Samantha no longer wears or has access to the jewellery from this date ie the reservation is released (a deemed PET).

Samantha dies in September 2008.

As Cynthia (the donee) gains full possession and enjoyment of the jewellery more than seven years before Samantha's death the PET originally made by Samantha and the deemed PET made by Samantha on the release of the reservation in June 2000 are no longer chargeable and the jewellery is not included as part of Samantha's estate on her death as at that time no reservation applies to the gift.

If Samantha's deemed PET occurs in, say, September 2006 although the original PET does not fall within the charge to IHT on her death, the deemed PET does now fall within the charge and the jewellery continues to form part of Samantha's estate as a GWR. Double tax arises subject to the relief provided for in *SI 1987/1130*.

12.10 If, however, the donor survives for seven years from the date of release of the reservation no IHT charge arises on the PET (ie the PET arising due to the release) or on death (as the property ceased to be subject to a reservation at least seven years prior to death).

12.11 It is thus possible for the following to arise. A GWR is initially made which constitutes a PET/CLT by the donor. The reservation subsequently ceases (ie a PET is deemed to have been made by the donor) and the donor dies within seven years of the date of the release of the reservation and of the original GWR. IHT thus, in principle, applies to the original CLT/PET GWR; the subsequent deemed PET; and the donor's estate. Provisions exist under which such double tax is prevented (*FA 1986 s 104*; *SI 1987/1130*).

12.12 The GWR provisions do not apply (*FA 1986 s 102*) if one or more of the following exemptions applies to the gift:

- the inter-spouse exemption (except where the donee is a non-UK domiciled spouse and the donor spouse is UK domiciled) (*IHTA 1984 s 18*);

- small gifts (*IHTA 1984 s 20*);
- gifts in consideration of marriage (*IHTA 1984 s 22*); and
- gifts to charities; political parties; and for national purposes (*IHTA 1984 ss 23, 24* and *25*).

However, gifts within the normal expenditure out of income exemption may be caught under the GWR provisions (*IHTA 1984 s 21*).

Land and chattels 'let-out'

12.13 Two exceptions to the GWR provisions relate to land and chattels (but not other property (eg intangibles))(*FA 1986 ss 102A, 102B* and *102C* and *Sch 20*).

The first exception provides that the GWR provisions do not apply where the donor provides full consideration (in money or money's worth) for any right of occupation or enjoyment retained of the land or chattel. Gifts of an undivided share in land where thereafter both donor and donee occupy the property, subject to satisfaction of certain conditions, also circumnavigates the GWR provisions (see paragraphs 12.15 and 20.109).

The second exception relates only to land and is only applicable where the donee is a relative of the donor or the donor's spouse. If the donor occupies the property which results from a change in circumstances since the time of the gift, being a change which was unforeseen at that time, and was not brought about by the donor to avoid the GWR provisions from applying and it occurs at a time when the donor is unable to maintain himself through old age, infirmity or otherwise and any benefits provided by the donee are restricted to reasonable provision for his care and maintenance the GWR provisions do not apply.

12.14 With respect to the first exceptions (see paragraph 12.13) full consideration needs to be provided throughout the period of occupation by the donor and should be on arm's-length terms (ie as if between third parties) preferably in writing (eg a tenancy agreement). Where full consideration ceases at any time to be provided by the donor the GWR provisions apply. Any rents paid by donor to donee are, of course, subject to income tax on the part of the donee.

Example 7

Bob and Myrtle Orange own their own home, which is mortgage free, and worth £850,000. They decide to gift it to their two sons, Harry and Tony, but remain in occupation.

12.15 *Inheritance tax: gifts with reservation*

Bob and Myrtle are aware of the GWR provisions and agree with their sons to pay a market rent in return for continuing to live there.

The gift is not treated as a GWR.

12.15 The gift of an individual share in land is a GWR if the donor continues in occupation. However, where following the gift, both donor and donee occupy the gifted property and the donor receives no benefit provided by or at the expense of the donee connected with the gift, the GWR provisions do not apply to the donor's gift.

Example 8

Ted Cup decides to gift a 30% share interest in his home to his daughter, Cheryl. Cheryl moves into the property to live with Ted.

Ted agrees to continue to pay all the running costs (eg gas, electricity etc) of the property but any major capital expenditure (eg roof repairs) is to be split 70/30.

As Ted receives no benefit from Cheryl (the donee) the GWR provisions do not apply to the gift of the 30% interests in the property.

As both live in the property even if Cheryl pays for 50% of the running expenses instead of Ted paying for all such expenses this should not cause the GWR provisions to apply.

However, in the event that the donee moves out of the property the donor is, at the time, treated as having made a GWR. Thus, short-term occupation of the property by the donee jointly with the donor achieves little *vis à vis* any IHT saving.

Tracing

12.16 To ascertain if a GWR occurs there is no tracing of cash. Thus, if a gift of cash is made which is then used by the donee to purchase property in which the donor then lives no GWR is made.

Example 9

Marianne gifts £200,000 to her son, Michael, who uses the cash to purchase a property in which she then allows Michael to live.

The gift of cash is not a GWR.

It is, however, important that the gift of cash is not made on condition that it is to be used to purchase property in which the donor intends to live.

Joint bank accounts

12.17 Joint bank accounts are particularly problematic. The precise IHT treatment depends upon the true nature of the bank account (eg who makes the deposits; the bank mandate with respect to the account including conditions of withdrawal; the understanding and intention of the parties etc). It is possible that each account holder, whether or not such holder contributes monies to the account has, de facto, a general power over the whole account in which case the monies in the account form part of each holder's estate on death (*IHTA 1984 s 3*; see paragraphs 10.61 and 10.66). It is also possible that deposits into the account are GWR.

There is therefore a very strong risk that each account holder is liable to IHT on death on the entire balance in the account.

Trusts

12.18 Where the settlor of a discretionary trust falls within the class of beneficiaries (or may be added into such class; although in this case the position is less clear) gifts by him into trust fall within the GWR provisions despite the fact that he may never in fact benefit from the trust (*FA 1986 Sch 20*). However, the GWR provisions do not apply if the settlor does not fall (and may not be added) within the class of beneficiaries even if his spouse does fall within the class.

Where the provisions apply the whole of the trust fund is treated as part of the settlor's estate on death.

12.19 There is no GWR where the settlor gifts property into trust in which he then possesses a qualifying interest in possession. A qualifying interest in possession is one created in lifetime where the trust is created before 22 March 2006 (or created by will where the trust is created on or after or before 22 March 2006; see Chapter 16). For IHT purposes the beneficiary possessing the qualifying interest is treated as entitled to the underlying property in the trust in which the interest subsists which thus forms part of his estate on death and the GWR provisions are not necessary.

12.20 Following *FA 2006* (ie effective 22 March 2006), the termination of all qualifying interests in possession created prior to 22 March 2006 (and not terminated by this date) and the termination of all interests in possession created

12.21 Inheritance tax: gifts with reservation

by will on or after this date are treated as gifts at that time by the individual possessing the interest (*FA 1986 s 102ZA*). The gift is treated as a gift of the property in the trust in which the interest subsists. This represents a change to the pre-*FA 2006* position where termination of a qualifying interest by the trustees (and not by the qualifying interest in possession beneficiary) was not regarded as a gift by the beneficiary (and thus the GWR provisions could not be in point).

12.21 From 22 March 2006, the termination of a qualifying interest in possession (irrespective of the manner of its termination) pursuant to which the beneficiary may continue to benefit under the trust is a GWR. Where, however, the individual's qualifying interest in possession terminates in favour of, for example, the spouse who takes a qualifying interest in possession the GWR provisions do not apply (*FA 1986 s 102*).

Example 10

Brian Blue under his will leaves the residue of his estate on qualifying interest in possession trust (an IPDI) for his spouse.

No IHT arises due to the inter-spouse exemption.

The trustees subsequently terminate the spouse's interest in possession and the trust property is then held on discretionary trust of which the spouse is one of the potential beneficiaries.

The spouse is treated as making a GWR. The gift is of the property in which her interest in possession subsists.

Pre-owned assets

12.22 This legislation was introduced to combat situations where a donor gifts property to a donee and the donor continues to benefit from the property yet due to the structuring of the arrangements it falls outside the GWR provisions (*FA 2004 s 84* and *Sch 15*).

Where the legislation applies the donor is subject to an annual income tax charge on the 'benefit' he derives from the property.

The legislation became effective on 6 April 2005 (*FA 2004 s 84*) but does not apply to cash gifts made prior to 6 April 1998 or to arrangements made before 18 March 1986. In effect, although a charge may only arise on or after 6 April 2005, this may be due to transactions entered into prior thereto.

12.23 The legislation applies for a tax year only to individuals who are resident for that tax year. For non-UK domiciled but UK resident individuals the legislation only applies to UK situs property; excluded property is thus outside the ambit of the pre-owned asset (POA) legislation.

12.24 Where property is part of an individual's estate or where it constitutes a GWR (and thus is included in the individual's estate) the POA legislation does not apply.

12.25 The income tax charge levied under the legislation applies to:

- land;
- chattels (ie movable tangible property); and
- intangible property.

Chattels include paintings, antique furniture, vintage wines, etc. and intangible property includes life policies and shares.

12.26 The legislation provides for an extensive range of exceptions and exemptions; typically, exemptions granted under the GWR provisions are replicated in the POA legislation.

Land

12.27 The POA legislation applies to land where the donor occupies the property (not necessarily all the time). In addition the 'disposal' or 'contribution' condition must be satisfied.

The disposal condition applies where on or after 18 March 1986 the donor owns an interest in land and disposes (either in whole or in part) of that interest (and the disposal is not an excluded transaction; *FA 2004 Sch 15*. It also applies where the donor owns interest in other property (ie not just land) on or after 18 March 1986 and disposes of the interest (either in whole or in part) otherwise than by an excluded transaction and the proceeds are applied by another person in acquiring an interest in land which the donor then occupies.

The contribution condition applies where on or after 18 March 1986 the donor provides (otherwise than as an excluded transaction) all or part of the consideration for the acquisition by another person of an interest in land which the donor occupies.

12.28 A typical example of a transaction falling within the disposal condition is the disposal by one individual to another (whether by gift or sale; assuming the transaction is not an excluded transaction) of an interest in land pursuant to

12.29 *Inheritance tax: gifts with reservation*

which the donor then occupies the land (assuming that the structuring was such as to circumnavigate the GWR provisions).

A typical example of a transaction falling within the contribution condition is the simple gifting of cash by one individual to another, the donee purchasing an interest in land and the donor then occupies the land (note, the GWR provisions do not permit tracing to apply to cash gifts which thus circumnavigate the GWR provisions; see paragraph 12.16).

12.29 The measure of the benefit where land is subject to the POA charge is the appropriate rental value of the land less any payments made by the donor (but only payments made under a legal obligation) Broadly, the appropriate rental value is the rent which might be expected on a year to year letting adjusted by a fraction which is determined slightly differently depending upon whether the disposal or contribution condition is in point.

Where occupation is not for a complete tax year any charge is based upon the period of occupation only.

Example 11

Thomas Cup gifts cash of £150,000 to his daughter Isabella.

Isabella purchases a property for £600,000 which Thomas occupies from 6 April 2010. At the date of occupation the annual rental value of the property is £40,000.

The proportion of the purchase price of £600,000 attributable to Thomas' contribution is:

£150,000/£600,000

The appropriate rental value is [[£150,000/£600,000] x £40,000]

(ie £10,000 p.a.)

Thomas is thus assessed to income tax at his marginal rate each tax year of occupation on £10,000 pa.

Chattels

12.30 The POA legislation applies to chattels in basically the same manner as it applies to land.

12.31 The quantum of the charge, however, is calculated by applying the official rate of interest to the value of the chattel and adjusting this amount by the appropriate fraction. An adjustment for contributions made under a legal obligation is also made as above.

12.32 For the tax year 2010–2011 the official rate of interest is 4% (*SI 2010/415*) reduced from 4.75% for 2009–2010 (*SI 2009/199*).

Intangible assets

12.33 The ambit of the POA legislation with respect to intangible assets is narrower than applies to land and tangible assets (*FA 2004 Sch 15*).

12.34 The legislation only applies to intangible assets which comprise settled property (ie in trust) where the property so settled is that of (or represents property settled by) the donor on or after 18 March 1986 and is a settlement in which the settlor has an interest (within *ITTOIA 2005 s 624*; namely, is settlor interested for income tax purposes although any interest of the spouse is excluded for this purpose).

12.35 The quantum of the charge is that found by applying the official rate of interest (see paragraph 12.32) to the value of the settlement as represents property settled by the donor.

12.36 Inevitably, the donor is assessable not only to a POA charge but also a charge under *ITTOIA 2005 s 624* (and possibly under *TCGA 1992 s 86* and *ITA 2007 ss 720 et al*). In all cases the amount of tax chargeable under these sections is deductible from the quantum of the charge levied by the POA legislation; note that this is not a 'tax credit' offset merely a deduction from the quantum of the amount chargeable under the POA legislation.

Exemptions

12.37 Where the property is either a GWR in relation to the donor or is comprised in the donor's estate (eg donor owns the property beneficially or has a qualifying interest in possession in the property *ab initio*) the POA legislation is inapplicable to land, chattels and intangibles.

12.38 In addition to the above, the POA legislation is also inapplicable to land and chattels (not intangibles) in the case of excluded transactions:

- where the whole of the donor's interest in the property is disposed of to a non-connected person in an arm's-length transaction (or to a

12.39 *Inheritance tax: gifts with reservation*

connected person which might be such as would apply to a non-connected person transaction) the POA legislation is inapplicable;

- inter-spouse transfers are outside the ambit of the POA legislation; as are transfers into trust where the spouse possesses an interest in possession *ab initio* (whether the interest is a qualifying interest or not; see Chapter 16). Termination of the interest, however, causes the settled gift to cease to qualify as excluded;

- gifts of cash if the gift is made at least seven years prior to the donor first occupying the land purchased with the cash (or first using the chattel); and

- disposals falling within the maintenance for the family exemption (*IHTA 1984 s 11*); the annual exemption (*IHTA 1984 s 19*); or the small gifts exemption (*IHTA 1984 s 20*).

Election

12.39 An individual can avoid a POA charge if an election is made under which the relevant property is brought back within the GWR provisions (ie the property then forms part of the individual's estate on death). If such an election is made the pre-owned asset provisions are no longer in point.

The election must be made on or before the 31 January following the *first* tax year in which the POA legislation would otherwise apply in respect of the relevant property. For those individuals in respect of property which fell within the POA legislation on its introduction (ie 6 April 2005) the requisite deadline was 31 January 2007; otherwise the deadline date for an election is the 31 January following the tax year in respect of which the POA legislation applies to a particular item of property.

The election is irrevocable and must be made on Form IHT500 (see *SI 2007/3000*).

12.40 The advisability of whether to make an election or not effectively involves a comparison of the respective consequences.

If no election is made then on death no IHT applies to the property gifted despite its subsequent enjoyment. On the other hand, for every tax year up to and including death, an income tax charge applies to the appropriate amount at the appropriate marginal tax rate.

If, however, an election is made the property in respect of which the election is made forms part of the individual's estate on death for IHT purposes. On the other hand, for every tax year up to and including death, an income tax charge is avoided.

12.41 *Prima facie*, if the donor of the gift is, relatively speaking, 'old' then it would seem that other things being equal no election should be made as the number of tax years in respect of which an income tax charge arises may be limited. If the donor is, relatively speaking, 'young' then the reverse (ie an election) *prima facie* seems appropriate.

De minimis let-out

12.42 If the aggregate quantum of charge with respect to land, chattels and intangibles for a tax year is £5,000 or less no POA charge applies (and no election is necessary). Over time the *de minimis* exemption may at some point cease to apply as the quantum of charge typically increases as, for example, where the rental value of land increases. The computation is made before any deduction for payments made under a legal obligation.

Summary

12.43 The GWR and POA provisions are extremely complex and it is easy for an individual to fall foul of them. Falling foul of them may prove costly in either income or IHT terms.

12.44 The GWR provisions in essence apply to what might loosely be termed 'conditional gifts' ie the donor makes a gift conditional on retaining enjoyment rights over the property gifted. The GWR provisions prevent attempts by an individual to gift property (so that it no longer forms part of the donor's estate) but still continue to enjoy the property thereafter. Where the GWR provisions apply, on death the property gifted is brought back into the donor's estate.

12.45 Where an individual manages to gift property yet still enjoy some benefit, but is not 'caught' by the GWR provisions, it is likely the gift will then be 'caught' by the POA provisions.

12.46 The POA provisions give rise to an income tax charge each tax year the donor enjoys the property gifted; it applies to land, chattels and intangibles albeit in slightly different ways.

Chapter 13

Inheritance tax: excluded property

Background

13.1 Chapter 11 examines the exemptions and reliefs available under the inheritance tax (IHT) legislation. This chapter examines the concept of 'excluded property'. Excluded property is of primary importance to the non-UK domiciled individual.

13.2 Excluded property (*IHTA 1984 s 6*) is property which is simply outside the scope of IHT whether in lifetime (*IHTA 1984 s 3*) or on death (*IHTA 1984 s 5*) (ie property not chargeable to IHT).

Thus, excluded property is generally ignored when ascertaining an individual's IHT liability whether on a lifetime gift and/or on death; similarly relevant property (ie property comprised in trust subject to ten-yearly and exit charges; but see paragraph 13.40) does not include excluded property.

13.3 Excluded property may comprise both settled and non-settled property.

Non-settled property

13.4 Property which is not settled property (typically property not held in trust for persons in succession; *IHTA 1984 s 43*) is excluded property if it is beneficially owned by a non-UK domiciled individual and the property is not situate in the UK.

Thus, two conditions need to be satisfied if non-settled property is to qualify as excluded property, namely:

- the individual must be non-UK domiciled under common law *and* not deemed UK domiciled for IHT purposes (*IHTA 1984 s 267*); and
- the property must be non-UK situs.

Thus, any UK situs property cannot qualify as excluded property irrespective of the domicile status of the beneficial owner (subject to one or two exceptions; see paragraph 13.23).

13.5 The situs of property for this purpose is determined by the common law rules (see Chapter 6).

Settled property

13.6 Despite the wide-ranging changes introduced in *FA 2006* concerning the IHT treatment of trusts no changes were made explicitly to the excluded property rules. The position, pre- and post-March 2006, re excluded property trusts (see paragraph 13.9) is thus in essence the same (however, because of some of the changes introduced by *FA 2006* an excluded property trust may lose this status in some, albeit, limited circumstances and account must be taken of this risk, however small; see paragraph 13.45).

13.7 With respect to settled property such property is excluded property if:

- the settlor is non-UK domiciled when the settlement is created; and
- the property (at the relevant time (ie when the charge to IHT needs to be considered)) is not situate in the UK.

13.8 Trusts set up by non-UK domiciled settlors comprising non-UK situs property are often referred to as 'excluded property trusts'. Strictly speaking, however, it is the non-UK situs property comprised in the trust which qualifies as excluded property. The trust, as such, is simply a trust and therefore to a degree the term 'excluded property trust' is misleading.

Relevant property trust

13.9 As indicated in paragraph 13.2 excluded property does not form part of the trust's relevant property. Most lifetime trusts created on or after 22 March 2006 qualify as relevant property trusts as do some trusts created before this date (mainly discretionary trusts). Relevant property trusts are trusts without a 'qualifying' interest in possession (*IHTA 1984 s 58*; see Chapter 16).

As a consequence, excluded property of a relevant property trust is not subject to the ten-yearly or exit charges which apply to other property of such trusts.

'Qualifying' interest in possession trust

13.10 In the case of a 'qualifying' interest in possession trust (typically one created pre-22 March 2006) the beneficiary possessing the interest in possession

13.11 *Inheritance tax: excluded property*

(regarded as owning the underlying trust assets in which the interest subsists and thus forming part of his estate on death) is not subject to IHT on death with respect to their interest in the excluded property.

13.11 A reversionary interest (broadly a future interest under a trust often arising on the termination of an interest in possession; *IHTA 1984 s 47*) is excluded property irrespective of the domicile status of the settlor and the domicile status of the holder of the interest (*IHTA 1984 s 48*).

An interest under a discretionary trust cannot, however, constitute a reversionary interest.

13.12 The excluded property rules apply in principle to settled property whether the trust is UK or non-UK resident although in practice such property tends to be comprised in non-UK resident trusts. This is usually to ensure advantageous CGT treatment for the trust (see Chapter 18).

Excluded property and the non-UK domiciled individual

Loss of excluded property status for settled property

13.13 Excluded property is central to most IHT planning for the non-UK domiciled individual. For the UK domiciled individual excluded property has in reality very little role to play (with perhaps one exception concerning UK gilts; see paragraph 13.25).

Example 1

Conswella Gomez, a non-UK domiciled individual, dies in 2008.

> Her estate comprises £600,000 of UK listed equities; a UK house worth £1.5 million; US listed equities worth £200,000 and a Spanish house worth £1 million.
>
> IHT on her estate is based on £2.1 million (ie the value of the UK situs assets).
>
> The non-UK situs assets (ie the US listed equities and the Spanish villa) qualify as excluded property.

Example 2

Helmut Brazil, a non-UK domiciled individual, on his death owns £100,000 of UK real estate; £75,000 of Brazilian real estate; £100,000 of cash in a bank account with a Swiss bank; and is the qualifying interest in possession beneficiary of a trust set up by his non-UK domiciled father in 2002 which, at Helmut's death, comprises exclusively US equities worth £1 million.

IHT on his estate on death is based on £100,000 only (ie. the value of the UK situs assets).

If, however, at Helmut's death the trust set up by his father comprises £1 million of UK equities, Helmut's estate for IHT purposes comprises the £100,000 of UK real estate (as above) and, in addition, comprises the assets in the trust of £1 million (as the property in which Helmut's qualifying interest in possession subsists is no longer excluded property).

13.14 Example 2 illustrates an important point.

As pointed out in paragraph 13.8 it is the property of the trust which is excluded, not the trust itself. Thus, where at the relevant time (ie on Helmut's death in Example 2) the property in his non-UK domiciled father's trust comprises UK situs property, such property no longer qualifies for excluded property treatment.

13.15 Although a change in the situs of trust property settled by a non-UK domiciled individual may affect its excluded property status, subsequent changes in the settlor's domicile status are ignored and have no such affect.

Thus, once set up, non-UK situs property of the trust remains excluded property (see paragraph 13.45, however, for one exception to this).

13.16 As one of the conditions of excluded property status with respect to settled property is a non-UK domiciled settlor a UK domiciled or deemed UK domiciled individual cannot set up an excluded property trust. Once a UK domiciled (or deemed UK domiciled) individual has set up a trust even if the individual subsequently becomes non-UK domiciled the property of that trust (even if non-UK situs) does not qualify as excluded property.

13.17 The following aspects have no impact upon an excluded property determination of settled property:

- the domicile status of the settlor at any other time (ie other than at the time the trust is created);
- the domicile status of the beneficiaries;
- the residence status of the trustees; and
- the type of trust (eg discretionary or interest in possession).

13.17 *Inheritance tax: excluded property*

Example 3

A non-UK domiciled individual settles shares held in a Liberian registered company (ie non-UK situs) on a non-UK resident trust. The trust is a discretionary trust whose beneficiaries comprise his two sons and one daughter.

The trust property (ie the shares) is excluded property, irrespective of the status of any of the beneficiaries, and neither the ten yearly nor exit charges apply to the shares held in the trust. Any appointment to the beneficiaries do not precipitate any exit IHT charges whether the beneficiaries are UK domiciled or not.

Example 4

A non-UK domiciled individual settles shares in a Liberian registered company (ie non-UK situs) on a non-UK resident trust pre-22 March 2006.

The trust is a qualifying interest in possession trust for his brother (ie the brother is entitled to the income of the trust for life).

On the termination of the brother's life interest, for whatever reason, no IHT charge arises on the shares (which qualify as excluded property).

Example 5

A non-UK domiciled individual settles shares in a Liberian registered company (ie a non-UK situs asset) on a non-UK resident trust pre-22 March 2006.

The trust property is excluded property.

The trustees decide after a period of time that it is preferable to hold shares in a UK registered company rather than one registered in Liberia. They therefore sell the shares in the Liberian company, subsequently purchasing shares in a UK registered company.

The trust is a qualifying interest in possession trust for his brother (ie the brother is entitled to the income for life of the trust).

The brother unexpectedly dies.

An IHT charge arises on the brother's death because the property in the trust at the time of his death comprises UK situs property (ie UK registered company shares) and thus no longer ranks as excluded property (and is treated as part of the brother's estate on death due to his qualifying interest in possession).

This follows despite the fact that the trust is created by a non-UK domiciled settlor and, despite the fact that for a time the trust assets are non-UK situs.

13.18 It is therefore crucial for an IHT charge to be avoided that the settled property is non-UK situs *at the time at which a possible IHT charge might arise,* for example, on the termination of a qualifying interest in possession (eg one arising on a pre-22 March 2006 trust); at the time of a ten-yearly anniversary or exit charge in the case of a relevant property trust (eg a discretionary trust).

13.19 It follows from the above that excluded property status can effectively be readily manipulated. For example, the trustees of a non-UK resident discretionary trust (set up by a non-UK domiciled settlor) decide that the greatest investment returns are obtainable on UK situs investments and thus so invests. As a ten-yearly anniversary approaches (ie a time at which the ten-yearly IHT charge arises on the trust property) the trustees are able to avoid such a charge by simply swapping the UK situs investments for non-UK situs investments to be held on the date of the ten-year anniversary charge; no ten-year IHT charge then arises.

Consider also the position where a lifetime qualifying interest in possession trust is set up by a non-UK domiciled settlor with a non-UK domiciled life tenant (ie the individual with the qualifying interest in possession). Assume the trust assets primarily consist of UK situs assets. It transpires that the life tenant has a terminal disease and is expected to die within the next six months. On the death of the life tenant an IHT charge arises on the UK situs assets which the life tenant is deemed to own and thus forms part of his estate on death.

However, by disposing of the UK situs assets in which the interest in possession subsists and acquiring non-UK situs assets, the property in which the interest subsists is then non-UK situs and thus excluded property; in which case, on the life tenant's death no IHT liability arises.

Deemed UK domicile risk

13.20 The situs of property is determined by the common law rules (see Chapter 6); where property is non-UK situs and is beneficially owned by the

13.21 *Inheritance tax: excluded property*

non-UK domiciled individual (ie the property is not held in trust) at the relevant time it is excluded property.

13.21 However, if the non-UK domiciled individual subsequently becomes deemed UK domiciled under the IHT deemed domicile rules (*IHTA 1984 s 267*) and/or under common law (eg acquires a UK domicile of choice; see Chapter 3) any non-UK situs property held by such individual no longer ranks as excluded property.

Example 6

Zizzi Schoneberg, a German (ie non-UK) domiciled individual, lives in the UK.

She owns various US equities; a house in Spain; cash held in a bank account in Liechtenstein; and various UK equities.

Apart from her holding of UK equities (which are UK situs) all the other property ranks as excluded property.

Should Zizzi die, IHT is only chargeable on the UK equities.

Example 7

Using the facts in Example 6, although Zizzi likes the UK very much she does eventually intend to return home to Germany (thus retaining her German domicile of origin).

However, in the tax year 2010–2011 she discovers that she has been UK resident for 17 tax years out of the last 20 tax years and is thus now deemed UK domiciled for IHT purposes (albeit still retaining her German domicile of origin under common law).

All her assets (both UK and non-UK situs) detailed in Example 10 are now subject to IHT on her death as none of them qualify as excluded property.

Minimum holding period

13.22 For assets to qualify as excluded property requires no minimum holding period either for individuals or trustees.

Thus if, for example, just prior to death a non-UK domiciled but UK resident individual who holds a large sterling (or foreign currency) deposit with a UK bank (a UK situs asset) transfers the monies to an account with an overseas-based bank (ie a non-UK situs asset) he would have converted non-excluded property into excluded property immediately.

UK situs assets

13.23 While it is primarily with non-UK situs assets that the concept of excluded property is concerned certain UK situs assets are specifically designated as excluded property (*IHTA 1984 s 6*; see also *IHTA 1984 s 157*). Such assets include:

- holdings in authorised unit trusts (AUTs);
- shares in open-ended investment companies (OEICs);
- UK Government securities (ie 'gilts'); and
- foreign currency (ie non-sterling) bank accounts

Non-settled property

Authorised unit trusts and open-ended investment companies

13.24 Despite being UK situs assets for IHT purposes units of an AUT or shares in an OEIC are excluded property if held beneficially by a non-UK domiciled individual.

However, if such individual becomes deemed UK domiciled (or UK domiciled under common law) for IHT purposes the assets no longer rank as excluded property.

UK Government securities

13.25 Despite being UK situs assets for IHT purposes UK Government securities or gilts are excluded property if they are issued on or after 29 April 1996 and are held beneficially by an individual who is *non-ordinarily resident* in the UK; the domicile status of such individual for such assets is irrelevant to excluded property status (this is unusual).

13.26 The condition of non-UK ordinary residence (rather than the usual non-UK domicile requirement) means that even a UK domiciled individual may

13.26 *Inheritance tax: excluded property*

take advantage of excluded property status *vis-à-vis* UK gilts in, for example, the following scenario.

A UK domiciled and UK resident individual emigrates from the UK and in so doing hopes to acquire a non-UK domicile of choice (under common law). However, even where the non-UK domicile of choice is in fact acquired, under the deemed UK domicile rules (*IHTA 1984 s 267*) the individual remains deemed UK domiciled for IHT purposes for three more years. During this three-year period the individual thus remains within the IHT charge on world-wide situs assets.

One option to minimise this three-year period of exposure is to liquidate various (otherwise inheritance taxable) investments and use the sale proceeds to purchase UK gilts which are held during this three-year period. The gilts rank as excluded property because, following emigration from the UK, the individual becomes both non-UK resident and (more importantly for present purposes) non-UK ordinarily resident (see paragraph 4.18).

Example 8

Albert Gross, who is aged 46 and possesses a UK domicile of origin, has decided to emigrate from the UK to Spain.

On 1 July 2007 HMRC accepts that he has acquired a Spanish domicile of choice from this date.

However, he remains UK deemed domiciled for IHT purposes for three more years ie until 30 June 2010.

His total estate comprises £525,000 of UK listed equities.

To avoid a potential IHT charge (which, assuming the availability of the nil rate band (NRB) of £325,000) is [£325 000 @ 0% plus £200,000 @ 40%] (ie £80,000) on the UK listed equities in the event of his death within the three-year deemed UK domicile period, Albert sells the equities reinvesting the proceeds in UK gilts to be held for the requisite three-year period as excluded property.

Due to his non-residence and non-ordinary residence status no CGT liability arises on any capital gains made on the sale of the UK equities.

Alternatively, Albert may choose not to liquidate his holding of the UK equities but to borrow, say, £200,000 secured against the equities. The £200,000 is then invested in UK gilts.

Should Albert die within the three-year period of deemed UK domicile status his IHT liability would be levied on his estate ie [£525,000 less £200,000] (ie £325,000 @ 0%, (ie nil)).

The £200,000 of UK gilts rank as excluded property.

13.27 It may be noted that in Example 8 if Albert has lived all of his life in the UK he in fact remains deemed UK domiciled up to and including 5 April 2011 (ie beyond the date of 30 June 2010 referred to in the example). The reason for this is that a UK domiciled individual remains deemed UK domiciled to the later date of three years from the date of acquisition of a new non-UK domicile of choice and 5 April of the tax year in which the individual satisfies the 17 tax years out of the last 20 tax years; which in Albert's case is 5 April 2011 (*IHTA 1984 s 267*; see paragraph 3.241).

Foreign currency bank accounts

13.28 A bank account in a currency other than sterling is excluded property if held beneficially by an individual who is non-UK domiciled *and* non-UK resident *and* non-UK ordinarily resident.

Thus, a foreign currency bank account held in the UK in a UK incorporated bank or the UK branch of an overseas incorporated bank can so qualify.

UK sterling deposits cannot qualify.

13.29 Excluded property treatment, however, only extends to the position on death. If a lifetime transfer is made of the foreign currency in a UK based account (ie UK situs) a potential IHT charge arises as in this case the account is not treated as excluded property.

Example 9

Abdul Mustapha is a non-UK domiciled individual who is neither UK resident nor ordinarily resident. He opens a US dollar bank account with a UK bank in London in which he keeps approximately $1 million at any one time.

On his death the account is not subject to IHT as it is excluded property.

On the other hand, if Abdul transfers $750,000 from his UK bank account to his daughter and her husband's joint dollar bank account in the same UK bank such a transfer is a PET and not a transfer of excluded property.

13.30 *Inheritance tax: excluded property*

Should Abdul die within seven years of making the transfer an IHT liability arises (subject to the NRB).

The charge, if this occurs, is the liability of the donees ie his daughter and her husband, not the donor, Abdul.

13.30 In Example 9, the exposure to IHT on the lifetime transfer could have been easily eliminated. If Abdul first transfers the monies to a non-UK bank account of his and then transfers the monies to the UK (or non-UK) bank account of his daughter and her husband, the transfer is then of non-UK situs property (ie the non-UK bank account) by a non-UK domiciled individual (ie excluded property).

Settled property

13.31 The assets referred to in paragraph 13.23 may also qualify as excluded property when settled.

Authorised unit trusts and open-ended investment companies

13.32 AUTs and OEICs held on a trust qualify as excluded property if at the time the trust is created the settlor is non-UK domiciled. No other factors are relevant.

UK Government securities

13.33 The rules here are relatively complex. The following are some of the key points to note:

- in the case of a relevant property trust (eg a discretionary trust) none of the beneficiaries of the trust must be ordinarily resident in the UK;
- in the case of a qualifying interest in possession trust the individual with the interest in possession must be non-ordinarily resident in the UK; and
- the domicile of the settlor is not relevant (and can thus be UK domiciled).

Foreign currency bank accounts

13.34 Three conditions need to be satisfied for such accounts to qualify as excluded property if comprised in a trust:

- the settlor is non-UK domiciled when the trust is created;
- the trustees are non-UK resident; and
- a qualifying interest in possession subsists in the trust where the individual so entitled is neither UK domiciled nor UK resident.

13.35 Apart from AUTs and OEICs the various conditions which need to be satisfied with respect to the other types of property referred to in paragraphs 13.33 and 13.34 when settled are less straightforward and, on balance, such investments should perhaps be avoided being held as trust assets.

Channel Islands and the Isle of Man

13.36 For a particular category of individual, namely, individuals domiciled in either the Channel Islands or the Isle of Man, certain types of savings are categorised as excluded property despite their UK situs (*IHTA 1984 s 6*)

13.37 These savings comprise:

- National Savings and Investment (NSI) premium bonds;
- NSI National savings certificates;
- NSI deposits with the National Savings Bank (or trustee savings bank);
- war savings certificates; and
- any certified contractual savings scheme (eg SAYE schemes).

13.38 Even if an individual domiciled in the Channel Islands or the Isle of Man becomes deemed UK domiciled for IHT purposes the above types of property remain excluded property (but this is not the case should the individual become UK domiciled under common law) (*IHTA 1984 s 6*).

13.39 Apart from the above, an individual domiciled in either the Channel Islands or the Isle of Man is treated in exactly the same manner as all other non-UK domiciled individuals.

Mixing UK and non-UK situs settled assets

13.40 As a general rule, trusts set up by the non-UK domiciled individual designed to hold property which qualifies as excluded property should avoid the trust comprising both UK and non-UK situs assets. It is preferable to segregate

13.41 *Inheritance tax: excluded property*

such assets into different trusts so as not to give rise to any issues or problems concerning the excluded property elements.

Two reasons for this are as follows.

First, if the trust is a relevant property trust, the inclusion of excluded property in addition to UK situs property has the effect of increasing the potential IHT charge levied (on the UK situs property) on ten-yearly anniversaries of creation of the trust and also on property leaving the trust (ie the exit charge) even though the excluded property itself is not subject to such charges.

Second, HMRC appear to be of the view that property which is non-UK situs but which is added to a trust at a time when the settlor is UK domiciled is not excluded property (even though at the date of creation of the trust, as required by the legislation, the settlor is non-UK domiciled). HMRC, however, appear to accept that the non-UK situs property added at a time when the settlor is non-UK domiciled qualifies as excluded property.

13.41 Regarding the first point made in paragraph 13.40 whilst excluded property (as non-relevant property) may not itself be subject to the ten-yearly or exit charges in the case of relevant property trusts it is taken into account when determining the quantum of charge on any relevant property (eg UK situs) within the trust (it is, of course, perfectly possible for relevant (eg UK situs) and excluded property (non-UK situs) to co-exist within the same trust).

A charge to IHT may thus arise even though the relevant property initially settled is, for example, within the NRB, of the settlor.

Example 10

On 1 January 1999 Helmut Dusseldorf, a non-UK domiciled individual, settles UK situs assets of an amount exactly equivalent to the then NRB (£223,000) and non-UK situs assets worth £500,000 on a non-UK resident discretionary trust.

Helmut has made no prior lifetime gifts.

The UK situs assets have grown over the first ten years to a value of £312,000 as at 1 January 2009 (ie the first ten-year anniversary). The non-UK situs assets have become worth £1 million.

Helmut believes that no ten-yearly charge arises as at 1 January 2009 because the UK situs assets fall within the then NRB.

However, although no charge arises on the excluded property (only relevant property is subject to charge), the £312,000 of UK situs assets at the ten-year anniversary is charged at 4.57% producing a charge of £14,258 because of the requirement in calculating the applicable rate applying at the date of the ten-year anniversary to include excluded property (ie the IHT on £1.312 million as at the date of the ten-year anniversary is [0% x £312,000 + 20% x £1million] (ie £200,000)).

The rate of IHT = [£200,000 / £1.312m] (ie 15.2439%)

The rate charged is then [30% x 15.2439%] (ie 4.57%)

(see paragraphs 16.28 and 16.29).

13.42 Keeping UK and non-UK situs assets in separate trusts is thus advisable where complete excluded property status is unambiguously required.

Excluded property and gifts with reservation

13.43 The gift with reservation rules (GWR) (*FA 1986 s 102*) are discussed in Chapter 12 and it may be preferable to read that chapter prior to reading this section. Suffice it to say, for present purposes, that a GWR is a gift which after having made it the donor continues to benefit from it. Where such a gift is made the donor is required to include the value of the gift (at the date of death) in his estate on which IHT is levied.

13.44 However, where an individual settles excluded property on trust but continues to benefit from it (eg individual settles excluded property on discretionary trust but is a possible beneficiary thereunder) no part of the excluded property so settled is included as part of the donor's estate on death (ie the excluded property rules override the GWR rules in such cases).

Even where the settlor becomes UK domiciled at a later date no part of the settled excluded property is included as part of the individual's estate on death.

Example 11

A non-UK domiciled individual, Milano, settles non-UK situs assets on a non-UK resident discretionary trust.

Milano is also one of the potential beneficiaries under the trust.

The settlement of the assets on trust thus constitutes a GWR by Milano as he may still possibly enjoy some benefit from the assets as he is one of the potential beneficiaries under the trust.

13.45 *Inheritance tax: excluded property*

However, as the excluded property rules override the GWR rules, on Milano's death none of the excluded property assets fall to be treated as part of his estate.

If prior to Milano's death the trustees sell the non-UK situs assets replacing them with UK situs assets the GWR rules apply and the UK situs assets are included as a part of Milano's estate and thus subject to IHT.

Excluded property trusts and *FA 2006*

13.45 Relevant property trusts are subject to ten-yearly and exit charges. Prior to 22 March 2006 where a settlor and/or the settlor's spouse has a qualifying interest in possession immediately after a trust is created (or successive such interests) the trust does not enter the relevant property regime until the later of the interests in possession terminate (*IHTA 1984 s 80*).

At the date of termination of the later interest the trust property is deemed to be held in a separate trust deemed created by the spouse who last held the interest. At this point the trust enters the relevant property regime (although the ten-yearly charge starts from the date the trust is initially created).

In effect a deferral of the time at which the trust enters the relevant property regime occurs.

13.46 For trusts created on or after 22 March 2006 the above 'deeming' in paragraph 13.45 only has application to such trusts where an immediate post death interest (IPDI) (see paragraph 16.80) subsists in the trust; an IPDI only arises under a trust created by will. Thus, no trust created in lifetime on or after 22 March 2006 is subject to the above deeming rule (because no qualifying interest in possession can subsist in such trusts as they are automatically relevant property trusts).

13.47 However, post-*FA 2006*, those trusts created pre-22 March 2006 continue to be affected by the deeming rules. This may adversely impact upon the excluded property status of the trust property

13.48 Where a trust is created before 22 March 2006 under which the settlor and/or spouse have a qualifying interest in possession (or successive interests in possession) and at the date of creation the settlor is non-UK domiciled excluded property status is lost with respect to the trust property if, at the date of termination of the later qualifying interest in possession of the spouses, the spouse (who holds this later interest) at that time possesses a UK or deemed UK domicile.

Inheritance tax: excluded property **13.49**

13.49 It is important to appreciate that the deeming only applies for the purposes of the relevant property regime, not for all IHT purposes.

Example 12

In 2000 Ferdinand Madrid settles non-UK situs property on a non-UK resident trust granting himself a qualifying life interest and his wife, Louise (non-UK domiciled) a successive qualifying life interest. Thereafter the property is to be held on discretionary trust.

Ferdinand dies in early 2005 and Louise dies in late 2005.

At her death, Louise has acquired a deemed UK domicile. As a consequence, on her death she is deemed to have settled the trust property which thus no longer qualifies as excluded property. The trust becomes a relevant property trust falling subject to future ten-yearly and exit charges.

However, the property still qualifies as excluded property on her death (and indeed on Ferdinand's death) and thus does not fall subject to an IHT charge on either death ie the deeming rules are applicable for the relevant property regime only.

Example 13

In 2000 Ferdinand Madrid settled non-UK situs property on a non-UK resident trust granting himself a qualifying life interest and his wife, Louise (non-UK domiciled) a successive qualifying life interest. Thereafter the property is to be held on discretionary trust.

Ferdinand dies in early 2007 and Louise dies in late 2009.

At her death, Louise has acquired a deemed UK domicile. As a consequence, on her death she is deemed to have settled the trust property which thus no longer qualifies as excluded property. The trust becomes a relevant property trust falling subject to future ten-yearly and exit charges.

However, the property still qualifies as excluded property on her death (and indeed on Ferdinand's death) and thus does not fall subject to an IHT charge on either death.

Although Ferdinand's death occurs after 22 March 2006 and his wife's interest in possession arises after this date, his wife's interest qualifies as a

13.50 *Inheritance tax: excluded property*

qualifying interest in possession as it is a transitional serial interest (TSI) (see paragraph 16.72).

The deed of variation and the mixed domiciled marriage

13.50 Inter-spouse transfers are exempt from IHT (except for transfers from a UK to a non-UK domiciled spouse where the exemption is restricted to £55,000) whether effected in lifetime or on death (*IHTA 1984 s 18*).

13.51 In the event that the first spouse to die is the non-UK domiciled spouse, UK and non-situs assets owned beneficially at death left to the surviving UK domiciled spouse lose the possibility of excluded property status for the future. Where this occurs the surviving spouse may execute a deed of variation (DoV) redirecting the UK situs assets onto trust; for IHT purposes the settlor is deemed to be the deceased non-UK domiciled spouse (not the UK domiciled spouse) and any subsequent conversion by the trustees of the UK situs assets into non-UK situs assets produces excluded property (see paragraph 28.57).

13.52 The execution of the DoV may, however, in this case precipitate an IHT charge on the deceased's estate which otherwise (due to the inter-spouse exemption) would have been avoided. This problem is solved by giving the surviving spouse an IPDI in the newly created trust (the IPDI constituting a qualifying interest in possession).

Unfortunately, in so doing another problem is created because excluded property status is eventually lost because on termination of the IPDI the trust is deemed to be created at that time under *IHTA 1984 s 80* (see paragraph 13.45), a time when the domicile of the spouse is UK; the trust will at that time become a relevant property trust (thus, subject to exit and ten-yearly charges).

There is thus a trade-off: create excluded property status forever (by not giving the surviving UK domiciled spouse an IPDI) but at the cost of creating an IHT charge (subject to the NRB) on the death of the first spouse.

13.53 Although the settlor for IHT under the DoV is the testator (who is non-UK domiciled), for income and CGT purposes it is the surviving UK domiciled spouse; thus if the trust created under the DoV is non-UK resident the income and CGT advantages which are normally available to such trusts if created by the non-UK domiciled individual are unavailable (see Chapter 18).

Summary

13.54 The term 'excluded property trust' refers to trusts comprised of non-UK situs assets set up by a non-UK domiciled settlor. The term is slightly misleading as it is the non-UK situs property within any trust that may qualify as excluded property, not the trust itself. Thus, for example, non-UK situs property of a UK resident trust may qualify as excluded property.

13.55 Excluded property is property which is not subject to IHT; it is simply outside the ambit of IHT.

13.56 Excluded property also comprises non-UK situs property beneficially owned by the non-UK domiciled individual. Certain limited categories of UK situs assets also qualify as excluded property.

13.57 As a general rule, non-UK and UK situs assets should not be settled by a non-UK domiciled individual on the same trust.

13.58 It is possible that although non-UK situs property once settled by the non-UK domiciled individual is likely to remain excluded property forever, there are limited circumstances under which this may not be the case; this is likely to be the case with respect to interest in possession trusts set up pre-22 March 2006.

13.59 Excluded property is very important for the non-UK domiciled individual.

Chapter 14

Inheritance tax administration

Background

14.1 The requirements with respect to the administration and collection of inheritance tax (IHT) are laid down in *IHTA 1984 Part VIII*. In particular, *IHTA 1984 s 216* requires the delivery of an 'account' to HMRC in certain specified circumstances including the death of an individual; where a chargeable lifetime transfer (CLT) has been made; and where a potentially exempt transfer (PET) proves to be chargeable (ie the donor dies within seven years of making the gift).

Provision is made for specifying the form and manner in which such accounts are to be supplied (*IHTA 1984 s 257*).

However, there are circumstances under which no account needs to be delivered including where an estate is an excepted estate or where a transfer is an excepted transfer (*SI 2008/605; SI 2008/606*).

14.2 Provision is made for HMRC to request (in writing) information and documents where necessary (*IHTA 1984 ss 219 and 219A*).

14.3 Provision is made with respect to the timing of making IHT payments (*IHTA 1984 s 226*); for IHT liabilities to be discharged by instalments (*IHTA 1984 s 227*); and for interest to be charged on late IHT payments (*IHTA 1984 s 223*).

14.4 *IHTA 1984 s 218* makes specific provision for information to be supplied where a UK-domiciled settlor settles property on a non-UK resident trust.

Lifetime transfers and trust property

14.5 Form IHT100 (HMRC 08/06) 'Inheritance tax account' is the form requiring completion where, *inter alia*, any of the following occur:

- gifts and other transfers of value including failed PETs;

Inheritance tax administration **14.9**

- ending of an interest in possession in settled property;
- assets in a discretionary trust ceasing to be relevant property (proportionate or exit charge); and
- discretionary trust ten-year anniversaries (principal charge).

14.6 There is thus no requirement for an individual to file an account with respect to a PET if the donor survives for seven years (ie the PET does not become chargeable).

14.7 It may also be necessary for various additional attaching forms to be filed which provide more details about the events identified on Form IHT 100; for example, Form IHT100a 'Gifts and other transfers of value' requires information about the identity of the transferor and transferee(s); the relationship between transferor and transferee; whether the transferor is paying the IHT charge; description of asset(s) received; etc.

14.8 However, no account is required where the transfer is an excepted transfer (or where it is an excepted termination) (*SI 2008/605*) or of property comprised in the trust defined as an excepted settlement (*SI 2008/606*).

14.9 *SI 2008/605* applies to lifetime transfers effected on or after 6 April 2007 and is applicable to actual (not deemed) CLTs made by an individual in one of two circumstances:

- where the value transferred is attributable to either cash or quoted shares/securities *and* that value together with the transferor's CLTs in the previous seven years does not exceed the threshold for payment of IHT for the year in which the transfer is made; or
- where the value of the CLT together with the transferor's CLTs in the previous seven years does not exceed 80% of the IHT threshold *and* the value of the transfer of value does not exceed that threshold less the value of the CLTs in the previous seven years.

It will be noted that the former of the two circumstances requires that the transfer consists only of cash and/or listed shares a restriction not applicable to the second of the two circumstances.

Example 1

In May 2010 Herbert, having made no earlier lifetime transfers, transfers £331,000 cash into a relevant property trust (eg a discretionary trust).

The transfer is an excepted transfer as the chargeable transfer comprises only cash and after the annual exemption amount of £6,000 (ie £3,000 for

14.10 *Inheritance tax administration*

the tax year 2010–2011 and the unused amount of £3,000 from the tax year 2009–2010) equals £325,000 (the nil rate band (NRB) for the tax year 2010–2011).

14.10 An excepted termination is the termination of an interest in possession in settled property of a specified trust (ie a trust in which the interest is a qualifying interest in possession) in one of three sets of circumstances; one such circumstance is if the value of the property in which the interest subsists is attributable to cash or quoted securities/shares and the value transferred in consequence of the termination, together with the values transferred by any previous CLT made by the transferor during the seven years preceding the transfer does not exceed the IHT threshold.

14.11 *SI 2008/606* applies to chargeable events occurring on or after 6 April 2007 with respect to property comprised in a class of trusts referred to as excepted settlements. There are five categories of excepted settlement all of which require there to be no qualifying interest in possession subsisting in the settled property.

One such category is where the settled property can comprise only cash, the trustees must be UK resident, the settlor must not have provided any additions to the settled property following the day of commencement of the settlement or have created any other settlements on the same day and the value of the settled property at the time of the chargeable event must not exceed £1,000 (so-called 'pilot trusts' qualify as falling within this category).

All other categories require that, *inter alia*, the settlor is UK domiciled at the commencement of the settlement and thereafter until the chargeable event (or his death if earlier); that the trustees are UK resident throughout the existence of the settlement; and there must be no related settlements.

Inheritance tax payable

14.12 IHT arising on a CLT is payable within six months of the end of the month in which it is made (if made after 30 September and before 6 April in any year) or on the 30 April in the following year where the transfer is made after 5 April and before 1 October in any year (*IHTA 1984 s 226*).

Any 'additional IHT' due to the death of the transferor within seven years thereof is due six months after the end of the month in which death occurs (*IHTA 1984 s 226*).

Any IHT liability arising on a PET due to the death of the transferor within seven years of the date of the transfer is due six months after the end of the month in which death occurs (*IHTA 1984 s 226*).

Inheritance tax administration **14.18**

Persons responsible for inheritance tax charge

14.13 The person primarily liable for any IHT arising on a CLT is the transferor (*IHTA 1984 s 199*).

However, his spouse may also be liable (treated as if she were the transferor); this is designed to preclude one spouse transferring property to the other spouse in an attempt to avoid any IHT payable (*IHTA 1984 s 203*).

Where the IHT remains unpaid other persons are also liable (to a limited extent) including the transferee, any person in whom the property has become vested and, where property is settled by the transfer, any person for whose benefit any of the property or income from it is applied (*IHTA 1984 s 199*).

14.14 Any additional IHT due to the death of the transferor within seven years of effecting the CLT is primarily the liability of the transferee. Similarly, where a PET falls chargeable due to the death of the transferor within seven years of the date of the transfer the liability is that of the transferee.

Where the IHT remains unpaid 12 months after death of the transferor the deceased's personal representatives (PRs) may be liable (*IHTA 1984 s 199*). This can present serious practical problems for PRs (in particular where the liability is discovered after the estate has been fully administered; one option is for the PRs to take out appropriate insurance cover; in this context the exposure of the PRs is limited to the value of the deceased's estate). The PRs are similarly exposed with respect to unpaid IHT liabilities in connection with gifts with reservation (GWR).

14.15 The person responsible for the delivery of the account (ie Form IHT 100) with respect to a CLT is the transferor. The account must be delivered within 12 months from the end of the month in which the transfer is made (although note that any IHT liability in respect thereof is due and payable much earlier) (see paragraph 14.12).

14.16 The person responsible for delivery of the account where the transferor dies within seven years of making a CLT is the transferee; similarly, in the case of a failed PET, the obligation to deliver the account is that of the transferee.

Where the transferor dies within seven years of making a CLT or PET the PRs (see paragraph 27.115) of the deceased are also under an obligation to deliver an account in respect of such CLTs and PETs.

14.17 HMRC have an automatic charge for unpaid IHT on the property transferred, including settled property (*IHTA 1984 s 237*). In the case of lifetime transfers (but not on death) the charge extends to personal property.

14.18 Where any IHT attributable to a CLT or failed PET is paid in

14.19 *Inheritance tax administration*

accordance with an account delivered to HMRC and HMRC accept such payment in full satisfaction HMRC cannot recover any further IHT in relation thereto after a period of four years (reduced from six years by *FA 2009 Sch 51*) in the absence of fraud, willful default or neglect (*IHTA 1984 s 240*).

Death estate

14.19 The executors of the deceased must deliver an account detailing all property which forms part of the deceased's estate immediately before death including property in trust in which the deceased has a qualifying interest in possession (eg an interest in possession under a pre-22 March 2006 trust). In addition, the executors are required to disclose details of any CLTs or PETs made by the deceased within seven years of death.

The account needs to be submitted within 12 months of the end of the month in which death occurs.

14.20 The PRs are liable to account for any IHT due on assets beneficially owned by the deceased (this excludes, for example, IHT arising with respect to GWRs; and qualifying interests in possession, see paragraph 14.31).

14.21 There are two main forms, namely, Form IHT 400 and Form IHT 205 (see paragraph 27.120).

14.22 Form IHT 400 (which replaced IHT 200 with effect from 9 June 2009 for deaths on or after 18 March 1986) requires completion where there is either IHT to pay *or* no IHT to pay but the estate does not qualify as an 'excepted estate' (see paragraph 14.25).

Accompanying Form IHT 400 is a suite of additional forms (Forms IHT 401 to 423 inclusive) on which further detailed information is required to be provided; such forms include IHT 404 'Jointly owned assets'; IHT 406 'Bank and building society accounts'; IHT 413 'Business or partnership interests and assets' and IHT 421 'Probate summary').

14.23 In certain cases a reduced Form IHT 400 may be completed. According to the 'IHT 400 Notes Guide to completing your inheritance tax account' (page 5) to file a reduced IHT 400 the deceased must have been UK domiciled at the date of death and there must be assets passing under a will to the deceased's surviving spouse; a UK charity; or a national body (eg British Museum). All such transfers constitute exempt transfers (ie no IHT charge arises).

If the total (before exemptions, reliefs etc) of assets passing to anyone other than the above exempt beneficiaries is less than or equal to the NRB (including the transferable NRB; see paragraph 11.44) a reduced IHT 400 may be completed.

The total referred to includes the deceased's share of jointly held assets; assets given away in the preceding seven years; GWR; and assets outside the UK not passing under the UK will.

14.24 Where a reduced IHT 400 may be completed boxes 1 to 28 need to be completed in full but boxes 29 to 48 require answers but it may not be necessary to fill in all the schedules (see pages 5 and 6 to the above referred to Guide).

Excepted estate

14.25 Form IHT205 (not Form IHT400) requires completion where the estate qualifies as an excepted estate. Typically, an excepted estate is an estate where there is no IHT to pay. However, even if there is no IHT to pay the estate may not be an excepted estate in which case Form IHT400 requires completion; this occurs where, for example, the whole of the estate passes to the surviving spouse but exceeds £1 million.

There are three types of excepted estate (*SI 2006/2141; SI 2004/2543*):

- low value estates;
- exempt estates; and
- foreign domiciliaries

Low value estates

14.26 The conditions for these estates are that:

- the person died on or after 1 September 2006, domiciled in the United Kingdom;
- the value of that person's estate is attributable wholly to property passing—
    - in connection with the distribution of profits of the company the taxpayer has received an abnormal amount by way of dividend which is then the subject of some form of tax relief (*ICTA 1988, s 704A* or *ITA 2007, s 686*);
    - under his will or intestacy,
    - under a nomination of an asset taking effect on death,
    - under a single settlement in which he was entitled to an interest in possession in settled property, or

14.27 *Inheritance tax administration*

- by survivorship in a beneficial joint tenancy or, in Scotland, by survivorship in a special destination;

• of that property —
  - not more than £150,000 represented value attributable to property which, immediately before that person's death, was settled property; and
  - not more than £100,000 represented value attributable to property which, immediately before that person's death, was situated outside the United Kingdom;
  - that person died without having made any chargeable transfers during the period of seven years ending with his death other than specified transfers where (BPR and APR are not to apply) the aggregate value transferred did not exceed £150,000; and

• the aggregate of—
  - the gross value of that person's estate,
  - the value transferred by any specified transfers made by that person (BPR and APR are not to apply), and
  - the value transferred by any specified exempt transfers made by that person,

did not exceed the IHT threshold.

Exempt estates

14.27 The conditions for these estates are that:

- the person died on or after 1 September 2006, domiciled in the United Kingdom;
- the value of that person's estate is attributable wholly to property passing—
  - under his will or intestacy,
  - under a nomination of an asset taking effect on death,
  - under a single settlement in which he was entitled to an interest in possession in settled property, or
  - by survivorship in a beneficial joint tenancy or, in Scotland, by survivorship in a special destination;
- of that property—

- not more than £150,000 represented value attributable to property which, immediately before that person's death, was settled property (other than settled property which is transferred on that person's death to a spouse or charity);
- not more than £100,000 represented value attributable to property which, immediately before that person's death, was situated outside the United Kingdom;
- that person died without having made any chargeable transfers during the period of seven years ending with his death other than specified transfers where (BPR and APR not to apply) the aggregate value transferred did not exceed £150,000;
- the aggregate of—
  - the gross value of that person's estate (i),
  - the value transferred by any specified transfers made by that person (BPR and APR not to apply) (ii), and
  - the value transferred by any specified exempt transfers made by that person, did not exceed £1 million (iii);
- and the aggregate of —

  A – (B + C) does not exceed the IHT threshold, where—

  A is the aggregate of the values in (i), (ii) and (iii),

  B is the total value transferred on that person's death by a spouse or charity transfer, and

  C is the total liabilities of the estate.

Foreign domiciliaries

14.28 The conditions for these persons are that:

- the person died on or after 1 September 2006;
- the person was never domiciled in the United Kingdom or treated as domiciled in the United Kingdom by *IHTA 1984 s 267*; and
- the value of that person's estate situated in the United Kingdom is wholly attributable to cash or quoted shares or securities passing under his will or intestacy or by survivorship in a beneficial joint tenancy the gross value of which does not exceed £150,000.

14.29 For each of the above categories of excepted estate the following definitions apply:

14.30 *Inheritance tax administration*

'Specified transfers' means chargeable transfers made by a person during the period of seven years ending with that person's death where the value transferred is attributable to—

- cash;
- personal chattels or corporeal moveable property;
- quoted shares or securities; or
- an interest in or over land.

'Specified exempt transfers' means transfers of value made by a person during the period of seven years ending with that person's death which are exempt transfers only by reason of, inter alia—

- *IHTA 1984 ss 18* (transfers between spouses);
- *IHTA 1984 ss 23* (gifts to charities); and
- *IHTA 1984 ss 24* (gifts to political parties).

Inheritance tax payable

14.30 The IHT is due within six months of the end of the month in which death occurs (*IHTA 1984 s 226*).

Persons responsible for inheritance tax charge

14.31 The PRs are liable to account for any IHT due on assets beneficially owned by the deceased. The person primary liable where the deceased has a qualifying interest in possession on death is the trustees thereof (*IHTA 1984 s 200*) and in the case of GWR, the transferee.

Clearance certificate

14.32 Provision is made for the PRs to apply for a clearance certificate or certificate of discharge once all the IHT attributable to the deceased's estate has been discharged (*IHTA 1984 s 239*). The application is made on Form IHT30.

Once obtained this alleviates any possible further charge to IHT on the part of the PRs with respect to the property comprised in the application.

Penalties

14.33 Provisions dealing with penalties are contained in *FA 2007 Sch 24*; *FA 2008 Sch 40*; *FA 2009 Sch 55* and *FA 2009 Sch 56*.

14.34 *FA 2009 Sch 55* contains provisions which lay down penalties for the late filing of IHT returns. A fixed penalty of £100 applies where a return is submitted after the due date for filing and, where the failure continues, additional penalties are leviable. For example, where a return is outstanding six months after the due filing date (and the return would have shown IHT payable) the penalty is the greater of £300 or 5% of the IHT liability which would have been shown in the return.

14.35 *FA 2009 Sch 56* contains provisions which lay down penalties for the late payment of IHT. Where the IHT due is not paid by thirty days after the due date for its payment the penalty is 5% of the amount of the unpaid IHT. Additional 5% penalties are levied where payment remains outstanding five and 11 months after the date when the first 5% penalty is due for payment.

14.36 *FA 2007 Sch 24*, as extended by *FA 2008 Sch 40*, provides for penalties to be made where reasonable care is not exercised in preparing IHT accounts and as a consequence an understatement of any IHT liability occurs. Failure to correct an inaccuracy may also precipitate the levying of a penalty.

The level of any penalties levied depends upon whether the error or failure is careless, deliberate or deliberate and concealed and whether the error or failure is disclosed unprompted as opposed to prompted. Accordingly, minimum penalties vary from 0% to 50% and maximum penalties from 30% to 100% of the loss of IHT due.

14.37 Appeals against the imposition of any penalties and the amounts thereof may be made but there is no need to make a payment thereof prior to a determination. A 'reasonable excuse' for the failure precludes a penalty from being levied.

Interest on unpaid inheritance tax

14.38 Interest on unpaid IHT is charged from the due date of payment until the payment is received by HMRC (*FA 2009 s 101*). The rate of interest is laid down in regulations published by *HM Treasury (Taxes (Interest Rate) Regulations 1989 (SI 1989/1297)* as amended).

14.39 The rate of interest levied on late payments of IHT on or after 29 September 2009 is 3%. For the period from 24 March 2009 to 28 September

14.40 *Inheritance tax administration*

2009 the rate is 0% (and 1% for the period 27 January 2009 to 23 March 2009) (*IHTA 1984 s 233*).

The interest rate paid on repayments of IHT on or after 29 September 2009 is 0.5%. For the period 24 March 2009 to 28 September 2009 the rate is 0% (and 1% for the period 27 January 2009 to 23 March 2009) (*IHTA 1984 s 235*).

Assessment and claims

14.40 Schedule *FA 2008 s 39* amends from 1 April 2010, with transitional provisions from 1 April 2009, most of the time limits that apply to claims and assessments for income tax and CGT. The period for making claims is generally set at four years; similarly, the normal time limit for raising assessments also becomes four years.

FA 2009 s 99 and *Sch 51* make corresponding changes to the time limits that apply to claims and assessments for IHT.

Summary

14.41 The making of a transfer of value typically requires an appropriate account to be lodged with HMRC. Similarly, trustees of relevant property trusts may also be required to lodge an appropriate return where chargeable events occur (eg ten-yearly charge).

14.42 Statutory forms are provided for filing accounts including, in particular, Forms IHT 100, 205 and 400

14.43 Penalties and/or interest charges may be levied if information provided to HMRC is incorrect and/or late.

Part III

Trusts

Chapter 15

Trusts: an overview

Background

15.1 The concept of 'the trust' is not necessarily easily understood. The concept is alien to many civil law jurisdictions. Nevertheless, trusts are widely used in effecting tax efficient family planning even by those individuals who are in fact nationals of civil law jurisdictions (the latter typically creating their trusts under 'offshore' jurisdictions (see Chapter 25) which recognise the trust concept).

15.2 The following three chapters concentrate on, and examine, the tax issues associated with trusts. It is important therefore that a basic grasp of the trust concept is obtained before reading the next three chapters (those familiar with the concept may skip this chapter).

Trust definition

15.3 There is no one universally recognised definition of the trust. As a consequence, most textbooks tend to explain what a trust *is* rather than seeking to define it.

15.4 A trust may be thought of as comprising an arrangement where one person gives property to another person(s) for the benefit of a third party or parties which may include the person to whom the property is transferred

Example 1

John Smith who owns 100 ordinary shares in XYZ Ltd gives the shares to his brothers, Bill and Tom Smith, for Bill and Tom to hold for the benefit of his (ie John's) two children, Henry and Mary.

15.5 In Example 1 John Smith is the settlor; Bill and Tom Smith are the

15.6 *Trusts: an overview*

trustees; and Henry and Mary are the beneficiaries. Legal ownership of the trust property is vested in the trustees and beneficial (or equitable) ownership is vested in the beneficiaries.

It is the splitting of legal and beneficial ownership of property which is the essence of the trust.

15.6 Trustees' duties and responsibilities are laid down by the settlor in the trust deed (ie the documentation which establishes the trust and sets out the terms and conditions of the trust) but the trustees are also subject to the general law of trusts and various statutes (eg *TA 2000*).

15.7 Beneficiaries of the trust are the persons to whom the income of the trust and all trust property belongs.

15.8 Trusts, generally speaking, cannot be set up for specific purposes but only to benefit human beings; perhaps, the major exception to this rule is that of the charitable trust. Typically, charitable trusts are set up for the purpose of public benefit, for example, to help the poor.

Equity

15.9 The trust is a creature of equity.

15.10 Equity is a body of rules which have evolved over time and originally emerged due to the perceived unfairness of the system of common law. Where it was perceived that the consequences of applying the common law could be said to be unfair equity then sought to take a more perceived just and fair approach.

15.11 As part of these attempts to ensure fairness and just consequences for all parties the trust concept emerged. It was used at the time to resolve a number of issues. For example, the trust concept enabled a landowner to leave his land under his will which common law did not permit; under common law a married woman was not entitled to her own separate property such property being under the control of her husband; the trust effectively permitted a married woman to own her own property.

15.12 Over time a body of general principles has emerged, referred to as the maxims of equity. Such maxims include equity looks to the substance rather than form; equity will not permit a statute to be used as an instrument of fraud; equity regards as done that which ought to be done; and he who comes to equity must come with clean hands. Where appropriate these maxims are applied by the courts.

In addition to this body of equitable principles various statutes have been passed which also impinge on the operation of trusts (eg *TA 2000; TLATA 1996*).

Trust creation

15.13 Trust may be created in lifetime (ie *inter vivos*) or by will (ie will trusts); by deed or by writing or by will or even orally.

15.14 The settlor may transfer his property to trustees instructing them to hold the property so transferred on appropriate trusts or he may simply declare (possibly orally) that his property is henceforth to be held by him as trustee on appropriate terms. As a general rule, the former approach is normally adopted.

15.15 The transfer of property to trustees involves the transfer of the legal and beneficial interests of the settlor in the property. The transfer of the legal title may require consent from third parties prior to transfer; for example, the transfer of property subject to mortgage typically requires the consent of the mortgagee and the transfer of shares in private companies often requires the consent of the other shareholders.

Trust classification

15.16 Trust law generally classifies trusts into various categories although for tax purposes these categories are not the ones generally adopted. The typical classification is as follows:

- express trusts;
- implied/resulting trusts;
- constructive trusts; and
- bare trusts.

This compares with the classification for tax purposes, namely:

- trusts in which an interest in possession subsists;
- trust in which no interest in possession subsists; and
- settlor-interested trusts.

Express trust

15.17 The express trust arises where, generally speaking, the settlor (or testator) makes a deliberate and conscious decision to transfer property on to trust. Where there is some ambiguity as to the settlor's (or testator's) intention the courts may hold that an express trust has been created.

15.18 *Trusts: an overview*

Implied/resulting trust

15.18 The implied/resulting trust arises where the courts infer from the actions of the settlor (or testator) that a trust is created. A typical example, is the transfer of property from one person (X) to another person (Y) where the latter person (Y) pays for the purchase of the property but the property is vested in the name of another person (Z); in such circumstances it is implied that the name of the person in whom the property is vested (Z) holds the property on trust for the payer (Y); albeit that such a presumption may be rebutted.

Constructive trust

15.19 The constructive trust is imposed exclusively by the courts irrespective of the intention of any of the parties involved. A typical example is where the person (X) exerts undue influence over another person (Y) to transfer property to, say, X. In this case X would be held to hold the property received from X on constructive trust for X.

Bare trust

15.20 The bare trust is not strictly speaking a trust to the same extent as those just described. The bare trust is a trust where the trustees hold the trust property on trust for the beneficiaries absolutely; the beneficiaries are entitled to the capital and income of the trust and the entitlement is not subject to any contingency (eg the beneficiaries only become absolutely entitled to the trust property on attaining 18 represents a contingency)

Trusts today

15.21 Today, the use of trusts is extremely wide ranging and their use extends to:

- trusts for charitable purposes;
- pension scheme trusts;
- trusts to protect minors, spendthrifts and persons of unsound mind;
- tax liability mitigation trusts;
- protection from creditor trusts; and
- trusts to provide anonymity in business dealings.

Protection of minors

15.22 A discretionary trust enables a settlor to benefit his minor children whilst at the same time preventing them from gaining direct access to the underlying trust property (and possibly squandering it unwisely or foolishly).

Bankruptcy protection

15.23 A discretionary trust may be used to protect the individual's assets from creditors in the event of the individual's bankruptcy. On the other hand, if a beneficiary possesses a fixed interest in the trust (eg a life interest in the trust income for life), in the event of bankruptcy the fixed interest (ie the income arising therefrom) will effectively become available to the creditors.

Will substitute

15.24 A trust can also be used as a substitute will. An individual during his lifetime might settle the major portion of his property on trust. The trust will continue after his death on the terms set out in the trust deed.

The use of the trust in this manner may be to mitigate inheritance tax (IHT) in particular and/or enable the trustees to take into account circumstances after the settlor's death when considering application of the trust property for the benefit of one or more beneficiaries.

15.25 A trust document (unlike a will) is a confidential document and does not need to be filed with any authority and is thus not available for inspection by the public.

The Perpetuities and Accumulations Act 2009

15.26 The *PAA 2009* came into effect on the 6 April 2010.

15.27 It replaces the previous rules with respect to perpetuities and accumulations which were perceived to be complex and no longer in keeping with the modern world; many offshore jurisdictions have amended the UK's rules in this regard (see paragraphs 25.29, 25.30 and 25.31).

15.28 The new rules apply to trusts which take effect on or after 6 April 2010 and to will trusts where the will is made on or after 6 April 2010.

However, will trusts created under wills executed before 6 April 2010, are governed by the pre-*PAA 2009* rules (even if the testator is alive on or after 6 April 2010).

15.29 *Trusts: an overview*

15.29 The two main changes introduced are:

- the perpetuity period is fixed at 125 years in all cases (*PAA 2009 s 5*); and

- the rule against accumulations is abolished (*PAA 2009 ss 13* and *14*; except for charitable trusts).

15.30 Trusts created before 6 April 2010 continue to be subject to the pre-*PAA 2009* rules as are will trusts created under wills executed before 6 April 2010.

Tax aspects

15.31 For tax purposes the trustees of the trust may be subject to income tax (on income arising to the trust) and capital gains tax (CGT) (arising on disposals of trust assets). They may also be responsible for discharging IHT liabilities arising on trust property.

15.32 The settlor and/or beneficiaries of the trust may also be exposed to such taxes with respect to the trust property.

15.33 As indicated in paragraph 15.16, there is no single classification of trusts applicable to income tax, CGT and IHT.

However, a convenient but somewhat broad classification is to divide trusts into discretionary and fixed interest (or interest in possession) trusts.

Discretionary trust

15.34 The key difference between these two types of trust is that in the case of a discretionary trust the beneficiaries have no *right* to obtain any current or future benefit from the trust; such beneficiaries can only *hope* that the trustees will exercise their (ie the trustees') discretion (hence the term discretionary) in their favour.

15.35 The extent of the trustees' discretion may vary. Thus, for example, their discretion may extend to allocating the income of the trust amongst the beneficiaries as they think fit or, alternatively, it may extend to including whether in the first instance they wish to allocate any of the income to the beneficiaries.

Interest in possession trust

15.36 An interest in possession trust is one under which the beneficiary(ies) possessing the interest has a current fixed entitlement to the income of the trust as it arises. The trustees, with this type of trust, cannot deny the beneficiary(ies) his right to the trust income as it arises; thus the beneficiary(ies) is not dependent upon the trustees exercising any discretion.

15.37 Often (although not necessarily so) the interest in possession subsists for the lifetime of the beneficiary and in such a case the beneficiary is commonly referred to as the life tenant of the trust; alternatively it may subsist until, for example, the beneficiary remarries or attains age 25.

The Hague Convention

15.38 The split of ownership of property into legal and beneficial ownership is unique to common law jurisdictions and is not, as a general principle, recognised in civil law systems (ie most countries in mainland Europe). Although civil law jurisdictions' own domestic legal systems do not recognise trusts as such, a number of these countries are signatories to the *HCLAT 1986*. In the United Kingdom, *HCLAT 1986* is given effect by the *RTA 1987*. Initially, only three countries signed *HCLAT 1986* namely, Australia, Italy and the UK where it came into effect in 1992. Under *HCLAT 1986* the signatory territories agree in principle to recognise the trust concept.

However, *HCLAT 1986* only applies to trusts created voluntarily and evidenced in writing and thus not all types of trust are covered by it (eg constructive trusts).

Summary

15.39 Trusts may be created in lifetime or on death by will.

15.40 The essence of the trust is the splitting of legal and beneficial ownership. The former resides with the trustees and the latter with the beneficiaries. The trustees' duties are governed by the trust deed, general trust law and statute.

15.41 For tax purposes the two main types of trust are the discretionary trust and the interest in possession trust. The beneficiaries of the discretionary trust benefit under the trust as and when the trustees exercise their discretion whereas the beneficiary with the interest in possession has an automatic entitlement to the income (not capital) of the trust.

15.42 Trusts are also used for non-tax reasons including provision for minor children; asset protection in the event of bankruptcy; and charitable purposes.

15.43 The trust, unlike a will, is confidential and may to some degree be used as a form of substitute will.

Chapter 16

Inheritance tax: trusts

Background

16.1 Inheritance tax (IHT) applies not only to individuals but also to property held on trust. It applies when property is settled on trust and when property leaves a trust. IHT may also be levied every ten years during the life of the trust depending upon the type of trust.

16.2 *FA 2006* made significant changes to the IHT treatment of trusts. The changes brought in by *FA 2006* apply not only to trusts set up on or after 22 March 2006 but also to trusts set up before this date albeit subject to transitional provisions.

16.3 The major impact of *FA 2006* is to treat most lifetime trusts created on or after 22 March 2006 as 'relevant property trusts'. A relevant property trust is one in which no 'qualifying interest possession' subsists (*IHTA 1984 ss 58* and *59*); classically, a discretionary trust.

16.4 A 'qualifying interest in possession' is an interest in possession to which an individual becomes entitled pre-22 March 2006.

A 'qualifying interest in possession' is an interest in possession to which an individual becomes entitled on or after 22 March 2006 if it is:

- an immediate post-death interest (IPDI) (*IHTA 1984 s 49A*);
- a transitional serial interest (TSI) (*IHTA 1984 s 49C*); or
- a disabled person's interest (*IHTA 1984 s 89B*).

(IHTA 1984 s 58)

Any other interest in possession is a non-qualifying interest.

An interest in possession is an interest in trust property by virtue of which the individual has an immediate entitlement to the income from the trust property in which the interest subsists (HMRC *Press Release 12 February 1976; SP10/79* and *Pearson v IRC (1981);* see paragraph 16.46).

16.5 The qualifying interest in possession may arise in lifetime or on death. However, post-*FA 2006* lifetime creation of such an interest is not possible unless the trust qualifies as a disabled trust (*IHTA 1984 s 89*).

16.6 The basic thrust of the changes introduced by *FA 2006* is to charge trusts created in lifetime on or after 22 March 2006 to IHT in the same manner as applies to relevant property trusts pre- (and indeed post-) 22 March 2006 (ie to bring within the ambit of the relevant property trust charges newly created lifetime interest in possession trusts).

16.7 Relevant property trusts are subject to a charge to IHT on trust property every ten years and when trust property leaves the trust. In addition, property settled on such trusts constitutes chargeable lifetime transfers (CLTs) thus precipitating an IHT charge at the date of settling the property; the charge is levied at 20% (subject to the availability of the nil rate band (NRB)).

16.8 Qualifying interest in possession trusts, on the other hand, are not subject to the ten-yearly charge nor any charge when property leaves the trust. Property settled on such trusts constitutes potentially exempt transfers (PETs) (not CLTs).

However, on the death of an individual possessing a qualifying interest in possession, the trust assets in which the interest subsists are treated as part of the deceased's estate (ie IHT is levied thereon; *IHTA 1984 s 49*). The death of a beneficiary under a relevant property trust has, by comparison, no such impact for IHT purposes.

Post-*FA 2006*, it is therefore possible for an interest in possession to be either a qualifying or non-qualifying interest.

Relevant property trusts

Creation of the trust

16.9 As indicated in paragraph 16.7 the creation of a relevant property trust is a CLT by the settlor. The NRB available for offset against the CLT in calculating the IHT charge thereon is determined by the cumulative total of CLTs the settlor has made in the previous seven years (PETs are ignored unless the settlor having made the PET dies within seven years thereafter; see paragraph 16.11).

The cumulative total of CLTs made by the settlor in the seven years prior to the trust creation is also critical in determining all future exit and ten-yearly charges; this total continues to be relevant even after seven years.

16.10 *Inheritance tax: trusts*

16.10 Grossing-up (see paragraph 10.54) is also relevant if the IHT arising on the CLT is to be paid by the transferor and not out of the settled property by the transferee (ie the trustees).

16.11 If the settlor dies within seven years of creation of the trust any PETs made within seven years of death become chargeable. This means that the IHT charged on the CLT on creation of the trust may need to be recalculated where the PETs are made prior to the creation of the trust but within seven years of death.

It also means that any exit charge(s) (see paragraph 16.23) calculated on property ceasing to be relevant property between the date of creation of the trust and the date of death may also need to be recalculated.

Any extra IHT that becomes payable on the CLT on creation of the trust and/or the exit charge(s) due to the settlor's death is that of the trustees.

Example 1

Steven Computer settles £450,000 on a discretionary trust on 1 March 2007. In the previous seven years he has made CLTs and PETs as follows:

January 2002	£100,000	CLT1
March 2004	£75,000	CLT2
October 2005	£150,000	PET1
August 2006	£125,000	CLT3

On 1 December 2010 the trustees appoint £80,000 to one of the trust beneficiaries.

Creation of the trust

Steven's aggregate CLTs made within seven years of creation of the trust is £300,000. Thus, the whole of the £285,000 NRB for 2006–2007 (ie the tax year of the creation of the trust) is utilised.

Assuming the trustees agree to pay the IHT charge on the CLT of £450,000 the charge thereon is 20% of £450,000 (ie £90,000).

If Steven agrees to pay the IHT the charge is:

[£450,000/0.8] x 20% ie £112,500.

The aggregate CLT is then £562,500 [ie £450,000 + £112,500].

(See Examples 2 and 3 paragraph 16.25 for the exit charge calculation and the need to then re-calculate this exit charge).

Principles underlying the ten-yearly and exit charges

16.12 The rules discussed here only apply to relevant property trusts created on or after 27 March 1974.

16.13 The relevant property regime applies to discretionary trusts and trusts with non-qualifying interests in possession (typically most, but not all, trusts created in lifetime on or after 22 March 2006).

16.14 On the tenth anniversary of the commencement (see paragraph 16.15) of the trust (and every subsequent tenth anniversary) a charge to IHT arises on the value of relevant property (ie property in which no qualifying interest in possession subsists; *IHTA 1984 s 58*) held in the trust at the anniversary (*IHTA 1984 s 64*).

The relevant property includes any income of the trust which has been 'accumulated'; thus, income which has not been accumulated is not subject to the ten yearly charge (SP8/86). Income is accumulated either by positive action on the part of the trustees to effect accumulation or it may, de facto, be treated as accumulated (eg if trustees take no positive action and significant time has passed since the income first arose, although this does not necessarily follow).

16.15 The date on which the trust commences (*IHTA 1984 s 61*) is the date on which property first becomes comprised in the trust.

16.16 The charge is payable by the trustees (and no grossing-up is necessary).

16.17 The underlying method of computation and the applicable rates mean that the maximum rate applicable on any ten-year anniversary is 6% (see paragraph 16.29).

16.18 A charge also arises when property ceases to be relevant property (*IHTA 1984 s 65*). This charge is commonly referred to as an 'exit' charge.

The measure of the quantum of property ceasing to be relevant property is the difference between the value of the relevant property in the trust before the exit charge arises and the value of the relevant property remaining in the trust immediately after the exit charge arises (*IHTA 1984 s 65*).

If the exit charge arising is paid by the beneficiary, (as opposed to the trustees), who is the recipient of the relevant property no grossing-up is necessary;

16.19 *Inheritance tax: trusts*

however, if the charge is to be borne by the relevant property remaining in the trust (ie by the trustees) grossing-up is necessary.

No exit charge arises on property ceasing to be relevant property in the first quarter beginning with the day on which the settlement commences or beginning with a ten-year anniversary often referred to as the 'Frankland trap' after the case of *Frankland v IRC* (1997) (*IHTA 1984 s 65;* see paragraph 28.89).

16.19 The maximum rate applicable to an exit charge is 5.85% (ie 39/40s of 6% (the maximum rate applicable to the previous ten-year anniversary)) (see paragraph 16.29).

16.20 An exit charge may arise, for example, where trustees of a relevant property trust appoint trust capital to one or more beneficiaries or where, under the terms of the trust, a beneficiary becomes absolutely entitled to trust capital.

Property may also cease to be relevant property if it is appointed on a fixed interest trust (ie an interest in possession is created in respect of some or all of the property comprised in the trust). This, however, does not apply with respect to fixed interests created on or after 22 March 2006 as such interests are not qualifying interests in possession (*IHTA 1984 ss 49* and *59*) and thus the property so appointed simply remains relevant property within the trust.

Computational principles of the exit and ten-yearly charges

16.21 The mechanics of computation to arrive at an IHT charge associated with a relevant property trust are complex.

16.22 Examples below illustrate the principles underlying the following:

- the computation of the exit charge which arises before the first ten-year anniversary;
- the computation of the first ten-year anniversary charge;
- the computation of the exit charge which arises after the first ten-year anniversary;
- the computation of the second ten-year charge; and
- the computational effects of adding property to the trust after its commencement.

Exit charge before the first ten-year charge

16.23 The rate of IHT applicable in calculating the exit charge is a 'fraction' of the 'effective rate' applicable to a 'hypothetical transfer' (*IHTA 1984 s 68*).

Inheritance tax: trusts **16.23**

The fraction is equal to 'three-tenths (ie 30%) multiplied by one-fortieth for each complete successive quarter that has elapsed between the date of creation of the trust and the date of the exit' (note there are forty quarters in a ten-year period).

The effective rate is the rate of IHT applied to the hypothetical transfer; the hypothetical transfer is the aggregate of the following constituent elements (*IHTA 1984 s 68*):

- the value of the property in the trust immediately after it commences (1);
- the value of any property added to the trust after commencement and before the exit charge arises (the value used is the value at the date of the addition) (2); and
- the value of any property comprised in a 'related trust' immediately after the related trust commenced (a related trust is one created by the same settlor on the same day; *IHTA 1984 s 62*) (3).

(The above numbers (1), (2) and (3) are used in the examples below as reference points).

The property to be included in the above aggregate amount (ie property within any of the above three components) calculation is not restricted to 'relevant property'. Thus, excluded property (*IHTA 1985 s 6*; see paragraph 13.41) is included for calculation purposes as is property subject to a qualifying interest in possession.

Where on the initial creation of the trust the trustees bear the IHT charge this reduces the value of property in the trust which is not the case if the settlor agrees to discharge the charge. Similarly, if the trustees bear the exit charge grossing-up is necessary and it is the gross amount which depletes the trust property.

The value of the trust property immediately after the trust commences includes the full value of any property settled which is eligible for business property relief (BPR) (or agricultural property relief (APR)). Thus, whilst such relief reduces the amount of the CLT (by 50% or 100%) made by the settlor on settling the property in computing his IHT liability on the CLT, it is the value pre-reliefs which is its value immediately after it is settled for the purposes of (1) above (*IHTA 1984 s 68*). However, the value of such property at the ten-year anniversaries is the value after BPR (or APR).

In arriving at the rate applicable to the hypothetical transfer it is necessary to take into account CLTs of the settlor in the seven years before he creates the trust (ie such CLTs made by the settlor will absorb some of the appropriate NRB applicable to the hypothetical transfer).

16.23 *Inheritance tax: trusts*

Any CLTs made by the settlor on the same day as the trust commences are ignored. Whilst this may be unlikely (although of course possible) where a lifetime trust is created, on death where the deceased settles property on trust (ie a will trust) any other gifts made in the will are made on the same day; however, such gifts are ignored.

Nevertheless, more than one trust created on death are related trusts (*IHTA 1984 s 62*) unless one of them creates an immediate post-death interest in possession (IPDI) for the surviving spouse in which case, due to the effect of *IHTA 1984 s 80,* the trusts are not related (see paragraph 13.45).

The relevant NRB is that applicable in the tax year of the exit charge.

Example 2

Using the facts of Example 1 above set out below for ease of reference.

Calculation of exit charge

Aggregate amount of CLTs made by Steven within seven years of creation of the trust £300,000.

The hypothetical transfer is the aggregate of components (1), (2) and (3) (see paragraph 16.23) and is [£450,000 − £90,000] ie £360,000 (of the £450,000 settled on trust £90,000 is the IHT paid by the trustees thus leaving only £360,000 cash in the trust) namely:

(1) £360,000 (on 1 March 2007)

(2) Nil (no additions made to the trust).

(3) Nil (assume Steven creates no 'related trusts').

An appointment of £80,000 occurs on 1 December 2010 (thus the applicable NRB is that of tax year 2010–2011 (ie £325,0000)).

The aggregate £300,000 of CLTs made in the seven years before the creation of the trust leaves £25,000 (ie £325,000 less £300,000) of the NRB available for use against the hypothetical transfer of £360,000.

Thus, the IHT charge on the hypothetical transfer of £360,000 is:

[0% x £25,000 + 20% x £335,000] = £67,000

The percentage rate applicable (ie the effective rate) is thus [£67,000/£360,000] (ie 18.6111%).

The appropriate fraction of the effective rate is then:

[30% x 15/40] x 18.6111% ie 2.0937%

(Between the date of creation of the trust 1 March 2007 and the date of the exit charge 1 December 2010 there are 15 complete quarters).

The IHT charge on the appointment of the £80,000 (ie the exit charge) is thus:

2.0937% of £80,000 (ie £1,675) (this assumes the recipient beneficiary discharges the liability).

If the trustees are to discharge the liability out of the remaining relevant property in the trust the IHT charge becomes:

[£80,000/0.9791] x 0.020937 = £1,711.

(note: 0.9791 is derived from [1 – 0.020937]).

Nil rate band discretionary trust (exit charge)

16.24 It may be observed that if the settlor has made no CLTs within the seven years prior to setting up a relevant property trust and the amount settled equals the then NRB, no exit charge can arise on any appointments out of the trust in its first ten years. This is because the 'effective rate' will be 0% due to the applicability of a full NRB (see also paragraph 16.30 with respect to the first ten-yearly charge on a NRB discretionary trust which may also be nil) and thus the rate applicable in calculating the exit charge will be 0% (ie 30% x 0%).

16.25 If in Example 1 Steven dies on 1 March 2011 this precipitates the following consequences:

- any lifetime CLTs made within seven years of death are subject to an 'additional' IHT charge which includes the initial amount settled on trust;
- any PETs made within seven years of death now become subject to an IHT charge; and
- the IHT charge on any exit charge needs to be recomputed (due to the change in the aggregate amount of CLTs now made in lifetime before creation of the trust).

16.25 *Inheritance tax: trusts*

The impact on the exit charge (only) originally computed in Example 2 is shown in Example 3:

Example 3

Aggregate amount of CLTs made by Steven within seven years of creation of the trust is now £450,000 (previously £300,000) due to the PET of £150,000 now becoming chargeable due to the death.

Aggregate of components (1), (2) and (3) is £360,000 (remains the same) namely:

(1)   £360,000 (on 1 March 2007)
(2)   Nil (no additions made to the trust).
(3)   Nil (assume Steve created no 'related trusts').

An appointment of £80,000 occurs on 1 December 2010 (thus the applicable NRB is that of tax year 2010–2011 ie £325,000).

The aggregate £450,000 (previously £300,000) of CLTs made in the seven years before the creation of the trust leaves no part of the £325,000 NRB (previously £25,000 left) for use against the hypothetical chargeable transfer of £360,000.

Thus, the IHT charge on the hypothetical transfer of £360,000 is:

20% x £360,000 = £72,000 (previously £67,000)

The percentage rate applicable (ie the effective rate) is thus [£72,000/ £360,000] (ie 20%).

The appropriate fraction of the effective rate is then:

[[30% x 15/40] x 20%] ie 2.25% (previously 2.0937%).

(Between the date of creation of the trust 1 March 2007 and the date of the exit charge 1 December 2010 there are 15 complete quarters).

The IHT charge on the appointment of the £80,000 (ie the exit charge) is thus:

2.25% of £80,000 ie £1,800 (previously £1,675) (this assumes the recipient beneficiary discharges the liability).

Inheritance tax: trusts **16.28**

If the trustees are to discharge the liability out of the remaining relevant property in the trust the IHT charge becomes:

[£80,000/0.9775] x 0.0225 = £1,841 (previously £1,711).

Example 3 reveals that Steven's death within seven years of creating the trust has increased the amount of the exit charge (albeit in this particular example not significantly). Had Steven died more than seven years after the creation of the trust, re-computation would not have been necessary as the PET he made in October 2005 would not then have become chargeable.

First ten-year charge

16.26 A charge to IHT arises on each tenth anniversary of the trust's commencement. The charge is applied to the relevant property held in the trust at the anniversary date (*IHTA 1984 s 64*).

16.27 The calculation in principle follows that applicable to calculating an exit charge.

16.28 The rate of IHT applicable in calculating the ten-yearly charge is a fraction of the effective rate applicable to a hypothetical transfer (*IHTA 1984 s 68*).

The fraction is equal to 'three-tenths' (ie 30%).

The effective rate is that which would be charged on the hypothetical transfer which is the aggregate of the following constituent elements (*IHTA 1984 s 66*):

- the value of relevant property comprised in the trust at its value the day before the anniversary (A);
- the value of any non-relevant property comprised in the trust immediately after it became comprised in the settlement (ie between creation of the trust and the ten-year anniversary) which has not subsequently become relevant property (B); and
- the value of property comprised in any related trust immediately after it commenced (C).

(The above letters (A), (B), (C) and (D), below, are used in the examples below as reference points.)

In arriving at the rate applicable to the above aggregate amount it is necessary to take into account CLTs (and failed PETs) of the settlor in the seven years before he creates the trust and any amounts in respect of which an exit charge has arisen within the previous ten (ie not seven) years (D). The latter requirement, to take into account property which ceases to be relevant property (ie in respect of which an exit charge arises), is to prevent the simple expedient of transferring property out of the trust just prior to the ten-year anniversary in order to reduce the value of relevant property subject to charge on the ten-year anniversary.

The relevant NRB to apply in the above calculation is that applicable in the tax year in which the tenth anniversary falls.

16.29 The maximum rate applicable on the tenth anniversary is 6% (ie 30% of 20%).

Example 4

Belinda York settles £365,000 on a discretionary trust on 5 October 1999.

In the immediately preceding seven years she has made CLTs of £55,000.

On 18 November 2003 and 23 March 2004 appointments totalling £100,000 are made to beneficiaries of the trust and the beneficiaries agree to pay any IHT (ie no grossing up necessary).

On the tenth anniversary (ie 5 October 2009), the value of relevant property in the trust is £500,000.

The hypothetical transfer is £500,000 comprised of:

(A) £500,000

(B) Nil

(C) Nil

The CLTs made by the settlor in the seven years preceding the creation of the trust amount to £55,000 and the amount on which exit charges have been levied is £100,000 (D).

Thus, of the £325,000 NRB (applicable for tax year 2009–2010 the tax year of the tenth anniversary) £155,000 has been utilised which leaves £170,000 unused.

IHT on the hypothetical transfer of £500,000 is thus:

0% x £170,000 + 20% x £330,000 = £66,000

This represents a percentage rate of [£66,000/£500,000]

(ie 13.20% (the effective rate)).

Thus, the rate applicable at the first tenth anniversary is:

30% x 13.20% (ie 3.96%).

Inheritance tax: trusts **16.30**

IHT levied on first tenth anniversary (and payable by the trustees) is 3.96% of £500,000 (ie £19,800).

Nil rate band discretionary trust (ten-year charge)

16.30 It may thus be observed that if no CLTs are made by the settlor within the seven years prior to setting up the discretionary trust and no appointments are made out of the trust prior to the first ten-year anniversary (and the amount initially settled in the trust equals the then NRB (ie the NRB at the time of initial creation)) no IHT charge arises on the first tenth anniversary.

This assumes, however, that the value of the relevant property in the trust on the tenth anniversary is no greater than the then NRB (ie the growth in value of the trust assets (initially equal to the then NRB) is exactly in line with the increase over the ten-year period of the NRB itself (see paragraph 16.24)).

Even where the growth over the ten-year period of the trust relevant property is in excess of the corresponding growth in the NRB, the IHT payable on the ten-year anniversary may still be relatively small.

Example 5

Belinda York creates a discretionary trust on 5 October 1998 settling property of value equal to the then NRB of £223,000 having made no earlier CLTs. She agrees to pay the IHT on the £223,000 but no grossing up occurs as there is no IHT to pay.

In the immediately preceding seven years she has made no CLTs.

No appointments are made to beneficiaries out of the trust in the first ten years.

On the tenth anniversary, (ie 5 October 2008) the value of the trust assets is £312,000.

The hypothetical transfer is £312,000.

The NRB available in calculating IHT on the hypothetical transfer is £312,000 (the NRB for tax year 2008–2009).

20% x [£312,000 – £312,000] (ie nil).

The rate applicable to the hypothetical transfer is thus 0% (the effective rate).

16.31 *Inheritance tax: trusts*

The rate applicable to the relevant property comprised in the trust on the ten-year anniversary is thus 30% of 0% (ie 0%).

No IHT is charged on the tenth anniversary.

Assume, however, at the tenth anniversary the relevant property is valued at £412,000.

The hypothetical transfer is £412,000.

The NRB available in calculating IHT on the hypothetical transfer is £312,000 (the NRB for tax year 2008–2009):

20% x [£412,000 – £312,000] (ie £20,000).

The rate applicable to the hypothetical transfer is thus [£20,000/ £412,000] (ie 4.8544% – the effective rate).

The rate applicable to the relevant property comprised in the trust on the ten-year anniversary is thus 30% of 4.8544% (ie 1.4563%).

IHT charge on ten-year anniversary is:

1.4563% × £412,000 = £5,999.

Exit charge arising between ten-year anniversaries

16.31 The calculation in respect of an exit charge arising after a ten-year anniversary is similar, but not identical, to the calculation of the exit charge arising within the first ten years of commencement of the trust.

16.32 The rate of IHT used to calculate the exit charge is the appropriate fraction of the rate which applies at the immediately preceding ten-year anniversary.

The appropriate fraction is one fortieth for each complete quarter between the date of the preceding ten-year anniversary and the date of the exit charge (note, however, the lack of exit charge where property ceases to be relevant property in the first quarter after the date of a ten-year anniversary; see paragraph 16.18).

However, it may first be necessary to re-compute the rate which applies at the previous ten-year anniversary if between the date of the latter and the date of the exit charge the rates of IHT have fallen ie reduced (eg the NRB applicable at the two dates has increased).

16.33 The measure of the quantum of property ceasing to be relevant property is the difference between the value of the relevant property in the trust before the exit charge arises and the value of the relevant property remaining in the trust immediately after the exit charge arises (*IHTA 1984 s 65*).

Example 6

Harold Car sets up a discretionary trust on 1 January 1997. He has made CLTs in the previous seven years of £100,000.

In the first ten years of the trust appointments of capital amount to £125,000 and the beneficiaries agree to pay any IHT arising.

At the ten-year anniversary the relevant property is worth £425,000.

On 15 June 2010 the trustees appoint £11,000 to one of the beneficiaries who agrees to pay any IHT due (ie no grossing up is necessary).

First ten-year anniversary charge

The relevant property at 1 January 2007 is valued at £425,000.

The hypothetical transfer amounts to £425,000.

Harold's CLTs in the seven years prior to creating the trust are £100,000 and the value of property ceasing to be relevant property (ie where an exit charge arises) within the first ten years is £125,000.

Thus, £225,000 of the £285,000 NRB (for tax year 2006–2007) is utilised.

The IHT charge on the hypothetical transfer is thus:

0% x £60,000 + 20% x £365,000 = £73,000.

This gives a rate of [£73,000/£425,000]:

17.1765% (the effective rate).

The rate applicable on the ten-year anniversary is therefore:

17.1765% x 30% ie 5.1529%.

The IHT charge arising on the tenth anniversary is:

5.1529% x £425,000 = £21,899.

Exit charge

The appointment of the £11,000 on 15 June 2010 precipitates an exit charge. This charge is computed using the rate charged at the previous ten-year anniversary (ie the rate of 5.1529%).

16.34 *Inheritance tax: trusts*

However, the NRB increases between the tax year in which the date of the ten-year anniversary (2006–2007) falls and the tax year in which the exit charge arises (2010–2011). Accordingly it is necessary to recompute the ten-year anniversary charge using the rates of the tax year 2010–2011.

The relevant property at 1 January 2007 is valued at £425,000.

The hypothetical transfer amounts to £425,000.

Harold's CLTs in the seven years prior to creating the trust are £100,000 and the value of property ceasing to be relevant property (ie where an exit charge arises) within the first ten years is £125,000.

Thus, £225,000 of the £325,000 NRB (for tax year 2010–2011) is utilised.

The IHT charge on the hypothetical transfer is thus:

0% x £100,000 + 20% x £325,000 = £65,000.

This gives a rate of [£65,000/£425,000] (ie 15.2941%).

The exit charge is therefore:

[15.2941% x 30% x 13/40] x £11,000 = £164.

(Number of complete quarters between 1 January 2007 (the first ten-year anniversary) and 15 June 2010 (the date of the appointment of property out of the trust) is 13.)

Charges after the first ten years

16.34 A ten-yearly charge arises on each ten-year anniversary of the commencement of the trust.

16.35 For second and subsequent anniversaries the computation of the charge in principle follows that set out in computing the charge on the trust's first anniversary (see paragraph 16.26) which it will be recalled includes:

'In arriving at the rate applicable to the above aggregate amount it is necessary to take into account CLTs (and failed PETs) of the settlor in the seven years before he created the trust and any amounts in respect of which an exit charge has arisen within the previous ten (ie not seven) years (D) (see paragraph 16.28).'

In computing the charge on second and subsequent anniversaries it is amounts in respect of which an exit charge has arisen within the ten years prior to the anniversary under consideration which is now to be ascertained and included in the above total (not the exit charges arising in the first ten years). The settlor's CLTs made within the seven years before the trust is created remain in the calculation as above.

Addition of property after the trust commences

16.36 Additions of property to a relevant property trust after its commencement add complexity to the calculations and affect the computation of the ten-yearly and exit charges.

16.37 The effect of additions of property is as follows:

- the quantum of the exit charge within the first ten years is affected as the computation of such exit charges includes in the hypothetical transfer additions of property (see paragraph 16.23);

- the aggregate amount of CLTs made by the settlor within seven years prior to the creation of the trust may need to be substituted with the aggregate amount of CLTs made within the seven years prior to the date of the addition of the property if the latter aggregate is greater than the former aggregate;

- where more than one addition has occurred at different times the seven-year period prior to any addition which produces the greatest total of CLTs is adopted;

- however, if in calculating the aggregate amount of CLTs in any seven-year period prior to the addition of property this amount includes transfers to the trust itself (as opposed to CLTs which are made in this period by the settlor but not to the trust) the aggregate total is to be reduced by the net amounts of these transfers into trust;

- similarly, if in calculating the aggregate amount of CLTs in any seven-year period prior to the addition of property this amount includes property which has ceased to be relevant property at the date of the ten-year charge and has been subject to an exit charge the aggregate total is to be reduced by the value attributable to the relevant property comprising the exit charge; and

- where added property comprises property subject to the ten-year charge a reduction applies to the rate applicable at the ten-year anniversary to this added property which is equal to one-fortieth for each complete quarter that the added property was not comprised in the trust commencing at the date of the immediately preceding ten-year anniversary.

16.37 *Inheritance tax: trusts*

Example 7

Bobby Tool sets up a discretionary trust on 10 August 1998 settling £75,000 and the trustees agree to pay any IHT.

His CLTs in the previous seven years amount to £40,000, £30,000 made on 12 October 1992 and £10,000 on 14 November 1997 (the donees agree to pay any IHT payable ie no grossing up necessary).

Bobby adds further property to the trust of £60,000 on 15 June 2007 and the trustees agree to pay any IHT (ie no grossing up necessary).

Within the seven years prior to the addition of the property into the trust on 15 June 2007, Bobby makes CLTs of £15,000 on 6 November 2006 and £40,000 on 19 November 2000 amounting to £55,000 in total (the donees agree to pay any IHT).

As the total (£55,000) of Bobby's CLTs in the seven years preceding the addition of the property on 15 June 2007 to the trust is greater than his CLTs in the seven years prior to the creation of the trust (£40,000), the £55,000 figure is used in calculating the ten-year charge on 10 August 2008.

Example 8

Using the facts from Example 7 above but assuming the addition of the £60,000 property occurred on 7 May 2003 (ie not 15 June 2007).

Within seven years of the addition of the property into the trust on 7 May 2003 Bobby makes CLTs amounting to £125,000 made up of £10,000 (14 November 1997), £75,000 (10 August 1998) and £40,000 (19 November 2000).

However, of this £125,000 the £75,000 relates to the creation of the settlement itself and thus should be excluded producing a figure of £50,000 which is in fact still greater than the £40,000 figure for CLTs made within seven years prior to the creation of the settlement.

As the total (£50,000) of Bobby's CLTs in the seven years preceding the addition of the property to the trust is greater than his CLTs in the seven years prior to the creation of the trust (£40,000), the £50,000 figure is used in calculating the ten-year charge on 10 August 2008.

Additions of property and the ten-year charge

16.38 As indicated in paragraph 16.37 the effect of additions of property to the trust is that the ten-year charge accommodates these additions by allowing a reduction in the effective rate applying to these additions by applying the reducing factor based on fortieths).

Additions of property and the exit charge

16.39 When property is subject to an exit charge it is necessary in calculating the charge to ascertain from which relevant property in the trust it is appointed as this impacts upon the amount of the charge. The property appointed may thus be attributed to the initial property settled in the trust (or property held at a previous ten-year anniversary) and/or additions of property to the trust thereafter.

Example 9

Trevor Smith sets up a discretionary trust on 9 November 2000 settling £550,000 and the trustees agree to pay any IHT due.

Tevor's CLTs in the seven years prior to creating the trust amount to £75,000 and the donees agree to pay any IHT due.

On 23 April 2008 Trevor adds further property to the trust of £400,000 and the trustees agree to pay any IHT due.

On 7 July 2010 the trustees appoint £160,000 out to one of the beneficiaries who agrees to pay any IHT due.

Creation of trust

The CLT of £550,000 settled on the trust precipitates an IHT liability (paid by the trustees, hence no grossing-up) of:

0% x [£234,000 – £75,000] + 20% x £391,000 = £78,200.

(NRB for tax year 2000–2001 is £234,000).

Addition of £400,000

In the seven years prior to the addition of the property of £400,000 Trevor has made no CLTs; thus, the whole of the NRB of £312,000 (for tax year 2008–2009) is available.

The IHT charge arising (paid by the trustees) is:

0% x £312,000 + 20% x [£400,000 – £312,000] = £17,600.

16.39 *Inheritance tax: trusts*

Exit charge

The appointment of £160,000 out of the trust creates an exit charge (the recipient beneficiary agrees to pay the IHT liability arising).

The exit charge arises in the first ten years of commencement of the trust. The hypothetical transfer consists of:

the value of the trust immediately after it commenced (ie [£550,000 – £78,200] = £471,800)

and

the value of any added property (ie [£400,000 – £17,600] = £382,400).

Hypothetical transfer is thus £854,200.

The IHT charge on the hypothetical transfer is:

0% x [£325,000 – £75,000] + [20% x £604,200] = £120,840.

(NRB for tax year 2010–2011 of £325,000; of this NRB £250,000 is left for offset against the £854,200 as £75,000 has been used by the CLTs made by Trevor in the seven years prior to commencement of the trust).

This gives a rate (the effective rate) of:

[£120,840/£854,200] = 14.1466%.

If the appointment of £160,000 is made out of the property originally settled by Trevor the effective rate of 14.1466% is adjusted by [30% x 38/40] producing a rate of 4.0318%.

The exit charge is then:

4.0318% x £160,000 = £6,451.

If the appointment of £160,000 is made out of the property of £400,000 subsequently added by Trevor the effective rate of 14.1466% is adjusted by [30% x 8/40] producing a rate of 0.8488%.

The exit charge is then:

0.8488% x £160,000 = £1,358.

Life and death rates versus relevant property rates

16.40 The major drawback from an IHT perspective with respect to relevant property trusts is normally the 20% 'up-front' charge applicable when the trust is created. This charge applies unless the NRB is available to the settlor.

16.41 This problem has become much more acute following *FA 2006*.

16.42 Nevertheless, the charges to IHT which apply once the trust is 'up and running' are, relatively speaking, much lower than the rate applicable on death (ie 40%); the maximum rate applicable to an exit charge is 5.85% (ie 39/40ths of 6%) and that applicable to the ten-yearly anniversary charge, 6%.

16.43 Taking a simple example; if £1 million is settled (assume no NRB available; no growth in the monies settled; and ignoring the time value of money) the 'up-front' cost is £200,000. Assuming the trust pays the £200,000 it is left with £800,000. The ten-yearly anniversary charges are £48,000 (ie £48,000 every ten years). To equate to the £400,000 charge (ie 40% on £1 million) that arises on death requires the trust to subsist for a little over 40 years (ie four amounts of £48,000 plus the initial 'up front' charge of £200,000).

16.44 Times, however, change and the IHT treatment for individuals and trusts in the future is impossible to predict (note the surprising changes made to the IHT treatment of trusts unannounced in *FA 2006*).

Interest in possession trusts

16.45 It is perhaps worth observing that the distinction between a 'qualifying interest in possession' and a 'non-qualifying interest in possession' is of relevance only for IHT purposes. It has no significance for general trust law purposes or for either income tax or capital gains tax (CGT).

Interests in possession may be, and often are, for the lifetime of the individual beneficiary or shorter periods (eg to terminate on marriage or on attaining a certain age). Where the interest is for the lifetime of the individual beneficiary the individual is often referred to as the life tenant.

16.46 Despite its significant importance the term 'interest in possession' is not defined in the legislation. It is a present right to present enjoyment *(Pearson v IRC (1980); SP10/79* and *IR Press Release* 12 February 1976). However, if the trustees have a power to accumulate the income of the trust (unless the accumulation must be held solely for the person having the interest in possession) this precludes an interest in possession from arising (because the present right to present enjoyment does not arise as it is dependent upon the trustees'

16.47 *Inheritance tax: trusts*

decision as to whether to accumulate or not). Similar powers over the capital of the trust should not preclude an interest in possession from arising.

16.47 A qualifying interest in possession is an interest to which an individual becomes entitled on or after 22 March 2006 and is:

- an IPDI (*IHTA 1984 s 49A*);
- a TSI (*IHTA 1984 s 49C*); or
- a disabled person's interest (*IHTA 1984 s 89B*).

(*IHTA 1984 s 58*)

An interest in possession to which an individual became entitled pre-22 March 2006 is also a qualifying interest in possession.

16.48 The only lifetime trusts created on or after 22 March 2006 which are qualifying interests in possession trusts are for the disabled (*IHTA 1984 s 89*). Trusts created by will, on or after 22 March 2006, may qualify as qualifying interests in possession trusts (ie where the interest in possession is an IPDI).

16.49 Two critical attributes of the qualifying interest in possession trust are, first, that the individual beneficially entitled to the interest is treated, for IHT purposes, as beneficially entitled to the underlying property in which the interest subsists (*IHTA 1984 s 49*). Thus, the property in which the interest subsists is treated as part of the individual's estate on death and may constitute a CLT or PET should the interest be terminated (or treated as terminated) during the individual's lifetime.

Second, the transfer of property by the settlor on creation of the trust qualifies as a PET (not a CLT). Thus, survival by the settlor for at least seven years after settling the property ensures no IHT charge arises on the gift into trust.

16.50 Should the individual die the IHT liability which arises on the property of the trust in which the qualifying interest in possession subsists is the liability of the trustees not the individual. However, the quantum of the charge is determined by the circumstances of the individual (not the trust).

Example 10

Raymond Car dies in June 2010 with a free estate of £500,000 never having made any lifetime gifts.

The IHT liability on Raymond's death is:

40% x [£500,000 – £325,000] = £70,000.

Raymond's brother, Sam, also dies in June 2010 with a free estate of £500,000 but also has a qualifying interest in possession worth £300,000 on his death.

The IHT liability on Sam's death is:

40% x [[£500,000 + £300,000] – £325,000] = £190,000

The estate rate is:

[£190,000/£800,000] (ie 23.75%).

On Sam's free estate his liability is:

23.75% of £500,000 (ie £118,750).

The charge on the trustees is:

23.75% of £300,000 (ie £71,250).

16.51 On the death of the individual with the qualifying interest in possession if the property in which the interest subsists passes to the spouse absolutely the inter-spouse exemption applies and no IHT charge arises (*IHTA 1984 s 18*). If, on the other hand on death, the spouse becomes entitled to a successive interest in possession which qualifies as a TSI (requiring, *inter alia*, that the deceased spouse's interest arose pre-22 March 2006; see paragraph 16.72) the inter-spouse exemption also applies (*IHTA 1984 s 18;* see paragraph 11.42) and no IHT arises.

Non-qualifying interest in possession

16.52 An individual beneficially entitled to a non-qualifying interest in possession is not treated as owning the underlying trust property in which the interest subsists and thus neither of the consequences in paragraph 16.49 follow.

Example 11

Hubert Grey having discussed matters with his wife, Mildred, decides to set up a lifetime trust under which Mildred is to have a life interest.

16.53 *Inheritance tax: trusts*

Hubert has been thinking about setting up the trust in early 2006. However, it is not until June 2006 that the trust is set up.

The interest of Mildred is a non-qualifying interest in possession.

Thus, the consequences for Hubert are:

the gift of assets into the trust is a CLT on which an IHT charge arises at 20% if the value of the gift, either in whole or in part, exceeds the NRB of £285,000;

the trust is governed by the relevant property regime and thus ten-yearly and exit charges arise; and

on Mildred's death, no part of the trust assets in which her interest subsists will form part of her estate.

Had Hubert set up the trust pre-22 March 2006 the consequences would have been:

the gift of assets into the trust would have qualified as a PET (not CLT);

the trust would not be governed by the relevant property regime and thus ten yearly and exit charges would not arise; and

on Mildred's death, the trust assets in which her interest subsisted would have formed part of her estate.

Lifetime termination of qualifying interests in possession

16.53 The qualifying interest in possession of a beneficiary may be assigned or surrendered by the beneficiary during the beneficiary's lifetime; the assignment or surrender may occur by way of gift or sale.

The trustees may not, of course, effect such an assignment or surrender as the interest is not the trustees to assign/surrender. However, the trustees (if they possess the appropriate powers) can, for example, simply terminate the beneficiary's interest and/or appoint additional such interests (which may or may not be qualifying interests in possession).

Assignment/revocation

16.54 The assignment of the interest by the beneficiary may be made to any person; thus, the assignment may be to another beneficiary under the trust or to a non-beneficiary. In either case the assignor is assigning his right to receive income on the relevant trust property in which his interest subsists to the assignee. If the original beneficiary's interest is, for example, a life interest the assignee's right to receive the income continues until the death of the assignor (the assignee becomes 'a tenant *pur autre* vie' (ie a tenant based on the life of another)). The death of the assignee does not precipitate the termination of the interest (assuming, of course, the assignor is still alive) but falls into his (ie the assignee's) estate.

Thus, whilst the assignor beneficiary's interest is terminated following the assignment the trust property in which the assignor beneficiary's interest subsisted continues to be subject to an interest in possession albeit with the right thereto now belonging to the assignee beneficiary.

16.55 The trustees, on the other hand, cannot assign the beneficiary's interest to another beneficiary but may, *inter alia*, terminate the interest by revocation and grant a new interest to a new beneficiary or appoint trust capital to a beneficiary.

Assignment and inheritance tax

16.56 An assignment in lifetime of a qualifying interest in possession by the beneficiary entitled thereto is a deemed (not an actual) termination (*IHTA 1984 s 51*). The assignment is a disposal of the beneficiary's interest in possession.

16.57 The beneficiary is regarded as having made a transfer of value equal to the value of the underlying property in which his interest subsists.

16.58 An assignment effected pre-22 March 2006 results in the beneficiary making a PET.

16.59 An assignment on or after 22 March 2006 and pre-6 October 2008 of a pre-22 March 2006 interest results in the beneficiary making a PET (as the assignee acquires a TSI; *IHTA 1984 s 49B to 49E*).

16.60 An assignment on or after 6 October 2008 of a pre-22 March 2006 interest results in the beneficiary making a CLT.

16.61 The assignment of an interest in possession which arises on or after 22 March 2006 which is a non-qualifying interest in possession precipitates no IHT consequences. Where, however, the interest is a qualifying interest (ie an IPDI) the assignment thereof on or after 6 October 2008 is a CLT (an assignment before 6 October 2008 of the interest which arises on or after 22 March 2006 which is a qualifying interest in possession is also a CLT).

16.62 *Inheritance tax: trusts*

Unlike the surrender of a qualifying interest in possession which may result in the termination of the trust, following an assignment the trust simply continues.

Surrender

16.62 A surrender is different from an assignment. Under a surrender, not only does the surrendering beneficiary's interest terminate but the trust property in which the interest subsists is no longer subject to that interest; any succeeding interests thus falls in. Typically, the interests following those of the now terminated earlier interest in possession are often those of the remainderman who take the trust property, in which the earlier interest subsisted, absolutely. However, this is not necessarily the case and it may be that the succeeding interests are further (ie new) interests in possession (whether qualifying interests or not) or discretionary in nature.

16.63 The trustees cannot surrender the beneficiary's interest (in the same way that they cannot effect an assignment thereof; see paragraph 16.55 above) but, as above, may terminate the interest by revocation and grant a new interest to a new beneficiary or appoint trust capital to a beneficiary.

Surrender/revocation and inheritance tax

16.64 The surrender in lifetime of a qualifying interest in possession by the beneficiary entitled thereto constitutes an actual (as opposed to a deemed) termination of that interest.

16.65 The beneficiary is regarded as having made a transfer of value equal to the value of the underlying property in which his interest subsists (*IHTA 1984 s 52*). Following the surrender the trust may continue or it may terminate.

Trust continues after termination of qualifying interest in possession

16.66 Where the trust continues after the surrender of the interest in possession the interest in possession beneficiary makes a PET if the termination of the interest occurs pre-22 March 2006 and a succeeding interest in possession arises (unless the spouse takes the succeeding interest in which case the surrender is exempt) or a beneficiary becomes absolutely entitled as against the trustees; if however, on the termination of the interest the trust property is held on discretionary trust the beneficiary makes a CLT.

16.67 Where the termination of the pre-22 March 2006 interest occurs on or after 22 March 2006 but prior to 6 October 2008 the same consequences as outlined in paragraph 16.66 arise (any succeeding interest qualifies as a TSI).

16.68 Where the termination of the pre-22 March 2006 interest occurs on or after 6 October 2008 the beneficiary makes a CLT.

16.69 The surrender of an interest in possession which arises on or after 22 March 2006 which is a non-qualifying interest in possession precipitates no IHT consequences. Where, however, the interest in possession is a qualifying interest in possession (ie an IPDI) the surrender on or after 6 October 2008 is a CLT (a surrender before 6 October 2008 of the interest which arises on or after 22 March 2006 which is a qualifying interest in possession is a CLT).

Trust ends after termination of qualifying interest in possession

16.70 Where the trust terminates after the surrender of the pre-22 March 2006 interest in possession and a beneficiary becomes absolutely entitled us against the trustees the surrender is a PET. This applies whether the surrender occurs pre- or on or after 22 March 2006.

16.71 The surrender of an interest in possession which arises on or after 22 March 2006 which is a non-qualifying interest in possession precipitates no IHT consequences (although the trustees may face an exit charge) Where, however, the interest in possession is a qualifying interest in possession (ie an IPDI) the surrender whether before or on or after 6 October 2008 is a PET where a beneficiary becomes absolutely entitled as against the trustees.

Transitional serial interest

16.72 A transitional serial interest (TSI) qualifies as a qualifying interest in possession (see paragraph 16.47; *IHTA 1984 s 49C*).

16.73 The concept of the TSI was introduced as a transitional measure due to the *FA 2006* changes under which the termination of a qualifying interest in possession on or after 22 March 2006 is no longer automatically treated as a PET which had in principle been the position prior to this date (unless on termination of the qualifying interest in possession the trust property was held on a discretionary trust).

16.74 The transitional period was originally set to expire on 5 April 2008, but *FA 2008* extended the deadline to 6 October 2008.

16.75 A TSI arises where a pre-22 March 2006 qualifying interest in possession terminates on or after 22 March 2006 but before 6 October 2008 (whether in lifetime or on death) and, on the termination, another person immediately becomes entitled to an interest in possession; the latter interest in possession is the TSI (a qualifying interest in possession) (*IHTA 1984 s 49G*). The lifetime

16.76 *Inheritance tax: trusts*

termination of the qualifying interest in possession pursuant to which a TSI arises constitutes a PET by the individual owning the former interest.

On the subsequent termination of the TSI, in lifetime, if the individual with the TSI becomes absolutely entitled to the property in which the interest subsists no IHT charge arises (or if it is their spouse who becomes absolutely entitled the inter-spouse exemption applies). Where another individual becomes absolutely entitled the individual with the TSI makes a PET.

In all other cases the lifetime termination of a TSI constitutes a CLT.

16.76 The manner in which the termination of the pre-22 March 2006 qualifying interest occurs where this is prior to 6 October 2008 is irrelevant. Thus, a TSI arises whether the termination is as a result of the trustees exercising an overriding power of appointment or the individual entitled to the interest assigns or surrenders it.

16.77 In one circumstance a TSI can also arise on or after 6 October 2008. If on the death of a spouse, on or after 6 October 2008, who possesses a pre-22 March 2006 qualifying interest in possession the surviving spouse becomes entitled to an interest in possession the latter qualifies as a TSI (*IHTA 1984 s 49D*). The surviving spouse's interest must, however, arise on death.

The inter-spouse exemption (*IHTA 1984 s 18*) applies.

16.78 The replacement of a TSI by a subsequent interest in possession cannot itself qualify as a TSI (even if the subsequent interest in possession arises before 6 October 2008). The succeeding interest in possession is a non-qualifying interest in possession. The TSI beneficiary thus makes a CLT.

16.79 The underlying property in which a beneficiary's TSI subsists forms part of his estate on death; the TSI being a qualifying interest in possession.

Example 12

Joshua Tree sets up a trust in 2000 under which his son, Gerard, is entitled to an interest in possession which, as a pre-22 March 2006 interest, qualifies as a qualifying interest in possession.

On Gerard's death his sister, Cynthia, acquires a succeeding interest in possession.

If Gerard's death occurs before 6 October 2008 Cynthia's interest qualifies as a TSI; however, should Gerard's death occur on or after 6 October 2008 Cynthia's interest would not qualify as a TSI.

On Gerard's death the trust property in which his interest subsists forms part of his estate.

Immediate post-death interest in possession

16.80 An immediate post-death interest in possession (IPDI) qualifies as a qualifying interest in possession (see paragraph 16.47; *IHTA 1984 s 49A*).

16.81 An IPDI is an interest in possession which arises under a trust created by will (ie on death) and the person entitled to the interest becomes beneficially entitled to it on the testator's death (*IHTA 1984 s 49A*). If the interest arises at a later point in time (ie not immediately on the death of the testator) it does not qualify as an IPDI.

16.82 As the IPDI is a qualifying interest in possession on the death of the beneficiary entitled to the IPDI the trust property in which the IPDI subsists is included as part of the beneficiary's estate.

16.83 Where, on the lifetime termination of an IPDI, the individual with the IPDI becomes absolutely entitled to the property in which the interest subsists no IHT charge arises (or if it is their spouse who becomes absolutely entitled the inter-spouse exemption applies). Where another individual becomes absolutely entitled the individual with the IPDI makes a PET.

In all other cases the lifetime termination of an IPDI constitutes a CLT; any succeeding interest in possession arising on the IPDI's termination is non-qualifying and cannot itself qualify as an IPDI (as the interest has not arisen on the death of an individual under a will created by such individual).

Example 13

Cary Grunt dies in July 2008 and his will provides for an interest in possession for his son, Egbert, as life tenant with remainder to his three sisters.

Egbert's interest qualifies as an IPDI.

If during Egbert's lifetime his interest is terminated by the trustees (eg under an overriding power of appointment) and property is appointed out to one of Cary's sisters, Egbert makes a PET.

16.84 The execution of a deed of variation (DoV) following death can give rise to an IPDI (see paragraph 28.84).

16.85 *Inheritance tax: trusts*

Accumulation and maintenance trusts

16.85 Accumulation and maintenance (A&M) trusts are a form of discretionary trust and thus technically fall within the relevant property regime. However, trusts set up pre-22 March 2006 which qualified as A&M trusts were subject to favourable IHT treatment. This favourable treatment precluded ten-yearly and exit charges from arising on trust property and transfers into such trusts were treated as PETs not CLTs (despite the trust technically falling within the relevant property regime).

16.86 However, it is no longer possible to set up, on or after 22 March 2006, an A&M-type trust which qualifies for the pre-22 March 2006 favourable treatment; such trusts set up on or after 22 March 2006 are now subject to the relevant property regime.

16.87 In order to qualify as an A&M trust (and thus receive the favourable IHT treatment) one or more beneficiaries on or before attaining age 25 had to become absolutely entitled to the property settled on trust or to an interest in possession in the trust property (*IHTA 1984 s 71*).

16.88 For those trusts which qualified as A&M trusts pre-22 March 2006 to remain outside the relevant property regime (on or after 22 March 2006) requires that on or before 6 April 2008 their terms be amended (if necessary) to provide that beneficiaries must obtain an absolute interest in trust property on or before attaining age 18 or, alternatively, before attaining age 25 (ie the acquisition of an interest in possession is no longer sufficient).

Where the age of vesting of trust property is to be 25 (and not 18) it is also necessary that any income of the trust must be either accumulated or applied for the maintenance, education or benefit of the beneficiaries (note that *TA 1925 s 31* provides that when a beneficiary has a contingent right to capital of the trust on reaching a specified age (eg 25), on attaining age 18 the beneficiary acquires an interest in possession and thus becomes entitled to the income of the trust at age 18; any accumulations of income prior to attaining age 18 become payable when the contingency is satisfied (ie age 25 in this example)). The provisions of *TA 1925 s 31* are often amended/excluded under the terms of a trust, as are *TA 1925 s 32*.

16.89 For those pre-22 March 2006 A&M trusts whose provisions provided for absolute entitlement or interests in possession at age 25 and whose provisions were not changed prior to 6 April 2008 such trusts enter the relevant property regime as at 6 April 2008 with the attendant consequences. The ten-year anniversary charge applies ten years from the date of commencement of the trust, not ten years from 6 April 2008.

Relevant property versus qualifying interest in possession trusts

Pre-FA 2006

16.90 One of the major distinctions between the two types of trust is that on creation in lifetime, transfers into relevant property trusts are CLTs thus precipitating the 20% IHT charges (subject to NRB availability). Transfers into qualifying interest in possession trusts are PETs and no IHT liability occurs if the settlor survives seven years. In principle, the latter type of trust is therefore less costly on set-up in lifetime.

16.91 On the other hand, on the death of the beneficiary with the qualifying interest in possession the trust property in which the interest subsists forms part of the beneficiary's estate and falls liable to IHT at 40%. The use of the qualifying interest in possession trust may thus have removed property from the settlor's estate but simply causes it to form part of the estate of the relevant beneficiary on death (albeit that the primary responsibility to discharge the liability falls to the trustees). The death of the beneficiary of a relevant property trust precipitates no such charge.

16.92 The relevant property trust is, however, subject to ten-yearly and exit charges which are inapplicable to the qualifying interest in possession trust although the maximum rate applicable is 6% (which compares extremely favourably with the 40% rate applicable to the estate of the individual on death).

Post-FA 2006

16.93 For the relevant property trust nothing has changed post-*FA 2006*. All the comments made above with respect to such trusts thus continue to apply.

16.94 However, for the interest in possession trust created in lifetime post-*FA 2006*, the regime applicable to that of the relevant property trust now applies. The cost of set-up in IHT terms has thus increased as transfers into such trusts are now CLTs precipitating a 20% charge (subject to availability of the NRB) as opposed to PETs which applied pre-*FA 2006*. Nevertheless, on the death of the interest in possession beneficiary no part of the trust assets now form part of the beneficiary's estate.

The decision over the creation of a lifetime relevant property trust or interest in possession trust, post-*FA 2006*, is thus IHT 'neutral'.

16.95 For the qualifying interest in possession trusts created pre-*FA 2006* the pre-*FA 2006* rules continue in principle to apply. The termination of the qualifying interest in possession (subsisting before 22 March 2006) before 6 October 2008 and the substitution of a new such interest (which creates a TSI) may defer the time at which the trust falls into the relevant property regime if the new replacement beneficiary is significantly younger than the original beneficiary.

16.96 In the case of will trusts the inter-spouse exemption applies if the trust created by will gives rise to an IPDI for the surviving spouse. On the surviving spouse's death the trust assets in which the IPDI subsists forms part of his estate. However, on termination of the IPDI in the surviving spouse's lifetime, the termination constitutes a CLT if the trust continues as the trust at that time falls within the relevant property regime.

Excluded property trusts

16.97 'Excluded property' trusts are not directly affected by *FA 2006* although they are possibly affected indirectly and possibly adversely (see paragraph 13.45) *(IHTA 1984 ss 6 and 48)*. However, in principle, non-UK situs property settled by an individual who at that time is non-UK domiciled (nor deemed UK domiciled) continues to fall outside any IHT charge. This applies irrespective of whether the trust is a discretionary, interest in possession or A&M trust (see Chapter 13).

Summary

16.98 *FA 2006* changed the IHT treatment of trusts markedly.

16.99 The creation of the IHT-efficient A&M trust is no longer possible on or after 22 March 2006. To ensure such tax advantages are maintained on or after 22 March 2006 (with respect to pre-22 March 2006 A&M trusts) amendment to the terms of the trust need to have been made before 6 April 2008.

16.100 Lifetime interest in possession trusts which are created on or after 22 March 2006 automatically fall within the relevant property regime. Such trusts created before this date, however, continue in principle to be subject to the rules applicable before 22 March 2006.

16.101 The concepts of the IPDI and TSI, introduced in *FA 2006*, effectively extend qualifying interest in possession treatment to such interests. TSIs, however, cannot be created on or after 6 October 2008 unless the successive interest in possession is the spouse of the prior interest and it arises on death.

16.102 For the non-UK domiciled individual the non-UK resident 'exempt property trust' continues, post-*FA 2006*, to offer an IHT attractive vehicle.

Chapter 17

UK resident trusts: income and capital gains taxation

Background

17.1 Chapter 15 provides a brief overview of the trust concept and Chapter 16 discusses the inheritance tax (IHT) implications of the different types of trust.

17.2 This chapter looks at the income tax and capital gains tax (CGT) aspects of UK resident trusts. While the trust is a separate taxable entity certain anti-avoidance provisions may apply, the consequences of which are that it is the settlor, and not the trust, who is subject to tax on the trust's income and/or capital gains.

The approach adopted in this chapter is to first consider the tax treatment of UK resident trusts (non-UK resident trusts are considered in Chapter 18) ignoring the possible application of these various anti-avoidance provisions and, second, to then consider the impact of these provisions on the trust's tax treatment.

17.3 The taxation of a trust depends upon the following factors:

- residence of the trust (ie UK resident or non-UK resident);
- type of trust (eg discretionary or interest in possession);
- residence status of the settlor;
- domicile status of the settlor;
- residence status of the beneficiaries;
- domicile status of the beneficiaries; and
- UK or non-UK source income/gains.

Strictly speaking, it is the trustees of the trust (not the trust, per se) who are liable to any income and/or CGT charges. Trustees are treated as a single

17.4 *UK resident trusts: income and capital gains taxation*

person, or single body, distinct from the persons who are in fact the trustees (companies and individuals may be trustees) (*ITA 2007 s 474; TCGA 1992 s 69*).

Trust residency

Pre-6 April 2007

Capital gains tax

17.4 Prior to 6 April 2007, a trust was non-UK resident if:

- all or a majority of the trustees were neither resident nor ordinarily resident in the UK; *and*
- the general administration of the trust was ordinarily carried on outside the UK.

A UK resident professional trustee (broadly, a person carrying on the business of trust management) was, however, deemed to be resident outside the UK if the whole of the settled property consisted of property provided by someone who at that time was neither UK domiciled, resident nor ordinarily resident. The general administration of the trust was regarded as carried on outside the UK if a majority of the trustees were non-UK resident.

However, the professional trustee 'let-out' did not apply for income tax purposes.

Income tax

17.5 A trust was UK resident for income tax purposes if there was a sole trustee who was UK resident or, if there was more than one trustee, all were UK resident.

If one or more trustees were UK resident and one or more were not (ie mixed residence trust) then the trust was UK resident if the settlor was domiciled or resident or ordinarily resident in the UK when the funds were provided.

Post-5 April 2007

17.6 The consequence of the changes introduced by *FA 2006* (effective 6 April 2007) is that the test for residence of trustees is now the same for income tax and CGT. The pre-6 April 2007 income tax rules now apply.

17.7 The trust is treated as resident and ordinarily resident in the UK at any time if:

- all the trustees are resident in the UK; *or*
- at least one trustee is resident in the UK and at least one trustee is not resident in the UK and the settlor is resident *or* ordinarily resident *or* domiciled in the UK when the trust is made (whether in lifetime or on death)

(*ITA 2007 ss 475* and *476; TCGA 1992 s 69*)

Thus, a trust where all of the trustees are non-UK resident will be non-UK resident irrespective of the domicile and/or residence status of the settlor.

17.8 Where the settlor is non-UK resident, not ordinary resident and non-UK domiciled at the time the trust is made the trust is non-UK resident so long as at least one trustee is non-UK resident.

17.9 The professional trustee let-out referred to above (see paragraph 17.4) has been abolished (regarded as State Aid under EU competition law) and the place of administration of the trust is now also irrelevant (see paragraph 17.4).

Example 1

Bertrand Dublin, a non-UK domiciled but UK resident individual, is keen to set up a trust (post-6 April 2007) outside the UK for family planning purposes.

He is a little wary of the trust comprising exclusively non-UK resident professional trustees and suggests that in addition his UK domiciled and UK resident brother or his non-UK domiciled but UK resident sister (or both) should also act as trustees.

If either Bertrand's brother and/or sister act as trustees the trust is classified as UK resident.

17.10 The changes introduced in *FA 2006* (effective from 6 April 2007) align the CGT treatment for residence with that for income tax; in essence no change was made with respect to the income tax rules. However, the change to the CGT rules meant that it was possible for a trust which was non-UK resident under the pre-*FA 2006* rules to automatically fall to be treated as UK resident post-*FA 2006*. This could have disastrous CGT consequences where the trust is then re-exported.

17.11 *UK resident trusts: income and capital gains taxation*

17.11 The re-exportation of the trust's UK residence precipitates a CGT charge on the part of the trustees; this occurs because there is a deemed disposal by the trustees of all trust assets at their market value at the date of export and a deemed re-acquisition at the same values (*TCGA 1992 s 80*).

17.12 The situation postulated in paragraph 17.10 arises if, for example, pre-6 April 2007 the trust administration was carried on outside the UK, a majority of the trustees were non-resident and the settlor was resident in the UK but non-UK domiciled. Such a trust would have been UK resident for income tax but non-UK resident for CGT. However, on 6 April 2007 such a trust would, while remaining UK resident for income tax, become UK resident for CGT.

It was therefore important if any such UK CGT charges were to be avoided that steps were taken pre-6 April 2007 to ensure that the non-UK resident trust remained so for CGT under the new rules. In the scenario of paragraph 17.10, this required that all (not just a majority) of the trustees were non-UK resident.

17.13 Although the exportation (or re-exportation) of a UK resident trust may give rise to significant CGT liabilities the income tax effects are less likely to be so serious. The exportation, per se, precipitates no general income tax consequences although offshore income gains (OIGs) are precipitated (in the same manner as capital gains are precipitated; OFTR 2009 *SI 2009/3001 reg 20* (see paragraph 18.139)). Any non-UK source income arising to the trust in the period between exportation and the end of the tax year of exportation continues to fall within the charge to income tax (see paragraph 17.14).

17.14 A trust is UK resident for the whole of a tax year for CGT if it is resident in any part of that year. ESC D2 provides split tax year treatment for CGT purposes only in the case of individuals, not trustees (see paragraph 4.64; see also *SP5/92*).

Similarly, ESC A11 provides for split tax year treatment for income tax purposes only in the case of individuals, not trustees (see paragraph 4.56).

Income tax

17.15 The income tax consequences for the UK resident trust are the same whether the trust is set up by a UK domiciled and UK resident individual or a non-UK domiciled but UK resident individual. This is the position with respect to both UK and non-UK source income accruing to the trust.

17.16 UK resident trustees are liable to self-assessment in the same manner as individuals (albeit with their own designed tax return; SA900 'Trust and estate tax return') and make payments on account in the same way. They are liable to income tax on worldwide income on the arising basis (ie whether such income is remitted to the UK or not).

17.17 However, there are differences between the income (and capital gains) tax treatment of individuals and of trusts:

- trustees are liable to income tax at the basic rate with respect to both savings and non-savings income (ie 20% for the tax year 2008–2009 and later tax years) or, in the case of dividends, the dividend ordinary rate (10% for tax year 2008–2009 and later tax years); for the tax year 2007–2008 and earlier tax years rates of 10%, 20% and 22% applied to income according to the category of income;

- the rates of 32.5% and 40% applicable to individuals only apply to certain trusts, primarily discretionary trusts (*ITA 2007 ss 9* and *479*); both these rates are increased to 42.5% and 50% respectively for the tax year 2010–2011 for discretionary trusts;

- trustees were not entitled to the 10% starting rate band (applicable for tax years 2007–2008 and earlier tax years);

- trustees are not entitled to the 'new' 10% 'starting rate for savings' available to individuals (*ITA 2007 s 12*);

- trustees are not entitled to any personal allowances; and

- trustees are entitled to 50% of the normal annual exempt amount applicable to individuals in respect of any liability to CGT; for the tax year 2010–2011 the annual exempt amount available to trustees is 50% of £10,100 (*TCGA 1992 Sch 1*).

Discretionary (and accumulation and maintenance) trusts

Trustees' liability to income tax

17.18 Accumulation and maintenance trusts (A&M) are a form of discretionary trust and thus the term 'discretionary trust' is used to encompass both types of trust. The concept of the A&M trust is primarily of value with respect to IHT (not income tax or CGT) as it receives favourable IHT treatment (see paragraph 16.85). However, following the significant changes to IHT introduced in *FA 2006* no new A&M trusts can be created for IHT purposes on or after 22 March 2006 although A&M trusts created pre-22 March 2006 may in principle continue to benefit from the favourable treatment.

17.19 The trustees of a discretionary trust are subject to income tax at the rate of 50% (the 'trust rate' effective 6 April 2010; previously the rate was 40% and was formerly referred to as the 'rate applicable to trusts') on any trust income

17.20 *UK resident trusts: income and capital gains taxation*

other than dividend income. Dividend income (whether UK source or not) is subject to income tax at 42.5% (the 'dividend trust rate' effective 6 April 2010; previously 32.5%).

Thus, the dividend ordinary rate of 10% and the basic rate of 20% (see paragraph 17.17) are inapplicable to the income of discretionary trusts.

17.20 Effective 6 April 2006 a new 'standard rate band' was introduced which applies to the income of discretionary trusts. Pre-*FA 2008*, the first £1,000 of taxable income was subject to tax at the 10% (ie dividend ordinary rate), 20% (ie the lower rate) or 22% (ie basic rate) rate depending upon the type of the income. Post- *FA 2008*, the first £1,000 of taxable income is subject to tax at the 20% basic rate of tax on income other than dividend income; in the case of dividend income the 10% (ie dividend ordinary rate) rate applies.

Where the trust receives more than one category of income the standard rate band is to be applied to income subject to income tax at the basic rate in priority to dividend income (*ITA 2007 s 491*).

17.21 Those trusts falling to be treated as discretionary trusts are those where income is payable at the discretion of the trustees or where income is to be accumulated (*ITA 2007 s 479*) and is not the income of any other person prior to distribution by the trustees (*ITA 2007 s 480*).

The income is that of another person if it is that of an interest in possession beneficiary (whether the interest in possession is 'qualifying' or not is irrelevant; this distinction is of relevance only for IHT purposes; see paragraph 16.4) or if the trust is settlor-interested (*ITTOIA 2005 Part 5 Ch 5*; see paragraph 17.66); in such cases the trust's income is not subject on the part of the trustees to either the trust rate (50%) or the dividend trust rate (42.5%) but only the basic rate (20%) and the dividend ordinary rate (10%) (ie even though the income is that of another person, as the trustees actually receive the income in the first instance they are subject to income tax thereon but not at the trust rate or the dividend trust rate). The income tax liability of the other person whose income it is then obtains a tax credit for any tax paid by the trustees, effectively on their behalf.

17.22 Expenses of the trust (ie the trust management expenses) are not deductible in computing the trust's income subject to the basic rate or dividend ordinary rate of income tax although are deductible in arriving at the amount of income subject to the trust rate or the dividend trust rate (the standard rate band (see paragraph 17.20) applies to trust income after the deduction of expenses). In order for trust expenses to rank as deductible for income tax purposes they must have been incurred wholly/solely with respect to the income of the trust (ie expenses incurred for the benefit of the whole trust fund are 'capital' and cannot be deducted; no apportionment of such expenses between trust income and trust capital is allowed; *RCC v Trustees of the Peter Clay Discretionary Trust* (2008)).

Expenses which are generally accepted as tax deductible are those of a recurrent nature and include the cost of trust account preparation and audit; preparation of trust tax returns; council tax and rates on land owned by the trust; rent payable in respect of leasehold property held by the trust; and interest on charges. Capital costs include capital expenditure on trust assets such as the cost of discharging any mortgage debt; cost of appointing new trustees; and the cost of taking legal advice as to the trustees' powers. Trustees' remuneration is generally incurred for the trust as a whole and therefore is not deductible.

Any determination as to the tax deductibility of trust expenses is made according to trust law and not according to any provisions in the trust deed in this regard.

17.23 Where trust expenses are deductible they are deductible against dividend income first; then savings income; and finally other income (ie non-savings income) (*ITA 2007 s 486*). This order of offset is beneficial as it maximises the tax paid by the trust which may then be passed on to the beneficiaries.

Appropriate 'grossing up' of the expenses is necessary to ascertain the amount to be deducted. This is because the trust rate and the dividend trust rate of income tax apply to the trust's income which is accumulated or payable at the trustees' discretion which is the trust income *after* deduction for expenses. Thus, expenses paid out of dividend income are grossed up at the dividend ordinary rate (10%) and those paid out of other income at the basic rate (20%).

Example 2

The Tom Smith discretionary trust receives the following income in tax year 2010–2011:

Bank interest (net of income tax @ 20%)	£2,400
Dividend income (net of the tax credit)	£90
Trust management expenses	£150
The expenses are deductible first against gross dividend income:	
Gross dividend income [£90/0.9] =	£100
Less: Grossed up expenses [£90/0.9] =	£100
Net income	nil

17.24 *UK resident trusts: income and capital gains taxation*

The balance of the trust expenses (ie £150 less £90) grossed up are then set against gross interest income:

Interest [£2,400/0.8]	£3,000
Less: Balance of grossed up expenses [£60/0.8]	£75
Net income	£2,925
The income tax liability is then:	
first £1,000 @ 20%	£200
balance of £1,925 @ 50%	£963
	£1,163
Less: 20% tax credit.	£233
(the £1,163 of bank interest has already suffered income tax of 20%)	
Trustees' net liability	£930

Thus, the income available for distribution at the trustees' discretion to the beneficiaries is [£2,490 less £150 less £930] (ie £1,410).

17.24 The trustees may make payments to a beneficiary out of the income of the trust or out of the trust capital. Under the former, the beneficiary receives income and is taxed accordingly; in the latter, generally, the receipt will be treated as capital and thus not subject to income tax. However, this may not always be so and a capital distribution may fall to be subject to income tax on the part of the beneficiary. For example, if the capital distribution is intended to supplement income for the beneficiary, such distribution is likely to be subject to income tax.

Trustees' position on income distributions to UK resident beneficiaries

17.25 Any payment made to a UK resident beneficiary of a discretionary trust, which is treated as income (and not capital) on the part of the beneficiary, is treated as if it has been made after the deduction of a sum representing income tax at the trust rate on the grossed-up amount of the payment (*ITA 2007 s 494*). The grossed up amount is the actual amount of the payment grossed up by reference to the trust rate (ie 50% for the tax year 2010–2011) (*ITA 2007 s 494*).

Even if the distribution out of the trust is made out of dividend income of the trust the rate of gross-up is at the trust rate and not the dividend trust rate. This is because the source of the income for the beneficiary is the trust itself and not the underlying income of the trust ie the nature of the trust's underlying income is irrelevant when determining the nature of the income the beneficiary receives from the trust (*Baker v Archer-Shee* (1927)).

17.26 On making the payment the trustees create a *'s 496'* (*ITA 2007*) liability for themselves which is treated as satisfied (in whole or in part) by the tax already paid by the trustees on trust income. Where the *s 496* liability exceeds the tax paid by the trustees on the trust income the shortfall is met out of the 'tax pool'.

The tax pool is the income tax *paid* over time by the trustees on the trust income; in effect, over time, the tax pool builds up and is reduced only when income distributions are made to trust beneficiaries (note that post-5 April 1999 the one-ninth tax credit attached to dividend income does not fall into the tax pool). Effectively the tax pool 'franks' the income distributions of the trustees.

Where, however, there is insufficient available income tax in the tax pool the trustees need to either reduce the amount of any income distributions to the beneficiaries so as to ensure they (ie the trustees) are able to discharge their own *s 496* tax liability in full or discharge their liability from other sources.

Example 3

The Bob Smith discretionary trust receives dividend income, bank interest income on bank deposits and rental income.

The tax pool of the trust amounts to £5,000.

In 2010–2011 the trustees make an income payment to Henry, one of the trust's beneficiaries of £1,600.

The payment of £1,600 is treated as a net payment after deduction of income tax of £1,600 from a grossed-up payment of £3,200 (ie £1,600 grossed-up at the trust rate of 50% applicable in 2010–2011). The £1,600 treated as income tax deducted from the £3,200 gross payment is the *s 496* tax liability on the part of the trustees.

The £1,600 *s 496* liability is met out of the tax pool thus reducing it to [£5,000 – £1,600](ie £3,400).

Had the payment of £1,600 to Henry been made in 2009–2010 the deduction for income tax would have been £1,067 from a grossed-up payment of £2,667 (ie £1,600 grossed-up at the trust rate of 40%) and the *s 496* liability would have been £1,067.

Example 4

The Albert Yellow discretionary trust is created in 2009–2010. Its income (non-dividend) for 2009–2010 is £2,000 creating an income tax liability for the trustees of 40% of £2,000 (ie £800), leaving net cash of £1,200 (ignoring trust expenses and the standard rate band).

17.27 *UK resident trusts: income and capital gains taxation*

In 2010–2011 the trust income amounts to £8,000 creating an income tax liability for the trustees of 50% of £8,000 (ie £4,000), leaving net cash of £4,000.

The tax pool amounts to [£800 + £4,000] (ie £4,800).

Total net cash is [£1,200 + £4,000] (ie £5,200).

The trustees are, however, unable to make an income distribution to the beneficiaries of the full £5,200. Assuming that £5,200 is paid to the beneficiaries (in 2010–2011) a *s 496* liability of £5,200 arises on the grossed-up amount of £10,400. However, the tax pool consists of only tax of £4,800 and thus a shortfall of £400 arises (and the trustees are unable to discharge their income tax liability).

The maximum income distribution which can be made is £5,000. This precipitates a *s 496* liability of £5,000 which can be settled out of the tax pool as to £4,800 and the balancing £200 from the cash retained by the trustees of £200 (ie £5,200 less £5,000 income distribution).

The problem arises due to the increase in the 'trust rate' between 2009–2010 and 2010–2011 from 40% to 50%.

17.27 The problem highlighted in Example 4 can also occur where, for example, a trust receives dividend income subject to the dividend trust rate of 42.5% (for the tax year 2010–2011; previously 32.5%) and effects income distributions to beneficiaries. The trustees' *s 496* liability in this case is greater than the income tax paid by the trustees on the dividend income.

Example 5

In 2010–2011 the Brian Mutter discretionary trust receives net dividend income of £900 to which is attached a one-ninth tax credit (the tax credit does not fall into the tax pool; see paragraph 17.26).

The income tax paid by the trustees (ignoring expenses and the standard rate band) on the income is [[42.5% x £1,000] – £100] (ie £325).

The tax pool amounts to £325.

Net cash is £575 (ie £900 – £325).

If the trustees make an income distribution of £575 this creates a *s 496* liability of £575. However, the tax pool consists of only £325.

UK resident trusts: income and capital gains taxation **17.31**

The maximum income distribution is thus £450. This creates a *s 496* liability of £450 which is satisfied as to £325 from the tax pool and the balancing £125 from the cash retained by the trustees of £125 (ie the £575 less the £450 income distribution).

17.28 Monitoring of the tax pool is thus necessary to ensure that the trustees' exposure to any income tax charge on distributions to beneficiaries can be discharged. Where a trust has accumulated trust income over many years the tax pool is likely to be significant.

Beneficiaries' position on income distributions to UK resident beneficiaries

17.29 A discretionary beneficiary has no rights to the trust income. A beneficiary only benefits from the trust as and when the trustees exercise their discretion in his favour. The source of the income received by a beneficiary is the trust itself, not the underlying trust income itself (see paragraph 17.25).

17.30 The beneficiary is subject to income tax on the income distribution under *ITTOIA 2005 s 683* as an annual payment.

17.31 The beneficiary's taxable income is the net amount distributed by the trustees grossed-up by the trust rate (ie 50% for the tax year 2010–2011). However, in computing the beneficiary's income tax liability on an income distribution the beneficiary is treated as having paid the income tax deemed to have been deducted by the trustees on making the payment (ie their *s 496* liability); in effect the beneficiary obtains a tax credit for the income tax paid by the trustees on the distribution.

For the beneficiary subject to income tax at the marginal rate of 50% no additional income tax liability arises; for the 40% or basic rate taxpayer an income tax refund (from HMRC) arises.

Other things being equal, this suggests that tax mitigation is maximised where discretionary payments are made to basic rate taxpayer (or even non-taxpayer) beneficiaries.

Example 6

Homer Springfield sets up a discretionary trust for his three adult children, Clarissa, Tig and Bro.

The trust's income for the tax year 2010–2011 is £75,000 and the trustees liability is 50% thereof (ie £37,500).

17.32 *UK resident trusts: income and capital gains taxation*

The trustees exercise their discretion in favour of Homer's children as follows:

£3,000 to Clarissa (who is a basic rate (20%) taxpayer);

£12,000 to Tig (who is a higher rate (40%) taxpayer);

£24,000 to Bro (who is an additional rate (50%) taxpayer).

Each of the beneficiaries is in principle liable to income tax at their applicable marginal rate on the 'grossed-up' amount received from the trust (ie £6,000 re Clarissa; £24,000 re Tig and £48,000 re Bro).

Clarissa is a basic rate taxpayer and therefore has no liability on the income and may apply to HMRC for a refund of £1,800 tax paid by the trustees (ie £3,000 less 20% of £6,000).

Tig is a higher rate taxpayer and therefore has a liability on the income of 40% of £24,000 (ie £9,600) and thus may apply to HMRC for a refund of £2,400 tax paid by the trustees.

Bro is an additional rate taxpayer and therefore has a liability on the income of 50% of £48,000 (ie £24,000) which matches the income tax already paid by the trustees and thus no additional tax liability arises on the part of Bro, but neither is he entitled to any tax refund from HMRC.

Accumulated income

17.32 Trustees may decide to accumulate trust income (ie the income is not paid out to a beneficiary) which then forms part of the trust's capital. The effect is that if in due course the accumulated income is paid out to one or more beneficiaries no income tax liability arises on the part of the recipient beneficiaries but income tax paid by the trustees on the income is irrecoverable on the part of the beneficiary (however, the tax paid by the trustees on the income falls into the tax pool and is thus available to 'frank' future income distributions).

However, the terms of the trust may permit the trustees to apply all or a part of the accumulated income as if it was income arising in the relevant year. In this case the recipient beneficiaries are subject to income tax thereon and, where appropriate, income tax paid by the trustees is recoverable.

Non-UK source income

17.33 Non-UK source income, as indicated in paragraph 17.16, is subject to income tax on the part of the trustees on the arising basis. Such income may have borne some form of tax in the jurisdiction in which the income has arisen; for example, it is not unusual for some form of withholding tax to be levied by the country in which investment income arises including interest and dividends.

17.34 Where non-UK source income has suffered some form of foreign tax double tax relief is available to the trustees by way of a tax credit (ie the tax paid overseas reduces the UK income tax charge on the income typically resulting in a net UK income tax liability (in particular given the trust rate of 50% and the dividend trust rate of 42.5% for the tax year 2010–2011).

17.35 By concession the beneficiary receiving an income distribution is granted a tax credit for the foreign tax paid (ESC B18) to which the beneficiary, if the income had been received directly by him, would have been entitled under a double tax agreement. In determining the composition of the income distribution (ie whether the trustees have distributed the income out of UK or non-UK source income and out of which tax year) the distributions are treated as having been made by the trustees on a last in first out (LIFO) basis and pro rata in respect of the trust's UK and non-UK source income (ESC B18). Without concessional treatment the recipient beneficiary is not eligible for a tax credit for any foreign tax paid by the trustees on the trust income as the source of the receipt for the beneficiary is the trust and not the underlying income (see paragraph 17.25).

Inevitably the amount of UK tax paid by the trustees on the foreign income is reduced where foreign tax credits (if any) are available and thus the amount of UK tax entering the tax pool is correspondingly reduced; UK tax offset by the foreign tax credit does not enter the tax pool. However, the availability of the foreign tax credit to the beneficiary precludes any problems arising due to the reduced amount entering the tax pool.

Example 7

Mary Tree sets up a discretionary trust in 2010–2011 which receives foreign income of £700 after a foreign withholding tax of 30% is levied.

Trustees' income tax liability is:

Gross income [£700 + 300]	£1,000
UK tax charge (50%)	£500
Less: Foreign tax credit	(£300)
Net UK income tax liability	£200
Net cash in trust	£500

17.36 *UK resident trusts: income and capital gains taxation*

The tax pool consists of only £200. The trustees cannot meet their *s 496* liability if they distribute the whole £500. The maximum distribution possible is £350 if the trustees are to meet their s 496 liability out of the trust income for the tax year 2010 – 2011.

The trustees therefore make an income distribution of £350 to one of the beneficiaries who is subject to income tax at the 20% basic rate of income tax. The beneficiary's income tax liability is:

Gross income	£700
UK tax charge (20%)	£140
Less: Credit for *s 496* trustees' tax	£350
Net income tax refund	£210
Net cash receipt of beneficiary	[£350 + £210] (ie £560)

The trustees thus receive net cash of £700 of which £200 is their UK tax liability on the gross income of £1,000; £350 is paid to the beneficiary; the balance of £150 is then used to discharge their *s 496* liability of £350 (having offset the £200 in the tax pool)

Non-UK resident beneficiaries

17.36   For the non-UK resident beneficiary of a UK resident trust who receives an income distribution the source of the income distribution is the trust (ie the UK) as indicated in paragraph 17.25 (not the underlying trust income). The beneficiary is thus in principle exposed to a UK income tax charge on the distribution as an annual payment (*ITTOIA 2005 s 683*) albeit with a credit for any income tax paid by the trustees on the distribution.

17.37   Such an annual payment, however, qualifies as disregarded income (see paragraph 23.11) and thus any income tax charge which arises on the part of the recipient beneficiary may be limited (*ITTOIA 2005 s 683; ITA 2007 ss 813* and *826*). A claim for repayment of any income tax paid by the trustees on the income distribution may be lodged with HMRC.

Non-UK domiciled beneficiaries

17.38   A non-UK domiciled but UK resident individual beneficiary in receipt of an income distribution from a UK resident trust is subject to income tax thereon.

17.39   Even where the trust income arises outside the UK and an income distribution is then made out of this income to a non-UK domiciled but UK resident beneficiary (with the income remaining outside the UK) the remittance basis is inapplicable as the source of the receipt by the beneficiary is the trust (which is UK resident) and not the underlying income (see paragraph 17.25).

Income distributions to a non-UK domiciled and non-UK resident individual beneficiary are treated in the same manner as such distributions to a UK domiciled and non-UK resident individual (see paragraph 17.36).

Interest in possession trusts

17.40 The distinguishing feature of the interest in possession trust is that one (or possibly more) beneficiary is entitled to the trust income as it arises. The interest in possession beneficiary is thus not dependent upon the trustees exercising their discretion in his favour.

As the interest in possession beneficiary is entitled to the trust income as it arises, the source of his income is the underlying income of the trust not the trust itself (see paragraph 17.25). Thus, his income tax liability is based upon the particular category of income to which he is entitled.

Trustees' and beneficiaries' tax position

17.41 The liability to income tax on the trust income is that of the interest in possession beneficiary to whom the income belongs and this liability arises for the tax year in which the income arises to the trust (not the tax year when it may be physically paid to the beneficiary by the trustees). However, the trustees are also liable thereon on the ground that they initially receive the income (ie prior to paying out to the beneficiary).

The income tax paid by the trustees on the income to which the interest in possession is entitled is then creditable against the interest in possession beneficiary's own income tax liability on the income; the beneficiary is able to reclaim any excess income tax paid by the trustees.

17.42 The income to which the interest in possession beneficiary is entitled is the trust income less trustees' management expenses and the trustees' income tax liabilities whether UK or foreign (see paragraph 17.44).

17.43 The trustees are liable to income tax at the basic rate (ie 20% for the tax year 2010–2011) and the dividend ordinary rate (ie 10% for the tax year 2010–2011) (*ITA 2007 ss 479* and *480*).

17.44 *UK resident trusts: income and capital gains taxation*

Thus, the trust rate (50%) and dividend trust rate (42.5%) do not apply to the income of the trustees of interest in possession trusts.

The standard rate band (see paragraph 17.20) does not apply to the trust income.

17.44 No deduction for trustee management expenses is allowed in computing the trustees' liability to income tax on the trust income (see paragraph 17.22). However, the expenses are deductible in arriving at the net trust income to which the interest in possession beneficiary is entitled (see paragraph 17.42). Such expenses may include those which, in addition to those provided by law (see paragraph 17.22), are deductible under the terms of the trust deed even if such provisions include capital expenses (*ITA 2007 s 500*).

The deduction of expenses is to be made first against dividend income, then savings income and then non-savings income (*ITA 2007 s 503*).

Example 8

Jenny Chair is an interest in possession beneficiary of a trust set up by her great grandfather about five years ago. She is a 50% taxpayer.

In the tax year 2010–2011 income arising to the trust comprises net dividend income of £18,000 and interest income (after tax has been deducted at source, at 20%, by the bank) of £64,000.

Trustee management expenses are £7,000.

The trustees' liability is 10% on the gross dividend income and 20% on the gross bank interest:

10% on [£18,000 +£2,000] + 20% on [£64,000 + £16,000]

The liability of £2,000 on the dividend income is offset by the dividend tax credit of £2,000 and thus no net tax liability arises on the trustees on this income.

The liability of £16,000 on the bank interest is offset by the £16,000 of tax which the bank deducted before paying the interest and thus no net tax liability arises on the trustees on this income.

The trust net income is thus £18,000 of net dividend income and £64,000 of bank interest.

Jenny is not entitled to these amounts as the trustee management expenses need to be deducted; these expenses are deducted from the net dividend income first leaving £11,000.

Jenny's income tax liability is computed on the net £11,000 of dividend income grossed-up at 10% and the £64,000 bank interest grossed-up at 20% producing gross income of £12,222 and £80,000 respectively.

Jenny is liable at 42.5% on the 'gross' dividend of £12,222 less a tax credit of £1,222 producing a net income tax liability on the dividends of £3,972 and liable at 50% on the 'gross' bank interest of £80,000 less the credit for the tax deducted by the bank of £16,000 producing a net income tax liability of £24,000.

17.45 Some receipts by the trustees are by trust law capital and thus not amounts to which the interest in possession beneficiary is entitled (and thus in respect of which he has no liability to income tax). Some such receipts are classified as income for income tax purposes and taxed accordingly albeit only on the trustees (such income does qualify for the standard rate band and the trustees are subject to income tax at the trust rate and the dividend trust rate on this income as such income is not that of the interest in possession beneficiary and falls within *ITA 2007 s 479*; see paragraph 17.21; *ITA 2007 ss 481* and *482*).

Examples of capital receipts treated as income for income tax purposes include offshore income gains (*FA 2008 ss 40A* to *42A*) and gains arising on non-qualifying life policies (*ITA 2007 ss 481* and *482* and *ITTOIA 2005 s 461*).

Non-UK source income

17.46 Non-UK source income, as indicated in paragraph 17.16, is subject to income tax on the part of the trustees on the arising basis. It is likely that such income will have borne some form of tax in the jurisdiction in which the income has arisen often (in the case of investment income (eg interest, dividends) a withholding tax). Typical rates of foreign domestic withholding tax are in the range of 0% to 30%.

17.47 Double tax relief is available to the trustees by way of a tax credit (ie the tax paid overseas reduces the UK income tax on the income). As the rates of income tax on the part of the trustees is either the basic rate of 20% (for the tax year 2010–2011) or the dividend ordinary rate of 10% (for the tax year 2010–2011) it may be that no net UK income tax liability arises due to a foreign tax credit of equal magnitude (this is perhaps different from that for the discretionary trust; see paragraphs 17.33 and 17.34).

17.48 The interest in possession beneficiary who is subject to income tax on the income as it arises is entitled to the foreign tax credit and also a credit for any income tax paid by the trustees on the income.

17.49 *UK resident trusts: income and capital gains taxation*

Non-UK resident beneficiaries

17.49 Non-UK resident individuals are in principle liable to income tax on UK source income. However, such liability may be limited if the UK source income is disregarded income (see paragraph 23.11).

Thus, for the non-UK resident interest in possession beneficiary exposure to UK income tax on the underlying trust income which qualifies as disregarded income may thus be limited.

17.50 Where the trust income does not so qualify the non-UK resident interest in possession beneficiary's liability to UK income tax is at the normal rates of income tax applicable to individuals (ie marginal rates of 50% for non-dividend income and 42.5% for dividend income for the tax year 2010–2011). However, any income tax paid by the trustees can be offset against such liability.

Non-UK domiciled beneficiaries

17.51 A non-UK domiciled but UK resident individual interest in possession beneficiary is subject to income tax on trust income in the same manner as the UK domiciled and UK resident beneficiary.

However, if the trust income arises outside the UK and remains outside the UK no income tax liability arises at that time on the part of the beneficiary (assuming remittance basis treatment; see paragraph 24.7).

Any subsequent remittance of the income to the UK by or for the benefit of a relevant person (*ITA 2007 s 809M*; assuming the income of the trust arises on or after 6 April 2008) precipitates, at that time, an income tax charge on the part of the beneficiary. Pre-6 April 2008 trust income which remains outside the UK is subject to income tax only if the trustees or the interest in possession beneficiary remits the income to the UK or another person remits it to the UK and the beneficiary benefits therefrom. This contrasts with the tax treatment of the non-UK domiciled discretionary beneficiary (see paragraph 17.38).

Example 9

Jonathan White sets up an interest in possession trust in the tax year 2010–2011 with his mother, Sophia Roma, as the interest in possession beneficiary for life, remainder to Jonathan's four children.

Sophia is non-UK domiciled but UK resident.

In the tax year 2010–2011 the trust receives UK source income of £20,000 and non-UK source income of £40,000. The UK source income is credited directly to the UK bank account of the trustees and the non-UK source income is credited directly to the non-UK bank account of the trustees before transfer to Sophia's non-UK bank account.

Sophia is liable to income tax on the UK source income on the arising basis but no income tax liability arises on her part on the non-UK source income unless it is remitted to the UK.

If, unknowingly, the trustees arrange for the non-UK source income to be credited to their (ie the trustees') UK bank account a remittance of the income occurs at that time on the part of Sophia because the income is that of Sophia as soon as it arises; Sophia is therefore subject to income tax thereon (the fact that Sophia did not personally remit the income is irrelevant for ascertaining whether a remittance to the UK occurs on her part; the trustees are 'relevant persons'; *ITA 2007 s 809M*).

Capital gains tax

Discretionary trusts and interest in possession trusts

17.52 Trustees of UK resident trusts are liable to CGT on actual disposals and deemed disposals. An actual disposal is, for example, the simple disposal by way of a sale of a trust asset (eg an antique painting). A deemed disposal, for example, is where a beneficiary of the trust becomes absolutely entitled as against the trustees with respect to trust property; in which case the trustees are deemed to have made a disposal of the trust assets at market value to the beneficiary (*TCGA 1992 s 71;* see paragraph 8.64).

There is no distinction between discretionary and interest in possession trusts for CGT purposes.

Rates of capital gains tax

17.53 CGT applies to trustees of discretionary or interest in possession trusts in the same manner and at the same rates.

17.54 Disposals effected on or after 23 June 2010 are subject to a flat rate of CGT of 28% (*F (No 2) Act 2010 s 2* and *Sch 1*).

Disposals effected prior to 23 June 2010 and on or after 6 April 2010 are subject to a flat rate of 18% (this rate also applies to disposals effected on or after 6 April 2008).

17.55 *UK resident trusts: income and capital gains taxation*

17.55 Disposals effected prior to 6 April 2008 (and from 6 April 2004) are subject to CGT at a flat rate of 40% (34% prior to 6 April 2004 and post-6 April 1998).

17.56 Disposals of business assets effected on or after 6 April 2008 may qualify for entrepreneur relief (ER) at an effective rate of 10% although such relief is inapplicable to asset disposals by the trustees of a discretionary trust (see paragraph 8.96). The method of computing the capital gain subject to ER changes with respect to disposals on or after 23 June 2010 but the effective rate is still 10% (*F (No2) Act 2010 s 2* and *Sch 1;* see paragraph 8.90).

17.57 Indexation allowance and taper relief cease to apply for CGT purposes on trust asset disposals on or after 6 April 2008 (see Appendix 2).

Annual exempt amount

17.58 Trustees are only entitled to one-half of the annual exempt amount available to individuals (*TCGA 1992 s 3* and *Sch 1*). Where a settlor creates a number of trusts (on or after 5 June 1978) the trustees of each trust are entitled to the greater of 10% of one-half of the annual exempt amount or one-half of the annual exempt amount divided by the number of trusts (*TCGA 1992 Sch 1*). Non-UK resident trusts are ignored in the calculation but lifetime trusts, will trusts and settlor-interested trusts are included.

Capital losses

17.59 The principles of capital loss offset are those applicable to the individual (see paragraphs 9.7 and 9.8). *Inter alia*, the trustees' annual exempt amount may thus be wasted as can occur with respect to the individual (see paragraphs 9.7 and 9.9).

Example 10

The Barker Smith discretionary trust has the following capital gains and losses:

	2008–09	2009–10	2010–11
Capital gains	£23,000	£20,000	£35,000
Capital losses	£27,000	£12,000	£5,000
Annual exempt amount 2008–2009	£4,800	£5,050	£5,050

Capital losses of £27,000 reduce capital gains of £23,000 to nil with carry-forward losses of £4,000. The annual exempt amount of 2008–2009 is wasted. It would, if possible, have been better to delay realising £8,800 of capital losses until 2009–2010 thus reducing net capital gains in 2008–2009 to £4,800 then reduced to nil by the annual exempt amount, thus not wasting the 2008–2009 annual exempt amount.

2009–2010

Capital losses of £12,000 are offset first against the capital gains of £20,000 producing net gains of £8,000. Of the 2008–2009 capital loss brought forward of £4,000, £2,950 may be used to reduce net gains to £5,050 which, after the annual exempt amount, is nil (ie no CGT charge).

2010–2011

Capital losses of £5,000 reduce capital gains of £35,000 to £30,000. This figure of £30,000 is further reduced by the remaining capital loss carry forward of £1,050 (ie £4,000 less £2,950) producing net gains of £28,950.

The net gains of £28,950 are then reduced by the annual exempt amount of £5,050 to £23,900.

Hold-over relief

17.60 Hold-over relief for CGT purposes applies where disposals are made either in the form of outright gifts or at sales at below market value. The broad effect of the relief is that the CGT charge, which otherwise arises on the disposal, is deferred (see paragraph 8.45).

17.61 The relief applies to trustees (as well as individuals) and in particular may be in point where the trustees of a discretionary trust appoint trust property out to a beneficiary. The relief also applies to transfers of assets into trust by the settlor (see paragraph 8.73).

17.62 Requirements of the relief are that, *inter alia*, the disposal is either of a business asset (*TCGA 1992 s 165*) or precipitates an immediate charge to IHT (*TCGA 1992 s 260*). It is normally the latter requirement that is more likely to be satisfied where trust disposals are effected.

17.63 For a detailed discussion of the principles of hold-over relief as it applies to transactions involving trusts see Chapter 8.

Anti-avoidance provisions

17.64 The above discussion considered the income tax and CGT implications for trustees and beneficiaries of UK resident trusts, be they discretionary or interest in possession in nature.

17.65 *UK resident trusts: income and capital gains taxation*

17.65 Unfortunately, the perception of successive governments that trusts are utilised for tax avoidance purposes has led to a proliferation of measures designed to remove or mitigate their perceived tax advantages. The broad thrust of these measures has been to effectively treat the trust as transparent and subject the settlor to both income tax and CGT as if the trust did not exist. These measures are usually referred to somewhat generically as the 'settlor-interested' provisions.

Income tax

17.66 The anti-avoidance provisions which deal with income tax are contained in *ITTOIA 2005 Part 5 Ch 5* and comprise three separate sets of provisions each of which have the effect of charging the settlor on the trust's income; however, the precise application of *ITTOIA 2005 s 633* (one of the sets of provisions) is slightly different from that of *ITTOIA 2005 ss 624* and *629* (the other two sets of provisions).

The three sets of provisions are:

- where the settlor retains an interest in the trust (*ITTOIA 2005 s 624*);
- where trust income is paid to or for the benefit of a minor child (ie a child under 18) of the settlor (*ITTOIA 2005 s 629*); or
- where a capital sum is paid by the trustees of the trust to the settlor (*ITTOIA 2005 s 633*).

Settlor-interested (ITTOIA 2005 s 624)

17.67 *FA 2006 s 89* made changes to the way trustees of settlor-interested discretionary/accumulation trusts are taxed. Effective 6 April 2006, the income of the trust subject to income tax on the part of the settlor retains its original character.

Discretionary payments to non-settlor beneficiaries are outside the tax pool arrangements (see paragraph 17.26) and thus do not carry a repayable tax credit for the beneficiary. Equally, the trustees are under no obligation to account for income tax on the grossed-up payments (see paragraph 17.25).

The discussion below is based on the post-*FA 2006* position (see '*IHT and Trust Newsletter*' December 2007).

17.68 A settlor retains an interest in a trust if the trust property is or may become payable for his benefit or that of his spouse at anytime whatsoever and under any circumstances (*ITTOIA 2005 s 625*). This encompasses the position where the settlor (or spouse) is, or may become, a beneficiary of a discretionary trust. It also encompasses any revocable trust under which trust property reverts to the settlor (or spouse). Thus, any income of the trust arising on trust property in respect of which the settlor or his spouse cannot benefit is not subject to income tax on the part of the settlor (see paragraph 17.102).

In certain cases even where the settlor or spouse may benefit under the trust the settlor is deemed not to have an interest in the trust property. Thus, for example, where the settlor or his spouse can only benefit in the event of the bankruptcy of a beneficiary or where they can benefit only on an assignment or charge by a beneficiary of the beneficiary's interest the settlor is deemed not to have an interest in the trust property (*ITTOIA 2005 s 625*).

17.69 The reference to property of the trust includes income from the property and/or replacement property (*ITTOIA 2005 s 625*).

17.70 The term 'spouse' does not include a spouse from whom the settlor is separated under an order of the court, separation agreement or where the separation is likely to be permanent or any former spouse or widow or widower of the settlor (*ITTOIA 2005 s 625*).

Thus, a trust under which the spouse of the settlor (but not the settlor) may benefit only in the event of the settlor's death is not 'caught' under these provisions.

17.71 Where the provisions apply 'income which arises under [the] trust' is treated as the income of the settlor 'and of the settlor alone' during the life of the settlor (*ITTOIA 2005 s 624*) and is treated as the highest part of the settlor's income (*ITTOIA 2005 s 619A*). The settlor is subject to income tax as if the trust income is his and is thus charged under the relevant provisions; *inter alia*, he is subject at the normal individual dividend rates (10%, 32.5% and 42.5% for the tax year 2010–2011) with respect to dividend income received by the trustees and is entitled to any attaching tax credit (*ITTOIA 2007 s 397A*).

OIGs arising to a UK resident trust are subject to income tax at the trust rate irrespective of the nature of the trust (ie whether discretionary or interest in possession) (*ITA 2007 ss 481* and *482*). The settlor-interested provisions also apply but only where the OIGs arise to a UK resident trust (*ITTOIA 2005 s 624*). The settlor-interested provisions do not, however, apply to OIGs accruing to non-UK resident trusts (see paragraph 18.150).

17.72 However, despite the settlor's liability on the trust income the trustees are also liable thereon with the trustees' liability offsetting by way of credit the charge on the settlor (*ITTOIA 2005 s 646*). The trustees' liability depends upon whether the trust is discretionary or interest in possession (see paragraphs 17.19 and 17.43).

17.73 *UK resident trusts: income and capital gains taxation*

Example 11

Dick Horse settles property on an interest in possession trust for his adult son, Matthew with remainder split equally between to his brother, Harry and his sister, Clarissa.

As neither Dick nor his spouse can benefit under the trust it is not settlor-interested and thus the income of the trust is not subject to income tax on Dick's part; Matthew, as the interest in possession beneficiary, is liable thereon.

Example 12

Following on from Example 11

One year later Dick Horse settles further property on another trust but decides to split the trust property into two funds. Matthew is given an interest in possession in one of the funds with remainder to Dick's brother Harry.

The other fund is discretionary in nature and includes Dick's wife Harriet.

Dick is subject to income tax under the settlor-interested provisions on income arising only to the latter fund due to his spouse being able to benefit therefrom. However, neither Dick nor his wife can benefit from the former fund and thus the settlor-interested provisions are inapplicable to income arising on that fund.

Discretionary trusts

17.73 In the case of a discretionary trust the trustees are liable at the trust rate (50% for the tax year 2010–2011) and the dividend trust rate (42.5% for the tax year 2010–2011). The standard rate band of £1,000 (for the tax year 2010–2011) is subject to income tax at 20% or 10% depending upon if the income is non-dividend income or dividend income respectively. Their liability is after deduction for trust management expenses. However, the settlor is liable on the trust's gross income without deduction for such expenses.

17.74 Where the income tax paid by the trustees exceeds the liability of the settlor a reclaim (from HMRC) for the excess may be lodged by the settlor. Where, however, the settlor's liability is greater than that of the trustees the settlor must discharge the excess (but has the right to reclaim any such excess paid from the trustees; *ITTOIA 2005 s 646*), (see paragraphs 18.62 and 25.56).

17.75 *Prima facie*, for many settlors who are subject to income tax at the basic rate (20% for the tax year 2010–2011) or the higher rate (40% for the tax year 2010–2011) but not the additional rate (50% for the tax year 2010–2011), reclaims (from HMRC) by the settlors with respect to income tax overpaid by the trustees seems likely.

For the settlor who is liable at the additional (50%) rate (for 2010–2011) the fact that the settlor's liability is based upon gross trust income whereas the trustees' liability (at 50%) is based upon gross income less expenses is likely to produce a liability for the settlor higher than that for the trustees; in which case claims against the trustees for any excess income tax paid seems highly likely.

17.76 Although the end result of the above mechanics is that the ultimate income tax liability is that of the settlor, not the trustees, the requirements for trustees of discretionary trusts to initially account for income tax at the trust rate and dividend trust rate on the trust income and to file relevant tax returns makes the use of such trusts particularly unattractive from a cash flow perspective.

17.77 Where a discretionary trust effects income distributions to its beneficiaries (other than the settlor) the recipient beneficiary is treated as having paid income tax at the higher rate (ie 40%) where the income distribution is received before 6 April 2010 or the additional rate (50%) where the income distribution is received on or after 6 April 2010; this however is a notional tax credit which cannot be reclaimed by the beneficiary (*ITTOIA 2005 s 685A*).

Distributions to the settlor are not treated as income and thus no further income tax charge arises thereon (*ITTOIA 2005 s 685A*).

Where *ITTOIA 2005 s 685A* applies neither *ITA 2007 ss 494* nor *495* apply (see paragraph 17.25).

Example 13

Henry Taxation set up a discretionary trust for his three adult children, Clarissa, Tig and Bro, but also includes as a beneficiary his wife, Meridian.

The trust's income (non-dividend) for the tax year 2010–2011 is £75,000.

The trustees' liability is thus 50% of £75,000 (ie £37,500) (ignoring trust expenses and the standard rate band).

The trustees pay out the following income:

£3,000 to Clarissa (who is a basic rate (20%) taxpayer);

£12,000 to Tig (who is a higher rate (40%) taxpayer);

£24,000 to Bro (who is an additional rate (50%) taxpayer).

17.78 *UK resident trusts: income and capital gains taxation*

As Henry's wife is within the class of beneficiaries the trust is settlor-interested. The trust income is thus treated as that of Henry even though he cannot personally benefit under the trust.

Assuming Henry is an additional rate (50%) taxpayer his income tax liability is 50% of £75,000 (ie £37,500). This liability is offset by that of the trustees and thus Henry has no additional income tax to pay.

The three children are not subject to income tax on their income receipts.

Interest in possession trusts

17.78 The income tax position of the parties depends upon whether the interest in possession beneficiary is the settlor or another person.

Where the beneficiary is the settlor he is subject to income tax, qua beneficiary, not qua settlor (the settlor-interested provisions in such cases being superfluous).

Where the beneficiary is not the settlor the settlor-interested provisions apply and the settlor is subject to income tax on the trust income but the beneficiary is not subject to income tax on his income entitlement.

17.79 As the trust is not a discretionary trust the trustees are liable to income tax at the basic rate (20% for the tax year 2010–2011) and the dividend ordinary rate (10% for the tax year 2010–2011); no deduction for trust expenses is allowed (see paragraphs 17.43 and 17.44).

17.80 Where the settlor is subject to income tax, qua beneficiary (ie not under the settlor-interested provisions), any income tax paid by the trustees is offsettable as a tax credit against the settlor beneficiary's liability qua beneficiary. However, any excess income tax which may have been paid by the trustees cannot be reclaimed by the settlor qua beneficiary.

The liability qua beneficiary is on the gross trust income less expenses and the income tax liability of the trustees (see paragraph 17.42). This means that, qua beneficiary, no income tax charge arises on the trust expenses and the trustees' income used to settle their tax liability; accordingly, the settlor is then charged under the settlor-interested provisions on this trust income (any tax arising thereon is reclaimable from the trustees).

Where the beneficiary is other than the settlor the settlor is subject to income tax on the gross trust income (ie no deduction for trust expenses) and any income tax paid by the trustees is offsettable as a tax credit; any excess tax paid by the trustees is recoverable (from HMRC). Where the settlor's liability exceeds that of the tax paid by the trustees the excess may be reclaimed from the trustees.

UK resident trusts: income and capital gains taxation **17.84**

Underlying companies

17.81 A not untypical structure is ownership of a company by trustees. The income of the company is not, however, 'income which arises under [the] trust' (see paragraph 17.71 and thus the settlor of the trust is not subject to income tax on the company's income under *ITTOIA 2005 s 624* (where the company is non-UK resident the transfer of asset provisions are in point and it is likely that the company's income will be subject to income tax on the part of the settlor/transferor under these provisions; see paragraph 18.69).

Non-UK domiciled but UK resident settlors

17.82 For the non-UK domiciled but UK resident settlor 'income which arises under a trust' does not include income (ie non-UK source income) which is not remitted to the UK (assuming the settlor claims remittance basis treatment, see paragraph 24.7) (*ITTOIA 2005 s 648*). However, as and when such income is remitted, the remitted income is treated at that time as 'income which arises under a trust' and thus falls subject to income tax at that time on the settlor.

17.83 A remittance of the non-UK source income (arising on or after 6 April 2008) occurs where it is effected by or for the benefit of a relevant person; this includes, *inter alia*, the settlor, the settlor's spouse and almost certainly the trustees (see paragraph 24.50). With respect to non-UK source income arising before 6 April 2008 the transitional provisions contained in *FA 2008* are applicable (see paragraph 24.70)

17.84 The above applies to relevant foreign income (RFI) which primarily includes foreign rental income, dividends and interest (*ITTOIA 2005 s 830*). Thus, income other than RFI arising to the trust is subject to income tax on the part of the settlor on the arising basis.

Example 14

Jonathan White sets up a UK resident interest in possession trust in 2008–2009 with his wife, Claudia Roma, as the life tenant remainder to their four children.

Jonathan is UK domiciled and UK resident. Claudia is non-UK domiciled but UK resident.

In the tax year 2010–2011 the trust receives UK source income of £20,000 and non-UK source income of £40,000. The UK source income is credited directly to the UK bank account of the trustees and the non-UK

17.85 *UK resident trusts: income and capital gains taxation*

source income is credited directly to the non-UK bank account of the trustees.

As the interest in possession beneficiary, Claudia is in principle liable to income tax thereon. However, the trust is settlor-interested as Jonathan's wife can (and as interest in possession beneficiary does) benefit under the trust.

Thus Jonathan, as UK domiciled settlor, is liable to income tax on all the trust income and Claudia is no longer subject to income tax thereon.

Although as a non-UK domiciled but UK resident individual Claudia is entitled to remittance basis treatment, as the trust is settlor-interested and John is UK domiciled the remittance basis is inapplicable to the trust's income.

Income paid to minor children (ITTOIA 2005 s 629)

17.85 Income of a UK resident trust which is paid to, or for the benefit of, an unmarried child under age 18 of the settlor is treated as income of the settlor during the settlor's lifetime (*ITTOIA 2005 s 629*). The section applies for a tax year where a payment is made in that tax year to the child if at any point in the tax year the child is under 18.

Thus, payments of income to the child in the tax year following the child attaining the age of 18 (and thereafter) cannot be treated as that of the settlor.

17.86 If the income of the trust is that of the settlor under the settlor-interested provisions (*ITTOIA 2005 s 624*; see paragraph 17.67) *ITTOIA 2005 s 629* is inapplicable.

17.87 The term 'child' includes a step-child (*ITTOIA 2005 s 629*).

17.88 A *de minimis* provision applies pursuant to which any income paid to a beneficiary which does not exceed £100 in a tax year is not subject to income tax on the part of the settlor (*ITTOIA 2005 s 629*).

17.89 A capital distribution (eg of accumulated income) to the child of the settlor (assuming the child is under 18) is treated as income of the settlor. It is so treated if there is sufficient retained income within the trust; retained income is the gross amount of the trust's income since creation less, *inter alia*, income which has already been treated as the settlor's or has been applied in meeting trust expenses or has been paid to a beneficiary (whether as income or capital) other than a minor child of the settlor or has been treated as income of a minor child of the settlor (*ITTOIA 2005 s 631*).

UK resident trusts: income and capital gains taxation **17.92**

Any initially untaxed element of the capital distribution (due to insufficient retained income) is carried forward and later treated as the settlor's income as and when further retained income becomes available.

The settlor is able to recover any income tax paid from the trustees.

Bare trusts for unmarried minors

17.90 Pre-9 March 1999 it was possible for a parent to settle property on bare trust (ie a trust in respect of which the beneficiary has the immediate right to both the trust capital and income and where such right is not subject to any contingency) for his children yet still avoid an income tax charge on the parent. The income of the trust property was that of the child and taxed accordingly; this applied so long as the income was not paid out to the child (which was often the case as a child under 18 was/is not capable of providing the trustees with a valid receipt; see paragraph 27.70).

Such trusts continue to be effective assuming that no additions to the trust have been made post- 8 March 1999. Where additions have been made to such trusts it is only the income which arises from the added capital which is subject to income tax on the part of the parent settlor when paid to the child. Thus, assuming the income from the pre-9 March 1999 trust property is not paid out to the child this income will continue to be treated as the child's and not that of the settlor.

However, for parental bare trusts set up on or after 9 March 1999 the income of such trusts is subject to income tax on the part of the parent settlor whether paid out to the child or not (assuming the income of the trust exceeds £100 per tax year) (*ITTOIA 2005 s 629*).

Capital sums paid to the settlor (ITTOIA 2005 s 633)

17.91 Where the settlor (or spouse) receives a capital sum from the trustees in a tax year the settlor is subject to income tax on an equivalent sum of available income to the extent that the amount of the capital sum falls within the amount of income available in the trust up to the end of the tax year (*ITTOIA 2005 ss 633 and 634*).

The capital sum is first grossed-up at the trust rate for the tax year in which the capital sum is made ie it is the grossed-up capital sum in respect of which the settlor is subject to income tax (*ITTIOA 2005 s 640*).

17.92 However, where the trust is an interest in possession trust (ie the trust's income is subject to income tax on the interest in possession beneficiary on the

17.93 *UK resident trusts: income and capital gains taxation*

arising basis) there can be no available income to which any capital sum can be matched; the income of the trust belonging to the interest in possession beneficiary. *ITTOIA 2005 s 633* is thus only of relevance in the case of discretionary trusts.

In addition, if the trust is settlor-interested *ITTOIA 2005 s 624* applies and thus the trust has no available relevant income. *ITTOIA 2005 s 633* thereon only appears to be of relevance to non-settlor-interested discretionary trusts.

17.93 The income which is regarded as available is the undistributed income of the trust less such income which has been treated as the settlor's under *ITTOIA 2005 ss 624* or *s 629* or has already been taken into account under *ITTOIA 2005 s 633* (with respect to the particular capital sum and/or earlier capital sums) or has been used to discharge trust expenses; in addition, an amount equal to the aggregate of tax at the trust rate on undistributed income of each tax year is also deducted in arriving at the available income (the appropriate trust rate is that applicable in the tax year in which the calculation is being carried out; for the tax year 2010–2011 the trust rate is 50%).

17.94 The matching of available income against the capital sum is carried out on a tax year by tax year basis taking earlier tax years first (*ITTOIA 2005 s 640*).

17.95 Any remaining unmatched part of the capital sum at the end of the tax year in which the sum is paid is carried forward for future matching (*ITTOIA 2005 s 633*).

17.96 The settlor's liability to income tax on the matching of the available income is at his marginal rate albeit with an offsetting tax credit for income tax paid on the available income by the trustees. The income tax paid by the trustees on the available income is the trust rate which was applicable in the tax year when the income arose to the trustees (eg 34% for tax years pre-2004–2005; 40% for tax years 2005–2006 to 2009–2010; and 50% for tax year 2010–2011).

The combination of matching on a tax year by tax year basis taking, earlier tax years first, and changes in the trust rate over time means that any matching in, say, 2010–2011 (in which a capital sum is made) with trust income which arose between 2004–2005 and 2009–2010 inclusive will precipitate a net income tax charge on the settlor if he is subject to income tax at the 50% additional rate. If in 2010–2011 the settlor's marginal rate of income tax is 40% a net income tax liability is precipitated if the matching is with trust income which arose pre-2004–2005 (then taxed at 34%).

17.97 There is no facility for the settlor to recover any net income tax liability from the trustees (*ITTOIA 2005 s 646*).

17.98 The term 'capital sum' refers to any sum paid by way of loan (to the settlor or settlor's spouse) or repayment of a loan (by the trustees on a loan to them from the settlor or settlor's spouse) or any other sum which is not paid as income and is not paid for full consideration (*ITTOIA 2005 s 634*).

Whether any such loan is on arm's-length terms or not is irrelevant.

Capital gains tax

17.99 Whereas the above anti-avoidance provisions on the treatment of trust income of UK resident trusts for income tax purposes continue to apply post-*FA 2008* this is not the position for CGT purposes.

In short, the 'settlor-interested' anti-avoidance provisions applicable to the CGT treatment of UK resident trusts have been abolished from 6 April 2008. Thus, any capital gains made by trustees of UK resident trusts on or after 6 April 2008 are subject to CGT on the part of the trustees only (ie the settlor is no longer subject to CGT thereon on the arising basis).

17.100 The reason for the repeal of these anti-avoidance provisions is that for disposals pre-*FA 2008* the rate of CGT was 40% if the disposal was made by the trustees of the trust which was also the applicable rate if the higher rate (ie 40%) taxpayer had made the disposal. Thus, no avoidance of CGT arose by the use of a UK resident trust. Similarly, for disposals on or after 6 April 2008 and pre-23 June 2010, the rate of CGT is the same (ie 18%) whether the sale is effected by a UK resident individual or a UK resident trust (*F (No 2) 2010 s 2* and *Sch 1*).

However, with respect to disposals on or after 23 June 2010, UK resident trusts are subject to CGT at a rate of 28% but for the individual the rate of CGT is either 18% or 28% (*F (No 2) 2010 s 2* and *Sch 1*; see paragraphs 8.17 and 8.22)

Settlor-interested trusts pre-FA 2008 (now abolished)

17.101 Chargeable gains accruing to a UK resident trust were, pre-*FA 2008*, treated as those of the settlor if the trust was 'settlor-interested' (*TCGA 1992 s 77*).

The definition of a 'settlor-interested' trust for CGT purposes was different to the definition which applied (and still applies post-*FA 2008*) for income tax purposes. A trust was deemed to be a settlor-interested trust for CGT if the settlor (or spouse) could benefit from the trust in any circumstances whatsoever (*TCGA 1992 s 169F*). This definition was then widened by the provisions of *FA 2006*.

17.102 *UK resident trusts: income and capital gains taxation*

With effect from 6 April 2006 a settlor was deemed to have an interest in a trust if, in addition to the possible benefit from the trust by the settlor or spouse, any dependent children of the settlor could benefit (*TCGA 1992 s 77*). For this purpose, a dependent child of the settlor was an unmarried living child under 18; child included step-child.

17.102 The above change effective 6 April 2006 applied to all trusts including those created prior to 6 April 2006.

Where the settlor-interested provisions applied the settlor would be charged to CGT on the trust gains and any such tax paid could be reclaimed from the trustees. Unlike the position with respect to the income tax settlor-interested provisions, all the trust gains were charged on the settlor whether or not the settlor (or spouse) could benefit from all the trust property. To this extent, the capital gains settlor-interested provisions were more penal than those which applied for income tax purposes.

Where the settlor was non-UK domiciled but UK resident, the remittance basis was inapplicable to capital gains arising even on the disposal of non-UK situs assets

17.103 The rules applicable to ascertaining the amount of capital gains of the trust to be charged on the settlor were changed from 6 April 2003. For the tax year 2003–2004 and later tax years trust gains charged on the settlor were the trust gains after the offsetting of any trust capital losses (pre-taper relief). Any surplus of capital losses of the settlor personally (ie after offset against the settlor's own capital gains) could then be used to reduce the pre-taper relief gains of the trust apportioned to the settlor (after which such net gains could be reduced by the taper relief to which the trust would have been entitled).

A surplus of trust capital losses (ie the surplus after the offset of trust losses against trust gains) was not, however, available for use by the settlor for offset against the settlor's personal capital gains.

17.104 As stated in paragraph 17.99 with effect from 6 April 2008 the capital gains made by UK resident trusts are no longer assessable on the settlor (but the position with respect to non-UK resident trusts is different ie settlor-interested provisions apply both pre- and post-*FA 2008*; see paragraph 18.99).

UK resident trusts: some concluding comments

Income tax

17.105 The trustees of a UK resident discretionary trust are liable to an income tax charge of 50% on non-dividend income and 42.5% on dividend income (for the 2010–2011 tax year). Thus, for the settlor who is UK domiciled and UK resident and who is subject to income tax at the basic rate (20% for the 2010–2011 tax year) or even the higher rate (40% for the 2010–2011 tax year) the discretionary trust (which is not settlor-interested) is tax inefficient even though on distributions of income the recipient beneficiary may be able to reclaim some part of this tax from HMRC depending upon his own income tax status. There is nevertheless a cash flow disadvantage.

17.106 In addition, even for the settlor-interested discretionary trust, the trustees are still required to file tax returns and make appropriate income tax payments albeit in respect of which the settlor may lodge tax refund claims where necessary (eg where settlor's income tax liability is less than that of the trustees) thus producing a cash flow disadvantage and extra administrative costs.

17.107 Dividend income arising to a discretionary trust is undesirable due to the mismatch between the income tax liability thereon at 42.5% (for the tax year 2010–2011) and the *s 494* income tax liability (50% on distributions in 2010–2011) on distributions to beneficiaries. The net cash receipt for the beneficiary is less than if the dividends had been received directly by him and not via an intermediary trust.

17.108 The interest in possession trust may be less cash flow disadvantageous as the trustees' income tax exposure is limited to the basic rate (20% for the tax year 2010–2011) and/or the dividend ordinary rate (10% for the tax year 2010–2011). However, administrative costs are still incurred in filing trust tax returns.

17.109 Trust expenses inevitably reduce the amount of income available to either the interest in possession beneficiary or beneficiaries of the discretionary trust.

17.110 There is thus no real income tax incentive for UK resident interest in possession or discretionary trusts to be set up by UK domiciled and resident individuals.

17.111 Similarly there is no real income tax incentive for non-UK domiciled but UK resident individuals to form such trusts although non-UK source income is subject to remittance basis treatment on the part of such individuals.

Capital gains tax

17.112 The rate of CGT (ie 18%) for disposals on or after 6 April 2008 and pre-23 June 2010 is the same for trusts and individuals. However, for disposals

17.113 *UK resident trusts: income and capital gains taxation*

effected on or after 23 June 2010 the rates of CGT for the individual are 18% or 28% whereas for the trustees the rate is a flat 28%.

In principle utilising a UK resident trust thus seems inadvisable from the CGT perspective.

17.113 The annual exempt amount for trustees is only one-half of that applicable to individuals.

17.114 There appears to be no CGT advantages for the UK domiciled and resident individual in using UK resident trusts of any description.

17.115 For the non-UK domiciled but UK resident individual, the use of a UK resident trust makes the CGT position worse with respect to non-UK source capital gains; (whereas the individual is able to claim remittance basis treatment, the UK resident trustees are not able to so claim).

Inheritance tax

17.116 UK resident trusts, whether relevant property trusts or qualifying interest in possession trusts, are within the ambit of IHT where created by UK domiciled individuals.

17.117 However the relevant property trust, while possibly giving rise to a 20% IHT charge on creation (unless the NRB is available to the settlor), is only subsequently subject to ten-yearly charges at the maximum rate of 6% (or exit charges of slightly less than 6%) which compares extremely favourably with the 40% rate applicable to individuals on death (see paragraphs 16.42 and 16.43).

Interest in possession trusts created in lifetime on or after 22 March 2006 are treated in the same manner (the position for qualifying interest in possession trusts, basically trusts created pre-22 March 2006, is different).

17.118 The NRB discretionary trust may be particularly attractive due to its minimal, if any, ten-yearly and exit charges (see paragraph 16.24).

17.119 The UK resident trust may also offer non-tax advantages in particular in relation to their use to avoid probate and/or as substitute wills.

17.120 Thus, despite UK resident trusts not giving rise to favourable income tax or CGT consequences, such trusts may offer IHT advantages.

17.121 The key to IHT planning for non-UK domiciled individuals is the retention or creation of excluded property. Whilst non-UK situs property of a UK resident trust created by such individuals constitutes excluded property such trusts are not favoured due to the negative income tax and CGT effects which are overcome by the use of non-UK resident trusts.

Summary

17.122 Trustees of UK resident trusts are liable to income tax on trust income and CGT on trust capital gains. The trust in this regard is a distinct and separate person from either its settlor or its beneficiaries.

17.123 The rates of income tax on trust income vary according to whether the trust is a discretionary trust or an interest in possession trust.

17.124 Pre-23 June 2010 and post-6 April 2008, the rate of CGT applicable to trusts is the same (ie 18%) irrespective of the type of trust. On or after 23 June 2010 the rate of CGT is 28%.

17.125 The settlor-interested trust provisions applicable to income tax continue to apply in the same manner pre-and post-*FA 2008*. *FA 2008* had no impact on these provisions. Broadly, such provisions subject the settlor to income tax on trust income as it arises; however, this does not preclude the trustees from liability on the trust income.

17.126 The settlor-interested trust provisions no longer apply to the capital gains of UK resident trusts following their abolition by *FA 2008*. Accordingly, all trust gains of a UK resident trust arising on or after 6 April 2008 are subject to CGT on the part of the trustees (not the settlor).

17.127 UK resident trusts are of limited value both for the UK and non-UK domiciled individual with respect to income tax and CGT although there may be IHT advantages for the UK domiciled individual.

Chapter 18

Non-UK resident trusts: income and capital gains taxation

Background

18.1 Chapter 15 provides a brief overview of the trust concept; Chapter 16 discusses the inheritance tax (IHT) implications of different types of trust; and Chapter 17 analyses in detail the income tax and capital gains tax (CGT) implications of UK resident trusts.

18.2 This chapter looks at the income tax and CGT aspects of non-UK resident trusts. While the trust is a separate taxable entity certain anti-avoidance provisions may apply the consequences of which are that it is the settlor and or the beneficiaries, and not the trust, who is subject to tax on the trust's income and/or capital gains.

The approach adopted in this chapter is the same as that adopted in Chapter 17 (ie first the tax treatment of non-UK resident trusts is discussed ignoring the possible application of these various anti-avoidance provisions and, second, the impact of these provisions on the trust's tax treatment is then discussed).

18.3 The taxation of a trust depends upon the following factors:

- residence of the trust (ie UK resident or non-UK resident);
- type of trust (eg discretionary or interest in possession);
- residence status of the settlor;
- domicile status of the settlor;
- residence status of the beneficiaries;
- domicile status of the beneficiaries; and
- UK or non-UK source income/gains.

Strictly speaking, it is the trustees of the trust (not the trust, per se) who are liable to any income and/or CGT charges. Trustees are treated as a single person, or single body, distinct from the persons who are in fact the trustees (companies and individuals may be trustees) (*ITA 2007 s 474; TCGA 1992 s 69*).

For ease, the section on trustee residence in Chapter 17 is repeated here.

Trust residency

Pre-6 April 2007

Capital gains tax

18.4 Prior to 6 April 2007, a trust was non-UK resident if:

- all or a majority of the trustees were neither resident nor ordinarily resident in the UK; *and*
- the general administration of the trust was ordinarily carried on outside the UK.

A UK resident professional trustee (broadly, a person carrying on the business of trust management) was, however, deemed to be resident outside the UK if the whole of the settled property consisted of property provided by someone who at that time was neither UK domiciled, resident nor ordinarily resident. The general administration of the trust was regarded as carried on outside the UK if a majority of the trustees were non-UK resident.

However, the professional trustee 'let-out' did not apply for income tax purposes.

Income tax

18.5 A trust was UK resident for income tax purposes if there was a sole trustee who was UK resident or, if there was more than one trustee, all were UK resident.

If one or more trustees were UK resident and one or more were not (ie a mixed residence trust) then the trust was UK resident if the settlor was domiciled or resident or ordinarily resident in the UK when the funds were provided.

Post-5 April 2007

18.6 The consequence of the changes introduced by *FA 2006* (effective 6 April 2007) is that the test for residence of trustees is now the same for income tax and CGT. The pre-6 April 2007 income tax rules now apply.

18.7 *Non-UK resident trusts: income and capital gains taxation*

18.7 The trust is treated as resident and ordinarily resident in the UK at any time if:

- all the trustees are resident in the UK; *or*
- at least one trustee is resident in the UK and at least one trustee is not resident in the UK and the settlor is resident *or* ordinarily resident *or* domiciled in the UK when the trust is made (whether in lifetime or on death).

(*ITA 2007 ss 475* and *476; TCGA 1992 s 69*)

Thus, a trust where all of the trustees are non-UK resident will be non-UK resident irrespective of the domicile and/or residence status of the settlor.

18.8 Where the settlor is non-UK resident, not ordinary resident and non-UK domiciled at the time the trust is made the trust is non-UK resident so long as at least one trustee is non-UK resident.

18.9 The professional trustee let-out referred to above (see paragraph 18.4) has been abolished (regarded as State Aid under EU competition law) and the place of administration of the trust is now also irrelevant (see paragraph 18.4).

Example 1

Bertrand Dublin, a non-UK domiciled but UK resident individual, is keen to set up a trust (post-6 April 2007) outside the UK for family planning purposes.

He is a little wary of the trust comprising exclusively non-UK resident professional trustees and suggests that in addition his UK domiciled and UK resident brother or his non-UK domiciled but UK resident sister (or both) should also act as trustees.

If either Bertrand's brother and/or sister act as trustees the trust is classified as UK resident.

18.10 The changes introduced in *FA 2006* (effective from 6 April 2007) align the CGT treatment for residence with that for income tax; in essence no change was made with respect to the income tax rules. However, the change to the CGT rules meant that it was possible for a trust which was non-UK resident under the pre-*FA 2006* rules to automatically fall to be treated as UK resident post-*FA 2006*. This could have disastrous CGT consequences where the trust is then re-exported.

18.11 The re-exportation of the trust's UK residence precipitates a CGT charge on the part of the trustees; this occurs because there is a deemed disposal by the trustees of all trust assets at their market value at the date of export and a deemed re-acquisition at the same values (*TCGA 1992 s 80*).

18.12 The situation postulated in paragraph 18.10 arises if, for example, pre-6 April 2007 the trust administration was carried on outside the UK, a majority of the trustees were non-resident and the settlor was resident in the UK but non-UK domiciled. Such a trust would have been UK resident for income tax but non-UK resident for CGT. However, on 6 April 2007 such a trust would, while remaining UK resident for income tax, become UK resident for CGT.

It was therefore important if any such CGT charges were to be avoided that steps were taken pre-6 April 2007 to ensure that the non-UK resident trust remained so for CGT under the new rules. In the scenario of paragraph 18.10 this required that all (not just a majority) of the trustees were non-UK resident.

18.13 Although the exportation (or re-exportation) of a UK resident trust may give rise to significant CGT liabilities the income tax effects are less likely to be so serious. The exportation, per se, precipitates no general income tax consequences although offshore income gains (OIGs) are precipitated (in the same manner as capital gains are precipitated; *OFTR 2009 SI 2009/3001 reg 20*; see paragraph 18.139)). Any non-UK source income arising to the trust in the period between exportation and the end of the tax year of exportation continues to fall within the charge to income tax (see paragraph 18.14).

18.14 A trust is UK resident for the whole of a tax year for CGT if it is resident in any part of that year. ESC D2 provides split tax year treatment for CGT purposes only in the case of individuals, not trustees (see paragraph 4.64; see also *SP5/92*).

Similarly, ESC A11 provides for split tax year treatment for income tax purposes only in the case of individuals, not trustees (see paragraph 4.56).

Income tax

18.15 The income tax consequences for the non-UK resident trust are the same whether the trust is set up by a UK domiciled and UK resident individual or a non-UK domiciled but UK resident individual. This is the position with respect to both UK and non-UK source income accruing to the trust.

18.16 Non-UK resident trustees are liable to self-assessment in the same manner as individuals and trustees of UK resident trusts (albeit with their own designed tax return; see paragraph 17.16) and make payments on account in the

18.17 *Non-UK resident trusts: income and capital gains taxation*

same way. However the non-UK resident trust, unlike the UK resident trust, is not liable to income tax on worldwide income but only liable to income tax on UK source income.

18.17 However, there are differences between the income (and capital gains) tax treatment of individuals and of trusts (whether UK or non-UK resident):

- trustees are liable to income tax at the basic rate with respect to both savings and non-savings income (ie 20% for the tax year 2008–2009 and later tax years) or, in the case of dividends, the dividend ordinary rate (10% for tax year 2008–2009 and later tax years); for the tax year 2007–2008 and earlier tax years rates of 10%, 20% and 22% applied to income according to the category of income;
- the rates of 32.5% and 40% applicable to individuals only apply to certain trusts, primarily discretionary trusts (*ITA 2007 ss 9* and *479*); both these rates are increased to 42.5% and 50% respectively for the tax year 2010–2011 for discretionary trusts;
- trustees were not entitled to the 10% starting rate band (applicable for tax years 2007–2008 and earlier tax years);
- trustees are not entitled to the 'new' 10% 'starting rate for savings' available to individuals (*ITA 2007 s 12*);
- trustees are not entitled to any personal allowances; and
- trustees are entitled to 50% of the normal annual exempt amount applicable to individuals in respect of any liability to CGT; for the tax year 2010–2011 the annual exempt amount available to trustees is 50% of £10,100 (*TCGA 1992 Sch 1*). *Note, however, that non-UK resident trustees are not subject to CGT even on UK situs assets (subject to one or two exceptions)* (see paragraph 18.54).

Discretionary (and accumulation and maintenance) trusts

Trustees' liability to income tax

18.18 Accumulation and maintenance trusts (A&M) are a form of discretionary trust and thus the term 'discretionary trust' is used to encompass both types of trust. The concept of the A&M trust is primarily of value with respect to IHT (not income tax or CGT) as it receives favourable IHT treatment (see paragraph 16.85). However, following the significant changes to IHT introduced in *FA 2006* no new A&M trusts can be created for IHT purposes on or after 22 March 2006 although A&M trusts created pre-22 March 2006 may in principle continue to benefit from the favourable treatment.

Non-UK resident trusts: income and capital gains taxation 18.22

18.19 Trusts falling to be treated as discretionary trusts are those trusts where income is payable at the discretion of the trustees or where income is to be accumulated (*ITA 2007 s 479*) and is not the income of any other person prior to distribution by the trustees (*ITA 2007 s 480*). The income is that of another person if it is that of an interest in possession beneficiary (whether the interest in possession is 'qualifying' or not is irrelevant; this distinction is of relevance only for IHT purposes; see paragraph 16.4) or if the trust is settlor-interested (*ITTOIA 2005 Part 5 Chapter 5*; see paragraph 18.60).

18.20 Whilst trustees of non-resident discretionary trusts are exposed to income tax, albeit on UK source income only, the extent of their liability depends upon whether there are one or more beneficiaries who is/are ordinarily resident in the UK (see paragraph 18.21). A person is a beneficiary for this purpose if he is an actual or potential beneficiary who is, or may become, entitled to receive some or all of the trust's income or where any income of the trust may be paid (or used) for the benefit of the beneficiary pursuant to the exercise of the trustees' discretion (*ITA 2007 s 812*).

18.21 Where one or more of the trust beneficiaries are UK ordinarily resident the trustees of a discretionary trust are subject to income tax at the same rates as those applicable to the resident discretionary trust ie a rate of 50% (the 'trust rate' effective 6 April 2010; previously the rate was 40% and was referred to as the 'rate applicable to trusts') on any UK source trust income other than UK source dividend income. UK source dividend income is subject to income tax at 42.5% (the 'dividend trust rate' effective 6 April 2010; previously 32.5%).

Although non-resident trustees are not entitled to the tax credit attached to UK source dividends (*ITTOIA 2005 s 397*) they are deemed to have discharged any liability thereon at the dividend ordinary rate (*ITTOIA 2005 s 399*). The effect is that the trustees' liability amounts to 42.5% on the gross dividend less the 10% tax credit producing a net income tax liability of 32.5% of the gross dividend.

18.22 Where, however, no UK ordinarily resident beneficiaries exist under the trust for the tax year concerned the trustees are subject to income tax on UK source income but such liability is limited where the UK source income qualifies as 'disregarded income'; the liability is limited to the amount of income tax withheld or deducted at source on the UK source income (*ITA 2007 ss 811* and *825*).

Disregarded income includes UK source dividend and interest income. Thus, with respect to UK source dividend income effectively no liability to income tax arises on the part of the trustees (this is because although the trustees are not entitled to any tax credit attaching to the dividend (*ITTOIA 2005 s 397*) the trustees are deemed to have discharged any liability at source at the dividend ordinary rate which is the limit of their liability (*ITTOIA 2005 s 399*)).

With respect to UK source bank/building society interest a withholding tax at the basic rate normally applies ie income tax at 20% (for the tax year 2010–

18.23 *Non-UK resident trusts: income and capital gains taxation*

2011) is deducted from the interest when credited to any account (*ITA 2007 s 851*). However, where the trustees of a non-resident trust make the requisite declaration to the bank any interest may then be credited gross (ie without levying the withholding tax). The declaration requires confirmation from the trustees that no beneficiaries who may receive income under the trust are UK ordinarily resident (*ITA 2007 s 858*). The consequence is that the trustees suffer no liability to income tax on the UK source interest.

18.23 Any UK source income not categorised as disregarded income (eg UK source rental income or UK source trading profit) is subject to income tax on the part of the trustees at the trust rate.

18.24 Effective 6 April 2006 a new 'standard rate band' was introduced which applies to the income of discretionary trusts including non-resident trusts. Pre-*FA 2008*, the first £1,000 of taxable income was subject to tax at the 10% (ie dividend ordinary rate), 20% (ie the lower rate) or 22% (ie basic rate) rate depending upon the type of the income. Post-*FA 2008*, this first £1,000 of taxable income is subject to tax at the 20% basic rate of tax on income other than dividend income; dividend income within the band is subject to the 10% (ie dividend ordinary rate) rate.

Where the trust receives more than one category of income the standard rate band is to be applied to income subject to income tax at the basic rate in priority to dividend income (*ITA 2007 s 491*).

The standard rate band is available for utilisation exclusively against the trust's UK source income only ie there is no requirement (as applies to the deductibility of trustee expenses; see paragraph 18.26) to pro-rata the standard rate band between the trust's UK and non-UK source income.

Example 2

The Raphael Niddle non-UK resident discretionary trust receives gross UK source income of £55,000 and gross non-UK source income of £45,000. The trust has within its class of beneficiaries UK ordinarily resident individuals (thus the trust rate and dividend trust rate apply to all the UK source income).

Trust expenses amount to £15,000.

The standard rate band can be utilised solely by the £55,000 of UK source income (after the deduction for appropriate expenses).

18.25 Expenses of a trust (ie the trust management expenses) are not deductible in computing the trust's income subject to the basic rate or dividend ordinary rate of income tax although are deductible in arriving at the amount of income subject to the trust rate or the dividend trust rate (the standard rate band (see paragraph 18.24) applies to trust income after the deduction of expenses). In order for trust expenses to rank as deductible for income tax purposes they must have been incurred wholly/solely with respect to the income of the trust (ie expenses incurred for the benefit of the whole trust fund are 'capital' and cannot be deducted; no apportionment of such expenses between trust income and trust capital is allowed; *RCC v Trustees of the Peter Clay Discretionary Trust* (2008)).

Expenses which are generally accepted as tax deductible are those of a recurrent nature and include the cost of trust account preparation and audit; preparation of trust tax returns; council tax and rates on land owned by the trust; rent payable in respect of leasehold property held by the trust; and interest on charges. Capital costs include capital expenditure on trust assets such as the cost of discharging any mortgage debt; cost of appointing new trustees; and the cost of taking legal advice as to the trustees' powers. Trustees' remuneration is generally incurred for the trust as a whole and therefore is not deductible.

Any determination as to the tax deductibility of trust expenses is made according to trust law and not according to any provisions in the trust deed in this regard.

18.26 Trust expenses which are deductible against trust income are pro-rated between the trust's UK and non-UK source income (*ITA 2007 s 487*). Thus, in computing the trustees' income tax liability only a proportion of the trust's expenses are deductible. Those expenses which are so deductible are deductible against the following UK sources, namely, dividend income first; then savings income; and finally other income (ie non-savings income) (*ITA 2007 s 486*). This order of offset is beneficial as it maximises the tax paid by the trust which may then be passed on to the beneficiaries

Where there are no UK ordinarily resident beneficiaries within the class of beneficiaries and the trust receives both UK source disregarded and non-disregarded income the expenses of the trust which have initially been pro-rated to the trust's UK source income are again pro-rated between the disregarded and non-disregarded UK source income (*ITA 2007 s 487*). Effectively in this case (ie no UK ordinarily resident beneficiaries) any expenses pro-rated to the disregarded income (which is in any event not subject to income tax) are simply 'wasted'.

Appropriate 'grossing up' of the deductible expenses is necessary to ascertain the amount to be deducted. This is because the trust rate and the dividend trust rate of income tax apply to the trust's income which is accumulated or payable at the trustees' discretion which is the trust income *after* deduction for expenses. Thus, expenses paid out of dividend income are grossed up at the dividend ordinary rate (10%) and those paid out of other income at the basic rate (20%).

18.27 *Non-UK resident trusts: income and capital gains taxation*

Example 3

The Heinrich Smith non-resident discretionary trust receives gross UK source income of £25,000 of which £20,000 (gross) is disregarded income and non-UK source income of £75,000. Trust management expenses amount to £10,000.

The trust has no UK ordinarily resident beneficiaries.

The £10,000 expenses are allocated as to:

[[£25,000/£100,000] x £10,000] (ie £2,500 to UK source income).

[[£75,000/£100,000] x £10,000] (ie £7,500 to non-UK source income).

Of the £2,500 expenses [[£5,000/£25,000] x £2,500] (ie £500) is deductible against the £5,000 of UK source non-disregarded income and the balancing £2,000 is deductible against the disregarded income.

The £1,000 standard rate band is utilised solely against the £5,000 of UK source non-disregarded income (after expenses) in computing the trustees' liability to income tax (the £20,000 of disregarded income is not subject to income tax and neither is the £75,000 of non-UK source income).

18.27 The trustees may make payments to a beneficiary out of the income of the trust or out of the trust capital. Under the former, the beneficiary receives income and is taxed accordingly; in the latter, generally, the receipt will be treated as capital and thus not subject to income tax. However, this may not always be so and a capital distribution may fall to be subject to income tax on the part of the beneficiary. For example, if the capital distribution is intended to supplement income for the beneficiary, such distribution is likely to be subject to income tax.

Trustees' position on income distributions to UK resident beneficiaries

18.28 Any payment made to a UK resident beneficiary of a *UK resident* discretionary trust, which is treated as income (and not capital) on the part of the beneficiary, is treated as if it has been made after the deduction of a sum representing income tax at the trust rate on the grossed-up amount of the payment (*ITA 2007 s 494*). The grossed up amount is the actual amount of the payment grossed up by reference to the trust rate (ie 50% for the tax year 2010–2011) (*ITA 2007 s 494*).

Non-UK resident trusts: income and capital gains taxation 18.32

Even if the distribution out of the trust is made out of dividend income of the trust the rate of gross-up is at the trust rate and not the dividend trust rate. This is because the source of the income for the beneficiary is the trust itself and not the underlying income of the trust ie the nature of the trust's underlying income is irrelevant when determining the nature of the income the beneficiary receives from the trust (*Baker v Archer-Shee (1927)*).

18.29 However, with respect to payments to a UK resident beneficiary of a non-UK resident discretionary trust the *ITA 2007 s 494* procedure referred to in paragraph 18.28 does not apply (*ITA 207 s 494*). There is thus no deemed grossing-up of the payment in respect of which the trustees have an obligation to account for income tax deemed deducted (*ITA 2007 ss 494* and *496*). It then naturally follows that there is no corresponding grossing-up of the amount received by the beneficiary (as applies to income distributions from UK resident trusts).

18.30 The concept of the 'tax pool' applicable for UK resident trusts (see paragraph 17.26) is thus not relevant to non-UK resident trusts (ie on the making of an income distribution to a beneficiary the non-UK resident trustees are not under any obligation to operate the deduction at source mechanism required by *ITA 2007 s 494* and offset the tax so deemed deducted against tax in the trustees' tax pool).

Beneficiaries position on income distributions: UK domiciled and resident

18.31 In the light of the comments in paragraph 18.29 the recipient beneficiary is subject to income tax on the income received (ie no grossing up applies). This has the effect of producing double tax (ie tax at the level of the trustees on trust income plus tax on the part of the beneficiary on income received without any offsetting tax credit).

ESC B18 however addresses this issue.

18.32 Under ESC B18 the beneficiary is able to claim appropriate credit for tax actually paid by the trustees on the income out of which the payment is made as if the payment out of UK income was from a UK resident trust and within *ITA 2007 s 494*; in essence the amount received by the beneficiary is grossed-up and a credit received in respect to tax paid on the income by the trustees. Where the trust income includes UK source dividend income only tax paid by the trustees thereon is creditable for the beneficiary (thus the one-ninth tax credit attaching to the net dividend received by the trustees is not creditable as it is not literally paid by the trustees).

ESC B18 does not apply to non-UK tax paid by the trustees on non-UK source income and thus the beneficiary in respect of income distributions out of such

18.33 *Non-UK resident trusts: income and capital gains taxation*

income does not obtain a credit for such tax; he is subject to income tax on the net distribution.

18.33 ESC B18 also states that the trust income is offset against income distributions on a last in first out (LIFO) basis and on a pro-rata basis as between UK and non-UK source income.

Example 4

The income of a non-UK resident discretionary trust (after expenses and the trustees' tax liability) for the tax years 2009–2010 and 2010–2011 is £50,000 and £10,000 respectively. Of the £50,000 UK source income amounts to £40,000 and non-UK source income £10,000. For 2010–2011 the corresponding figures are £6,000 and £4,000 respectively.

At the end of 2010–2011 an income distribution of £20,000 is made to a UK resident beneficiary.

This figure of £20,000 is deemed to be made up of £6,000 of UK source income and £4,000 of non-UK source income of the 2010–2011 tax year; and [[£10,000/£50,000] x £40,000] (ie £8,000 of UK source income) and [[10,000/£50,000] x £10,000](ie £2,000) of non-UK source income of the 2009–2010 tax year).

18.34 It is important to bear in mind that the computation under ESC B18 (see paragraph 18.33) requires income distributions to be matched with the income of the trust (ie both UK and non-UK source) on a LIFO basis (ie trust income of later tax years is matched before trust income of earlier tax years). This inevitably affects the extent of any tax credit available to the beneficiary in respect of income tax paid on UK source income by the trustees (as the trust rate and the dividend trust rate have varied over time).

18.35 Strict conditions are laid down for ESC B18 to apply. The conditions are that the trustees must be completely up to date with respect to their tax returns and all income tax due on UK source income must have been paid. It is not unusual for non-resident trusts to fail to file UK tax returns for whatever reason and to also fail to discharge their income tax liabilities at the trust rate and dividend trust rate on UK source income (in particular where their sole source of UK source income is bank interest and/or dividend income and the disregarded income rules do not apply due to UK ordinarily resident beneficiaries).

In such cases UK resident beneficiaries in receipt of income distributions are not in a position to invoke ESC B18 and thus are simply subject to income tax at their marginal rate of income tax on the income distribution.

Non-UK resident trusts: income and capital gains taxation **18.39**

18.36 For the beneficiary subject to income tax at the marginal rate of 50% (for the tax year 2010–2011) no additional income tax liability arises in respect of distributions out of UK source non-dividend income which arises to the trust in that tax year (2010–2011); for the 40% taxpayer an income tax refund (from HMRC) arises as also is the case for the basic rate taxpayer.

Accumulated income

18.37 Trustees may decide to accumulate trust income (ie the income is not paid out to a beneficiary) which then forms part of the trust's capital. The effect is that if in due course the accumulated income is paid out to one or more beneficiaries no income tax liability arises on the part of the recipient beneficiaries but income tax paid by the trustees on the accumulated income is irrecoverable (see paragraph 17.32).

Non-UK source income

18.38 Non-UK source income is not subject to income tax on the part of the non-resident trustees. Such income may, however, have been subject to foreign income taxes either in the territory of residence of the trustees and/or the country in which the income arises.

18.39 An income distribution out of such foreign income to a beneficiary is subject to income tax on the amount of the receipt; there is no grossing-up as the foreign income tax is not creditable against the beneficiary's income tax liability (either by law or under ESC B18). To this extent an element of double tax arises.

Example 5

The Mary Tree non-resident discretionary trust in 2010–2011 receives foreign interest income of £800 after a foreign withholding tax of 20% is levied. The trustees are not liable to any additional income taxes in their jurisdiction of residence.

The trustees make an income distribution to a UK resident beneficiary of £600. The beneficiary is subject to income tax at the 50% marginal rate. The beneficiary's income tax liability is thus:

50% of £600 (ie £300 leaving net cash of £300).

If, however, the trustees had received UK source interest income of £800 less the deduction of £200 income tax deducted at source out of which

18.40 *Non-UK resident trusts: income and capital gains taxation*

£600 had been made as an income distribution the beneficiary's income tax liability would have been:

50% of [£600/0.8] less tax credit of £150 (ie [[£600/£800] x £200] ((ie £125)).

This leaves net cash of £475.

Non-UK resident beneficiaries

18.40 Non-UK resident individuals receiving any form of distribution from a non-resident trust are not liable to income tax thereon. If, however, the distribution is out of the trust's UK source income ESC B18 applies and the beneficiary may be able to reclaim some part of the UK tax paid by the trustees on the income.

Non-UK domiciliary beneficiaries

18.41 A non-UK domiciled but UK resident individual beneficiary in receipt of an income distribution from a non-resident trust is not subject to income tax thereon assuming the remittance basis applies (see paragraph 24.7) to the individual and assuming the income distribution is made outside the UK. An income distribution is made outside the UK so long as the trustees appoint the income directly to an overseas bank account of the beneficiary. Until the income distribution is made by the trustees to the beneficiary the income is not that of the beneficiary.

18.42 However, if the trustees effect a distribution out of UK source income (which resides in the UK bank account of the trustees) directly to the UK bank account of the beneficiary a remittance of the income occurs; similarly, if the trustees effect a distribution out of non-UK source income (which resides in the non-UK bank account of the trustees) directly to the UK bank account of the beneficiary a remittance occurs. This arises where the income distribution is out of trust income which has arisen on or after 6 April 2008. In such cases as the trustees are relevant persons the remittance by them causes the beneficiary to have deemed to have remitted the income; *(ITA 2007 s 809M)*; see paragraph 24.50.

With respect to income distributions on or after 6 April 2008 out of pre-6 April 2008 trust income a remittance on the part of the beneficiary arises only if it is effected by the beneficiary or some third party (eg the trustees) and for the beneficiary's benefit (see paragraph 24.70).

Compare this discussion with that applicable to the UK resident where the remittance basis is not in point (see paragraphs 17.39).

Interest in possession trusts

18.43 The distinguishing feature of the interest in possession trust is that one (or possibly more) beneficiary is entitled to the trust income as it arises. The interest in possession beneficiary is thus not dependent upon the trustees exercising their discretion in his favour.

As the interest in possession beneficiary is entitled to the trust income as it arises, the source of his income is the underlying income of the trust not the trust itself (see paragraph 18.28). Thus, his income tax liability is based upon the particular category of income to which he is entitled.

Trustees' and beneficiaries' tax position

18.44 The liability to income tax on the trust income is that of the interest in possession beneficiary to whom the income belongs and this liability arises for the tax year in which the income arises to the trust (not the tax year when it may be physically paid to the beneficiary by the trustees). However, the trustees are also liable with respect to UK source income on the ground that they initially receive the income (ie prior to paying out to the beneficiary).

The income tax paid by the trustees on the income to which the interest in possession is entitled is then creditable against the interest in possession beneficiary's own income tax liability on the income; the beneficiary is able to reclaim any excess income tax paid by the trustees.

18.45 The income to which the interest in possession beneficiary is entitled is the trust income less trustees' management expenses and the trustees' income tax liabilities (whether UK or foreign) (see paragraph 18.47).

18.46 The trustees are liable to income tax at the basic rate (ie 20% for the tax year 2010–2011) and the dividend ordinary rate (ie 10% for the tax year 2010–2011) on UK source income (*ITA 2007 ss 479* and *480*).

Thus, the trust rate (50% for the tax year 2010–2011) and dividend trust rate (42.5% for the tax year 2010–2011) do not apply to the income of the trustees of interest in possession trusts.

The standard rate band (see paragraph 18.24) does not apply to the trust income.

18.47 No deduction for trustee management expenses is allowed in computing the trustees' liability to income tax on the trust income (see paragraphs 17.44 and 18.25).

18.48 *Non-UK resident trusts: income and capital gains taxation*

Example 6

Jenny Chair is a UK resident, interest in possession beneficiary of a non-resident trust set up by her great grandfather about five years ago. She is a 50% taxpayer.

In the tax year 2010–2011 the trustees receive UK source net dividend income of £18,000 and UK source interest income (after tax has been deducted at source, at 20%, by the bank) of £64,000.

Trustee management expenses are £7,000.

The trustees' liability is 10% on the gross dividend income and 20% on the gross bank interest:

ie 10% on [£18,000 +£2,000] + 20% on [£64,000 + £16,000]

The liability of £2,000 on the dividend income is deemed to be offset by the dividend tax credit of £2,000 and thus no net tax liability arises on the trustees.

The liability of £16,000 on the bank interest is offset by the £16,000 of tax which the bank deducted before paying the interest; thus no net tax is due by the trustees.

The trust net income is thus £18,000 of net dividend income and £64,000 of net bank interest.

Jenny is not entitled to these specific amounts as the trustee management expenses need to be deducted; these expenses are deducted from the net dividend income first leaving £11,000.

Jenny's income tax liability is computed on the net £11,000 of dividend income grossed-up at 10% and the £64,000 of bank interest grossed-up at 20% producing gross income of £12,222 and £80,000 respectively.

Jenny is liable at 42.5% on the 'gross' dividend of £12,222 less a tax credit of £1,222 producing a net income tax liability on the dividends of £3,972 and liable at 50% on the 'gross' bank interest of £80,000 less the credit for the tax deducted by the bank of £16,000 producing a net income tax liability of £24,000.

18.48 Some receipts by the trustees are by trust law capital and thus not amounts to which the interest in possession beneficiary is entitled (and thus in respect of which he has no liability to income tax). Where such receipts are classified as income for income tax purposes the trustees are subject to income tax thereon, assuming UK source income, at the trust rate (50%) and the dividend trust rate (42.5%) as such income is not that of the interest in possession beneficiary and falls within *ITA 2007 s 479* (see paragraph 18.19; such income qualifies for the standard rate band (see paragraph 18.24)).

An example of a UK source capital receipt treated as income for income tax purposes and subject to income tax on the part of the non-resident trustees is a gain arising on a non-qualifying life policy issued by a UK (or non-UK; but in this case the trustees have no income tax liability thereon) based life insurance company (*ITA 2007 ss 481* and *482* and *ITTOIA 2005 s 461*).

Non-UK source income

18.49 The trustees are not subject to UK income tax on non-UK source income of the trust although may have exposure to foreign taxes.

The interest in possession beneficiary who is subject to income tax on the non-UK source income as it arises is entitled to credit for any foreign tax which the trustees may have paid.

Non-UK resident beneficiaries

18.50 Non-UK resident individuals are in principle liable to income tax on UK source income. However, such liability may be limited if the UK source income is disregarded income on the part of the individual (see paragraph 23.11).

For the non-UK resident interest in possession beneficiary this exposure to UK income tax on the underlying income which qualifies as disregarded income may be limited.

18.51 Where the income does not so qualify the non-UK resident interest in possession beneficiary's liability to UK income tax is at the normal rates of income tax applicable to individuals (ie marginal rates of 50% for non-dividend income and 42.5% for dividend income for the tax year 2010–2011). However, any income tax paid by the trustees can be offset against such liability.

Non-UK domiciled beneficiaries

18.52 A non-UK domiciled but UK resident individual interest in possession beneficiary is subject to income tax on trust income in principle in the same manner as the UK domiciled and UK resident beneficiary.

18.53 *Non-UK resident trusts: income and capital gains taxation*

18.53 However, if the trust income arises outside the UK and remains outside the UK no income tax liability arises at that time on the part of the beneficiary (assuming remittance basis treatment; see paragraph 24.7).

Any subsequent remittance of the income to the UK by the beneficiary or the trustees precipitates at that time an income tax charge computed in the same manner as for the UK domiciled beneficiary (the trustees qualifying as relevant persons; *ITA 2007 s 809M*). Income of the trust, which arises pre-6 April 2008 outside the UK, is subject to income tax if the beneficiary remits the income or a third party (eg the trustees) brings the income to the UK for the benefit of the beneficiary. This contrasts with the treatment of the discretionary beneficiary (see paragraph 18.42).

Example 7

Jonathan White sets up a non-resident interest in possession trust in the tax year 2010–2011 with his mother, Sophia Roma, as the interest in possession beneficiary for life, remainder to Jonathan's four children.

Sophia is non-UK domiciled but UK resident.

In the tax year 2010–2011 the trust receives UK source income of £20,000 and non-UK source income of £40,000. Both sources of income are credited directly to the non-UK bank account of the trustees before transfer to Sophia's non-UK bank account.

Sophia is liable to income tax on the UK source income on the arising basis but no income tax liability arises on her part on the non-UK source income unless it is remitted to the UK.

If, unknowingly, the trustees arrange for the non-UK source income to be credited to their (ie trustees') UK bank account a remittance of the income occurs at that time by Sophia because the income is that of Sophia as soon as it arises; Sophia is therefore subject to income tax thereon (the fact that Sophia did not personally remit the income is irrelevant for ascertaining whether a remittance to the UK has occurred on her part; the trustees are 'relevant persons'; *ITA 2007 s 809M*).

Even though the UK source income is credited to a non-UK bank account of Sophia, it is still subject to income tax on the arising basis on Sophia's part as the income is UK source and thus remittance basis treatment is precluded.

Capital gains tax

Trustees

18.54 Trustees of non-UK resident trusts (whether discretionary or interest in possession) are not liable to CGT even on UK situs assets (unless the trustees are carrying on a business/trade in the UK through a branch/agency in which case assets comprised in the UK business are subject to CGT on disposal; *TCGA 1992 s 10*).

Beneficiaries

18.55 Beneficiaries of non-resident discretionary trusts or interest in possession beneficiaries of non-UK resident trusts are not liable to CGT on trust assets. Interest in possession beneficiaries are entitled to trust income as it arises but there is no CGT equivalent.

18.56 Anti-avoidance provisions may, however, precipitate CGT charges on UK domiciled and resident settlors (but not non-UK domiciled but UK resident settlors) of non-UK resident trusts (whether discretionary or interest in possession trusts) and/or beneficiaries (both UK and non-UK domiciled) of non-UK resident trusts (whether discretionary or interest in possession trusts).

Anti-avoidance provisions

18.57 The above discussion considered the income tax and CGT implications for trustees and beneficiaries of non-UK resident trusts be they discretionary or interest in possession in nature.

18.58 Unfortunately, the perception of successive governments that trusts are utilised for tax avoidance purposes has led to a proliferation of measures designed to remove or mitigate their perceived tax advantages. The broad thrust of these measures has been to effectively treat the trust as transparent and subject the settlor to both income tax and CGT as if the trust did not exist. These measures are usually referred to somewhat generically as the 'settlor-interested' provisions (see paragraphs 18.60 and 18.99).

18.59 With respect to income tax the settlor-interested provisions apply to both UK (see paragraph 17.66) and non-UK resident trusts (see paragraph 18.60) but those which target CGT are applicable only to non-UK resident trusts (effective 6 April 2008; prior to this date CGT anti-avoidance provisions applied to UK resident trusts (*TCGA 1992 s 77*, now repealed; see paragraph 17.99)).

18.60 *Non-UK resident trusts: income and capital gains taxation*

Income tax

18.60 The anti-avoidance provisions which apply for income tax purposes are contained in *ITTOIA 2005 Part 5 Chapter 5* and comprise three separate sets of provisions each of which have the effect of charging the settlor on the trust's income; however, the application of *ITTOIA 2005 s 633* is slightly different to that where *ITTOIA 2005 ss 624* and *629* apply. The three sets of provisions are:

- where the settlor retains an interest in the trust (*ITTOIA 2005 s 624*);
- where trust income is paid to or for the benefit of a minor child (ie a child under 18) of the settlor (*ITTOIA 2005 s 629*); and
- where a capital sum is paid by the trustees of the trust to the settlor (*s ITTOIA 2005 s 633*).

These provisions apply to both UK and non-UK resident trusts.

In addition, *ITA 2007 Part 13 Chapter 2* applies for income tax purposes, (although not to UK resident trusts) and comprises two separate but related sets of provisions (commonly referred to as the 'transfer of asset' provisions); one set of provisions subjects the 'transferor' (broadly, the same as 'settlor' but wider in application) to income tax on the arising basis on income which arises to a non-UK resident person (eg trust or company); and the other set of provisions subjects 'non-transferors' to income tax on benefits they receive from the non-UK resident person. The transfer of asset provisions apply to non-UK resident companies (as well as non-UK resident trusts) whereas the settlor-interested provisions only apply to trusts (UK and non-UK resident).

18.61 There is a high degree of overlap between the settlor-interested and transfer of assets provisions. However, where both sets of provisions apply to the settlor/transferor the former takes precedence (see paragraph 18.63).

18.62 As indicated in paragraph 18.60 the settlor-interested provisions apply to both UK and non-UK resident trusts. Chapter 17 addresses in detail these provisions as they apply to UK resident trusts. Their application to non-UK resident trusts is, in principle, the same and thus is not addressed again here; reference should be made to paragraphs 17.66 *et seq*.

However, one point of difference in practice, if not in theory, is that any income tax paid by the settlor is recoverable from the trustees (see paragraph 17.74). Where trustees are non-UK resident there are likely to be serious problems with respect to the enforcement of this statutory right (see paragraph 25.56).

Transfer of asset provisions

18.63 The transfer of asset provisions are extremely complex. They are designed to prevent an individual from avoiding UK income tax by utilising

Non-UK resident trusts: income and capital gains taxation 18.68

structures (eg trusts and/or companies) set up outside the UK to receive, in particular, non-UK source income. In part these provisions operate in a not dissimilar (but not identical) manner to the settlor-interested provisions discussed in Chapter 17 (see paragraph 17.66; in particular *ITTOIA 2005 s 624*). However, they are much wider albeit they do not apply to UK resident entities (trust or company).

Where the transfer of asset and the settlor-interested provisions apply to the settlor/transferor (*ITTOIA 2005 ss 624 and 633*, but not *s 629*) the latter take priority; this is because under *ITTOIA 2005 ss 624 and 633* the income is deemed to be 'the income of the settlor alone' and thus it cannot be the income of anyone else including the person abroad (re the transfer of asset provisions).

18.64 The charges levied under the transfer of asset provisions are split into the provisions which levy income tax on the 'transferor' and those which levy income tax on the 'non-transferors'. The three main charging sections are *ITA 2007 ss 720, 727* and *731*.

Sections 720 and *727* are the charging provisions which charge the transferor and *s 731* charges non-transferors.

18.65 For any of the above provisions to apply it is necessary in the first instance for a transfer of assets (whether UK or non-UK situs) to have occurred, effected by an individual, as a consequence of which income becomes payable to a person abroad (*ITA 2007 s 716*).

For the charge to apply the individual concerned must be ordinarily resident in the UK (residency, per se, is thus insufficient) in the tax year of charge. The ordinary residency of the individual at the time of the transfer is irrelevant (*ITA 2007 s 731*).

18.66 A person (ie individual, trust or company) is abroad if he is resident or domiciled outside the UK (*ITA 2007 s 718*).

18.67 Where a transfer of assets occurs but no income arises to the person abroad (eg the assets are not income producing or have as yet not produced such income) the transfer of asset provisions do not at that time apply.

Income subject to charge includes, *inter alia*, OIGs (*OTFR 2009 reg 21*; see paragraph 18.139) and gains arising on non-qualifying life policies (*ITTOIA 2005 s 461;* see paragraph 19.44).

18.68 None of the provisions apply where the so-called 'motive defence' applies (*ITA 2007 s 737*). Broadly, satisfaction of the motive defence requires that the individual is able to show that it would not be reasonable to conclude from all the circumstances of the case that the avoidance of tax was the purpose

18.69 *Non-UK resident trusts: income and capital gains taxation*

or one of the purposes for which the relevant transactions were effected or that all the transactions were genuine commercial transactions and it would not be reasonable to conclude that any of the transactions was more than incidentally designed for the purposes of avoidance (a slightly different but in principle not all that dissimilar motive test applies to pre-5 December 2005 transactions; *ITA 2007 s 739*).

The term 'tax' is not restricted to income tax but extends to any form of tax including CGT, IHT and national insurance contributions albeit not foreign taxes (*ITA 2007 s 737*).

Example 8

Terry Harbour is ordinarily resident in the UK and decides to purchase a holiday villa in Spain which he intends to let out. He has been advised that it would be sensible to purchase the property through a Gibraltar-based company.

The transfer of asset provisions will apply and the income of the company will be treated as that of Terry (note that *ITA 2007 s 624* does not apply as the vehicle used is a company and not a trust).

Transferor provisions

ITA 2007 s 720

18.69 The *ITA 2007 s 720* charge applies for a tax year where the transferor has power to enjoy the income of a non-UK resident person (eg trust and/or company) as a consequence of a transfer of assets effected by the individual and the income would be chargeable if it had been received by the individual in the UK (*ITA 2007 s 721*). Where it applies the income of the non-UK resident person is attributed to the transferor and the transferor is then liable to income tax on the income. It is necessary that the individual has power to enjoy in the tax year concerned if a liability is to arise.

Under *ITA 2007 s 714*:

'... references to individuals include their spouses ...'

Thus, any reference throughout the following discussion on the transfer of asset provisions to the individual (whether transferor or non-transferor) automatically includes a reference to the spouse.

18.70 'Power to enjoy' is very broadly defined (*ITA 2007 s 723*). Examples of power to enjoy include: where income is in fact so dealt with so as to be calculated at some time to enure for the benefit of the transferor whether in the form of income or not; where the transferor receives or is entitled to receive at any time any benefit provided or to be provided out of the income (or related money); or if the transferor is able in any manner to control directly or indirectly the application of the income.

The effect of the above is that the transferor of most typical non-UK structures used for tax planning purposes will have power to enjoy the structure's income unless he is explicitly excluded from such enjoyment.

Example 9

James Structure settled various non-UK situs assets, which included shares held in an Isle of Man company, on a Cayman Island discretionary trust.

James is excluded from benefit under the trust but his wife, Leona, is not.

The trust is settlor-interested (ie *ITTOIA 2005 s 624*) and James has power to enjoy the trust's income (due to his wife's ability to benefit); in practice the settlor-interested provisions take priority.

However, the settlor-interested provisions are inapplicable to the income of the underlying company (see paragraph 17.81), but the transferor transfer of asset provisions apply as Leona has the power to enjoy the company's income and thus James is subject to income tax thereon.

18.71 Where *ITA 2007 s 720* applies the transferor is subject to income tax on the income of the person abroad computed under normal income tax rules (ie those of the UK). Accordingly, the same deductions and reliefs are allowed as would have been allowed if the income treated as arising to the transferor had actually been received by the individual (*ITA 2007 s 746*). Trust management expenses or management expenses of an investment company are thus not deductible; where the person abroad is a company carrying on a trade the income subject to income tax on the part of the transferor is the trading profit as computed under UK tax principles (not the gross trading receipts).

18.72 UK income tax levied at the basic rate, the starting rate for savings and the dividend ordinary rate is not charged on the transferor in respect of any income so far as it has borne UK income tax at that rate by deduction or otherwise (*ITA 2007 s 745*); in essence, these rates apply to any UK source income of the person abroad. It is understood, however, that HMRC permit

18.73 *Non-UK resident trusts: income and capital gains taxation*

credit to be given for any UK income tax levied on the person abroad (ie including other rates of income tax).

With respect to foreign tax levied on the income of the person abroad credit is available to the transferor against his income tax liability thereon (*ITA 2007 s 746*).

18.73 The general charge (see paragraph 18.71) is superseded where the transferor has power to enjoy the income of the person abroad but only by reason of the receipt of a benefit provided out of the income (*ITA 2007 s 724*). The transferor is liable to income tax on the amount or value of that benefit in the tax year of receipt (but is not liable to income tax on the whole of the income of the person abroad). The charge to income tax is thus restricted.

Where it is shown that the benefit derives directly or indirectly from income in respect of which the transferor has already been charged to income tax for that tax year (ie the tax year of receipt of the benefit) or a previous tax year no charge arises on the amount or value of the benefit. This would apply where the individual has power to enjoy the income of the person abroad (the general charge (see paragraph 18.71) then applying) in which case the provision of any subsequent benefit out of such income is not then subject to income tax (thus avoiding double tax).

Example 10

Hector Tax settles a flat owned by him on a non-UK resident discretionary trust under which he has power to enjoy the income of the trust only to the extent that a benefit is provided to him and/or his wife. The flat is made available to Hector and Helen rent free for the tax years 2009–2010 and 2010–2011.

However, as Hector has power to enjoy the income of the trust only where a benefit is provided the general charge under *ITA 2007 s 720* is inapplicable but *ITA 2007 s 724* applies because the provision of the flat rent free is a benefit.

Hector is thus subject to income tax on the value of the benefit for the two tax years; the value of the benefit is likely to be the market rent which is payable on the property.

If, however, the 'benefit' is also a 'capital sum' the transferor is then liable on the whole of the income of the person abroad, not just the value of the benefit (*ITA 2007 s 727*; see paragraph 18.75). *Prima facie*, a 'capital sum' refers to monies,

Non-UK resident trusts: income and capital gains taxation **18.78**

not non-monetary benefits, and thus the benefit provided in Example 10 should not fall within *ITA 2007 s 727*.

18.74 Inevitably at some point the income of the person abroad is likely to be utilised in some manner for the benefit of the transferor whether as a distribution of the income or the provision of some form of benefit. However, no amount of income may be taken into account more than once in charging income tax (*ITA 2007 s 743*). Thus, where income has been treated as that of the transferor and taxed accordingly (under *ITA 2007 s 720*) any subsequent receipt of that income (or provision of any benefit out of the income) by the individual is treated as not being that of the individual for income tax purposes (*ITA 2007 s 743*).

ITA 2007 s 727 capital sums

18.75 Where the transferor receives or is entitled to receive a capital sum in a tax year (or in an earlier tax year has received a capital sum) income of the person abroad is treated as arising to the transferor (*ITA 2007 ss 727* and *728*). Where the capital sum is received by another person at the transferor's direction it is treated as received by the transferor (*ITA 2007 s 729*). The reference to entitlement to receive a capital sum does not extend to the possibility of receiving a capital sum qua discretionary beneficiary; a discretionary beneficiary has no 'entitlement' to trust property merely a hope that he may benefit.

18.76 A capital sum is any sum paid to the transferor by way of loan; any sum paid to him by way of repayment of loan; or any other sum paid or payable otherwise as income and not for full consideration (*ITA 2007 s 729*).

The application of the section requires, *inter alia*, that the individual receives a 'capital sum'. This suggests the receipt of monies and not some non-monetary benefit (eg the provision of rent-free accommodation; see Example 10).

18.77 The capital sum is not itself treated as the income but causes income of the person abroad to be treated as that of the transferor. Once a transferor has received a capital sum it is the whole of the income of the person abroad that is treated as the transferor's income (ie it is not just income of the person abroad up to the equivalent of the amount of the capital sum which is treated as the transferor's income (compare paragraph 18.73)). Thus, even the receipt of a small capital sum may cause significant income of the person abroad to be taxed on the part of the transferor.

Furthermore, there is no time limit to the application of *ITA 2007 s 727* once it applies (ie it applies, literally, forever).

18.78 However, it is understood that HMRC do not in practice invoke the section for tax years after the transferor has repaid a loan originally granted to him by the trustees.

18.79 *Non-UK resident trusts: income and capital gains taxation*

18.79 ITA 2007 s 727 applies whether or not the transferor has power to enjoy the income of the person abroad; all that is required is that, *de facto*, he receives a capital sum. However, if the transferor has power to enjoy the income, *ITA 2007 s 727* appears superfluous; it is in point if the transferor receives a capital sum but neither he nor his spouse have power to enjoy the income of the person abroad.

'Non-transferor' provisions

18.80 An individual, who has not effected any transfer of assets (ie is a non-transferor) pursuant to which income arises to a person abroad, may still receive some form of benefit out of the income of the person abroad. However, as the individual is not the transferor the 'transferor' transfer of asset provisions discussed above do not apply.

18.81 In such cases a charge may arise on the non-transferor under different provisions (*ITA 2007 s 731*).

18.82 For the charge to arise on the non-transferor he must receive a benefit when he is ordinarily resident in the UK; not be subject to income tax under *ITA 2007 ss 720* or *727* on the benefit; and not be otherwise subject to income tax on the benefit (*ITA 2007 s 732*).

18.83 Thus, a transferor cannot be subject to income tax under *ITA 2007 s 731*. However, this does not preclude the spouse of a transferor being subject to income tax under *ITA 2007 s 731*.

18.84 Although the term 'benefit' is not defined it, *prima facie*, encompasses transfers of assets *in specie*; loans at less than market rates; and rent-free occupation of property. However, as noted in paragraph 18.82, the benefit must not otherwise to be subject to income tax (thus, for example, if the provision of rent-free occupation of property falls to be regarded as an employee benefit in kind and thus subject to income tax under *ITEPA 2003* no charge arises under *ITA 2007 s 731*).

18.85 Whilst the non-transferor is in principle subject to income tax in the tax year of receipt of the benefit (assuming UK ordinary residence) an actual charge to income tax only arises as and when 'available relevant income' of the person abroad exists which can be 'matched' to the value or amount of the benefit (*ITA 2007 ss 732* and *733*).

The available relevant income may include that which has arisen in previous tax years (ie prior to the tax year in which the benefit is provided to the beneficiary) which has not been matched to any earlier benefit.

18.86 A benefit may be provided to a non-transferor who is UK ordinarily

Non-UK resident trusts: income and capital gains taxation **18.88**

resident in a tax year when in fact no available relevant income exists (ie no available relevant income arises in the tax year of provision of the benefit nor has any such income arisen in earlier tax years which has not been matched). Thus, *de facto*, in that tax year no actual income tax charge arises as no available relevant income exists for matching. In this case the value or amount of the benefit is effectively carried forward to future tax years and then matched to any available relevant income which arises in the future until the benefit has been completely matched (ie has been completely subject to income tax).

Even if in the tax year in which available relevant income is available for matching the non-transferor is no longer UK ordinarily resident matching is still applied and a charge to income tax arises in that tax year; it is the ordinary residence status of the non-transferor in the tax year of receipt of the benefit which precipitates the charge.

18.87 Two subtle points need to be made with respect to the calculation of available relevant income and the matching process (*ITA 2007 s 733*).

First, in carrying out the matching process it is often suggested that the benefit is matched to a 'pool' of available relevant income which has arisen over time to the person abroad. However, this is not strictly technically correct. A determination of the amount of available relevant income is in fact a determination only of the available relevant income which may be used to provide a benefit to the specific non-transferor under consideration. It may be that only some (ie not all) of the income which arises to the person abroad can be so used (although perhaps in most cases all the income of the person abroad may in fact be so used).

Second, the available relevant income for matching is that which arises as a consequence of a particular transfer of assets to the person abroad out of which the benefit is provided. Thus, not all income arising from all transfers to the person abroad is available for matching to a particular benefit (ie a single aggregate pool of income is not created). Thus, for example, over time the same transferor may make a number of separate transfers to the person abroad. Each such transfer may or may not subsequently give rise to income. As and when a benefit is provided to a non-transferor it is important to identify out of which of the various transfers the benefit is provided. Available relevant income for matching is then only that income which has arisen over time from that particular transfer (ie income arising from the other transfers out of which the benefit is not provided is not available relevant income for matching).

18.88 As indicated above, in order to ascertain the income tax liability of the non-transferor who receives a benefit, it is necessary to identify and calculate for that particular non-transferor the available relevant income out of which a benefit may be provided to him. The computation involves aggregation carried out for the tax year in which the benefit is provided and earlier tax years

18.88 *Non-UK resident trusts: income and capital gains taxation*

(following tax years are involved only where some benefits remain untaxed). The computation involves the following stages:

(1) calculate his 'total untaxed benefits' (ie (a) the total benefits received by him in the tax year and earlier tax years less (b) the total amount of income treated as arising to him with respect to benefits provided only in earlier tax years);

(2) calculate the 'total relevant income' of the individual (ie the total amount of income which can be used to provide the individual with benefits in the tax year and earlier tax years);

(3) calculate the 'available relevant income' (ie deduct from 'total relevant income' in (2) the total amount of income treated as arising to him with respect to benefits provided only in earlier tax years (ie (b) in (1)); and

(4) finally, compare the 'total untaxed benefits' with 'available relevant income' (if the former is smaller than the latter the income tax liability is based upon the former; if the former is greater than the latter the income tax liability is based upon the latter).

(ITA 2007 s 733)

In determining the available relevant income with respect to the non-transferor such income may have already been subject to income tax on the part of the transferor; in which case it is not available to 'match' to benefits received by the non-transferor. Where the person abroad is a trust, the income of which the transferor has power to enjoy, the trust also qualifies as settlor-interested and the latter provisions apply (see paragraph 18.61); nevertheless such income is no longer available income with respect to the non-transferor.

The position is slightly different where, for example, the person abroad is a company owned by a trust. In this case the company's income is not subject to income tax under the settlor-interested provisions (see paragraph 17.81). However, it is subject to income tax on the transferor (assuming power to enjoy) under the transferor transfer of asset provisions and is thus not available for matching to benefits provided to the non-transferor unless in the tax year in which the income arises to the company a benefit is provided to the non-transferor. In this case the income is allocated between transferor and non-transferor in 'just and responsible' manner as HMRC may determine *(ITA 2007 s 743)*.

Example 11

Teresa is a non-transferor beneficiary (who is ordinarily resident in the UK) of a non-UK resident trust (the transferor has no power to enjoy the income) which is set up on 6 April 2007. The trust has no OIGs or capital

Non-UK resident trusts: income and capital gains taxation 18.88

gains, only income. Teresa receives benefits from the trust in the following tax years worth:

Tax Year			
2007–2008	2008–2009	2009–2010	2010–2011
Benefit:			
£10,000	£6,000	£25,000	£16,000
Income of trust:			
£12,000	£4,000	£15,000	£30,000

It is necessary to calculate Teresa's income tax liability for each tax year in which she receives a benefit.

Using the numbered steps in paragraph 18.88 for each tax year:

2007–2008

(1) (a)	£10,000	
(b)	nil	
[(a)–(b)]	£10,000	
(2)	£12,000	
(3)	£12,000	[2 – 1(b)]
(4)	£10,000	[c.p. 3 and [(a) – (b)] of 1]

2008–2009

(1) (a)	£16,000	[£10,000 + £6,000]
(b)	£10,000	
[(a)–(b)]	£6,000	
(2)	£16,000	[£12,000 + £4,000]
(3)	£6,000	[ie (2 – 1 (b)]
(4)	£6,000	[c.p. 3 and [(a) – (b)] of 1]

2009–2010

(1) (a)	£41,000	[£10,000 + £6,000 +25,000]
(b)	£16,000	
[(a)–(b)]	£25,000	
(2)	£31,000	
(3)	£15,000	[ie (2 – 1 (b)]
(4)	£15,000	[c.p. 3 and [(a) – (b)] of 1]

etc.

18.89 *Non-UK resident trusts: income and capital gains taxation*

18.89 It may be that the 'benefit' received by the non-transferor also falls to be treated as a 'capital payment' (*TCGA 1992 s 97*) for CGT purposes.

A 'capital payment' is defined as:

> '... any payment which is not chargeable to income tax on the recipient or, in the case of a recipient who is neither resident nor ordinarily resident in the UK, any payment received otherwise as income ... '

A capital payment is not restricted to a literal payment. The term includes:

> '... references to the transfer of an asset and the conferring of any other benefit ...'

(*TCGA 1992 s 97*; see paragraph 18.109)

18.90 Thus, for the UK resident beneficiary, if in the tax year of receipt of the benefit there is sufficient available relevant income to match to the benefit a charge to income tax arises; in such cases the benefit does not fall within the definition of a capital payment. However, if the quantum of available relevant income is less than the benefit in the tax year of receipt of the benefit, some part of it has not been subject to income tax.

This element of the benefit thus falls to be treated as a capital payment. Accordingly, under *TCGA 1992 s 87* (see paragraph 18.108) any OIGs and capital gains of the trust out of which the benefit is provided are matched to the capital payment (to the extent that the trust contains OIGs and/or capital gains available for matching at that time).

18.91 Where part of the benefit is treated as a capital payment and is matched to OIGs and/or capital gains in the tax year of receipt of the benefit, that part of the benefit so matched cannot then be subsequently matched to future available relevant income.

18.92 In the tax year of receipt of the benefit there may be insufficient available relevant income for matching and no OIGs or capital gains available for matching. In this case the amount of the benefit unmatched is effectively carried forward to future tax years and matched adopting the same procedure.

Example 12

In Example 11 in the tax years 2007–2008 and 2008–2009 there is sufficient available relevant income to match the benefits provided to Teresa in respect of which she suffers an income tax charge.

However, in the tax year 2009–2010 there is a deficiency in available relevant income and, as a consequence, of the benefit provided in that tax year of £25,000 only £15,000 is matched and subject to income tax in that tax year. The unmatched £10,000 is carried forward to future tax years for later matching.

If, however, the trust has OIGs of, say, £3,000 and capital gains of, say, £7,000 which arise in 2009–2010 (or earlier tax years assuming the amounts have not been matched) the £10,000 of unmatched benefits are matched to the £3,000 of OIGs and then the £7,000 of capital gains.

In 2009–2010 Teresa is thus exposed to an income tax charge on the matching of income of £15,000; an income tax charge on the matching of £3,000 of OIGs; and a CGT charge on the matching of £7,000 of capital gains.

None of the £25,000 benefit remains unmatched and is thus not carried forward for future matching for transfer of asset or other matching purposes.

Non-UK domiciled individuals

Transferors

18.93 Non-UK domiciled but UK resident individuals are in principle subject to income tax on the remittance basis (*ITA 2007 s 809B*; see paragraph 24.7) on relevant foreign income (RFI) (*ITTOIA 2005 s 832;* see paragraph 24.1). For transferor transfer of asset purposes any income which is treated as that of the transferor (under *ITA 2007 s 720*) is regarded as 'deemed income' (*ITA 2007 s 726*). Where the deemed income is UK source the normal arising basis applies to the transferor; where, however, the deemed income is non-UK source it is treated as RFI of the transferor and thus subject to remittance basis treatment (under *ITTOIA 2005 s 832*) assuming if the transferor had received the income directly it would have qualified as RFI. Once RFI is treated as that of the transferor, even where such income is not remitted (and thus no income tax charge has arisen), it is no longer available for matching when ascertaining any income tax charge on the non-transferor (see paragraph 18.98).

18.94 Deemed income, however, cannot be remitted and thus it is the remittance of RFI of the person abroad which determines whether a remittance on the part of the transferor occurs (*ITA 2007 s 726*).

Whether the RFI is remitted to the UK is determined under the rules in *ITA 2007 Part 14 Chapter A1* (see paragraph 24.36) assuming the trust income arises on or after 6 April 2008 and thus if, *inter alia*, the person abroad brought the trust

18.95 *Non-UK resident trusts: income and capital gains taxation*

income to the UK the transferor is subject to income tax thereon if the person abroad qualifies as a relevant person (eg *ITA 2007 s 809M*; see paragraphs 24.50 and 24.54; where the person abroad is a non-UK resident trust, the trustees thereof typically qualify as a relevant person).

A remittance of RFI on or after 6 April 2008 of income which arises pre-6 April 2008 to the person abroad is not subject to income tax on the part of the transferor assuming it is remitted by anyone other than the transferor and is not for his benefit (see paragraphs 24.43 and 24.70).

Thus, RFI arising on or after 6 April 2008 to the person abroad (eg trust) is treated as remitted by the transferor (and thus subject to income tax on his part) if the trustees bring that income into the UK even if not appointed out to the transferor. If the trustees appoint the income out to the transferor outside the UK no remittance at that time occurs; whether any remittance occurs thereafter is determined under *ITA 2007 Part 14 Chapter A1* (see paragraph 24.36).

Non-transferors

18.95 The remittance basis also in principle applies to non-transferors (*ITA 2007 ss 735* and *735A*).

18.96 Any income of the person abroad which may be used to benefit the non-transferor is treated as RFI assuming it would have been so classified if the non-transferor had received the income directly. The non-transferor is thus subject to income tax where the actual RFI of the person abroad matched to the benefit provided is remitted to the UK *or* where the benefit provided out of such income is itself brought to the UK (*ITA 2007 s 735*).

Where the benefit itself is provided outside the UK an income tax charge arises if UK source income arises to the person abroad and is matched thereto (ie the remittance basis is applicable).

18.97 It thus becomes necessary to determine whether the income of the person abroad which is matched to the benefit received by the non-transferor is UK source or RFI. The matching rules are laid down in *ITA 2007 s 735A*. Broadly, income of earlier tax years arising to the person abroad is matched before such income of later tax years; within the same tax year income from within the UK is matched before RFI and income from within the UK is matched in the order it has been received (as is RFI).

Example 13

Nomura Tokyo, a non-UK domiciled but UK resident individual, sets up a non-UK resident trust for his three non-UK domiciled but UK resident children, all aged over 18, Fuji, Nippon and Mazda. Neither Nomura nor his wife can benefit under the trust.

In the tax year 2010–2011 the trust receives income of £80,000 of which £15,000 arises in the UK and the balance of £65,000 arises outside the UK.

The trust owns a UK property in which for the whole of 2010–2011 one of the children, Fuji, lives rent free although the child does pay all the house running costs. The trust also owns a non-UK property (worth £40,000) which is appointed out to Mazda.

The rent-free accommodation benefit is enjoyed in the UK by Fuji (say, value £20,000); the non-UK property benefit is enjoyed by Mazda outside the UK.

Under the ordering rules (see paragraph 18.97) the UK source income is matched first. As there is insufficient income to match the benefits to Fuji and Mazda it is suggested that such income is apportioned: Fuji is treated as receiving £5,000 of UK source income (ie £20,000/£60,000 of the £15,000) and Mazda is treated as receiving the balance of £10,000 of the UK source income.

The appropriate amount of the RFI is then matched: £15,000 of non-UK source income to Fuji and £30,000 of the non-UK source income to Mazda.

Fuji is subject to income tax on the whole £20,000 as her benefit is enjoyed in the UK. Mazda is subject to income tax on £10,000 on the arising basis but the £30,000 is subject to remittance basis treatment as his benefit is enjoyed outside the UK.

18.98 In determining the amount of income which is treated as available for matching to a non-transferor any income which has been matched previously even if such has not been remitted (and thus has not fallen subject to income tax on the part of the non-transferor) is unavailable for matching. Similarly, any income which has been treated as the transferor's income, even if not remitted by him, is unavailable for matching.

Example 14

Nomura Tokyo, a non-UK domiciled but UK resident individual, sets up a non-UK resident trust for his three non-UK domiciled but UK resident children, all aged over 18, Fuji, Nippon and Mazda. Neither Nomura nor his wife can benefit under the trust.

18.99 *Non-UK resident trusts: income and capital gains taxation*

The income of the trust is £80,000 (all UK source) for the tax year 2009–2010 and nil for the tax year 2010–2011.

The trust owns three properties in the UK one of which Fuji occupies rent free for 2010–2011 only. The other two properties are each occupied by Nippon and Mazda rent free for 2009–2010 only.

Nippon and Mazda are subject to income tax in 2009–2010 on the benefit they receive from the trust. Assuming that each benefit is £40,000, each of them is subject to income tax on the arising basis on £40,000 (this amount being matched with the trust's £80,000 income).

In 2010–2011 Fuji's benefit (say, £20,000) is in principle subject to an income tax charge. However, there is no income of the trust which can be treated as his income and thus no income tax charge arises for the 2010–2011 tax year.

If the trust income in 2011–2012 is £20,000 (and assuming none of the children occupy any of the properties any longer) Fuji is subject to income tax on the arising basis on £20,000 for 2011–2012.

Capital gains tax

Settlor-interested charge (TCGA 1992 s 86)

18.99 Non-UK resident trusts are not within the charge to CGT (see paragraph 18.54). However, capital gains of a non-UK resident trust are treated as accruing to the settlor where the settlor is UK domiciled and UK resident and the settlor has an interest in the trust (*TCGA 1992 s 86* and *Sch 5*). *TCGA 1992 s 86* does not apply to the non-UK domiciled individual settlor (see paragraph 18.104).

Where these conditions are satisfied the settlor is subject to CGT on the trust's capital gains treated as accruing to him (where *TCGA 1992 s 86* applies, any capital gains subject to charge on the part of the settlor for the tax year 2010–2011 are treated as arising before 23 June 2010 (*F (No 2) 2010 s 2* and *Sch 1*) and are thus charged at the 18% (not 28%) rate).

OIGs of a non-UK resident trust are not attributed to the settlor (irrespective of the settlor's status) under *TCGA 1992 s 86* (see paragraphs 18.147 and 18.150).

Capital losses of the trust are not apportioned under *TCGA 1992 s 86* but are utilised within the trust by way of offset against trust capital gains to give rise to the net capital gains that are then apportioned (see paragraph 18.106).

Non-UK resident trusts: income and capital gains taxation 18.102

Capital gains of non-UK resident close companies (*TCGA 1992 s 288;* see paragraph 8.99) are attributed to non-UK resident trust shareholders (in proportion to the trust's shareholding) and thus form part of trust capital gains subject to *TCGA 1992 s 86 (TCGA 1992 s 13*; see paragraphs 8.99 and 8.108). Each capital gain of the company is apportioned to the trust as is each capital loss (see paragraph 8.107); the company's capital losses apportioned can be offset only against apportioned capital gains of the same tax year but cannot be offset against other trust capital gains (nor can any unrelieved capital losses apportioned by carried forwards or backwards) (see paragraph 8.107).

However, no such apportionments are made if the trust's shareholding is ten percent or less of the company, (*TCGA 1992 s 13*) (see paragraph 8.104).

18.100 If the trustees are UK resident in any part of the tax year the capital gains are those of the trustees not the settlor (ie *TCGA 1992 s 86* does not apply).

18.101 A settlor has an interest in the trust in the tax year concerned if property (settled by the settlor) or income of the trust may be applied in any circumstances whatsoever for the benefit of a 'defined person' (*TCGA 1992 Sch 5*).

A defined person includes, *inter alia*:

- the settlor;
- the settlor's spouse;
- any child of the settlor or of the settlor's spouse;
- the spouse of any such child;
- any grandchild of the settlor or of the settlor's spouse; or
- the spouse of any such grandchild.

18.102 A settlor does not have an interest in the trust if the trust was created before 17 March 1998 and all of the above defined persons are excluded from benefit other than the grandchildren and their spouses. Thus, a trust created prior to 17 March 1998 for the benefit of, say, grandchildren, their spouses and issue is not subject to the *TCGA 1992 s 86* regime.

Example 15

Ted News, a UK domiciled and UK resident individual, sets up a non-UK resident discretionary trust in 2008 for his children and grandchildren. In the tax year 2008–2009 and 2009–2010 the trust's capital gains are £33,000 and £40,000 and for 2010–2011 capital losses are £15,000.

455

18.103 *Non-UK resident trusts: income and capital gains taxation*

As Ted has an interest in the trust he is subject to CGT on capital gains of £33,000 and £40,000 for the tax years 2008–2009 and 2009–2010 respectively. Apportioned capital losses cannot be carried back, only forwards.

If in the tax year 2011–2012 trust capital gains are £26,000 Ted is subject to CGT on capital gains of £11,000 (ie £26,000 less the £15,000 of losses carried forward within the trust).

18.103 In principle, only trusts created on or after 19 March 1991 are subject to the *TCGA 1992 s 86* regime; thus, trusts created before this date escape the *TCGA 1992 s 86* charge (often referred to as 'golden trusts'). However, where a pre-19 March 1991 trust is subject to later 'tainting' it then falls within the *TCGA 1992 s 86* regime; thus tainting, wherever possible, should be avoided.

'Tainting' occurs where, *inter alia*, on or after 19 March 1991 property or income is added to the trust by any person; or the trust was UK resident but becomes non-UK resident; or the terms of the trust are varied so that a defined person (see paragraph 18.101) becomes for the first time a person who will or might benefit from the trust; or, a defined person enjoys a benefit from the trust for the first time but who could not benefit from the trust before 12 March 1991 (see SP5/92).

18.104 Where the settlor is non-UK domiciled but UK resident, the capital gains of the trust are not treated as those of the settlor (this is the case whether the non-UK domiciled has claimed remittance basis treatment or not; see paragraph 24.7).

Example 16

Kitty Kenya is a non-UK domiciled, but UK resident individual.

After arriving in the UK in 2003 she sets up a trust in the Cayman Islands to which she transfers £500,000 of her offshore cash. The trust invests in non-income producing capital growth shares. Kitty is a beneficiary under the trust.

In late 2008 the trust sells a significant part of its share portfolio realising £750,000 of capital gains.

As the trust is non-UK resident it is not subject to CGT. In addition, as Kitty is non-UK domiciled *TCGA 1992 s 86* does not apply and thus no CGT arises on her part with respect to the trust capital gains.

If, however, Kitty had been UK domiciled throughout, or had acquired a UK domicile of choice (see paragraph 3.74) by 6 April 2008, the £75,000 of trust capital gains would be subject to CGT on her part for the tax year 2008–2009.

18.105 Although *TCGA 1992 s 86* applies to the settlor only for a tax year in respect of which he is UK resident the section also applies where, *inter alia*, the settlor is non-UK resident for less than five complete tax years (*TCGA 1992 s 10A*; see paragraph 4.73) and during this period the trust (or any underlying company) realises capital gains which would have been apportioned under *TCGA 1992 ss 13* and *86* if the settlor had been UK resident (*TCGA 1992 s 86A*; see paragraph 8.125). On his re-acquiring UK residency the settlor is subject to CGT in the tax year of return on the trust (and/or the company) capital gains arising during the settlor's period of non-UK residency (as if he had remained UK resident).

Example 17

Peter Doubt sets up a non-UK resident discretionary trust in 2000. Having lived all his life in the UK, in July 2007 Peter becomes non-UK resident returning to the UK in May 2010. Peter is thus non-UK resident for the whole of the tax years 2008–2009 and 2009–2010.

In 2008–2009 and 2009–2010 trust capital gains are £15,000 and £21,000 respectively.

Peter is subject to CGT in the tax year of his return to the UK, (ie 2010–2011) on the trust capital gains of £36,000.

18.106 To determine the quantum of capital gains of the trust which are subject to CGT on the part of the settlor the capital gains of the trust are computed as normal (ie as if the trust is UK resident) and deducted therefrom are trust capital losses (ie both current and those brought forward) ie the trust's net capital gains are subject to CGT on the part of the settlor. If the net CGT position of the trust is a net capital loss, such capital loss is not apportioned to the settlor. The net capital loss remains in the trust for carry forward and offset against future trust capital gains.

No deduction for the annual exempt amount is permitted in arriving at the trust's net capital gains (*TCGA 1992 Sch 5*).

Capital losses of the settlor may be offset against apportioned capital gains of the trust subject to CGT on his part.

18.107 Where the settlor suffers a CGT charge on trust capital gains he has a

18.108 *Non-UK resident trusts: income and capital gains taxation*

statutory right to recover any such CGT from the trustees although in practice this may be problematic (see paragraphs 17.74, 17.102, and 25.56) (*TCGA 1992 Sch 5*).

Beneficiaries charge: capital gains tax (TCGA 1992 s 87)

18.108 Capital gains of non-UK resident trusts are treated as accruing to UK domiciled and UK resident beneficiaries to the extent that they receive 'capital payments' (*TCGA 1992 s 87*). However, any capital gains of the trust treated as those of the settlor under *TCGA 1992 s 86* are not subject to *TCGA 1992 s 87* (note, however, that a settlor-interested trust set up before 9 March 1991 and which has not subsequently been 'tainted' (see paragraph 18.103) is not subject to *TCGA 1992 s 86*; thus, capital gains of such trusts are not attributed to the settlor under *s 86* and are thus available for matching under *TCGA 1992 s 87*).

Trust capital gains are reduced by trust capital losses (current tax year losses and/or losses brought forward) but no deduction for the annual exempt amount is permitted (*TCGA 1992 s 87*). However, capital losses of a beneficiary to whom trust capital gains are attributed may not be offset against the attributed trust capital gains (*TCGA 1992 s 2*); contrast this with the position under *TCGA 1992 s 86* (see paragraph 18.106).

Capital gains (and capital losses) of companies in which the trust owns 10% or more are apportioned to the trust and thus available for attribution under *TCGA 1992 s 87* (as is applicable to *TCGA 1992 s 86*; see paragraph 18.99).

Example 18

Jake Window, a UK domiciled and UK resident individual, set up a non-UK resident trust two years ago for his two brothers and three sisters. Neither he nor his wife can benefit under the trust.

The trust is not settlor-interested for CGT purposes and thus *TCGA 1992 s 86* does not apply to the trust capital gains; *TCGA 1992 s 87* is in point.

18.109 A capital payment is any payment not chargeable to income tax on the recipient beneficiary or, in the case of a recipient beneficiary who is neither UK resident or ordinarily resident, any payment received otherwise than as income (*TCGA 1992 s 97*). Capital payment includes transfers of assets and the conferring of any other benefit; the term also applies where a beneficiary becomes absolutely entitled to trust property as against the trustees (*TCGA 1992 ss 60 and 97*).

18.110 *FA 2008* makes a number of changes to CGT including the manner in which *TCGA 1992 s 87* applies (ie the manner in which capital payments are matched against trust capital gains (*TCGA 1992 s 87A*)); the changes are effective from 6 April 2008. Broadly, matching now takes place on a LIFO rather than a first in first out (FIFO) basis (ie capital payments are, post-*FA 2008*, matched with later trust capital gains before matching with earlier trust capital gains).

18.111 The method of attribution of trust capital gains to capital payments received by beneficiaries is as follows.

In any tax year the trust capital gains are calculated for that tax year and the total capital payments made to all beneficiaries in that tax year ascertained. The capital gains are then matched to the capital payments; where the trust capital gains exceed the capital payments for the tax year a complete matching of the capital payments occurs and the surplus unmatched capital gains are available to match unmatched earlier tax year capital payments brought forward. Where, however, capital gains are less than capital payments for the tax year only a proportion of each of the capital payments is matched. In this latter case, the surplus unmatched capital payments are carried back to the preceding tax year and matched against any capital gains of that prior tax year which remain unmatched; if surplus capital payments still remain they are carried back to earlier tax years until a full matching occurs (or if this does not occur the resulting surplus is carried forward for future matching) (*TCGA 1992 s 87A*).

The trust capital gains of earlier or later tax years available for matching to surplus capital payments carried backwards or forwards are those remaining after matching to capital payments of those particular earlier or later tax years (or any intervening tax year) (*TCGA 1992 s 87A*).

18.112 The effect of the matching process described in paragraph 18.111 is that the beneficiary in receipt of a capital payment is subject to CGT on any trust capital gains matched to the capital payment. The charge to CGT arises in the tax year of the capital payment where there are sufficient capital gains of that tax year or earlier tax years to match to the capital payment. Where capital gains of tax years after the tax year of the capital payment are matched to the earlier capital payment the CGT charge arises in the later tax year of the matching.

In other words, the tax year of the capital payment is the tax year of the CGT charge unless the capital gains of that tax year together with earlier unmatched capital gains are insufficient to match the capital payment in full; a CGT charge then arises in a future tax year(s) to the extent that the surplus unmatched part of the capital payment is matched to future tax years unmatched capital gains.

For the tax year 2010–2011 where the receipt of capital payments in 2010–2011 results in capital gains being charged to beneficiaries for that tax year, the

18.113 *Non-UK resident trusts: income and capital gains taxation*

capital gains matched with each capital payment is treated as arising when the capital payment is received.

Thus capital gains matched with capital payments received between 6 April 2010 and 22 June 2010 are chargeable at the 18% rate of CGT. Capital gains matched with capital payments received on or after 23 June 2010 are chargeable at the 18% or 28% rate as appropriate (see paragraph 8.22). Capital payments made pre-6 April 2010 but matched to capital gains made between 6 April 2010 and 5 April 2011 are treated as accruing pre-23 June 2010.

18.113 In carrying out the matching process trust capital gains are matched to capital payments received by trust beneficiaries whether such beneficiaries are UK resident or non-UK resident and whether UK domiciled or not. However, for the non-UK resident beneficiary (whether UK domiciled or not) no CGT arises (due to non-UK residency). For the non-UK domiciled but UK resident beneficiary the remittance basis may apply to any CGT charge (see paragraph 18.116).

Example 19

A non-UK resident discretionary trust (non-settlor-interested) in the tax year 2009–2010 has capital gains of £20,000 and capital payments are made in that year of £15,000 to Bert and £10,000 to Sally both UK domiciled and UK resident individual beneficiaries of the trust. There are no prior unmatched capital gains or capital payments.

As the amount of capital payments (ie £25,000) exceeds the amount of capital gains (ie £20,000) not all the payments are matched.

The capital gain accruing to each beneficiary is as follows:

Bert:

£20,000 x [£15,000/£25,000] = £12,000.

Sally:

£20,000 x [£10,000/£25,000] = £8,000.

Thus, the capital gains treated as accruing in the tax year 2010–2011 to Bert is £12,000 and Sally £8,000.

The quantum of unmatched capital payments is Bert £3,000 and Sally £2,000.

Example 20

A non-UK resident discretionary trust (non-settlor-interested) has the following capital gains and capital payments made:

	Capital payments	Capital gains
2008–2009	£10,000	£nil
2009–2010	£15,000	£nil
2010–2011	£2,000	£24,000

2008–2009

At the end of the tax year no matching of capital gains to capital payments occurs; thus no CGT charge arises.

2009–2010

At the end of the tax year no matching of capital gains to capital payments occurs; thus no CGT charge arises.

2010–2011

In the tax year the capital payments of £2,000 are matched with £2,000 of capital gains out of the £24,000 capital gains of that tax year. Thus £2,000 of capital gains is treated as accruing to the recipient beneficiary in 2010–2011.

The unmatched capital gains of [£24,000 − £2,000] is matched with the 2009–2010 capital payments of £15,000 giving rise to a capital gain of £15,000 treated as accruing to the recipient beneficiary in 2010–2011.

The unmatched capital gains of [£24,000 − £2,000 − £15,000] is matched to the 2008–2009 capital payments of £10,000 giving rise to a capital gain of £7,000 treated as accruing in 2010–2011.

The total capital gains for the tax year 2010–2011 subject to CGT on the part of the beneficiary is [£2,000 + £15,000 + £7,000] (ie £24,000). The applicable rates of CGT are determined by the dates of the capital payments (see paragraph 18.112).

Unmatched capital payments are £3,000 for 2008–2009 which may be matched with capital gains arising in future tax years.

18.114 *Non-UK resident trusts: income and capital gains taxation*

Example 21

A non-UK resident discretionary trust (non-settlor-interested) has the following capital gains and capital payments made:

	Capital payments	Capital gains
2008–2009	£nil	£12,000
2009–2010	£nil	£15,000
2010–2011	£43,000	£4,000

2008–2009

No matching occurs and thus no CGT charge arises.

2009–2010

No matching occurs and thus no CGT charge arises.

2010–2011

The capital payments of £43,000 are matched with the capital gains of £4,000 and thus £4,000 of capital gains is treated as accruing in 2010–2011.

The unmatched capital payments of [£43,000 – £4,000] (ie £39,000 is matched with the capital gains of £15,000 of 2009–2010). Thus, capital gains of £15,000 are treated as accruing in 2010–2011.

The unmatched capital payments of [£43,000 – £4,000 – £15,000] (ie £24,000 is matched with the capital gains of £12,000 of 2008–2009. Thus, capital gains of £12,000 are treated as accruing in 2010–2011).

The total capital gains for the tax year 2010–2011 is [£4,000 + £15,000 + £12,000] (ie £31,000). The applicable rates of CGT are determined by the dates of the capital payments (see paragraph 18.112).

Unmatched capital payments are £12,000 which may be matched with capital gains arising in future tax years.

18.114 The new rules introduced by *FA 2008*, as indicated in paragraph 18.110, are effective from 6 April 2008. However, there may be unmatched capital payments or unmatched capital gains which arose pre-6 April 2008. *FA 2008*, which introduced the new rules (now contained in *TCGA*

1992 s 87A), provides the manner in which the quantum of pre-6 April 2008 unmatched capital payments and unmatched capital gains is to be determined.

The reason for the necessity for rules to deal with interaction of the pre- and post-6 April 2008 periods is due to the FIFO basis applying before this date but the LIFO basis applying after this date.

18.115 The approach adopted is to apply the FIFO basis to the pre-6 April 2008 period (as far back as the tax year 1981–1982 where necessary (ie capital payments made before 10 March 1981 are ignored and some capital payments made before 1983–1984 are also ignored)) to identify the unmatched positions as at 6 April 2008.

The LIFO rules are then applied to the unmatched amounts when matching is required to be carried out on or after 6 April 2008.

Example 22

A non-UK resident discretionary trust (non-settlor-interested) set up on 6 April 2005 has the following capital gains and capital payments made:

2005–2006	2006–2007	2007–2008	2008–2009
Capital payments:			
£16,000	£12,000	£14,000	£3,000
Capital gains:			
£ Nil	£24,000	£10,000	£17,000

Under the FIFO rule the capital payments of £16,000 of 2005–2006 are matched with the £24,000 of capital gains of 2006–2007. The balancing £8,000 of unmatched capital gains is matched to the £12,000 of capital payments of 2006–2007.

The remaining unmatched £4,000 of capital payments is matched with the £10,000 of capital gains of 2007–2008 and the balancing £6,000 of unmatched capital gains is matched to the capital payment of £14,000 of 2007–2008.

This leaves for future matching, on or after 6 April 2008, unmatched capital payments of £8,000.

The capital payments of 2008–2009 of £3,000 are matched to the capital gains of £17,000 of that tax year (on a LIFO basis). The unmatched

18.116 *Non-UK resident trusts: income and capital gains taxation*

capital gains of £14,000 are then matched to the unmatched capital payments of £8,000 brought forward.

Non-UK domiciled but UK resident individuals

18.116 *FA 2008* made significant changes to the treatment of non-UK domiciled but UK resident individual beneficiaries receiving capital payments from non-UK resident trusts.

18.117 Prior to 6 April 2008 such individuals were not subject to *TCGA 1992 s 87* and thus effectively were able to receive capital payments without any UK tax charges arising (although matching was still carried out, thus reducing the amount of trust capital gains available for matching to UK domiciled beneficiaries). This exemption no longer applies where such individuals receive capital payments on or after 6 April 2008.

18.118 The receipt on or after 6 April 2008 of a capital payment by a non-UK domiciled but UK resident individual is subject to CGT under *TCGA 1992 s 87*; however, the remittance basis applies where the individual claims remittance basis treatment (*TCGA 1992 s 87B*). If no such claim is made the individual is subject to *TCGA 1992 s 87* in the same manner as a UK domiciled and UK resident individual (albeit that transitional reliefs (*FA 2008 Sch 7*) are available to the non-UK domiciled individual (whether a remittance basis claim is lodged or not) with respect to capital payments and trust capital gains made prior to 6 April 2008 but matched to capital payments or capital gains arising on or after 6 April 2008; rebasing of trust assets may also apply (see paragraph 18.126)).

18.119 The capital gains of the trust which are matched to capital payments received by the non-UK domiciled individual are characterised as 'foreign chargeable gains' (*TCGA 1992 s 87B*). This characterisation applies whether the trust capital gains arise on UK or non-UK situs assets (thus, for the individual claiming remittance basis treatment trust capital gains arising even on UK situs assets are subject to remittance basis treatment (see paragraph 24.7) where matched for *TCGA 1992 s 87* purposes).

18.120 For the remittance basis to apply it must apply in the tax year in which the trust capital gains are treated as accruing to the individual (which is not necessarily the tax year in which the individual receives a capital payment; *TCGA 1992 s 87A*). The tax year in which trust capital gains are treated as accruing to the individual is the tax year in which any part of, or the whole of, the capital payment received is matched to the trust gains under *TCGA 1992 s 87A*.

Example 23

Charles Brasil is a non-UK domiciled but UK resident individual. In the tax year 2008–2009 he receives a capital payment of £45,000 outside of the UK.

Non-UK resident trusts: income and capital gains taxation **18.122**

There are no trust capital gains to attribute to the payment in 2008–2009 or 2009–2010. In the tax year 2010–2011 trust capital gains of £45,000 arise to the trust.

The unmatched capital payments of £45,000 is matched to the £45,000 trust capital gains in 2010–2011.

Charles is subject to remittance basis treatment with respect to the £45,000 capital gains matching if in the tax year 2010–2011 (in which the trust capital gains are deemed to accrue) he claims remittance basis treatment.

18.121 The concept of remittance is applied to the capital payment (whether the underlying capital gains of the trust which are attributed to the capital payment of the individual are remitted to the UK by the trustees is irrelevant for this purpose).

To determine whether the capital payment is remitted the provisions of *ITA 2007 Part 14 Chapter A1* apply to capital payments made on or after 6 April 2008 (see paragraph 24.36).

18.122 As non-UK domiciled but UK resident individuals prior to *FA 2008* were not subject to *TCGA 1992 s 87* transitional provisions are included in *FA 2008* which retain this position (*FA 2008 Sch 7*). These provisions thus provide that any capital payment made to the individual prior to 6 April 2008 is not subject to CGT under *TCGA 1992 s 87* and any capital payment made on or after this date, but matched to trust capital gains which arose before this date, are similarly not subject to CGT under *TCGA 1992 s 87*.

For these transitional provisions to apply all that is required is that the individual is non-UK domiciled (whether or not he claims remittance basis treatment) in the tax year in which the trust capital gains are deemed to accrue (ie the tax year of the matching; see paragraph 18.112).

Example 24

Harry Spain, a non-UK domiciled but UK resident individual, receives capital payments from a non-UK resident discretionary trust (non-settlor-interested) of £160,000 on 10 February 2008.

Trust capital gains for 2007–2008 are £75,000 and for 2008–2009 are £65,000.

The capital payments are matched to the trust capital gains of £75,000 for 2007–2008 (under the FIFO basis). However, no CGT charge arises (as

18.123 *Non-UK resident trusts: income and capital gains taxation*

TCGA 1992 s 87 is inapplicable to non-UK domiciled individuals pre-6 April 2008).

The unmatched capital payments of £85,000 are matched with the trust capital gains of £65,000 in 2008–2009 but no CGT arises on the matching of the capital payments due to the transitional provisions.

18.123 Although no actual CGT charge arises under the transitional provisions, the matching process is still carried out and trust capital gains are attributed to capital payments thus reducing the trust capital gains available for other matching (eg to a UK domiciled and UK resident individual). This is subject to any capital payments made between 12 March 2008 and 5 April 2008 inclusive.

Capital payments received in this period by non-UK domiciled but UK resident individuals are ignored (ie no matching takes place) where the trust capital gains accrue to the individual in the tax year 2008–2009 or later. Matching does, however, take place if the capital payment paid in this period is matched to pre-6 April 2008 trust capital gains.

18.124 The reason for the 12 March 2008 to 5 April 2008 provisions was to discourage trustees making large capital payments in this period which could then have been matched with post-5 April 2008 trust capital gains without precipitating any CGT liabilities (note the new measures were announced in the Budget 2008 on 12 March 2008). This, would then have permitted further capital payments to be made on or after 6 April 2008 in respect of which large amounts of trust capital gains would have been removed (due to the 12 March 2008 to 5 April 2008 matching) thus providing an element of CGT deferral pending the creation of additional trust capital gains.

Thus, if in Example 24 the £160,000 capital payment is made on, say, 15 March 2008 it is first matched to the trust capital gains of £75,000 for 2007–2008 (under the FIFO basis) but precipitating no CGT charge. The unmatched capital payments of £85,000, however, are not matched to the trust capital gains of £65,000 in 2008–2009 and simply ignored. The £65,000 of capital gains thus remains unmatched and available for future matching.

18.125 With respect to non-UK resident trusts created by non-UK domiciled settlors only trust capital gains arising on or after 18 March 1998 and capital payments made on or after 18 March 1998 are available for matching (*FA 2008 Sch 7*).

18.126 Further relief is also available to the non-UK domiciled but UK resident beneficiary (whether claiming remittance basis treatment or not) receiving capital payments due to 'rebasing' (*FA 2008 Sch 7*).

18.127 Re-basing refers to the option of the non-UK resident trustees to elect that all (not just some; it is an 'all or nothing' election) trust assets are rebased at their respective market values as at 6 April 2008 (the rebasing also applies to assets held by any underlying companies subject to *TCGA 1992 s 13* apportionment). The effect of the rebasing is that on a disposal on or after 6 April 2008 the element of the trust capital gains accruing pre-6 April 2008 but matched to a capital payment made on or after 6 April 2008 is not subject to CGT. However, the post-6 April 2008 element matched to the capital payments is subject to CGT.

In such cases it is necessary to pro-rata the elements of the trust capital gains to the pre-and post-6 April 2008 periods when matching to the capital payments.

Example 25

Placido Spain, a non-UK domiciled but UK resident individual, receives capital payments of £63,000 in the tax year 2010–2011.

Trust assets owned prior to 6 April 2008 have a base cost of £10,000 and are sold in 2010–2011 for £100,000 producing capital gains of £90,000.

The trust assets as of 6 April 2008 have a market value of £50,000.

In the absence of an election £63,000 of the £90,000 trust capital gains is matched to Placido's £60,000 capital payments and thus subject to a CGT charge (subject to remittance treatment).

If the trustees make the election, four-ninths of the trust capital gains (ie £40,000 out of £90,000) are attributable to the post-6 April period and five-ninths (ie £50,000 out of £90,000) are attributable to the post-6 April 2008 period.

Thus, £63,000 of trust capital gains are matched to the £63,000 capital payments.

Of this amount, £28,000 (ie 4/9ths) of the capital gains matched are attributable to the pre-6 April 2008 period and £35,000 (five-ninths) of the capital gains matched are attributable to the post-6 April 2008 period.

CGT thus arises on the £35,000 of trust capital gains matched to the £63,000 capital payments. No CGT arises with respect to the £28,000 of matched trust capital gains.

18.128 The election is an irrevocable election and must be made in the way and form specified by HMRC (*FA 2008 Sch 7*); Form RBE1 is the relevant form

18.129 *Non-UK resident trusts: income and capital gains taxation*

on which to make the election. It must be made on or before the 31 January following the first tax year (ie 2008–2009 or later) in which a capital payment is made to a UK resident beneficiary (UK domiciled or not) as a consequence of which trust capital gains are 'matched' under *TCGA 1992 s 87* (*FA 2008 Sch 7*). Thus, a capital payment made in a tax year (to a UK resident beneficiary) which is not matched to any trust capital gains does not trigger the need to make an election.

For those trusts making regular capital payments the first tax year is thus likely to be 2008–2009 requiring an election to have been filed on or before 31 January 2010. However, where the trust has significant unmatched income any capital distribution made is matched to this income (under *ITA 2007 ss 731 to 735*) in priority to any trust capital gains (see paragraph 18.170) in which case an income tax charge arises on the part of the beneficiary and thus the capital distribution does not qualify as a capital payment (see paragraph 18.109). In such cases the date for making the election is later than 31 January 2010.

In view of the adverse consequences of failing to file a timely election it may be advisable for an election to be lodged sooner rather than later even if it is not strictly necessary. HMRC have confirmed that such action is acceptable (see paragraph 18.130).

18.129 The rebasing election does not impact on the matching rules, per se. The matching process follows the normal approach reducing both the quantum of capital payments matched and the trust capital gains available to be matched. The effect of the rebasing election is merely to reduce the quantum of any matched trust capital gains which is subject to CGT on the part of (only) non-UK domiciled beneficiaries.

There is thus no effect on UK domiciled but UK resident beneficiaries which arises from the rebasing election.

18.130 In general terms, filing an election is probably advisable as for non-UK domiciled individuals the CGT position cannot be made worse than that which applies in the absence of an election (*FA 2008 Sch 7*).

18.131 Overall, for the non-UK domiciled but UK resident beneficiary of a non-UK resident trust the CGT position is significantly worse post-*FA 2008*. Previously, neither *TCGA 1992 s 86* nor *TCGA 1992 s 87* applied to such individuals. Whilst this continues to be the position with respect to *TCGA 1992 s 86*, post-*FA 2008*, *TCGA 1992 s 87* now applies to such individuals (albeit subject to transitional reliefs) precipitating CGT charges where, previously, none would have arisen.

Additional CGT charge (effectively an 'interest' charge)

18.132 The effect of *TCGA 1992 s 87* is that any CGT liability only arises as and when a beneficiary receives a capital payment and trust capital gains are matched thereto. The matching of any capital payment with trust capital gains of earlier tax years thus effectively permits a deferral of the CGT charge. Accordingly provision is made (*TCGA 1992 s 91*) under which additional CGT is charged which purports to represent interest and is determined as a percentage of the CGT charge.

18.133 The additional charge arises where a capital payment is matched against trust capital gains of earlier tax years and the payment is received more than one year after the end of the tax year in which the trust capital gains accrues (*TCGA 1992 s 91*).

18.134 The time period in respect of which the additional charge may be levied is subject to a maximum period of six years. The relevant time period commences on the later of the 1 December in the tax year following the tax year in which the trust disposal occurs and the 1 December six years before the 1 December in the tax year of assessment following that in which the capital payment is made and ends on the 30 November in the tax year of assessment following that in which the capital payment is made.

18.135 The rate used to determine the additional charge is currently (ie for tax year 2010–2011) ten percent per annum (*TCGA 1992 s 91*).

Example 26

Non-UK resident trust capital gains of £50,000 arise in the tax year 2008–2009.

Capital payments are made to a UK domiciled and UK resident beneficiary in 2009–2010, 2010–2011 and 2011–2012 of £10,000 £15,000 and £25,000 respectively.

The trust capital gains are matched to the capital payment as to £10,000 £15,000 and £25,000 in respect of tax years 2009–2010, 2010–2011 and 2011–2012 respectively.

A CGT charge arises in each of the tax years.

The capital payment of 2009–2010 is within one year of the end of 2008–2009 (ie the tax year in which the trust capital gains arose) and thus no additional CGT charge arises thereon.

The capital payment of 2010–2011 is not within one year of the end of 2008–2009 (ie the tax year in which the trust capital gains arose) and thus an additional CGT charge arises thereon. The amount of the additional

18.136 *Non-UK resident trusts: income and capital gains taxation*

charge is 10% per annum of the CGT charge on the matched trust capital gains of £15,000 for the period 1 December 2009 to 30 November 2011 (ie two years). This gives a CGT charge on the £15,000 of [18% + (10% x 18% x 2)] (ie 21.6% (assuming the applicable rate of CGT for the individual is 18%)).

The capital payment of 2011–2012 is not within one year of the end of 2008–2009 (ie the tax year in which the trust capital gains arose) and thus an additional CGT charge arises thereon. The amount of the additional charge is 10% per annum of the CGT charge on the matched trust capital gains of £25,000 for the period 1 December 2009 to 30 November 2012 (ie three years). This gives a CGT charge on the £25,000 of [18% + (10% x 18% x 3)] (ie 23.4% assuming the applicable rate of CGT for the individual is 18%).

18.136 The minimum period over which an additional charge may be made is two years (ie 2 x 10% – 20%) with a maximum of six years (ie 6 x 10% – 60%). Based upon a CGT rate of 18% the minimum and maximum CGT charges are 21.6% and 28.8% respectively. Based upon a CGT rate of 28% (applicable on or after 23 June 2010) the corresponding figures are 33.6% and 44.8%.

18.137 The matching process (post-*FA 2008*) is that provided in *TCGA 1992 s 87A* (ie a LIFO basis (see paragraph 18.111)). Pre-*FA 2008* a FIFO basis of matching applies. Other things being equal, the new LIFO matching is likely to cause trustees to make capital payments thus mitigating any *TCGA 1992 s 91* charge.

18.138 If the trust has significant pre-6 April 2008 unmatched capital gains it may make sense for the trustees to effect capital payments to non-UK resident beneficiaries (whether UK or non-UK domiciled). Such capital payments are matched to trust capital gains on the LIFO basis thus 'washing out' the most recent (ie post-5 April 2008) trust capital gains first without precipitating any CGT charge (due to the beneficiaries' non-residence status).

Capital payments can then be made to non-UK domiciled but UK resident beneficiaries which are matched to pre-6 April 2008 trust capital gains in respect of which no CGT arises (due to the *FA 2008* transitional provisions; see paragraph 18.122).

Offshore income gains

18.139 Offshore income gains (OIGs) are a 'mix' of 'capital' and 'income' and in a sense a form of hybrid. OIGs are subject to income tax but the computation

Non-UK resident trusts: income and capital gains taxation **18.144**

is based on CGT principles. The normal income tax and CGT anti-avoidance provisions apply albeit in a somewhat unique manner.

OIGs constitute deemed income for all tax purposes (*OFTR 2009 reg 18*) although for trust law purposes they are capital (thus, for example, an interest in possession beneficiary is not entitled to OIGs arising within the trust).

18.140 The primary legislation in relation to OIGs is now contained in *FA 2008 ss 40A to 42A* (following amendments made by *FA 2009 Sch 22 to FA 2008 ss 41* and *42*). The legislation provides for the making of regulations and such regulations have been issued under the *OFTR 2009*; see paragraph 18.13). The Regulations repeal and replace the earlier legislation contained in *ICTA 1988 ss 756A to 763*.

Offshore funds are typically structured as unit trusts or companies which are non-UK resident. To qualify as an OIG, the gain must arise on a disposal of an interest in a non-reporting (prior to December 2009 referred to as non-distributing) fund; disposals of interests in reporting funds (prior to December 2009 referred to as distributing funds) do not qualify as OIGs and are subject to CGT in the normal manner.

18.141 Although an OIG is subject to income tax, it is the legislation applicable to capital gains which is primarily of relevance. In particular, the computation of the OIG is based upon CGT principles (*OFTR 2009 regs 38* and *39*) although no annual exempt amount (*TCGA 1992 s 3*) is available to reduce the amount of OIGs subject to income tax.

Losses arising on disposals are not available for offset against OIGs but are offsettable against capital gains in the normal manner (*OFTR 2009 reg 42*).

18.142 For CGT purposes, on death the deceased is not deemed to have made a disposal of assets owned by him at the date of death (*TCGA 1992 s 60*); thus no CGT liability arises on death (see paragraph 8.40). However, interests in non-reporting offshore funds are deemed to have been disposed of by the individual on death thus precipitating OIGs and consequent income tax charges thereon (*OFTR 2009 reg 34*).

18.143 The temporary non-UK residence CGT provisions (*TCGA 1992 s 10A;* see paragraph 4.73) apply to OIGs in the same manner as they apply with respect to CGT. Thus, an absence from the UK of less than five complete tax years may result in OIGs arising during the period of non-UK residence falling subject to income tax on the part of the individual in the tax year of resumption of UK residence (*OFTR 2009 reg 23*; see paragraph 8.125).

18.144 Under *TCGA 1992 s 87* capital gains of non-UK resident trusts are matched to non-UK resident beneficiaries in receipt of capital payments. Where

18.145 *Non-UK resident trusts: income and capital gains taxation*

the matching occurs during the period of non-UK residency (for less than five complete tax years) a CGT charge arises on the part of the beneficiary in the tax year of resumption of residence. However, *TCGA 1992 s 10A* does not apply to OIGs subject to matching under *TCGA 1992 s 87*; this does not, however, preclude an income tax charge arising where a capital payment is made whilst the individual is non-UK resident (at a time when there are no OIGs available for matching) but on the resumption of residency OIGs arise which are then matched to the capital payment.

The 'additional CGT charge' provisions (*TCGA 1992 s 91*) which effectively levy an interest charge where a non-UK resident trust makes capital payments to UK resident beneficiaries do not apply to OIGs (see paragraph 18.132).

18.145 Non-UK domiciled but UK resident individuals are subject to income tax on OIGs on the remittance basis (assuming a claim for remittance basis treatment has been made; see paragraph 24.7) (*OFTR 2009 reg 19*).

UK resident trust

18.146 UK resident trustees are subject to income tax on trust OIGs at the trust rate irrespective of the nature of the trust (ie whether discretionary or interest in possession) (*ITA 2007 s 482*).

18.147 Where the UK resident trust is a settlor-interested trust (see paragraph 17.66) the settlor is subject to income tax on the trust OIGs as OIGs are treated as income for all tax purposes (*OFTR 2009 reg 18*); however, with respect to non-UK resident trusts the settlor-interested provisions (of *ITTOIA 2005 Chapter 5 Part 5*) do not apply (*OFTR 2009 reg 20*).

If the OIGs arise to non-UK resident companies owned by UK resident trusts the settlor is not liable thereon as such OIGs are not trust income (see paragraph 17.71). However, under *TCGA 1992 s 13* the OIGs of the underlying company are apportioned to the UK resident trust (*OFTR 2009 reg 24*). Nevertheless, such apportioned OIGs whilst subject to income tax on the part of the trustess at the trust rate (*OFTR 2009 reg 24*) are not subject to income tax on the part of the settlor under *ITTOIA 2005 Part 5 Chapter 5* (*OFTR 2009 reg 20*).

18.148 The remittance basis applies to non-UK domiciled, but UK resident settlors (assuming a claim is lodged; see paragraph 24.7); thus, trust OIGs are not subject to income tax on the part of the settlor unless the OIGs are remitted (see paragraph 17.83).

Non-UK resident trusts

18.149 As a non-UK resident trust, CGT does not apply to trust capital gains and non-UK source income of the trust, including OIGs, is not subject to income tax. However, anti-avoidance provisions may cause such income and capital gains to fall subject to CGT on the part of the settlor and/or the beneficiaries.

18.150 The settlor-interested provisions (*ITTOIA 2005 Part 5 Chapter 5*) in relation to income tax are inapplicable to OIGs of non-UK resident trusts and thus there is no attribution of the trust income to UK resident settlors (*OFTR 2009 Reg 20;* see paragraph 18.60).

The settlor-interested provisions (*TCGA 1992 s 86*) in relation to CGT are inapplicable to OIGs of non-UK resident trusts and thus there is no attribution of trust OIGs to UK resident settlors (see paragraph 18.99).

It thus also follows that OIGs of a non-UK resident underlying company apportioned under *TCGA 1992 s 13* are not subject to income tax on the part of the settlor under the settlor-interested provisions.

18.151 The relevant anti-avoidance provisions applicable to OIGs are those contained in *TCGA 1992 s 87* (see paragraph 18.108) and the transfer of asset provisions of *ITA 2007 ss 714* to *751* (see paragraph 18.63).

The application and interaction of these anti-avoidance provisions is somewhat complex.

18.152 The basic rule is that in the first instance *TCGA 1992 s 87* applies to OIGs of the non-UK resident trust (including any OIGs of a non-UK resident company in which the trust is a shareholder which, under *TCGA 1992 s 13*, are apportioned to the trust (*OFTR 2009 reg 24*)).

Thus, where a trust beneficiary receives a capital payment (*TCGA 1992 s 97*) OIGs of the trust are matched thereto. The matching process is identical to that applicable to trust capital gains (*TCGA 1992 s 87A;* see paragraph 18.111). In essence, therefore, trust OIGs are matched on a LIFO basis to the capital payment received by the beneficiary whether the beneficiary is UK resident or not and whether he is UK domiciled or not (subject to the transitional and rebasing provisions; see paragraphs 18.122 and 18.126).

For the non-UK domiciled but UK resident beneficiary the remittance basis applies (see paragraph 24.7) and a remittance occurs if the capital payment is remitted to the UK (see paragraph 18.121). This is different from the ascertainment of whether a remittance occurs where the capital payment is matched to OIGs which fall to be treated as income for transfer of asset purposes (see paragraph 18.157).

18.153 The non-UK resident trust, in addition to having made OIGs, may also have made normal capital gains. In this case any capital payments are also to be

18.153 *Non-UK resident trusts: income and capital gains taxation*

matched to the trust capital gains but trust OIGs are matched in priority to trust capital gains (*OFTR 2009 reg 20*). The matching process requires that OIGs of the current tax year in which the capital payment is received by the beneficiary are matched first and if some part of the capital payment remains unmatched OIGs of earlier tax years are then matched (ie LIFO basis applies); once all OIGs are matched any remaining unmatched capital payments are then matched in the same manner to unmatched trust capital gains.

Example 27

Harry Bush is a UK domiciled and UK resident individual. He sets up a non-UK resident discretionary trust for his nephews and nieces, Tom, Dick, Mary and Joan, all aged over 18, UK domiciled and UK resident.

The trust makes OIGs as follows:

2008–2009	£50,000
2009–2010	£65,000
2010–2011	£90,000

The trust has received no income.

The trust makes a capital payment to Mary of £75,000 in 2009–2010 and £70,000 to Joan in 2010–2011.

2009–2010

The capital payment of £75,000 to Mary in 2009–2010 is matched to £65,000 OIGs of 2009–2010 and £10,000 OIGs of 2008–2009 (ie LIFO basis). Thus, Mary is subject to income tax in the 2009–2010 tax year on OIGs of £75,000.

2010–2011

The capital payment to Joan of £70,000 in 2010–2011 is matched to £70,000 OIGs of 2010–2011. Thus, Joan is subject to income tax in the tax year 2010–2011 on OIGs of £70,000.

This leaves unmatched OIGs of £40,000 in 2008–2009 and £20,000 in 2010–2011.

Example 28

Harry Bush is a non-UK domiciled but UK resident individual. He sets up a non-UK resident discretionary trust for his nephews and nieces, Tom, Dick, Mary and Joan, all aged over 18, each of whom are non-UK domiciled but UK resident.

The trust makes OIGs and capital gains as follows:

	OIGs	Capital gains
2008–2009	£30,000	£15,000
2009–2010	£35,000	£30,000
2010–2011	£40,000	£50,000

The trust makes a capital payment in the UK to Mary of £115,000 in 2009–2010 and £85,000 to Joan outside of the UK in 2010–2011.

2009–2010

The capital payment of £115,000 to Mary in 2009–2010 is matched first to OIGs on a LIFO basis (ie £35,000 OIGs (2009–2010) and then £30,000 OIGs (2008–2009)). The remaining unmatched £50,000 of capital payment is then matched to £30,000 capital gains (2009–2010) and then £15,000 capital gains (2008–2009). This leaves £5,000 of unmatched capital payment which is thus carried forward for offset against future OIGs and capital gains (see tax year 2010–2011).

Mary is thus subject to income tax on £65,000 OIGs and CGT on £45,000 capital gains in the tax year 2009–2010. As the capital payment is made in the UK the remittance basis is inapplicable.

2010–2011

The capital payment of £85,000 to Joan in 2010–2011 is matched first to OIGs on a LIFO basis (ie £40,000 OIGs (2010–2011)). There are no OIGs remaining unmatched. Thus, the remaining unmatched £45,000 of capital payment is then matched to £45,000 capital gains (2010–2011).

Joan is thus subject to income tax on £40,000 OIGs and CGT on £45,000 capital gains in the tax year 2010–2011. However, as the capital payment is made outside the UK, the remittance basis is applicable and thus no charges arise unless the capital payment is remitted.

Mary's unmatched £5,000 capital payment which is brought forward to 2010–2011 is now matched with £5,000 capital gains of the tax year 2010–2011 and thus Mary is subject to CGT on £5,000 in 2010–2011.

(See paragraph 18.154.)

18.154 *Non-UK resident trusts: income and capital gains taxation*

18.154 Under the LIFO basis later capital payments are matched to trust OIGs and trust capital gains before any unmatched capital payments brought forward are matched. Thus, in Example 28, the capital payment made to Joan in 2010–2011 is matched in priority to the brought forward (ie £5,000) unmatched capital payment of Mary.

18.155 Trust OIGs may also fall to be treated as income for the purposes of the transferor and non-transferor transfer of asset provisions. However, to the extent that trust OIGs are matched to capital payments made to UK resident trust beneficiaries (whether UK domiciled or not) this then precludes such OIGs from being treated as income for transfer of asset purposes (*reg 21*).

18.156 Thus, where any trust OIGs for a tax year are not matched to any capital payments, whether of that tax year or brought forward unmatched from prior tax years, or are matched to capital payments made to non-UK resident beneficiaries such OIGs fall to be treated as income under the transferor transfer of asset provisions. The transferor is then immediately subject to income tax on the OIGs under the transferor transfer of asset provisions.

The matching of capital payments to non-UK residents, whilst causing such OIGs to fall to be treated as income under the transferor transfer of asset provisions, nevertheless removes such matched OIGs from any future matching under *TCGA 1992 s 87*.

Example 29

Herbert England, a UK domiciled and UK resident individual, sets up a non-UK resident trust under which both him and his wife, Cheryl, can benefit.

The trust makes the following OIGs and capital payments to their daughter, Helen, a UK domiciled and UK resident individual:

2008–2009	2009–2010	2010–2011	2011–2012
OIGs:			
£30,000	£35,000	£40,000	£25,000
Capital payments:			
£20,000	£10,000	£50,000	£5,000

2008–2009

The capital payments of £20,000 are first matched under *TCGA 1992 s 87* to OIGs of £20,000 (2008–2009) and Helen has an income tax liability on the OIGs of £20,000.

This leaves £10,000 of OIGs (2008–2009) unmatched which are then treated as income and subject to income tax on the part of the transferor, Herbert, under the transferor transfer of asset provisions.

2009–2010

The capital payments of £10,000 are matched under *TCGA 1992 s 87* to OIGs of £10,000 (2009–2010) and Helen has an income tax liability on the OIGs of £10,000.

This leaves £25,000 of OIGs unmatched which are then treated as income and subject to income tax on the part of the transferor, Herbert.

2010–2011

Of the capital payments of £50,000 only £40,000 is matched under *TCGA 1992 s 87* to OIGs of £40,000 (2010–2011) and Helen has an income tax liability on the OIGs of £40,000.

There are no unmatched OIGs from earlier tax years and thus the balancing £10,000 of unmatched capital payments is carried forward for future matching.

Herbert has no income tax liability in 2010–2011.

2011–2012

The capital payments of £5,000 are matched under *TCGA 1992 s 87* to OIGs of £5,000 (2011–2012). The unmatched capital payments of £10,000 carried forward from 2010–2011 are then matched to £10,000 of OIGs (2011–2012). Helen has an income tax liability on the OIGs of £15,000.

This leaves £10,000 of unmatched OIGs (2011–2012) which are then treated as income and subject to income tax on the part of Herbert, the transferor.

18.157 Where the capital payments remain unmatched and are thus treated as income for transfer of asset purposes and are attributed to the non-UK domiciled but UK resident transferor, the remittance basis applies. A remittance arises where the OIGs are bought to the UK (ie the remittance rules applicable to the transferor transfer of asset provisions apply; *ITA 2007 s 726;* see paragraphs 18.93 and 18.152).

Unfortunately, the 'reclassification' of the OIGs as income for transferor transfer of asset provision purposes precludes the OIG rebasing provisions from

18.158 *Non-UK resident trusts: income and capital gains taxation*

applying (see paragraph 18.126). This is in principle undesirable as any pre-6 April 2008 accrual of any OIG arising on a post-5 April 2008 disposal is then subject to income tax on the part of the transferor (otherwise exempt if matched under *TCGA 1992 s 87*).

18.158 Assuming the transferor transfer of asset provisions are in point it is thus preferable if trust OIGs arising on or after 6 April 2008 but containing an element of pre-6 April 2008 accrued gain are matched immediately to capital payments to UK resident beneficiaries so that advantage can be taken of the rebasing provisions (thus reducing any resulting income tax charge on the recipient beneficiary).

18.159 Where trust OIGs are reclassified as income for the transferor transfer of asset provisions they are no longer eligible for matching to future capital payments to trust beneficiaries under *TCGA 1992 s 87* (see paragraph 18.156).

18.160 Where the transferor transfer of asset provisions do not apply (ie where neither the transferor nor the transferor's spouse can benefit from the trust) any unmatched OIGs do not fall to be treated as income for the non-transferor transfer of asset provisions. Unmatched OIGs are then simply available for matching against future capital payments under *TCGA 1992 s 87*.

18.161 However, matching trust OIGs to non-UK resident beneficiaries whilst removing the OIGs from future matching under *TCGA 1992 s 87*, results in the OIGs becoming income for the non-transferor transfer of asset purposes. Future benefits made to UK resident (but not non-UK resident) beneficiaries may thus be matched to such income precipitating an income tax charge; future benefits are in the first instance matched against income under the non-transferor transfer of asset provisions before any matching to OIGs and then capital gains.

Example 30

Sammy Shed, a UK domiciled and UK resident individual, sets up a non-UK resident discretionary trust under which neither he nor his wife can benefit.

The trust makes the following OIGs and capital payments:

2008–2009	2009–2010	2010–2011	2011–2012
OIGs			
£30,000	£35,000	£40,000	£25,000
Capital payments:			
£20,000	£10,000	£50,000	£5,000

The £20,000 and £10,000 capital payments made in 2008–2009 and 2009–2010 respectively are made to a non-UK resident beneficiary, Antoine. The other capital payments are made to a UK domiciled and UK resident beneficiary, Michael.

2008–2009

The £20,000 capital payments are matched to £20,000 OIGs although no income tax charge arises due to Antoine's non-UK residency. The £20,000 of OIGs as a consequence fall to be treated as income for non-transferor transfer of asset provisions.

2009–2010

The £10,000 capital payments are matched to £10,000 OIGs although no income tax charge arises due to Antoine's non-UK residency. The £10,000 of OIGs as a consequence fall to be treated as income for non-transferor transfer of asset provisions.

2010–2011

The £50,000 capital payments to Michael are first matched with any income available for matching on a FIFO basis (see paragraph 18.88). Thus, £10,000 of 2008–2009 income is matched; £25,000 of 2009–2010 income is matched; and, as there is no other available income for matching, the balancing £15,000 capital payment is matched to £15,000 of OIGs (of 2010–2011).

Michael is thus subject to income tax on £50,000 of income.

2011–2012

The capital payments of £5,000 are matched under *TCGA 1992 s 87* to OIGs of £5,000 giving rise to an income tax charge on the part of Michael (as there is no income left for matching).

18.162 For the non-UK domiciled but UK resident beneficiary the reclassification of OIGs as income for transfer of asset purposes means that neither the rebasing provisions nor the other transitional reliefs (*FA 2008 Sch 7*) apply as and when a benefit is provided (as such reliefs only apply to matching of OIGs and capital gains).

It is therefore preferable for OIGs which arose pre-6 April 2008 or which arise thereafter but contain an element of pre-6 April 2008 accrued gains to be matched to capital payments to UK resident beneficiaries under *TCGA 1992*

18.162 *Non-UK resident trusts: income and capital gains taxation*

s 87 (enabling advantage to be taken of the rebasing/transitional provisions); matching such OIGs to capital payments to non-UK resident beneficiaries causes the OIGs to then fall to be treated as income for non-transferor transfer of asset purposes without any benefit under the rebasing/transitional provisions.

Where the capital payment is matched to income then a remittance occurs if either the capital payment or the OIGs are brought to the UK (ie the remittance rules applicable to the non-transferor transfer of asset provisions apply; *ITA 2007 s 735*).

Example 31

Francesca Italy, a non-UK domiciled but UK resident individual, sets up a non-UK resident discretionary trust under which neither she nor her husband can benefit.

Francesca has two nieces Hermoine (non-UK domiciled and non-UK resident) and Shelly (non-UK domiciled but UK resident). The following OIGs and capital payments are made by the trust:

2007–2008	*2008–2009*
OIGs:	
£30,000	£35,000
Capital payments:	
£20,000	£25,000

The £20,000 capital payments made in 2007–2008 (outside the UK) are made to Hermoine and the £25,000 capital payments made in 2008–2009 (within the UK) are made to Shelly.

2007–2008

The £20,000 capital payments to Hermoine are matched under *TCGA 1992 s 87* to the OIGs of £20,000. As a non-UK resident no income tax charge arises on Hermoine. The £20,000 of OIGs fall to be treated as income.

2008–2009

The £25,000 capital payments to Shelly are matched first with the £20,000 of income of 2007–2008 and then to OIGs of £5,000 of 2008–2009. As the capital payments are made in the UK the remittance basis cannot apply to either the OIGs or the income matched to the capital payments. Shelly is subject to income tax on the £20,000 of income and on the £5,000 of OIGs in 2008–2009.

However, if no capital payments had been made to Hermoine the capital payments of £25,000 to Shelly would have been matched under *TCGA 1992 s 87* (only) to the OIGs of £5,000 in 2008–2009 and the OIGs of £20,000 in 2007–2008. Only the £5,000 OIGs are subject to income tax charge on Shelly as, under the transitional provisions, the matching of post-6 April 2008 capital payments to pre-6 April 2008 OIGs do not precipitate an income tax charge.

18.163 With respect to the transitional provisions capital payments made in the period 12 March 2008 to 5 April 2008 inclusive are matched to OIGs whether arising on or after 6 April 2008 albeit that no income tax charge arises (this is different from that applicable to capital gains where no such matching occurs to post-5 April 2008 capital gains; see paragraph 18.123). This does, however, mean that post-5 April 2008 OIGs, so matched, cannot fall to be treated as income for the non-transferor transfer of asset provisions, (unless the capital payment is to a non-UK resident beneficiary (see paragraph 18.162)).

18.164 The transfer of asset provisions are generally inapplicable where the motive test applies (see paragraph 18.68). Where the transferor transfer of asset provisions are in point and OIGs are not matched to capital payments made to UK resident beneficiaries (ie because no capital payments are made) or are made to non-UK resident beneficiaries they fall to be treated as income (see paragraphs 18.156 and 18.157). However, if the motive test applies no income tax charge arises on the part of the transferor under the transferor transfer of asset provisions on the income; in fact, in such cases, the transferor escapes any charge on the trust OIGs either under *TCGA 1992 s 87* or the transferor transfer of asset provisions.

If the transferor transfer of asset provisions are not in point (but the non-transferor provisions are in point) and the motive test applies trust OIGs matched to capital payments to non-UK resident beneficiaries under *TCGA 1992 s 87* are not subject to income tax (due to the non-UK residency) and although the OIGs then fall to be treated as income the motive test precludes any income tax charge under the non-transferor transfer of asset provisions. As a consequence, any capital payments subsequently made to a UK resident beneficiary matched to the income are not subject to income tax.

Example 32

Francesca Italy, a non-UK domiciled but UK resident individual, sets up a non-UK resident discretionary trust under which neither she nor her husband can benefit.

The motive test applies to the trust.

18.165 *Non-UK resident trusts: income and capital gains taxation*

Francesca has two nieces Hermione (non-UK domiciled and non-UK resident) and Shelly (non-UK domiciled but UK resident). The following OIGs and capital payments are made by the trust:

2007–2008	2008–2009
OIGs:	
£30,000	£5,000
Capital payments:	
£20,000	£25,000

The £20,000 capital payments made in 2007–2008 (outside the UK) are made to Hermione and the £25,000 capital payments made in 2008–2009 (within the UK) are made to Shelly.

2007–2008

The £20,000 capital payments to Hermione are matched under *TCGA 1992 s 87* to the OIGs of £20,000. As a non-UK resident no income tax charge arises on Hermione. The £20,000 of OIGs fall to be treated as income.

2008–2009

The £25,000 capital payments to Shelly are matched first with the £20,000 of income of 2007–2008 and then to OIGs of £5,000 of 2008–2009. As the capital payments are made in the UK the remittance basis cannot apply. However, Shelly is not subject to income tax on the £20,000 of income as the motive test applies but she is subject to income tax on the £5,000 of OIGs.

Irish offshore funds

18.165 Pre-*FA 2008* a non-UK domiciled but UK resident individual was subject to income tax on the arising, not remittance, basis with respect to Irish source income (eg dividends on Irish investments) although for CGT purposes the remittance basis applied.

Despite this, any gain on the disposal of an investment in a non-distributor Irish-based fund was still subject to tax on the remittance basis despite being treated as income.

18.166 Post-*FA 2008* there is no longer a distinction between Irish source income and income from other countries (ie the remittance basis applies (this change was implemented following a ruling by the EU that it was discriminatory)).

18.167 One impact of this change is that for the non-UK domiciled but UK resident individual there is no (tax) distinction between investing in an Irish-based fund versus a Luxembourg based fund. Pre-*FA 2008*, the dividend income from the Irish fund would have been subject to income tax on the arising basis whereas the corresponding income from the Luxembourg fund would have been subject to income tax on the remittance basis; thus, favouring Luxembourg-based funds. This distinction has now disappeared.

Trust income, offshore income gains and capital gains interaction

18.168 In many non-UK resident trusts income, OIGs and capital gains are likely to arise to the trustees.

18.169 In some cases the settlor (and/or his spouse) may benefit from the trusts whereas in others this may not be so. Invariably, at some point, one or more of the trust's beneficiaries are likely to receive some form of capital payment/benefit from the trust whether in the form of capital or income. The settlor, his spouse and the beneficiaries may be a mixture of UK and non-UK domiciled and UK and non-UK resident individuals.

The interaction of the various tax provisions is extremely complex.

18.170 Where, however, a non-UK resident trust effects capital distributions to trust beneficiaries (assuming the settlor/transferor cannot benefit under the trust) the distribution is matched:

- *first*, to available relevant income of the trust;
- *second*, to OIGs of the trust; and
- *third*, to capital gains of the trust.

18.171 Available relevant income of the trust is effectively matched on a FIFO basis (see paragraph 18.88) whereas both trust OIGs and capital gains are matched on a LIFO basis (see paragraph 18.111).

18.172 OIGs, however, may be reclassified as available relevant income and thus the matching rules of the latter apply.

18.173 *Non-UK resident trusts: income and capital gains taxation*

Non-UK resident trusts for UK domiciled and UK resident individuals: some general comments

Income tax

18.173 A non-UK resident discretionary trust is in principle liable to an income tax charge of 50% on non-dividend UK source income and 42.5% on UK source dividend income (for the tax year 2010–2011). No such liabilities arise on non-UK source income. However, UK source income may qualify as disregarded income for the trust thus precipitating no UK income tax liability thereon.

18.174 If the trust is settlor-interested UK and non-UK source income of the trust is subject to income tax on the part of the settlor.

Where the settlor is an interest in possession beneficiary of the trust the income of the trust is subject to income tax on his part as it arises (the settlor-interested provisions do not apply).

18.175 For the settlor who is subject to income tax at the basic rate of 20% (ie not the higher or additional rate taxpayer) the discretionary trust, which is not settlor-interested, may be (eg if disregarded income treatment is inapplicable) tax inefficient even though on income distributions out of the trust the recipient beneficiary may be able to reclaim some part of the tax paid by the trustees from HMRC (eg if the beneficiary is a nil rate or basic rate taxpayer); there is, however, still a cash-flow disadvantage.

18.176 Where the trust is not settlor-interested the provision of any capital payments/benefits by the trustees to UK or non-UK domiciled but UK resident beneficiaries provided in the UK (eg rent-free house in the UK; provision of assets *in specie*) is likely to precipitate an income tax or CGT charge on the part of the beneficiary. As to whether the charge is an income tax or CGT charge depends upon the extent of available relevant income and/or OIGs and/or capital gains within the trust at the time of the capital payment/benefit.

The provision of capital payments/benefits outside the UK to non-UK domiciled but UK resident beneficiaries avoids the above charges if the trust receives no UK source income and none of the non-UK source income (including OIGs) is remitted to the UK.

18.177 For income tax purposes the non-UK resident trust set up by the UK domiciled settlor does not offer any particular income tax advantages (and may in some circumstances be cash flow disadvantageous if UK source income is in point). Such trusts may, however, offer some flexibility and tax deferral where beneficiaries of the trust include UK domiciled and UK resident individuals.

Outright gifts of non-UK situs property from the UK domiciled individual to UK domiciled members of the family cause any income from such property to continue to fall within an income tax charge on the arising basis (and indeed such property similarly falls within the CGT provisions on the arising basis). By settling such property into a non-UK resident trust for the benefit of such family members allows income of the trust and/or the trust property to be appointed to the family members when necessary but in the meantime no UK income tax or CGT charges arise or may be deferred (where the trust is not settlor-interested).

18.178 It is tax efficient to utilise different trusts where property comprises income producing and capital growth property and separation of UK and non-UK situs property into different trusts may also be advisable.

This enables greater control over whether income tax or CGT charges arise and the timing thereof.

Capital gains tax

18.179 Neither UK nor non-UK source capital gains of non-UK resident trusts are subject to CGT on the part of the trustees. Thus non-UK resident trusts offer CGT advantages for the UK domiciled individual (assuming the trust is not settlor-interested; the settlor CGT interested provisions apply to UK domiciled settlors). Thus, even UK situs assets may be settled in non-UK resident trusts insulating them from a CGT charge which otherwise arises.

18.180 Assuming the trust is not settlor-interested any capital payments provided by the trustees to UK or non-UK domiciled but UK resident beneficiaries in the UK is likely to precipitate either an income tax or CGT charge depending upon the extent of the trust's income (and OIGs) and capital gains. However, flexibility as to the timing of the provision of such capital payments (and thus the tax charge) remains with the trustees.

For UK domiciled beneficiaries the provision of capital payments outside the UK still precipitate the above charges.

18.181 The 'additional CGT charge', whilst arguably post-*FA 2008* perhaps less penal, is still important resulting in effective rates of CGT from 18% to 28.8% or 28% to 44.8% depending upon whether the individual is subject to the 18% or 28% rate of CGT. However, both these maxima are below the additional rate of income tax (ie 50% for the tax year 2010–2011).

Inheritance tax

18.182 Excluded property treatment is inapplicable to trust property where the settlor is UK domiciled at the date of creation of the trust.

18.183 *Non-UK resident trusts: income and capital gains taxation*

18.183 However, relevant property trusts (eg discretionary trusts) are only subject to IHT at ten-yearly intervals at the maximum rate of 6% which compares extremely favourably with the 40% rate applicable to individuals on death (assuming the settlor cannot benefit from the trust; otherwise the gift with reservation rules apply). Exit charges may also be levied, but again at a maximum rate of 5.85% (ie 39/40ths of 6%).

Interest in possession trusts, created in lifetime on or after 22 March 2006 are treated in the same manner (trusts created pre-22 March 2006 are not subject to these charges).

The NRB discretionary trust may be particularly attractive (in particular giving rise to no IHT on the trust's creation).

Non-UK resident trusts for non-UK domiciled but UK resident individuals; some general comments

Income tax

18.184 A non-UK resident discretionary trust is in principle liable to an income tax charge of 50% on non-dividend UK source income and 42.5% on UK source dividend income (for the tax year 2010–2011). No such liabilities arise on non-UK source income. However, UK source income may qualify as disregarded income for the trust thus precipitating no UK income tax liability thereon.

18.185 If the trust is settlor-interested UK source income of the trust is subject to income tax on the part of the settlor although any non-UK source income of the trust is subject to income tax on the settlor on the remittance basis.

Where the settlor is an interest in possession beneficiary of the trust (the settlor-interested provisions do not apply) the income of the trust is subject to income tax on his part as it arises unless the income is non-UK source and is retained by the trustees (and the beneficiary) outside the UK in which case the remittance basis applies.

18.186 For the settlor who is subject to income tax at the basic rate of 20% (ie not the higher or additional rate taxpayer) the discretionary trust, which is not settlor-interested, may be (eg if disregarded income treatment is inapplicable) tax inefficient even though on income distributions out of the trust the recipient beneficiary may be able to reclaim some part of the tax paid by the trustees from HMRC (eg if the beneficiary is a nil-rate or basic rate taxpayer); there is, however, still a cash flow disadvantage.

18.187 Where the trust is not settlor-interested the provision of any capital payments/benefits by the trustees to non-UK domiciled but UK resident beneficiaries provided in the UK (eg rent-free house in the UK; provision of assets in specie) is likely to precipitate an income tax or CGT charge on the part of the beneficiary. As to whether the charge is an income tax or CGT charge depends upon the extent of available relevant income and/or OIGs and/or capital gains within the trust at the time of the capital payment/benefit.

The provision of capital payments/benefits outside the UK to non-UK domiciled but UK resident beneficiaries avoids the above charges if the trust receives no UK source income and none of the non-UK source income (including OIGs) is remitted to the UK.

18.188 For income tax purposes the non-UK resident trust set up by the non-UK domiciled settlor does not offer any particular income tax advantages (and may in some circumstances be cash flow disadvantageous if UK source income is in point). Such trusts may, however, offer some flexibility and tax deferral where beneficiaries of the trust include UK domiciled and UK resident individuals.

Outright gifts of non-UK situs property from the non-UK domiciled individual to UK domiciled members of the family cause any income from such property to then fall within an income tax charge on the arising basis (and indeed such property similarly falls within the CGT provisions on the arising basis). By settling such property into a non-UK resident trust for the benefit of such family members allows income of the trust and/or trust property to be appointed to the family members when necessary but in the meantime no UK income tax or CGT charges arise or may be deferred (ie where either the trust is not settlor-interested).

18.189 It is tax efficient to utilise different trusts where property comprises income producing and capital growth property and separation of UK and non-UK situs property into different trusts may also be advisable.

This enables greater control over whether income tax or CGT charges arise and the timing thereof.

Capital gains tax

18.190 Neither UK nor non-UK source capital gains of non-UK resident trusts are subject to CGT on the part of the trustees. Thus, non-UK resident trusts offer CGT advantages for the non-UK domiciled individual (even if the trust is settlor-interested as the settlor-interested CGT provisions do not apply to non-UK domiciled settlors whether the remittance basis has been claimed or

18.191   *Non-UK resident trusts: income and capital gains taxation*

not). Thus, even UK situs assets may be settled in non-UK resident trusts insulating them from a CGT charge which otherwise arises.

18.191   Although the settlor-interested CGT provisions are not applicable to the non-UK domiciled settlor any capital payments provided by the trustees to non-UK domiciled but UK resident beneficiaries in the UK is likely to precipitate either an income tax or CGT charge depending upon the extent of the trust's income (and OIGs) and capital gains. However, flexibility as to the timing of the provision of such capital payments (and thus the tax charge) remains with the trustees.

18.192   The 'additional CGT charge' represents an additional CGT burden for the beneficiary in receipt of any capital payments from the trust (although arguably less so post-*FA 2008*) producing an overall effective rate of CGT of 18% to 28.8% or 28% to 44.8%; however, both these maxima are below the additional rate of income tax (ie 50% for the tax year 2010–2011).

Inheritance tax

18.193   If the settlor is non-UK domiciled at the date of creation of the trust, trust property which is non-UK situs qualifies as excluded property for IHT purposes. Whilst it is not necessary for the trust to be non-UK resident for its property to so qualify it is almost universally a preferable option for the non-UK domiciled individual; primarily because of the advantages the non-UK resident trust offers with respect to income tax and CGT.

Summary

18.194   The tax provisions which apply to non-UK resident trusts are extremely complex. In part this is due to the overlap of the various applicable provisions.

18.195   Non-UK resident trusts are not liable to CGT even on UK situs assets and are only liable to income tax on UK source income.

18.196   The basic thrust of the settlor-interested (and transfer of asset) anti-avoidance provisions is to charge the UK domiciled and UK resident settlor on the income and capital gains of the trust as if the income and capital gains had been made directly by the settlor; in effect looking through the trust. However, these provisions only apply if the trust is settlor-interested' which broadly means that the settlor or spouse (and in some cases other members of the family) can benefit under the terms of the trust. Where this is not the case the setting up of such a trust enables UK tax to be deferred.

18.197 For non-UK domiciled but UK resident settlors the anti-avoidance provisions with respect to the settlor-interested provisions apply with respect to income tax but not CGT; the transfer of asset provisions also apply.

18.198 For non-UK resident trusts which are not settlor-interested for either income tax or CGT purposes, beneficiaries of the trust are likely to be subject to income tax or CGT on any capital payments/benefits provided out of the trust. This applies to both UK and non-UK domiciled but UK resident beneficiaries.

18.199 Non-UK domiciled but UK resident individuals are generally able to utilise the remittance basis.

Part IV

Investments and main residence

Chapter 19

Investments

Background

19.1 For the individual investor the range of possible investments continues to grow at a pace. This chapter is concerned with identifying the tax treatment of the more common investments. The tax treatment of products such as bond futures, interest rate swaps and index futures contracts are not addressed.

19.2 The tax treatment of investments undertaken by individuals varies and will depend upon, *inter alia*, the nature of the investment (eg a capital growth investment versus an income producing investment); the domicile and residence status of the investor; whether the investment is a UK or non-UK situs investment; and whether or not anti avoidance provisions (ie provisions which may reclassify an investment return from, say, capital to income for tax purposes) are in point.

19.3 For the individual investor some or all of the following tax-related factors will need to be taken into account when considering a particular investment:

- whether the return is subject to income or capital gains tax (CGT);
- whether inheritance tax (IHT) is applicable on death and/or a lifetime gift;
- whether loss relief is available on a disposal;
- what constitutes a disposal for tax purposes;
- what restrictions (if any) apply where favoured tax status is granted;
- whether double tax issues arise;
- whether any tax exemptions are applicable;
- the timing of any tax liability; and
- whether remittance basis treatment applies to returns from non-UK investments for non-UK domiciled but UK resident individuals.

19.4 *Investments*

The tax treatment of some of the more common types of investment is considered below.

Deposit-based investments

19.4 Straightforward deposit type investments are primarily the province of both banks and building societies. In return for placing money on deposit, interest is paid thereon. The level of interest will typically vary depending upon the amount of the deposit and the length of time the deposit is to be tied up. At the end of the period the deposit is simply repaid.

19.5 Such investments thus offer no capital growth potential.

19.6 The interest credited is subject to income tax at the marginal rate of the investor in the tax year the interest is credited to the account (*ITTOIA 2005 s 370;* interest income for individuals is not taxed on the accruals basis).

19.7 In the case of deposits with UK based banks or building societies income tax at the basic rate in force (the current rate is 20% for the tax year 2010–2011) is required to be deducted prior to crediting the interest (*ITA 2007 ss 850* and *851*). This applies to deposits made by individuals and trustees of a discretionary or accumulation trust (*ITA 2007 ss 850, 856* and *873*).

However, provision is made under which no income tax is deducted if an appropriate declaration is made to the bank/building society (*ITA 2007 s 858*).

19.8 Thus, where an individual who is beneficially entitled to the interest declares that at the time the declaration is made he is not ordinarily resident in the UK no income tax at source is deducted; in the case of joint accounts held by individuals all such individuals must so declare (ie if only one such individual is ordinarily resident in the UK no such declaration can be made and income tax at source is deducted from the interest payments (*ITA 2007 s 858*)).

Trustees of a discretionary or accumulation trust may similarly make a declaration where the trustees are non-UK resident and all the beneficiaries are not ordinarily resident in the UK (*ITA 2007 ss 858* and *861*).

For the interest in possession trust the interest in possession beneficiary must declare that he is not ordinarily resident in the UK (*ITA 2007 s 858*).

19.9 The declaration is made to, and lodged with, the bank/building society not HMRC although HMRC have the rights of inspection (*ITA 2007 s 862*).

19.10 The declaration is required to be made on Form R85 (2010) 'Getting your interest without tax taken off'.

19.11 Many UK individuals have left the UK to live/retire in countries such as France, Italy and Spain and are no longer ordinarily resident in the UK but have retained UK bank/building society accounts. For such individuals completing the declaration is advisable.

19.12 The 20% income tax withheld at source can be reclaimed if, for example, the depositor is an individual whose income tax liability is less than the income tax withheld. This might be the case for a UK resident individual whose personal allowance is equal to or greater than the amount of interest credited (assuming no other income) or where the interest is the individual's sole income and the income tax exposure thereon is at the new 10% starting rate for savings (see paragraph 2.27; applicable in tax year 2008–2009 and thereafter).

19.13 No CGT consequences arise with respect to such deposits unless the deposit is in a foreign currency (ie not sterling). Foreign currency bank deposits are chargeable assets for CGT purposes and thus fluctuations in the foreign currency/sterling rate of exchange may precipitate either capital gains or capital losses (see paragraph 6.39).

Foreign currency deposits with UK banks/building societies are UK situs for CGT purposes.

19.14 Such deposits are UK situs for IHT purposes and thus fall within the charge on death or on lifetime gifting (subject to the nil rate band (NRB)). For non-UK domiciled individuals, however, foreign currency deposits with UK banks/building societies may fall outside the charge to IHT (see paragraph 13.28).

Offshore deposits

19.15 Interest bearing deposits of UK resident individuals (or UK resident trusts) with 'offshore' (ie non-UK) banks/building societies often suffer no deduction of income tax at source when interest is credited. However, it is important to appreciate that such interest is still subject to UK income tax on the part of UK domiciled and UK resident individuals and UK resident trusts (*ITTOIA 2005 s 370*).

However, effective 1 July 2005, the EU Savings Directive (see Chapter 26) has resulted in many offshore banks now having to deduct income tax at source (as do UK based banks) prior to crediting any interest. This deduction is referred to as a 'retention' tax and prior to 30 June 2008 was at a rate of 15%; effective 1 July 2008 the rate has increased to 20%. Not surprisingly, to avoid this retention tax, monies have moved to non-EU destinations such as Dubai, Hong Kong and Singapore.

19.16 *Investments*

Offshore foreign currency deposits are, for CGT purposes, UK situs for UK domiciled and UK resident individuals but non-UK situs for the non-UK domiciled individual (see paragraph 6.40). Offshore sterling deposits are UK situs for UK and non-UK domiciled individuals.

Offshore foreign currency (and sterling) deposits are non-UK situs for IHT purposes.

Money market accounts

19.16 Money market accounts are available where the amount of the deposit is above a certain size. Such monies are typically invested for short terms (eg sometimes overnight). Where the deposit is for at least £50,000 repayable within five years such accounts typically qualify as 'qualifying time deposits' and no income tax at source is deducted when interest is credited (*ITA 2007 s 866*).

19.17 The CGT and IHT consequences are the same as those for deposit-based investments.

National savings income

19.18 No liability to income tax arises for an individual in respect of interest on deposits in ordinary accounts with the National Savings Bank if the interest for the tax year does not exceed £70 (*ITTOIA 2005 s 69*). Where the interest exceeds £70 only the excess is subject to income tax.

19.19 No liability to income tax arises in respect of income from authorised National Savings certificates.

SAYE interest

19.20 No liability to income tax arises in respect of interest payable under a certified SAYE savings arrangement (*ITTOIA 2005 s 702*).

Ordinary shares

19.21 Equity investments (eg ordinary shares; zero coupon preference shares) are either listed or unlisted on which, typically, dividends are paid.

19.22 Dividend income arising on UK equities is subject to income tax at a rate of 10%, 32.5% or 42.5% (for the tax year 2010–2011) depending upon the investor's income tax position (*ITTOIA 2005 s 383*). However, any such liability is reduced by a tax credit which attaches to a net dividend; this tax credit is equal to one-ninth of the net dividend (*ITTOIA 2005 s 397*).

Unlike the income tax withheld from interest credited to a bank/building society deposit account, which is potentially reclaimable by the individual (see paragraph 19.12), the tax credit attaching to a net dividend is not reclaimable.

19.23 Following *FA 2008*, dividends from equity investments in non-UK resident companies paid to UK resident individuals now give rise to a dividend tax credit of one-ninth of the 'gross' dividend (*FA 2008 s 34*). Effective 6 April 2008 individuals owning less than 10% in the non-UK resident company are entitled to the tax credit provided the non-UK resident company was not an offshore fund (*ITTOIA 2005 s 397A*).

19.24 *FA 2009* (*s 40* and *Sch 19*) extends the entitlement to the tax credit. UK resident individuals in receipt of dividends paid on or after 22 April 2009 where, *inter alia*, they own 10% or more of the foreign company, the territory of the dividend paying company is a 'qualifying territory' and the foreign company is not an 'excluded company' are entitled to a tax credit of one-ninth. In addition, dividends paid on or after 22 April 2009 to UK resident individuals by offshore funds also attract the one-ninth tax credit (*ITTOIA 2005 s 397A*).

A 'qualifying territory' is defined as a territory with which the UK has a double tax agreement which contains a 'non-discrimination article' and an 'excluded company' is a company which is excluded from the benefits of the relevant double tax agreement (see *Revenue & Customs Brief 76/09*).

19.25 Examples of qualifying territories include: Australia, Canada, France, Germany, Japan, Switzerland and the USA. Examples of excluded companies include: certain companies resident in Barbados, Cyprus, Luxembourg, Malaysia and Malta.

19.26 Thus, on or after 22 April 2009, shareholdings of less than 10% automatically qualify for the one-ninth dividend tax credit; shareholdings of 10% or greater so qualify subject to the conditions set out in paragraph 19.24; and all shareholdings in offshore funds automatically qualify.

Example 1

Fred Gutter, a higher rate (40%) taxpayer, owns a 15% shareholding in ABC Ltd a non-UK resident company which is resident in a qualifying territory and is not an excluded company.

19.27 *Investments*

In the tax year 2010–2011 he receives a cash dividend of £8,100 after foreign local withholding tax at 10% has been applied.

For UK income tax purposes Fred's tax position 2010–2011 is as follows:

Net dividend received	£8,100
Plus local w/tax	£900
	£9,000
Plus UK tax credit (1/9th)	£1,000
Gross dividend	£10,000
UK income tax at 32.5%	£3,250
Less tax credits	£1,900
Net UK tax liability	£1,350

The original 'gross' foreign dividend was £9,000 from which 10% (ie £900) local withholding tax is levied resulting in Fred actually receiving £8,100.

Fred's UK income tax liability is £1,350 so that Fred's net cash receipt after all taxes is £6,750.

Had Fred received the same cash dividend in the tax year 2007–2008 (ie prior to the introduction of any tax credit for foreign dividends) his tax position would have been as follows:

Net dividend received	£8,100
Plus local w/tax	£900
Gross dividend	£9,000
UK income tax at 32.5%	£2,925
Less tax credits	£900
Net UK tax liability	£2,025

Fred's UK income tax liability is £2,025 so that Fred's net cash receipt after all taxes is £6,075 (compared to a net cash receipt in 2010–2011 of £6,750).

19.27 As is evident from Example 1 the granting of a UK tax credit on foreign dividend income has improved the attractiveness of equity investments in non-UK resident companies (which extends to investments in offshore funds post-22 April 2009).

19.28 Disposals of equity investments (UK or non-UK) precipitate charges to CGT although a reduced 10% rate may apply where entrepreneur relief (ER) is applicable (see paragraph 8.79).

19.29 Equity investments (UK or non-UK) are in principle subject to IHT although business property relief (BPR) may significantly reduce the amount of IHT thereon (see paragraph 11.61).

Alternative Investment Market shares

19.30 Investment in Alternative Investment Market (AIM) shares tends to be dominated by the Enterprise Investment Schemes (EIS) and Venture Capital Trusts (VCT) funds and institutional investors although individuals may also subscribe to such shares.

The tax treatment of dividends arising on AIM shares is exactly the same as described above with respect to a UK equity investment. Similarly, on a disposal, a CGT liability arises.

19.31 Pre-*FA 2008* one of the key tax attractions of AIM (most but not all AIM companies) shares was that they would typically qualify for business asset taper relief for CGT purposes which, after a holding period of two years, reduced any capital gain by 75% producing an effective CGT rate for the higher rate taxpayer of 10% (see Appendix 2).

Post-*FA 2008*, taper relief for CGT purposes has been abolished and replaced by entrepreneur relief. The rate of ER is an effective 10% rate, irrespective of the rate of income tax applicable to the individual investor (see paragraph 8.79).

One category of investor whose CGT position has worsened post-*FA 2008* is that of the passive investor. To qualify for ER requires that the passive investor holds a minimum 5% shareholding and is also a full-time employee of the company. Thus, the 18% or 28% rate of CGT (for the tax year 2010–2011) is likely to apply to many shareholding held as investments.

Other things being equal, the *FA 2008* changes have made investment in AIM shares less CGT attractive.

However, with respect to IHT, many AIM investments qualify for BPR at the 100% rate (both pre- and post-*FA 2008*).

Individual Savings Accounts

19.32 Individual Savings Accounts (ISAs) became available on 6 April 1999 and were a replacement for Personal Equity Plans (PEPs) and Tax Exempt Special Savings Accounts (TESSAs).

19.33 *Investments*

The rules and regulations for the ISA scheme are contained in *'The Individual Savings Account Regulations 1998'* (*SI 1998/1870*) as provided for by *ITTOIA 2005 s 694*.

19.33 ISAs are available for subscription only by individuals aged over 18 who are UK resident *and* ordinarily resident (although post-5 April 2001 individuals aged 16 and 17 could subscribe to a cash mini-account or the cash component of a maxi-account, subject to limits, now referred to as 'cash accounts').

The terms 'maxi-account' and 'mini-account', applicable pre-*FA 2008*, were replaced with the terms 'stocks and shares account' and 'cash account' from 6 April 2008.

19.34 The key attributes of ISAs include:

- no statutory 'lock-in' period;
- no minimum subscription;
- no minimum holding period; and
- withdrawals without loss of tax relief.

19.35 Interest and dividends arising on the 'cash account' and/or the 'stocks and shares account' are not subject to income tax and any capital gains arising on the sale of shares in the stocks and shares account are not subject to CGT (correspondingly, no losses are allowable for CGT purposes).

19.36 Where an individual who was previously UK resident and ordinarily resident becomes non-UK resident any ISAs previously subscribed for may be retained (with the accompanying tax benefits) but no further subscriptions may be made until UK residency and ordinary residency are reacquired.

19.37 All subscriptions to an ISA must be made in cash (it is possible for certain employee acquired shares to be transferred to a stocks and shares component without tax effect) and must be made by individuals (ie subscriptions by trustees of a trust (whether UK resident or not) are not permitted).

19.38 Individuals are allowed to subscribe for two ISAs in a tax year: one 'cash' ISA and one 'stocks and shares' ISA. The maximum annual ISA investment allowance was increased to £7,200 for the tax year 2008–2009 (previously, £7,000 for tax year 2007–2008).

Accordingly, up to £3,600 per tax year could be invested in a cash ISA with one provider with the balance (ie £7,200 less £3,600) available for investment in the tax year in a stocks and shares ISA (whether with the same or another provider).

Alternatively, the whole of the tax year allowance of £7,200 could be invested in a stocks and shares ISA.

Transfers between accounts of the same type are permitted and transfers between cash ISAs and stocks and shares ISAs are also permitted.

19.39 The limits referred to in paragraph 19.38 were again increased for the tax year 2009–2010. For individuals who were aged 50 or over no later than 5 April 2010 the subscription limits were increased to £10,200 (the annual overall limit) of which up to £5,100 could be invested in a cash ISA; these new limits took effect from 6 October 2009 (*SI 2009/1550*).

These new limits now apply to all ISA investors (ie not just those aged 50 or over) from 6 April 2010 (except for those between the ages of 16 and 18 who may only invest in cash ISAs).

Insurance-based investments

19.40 Insurance serves a number of roles. It can, for example, provide financial support to the surviving spouse and family following the death of the 'breadwinner'; provide funds to meet an IHT liability, whether on death or on a lifetime gift due to the death of the donor; or be used as a so-called 'tax wrapper' for tax planning purposes (eg the single premium bond; see paragraph 19.46).

Term and whole of life assurance policies

Term assurance

19.41 Term assurance is probably one of the cheapest forms of life insurance. If the life assured survives the term of the policy no sum assured is payable. If, on the other hand, the life assured dies within the term of the policy the sum assured becomes payable. It is particularly ideal for a young married couple with young children; the policy is typically taken out by the 'breadwinner' for, say, a 15 to 20-year term for relatively low cost but a maximum sum assured. In the event of the breadwinner's death the sum assured is payable to the surviving spouse to be used to provide ongoing financial support thereafter (eg funding of mortgage; school fees; etc.) or to fund IHT liabilities arising on the breadwinner's death.

19.42 In order to mitigate any IHT exposure on the death of the breadwinner it is usual to write the policy in trust (from inception of the policy) for the surviving spouse/family. In addition to avoiding IHT thereon, the policy proceeds are not then subject to probate and thus the surviving spouse can readily

19.43 *Investments*

and speedily access the proceeds. If the policy is not written in trust the proceeds fall into the breadwinner's estate on death and thus subject to IHT (and probate).

Pre-22 March 2006 the typical trust used was a flexible qualifying interest in possession trust but such trusts cannot, post-21 March 2006, be set up in lifetime. Now such policies tend to be held on discretionary trusts thus, in principle, precipitating ten-yearly (and exit) IHT charges; however, the surrender values for term policies is usually very low and thus any ten-yearly charges are likely to be low. In the event of the death of the life assured the trust's value will significantly increase and any ten-yearly charge may thus not be insignificant. The appointment out of the trust of the monies will also in principle precipitate an IHT exit charge. However, such IHT charges are significantly less than the 40% charge which applies if the policy has not been written in trust.

19.43 Term assurance policies are also a useful method of funding the potential IHT liability which may arise on the death of the donor within seven years of making a PET. The term of the policy should of course be seven years with the sum assured equal to the IHT liability facing the donee (not donor). As the actual IHT liability reduces due to taper relief over the seven-year period a decreasing term policy (matching the actual IHT liability over the seven years) may be effected instead which will be cheaper.

Whole of life assurance

19.44 The whole of life policy is more expensive than a term assurance but in principle serves the same functions; surviving the term of a term assurance policy means that no amount is then paid out on death and to this extent the term assurance may be seen as a bit of a gamble. This problem does not arise with respect to whole of life policies.

Husband and wife

19.45 In the case of a husband and wife, a joint whole of life policy may be appropriate with payment on either the death of the first to die or on the surviving spouse's death. The choice will depend upon the particular facts including which of the two deaths is likely to produce the greater IHT liability.

Single premium bonds

19.46 Life policies fall to be treated as either qualifying or non-qualifying policies for tax purposes.

19.47 For qualifying life policies issued after 19 March 1968 and before

Investments **19.52**

13 March 1984 income tax relief is available on premiums paid and no liability to income tax arises on any gains made on the policy (*ICTA 1988 Sch 15*).

Income tax relief on premiums paid also requires that the policy has been effected with an insurance company legally established in the UK (or any branch of a non-UK insurance company lawfully carrying on life business within the UK); secures a capital sum on death; and is a policy effected by a husband on his own life or that of his spouse (and vice versa).

19.48 The *Finance Act 1984* withdrew income tax relief for premiums paid on life policies effected on or after 14 March 1984 or in respect of policies issued before this date if they have been subsequently varied (eg extension of its term or an increase in the benefits thereunder). Gains on qualifying policies remain tax exempt.

19.49 Gains arising on all life policies issued after 19 March 1968 which are non-qualifying are subject to income tax at an individual's marginal rate of income tax (ie 40% pre-6 April 2010 and 50% thereafter) (*ITTOIA 2005 s 465A*); such gains are thus not subject to CGT. Non-qualifying policies include so-called 'single premium bonds' (*ITTOIA 2005 Chapter 9 Part 4*).

19.50 A single premium bond (ie an investment bond or a unit-linked bond) is a non-qualifying single premium life policy. A single premium is normally paid at the commencement of the policy and a lump sum is paid out on maturity of the policy or in the event of the death of the life, or live(s), assured.

It may be possible to make further premium payments under the policy often at irregular intervals. During the period of the policy it may be sold, assigned or surrendered prior to maturity. In addition, sums may be withdrawn under the policy and/or loans made under it.

19.51 Single premium bonds can be written by UK-based life insurance companies or, more usually, by life insurance companies outside the UK. Little mortality risk is in fact necessary for qualification as a life policy and many of these bonds are written outside the UK in jurisdictions where the policyholder need not have an insurable interest in the life assured (a requirement under UK law).

19.52 Single premium bonds are not chargeable assets for CGT purposes and thus any gain arising is treated as an income gain not a capital gain. Whilst pre-6 April 2008 the marginal rates of income and CGT were the same (ie 40%), post-6 April 2008 and pre-6 April 2010 the comparable rates were 40% and 18%, respectively. Effective 6 April 2010, the marginal rate of income tax has increased to 50% and the rate of CGT, on or after 22 June 2010 is either 18% or 28% (*FA (No 2) 2010 s 2* and *Sch 1*).

19.53 *Investments*

The effect of these changes, post-6 April 2008, would appear to make the single premium bond significantly less attractive than was the case before this date as compared to those investments whose gains are subject to CGT (and not income tax at marginal rates).

19.53 The potential attractiveness of the single premium bond is that no tax liability arises unless or until the bond is cashed in (ie surrendered) *or* matures *or* the relevant life assured dies *or* it is assigned for money (an assignment for no consideration precipitates no tax charge; *ITTOIA 2005 s 484*). Thus, assuming none of these events occurs, the investment returns underlying the bond 'roll up' tax free. The bond, in this sense, acts as a tax efficient 'wrapper'.

19.54 On encashment/surrender (or partial encashment/surrender) or maturity or death or assignment for money, a 'chargeable event' for income tax purposes occurs and a potential charge to income tax arises (*ITTOIA 2005 s 484*).

The gain is not subject to basic rate income tax as the individual is treated as having paid income tax at this rate (*ITTOIA 2005 s 530*). Thus, a liability only arises where the individual's marginal rate is 40% or 50% (post-6 April 2010). *ITTOIA 2005 s 530* only applies to bonds issued by UK-based life insurance companies. In the case of bonds issued by non-UK life insurance companies the liability extends to both the basic and marginal rates of income tax (*ITTOIA 2005 s 531*).

In calculating the gain subject to income tax so-called 'top slicing relief' may apply (*ITTOIA 2005 s 535*; see paragraph 19.57).

19.55 In ascertaining the quantum of the gain slightly different rules apply depending upon the nature of the chargeable event which precipitates the charge (*ITTOIA 2005 s 491*).

Thus, where the chargeable event is death, the gain is measured against the surrender value immediately before death, not the policy proceeds, and thus the difference between these two amounts is effectively received tax free (although any difference is likely to be small due to the low life assurance element of the contract). In the case of maturity or full surrender the gain is measured against the amount payable under the policy.

Example 2

Harry Brewin invested £250,000 in an offshore single premium bond.

After seven years Harry decided to surrender the policy receiving £350,000.

The gain is [£350,000 − £250,000] = £100,000.

As a 40% taxpayer Harry's income tax charge is £40,000 (as a higher rate taxpayer no top-slicing relief applies; see paragraph 19.57).

To prevent certain abuses which were prevalent with respect to the sale of off-shore single premium bonds new measures were introduced (effective 22 March 2007 (ie new policies made on or after this date and existing policies if further premiums on or after this date are paid in respect thereof)). These new measures apply in connection with short-to medium-term life policies where a person invests premiums exceeding £100,000 per tax year. In calculating any gain arising on such policies the allowable amount of premium will be reduced by the amount of any commission rebated or any commission waived and reinvested in the policy.

19.56 One of the potential disadvantages of the single premium bond is that for the non-UK domiciled but UK resident individual the remittance basis is inapplicable to any gain arising on a chargeable event. If in Example 2 the investor had been a non-UK domiciled but UK resident individual, the income tax consequence would be the same as the remittance basis is inapplicable.

Top slicing relief

19.57 Top-slicing relief may apply to relieve any tax charge arising on a chargeable event. Top-slicing only applies to individuals (not trustees or executors). The effect of the relief is to reduce the amount of the gain subject to the marginal rate income tax. The relief is only applicable to individuals who, ignoring the gain on the policy, are not liable to a rate of income tax in excess of the basic rate on their income but who become liable to a rate in excess of the basic rate when the 'sliced gain' is added to the taxable income of the individual (the 'sliced gain' is the gain arising on the chargeable event divided by the number of years between effecting the policy and the chargeable event).

Example 3

Ben Trouble invests £75,000 in an offshore single premium bond.

After 10 years, in the tax year 2008–2009, Ben surrenders the policy receiving £125,000.

Ignoring the gain arising on the policy Ben does not pay income tax in excess of the basic rate of income tax. His taxable income (pre-the gain) amounts to £34,000.

The 'sliced gain' = [£125,000 − £75,000]/10 = £5,000.

19.58 *Investments*

The inclusion of the sliced gain with Ben's other taxable income results in Ben being charged to income tax in excess of the basic rate and thus entitles Ben to top-slicing relief. This involves the following:

Income tax liability on £39,000 of taxable income, (ie £8,640).

Income tax liability ignoring the 'sliced gain', (ie £6,800).

The income tax liability on the gain of £50,000 is thus [£8,640 − £6,800]×10 = £1,840 ×10 = £18,400.

Without top-slicing relief Ben's income tax liability on the gain is £19,840 (ie of the £50,000 gain some £800 falls within the basic rate band; the balancing £49,200 is subject to income tax at 40%).

Note:

For the tax year 2008–2009 the 40% rate applies on taxable income above £34,800.

Strictly speaking, gains arising on chargeable events are entitled to the 10% 'starting rate on savings income' applicable from 6 April 2008. However, this has been ignored in this example.

19.58 It also needs to be noted that there is no automatic 'tax-free' uplift on death as occurs with chargeable assets for CGT purposes; as indicated above, single premium bonds are not chargeable assets for CGT purposes. Thus, if the bond is held beneficially by the individual (or on trust created by the individual) on the individual's death a chargeable event occurs which results in the gain arising being treated as part of the deceased's (not the executor's income of the period of administration) income for the tax year of death and thus subject to income tax.

Non-UK domiciled individual

19.59 For the non-UK domiciled but UK resident individual the remittance basis does not apply to any gain arising outside the UK as a result of a chargeable event occurring. Thus, single premium bond investments by a non-UK domiciled but UK resident individual require careful thought (given that the remittance basis applies to virtually all other forms of non-UK investment). A chargeable event occurring while such individual is UK resident will thus precipitate an income tax charge on the arising basis.

Offshore issued life policies (eg single premium bonds) are treated as debts for IHT purposes and thus the location of the debtor determines its source (ie the residence of the life office). Thus, for the non-UK domiciled individual such bonds qualify as excluded property.

Trusts

19.60 Where the individual settles the bond on a UK resident trust any gain arising in the trust (eg on a surrender) will be subject to income tax on the part of the settlor assuming the latter is alive at this date (*ITTOIA 2005 s 467*). Otherwise, the trustees are liable to income tax at the trust rate (ie 50% for the tax year 2010–2011).

If the trust is a non-UK resident trust and the individual settlor is alive at the date of the chargeable event the settlor is liable to income tax on the gain (under *ITA 2007 s 720*). However, if the settlor is dead at the date of the chargeable event and the policy is held in a non-UK resident trust created by the individual, no income tax charge arises at that time. If and when the non-UK resident trust appoints any of the income arising from the chargeable event out to a beneficiary (which is a capital not an income distribution) the income gain which arose on the chargeable event is treated as available relevant income and can thus be matched under the non-transferor transfer asset provisions with the capital distribution thus precipitating an income tax charge at that time (see *ITTOIA 2005 s 468* and *ITA 2007 s 731*); this applies even if the beneficiary is non-UK domiciled but UK resident as the remittance basis is inapplicable. A UK or non-UK domiciled but non-UK resident beneficiary, however, could enjoy the income outside the UK free of income tax.

Partial surrenders

19.61 Two advantages of the single premium bond are that no income tax liability arises until a chargeable event occurs (and in the meantime the income/gains underlying the bond accrue UK tax free) and, second, the bond holder may effect tax deferred withdrawals of up to 5% each year of the amount of the one-off initial premium paid (referred to as partial surrenders).

Any such sum not withdrawn may be carried forward for withdrawal in future tax years. The maximum amount of such withdrawals in aggregate is the amount of the initial premium. Thus, if 5% is withdrawn each tax year, after 20 tax years no further withdrawals can be made without then precipitating a tax charge. Such withdrawals are not, as often thought, 'tax free'. They are treated as partial surrenders and are taken into account in determining any income tax liability on the occasion of a chargeable event.

Example 4

Mandy Purple invested £50,000 in an offshore single premium policy on 16 June 2006.

19.62 *Investments*

She withdrew £2,500 in each of the two years to 15th June 2007 and 2008, respectively. Neither withdrawal precipitates an income tax charge as Mandy is entitled to withdraw each year up to 5% of the initial premium (ie 5% of £50,000, namely, £2,500) without precipitating an income tax charge.

Example 5

Continuing Example 4, in the year to 15 June 2009 Mandy withdraws a further £4,000.

Mandy is entitled to withdraw 5% of the initial premium each year (ie 5%) for the years ended 15 June 2007, 2008 and 2009 (ie £7,500 in total).

However, her actual withdrawals amount to £9,000 in total.

A gain thus arises in the year ended 15 June 2009 of:

[£9,000 − £7,500] = £1,500.

Example 6

Continuing the facts from the Example 4 and 5, after 10 years Mandy decides to surrender the policy receiving £80,000. No further withdrawals were made after the £7,500 withdrawal in 2009.

The gain arising on surrender is:

[£80,000 + £2,500 + £2,500 + £4,000] − [£50,000 + £1,500] = £47,500

As can be seen, the 5% withdrawals which are treated as partial surrenders are eventually brought into account on the policy's surrender (ie they are not, as commonly thought, 'tax-free' withdrawals. In essence, they are a form of tax deferral).

19.62 For the non-UK domiciled but UK resident individual, however, care with respect to the 5% withdrawals is required. If such individual used non-UK source income or capital gains to fund the purchase of the bond, which if remitted to the UK would have fallen subject to income or CGT, the 5% withdrawals, if remitted to the UK, will be treated as if the monies used to fund the purchase had been remitted to the UK; an income tax or CGT charge will thus arise on the monies deemed to have been remitted. In effect, therefore, the

5% withdrawals although, per se, 'tax free' would in such cases precipitate a tax charge on the deemed remittance.

Example 7

Mandy Paris, a non-UK domiciled but UK resident individual, invested £50,000 in an offshore single premium policy on 16 June 2006.

She withdrew £2,500 in the years to 15 June 2007 and 2008, respectively, bringing the monies into the UK.

Neither withdrawal, per se, precipitates an income tax charge as Mandy is entitled to withdraw each year up to 5% of the initial premium (ie 5% of £50,000, namely, £2,500).

However, Mandy used her non-UK source earnings to fund the £50,000 purchase.

As a consequence, Mandy will be treated as if she had remitted part (ie £2,500) of her offshore earnings in each of the two tax years when she effected the withdrawals thus giving rise to an income tax charge on the deemed remitted non-UK source earnings.

19.63 Following the *FA 2008* changes regarding remittances (see paragraph 24.36) it has been suggested that if the non-UK domiciled but UK resident individual (having used non-UK source income or capital gains to effect the bond purchase) arranged for the 5% withdrawals to be paid outside the UK an income tax charge will still arise as the remittance basis is inapplicable to single premium bond investments. The contrary view is as follows.

The 5% withdrawals do not constitute 'chargeable events' for the purposes of the legislation as they are merely 'partial surrenders' (*ITTOIA 2005 s 484*). Hence no immediate charge to tax arises (although such are taken into account as and when a chargeable event occurs). However, as discussed above, it is possible to link the 5% withdrawals to the individual's non-UK source income/capital gains used to purchase the bond.

As the non-UK source income/capital gains used to effect the purchase is itself not subject to income tax unless remitted it is difficult to see how the 5% withdrawals, even if linked to such income/capital gains, can be subject to income tax if they are withdrawn outside the UK and retained outside the UK.

However, if the 5% is 'brought' to the UK then it would seem to be the case that 5% of the non-UK source income/capital gains used to fund the purchase would have itself then been remitted to the UK and accordingly taxable.

19.64 *Investments*

19.64 In short, the remittance basis does not apply to chargeable events (ie arising basis applies). A 'partial surrender' is not a chargeable event. The only difference between the pre-and post-*FA 2008* position in this regard is that post-*FA 2008* the definition of 'remittance' is much broader and thus may apply to a transaction which pre-*FA 2008* would not have been the case. However, even post-*FA 2008*, under the transitional rules if the individual who purchased the bond pre-*FA 2008* made a gift of the 5% withdrawals effected pre-*FA 2008* outside the UK to a 'relevant person' (see paragraph 24.50) who then brings the 5% monies into the UK it will not give rise to a taxable remittance of the original income or capital gains of the individual used to effect the purchase of the bond (unless the individual benefits from the remittance). If, however, the bond is purchased out of post-*FA 2008* non-UK source income or capital gains the position is different.

In this case to avoid a taxable remittance where the 5% withdrawal is to be enjoyed by the individual in the UK the purchase of the offshore bond should be effected using non-UK source 'pure' capital monies or UK source taxed income/capital gains.

New arrivals in the UK

19.65 A possible course of action for the non-UK domiciled individual intending to acquire UK residency is for any single premium bond already owned to be surrendered prior to the acquisition of UK residency (hence 'tax free') or, if surrendered shortly after arrival, significant non-resident relief should be available reducing any chargeable income gain arising (*ITTOIA 2005 s 528*).

Temporary non-UK residence

19.66 As CGT does not apply to gains on single premium bonds the temporary non-resident CGT provisions (*TCGA 1992 s 10A;* see paragraphs 4.73 and 8.125) do not apply to individuals disposing of them (eg surrender) while non-UK resident (ie the minimum five tax year non-UK residence period is not necessary to avoid an income tax charge).

However, *FA 2008* has introduced an equivalent provision which is applicable to non-UK domiciled but UK resident individuals for income tax purposes (*ITTOIA 2005 s 832A;* see paragraph 4.77). The new provision only applies to relevant foreign income (RFI) (which includes income gains arising on bonds) which arose in the tax year of departure (prior to the departure date) or in earlier tax years. Thus if the non-UK domiciled but UK resident individual becomes non-UK resident, surrenders the offshore bond and then remits the proceeds to the UK while non-UK resident a deemed income tax charge on reacquiring UK residency should not apply; the income gain not having arisen before departure.

Provision for children

19.67 A typical use of the offshore single premium bond is where parents or grandparents wish to provide funds for children/grandchildren in the future. One or more bonds are effected on the life or lives of the various children/grandchildren. The bonds could be settled on trust for the benefit of the children subject to attaining, say, age 18 or 21. Although the settlor interested provisions are in point (where the parent, but not grandparent has taken out the bond) no income arises on the bond and thus no actual charge occurs; once the child attains age 18 or over the settlor anti-avoidance provisions do not apply.

On attaining the relevant age the bond will pass to the beneficiary by way of assignment without tax charge (as no consideration passes). The beneficiary is then free to deal with the bond as appropriate. Should the bond be cashed in (ie surrendered) by the beneficiary an income tax charge will arise but at rates of income tax applicable to the beneficiary. Alternatively, the beneficiary could continue to hold the bond.

Enterprise Investment Schemes and Venture Capital Trusts

19.68 EISs and VCTs are designed to attract new investment into the unquoted trading company market. The approach of each varies slightly but each offers attractive (ie income and capital gains) tax reliefs to the individual investor.

Enterprise investment schemes

19.69 EISs involve the issue of ordinary shares to individual investors who subscribe for the shares on their own behalf (*ITA 2007 s 157*); thus relief is not available for investment by or via trusts or companies (*inter alia*, the individual investor must be unconnected with the company; broadly, an individual who is an employee or paid director of the company *or* the individual plus associates possess more than 30% of the voting power of the company is connected; *ITA 2007 ss 163* and *166*).

The individual need not, however, be UK resident but must be liable to income tax and the company issuing the shares does not itself need to be UK resident (although it must be carrying on its trade mainly in the UK).

19.70 *Investments*

Income tax relief

19.70 EIS income tax relief operates by way of a 'tax reducer' and is given for the tax year in which the shares are issued. In simple terms, an individual's income tax liability is calculated as normal for a particular tax year and any EIS income tax relief is then deducted directly therefrom (*ITA 2007 s 158*).

19.71 Income tax relief is granted at the 'EIS rate' ie 20% (*ITA 2007 s 158*). EIS relief is available at the lower of:

- 20% of the amount subscribed for the shares; and
- the individual's income tax liability for the tax year of the investment *after* deducting any VCT relief.

The 20% is applied up to a maximum subscription of £500,000 (for the tax year 2008–2009 and later tax years; *FA 2008 s 31*); earlier maxima were £400,000 for tax years 2006–2007 and 2007–2008 and £200,000 for earlier tax years.

19.72 Thus, if an individual subscribed for the full amount of £500,000 in the tax year 2010–2011 the individual's income tax liability for that tax year (after VCT relief, if any) would need to be at least £100,000 for full EIS relief to be obtained.

19.73 A carry-back option exists under which a subscription undertaken in a particular tax year before 6 October in that tax year may receive tax relief in the immediately preceding tax year (subject to that earlier tax year's relief not exceeding the limit for relief for that tax year). Up to one half of the subscription (made pre-6 October) in the tax year may be treated as if made in the immediately preceding tax year subject to an overall limit of £50,000 on the amount of the subscription which may be so treated (*ITA 2007 s 158*).

19.74 Income tax relief requires that the shareholding is held for a minimum holding period of three years (shares issued after 5 April 2000). Any disposal within this period will result in the income tax relief already granted being withdrawn either in whole or in part (which depends upon whether the disposal is at arm's length or not) (*ITA 2007 ss 209 and 158*).

19.75 Any dividends arising on the shares are subject to income tax in the normal manner.

Capital gains tax relief

19.76 Any disposal of the shareholding is exempt from a charge to CGT if the shares have been held for at least three years and income tax relief has not been withdrawn (*TCGA 1992 s 150A*). Perhaps surprisingly, any capital losses arising on such a disposal are available for offset; indeed, a disposal precipitating a capital loss even within the three-year period is also an allowable capital loss. In calculating the amount of any allowable capital loss, account must be taken of any income tax relief which has not been withdrawn (in effect reducing the quantum of the capital loss).

19.77 Any capital loss may be offset against the individual's 'income' of the tax year of sale and/or the preceding tax year (*ITA 2007 ss 131* and *133*); any remaining unrelieved loss is then eligible for capital gains offset. Given the difference in CGT and income tax rates offset against income is likely to prove more beneficial.

Venture Capital Trusts

19.78 Unlike the EIS which involves subscriptions for shares in individual unquoted trading companies, subscriptions to VCTs are subscriptions for shares in a listed company (ie the VCT) which in turn then subscribes for shares in unquoted trading companies. Accordingly, the shares in the VCT must be listed in the Official List of the Stock Exchange.

19.79 As in the case of the EIS any subscriptions must be by individuals beneficially.

Income tax relief

19.80 VCT income tax relief operates by way of a 'tax reducer'. An individual's income tax liability for a tax year is calculated as normal and any VCT income tax relief is deducted directly therefrom.

19.81 VCT relief is available as a tax reducer at the lower of:

- 30% of the amount subscribed for the shares (for shares issued on or after 6 April 2006); and
- the individual's income tax liability for the tax year of the investment.

(*ITA 2007 s 263*)

19.82 For shares issued prior to 6 April 2006 the applicable rate was 40% (*ITA 2007 Sch 2*).

19.83 The maximum subscription in any tax year is £200,000 (*ITA 2007 s 262*).

19.84 *Investments*

19.84 To qualify for income tax relief the shares must be held for a minimum holding period of five years where the shares are issued on or after 6 April 2006 (three years where shares were issued after 5 April 2000) (*ITA 2007 s 266*).

Any disposal within the five-year period will result in any income tax relief being withdrawn either in whole or part (depends if the disposal is arm's length or not).

19.85 Unlike the position with respect to EIS, dividend income arising on a subscription to a VCT is tax exempt (irrespective of any minimum holding period) (*ITA 2007 s 260*).

Capital gains tax relief

19.86 Any gain arising on a disposal of the shareholding in the VCT is exempt from CGT irrespective of the length of the ownership period prior to the disposal. Capital losses, however, are not allowable (*TCGA 1992 s 100*).

Chargeable gain deferment possibilities (EIS only)

19.87 Where an individual has a crystallised capital gain on a disposal of any chargeable asset, the whole or part of the gain may be deferred (ie held over) by matching the gain against a subscription for qualifying shares in an EIS (effective 6 April 2004, any deferment is no longer possible if the investment is into a VCT (ie for shares issued on or after 6 April 2004) (*TCGA 1992 s 150C* and *Sch 5B*).

19.88 This deferral is possible even where the vendor invests in his own company (although EIS income tax relief would be prohibited as he would typically (together with associates) own ≥ 30% and no CGT relief would be available on an ultimate sale) assuming that the shares in his company are 'qualifying shares' and his company is a 'qualifying company'.

19.89 The investment in the EIS must be made within one year before and three years after the chargeable event giving rise to the capital gain. There is no limit to the amount of chargeable gain which may be deferred (ie the £500,000 subscription limit re income tax relief does not apply to the deferral).

19.90 The deferral operates by holding over the gain (ie not levying CGT immediately) on the sale of the original asset until a disposal of the EIS shares occurs at which time the original gain held over will be subject to CGT at that time and at the rates, etc in force at that time. However, a disposal of the EIS shares to a spouse will not crystallise the held-over gain.

The held-over gain may also be crystallised if the shareholder becomes non-UK resident within three years of the issue of the EIS shares (unless the shareholder goes abroad under a full-time contract of employment for up to three years and retains the EIS shares until his return to the UK).

19.91 Any gain deferred does not become chargeable on the death of the investor (in effect the gain held over is wiped out as normal).

19.92 It is also possible to defer gains arising on the sale of EIS shares into further EIS investments.

19.93 Although trustees are not eligible for EIS income or CGT relief re EIS investments, trustees may still defer chargeable gains arising on trust asset sales by reinvesting in EIS investments.

Collective investments

19.94 Collective/pooled investments are simply an aggregation of individual investment monies which are pooled in a single investment vehicle. The investment vehicle may be a unit trust or an open-ended investment company (OEIC), commonly referred to as 'authorised funds', or an investment trust. Such vehicles may be UK or non-UK resident.

19.95 With respect to UK resident unit trusts, investment trusts and OEICs there are no particular tax advantages for the UK resident individual investor. Any income (dividend or interest) arising on the investment is subject to income tax in the normal manner. Any disposal of the investment will also be subject to CGT in the normal manner. Furthermore, none of the investments are likely to qualify for BPR for IHT purposes (see paragraph 11.61).

However, for the non-UK domiciled individual, investment in authorised unit trusts and UK OEICs although UK situs constitute excluded property for IHT purposes (*IHTA 1984 s 6;* see *Chapter 13*).

Offshore funds

19.96 See paragraph 18.139 for a detailed discussion on offshore funds.

Summary

19.97 For the individual investor it is important to identify the nature of any gain which may arise from the investment (ie is the gain to be taxed as an income gain, and thus subject to income tax, or capital gain, and thus subject to CGT?).

19.98 *Investments*

19.98 The extension of the tax credit to dividends received on equity investments in some non-UK situs equities (including offshore funds) has enhanced the attractiveness of such investments.

19.99 Despite the differential between the marginal rate of income tax and the rate of CGT on or after 6 April 2010, offshore single premium bonds offer an attractive form of investment in particular because of the 5% tax deferral withdrawal facility.

19.100 EIS and VCT schemes offer significant income tax and CGT reliefs but are high risk investments.

19.101 It is also particularly important for the non-UK domiciled but UK resident individual to ascertain if any gain and/or income arising from a non-UK situs investment is subject to remittance basis treatment.

19.102 The position with respect to the possible relief for any losses should also be ascertained. Following *FA 2008* relief for capital losses arising to non-UK domiciled but UK resident individuals on non-UK situs investments is now available.

Chapter 20

Main residence or home

Background

20.1 For many individuals the family home or main residence constitutes their most valuable asset. It is an asset in respect of which any capital gain arising on a disposal is in principle exempt from capital gains tax (CGT) (*TGCA ss 222* and *223*). There are, however, no corresponding tax reliefs/exemptions with respect to inheritance tax (IHT). Similarly, rental income which arises from the letting out of the home, during periods of absence, is subject to income tax (*ITTOIA 2005 Part 3*).

20.2 It is an asset that, for many, is held jointly whether by husband and wife, co-habitees, or just friends (see Chapter 7).

20.3 Nevertheless, while in principle any capital gain arising on a disposal of the property is exempt from CGT, the legislation is littered with caveats and thus not all disposals may necessarily be effected without a charge to CGT arising. Where a CGT charge arises, the annual exempt amount (*TCGA 1992 s 3*; £10,100 for the tax year 2010–2011; see paragraph 8.12) is available to reduce the charge.

20.4 Where an IHT charge arises it is likely to be relatively material due to the typical value of the home compared to other family assets. It is not therefore surprising that various 'schemes' have been developed designed to allow parents to gift the home, so as to exclude it from their estate on death for IHT purposes, yet still allow them to continue to live in it until death.

Unfortunately, a number of these schemes are no longer viable.

20.5 Inter-spouse transfers of interests in the home, as with other property, are exempt both for CGT and IHT purposes (*TCGA 1992 s 58* and *IHTA 1984 s 18*; see paragraphs 8.31 and 11.42).

20.6 This chapter examines the key CGT and IHT issues affecting planning for the family home including some of the associated tax issues arising on

20.7 *Main residence or home*

divorce. Chapter 7 discusses the issue of jointly held property and should be read in conjunction with this chapter.

20.7   Chapter 21 addresses the tax and structuring issues for the non-UK domiciled individual and the family home.

Capital gains tax

20.8   An overview of the key points applicable to the CGT issues relating to the main residence/home are set out below before a more detailed consideration of some of the points is undertaken.

For CGT purposes the date of disposal of land is the date of 'exchange of contracts' not the date of 'completion' (assuming the contract is not conditional which is usually the case for residential properties; *TCGA 1992 s 28*).

Overview

20.9   The CGT legislation (*TCGA 1992 Part VII*) uses the terms 'private residence', 'residence' and 'dwelling house'.

More specifically, the legislation refers to (*TCGA 1992 s 222*):

> 'an interest in ... a dwelling house or part of a dwelling house which is, or has at any time in his period of ownership been, his only or main residence'.

The statute continues (*TCGA 1992 s 223*):

> 'No part of a gain ... shall be a chargeable gain if the dwelling house or part of a dwelling-house has been the individual's only or main residence throughout the period of ownership or throughout the period of ownership except for all or any part of the last 36 months of that period'.

Any period of ownership of before 31 March 1982 is to be ignored (*TCGA 1992 s 223*) and, irrespective of all circumstances, the capital gain attributable to the last 36 months of ownership is always exempt from CGT.

20.10   The reference to any 'gain' not being a 'chargeable gain' means that the gain on disposal is exempt from CGT. This exemption extends to (*TCGA 1992 s 222*):

'land which he has for his own occupation and enjoyment with that residence as its garden or grounds up to the permitted area [ie 0.5 hectare]'.

The 'permitted area' may be greater than 0.5 hectare where the larger area is (*TCGA 1992 s 222*):

'required for the reasonable enjoyment of the dwelling house as a residence, having regard to the size and character of the dwelling house'.

Two or more residences of the individual

20.11 The use of the phrase 'only or main residence' (see paragraph 20.9) suggests that an individual may have more than one residence (which is in fact correct) and the term 'individual' which appears in the legislation (*TCGA 1992 ss 222 and 223*) suggests that perhaps only individuals may qualify for exemption from CGT (this is incorrect as trustees of a settlement and executors administering a deceased's estate may also qualify; *TCGA 1992 ss 225 and 225A*; see paragraphs 20.69 and 20.77).

20.12 Where an individual in fact has two or more residences it is possible to elect which of the various residences is to be treated as the main residence for CGT exemption purposes. Any such election can be varied at a later date depending upon circumstances (see paragraph 20.26).

Non-UK property

20.13 There is no apparent territorial restriction contained within the legislation and therefore a residence outside the UK may qualify as the individual's only or main residence in the same manner as a residence within the UK. This may, in particular, apply in the case of a non-UK domiciled but UK resident individual who may own at least two residences, one in the UK and one in the country of nationality.

However, for the UK domiciled and UK resident individual who owns a home in the UK and a holiday home in, say, Spain it is unlikely that the latter qualifies as a 'residence' and thus such individual does not have two 'residences' (this concept of a 'residence' is extremely important and is discussed below; see paragraph 20.20) and any election (see paragraph 20.27) is not then either necessary or possible.

20.14 *Main residence or home*

Example 1

Toby and Helen Blue own a detached property in Yorkshire where they, together with their three children, live for most of the time.

Three years ago they purchased an apartment in Marbella, Spain, which they tend to use for three months each summer.

Although Toby and Helen own two properties it is unlikely that the apartment in Marbella qualifies as a 'residence'.

Example 2

Tobias and Maria Barcelona are both non-UK domiciled but UK resident and jointly own a detached property in Barcelona, Spain.

Three years ago they purchased an apartment in London.

They spend roughly equal amounts of time in each property.

In this example it is likely that there are two 'residences'. If this is so then it becomes necessary for any periods of time to identify which of the two properties qualifies as their 'main' residence for CGT purposes.

Tobias and Maria can elect which of the two properties is, for CGT purposes, to be treated as their 'main' residence.

It is probably sensible for Tobias and Maria to elect for their UK property to be their main residence thus avoiding a CGT charge on sale. Any capital gain arising on the sale of their Spanish property is subject to CGT but as they are non-UK domiciled any such gain is only in fact taxable in the UK if and when any of the sale proceeds are remitted to the UK.

Married couple and cohabitees

20.14 A married couple who are living together can only have one main residence (*TCGA 1992 s 222*). Thus, a couple who are married but not living together (eg formally separated or divorced) may each have a main residence.

20.15 For cohabitees each cohabitee may have a main residence (perhaps this is one of the few tax advantages available to cohabitees compared to married couples).

Total v partial capital gains tax exemption

20.16 For the capital gain arising on the disposal of a sole or main residence to be completely exempt requires that the property is the sole or main residence throughout the whole period of ownership of the property (except for the last 36 months of ownership; see paragraph 20.9). In the event that this is not the case (eg for part of the ownership period the property is let; the individual perhaps lives elsewhere; or the property is left empty) some part of the capital gain on disposal may fall subject to CGT; typically, a time apportionment approach is adopted when computing any capital gain.

Example 3

Gregory Pick owned a UK property for 20 years following which the property was sold for £500,000 (purchase cost £100,000).

For eight years of this 20-year ownership period Gregory lived in his Florida villa letting out his UK property in the meantime.

On the sale of the UK property, of the 20-year period of ownership the property qualifies as Gregory's sole or main residence for 15 years (ie the 12 years of actual occupation plus the last 36 months). Thus:

Exempt capital gain = 15/20ths of £400,000 = £300,000.

Taxable capital gain = 5/20ths of £400,000 = £100,000.

However, in addition, certain periods of absence from the property may also be deemed to be periods of occupation and thus no loss of CGT exemption for such periods occurs; furthermore, where the home is let 'lettings relief' may be available (see paragraphs 20.53 and 20.63).

20.17 It is also necessary if the capital gain on disposal of the sole or main residence is to be completely exempt that the property is not either in whole or in part used exclusively for business purposes. If this is the case an apportionment of the capital gain on disposal is necessary with that relating to the business element constituting a capital gain subject to CGT.

20.18 *Main residence or home*

Profit motive

20.18 This issue is often overlooked. If an individual acquires a dwelling house for the purpose of disposing of it at a profit the sole or main residence (and lettings relief) CGT exemption is inapplicable. Thus, intention at the time of purchase is important. More specifically *TCGA 1992 s 224* provides that:

> '[an exemption from CGT is inapplicable if] the acquisition of the dwelling house or part of a dwelling house was made wholly or partly for the purpose of realising a gain from the disposal of it'.

20.19 The above topics are now discussed in more detail.

Residence

20.20 Unless a property is in fact an individual's residence no exemption on any gain arising on its disposal is possible. It is therefore important in the first instance to ascertain whether or not a particular property is, *de facto*, a residence of the individual.

20.21 Ownership, per se, is insufficient to cause a property to automatically qualify as an individual's residence and a property which an individual does not own, but in which he resides, may still constitute a residence.

20.22 This might arise where, for example, the individual purchases a property which he lets out whilst he continues to live with his mother in a property she owns. In this case, his sole residence is that of his mother's house (even though he owns no part of it) and the house he owns is not a residence of his, *per se*; in which case on disposal, a CGT charge arises.

20.23 In normal parlance a residence is, perhaps, a place where somebody lives on a day-to-day basis.

20.24 Whether a property is a residence of an individual is a question of fact to be determined in the light of all the surrounding circumstances.

Generally speaking, to qualify as an individual's residence the property must be occupied and must be occupied with some degree of permanence. It is not necessary for the individual to live in the property literally every day but some degree of permanence is required. If an individual purchases a property and never in fact actually lives in the property it almost certainly does not qualify as a residence (however, see paragraph 20.61 concerning job related accommodation). Spending only the odd night in the property may also fail to cause the property to qualify as a residence.

20.25 Matters likely to be important to any determination of whether a particular property qualifies as a residence (or main residence) may include:

- length of ownership;
- number of nights spent at the property;
- address used for council tax, passport, driving licence and car registration;
- location of children's school;
- location of workplace; and
- location of private possessions.

In the final analysis it is the 'quality' of the residence not 'quantity' which is important.

Example 4

Thomas Golding lives in a rented flat in London and the house which he owns in the country has been let out almost continually from the date of purchase. When the house has not been let, Thomas spends the odd night there.

Although Thomas does not own the flat, it qualifies as a residence.

The house is arguably not a residence of Thomas and thus on sale it is likely that the exemption from CGT will not apply.

Example 5

Thomas Golding's brother, Gerald, also lives in a rented flat in London but also spends virtually every weekend at his house which he owns in the country.

Although, like Thomas, Gerald does not own the flat it qualifies as a residence.

However, in Gerald's case, the house in the country is also a residence.

In this scenario Gerald has two residences and for CGT purposes it is necessary to ascertain which is his main residence (this is done by making an appropriate election; see paragraph 20.27).

20.26 *Main residence or home*

Two or more residences and the election

20.26 Example 5 illustrates that an individual may have more than one residence over the same time period. However, in such cases only the main residence qualifies for CGT exemption and thus such needs to be determined.

20.27 It is possible for an individual in such circumstances to simply make an election pursuant to which he selects which of the two (or possibly more) residence is to be regarded as his main residence (*TCGA 1992 s 222*). Such an election is simply made in writing, duly signed, to HMRC, *inter alia*, stating the date from which the chosen residence is to be regarded as the main residence. This election has to be made within two years of the date from which the individual has two (or more) residences (*TCGA 1992 s 222*).

Should the individual fail to lodge such an election within the time provided the determination as to the individual's main residence is determined by HMRC on the facts (which may produce a different, and possibly less favourable, result than if the individual had settled the matter by lodging an election).

Example 6

Barbara Tomkins owns a house in the country where she resides and which she regards as her home.

She also owns a flat in London which she permanently lets out.

Barbara owns two properties but only the house qualifies as a residence and thus an election is not possible or indeed needed.

Example 7

Barbara Tomkins' sister, Amelia, owns a house in the country where she spends every weekend.

She also owns a flat in London where she stays during the working week as she works in London and it is not possible to travel each day from her country house to London.

Amelia, unlike Barbara, owns two properties each of which qualifies as a residence.

Barbara would thus be well advised to make a formal election to determine which of her two residences she wants to be treated as her main residence.

Example 8

Alistair Duckling purchased his country house ten years ago in which he lives.

On 1 January 2006 he purchased a flat in London which he immediately let out on a two-year lease.

The acquisition of the flat in January 2006 has not given rise to Alistair having two residences (although he owns two properties) since he does not occupy the flat and thus no election is possible or needed.

On 1 January 2008, following the termination of the lease, Alistair begins to occupy the flat most days of the week as he now works in London but continues to spend weekends at his country house.

It is arguable that effective 1 January 2008 Alistair has two residences and it would thus be advisable that he lodges an election to determine which of the two residences is to be treated for CGT purposes as his main residence.

The election would need to be made on or before 31 December 2010.

20.28 Although the making of an election is to some extent a precautionary measure, and invariably in the individual's interest to so do, it can also be used as a planning device.

20.29 Once an election is made it is not irrevocable and it can thus be subsequently varied. On a variation the time period to which the variation relates cannot commence more than two years prior thereto (ie prior to the date of the variation).

Example 9

Simon Plus owns two properties: a house in the country and a flat in London. Both qualify as residences and Simon has made a timely election in favour of his country house (on which he anticipates will be the larger gain should a sale be effected).

On 1 August 2008 Simon sells his flat on which a capital gain arises with no exemption. Simon therefore lodges, on 1 August, a variation under which he elects that his flat, not his house, is to be regarded as his main residence.

20.30   *Main residence or home*

This later variation is effective from two years earlier (ie 1 August 2006). As the flat is now to be regarded as his main residence Simon is entitled to treat the last 36 months of ownership of the flat as his main residence. Thus, the capital gain attributable to the period 1 August 2005 to 1 August 2008 is exempt from CGT (whereas without the variation no part of the capital gain on sale of the flat would be exempt).

On, say, 7 August 2008 Simon varies the latest election and elects for the house to be his main residence; this applies from 7 August 2006 (ie two years earlier).

The effect of the above is that his house is no longer his main residence but only for the period 1 August 2006 to 7 August 2006. On an eventual sale of the country house only the capital gain pro-rated to this one week will be subject to CGT.

20.30   In Example 9 it may be noted that the third election (ie the last election) is in fact lodged when Simon only has the one property, his house (ie at this time he does not have two residences, having sold the flat).

The point is, however, that the election relates to a period commencing two years earlier during which Simon does have two residences and thus in respect of which a valid election is possible.

20.31   In order for an election to be made an individual in principle needs to occupy at least two properties as a residence; ownership is irrelevant. However, HMRC are of the view that for an election to be valid the possibility of a capital gain subject to CGT arising must apply to both properties. Where one of the properties is occupied under a mere licence (eg where an individual lives in their parents' house) HMRC's view is that this does not represent an interest which is capable of giving rise to a CGT charge on disposal and thus no election in respect thereof is possible; HMRC require that the interest must be either a legal or equitable interest (either of which may precipitate a capital gain subject to CGT on disposal).

20.32   There are various categories of licence including bare licences and contractual licences. The former is simply a personal permission granted by, say, X to, say, Y permitting Y to enter X's land; no consideration is provided by Y to X.

The latter differs from a bare licence as consideration passes from the licensee (Y in the above example) to licensor (X in the above example).

20.33   A licence is generally accepted as creating no interest in land; its creation transfers no interest in the land.

20.34 A lease (tenancy) on the other hand grants exclusive possession of the land (to the lessee or tenant); is for a fixed or periodic term; and under which the lessee (or tenant) pays to the lessor a premium (ie a lump sum) and/or periodical payments.

20.35 A lease, unlike a licence, creates a proprietary estate in the land on the part of the lessee and an election in respect thereof is possible.

20.36 An individual may thus have two residences one of which is owned and one of which is occupied under a short lease/tenancy agreement and thus a valid election is possible and indeed, in such situations, advisable. However, a short lease/tenancy agreement may have minimal value precipitating minimal (if not negligible) capital gain on disposal subject to CGT.

It may be that the individual is unaware of the need for an election where one property is occupied under a lease and its value is minimal and accordingly fails to lodge an election within the two-year time limit. HMRC provide by concession (ESC D21) that where this occurs the individual may still lodge an election (even if it is outside the two-year time limit) if it is lodged as soon as the individual realises that such an election is necessary (which normally arises on a disposal of the owned property).

Married couples

20.37 As indicated in paragraph 20.14, a married couple who are living together are permitted only one main residence (*TCGA 1992 s 222*). Where a married couple owns more than one property, each of which qualifies as a residence, a formal election is advisable (see paragraph 20.27). Any such election is required to be signed by both spouses (*TCGA 1992 s 222*).

20.38 It is important to note that a married couple who are not living together (ie are separated) may each possess a main residence (as indeed can cohabitees).

20.39 Prior to marriage it is not unusual for each of the two individuals to each own their own property with each property qualifying as the sole residence of the respective individual. On marriage one of the, now spouses, often moves into the residence of the other spouse with the property which is vacated no longer qualifying as a residence. However, this may not be the case and the married couple may continue to reside in both of the properties. Where it is arguable that both properties continue to qualify as residences an election should be made (and made within two years of the date of marriage (ie within two years of the commencement of the date both properties qualify as residences; see paragraph 20.27)).

20.40 Where one of the properties is vacated and no longer qualifies as a

20.41 *Main residence or home*

residence (thus precluding the need for an election) if it is sold within 36 months of vacation no CGT arises (as the last 36 months of ownership are always treated as periods of occupation; *TCGA 1992 s 223*; see paragraph 20.9).

However, where the sale occurs after the 36-month period some part of the capital gain will be subject to CGT.

20.41 An alternative to an immediate sale of the property is to initially let it out and to then sell it at a later date. Where the sale is made more than 36 months after it is vacated as a residence some part of the capital gain falls subject to CGT albeit lettings relief will be available in respect of the period of the letting (see paragraph 20.63 up to a maximum of £40,000; *TCGA 1992 s 223*).

Inter-spouse transfers

20.42 Inter-spouse transfers are generally not subject to IHT or CGT (see paragraph 20.5). However, inter-spouse transfers of interests are subject to special provisions (*TCGA 1992 s 222*).

20.43 The basic rule for CGT purposes is that inter-spouse transfers (assuming spouses are living together) take place at no gain/no loss and at the date of the transfer (although the transfer takes place at no gain/no loss a disposal for CGTV purposes still occurs; it is not an exempt transfer; *TCGA 1992 s 58*; see paragraph 8.31). The transferee spouse thus acquires the interest in the property at the original cost to the transferor spouse.

20.44 However, with respect to inter-spouse transfers of an interest in a sole or main residence, whilst the transfer takes place at no gain/no loss (as normal) under certain conditions (see paragraph 20.46) the recipient spouse's period of ownership is deemed not only to commence (not at the date of the transfer) at the date of the original acquisition by the transferor spouse but any period during which the property was the sole or main residence of the transferor spouse shall also be deemed to be that of the transferee spouse (*TCGA 1992 s 222*).

In essence, the transferee spouse 'stands in the shoes of the transferor spouse' (ie there is a 'backdating' effect to the transfer).

20.45 The 'deeming' referred to in paragraph 20.44 occurs irrespective of the real position and even applies where, at the date the transferor spouse initially acquires the property, the transferee spouse and transferor spouse are not in fact married (perhaps did not even know each other at that time). In effect, a CGT fiction is created for CGT purposes on inter-spouse transfers of an interest in a sole or main residence (subject to the transfer falling within specified conditions; see paragraph 20.46).

Main residence or home **20.47**

20.46 The conditions referred to in paragraph 20.45 which, if satisfied, result in the backdating effect are that *at the date of the transfer of the interest in the property:*

- the spouses are married and living together; and
- the property in which the interest is being transferred is their (ie both) sole or main residence.

20.47 Thus, even if at some time the property has been their sole or main residence, if at the date of the transfer the conditions in paragraph 20.46 are not satisfied no deemed 'backdating' arises. This may occur if, for example, the transfer takes place at a time when the property is let out or if another property is their main residence (possibly by election; see paragraph 20.26).

Example 10

Alice Spring acquires her house on 1 July 1999 for £200,000 and marries Jim Horse on 1 July 2002 when the house is worth £250,000.

As a wedding present Alice transfers (after they are married) a 50% interest in the house to Jim (prior to marriage Jim had lived with his brother in the latter's house) on 1 July 2002.

On 31 May 2010 they sell the house for £650,000.

On 1 July 2002 when Alice transfers 50% of her interest to Jim the house is their sole residence. He is thus deemed to have acquired that interest for £100,000 (ie 50% of the original cost to Alice) and at the date Alice bought the house (1 July 1999). As between July 1999 and the date of marriage the house has been Alice's sole residence and it is thus similarly treated as such for Jim.

On the sale on 31 May 2010 the capital gain each spouse makes is £225,000 (ie £325,000 less £100,000).

Throughout the period of ownership for each spouse the house is (or in Jim's case deemed to be) their sole residence and thus no CGT arises for either spouse.

Example 11

Assuming the same circumstances as Example 10 except Alice transfers the 50% interest in the house to Jim on 1 July 2001 (ie prior to their marriage (value £220,000)).

20.48 *Main residence or home*

At the date of the transfer Alice and Jim are not married and, in addition, Alice's house is not the sole or main residence of Jim as he does not reside there.

The relevant conditions (see paragraph 20.46) are not satisfied and thus no 'backdating' or 'standing in the shoes' occurs.

The 50% takes place at the date of transfer but at market value (*TCGA 1992 s 58* inapplicable; *TCGA 1992 s 17* applies). However, as the house has been Alice's sole residence throughout her ownership no CGT is precipitated at that time on the disposal by her of the 50% interest to Jim.

Jim is thus assumed to have acquired the 50% interest at the date of transfer for its then market value of £110,000.

On sale on 31 May 2010 no CGT arises on the part of Alice's 50% retained interest for the reasons in Example 10 (ie it is her sole residence).

However, between 1 July 2001 and 31 May 2010 (107 months) the property is Jim's sole residence only from 1 July 2002 (when he moves into the house). Jim's capital gain chargeable to CGT is thus:

$12/107 \times [£325,000 - £110,000] = £24,112$

$CGT = 18\% \times [£24,112 - £10,100] = £2,522$

(annual exempt amount for tax year 2010–2011 £10,100).

20.48 A comparison of Examples 10 and 11 reveals that Jim's CGT liability (ignoring the annual exempt amount) is avoidable by effecting the transfer of the interest in Alice's house after they are married (ie when the house qualifies as their sole residence).

20.49 There are, however, circumstances in which the 'backdating' referred to in paragraph 20.44 can be counter-productive.

Example 12

Alice Spring acquires her house on 1 July 1990 for £200,000 and married Jim Horse on 1 July 2006 when the house is worth £600,000.

Between 1 July 1991 and 30 June 2001 Alice leaves the house empty (ie it is not used by her as a residence) whilst she lives with her mother.

As a wedding present Alice transfers (after they are married in July 2006) a 50% interest in the house to Jim (prior to marriage Jim had lived with his brother in the latter's house) on 1 July 2006.

On 30 June 2010 they sell the house for £650,000.

On 1 July 2006 (market value £500,000) when Alice transferred 50% of her interest to Jim the house is their sole residence. He is thus deemed to have acquired that interest for £100,000 (ie 50% of the original cost to Alice) and at the date Alice bought the house (ie 1 July 1990). Between 1 July 1991 and 30 June 2001 the house is not Alice's sole or main residence and is thus similarly treated as such for Jim.

On the sale on 30 June 2010 the capital gain each spouse makes is £225,000 (ie £325,000 less £100,000).

The capital gain chargeable to CGT for each spouse is:

120/240 x [£325,000 − £100,000] = £112,500.

Now assume Alice transfers the 50% to Jim on 1 June 2006 (ie one day prior to marriage).

Jim is assumed to have acquired his interest on 1 June 2006 at the then market value (ie £250,000).

Jim's capital gain chargeable to CGT is in fact nil as he has lived in the property from the date of transfer to the date of sale (ie the whole of his period of ownership).

20.50 Example 12 illustrates that if the transferee (ie Jim in Example 12) is to live in the property as his sole residence from the date of transfer of an interest in the property (ie 50% in Example 12) and there is a long period of time for the transferor (ie Alice in Example 12) when the property does not comprise her sole residence (eg when it was left empty) it is preferable to effect the 50% transfer at a time when the property is not their sole or main residence.

This then breaches the conditions (see paragraph 20.46) which if satisfied result in backdating for the transferee spouse. The transferee spouse's ownership period is then not diluted/tainted by the transferor spouse's period during which the property is not the transferor spouse's sole or main residence.

20.51 The following example also illustrates this important point.

Example 13

Henry has been living overseas for many years but plans to return to the UK in the next ten years or so with his wife.

20.52 *Main residence or home*

Whilst outside the UK Henry and his wife plan to purchase a house in the UK (50/50) which they intend to let out prior to their return to the UK.

After their return, any future sale of the UK property is likely to precipitate a CGT charge for each spouse because for ten years prior to their return to the UK the property has not been either spouse's sole or main residence.

One option might therefore be for the husband to purchase the property 100% and to let it out as planned. Just prior to returning to the UK the husband transfers 100% of the property to his wife.

The transfer takes place at the date of the transfer and is at no gain/no loss but involves no backdating because at the time of the transfer the property is not their sole or main residence.

On any future sale by the wife 100% of the capital gain is exempt because throughout her period of ownership the house qualifies as her sole residence (the letting period of her husband is irrelevant).

20.52   The conditions of paragraph 20.46 and the backdating are also applicable to transfers on death. Where a transfer of an interest in a sole or main residence occurs on death, between a husband and wife who are living together, the surviving spouse is deemed to have acquired the interest at the date the deceased acquired the interest and any period during which the deceased's interest qualified as his sole or main residence is also attributed to the surviving spouse with respect to that interest (*TCGA 1992 s 222*).

However, the surviving spouse acquires the interest from the deceased spouse at probate value (ie market value) and not at the value at the date of the original acquisition by the deceased (*TCGA 1992 s 62*).

Deemed periods of residence

20.53   In ascertaining the capital gain subject to CGT (if any) on the sale of an interest in a sole or main residence any part of the capital gain attributable to periods of non-occupation (when the property is not used as a residence) would not on normal principles qualify for exemption. However, specific provision is made under which certain (not all) periods of absence (ie non-occupation) are treated as if during such periods the property is still the sole or main residence (*TCGA 1992 s 223*). These periods are:

- any period(s) of absence not exceeding three years;
- any period of absence throughout which the individual works in an office or employment all the duties of which are performed outside the UK; and
- any period(s) of absence not exceeding four years throughout which the individual is prevented from residing in the property in consequence of the situation of his place of work or in consequence of any condition imposed by his employer requiring him to reside elsewhere.

For the above periods of absence to so qualify it is necessary that:

- both before and after the period there is a time when the property is the individual's sole or main residence; and
- throughout the period of absence the individual has no sole residence or main residence eligible for relief.

20.54 Where any of the above periods are exceeded only the excess element fails to qualify (ie only the excess element is not regarded as qualifying as the individual's sole or main residence).

20.55 The individual may qualify for each of the three periods of absence (ie the periods are additive).

20.56 The above periods, if satisfied, are in addition to the last 36 months of ownership which are always treated as the individual's sole or main residence without qualification (see paragraph 20.9).

Example 14

Tommy Television purchases a property on 1 January 1990 moving in on that day.

Due to his occupation as a travel agent, Tommy often travels. In particular, he works abroad between 1 July 1995 and 30 June 2000 and between 1 August 2002 and 30 September 2004.

He is also required to work some 300 miles from his home for the period 1 May 2005 to 31 December 2005 and stays in a local hotel for this period.

He moves back into the property on 1 January 2006 and sells it on 15 August 2010.

20.57 *Main residence or home*

All the conditions for the property to be treated as Tommy's sole residence during each of the periods of absence are satisfied (see paragraph 20.53).

On sale the whole of the capital gain is thus exempt.

20.57 Some points to note with respect to satisfying the conditions relating to the periods of absence detailed in paragraph 20.53 are as follows:

- any failure to reoccupy the property after a period of absence precludes that period from qualifying (although see paragraph 20.58);
- for the period of absence outside the UK to qualify the individual must be an employee; thus a sole trader or partner in a partnership is not eligible;
- it is irrelevant whether the property is let or not during the periods of absence; and
- the existence of another residence qualifying for sole or main residence treatment during the period of absence precludes any of the periods of absence from qualifying (see paragraph 20.60).

20.58 Originally, by concession (ESC D4), but now statutorily provided (*SI 2009/730*; effective in relation to disposals on or after 6 April 2009), even where the individual does not resume residence in the property after a period of absence due to work the period is still treated as qualifying if the reason for the failure to reoccupy the property is due to the terms of the employment requiring the individual to work elsewhere (either overseas or elsewhere in the UK).

However, reoccupation of the property after an absence not exceeding three years, is required if the property during period of absence is to be treated as the sole or main residence.

20.59 Similarly, originally by concession (ESC D3) now statutorily provided (*SI 2009/730*; effective in relation to disposals on or after 6 April 2009), where one spouse satisfies the conditions relating to the periods of absence relating to work (whether in the UK or overseas), and both spouses are living together, the other spouse is treated as also satisfying those conditions.

20.60 However, as stated in paragraph 20.57, satisfaction of the conditions attaching to the periods of absence includes the need to satisfy the requirement that at no time during the period of absence has the individual another residence eligible for qualification as a sole or main residence. Thus, if the individual works overseas and/or elsewhere in the UK and, for example, leases a property this property is eligible for sole or main residence treatment (thus the condition is breached). In practice, HMRC do not appear to take this point; which arguably is a nonsensical condition.

However, for certainty, the individual should make an election in favour of the main home for the relevant period of absence (although arguably for the period of absence the main home is not in fact a residence due to its non-occupation!). Nevertheless, it is understood that HMRC allow an election in such circumstances.

20.61 Where an individual is required to live in job-related accommodation (eg a caretaker) any property he owns and which he intends to occupy as his sole or main residence is treated as if he has occupied the property as a residence (*TCGA 1992 s 222*). This applies even if, in the event, no actual occupation of the property prior to disposal occurs.

20.62 Where a property is purchased but due to work with respect to alterations etc immediate occupation of the property is prevented for a period of up to 12 months the first 12 months are nevertheless treated as a period of residence. This also applies if occupation is prevented due to the property being built.

Lettings relief

20.63 Lettings relief applies where the sole or main residence has during the period of ownership been let out either wholly or in part. On a disposal of the property any capital gain attributable to the period of the letting is subject to CGT as during this period the property cannot qualify as a residence. However, lettings relief provides for all, or some part, of the capital gain attributable to the period of letting to be exempt from CGT (*TCGA 1992 s 223*; see paragraph 20.64).

For this purpose a property is let, presumably, if a lease/tenancy or some form of contractual licence exists between the parties.

The relief appears to apply whether or not the property is let to 'connected persons' (*TCGA 1992 s 18*; see paragraph 8.29) and whether or not an arm's-length rent is payable (see paragraph 8.30). Whether a purely nominal rent is sufficient to constitute a 'letting' is unclear.

20.64 The capital gain attributable to the period of the letting which is exempt from CGT is the least of the following three amounts:

- £40,000;
- the capital gain attributable to the letting period; and

20.65 *Main residence or home*

- the amount of the capital gain which is exempt due to sole or main residence relief.

Example 15

Sonia Bird acquired her house 25 years ago and recently sold it making a capital gain of £275,000.

She occupies the house as her main residence for 15 years, letting it out for 10 years.

Capital gain	£275,000
Less:	
Exempt portion due to sole residence relief: 18*/25 of £275,000	(£198,000)
	£77,000
Less:	
Lettings exemption (ie least of):	
(i) £40,000	
(ii) £110,000 (10/25 of £275,000)	
(iii) £198,000	
	(£40,000)
Capital gain	£37,000

*includes last 36 months of ownership which is always treated as if the property has been the sole or main residence irrespective of the actual facts.

20.65 Lettings relief applies where the property has at any time in the period of ownership qualified as the individual's sole or main residence. Thus, even where the property is let prior to it becoming the individual's sole or main residence, lettings relief is still available.

The relief is, however, only available to the individual who lets the property. This may cause the lettings relief to be denied where, for example, one spouse transfers an interest in the property to their spouse after having let the property. In this case the transferee spouse could not have been a party to the letting of the property (as he/she did not own an interest therein at that time) and thus is denied lettings relief on a future disposal of the property.

Example 16

Doug buys a property in January 2000 which qualifies as his sole residence.

In March 2003 Doug lets out the property whilst he travels around the world returning to the property in July 2004.

He marries Lesley in December 2004 and in that month (following marriage) he transfers a 50% interest in the property to her.

The property is sold in August 2010.

The property qualifies as Doug's sole residence for the whole period of ownership except for the period of the letting (ie March 2003 to July 2004) in respect of which he receives lettings relief.

At the time the 50% interest is transferred to Lesley the property qualifies as their main residence (ie his and hers) and thus Doug's period prior thereto which qualifies as his sole residence is also deemed to be a sole residence of Lesley (ie the periods January 2000 to March 2003 and July 2004 to December 2004; see paragraph 20.44).

However, Lesley does not qualify for lettings relief as she is not a party to the letting at the time the property is let in March 2003.

20.66 Where spouses jointly own property and both are a party to any letting each spouse qualifies for lettings relief (ie each spouse is entitled to a maximum relief of £40,000).

20.67 There is no requirement for the property to be occupied after any letting period for lettings relief to be available (as applies to the 'periods of absence' reliefs; see paragraph 20.53) and the property may be let furnished or unfurnished.

20.68 The property may also be let on more than one occasion. In determining the quantum of lettings relief in such circumstances the separate periods of letting are simply aggregated (ie lettings relief is not computed for each separate period of letting).

Trusts and sole or main residence relief

20.69 Sole or main residence relief is not restricted to ownership by individuals but may be extended to ownership by trustees (*TCGA 1992 s 225*).

20.70 *Main residence or home*

20.70 The relief applies in the case of trustee ownership where one or more beneficiaries of the trust occupy the property as a residence and who are entitled to occupy the trust under the terms of the settlement. Entitlement to occupy under the terms of the settlement is satisfied where a beneficiary has an interest in possession in the property or where, under the terms of a discretionary trust, the trustees have power to allow a beneficiary under the trust to occupy the property.

The trustees must make a claim for the relief to apply (*TCGA 1992 s 225*).

20.71 The property occupied by the beneficiary must thus constitute his sole or main residence; where such beneficiary has more than one residence any election in favour of the trust property is to be signed by both trustees and beneficiary (*TCGA 1992 s 225*).

20.72 Where one or more beneficiaries possess interests in possession in the property, for main or sole residence relief to apply, it is sufficient that only one of the beneficiaries occupies the property as his sole or main residence (ie occupation by all of them is not necessary).

Trusts, sole or main residence relief and hold-over relief claims

20.73 For hold-over relief purposes UK resident trusts are settlor-interested if the settlor or the settlor's spouse may benefit under the trust or, from 6 April 2006, dependent children of the settlor may also benefit (*TCGA 1992 s 169F*; see paragraphs 8.45 and 8.73). A dependent child is a child who is under 18 and unmarried (*TCGA 1992 s 169F*).

The effect of including dependent children of the settlor in the definition of the settlor-interested probably caused many trusts already in existence at that time to become settlor-interested from 6 April 2006 not having so qualified prior thereto.

20.74 The effect of a trust qualifying as settlor interested is that transfers into trust by the settlor are not eligible for hold-over relief (ie hold-over relief under *TCGA 1992 ss165* and/or *260* cannot apply, *TCGA 1992 s 169B*; see paragraphs 8.45, 8.54, 8.67 and 8.73) although transfers out of such a trust may so qualify (see paragraph 8.73).

This applies to transfers into trust on or after 10 December 2003.

20.75 However, even where a trust is not settlor interested, and thus any capital gain arising on a transfer into trust by the settlor may in principle qualify for hold-over relief, it is not possible to combine such hold-over relief with sole or main residence relief on the capital gain accruing to the trustees on a future disposal (*TCGA 1992 s 226A*).

Thus, it is not possible for the trust to claim sole or main residence relief on the disposal of the trust property if a hold-over claim is lodged on the transfer of the property into the trust (*TCGA 1992 s 226A*). Such a claim to sole or main residence relief is only possible where no prior hold-over claim has been lodged (ie there are two options: no hold-over claim but sole residence relief; or hold-over claim but no sole or main residence relief).

The above applies to transfers into trust occurring on or after 10 December 2003. Transfers effected before this date qualify for partial sole residence relief (ie sole residence relief is available for the period up to 9 December 2003 but not thereafter (not even for any part of the 36 months which falls after 9 December 2003; see paragraph 20.9)).

20.76 The provisions referred to in paragraph 20.75 are primarily designed to prevent 'second homes' (which typically do not qualify for sole or main residence relief) being sold without any CGT charge arising.

Example 17

Joe Soap owns a house which qualifies as his main residence and a holiday cottage (any capital gain arising on the sale of the latter precipitating a CGT charge).

He accordingly transfers the cottage into a discretionary trust (non-settlor interested) and the trustees allow his adult son (one of the trust's beneficiaries) to occupy the cottage as his sole residence.

On transfer into trust Joe claims hold-over relief (*TCGA 1992 s 260*).

In due course, on sale by the trustees, the capital gain arising (which in fact comprises the held-over gain plus any gain which has arisen whilst the trustees owned the cottage) is exempt as sole residence relief applies (under *TCGA 1992 s 225*).

Thus, complete avoidance of a charge to CGT is achieved even though the property does not qualify for sole residence relief when owned prior to the transfer into trust.

However, this form of planning is no longer available for transfers into trusts effected on or after 10 December 2003 (transitional relief applies, for transfers before this date where the disposal by the trustees occurs after this date).

20.77 *Main residence or home*

Death and sole or main residence relief

20.77 Any capital gain made on the disposal of the former family home of the deceased by the executors during the administration period (see paragraph 28.28) is in principle subject to CGT.

Executors are liable to CGT on capital gains arising on disposals of property made during the administration period (any capital gain will be the difference between the probate value (ie market value at the date of death, and the disposal value)).

20.78 However, the disposal may qualify for sole or main residence relief (*TCGA 1992 s 225A*). The relief applies where the following conditions are satisfied:

- the disposal occurs on or after 10 December 2003;
- immediately before, and immediately after, the death of the individual the property is the sole or main residence of one or more individuals; and
- at least one of those individuals (or two or more of those individuals) has, under the will, an entitlement to at least 75% of the net proceeds of the disposal (broadly, sales proceeds less deductible expenditure; any IHT charge thereon or liabilities (eg mortgage) thereon are ignored for this purpose).

20.79 The entitlement to at least 75% of the net proceeds is an entitlement by those in respect of which the property, both before and after the death, qualifies as their sole or main residence.

This creates a problem where, for example, the property is not the sole or main residence of one or more of the beneficiaries who, under the will, are entitled to inherit a part of the property (if such beneficiaries' interests amount to more than 25% of the property).

Example 18

Eric Dunce is a widower and has two daughters, Louise and Clare.

Following the death of Eric's wife his daughter Louise, who is not married, sold her own property and moved in with Eric; the property thus becomes her sole residence.

Clare, who is married, continues to live in her family home with her husband and family.

Main residence or home **20.82**

Following Eric's death Louise continues to live in the property as her sole residence.

Under his will Eric leaves the property to each of his two daughters equally.

Eric's executors sell the property and distribute the sale proceeds equally between the two daughters.

However, as Louise is only entitled to 50% of the proceeds (ie less than 75%) a CGT charge arises on any capital gain arising on a disposal of the property (ie the difference between probate value and value at the date of sale) by the executors.

This reduces the amount of the inheritance of each daughter.

20.80 The CGT charge in Example 18 could have been avoided in one of two of the following circumstances.

If Eric had left the whole of the property to Louise (she would have been entitled to 100% of the proceeds on any subsequent sale by the executors and any capital gain on sale by them would have qualified for sole or main residence relief); alternatively, if following Eric's death Clare had, within two years, executed a deed of variation (DoV) in Louise's favour for CGT (and IHT) purposes Louise would be deemed to have inherited the property as to 100% from Eric and thus would be entitled to 100% of the sale proceeds on a sale by the executors; *IHTA 1984 s 142* and any capital gain on the sale would have qualified for sole residence relief.

20.81 With respect to the former suggestion in paragraph 20.80 Eric could have compensated Clare by leaving her other assets in his will, failing which Louise could, following the sale, compensate Clare (eg by giving 50% of the net proceeds to her; this would constitute a potentially exempt transfer (PET) for IHT purposes on the part of Louise; see paragraph 10.35).

With respect to the latter suggestion in paragraph 20.81 if Louise agreed to compensate Clare in exchange for Clare agreeing to execute the DoV the deed would be ineffective (see paragraph 28.74) and a CGT charge would arise on disposal by the executors; thus, no such arrangement would have to be agreed in advance between Louise and Clare. Alternatively, it would be acceptable, however, for Louise to also enter a DoV in favour of Clare with respect to any other property which Eric had left her (ie Louise).

20.82 The executors must make a claim for the relief to apply (*TCGA 1992 s 225A*).

20.83   *Main residence or home*

Divorce and separation

20.83   As indicated in paragraph 20.14 a married couple who are living together are entitled to one sole or main residence (*TCGA 1992 s 222*).

20.84   This does not apply where:

- the spouses are not living together; or
- following divorce.

In either of these two situations each spouse may possess their own sole or main residence.

20.85   Where one spouse is resident in the UK but the other spouse is non-resident they are still treated as living together (assuming that they are not either separated or, of course, divorced) *(Gubay v Kington* (1983)).

20.86   Spouses are treated as 'not living together' where they are separated in such circumstances that the separation is likely to be permanent (see paragraph 8.33). Although normally divorce follows a separation this is not strictly necessary. Spouses may be treated as separated for present purposes even though a decree of judicial separation (granted under *MCA 973 s 17*) is not in force or has been granted.

20.87   Where a decree of judicial separation is in force the will of either spouse is not affected (*MCA 1973 s 18*) although either spouse cannot succeed to the other's property on an intestacy (see paragraphs 27.36 and 27.38).

20.88   'Divorce' refers to 'annulment' or judicial separation' and the requisite law is contained in *MCA 1973* (*Part I* sets out the law with respect to obtaining a divorce and *Part II* deals with fiancé and property orders).

20.89   Following a petition for divorce, assuming the judge is satisfied that the case for divorce is made out, a 'decree nisi of divorce' is granted. Such a decree does not, however, terminate the marriage.

Only when a 'decree absolute' is granted is the marriage terminated/dissolved and both spouses are then free to re-marry.

20.90   Spouses may try and reach some form of divorce settlement without the need for the intervention of the courts other than to obtain a court order which, in essence, ratifies the agreement already reached. Alternatively, the court may impose a court order as it sees fit in the light of all the relevant circumstances.

Main residence or home **20.94**

However, the CGT (and IHT) implications of transfers of property between spouses (which may be agreed between them) varies according to whether the spouses are separated or divorced (ie grant of a decree absolute has been issued) at that time of the transfers. Care thus needs to be exercised if any adverse tax consequences are to be minimised.

20.91 Three possible scenarios arise:

- where spouses are married and living together transfers are effected at neither gain nor loss (*TCGA 1992 s 58*; see paragraph 8.31);

- where spouses are separated but not divorced (eg the decree nisi may be in force but the decree absolute has not been issued) transfers effected after the end of the tax year of separation are transfers between 'connected persons' (*TCGA 1992 s 286*; see paragraph 8.29) and thus are deemed to be made at market value; and

- where spouses are divorced (ie the decree absolute is in force) transfers effected are no longer between spouses (or connected persons; see paragraph 8.29) but between two independent individuals and actual consideration passing applies (ie no market value imputation; see paragraph 8.30).

20.92 Typically, on a separation/divorce one of the spouses leaves the matrimonial home (ie the sole or main residence) whilst the other spouse (often with children) continues to reside in it. If the departing spouse is to transfer his/her interest in the property to the other spouse avoidance of CGT requires that this interest is transferred within 36 months of departing the property (ie the last 36 months of ownership qualifies for sole residence treatment in all circumstances; see paragraph 20.9).

The recipient spouse (ie the spouse continuing to reside in the property) acquires this interest at the date of the transfer at market value (assuming the transfer occurs after the end of the tax year of separation and before the decree absolute; see paragraph 8.33); a transfer before the end of the tax year of separation but following separation is effected at no gain/no loss (ie recipient spouse acquires the interest at the departing spouse's original acquisition cost; see paragraphs 8.33 and 20.44).

20.93 Any transfer by the departing spouse after the 36-month period has expired precipitates a CGT charge on his/her part with respect to the capital gain attributable to the excess period.

However, this may not be the case where the conditions of ESC D6 apply.

20.94 Under ESC D6 the departing spouse may treat the time period from the date of departure to the date of the transfer of his/her interest in the property to

20.95 *Main residence or home*

the other spouse as a period of residence. The effect is therefore to permit the departing spouse to avoid a CGT charge arising on the transfer (even if it occurs after the 36-month period).

ESC D6 requires that:

- the transfer must be part of a financial settlement;
- the spouse remaining in the property must have continued to live in it; and
- the departing spouse must not have elected for some other property to qualify as his main residence for this period.

20.95 Where the departing spouse acquires another residence after leaving the matrimonial home in respect of which sole or main residence relief may be available the departing spouse may either invoke ESC D6 or, alternatively, ignore it and claim main residence relief on his/her newly acquired property.

The choice depends upon the amounts involved for the relevant time period.

20.96 On divorce the matrimonial home is often the couple's most valuable asset. There are a number of options open to the court with respect to the home; although various options appear to fall in and out of favour with the courts over time.

Two often used options are the so-called 'Mesher order' and the 'Martin order'.

20.97 Under a Mesher order the property is settled on trust for one or both spouses in appropriate shares and is to be sold when the youngest child attains, say, 18 or on ceasing full-time education. Historically, it also used to provide for sale if the spouse remaining in the property (typically the wife) died, remarried or co-habited although this is no longer a condition adopted.

For CGT purposes the spouses are treated as disposing of their respective interests in the property to the trust at market values (as at the time of disposal to the trustees the spouses and the trustees are connected persons; see paragraph 8.29) at the date of the order. No CGT charge arises on the spouse remaining in occupation and similarly no such charge arises to the departing spouse (assuming the transfer is effected within 36 months of leaving the property although HMRC appear to accept that ESC D6 may apply assuming, of course, that its conditions are satisfied).

When one of the events specified in the order occurs the trustees are deemed at that date to have sold and re-acquired the property at its then market value in principle precipitating a capital gain subject to CGT (*TCGA 1992 s 71*; effectively the trust terminates and the trustees henceforth hold the property as bare trustees for the spouses; see paragraph 8.64). However, on the deemed disposal by the trustees sole or main residence relief is available to the trustees as one of the beneficiaries (namely, the spouse who remains in the property) occupies the property under the terms of the trust (*TCGA 1992 s 225*; see paragraph 20.69).

As and when the trustees subsequently sell the property any appreciation in the value of the property between the date of termination of the trust and the date of sale is subject to CGT on the part of each spouse as appropriate (the trustees are not subject to charge as they are holding the property as bare trustees for the spouses); for the spouse remaining in the property sole residence relief applies to such gain on her interest but the departing spouse may suffer a CGT charge on such gain on his interest.

20.98 A Martin order is similar to a Mesher order. The difference is that the spouse remaining in the property is permitted to do so indefinitely subject to a sale being precipitated if the spouse dies, remarries or cohabits; however, no sale is precipitated due to the children either attaining a certain age or ceasing full-time education.

The CGT consequences are the same as those for the Mesher order (see paragraph 20.97).

20.99 Other options include an outright transfer from one spouse to the other; the granting of a life interest in the property to one spouse reverting to the other spouse (or possibly the children) on the death of the occupying spouse; or an outright transfer to one spouse but the transferring spouse retaining a right to share in the sale proceeds on the sale of the property on the occurrence of one of a number of specified events (the share of the sale proceeds may be based upon market value of the property at the date of the court order or date of sale; in the latter case some form of indexing linking may also apply).

20.100 For the departing spouse the date of the transfer of his/her interest is the date of the order for CGT purposes; thus, a CGT liability is crystallised at this point.

However, any such capital again is normally exempt either because the transfer occurs within 36 months of the departing spouse leaving the property or ESC D6 applies (see paragraphs 20.9 and 20.94). No allowance is made for CGT purposes due to the deferral of the receipt of any consideration from the sale (*TCGA 1992 s 48*; see paragraph 8.26).

Inheritance tax

Overview

20.101 The matrimonial home is invariably the most valuable asset owned by an individual and as a consequence may precipitate a significant IHT liability on death.

20.102 *Main residence or home*

20.102 In the early years of ownership any potential IHT liability is often materially reduced due to borrowings (eg a mortgage) secured against the property which reduce the value of the property for IHT purposes (see paragraph 10.60).

However, as the individual gets older, such borrowings reduce as repayments are effected until in later life the property becomes debt free whilst at the same time the market value of the property significantly increases. The potential IHT liability at this point becomes significant.

20.103 The individual's estate may be reduced for IHT purposes by making lifetime gifts (typically PETs; see paragraph 10.36). This is somewhat problematic in relation to the matrimonial home.

In particular, should a lifetime gift of the property be made (eg to the children or in trust) but the donor(s) continue to live in the property the gift qualifies as a gift with reservation (GWR) (see Chapter 12); the effect of a GWR is that on the death of the donor(s) the gifted property is regarded as still forming part of the donor(s)' estate and IHT is payable thereon (see paragraph 12.6).

20.104 'Schemes' have been designed which enable such gifting to occur whilst at the same time not falling foul of the GWR provisions. Under such schemes the donor(s) gifts the property yet still continues to live in it until death without the adverse IHT consequences referred to in paragraph 20.103 arising. However, a number of these schemes are no longer effective (due to changes in the law). Four such schemes commonly known as Ingram (*Ingram v IRC* (1995)), Eversden (*IRC v Eversden* (2002)), reversionary lease and home loan schemes are thus unlikely to be utilised in future.

One consequence of such schemes was the introduction of the pre-owned asset (POA) legislation (see paragraph 12.22) which applies where the GWR provisions fail to apply.

20.105 Nevertheless, some 'safer' planning options are available to mitigate the potential IHT liability on the matrimonial home as follows.

Downsizing

20.106 It is not unusual later in life, particularly when the children have left home, for the parents to contemplate so-called 'downsizing' which simply involves selling the home and purchasing a smaller home, thus releasing surplus cash.

This enables the surplus cash to be gifted to family members (constituting PETs; see paragraph 10.36) which is not subject to IHT so long as the donor survives at least seven years (see paragraph 10.35); at the same time a reduction in the parents' estate on death is also effected.

20.107 Alternatively, any surplus cash arising from the sale of the home can be invested in property that, on death, qualifies for business property relief (BPR) (eg certain shares listed on the Alternative Investment Market (AIM); see paragraph 11.61) at either the 50% or 100% rate thus mitigating the IHT liability on death.

Shared home arrangements

20.108 The existing owner of the property (the donor) gifts a share of the property (to the donee) and both donor and donee occupy the property thereafter.

The gifted interest in the property qualifies as a PET and in principle falls out of the donor's estate so long as the donor survives for seven years thereafter (see paragraph 10.35).

20.109 However, as the donor continues to reside in the property the gift qualifies as a GWR but if, *inter alia*, the donor does not receive any benefit from the donee in connection with the gift the GWR provisions do not apply (*FA 1986 s 102B*).

20.110 To prevent the donor from receiving any benefit from the donee the expenses of the property (ie heating, lighting, etc.) should be paid by both donor and donee reflecting their respective usage (not reflecting their respective ownership percentages). Thus if, for example, the donor has given a 75% interest in the property to the donee this does not mean that the expenses associated with the property need to be split 75/25. It is the respective usage of the facilities by the donor and donee which determine the payments by each. Assuming, the donor and donee live in the property on a day-to-day basis, other things being equal, the donor and donee should each contribute 50/50 towards the running costs of the property.

Arguably, with respect to non-recurrent expenditure (ie 'one-off' capital expenditure) the respective contributions should reflect in their respective beneficial ownership percentages. In the above example (ie gift of 75%), should the property subsequently, say, need re-roofing, *prima facie* each should contribute 75/25 not 50/50.

20.111 There is, however, nothing to prevent the donor despite having gifted some part of his interest in the property to the donee continuing to pay all the ongoing expenses of the property; the important point is that the donor (not donee) does not receive any benefit from the donee in relation to the gift.

20.112 *Main residence or home*

20.112 The gift by the donor cannot, however, be a gift of 100% of the property but must be a lesser percentage. HMRC appear to be of the view that a gift of no more than 50% is acceptable although there does not seem to be any legislative support for this stance.

20.113 This option is, perhaps, not suitable for most family situations although as children find it increasingly more difficult to fund their own property purchase, and parents find it more difficult to fund household running costs, perhaps sharing offers an increasingly realistic option.

Sharing may be particularly attractive where, following the death of one parent, a child moves back in with the surviving parent. Care needs to be exercised in such cases to ensure that HMRC cannot successfully argue that the parent (ie donor) has benefitted in some way at the expense of the child (ie donee); this might arise if a condition of the gift is that the child (ie donee) agrees to provide full caring facilities at their (ie the child's) expense.

20.114 Although an outright sale of a part of the property for market value followed by joint occupation cannot fall within the GWR provisions (as it is not a gift) it may precipitate other problems (see paragraph 12.22).

Cash gift

20.115 This option is perhaps of limited practical use.

20.116 The donor makes a gift of cash to the donee. The donee uses the cash to purchase a property in which the donor then resides. It is important that the gift of cash is not made on the condition that the donee purchases the property for the donor's occupation (otherwise there may be strong arguments that the effect is that the donor has in fact gifted an interest in land and not cash).

The gift does not constitute a GWR as the gift is of cash and not an interest in the matrimonial home (ie it is not a gift of an interest in land (*FA 1986 ss 102, 102B* and *Sch 20*).

20.117 Unfortunately, this option falls foul of the pre-owned assets provision (POA) legislation. As a consequence, the donor is assessed each tax year to income tax (at his marginal rate of income tax) on a deemed market rent of the property. This charge may be avoided if the donor elects to bring the property back into his estate for the purposes of IHT but this, of course, simply defeats the object of the exercise.

20.118 The POA charge may, however, also be avoided if, following the gift of cash, the donor does not occupy the property purchased within seven years of the date of making the gift.

Main residence or home **20.124**

Although of limited use, this 'let-out' might be useful where the donor has lived outside the UK for many years (perhaps in a 'tax-free' environment) and plans to return, say on retirement. The gift of cash to the donee may be made such that occupation of any property by the donor on return to the UK does not occur within the seven-year period.

Sale

20.119 The whole (not just a part; *FA 1986 Sch 15*) of the interest in the property is sold for market value (eg to one or more of the children). The child purchaser then allows the vendor parent to live in the property (no rent need be charged; see paragraph 20.123).

20.120 The lack of any gift precludes the application of the GWR provisions and an exemption from the POA legislation is specifically provided where a sale is of the whole of the interest in the property (*FA 1986 Sch 15*).

20.121 The purchase can be effected by cash or the purchase price may be left outstanding on loan account. In the latter case the loan must be on terms as would be agreed between third parties (thus, for example, it could not be 'interest free').

20.122 The preferred option is for an outright cash purchase as this is what typically applies with respect to sales to third parties; in addition, the cash received by the parents could be used to make gifts to family members (ie PETs) reducing the parents' estate on death or to invest in investments qualifying for BPR (see paragraph 11.61).

Gift plus rent payable

20.123 As stated in paragraph 20.103 a gift of the property by the parents followed by continued residence constitutes a GWR and no IHT is thus saved.

However, if following the gift the occupant parent pays a market rent to the donee, neither the GWR nor the POA legislation applies.

20.124 The recipient of the rent is subject to income tax each tax year on the part of the donee (eg the children) at his marginal rate, of income tax, possibly 40% or even 50% (post-6 April 2010).

In essence, there is thus a potential 'trade-off' (ie IHT at 40% on the property on the parents' death is avoided by the parent but during the parents' lifetime an

20.125 *Main residence or home*

annual 40%/50% income tax charge on the market rent from the property (broadly, say 5% of the property's market value) arises on the part of the donee.

Other things being equal, the older the parents at the time of effecting the gift the less the aggregate income tax charge on the part of the children and the greater the potential net tax saving.

General comments

20.125 Three points are perhaps worth noting:

- *first*, it is important to appreciate that in each of the above options where a gift is made from one individual to another individual the gift constitutes a PET whether or not it is treated as a GWR (see paragraph 12.6). In the event of the death of the donor within seven years of the gift the PET becomes chargeable and a possible double tax charge arises although relief is provided (see paragraph 12.6);

- *second*, where the property is owned by, say, a child of the parent (following a gift) but the parents alone continue to occupy the property, on any future sale of the property the child is subject to CGT on any capital gain. The exemption available with respect to ownership of a sole or main residence (see paragraph 20.9) is inapplicable as the property is not the residence of the child. However, if the child and parent each have an interest in the property and both live in it then the exemption from CGT applies to each individual with respect to their respective interests on any sale; and

- *third*, where a parent makes a gift either in whole or in part of their home to one or more of their children the parent to some degree loses control over the property. Should the child(ren) decide to sell the property against the wishes of the parent complications are likely to arise. The requirement to sell may be forced on the child following a 'messy' divorce or perhaps a business bankruptcy or simply following a 'fall-out' with the parent.

Thus, while some of the above options may offer effective IHT planning, regard must be had to all factors (ie non-tax as well as tax), in particular, given the importance (both fiscal and non-fiscal) attached to the family home.

Death and inheritance tax

20.126 For the individual who dies owning a part interest in the matrimonial home such interest forms part of the individual's estate which in principle is subject to IHT (see paragraph 10.61). Where the first spouse to die leaves their interest in the property to the surviving spouse the surviving spouse dies owning 100% of the property which is then subject to IHT.

20.127 Where the first spouse to die leaves their interest in the property to the surviving spouse it is possible that the whole, or part, of their nil rate band (NRB) is wasted (ie not used).

However, this risk is significantly reduced following the introduction in *FA 2008* of the concept of the 'transferable nil rate band' (*IHTA 1984 s 8A*; see paragraph 11.44) between spouses (applicable where one or both spouse deaths occur on or after 9 October 2007).

20.128 The effect of the transferable NRB is that if the whole, or part, of the NRB of the first spouse to die is unutilised the NRB of the second spouse to die is increased (by the percentage of the NRB of the first spouse to die which is unutilised; see paragraph 11.44).

Thus, in principle if the first spouse to die leaves the whole of his estate to the surviving spouse (thus utilising none of their NRB), on the death of the latter the NRB applicable is twice the amount of the NRB applying for the tax year of the latter's death; thus the NRB on the first spouse's death is not wasted.

20.129 Nevertheless, reliance upon this transferability to ensure efficient NRB utilisation may not necessarily be the best option to pursue in all cases.

20.130 Indeed before the introduction of the transferable NRB in *FA 2008* (*IHTA 1984 ss 8A to 8C*) it was (and still is) common practice for the first spouse to die to leave the whole of their interest (or that interest which equated to the then NRB, the balance of the interest left to the surviving spouse absolutely) in the property on discretionary trust for the surviving spouse and children (this requires that the spouses' interests in the property are held as tenants in common or severance followed by execution of a DoV is necessary; see paragraphs 7.8, 7.18 and 7.21). The use of such a trust ensured utilisation of the NRB.

20.131 Even where use may be made of the transferable NRB the NRB discretionary trust option allows a degree of flexibility to be retained for the future with respect to the settled interest. It may also be used, for example, by spouses of second marriages who have children from the first, or earlier, marriage(s) who do not wish to deprive their second marriage spouse from remaining in the marital home but who want their children to ultimately benefit on the death of the surviving spouse.

The trust may also be of help in preventing the interest in the property being 'charged' by local councils to secure the payment of care home fees for the surviving spouse.

20.132 *Main residence or home*

Unfortunately, the use of the discretionary will trust may precipitate adverse IHT consequences.

20.132 In the typical scenario each spouse has a 50% beneficial interest in the property. Where the interest of the first spouse to die is left on discretionary trust for the surviving spouse and children HMRC take the view that the surviving spouse acquires an interest in possession (see paragraphs 16.4 and 16.5) in the property under the trust.

If such interest arises pre-21 March 2006 such an interest is a qualifying interest in possession and thus on the surviving spouse's death (whether pre- or post-21 March 2006) included in the estate is the 50% owned absolutely plus the 50% interest in possession element; in short, the whole of the property falls subject to IHT on the death of the second spouse as opposed to just the surviving spouse's 50% absolute interest.

If the interest in possession arises on or after 21 March 2006 it is likely to qualify as an immediate post-death interest in possession (IPDI) (which is a qualifying interest in possession) and the above consequences still follow (see paragraph 16.80). Technically, an IPDI in this case only arises where the interest in possession arises within two years of death as it is then read back under the will (*IHTA 1984 s 144*; see paragraph 28.88).

20.133 With a view to trying to preclude the arising of a qualifying interest in possession, whether pre- or post-*FA 2006*, so-called 'debt' or 'charge' schemes are sometimes used. Under the former, the surviving spouse agrees to pay to the trustees of the discretionary trust (created under the will of the first spouse to die) a sum equivalent to the NRB. In exchange, the interest in the property equivalent to the NRB is left to the surviving spouse.

Under the latter, the executors effect a charge over the estate's interest in the matrimonial home (equivalent to the NRB) and then assent that interest to the surviving spouse (ie the surviving spouse acquires the deceased spouse's interest in the matrimonial home albeit subject to the charge).

For stamp duty land tax (SDLT) (see Chapter 22) purposes the latter (ie 'charge') option is probably preferable as under this option no SDLT arises. Under the former (ie 'debt') option as the surviving spouse effectively provides consideration by way of the debt given to the trustees in exchange for the interest in the property SDLT is payable.

20.134 The possibility of executing DoVs might also be considered where appropriate.

Divorce

20.135 The CGT position on separation and divorce is discussed in paragraph 20.83.

20.136 However, IHT issues should not be overlooked.

20.137 Where an outright transfer of a spouse's interest in the matrimonial home to the other spouse occurs whilst the spouses are married (whether living together or not so long as prior to the decree absolute) no IHT arises due to the inter-spouse exemption (*IHTA 1992 s 18*; see paragraph 11.42).

Such a transfer occurring after the decree absolute constitutes a PET although the transfer may fall within the 'disposition for maintenance of the family' exemption (*IHTA 1984; s 11*, see paragraph 11.34) or the 'dispositions not intended to confer gratuitous benefit' exemption (*IHTA 1984 s 10*; see paragraph 10.2).

20.138 The utilisation of trusts created post-21 March 2006 is less attractive as such trusts are relevant property trusts (see paragraph 16.9) and are thus subject to ten-yearly and exit charges (see paragraph 16.12) and the initial settlement of property on such trusts is a chargeable lifetime transfer (CLT) and thus precipitates an IHT charge (see paragraph 16.7).

Prior to 22 March 2006 typically a qualifying interest in possession trust would have been created for the spouse (ie before the decree absolute) which would have qualified as an exempt inter-spouse transfer avoiding the ten-yearly and exit charges; on the spouse's death the children would inherit the trust assets. Lifetime qualifying interest in possession trusts cannot be created post-21 March 2006.

Summary

20.139 An individual's sole or main residence is typically an extremely valuable asset. Thus, on death a significant IHT liability arises. Depending upon the circumstances, options exist which, if implemented, may mitigate such an IHT charge. Some of these options involve lifetime gifts while others involve arrangements effected on death.

20.140 CGT exemption applies to the capital gain on the sale of a sole or main residence. It is important, however, that the property owned constitutes a 'residence'; owning a property but not living there does not constitute a 'residence'.

20.141 Ownership of two or more residences requires a formal election in favour of one or the other for CGT purposes as only one property may qualify for sole or main residence exemption. In the absence of such a formal election the facts determine the matter.

20.142 *Main residence or home*

20.142 Divorce or separation may precipitate adverse CGT and IHT consequences for one or both spouses. The timing of any transfers between the spouses is critical to the tax consequences.

Chapter 21

Non-UK domiciliaries and UK homes

Background

21.1 For many non-UK domiciled individuals who are UK resident the purchase of a family home is generally inevitable. For those who remain non-UK resident but who visit the UK regularly a purchase often makes life easier.

It is assumed in this chapter that the non-UK domiciled individual is UK resident.

21.2 For many non-UK domiciled individuals the majority of the individual's wealth has been made and remains outside the UK. The simple expedient of bringing non-UK source funds into the UK to effect a UK property purchase precipitates an income tax and/or capital gains tax (CGT) charge if a remittance of the foreign income and/or capital gains occurs (see Chapter 24).

A remittance of the foreign income and/or capital gains occurs whether such income/gains arose prior to 6 April 2008 or on or after 6 April 2008 and the purchase is effected directly by the individual; through a non-UK resident company; through a non-UK resident trust; or some combination thereof (see paragraph 24.36).

To avoid income tax and/or CGT charges arising requires that the monies brought to the UK comprise, for example, inheritances, gifts from other family members (who are non-UK resident; otherwise the bringing in of the monies precipitates a remittance on their part if UK resident and they qualify as relevant persons; *ITA 2007 s 809M*; see paragraph 24.50); or monies generated by the individual prior to acquiring UK residence. Alternatively, already taxed UK source income and/or capital gains may be used.

21.3 The two primary issues for consideration on purchasing a UK home are:

- ownership structuring; and
- financing the purchase.

21.4 *Non-UK domiciliaries and UK homes*

Ownership structuring

21.4 The main structuring options appear to be:

- individual ownership;
- company ownership;
- trust ownership; and
- some combination thereof.

Individual ownership

21.5 This is the simplest of all the options; the individual simply purchases the property directly in his own name (and/or that of his spouse).

A joint purchase in the name of the individual and the individual's spouse (or other third party) requires consideration as to whether beneficial ownership should be as joint tenants or tenants in common (see paragraphs 7.17 and 7.45); as a broad general rule, ownership as tenants in common is preferable.

Capital gains tax

21.6 For CGT purposes, no CGT charge arises on any eventual sale effected after the individual has become non-UK resident or, if still resident, the property qualifies for sole or main residence relief (*TCGA 1992 s 223*; see paragraph 20.1). Such individual will also typically own one or more homes outside the UK which also probably qualify as residences (see paragraph 20.20). It is therefore sensible for an election to be lodged in favour of the UK property (*TCGA 1992 s 222*; see paragraph 20.26).

21.7 In the event that no lifetime sale is effected when the property passes on death no CGT charge arises and the person inheriting the deceased's interest in the property does so at the property's then market value (see paragraph 8.40). Thereafter, the CGT position depends upon who inherits and their CGT status (and that of the property) at the time of sale.

Thus CGT is, in general, not a serious problem under this option.

Inheritance tax

21.8 The property, as a UK situs asset (see paragraph 6.30), is within the charge to inheritance tax (IHT) on death and with respect to any lifetime gift (see paragraph 10.6). Where the deceased's interest in the property passes to the surviving spouse the inter-spouse exemption applies (*IHTA 1984 s 18*; see paragraph 11.42).

21.9 However, where the first spouse to die is UK or deemed UK domiciled (*IHTA 1984 s 267*; see paragraph 10.9) and the surviving spouse is non-UK domiciled (*IHTA 1984 s 18*) only the first £55,000 of transfer is exempt although the nil rate band (NRB) applies to the next £325,000 (for the tax year 2010–2011) of transfer; over and above this total of £380,000 IHT at 40% is charged.

21.10 The surviving spouse owns or continues to own a UK situs asset and thus in principle a further charge to IHT arises on death subject to the availability of the NRB. Gifting in lifetime to another family member (ie an individual) qualifies as a potentially exempt transfer (PET; see paragraph 10.36) and an IHT liability only arises should the spouse die within seven years of the gift (see paragraphs 10.35 and 10.36); settling the property on trust (whether a UK or non-UK resident trust; see Chapters 17 and 18) is a chargeable lifetime transfer (CLT) and thus is in principle chargeable to IHT subject to the availability of the NRB (see paragraphs 10.15 and 10.22).

21.11 Where a potential IHT exposure exists mitigation may be achieved by the use of insurance and/or debt.

21.12 Where the individual is young and healthy taking out appropriate life cover is probably the easiest, most cost effective and sensible option. Such insurance may be written in trust (see paragraph 19.38) and/or taken out offshore (offshore policies qualify as excluded property; *IHTA 1984 s 6*).

Where insurance cannot be obtained cost effectively, debt (eg a mortgage) incurred at the time of the purchase or created subsequently offsets the value of the property on death for IHT purposes (*IHTA 1984 s 5*; see paragraph 10.74).

Historically, such borrowing was usually incurred from a foreign bank because this enabled the individual's relevant foreign income (RFI) to be used to discharge the interest cost thereon without precipitating a taxable remittance of such RFI to the UK (see paragraphs 24.1 and 24.134). The use of such monies to effect repayments of capital, however, constituted a taxable remittance and generally no such repayments were made whilst the individual remained UK resident (or were effected out of monies which would not have given rise to a taxable remittance (eg so-called 'pure capital') see paragraph 24.134).

The changes introduced in *FA 2008* (effective 6 April 2008) have closed down this tax-effective option albeit subject to transitional provisions with respect to pre-12 March 2008 borrowings (see paragraph 24.136). Now, post-*FA 2008*, in order to avoid taxable remittances the discharge of interest and/or capital

21.13 *Non-UK domiciliaries and UK homes*

repayments out of foreign monies needs to be made out of, *inter alia*, gifts from family members; an inheritance; or UK source monies already taxed and transferred outside the UK.

21.13 The borrowing of monies from non-bank sources, such as friends and family or from non-UK structures created by the individual (eg non-UK resident trusts), is of course possible, but the issue of remittance remains the same. Indeed, if the lender is an individual or non-UK resident trust the debt is likely to constitute UK situs property for IHT purposes so the lender in principle falls within the charge to IHT.

21.14 The ownership of UK situs property requires probate to be obtained (see paragraph 27.114) in the event of the death of the individual unless the property is jointly owned, and if so, is held as joint tenants (see paragraphs 7.6 and 7.8); where the property is owned by a non-UK resident trust or company as no change in the legal ownership of the property occurs probate is not required.

Company ownership

Inheritance tax

21.15 The purchase of the UK property by a non-UK resident and registered company resolves the IHT issue associated with a direct purchase by the individual (as the asset held by the individual is now the shares in the company, not the underlying UK property, which qualify as excluded property; see Chapter 13).

Capital gains tax

21.16 A non-UK resident company is not within the charge to CGT (see paragraph 23.26). However, anti-avoidance provisions apportion any capital gain the company makes to the company's resident shareholders at that time thus precipitating a CGT charge on the gain (*TCGA 1992 s 13*; see paragraph 8.99); the remittance basis is unavailable to the individual as the property disposed of (ie the family home) is UK situs (see paragraph 8.111).

The apportionment problem only arises with respect to disposals made on or after 6 April 2008 following the major changes introduced in *FA 2008* pursuant to which *TCGA 1992 s 13* is extended to non-UK domiciled but UK resident individuals (see paragraph 8.110).

21.17 If the individual lives in the property sole or main residence relief is unavailable with respect to the apportioned gain as such relief only applies to property held by individuals or held in trust (*TCGA 1992 ss 223* and *225*; see paragraphs 20.1 and 20.69).

21.18 A sale of the property by the company after the individual becomes non-UK resident avoids the CGT charge.

Income tax

21.19 Corporate ownership of the property may precipitate an income tax charge on the part of the individual. This occurs if the individual is a director or employee of the company (which is probably unlikely) or is regarded as a so-called 'shadow director' of the company (which is more likely); the consequence of which is that the individual's occupation of the property is a benefit in kind subject to income tax (*ITEPA 2003 s 97*).

The measure of the benefit is obtained by applying the official rate of interest to the excess over £75,000 of the cost of the property (not its market value). For the tax year 2010–2011 the official rate of interest is 4% (*SI 2010/415*); for the tax year 2009–2010 it was 4.75%. The benefit is not a 'one-off' benefit but a benefit levied for each tax year the individual occupies the property.

Thus, for a property costing, say, £1 million the annual benefit in round figures (ie ignoring the deduction of £75,000) at the 2010–2011 rate is £40,000 which produces an income tax charge of £16,000 per tax year (for a 40% higher rate taxpayer) or £30,000 per tax year (for a 50% additional rate taxpayer).

21.20 Whether the individual is a director or employee of the company is readily ascertainable; however, whether he is a shadow director is more difficult to determine. In essence, a shadow director is someone upon whose instructions the directors of the company typically act.

In practice, where the individual owns the company (but is not a director or an employee) HMRC are likely to allege that the individual is in fact a shadow director.

21.21 Corporate ownership may thus precipitate a significant annual income tax charge unless the individual pays a market rent for occupation of the property. This then has the consequence that the recipient company is exposed to income tax at the basic rate of income tax (20% for the tax year 2010–2011; see paragraph 23.20); such income not constituting disregarded income (see paragraph 23.12).

Trust ownership

Capital gains tax

21.22 A non-UK resident trust is not within the charge to CGT (see paragraph 23.26). The *TCGA 1992 s 13* issue raised in paragraph 21.16, applicable to corporate ownership, is inapplicable to trust ownership.

21.23 *Non-UK domiciliaries and UK homes*

However, capital gains of non-UK resident trusts may be treated as accruing to beneficiaries of the trust who receive capital payments from the trust (*TCGA 1992 s 87*; see paragraph 18.108). The imputation of capital gains of non-UK resident trusts under *TCGA 1992 s 86* to the settlor of the trust is inapplicable to non-UK domiciled individuals (see paragraph 18.99).

21.23 Occupation of the property rent free by the individual constitutes a capital payment for each tax year the property is occupied; thus, in principle, the capital gain made on a disposal of the property by the trust (assuming no other property is held in the trust) is treated as that of the individual (in the tax year of sale) up to the aggregate quantum of capital payments received by matching the capital gain with the capital payments made to the individual (see paragraph 18.120).

Despite the non-UK domicile status of the individual the remittance basis is inapplicable to the matching of the capital gain to the quantum of the capital payments as the capital payments (ie the rent-free occupation of the property every tax year) are made in the UK; thus, a CGT charge arises in the tax year of sale of the property.

21.24 As the capital gain arising on the disposal of the property by the trust is likely to qualify for main residence relief (*TCGA 1992 s 225*; see paragraph 20.69) the capital gain is not matched with the capital payments under *TCGA 1992 s 87*; in which case no CGT charge arises on the disposal of the property on the individual. An election may be necessary where the individual has other residences (see paragraphs 20.20 and 20.26).

Under *TCGA 1992 s 87* any capital gains of the trust are matched with capital payments made by the trust; thus, if the trust made other capital gains such gains could then be matched to the capital payments made by the trust (ie the occupation of the property). However, where the trust's only asset is the UK property such matching cannot arise).

For this reason, it may be preferable that the only property of the trust is the UK property.

Inheritance tax

21.25 IHT, however, remains an issue.

Although non-UK situs property of non-UK resident trusts created by a non-UK domiciled settlor qualifies as excluded property (*IHTA 1984 s 6*; see paragraph 13.7), UK situs property does not so qualify.

21.26 To avoid any IHT charge arising on the creation of the trust (ie to avoid the transfer of the monies constituting a CLT; see paragraph 10.22) the monies used should be located outside the UK at the time of creation of the trust (see paragraph 6.28). The monies may then be used by the trustees to effect the purchase of the UK home.

21.27 Where the property is purchased by the trust prior to 22 March 2006 the individual occupying the property is likely to be treated as possessing a qualifying interest in possession (see paragraph 16.4); thus, on death the property is included as part of the estate of the individual and subject to IHT.

21.28 Where the trust is set up on or after 22 March 2006 (ie the property is purchased on or after this date) the individual's interest in possession is non-qualifying (see paragraph 16.4) and thus the IHT charge arising on death of the individual referred to in paragraph 21.27 is inapplicable. However, the gift with reservation (GWR) provisions apply and, as a consequence, the trust property (ie the property itself) forms part of the individual's estate on death (*FA 1986 s 102*; see paragraphs 10.61 and 12.6).

The trust qualifies as a relevant property trust (see paragraph 16.9) and is thus subject to both exit and ten-yearly IHT charges (see paragraph 16.12).

21.29 The benefit in kind problem raised in paragraph 21.19 is of no application where trust, as opposed to corporate, ownership is involved and to this extent the trust option is arguably the better of the two.

Combination structure

21.30 The typical such structure is a non-UK resident trust which owns the shares of a non-UK resident and registered company; the company effects the purchase of the UK property.

Capital gains tax

21.31 Whilst the company, as a non-UK resident company, is not subject to CGT any capital gain made is apportioned to its trust shareholder (*TCGA 1992 s 13*; see paragraph 21.16); such gain is then attributable to any beneficiaries of the trust who receive capital payments from the trust (*TCGA 1992 s 87*; see paragraph 21.22). Capital payments include, *inter alia*, benefits provided by a company of which the trustees have control (*ICTA 1988 s 416*) and thus occupation of the property by the individual constitutes receiving a capital payment (for each and every tax year occupation continues).

21.32 However, whereas in the case of direct and trust ownership of the property CGT relief is available with respect to any capital gain arising on

21.33 *Non-UK domiciliaries and UK homes*

disposal due to sole or main residence relief (*TCGA 1992 s 225*; see paragraphs 21.6 and 21.24) no such relief is available where corporate ownership subsists (as applies here).

21.33 Thus, a disposal of the property by the company whilst the individual is UK resident precipitates a CGT charge on the part of the individual (due to a combination of *TCGA 1992 s 13* and *s 87*); the remittance basis is inapplicable as the capital benefit is provided in the UK.

21.34 Thus, only by ensuring that the disposal of the property occurs when the individual is non-UK resident is the CGT charge on disposal avoided.

Inheritance tax

21.35 The shares of the company owned by the trust (created by the non-UK domiciled individual) qualify as excluded property (*IHTA 1984 s 6*; see paragraph 13.7) and thus the ten-yearly and exit charges are inapplicable (see paragraph 13.9).

21.36 To avoid any IHT charge arising on the creation of the trust (ie to avoid the transfer of the monies constituting a CLT; see paragraph 10.22) the monies used should be located outside the UK at the time of creation of the trust (see paragraph 6.28). The monies settled are then used by the trustees to subscribe for shares in the company and/or grant loans to the company.

21.37 The GWR provisions apply and, as a consequence, the trust property (ie the shares of the company) forms part of the individual's estate on death (*FA 1986 s 102*; see paragraphs 10.61 and 12.6).

Income tax

21.38 The issue of 'shadow director' (see paragraph 21.19) is equally applicable to this option. However, the risk under this option is arguably much reduced (if not entirely removed) as the individual is no longer a shareholder in the company and thus, arguably, is less able to instruct the directors thereof; any instructions emanating from the trustees. In the final analysis the matter is one of fact.

General comments

21.39 Prior to *FA 2008* (effective 6 April 2008) neither *TCGA 1992 s 13* nor *TCGA 1992 s 87* applied to non-UK domiciled individuals. Thus, prior to 6

April 2008, there was no risk of capital gains of the non-UK resident company or trust being attributed to the individual.

With respect to capital gains arising on or after 6 April 2008 both sections apply to non-UK domiciled individuals.

21.40 *TCGA 1992 s 86*, both before and after *FA 2008*, has no application to non-UK domiciled individuals (see paragraph 18.99).

21.41 The issue of remittance, briefly mentioned in paragraph 21.2, is likely to be problematic.

Pre-owned asset provisions

21.42 The pre-owned assets provisions (POA) do not apply where, *inter alia*, the GWR provisions apply or where the individual possesses a qualifying interest in possession (*FA 2004 Sch 15*; see paragraph 12.37); in both cases the property in which the GWR or interest in possession subsists are included as part of the individual's estate on death (see paragraph 10.61).

21.43 Where therefore a non-qualifying interest in possession arises and the GWR provisions do not apply the POA provisions are, *prima facie*, applicable.

Preliminary conclusions

21.44 None of the above options satisfactorily resolve all the tax issues. The choice of option depends upon many factors including the domicile status of both spouses; family arrangements; future plans as to the location of ultimate residence; etc.

21.45 If it is likely that the individual does not anticipate long-term residence in the UK (and death is, other things being equal, unlikely) and the property is likely to be sold direct ownership in the individual's (and/or the spouse's) name is probably the best option. If necessary any IHT exposure may be mitigated by effecting insurance.

21.46 If long-term residence is likely and it is unlikely that the property will be sold (as it is intended to retain it in the family) the combination structure is probably preferable (ie the trust/company structure).

Summary

21.47 Non-UK domiciled individuals purchasing a UK home need to consider the twin issues of ownership structure and finance.

21.48 *Non-UK domiciliaries and UK homes*

21.48 Non-UK resident trusts are an important vehicle in structuring ownership of UK situs assets for non-UK domiciled individuals but with respect to the family home direct ownership, on balance, may be the best option.

21.49 IHT and CGT are the two major taxes in respect of which consideration needs to be given, *vis-à-vis* death and disposal, but income tax charges may also apply where corporate ownership of the home is adopted.

21.50 Remittance of the individual's foreign income and/or capital gains to fund the purchase of the home, whether directly or indirectly, is likely to precipitate income tax and/or CGT charges.

21.51 Direct ownership by the individual does not avoid the need for probate on death.

Chapter 22

Stamp duty and stamp duty land tax

Background

22.1 When compared to rates of income tax, capital gains tax (CGT) and inheritance tax (IHT) those applicable to stamp duties are relatively much smaller; however, they are levied on the gross amount of consideration applicable to a particular transaction and thus in absolute terms may be very significant.

22.2 Historically stamp duties were levied on instruments and not transactions or persons. It was thus possible to avoid the charge to stamp duty by simply not having any instrument to stamp wherever possible.

Stamp duty and stamp duty reserve tax

22.3 Stamp duty was first levied under the *Stamp Act 1694* and has been amended over the years by various Finance Acts; however, a major overhaul of the stamp duty was implemented by *FA 2003*.

22.4 Under the reform, stamp duty was replaced by stamp duty land tax (SDLT) in connection with land transactions. In addition, stamp duty was abolished in connection with all documents and transfers other than transfers with respect to shares and marketable securities (indebtedness which is marketable).

22.5 Seven years earlier in 1986 stamp duty reserve tax (SDRT) had been introduced which levies charges where there is an agreement to transfer shares or marketable securities.

22.6 Stamp duty and SDRT are taxes on documents (basically, no document no tax) whereas SDLT is a transaction-based tax, applicable whether or not a document exists in connection with the transaction.

22.7 SDRT is levied at the *ad valorem* rate of 0.5% of the amount or value of the consideration and is payable by the purchaser.

22.8 *Stamp duty and stamp duty land tax*

Stamp duty is levied either at the *ad valorem* rate of 0.5% of the amount or value of the consideration or at a fixed amount of £5 and in either case is payable by the purchaser.

22.8 SDRT, as indicated above, is levied on agreements (eg contracts) for the sale of shares whereas stamp duty is levied on an actual transfer of the shares. Where payment of the stamp duty is made this cancels any charge to SDLT (ie in this case stamp duty takes priority).

Stamp duty land tax

22.9 Stamp duty land tax is a tax on land and applies from 1 December 2003. It replaces the former stamp duty which applied to land.

22.10 It applies to transactions relating to land (*FA 2003 s 43*) including those relating to freeholds, leaseholds and options over land. However, SDLT applies only to UK-situated land (*FA 2003 s 48*). Where the land is UK situated, SDLT applies, despite some views to the contrary, irrespective of whether or not the parties to the transaction and/or the instrument relating to the land are within the UK.

22.11 For a charge to SDLT to arise there must be chargeable consideration (*FA 2003 Sch 4*). Chargeable consideration includes money and money's worth provided by the purchaser or a person connected with him (*ICTA 1988 s 839*; broadly, a person is connected with an individual if that person is the individual's spouse, sister, brother, ancestor or lineal descendant; in addition, trustees of a settlement of which the individual is a settlor are connected). It may also include assumption by the purchaser of a debt obligation of the transferor (see paragraph 22.28).

22.12 The payment of SDLT is the responsibility of the purchaser (as is the reporting of the transaction) and the payment of any SDLT due must be made within 30 days of the transaction (*FA 2003 ss 43, 76* and *119*).

22.13 The rates of SDLT vary according to whether the land is residential or non-residential and according to the amount of the consideration. The rates prior to the amendments introduced by FA 2010 with respect to residential land are as follows:

- not more than £125,000   0%
- more than £125,000 but not more than £250,000   1%
- more than £250,000 but not more than £500,000   3%
- more than £500,000   4%

FA 2010 s 7 has introduced a new 5% rate for consideration over £1 million. The new 5% rate applies to transactions effected on or after 6 April 2011.

FA 2010 s 6 has introduced a temporary measure under which the 0% band will apply to purchases of residential property at up to £250,000 where the purchaser or purchasers are first-time buyers. The relief applies to transactions effected on or after 25 March 2010 but before 25 March 2012 (a similar temporary measure was introduced in *FA 2009 s 10* which applied to transactions made between 22 April 2009 and 31 December 2009 with respect to residential property; after that date the SDLT threshold for residential property reverted to £125,000).

22.14 Where the amount of the consideration falls into one of the bands the rate applicable for that band applies to the whole of the consideration. Thus, for example, a consideration of £1 million is subject to SDLT of 4% of £1 million (ie £40,000) not 4% of [£1 million less £500,000].

22.15 The appropriate rate is levied on the consideration with no discount applicable should the consideration be deferred.

Death

22.16 The executors are liable for any unpaid SDLT owed by the deceased at his date of death (*FA 2003 Sch 4*).

22.17 On the death of an individual the deceased's property vests in the executors (see paragraph 27.116). However, no SDLT arises on the vesting of land (eg the deceased's matrimonial home) in the executors even if the land is subject to a mortgage at the time of the testator's death (ie there is an assumption of the mortgage by the executors).

22.18 Any assent or appropriation by the executors of estate property to a beneficiary under the will does not precipitate an SDLT charge (assuming, as is invariably the case, that no consideration is provided by the beneficiary). This also applies if the land appropriated to the beneficiary is subject to mortgage (*AEA 1925 s 41* and *FA 2003 Sch 3*). The provision of any consideration (other than the assumption of any attaching mortgage) is subject to SDLT.

22.19 Variations entered into following death (see paragraph 28.71) are not subject to an SDLT charge (assuming the variation is within two years of the testator's death and no consideration is provided; *FA 2003 Sch 3*). However, an assumption of any debt attached to the property constitutes chargeable consideration in respect of which an SDLT charge arises.

Trusts

22.20 It is possible for SDLT to apply with respect to land transactions involving trusts.

22.21 *Stamp duty and stamp duty land tax*

22.21 A purchase of land by trustees is treated like any other purchase and thus where consideration is provided an SDLT charge arises.

22.22 An individual with an interest in possession constitutes a chargeable interest for SDLT purposes. Thus, if the interest in possession beneficiary assigns, releases or surrenders his interest for consideration SDLT is chargeable; similar consequences apply with respect to the interest of any remainderman.

However, the above does not apply to the interests of beneficiaries of discretionary trusts; such beneficiaries (unlike an interest in possession beneficiary) merely have a 'hope' that the trustees may exercise their discretion in their favour but do not have any interests in the trust property (see paragraph 15.34).

22.23 Generally speaking, on the exercise by trustees of a power of appointment (ie a right given to the trustees under the trust deed to appoint trust property to one or more beneficiaries) no SDLT charge arises as the exercise is normally effected without any form of consideration passing. However, should land be appointed to a beneficiary subject to mortgage then an SDLT charge arises.

Bare trust

22.24 A bare trust is basically a trust where the trustees hold the trust property on trust for one or more beneficiaries absolutely (see paragraph 15.20). Effectively, the trustees have no duties to perform apart from acting on instructions from the beneficiaries. For SDLT purposes it is the beneficial owners (ie the beneficiaries) who are liable for any SDLT on the trust property, not the bare trustees.

Non-UK resident trusts

22.25 Non-UK resident trusts are not outside the scope of SDLT as a matter of principle. Thus, for example, a disposal, whether by way of assignment, release or surrender by an interest in possession beneficiary of their interest in UK land for consideration precipitates an SDLT charge; such a charge applies irrespective of the residence (or domicile) status of the beneficiary concerned.

Matrimonial home

22.26 Inter-spouse transfers can usually be effected without income tax, CGT or IHT consequences as such transactions are typically treated as exempt. However, no such automatic exemption applies for SDLT purposes.

22.27 An SDLT charge only arises where there is chargeable consideration; thus, gifts do not precipitate SDLT charges. However, where a gift is made but an accompanying assumption or satisfaction of an attaching debt occurs SDLT is chargeable.

22.28 Where property is transferred subject to a charge and the transferee specifically agrees to discharge the debt and/or to indemnify the transferor the debt is treated as chargeable consideration. However, if the property is acquired (albeit subject to a charge) but the transferee neither provides an indemnification nor agrees to discharge the debt it is not included as part of the chargeable consideration.

An indemnification is necessary as liabilities are not capable of assignment.

22.29 It is important that on any transfer of property which is subject to charge that the transferor and transferee are clear as to whether the latter agrees to discharge the debt or agrees to indemnify the former; often unforeseen SDLT charges arise on such transfers.

For example, following marriage, an interest in a property (normally 50%) previously owned 100% by one of the spouses (the property having been purchased using a mortgage) is transferred to the other spouse. The transfer of the beneficial interest (say, 50%) by way of gift precipitates no SDLT charge; however, it often happens that the recipient spouse assumes joint liability for the mortgage debt and/or indemnifies the transferor spouse. Where this happens the assumption of joint liability constitutes consideration by the recipient spouse and an SDLT charge arises (payable by the recipient spouse).

The SDLT charge applies to that percentage of the mortgage which equates to the percentage beneficial interest acquired by the recipient spouse (eg if a 50% beneficial interest is acquired the assumption of the mortgage debt is regarded as an assumption of 50% of the amount outstanding at the date of the transaction).

22.30 Where on the transfer of the beneficial interest the 'old' mortgage is redeemed and a 'new' mortgage is taken out an SDLT charge arises as above on the part of the recipient spouse (albeit any percentage is based on the quantum of the redeemed mortgage, not the quantum of the newly taken out mortgage).

Matrimonial breakdown

22.31 Under certain conditions the transfer of an interest in the matrimonial home from one spouse to the other following a breakdown of the marriage may be effected without CGT charge even though at the time of the transfer the

22.32 *Stamp duty and stamp duty land tax*

property is no longer the main residence of the transferor spouse (see paragraph 20.83).

SDLT exemption may also apply to such transfers.

Thus, where an interest in the ex-matrimonial home is transferred in pursuance of an order of the court on the granting of a divorce decree or judicial separation (ie an order of the court pursuant to which the parties to the marriage no longer have to cohabit) no SDLT is charged. Similarly, no SDLT is charged if the transfer is in pursuance of an agreement between the parties made in contemplation of the divorce or judicial separation (*FA 2003 Sch 3*).

Chattels

22.32 Often the purchase price of a residential property includes a sum which represents chattels to be included in the sale. Chattels are not land and therefore not subject to SDLT. However, any attempt to allocate a disproportionate amount of the consideration to the chattels will fail as provisions exist under which only a reasonable proportion of the aggregate consideration may be so allocated.

Arm's-length provisions

22.33 If no consideration is provided (including no assumption of any debt) in respect of a land transaction no SDLT is payable.

There are no 'arm's-length' type provisions (with one exception; see paragraph 22.34) which impute a market value consideration. Thus, an outright gift of land will not give rise to an SDLT charge.

22.34 However, where the transfer of the land is by the individual to a 'connected company' the land will be treated as having been transferred for a consideration equal to the market value of the land at the date of the transfer (*FA 2003 s 53*). This rule applies irrespective of the actual consideration paid. For this purpose an individual is connected to a company if the individual 'controls' (broadly, owns more than 50% of the voting or share capital) of the company.

22.35 Such a transaction might arise where, for example, a non-UK domiciled but UK resident individual owns UK land in respect of which an IHT liability on death is to be avoided. This is achievable by simply transferring the land to a non-UK resident and non-UK registered company, the shares of which are non-UK situs (see paragraphs 6.30 and 6.37) and thus outside the charge to IHT.

In such cases there is a trade-off between a saving of IHT on death and the incurring of an SDLT charge (and where the company is non-UK resident, a CGT charge).

Linked transactions

22.36 The basic thrust of the 'linked transaction' provisions (*FA 2003 s 108*) is to prevent one potentially large transaction (subject to SDLT at, say, 4%) being broken down into smaller transactions (each subject to SDLT at, say, 1% or even 0%). The provisions treat the various separate transactions as if they were a single transaction (ie the separate considerations are simply aggregated into one sum).

Broadly, a linked transaction is a transaction or series of transactions between the same vendor and purchaser. Thus, if one purchaser effects a purchase of land from a number of unrelated vendors such transactions are not linked transactions; similarly, a sale of land by one vendor to a number of unrelated purchasers does not constitute linked transactions.

22.37 An example of a linked transaction is where an attempt is made to split a purchase of a residential property into two separate purchases; a purchase of the house and a separate purchase of the surrounding land/garden. Even if one of the purchases is by one spouse and the other purchase is effected by the other spouse the transactions would be linked. SDLT is then payable on the aggregate consideration, not on the two separate considerations.

Summary

22.38 Stamp duty, SDRT and, in particular, SDLT are commonly overlooked when analysing the tax consequences of a particular transaction. With a maximum rate of 5% on the gross consideration SDLT represents a serious cost.

22.39 Inter-spouse transfers and/or transfers to other members of the family and/or transfers into and out of trusts may involve the assumption by the transferee of borrowings attached to property. SDLT is in principle payable in such cases as the assumption of such debt is treated as chargeable consideration.

22.40 Transactions involving trusts and the estates of deceased individuals are typically exempt transactions in respect of which no SDLT arises.

22.41 The SDLT legislation contains anti-avoidance provisions designed to prevent attempts to reduce the charge by 'artificial' means. Such provisions apply to 'linked transactions' and transfers to companies.

Part V

The international dimension

Chapter 23

Non-UK resident taxation

Background

23.1 This chapter looks at the tax treatment of individuals and trusts who are not resident in the UK. Despite non-UK residency, exposure to UK income tax or capital gains tax (CGT) may still arise eg where UK source income arises or UK situs property is owned.

23.2 The terms of a double tax agreement to which the UK is a party may modify the normal UK domestic tax treatment of any UK source income/capital gains (see Chapter 26).

This chapter examines the UK domestic tax provisions and ignores the impact of any possible overriding double tax agreement provisions (see paragraph 23.34 for comments on the impact of such agreements).

23.3 Non-UK residents are not exposed to UK tax on non-UK source income or non-UK source capital gains. However, inheritance tax (IHT) is chargeable on any non-UK resident individual who is domiciled in the UK or deemed domiciled within the UK on worldwide property (*IHTA 1984 s 267*; see paragraphs 10.5 and 10.9). For the non-UK resident individual who is non-UK domiciled IHT is leviable on UK situs property only (see paragraph 10.6).

Property (whether UK situs or not) in a non-UK resident trust created by a UK domiciled settlor (irrespective of residency) falls within the charge to IHT; an IHT charge is also leviable on UK situs property (only) in a non-UK resident trust created by a non-UK domiciled settlor (irrespective of residency; see Chapter 16).

23.4 Whilst the non-UK resident person (ie company and trust) may in principle be outside the charge to CGT and possibly exempt from income tax (eg with respect to disregarded income) UK anti-avoidance provisions may impute/deem that person's income and/or capital gains to a UK resident individual thus precipitating a UK tax charge thereon (see Chapter 18).

23.5 The remittance basis of tax applicable to non-UK domiciled but UK resident individuals is of no application to non-UK residents.

23.6 *Non-UK resident taxation*

Income tax

Individuals

23.6 In principle a non-UK resident individual is exposed to income tax on UK source income at the rates applicable to the UK resident individual (ie 10%/20%/40%/50% in respect of non-dividend source income (eg rental income)) and 10%, 32.5% and 42.5% in respect of dividend income for the tax year 2010–2011; 10%/20%/40% in respect of non-dividend source income (eg rental income) and 10% and 32.5% in respect of dividend income for the tax year 2009–2010 (see Chapter 2).

23.7 However, with certain exceptions, the non-UK resident individual is not entitled to any of the normal personal allowances.

Commonwealth citizens have in the past been entitled to claim personal allowances purely on the grounds of such citizenship. However, personal allowances are no longer (ie from 6 April 2010) available to Commonwealth citizens purely on this ground alone (*FA 2009 s 5* and *Sch 1*). Those individuals primarily affected include citizens of the Bahamas, the Maldives, St Lucia, Tanzania, Tonga and Vanuatu.

Those non-UK resident individuals who continue to be entitled to personal allowances include (*ITA 2007 s 56*):

- nationals of the EEA state;
- residents of the Channel Islands and the Isle of Man;
- former UK residents who reside abroad due to health reasons or for health reasons of a family member who is resident with the individual; and
- those individuals who are, or have been, employed in the service of the Crown.

Non-UK domiciled but UK resident individuals in the past were entitled to personal allowances but following the major changes introduced in *FA 2008* those who claim remittance basis treatment (see paragraph 24.7; on or after 6 April 2008) for a particular tax year in respect of their non-UK source income/gains are denied entitlement to personal allowances for that tax year (*ITA 2007 ss 809B* and *809G*; see paragraph 24.15).

23.8 The categories of UK source income subject to income tax on the part of the non-UK resident individual include property income (eg rental income arising from UK situs land) (*ITA 2007 s 263*); employment income received in respect of duties performed in the UK (*ITEPA 2003 s 25*); UK pensions (*ITEPA*

2003 s 27); and trading income (*ITTOIA 2005 s 6*). All these categories of income are subject to income tax at the higher rates (40% and 50% or 32.5% and 42.5% for the tax year 2010–2011) as well as the basic rate (20% for the tax year 2010–2011) and dividend ordinary rate (10% for the tax year 2010–2011) (*ITA 2007 s 6*).

In addition, UK source interest and dividends are subject to income tax but the quantum of any liability thereon (unlike the above categories of income) is limited (see paragraph 23.11).

23.9 A non-UK resident individual letting out UK situs property is subject to income tax at the basic rate (20%), the higher rate (40%) and the additional rate (50%) for the tax year 2010–2011 (*ITTOIA 2005 Part 3; ITA 2007 s 6*). Payments of rental income by the tenant directly to a non-UK resident individual are subject to deduction of income tax at source at the basic rate (*ITA 2007 ss 971 and 972*). The tenant is then obliged to account to HMRC for any income tax so deducted. Where the tenant pays the rent to a UK letting agent the rent is paid gross and it is then the responsibility of the letting agent to deduct income tax at source and account to HMRC for the tax so deducted (in this case, however, the tax deducted is levied on gross rents less deductible expenses (eg interest on borrowings used to purchase the property)).

The withholding of income tax at source can be circumnavigated if the non-UK resident individual applies to Financial Intermediaries and Claims Office (FICO) for confirmation that such rental income can be paid without deduction of tax at source; this requires various conditions to be satisfied (*The Taxation of Income from Land (Non-residents) Regulations SI 1995/2902*).

In any event the non-UK resident individual is required to file a tax return of rental income received less relevant deductible expenses (see Supplementary Pages 'UK property SA105' to the tax return; as a non-UK resident it is also necessary to complete Supplementary Pages 'Residence, remittance basis etc'; see paragraphs 5.3 and 5.5).

23.10 Similar tax returns are also required with respect to any employment income arising from UK duties (see Supplementary Pages 'Employment SA102') and any UK source trading income (see Supplementary Pages 'Self employment income SA103F') (see paragraph 5.3).

Disregarded income

23.11 The non-UK resident individual's overall exposure to income tax on UK source income (namely, disregarded income) may in fact be limited (*ITA 2007 ss 811 and 812*).

The income tax liability on such income cannot exceed the sum of:

23.12 Non-UK resident taxation

- sums representing income tax deducted from 'disregarded income';
- sums representing income tax that are treated as deducted from or paid in respect of 'disregarded income'; and
- any tax credits in respect of 'disregarded income';

plus

- the income tax liability of the individual if the whole of the individual's income (excluding disregarded income) is subject to income tax without any deduction for personal allowances.

(ITA 2007 s 811)

23.12 'Disregarded income' primarily consists of:

- disregarded savings and investment income (which includes dividend and interest income) (ITA 2007 s 825);
- disregarded pension income (ITA 2007 s 826); and
- disregarded social security income.

(ITA 2007 s 813)

23.13 With respect to dividend income no withholding taxes apply and thus no income tax charge arises thereon. Where the recipient individual is entitled to a personal allowance and is thus entitled to a tax credit (equal to one-ninth of the net amount of the dividend) the tax credit satisfies any income tax liability. If there is no entitlement to the tax credit the individual is treated as having paid income tax at the dividend ordinary rate (ie 10%) on the amount of the dividend 'grossed up' at the dividend ordinary rate (ie 10% for the tax year 2010–2011) (ITA 2007 ss 397 and 399).

The effect of the limit on the total income tax liability means that no additional income tax liability arises on any dividend income.

Example 1

Terry Space is non-UK resident and his sole source of UK income is dividend income.

The net amount of dividends for the tax year 2010–2011 is £9,000.

Terry is entitled to a personal allowance and is thus entitled to the dividend tax credit of £1,000 (ie one-ninth of the net dividend). His liability cannot exceed the amount of the tax credit of £1,000 and thus no further income tax charge arises.

If Terry is not entitled to a personal allowance (and hence is not entitled to a tax credit on the dividends) his liability cannot exceed sums representing income tax treated as paid in respect of the income; Terry is treated (under *ITA 2007 s 399*) as having paid income tax of £1,000 and thus no further income tax charge arises.

23.14 With respect to interest income, income tax is withheld at source at the basic rate (ie 20% for the tax year 2010–2011) applying at the date of payment (*ITA 2007 s 874*) although interest paid by a bank or building society on deposits is subject to deduction (again at the basic rate) under *ITA 2007 851* (not *ITA 2007 s 874*). However, interest paid by a bank or building society may still be paid without deduction of income tax at source where the individual makes a declaration confirming that he is not ordinarily resident in the UK (at the time of the declaration) (*ITA 2007 s 858*). Where two or more individuals are entitled to the interest (eg a joint account) all must be not ordinarily resident in the UK (see Form R105 'Application for a not ordinarily resident saver to receive interest without tax taken off'). However, the banks/building societies are under no obligation to accept the Form.

In the event an individual subsequently becomes ordinarily resident in the UK the bank/building society must be notified (*ITA 2007 s 858*).

23.15 It is the individual's 'ordinary residence' status in the UK which is important, not that of 'residence' (see paragraph 4.7).

23.16 The effect of the limit on the total income tax liability means that no additional income tax liability can arise on any interest income over and above any income tax withheld (if no such income tax is withheld no income tax charge arises).

Example 2

Harry Blue is a non-UK resident and non-UK ordinarily resident individual whose sole source of UK income is interest credited to a UK bank account.

Harry files the declaration (*ITA 2007 s 858*) under which his interest is credited without any income tax withheld at source.

Harry's income tax liability is nil.

23.17 *Non-UK resident taxation*

If Harry fails to file the above declaration the bank deducts income tax at the basic rate (ie 20% for the tax year 2010–2011). Harry's income tax liability is restricted to this amount.

23.17 Where the non-UK resident individual has UK source non-disregarded income (eg rental income) in addition to disregarded income it may be that the limit under *ITA 2007 s 811* (see paragraph 23.11) does not in fact result in any restriction of the individual's income tax liability.

Example 3

Charles and Diane are non-UK resident and non-UK ordinarily resident and are each entitled to the personal allowance for 2010–2011.

Their UK income is as follows:

	Charles (£)	Diane (£)
Gross rental income	4,000	10,000
Gross dividend income	10,000	1,000
Gross interest income	7,000	400

Charles' 'normal' income tax liability is:

20% of [£21,000 – £6,435] = £2,905.

Diane's 'normal' income tax liability is:

20% of [£11,400 – £6,435] = £993.

Charles' limit is the income tax charge on £4,000 of gross rental income (ignoring the personal allowance and his disregarded income of £17,000), namely, 20% of £4,000 (ie £800).

Diane's limit is the income tax charge on £10,000 of gross rental income (ignoring the personal allowance and her disregarded income of £1,400), namely, 20% of £10,000 (ie £2,000).

Charles's income tax liability is thus limited to £800 but Diane's income tax liability is not limited and is thus £993.

Trusts

23.18 Detailed treatment of non-UK resident trusts is provided in Chapter 18.

In principle, non-UK resident discretionary trusts are liable to income tax on UK source income at the trust rate of 50% (effective 6 April 2010; previously 40%) and the dividend trust rate of 42.5% (effective 6 April 2010; previously 32.5%) (see paragraph 18.21).

However, where the disregarded income provisions apply, any UK income tax on the disregarded income is limited to the amount of income tax deducted at source (in the same manner as applies to individuals; see paragraph 23.11) (*ITA 2007 ss 811* and *813*).

23.19 The disregarded income provisions apply where none of the beneficiaries are UK ordinary resident; the term 'beneficiary' includes individuals who are (eg beneficiaries of interest in possession trusts), or may become (eg discretionary trust beneficiaries), entitled to trust income or some benefit in respect thereof (*ITA 2007 s 812*).

Where, however, at least one beneficiary of the trust is an individual who is ordinarily resident in the UK the disregarded income rules do not apply (*ITA 2007 s 812*).

Companies

23.20 Non-UK resident companies are liable to income tax on UK source income (other than dividends) at the basic rate only (ie 20% for the tax year 2010–2011; for earlier tax years such companies were liable to the then basic rate (22%) on non-savings income and 20% on savings income) (*ITA 2007 s 11*); dividend income is subject to income tax at the dividend ordinary rate (ie 10% for the tax year 2010–2011) (*ITA 2007 s 14*). The 40% and 50% rates applicable to individuals (effective 6 April 2010) do not apply to companies.

However, where the non-UK resident company carries on a part of its trade within the UK through a UK permanent establishment (broadly, a fixed place of business) it is liable to corporation tax on its profit attributable to the permanent establishment; this includes the trading income and capital gains accruing on assets attributable to the permanent establishment (*CTA 2009 s 5*).

23.21 The non-UK resident company's overall exposure to income tax on certain UK source income (namely, disregarded company income) may be limited (*ITA 2007 ss 815* and *816*).

The income tax liability on such income cannot exceed the sum of:

- any amounts representing income tax deducted from the non-UK resident company's disregarded company income;

23.22 *Non-UK resident taxation*

- any amounts representing income tax that are treated as deducted from or paid in respect of that income: and
- any tax credits in respect of that income.

(*ITA 2007 s 815*)

23.22 'Disregarded company income' primarily consists of:

- disregarded savings and investment income (which includes dividend and interest income; *ITA 2007 s 825*); and
- disregarded annual payments (*ITA 2007 s 826*).

23.23 Dividend income is effectively exempt from income tax as the company is deemed to have paid income tax at the dividend ordinary rate (*ITA 2007 s 14; ITTOIA 2005 s 399*).

23.24 No income tax at source is deducted from interest on deposits with banks and building societies (*ITA 2007 ss 851* and *856*). Thus, such interest is exempt from income tax.

23.25 UK source rental income which does not qualify as disregarded income is subject to income tax at the basic rate (*ITA 2007 s 11*).

Capital gains tax

23.26 Non-UK resident persons (ie individuals, trusts or companies) are not within the charge to CGT on UK situs assets unless the person is carrying on a trade, or part of a trade, within the UK through a branch or agency (see paragraph 8.2); in this case CGT is chargeable on a disposal of the UK situs assets used for the purposes of the trade (*TCGA 1992 s 10*).

Inheritance tax

23.27 IHT is levied according to the domicile status of the individual, not the individual's residence status (see paragraph 10.5). Thus, non-UK residence on the part of the individual does not remove an IHT charge on UK (or indeed non-UK) situs property (see paragraph 23.3).

23.28 Property held in relevant property non-UK resident trusts (eg discretionary trusts) is within the charge to IHT unless the property qualifies as excluded property (see Chapter 13).

23.29 UK situs property of non-UK resident trusts in which a qualifying interest in possession (see paragraph 16.4) subsists is within the charge to IHT. Non-UK situs property of a non-UK resident trust in which a qualifying interest in possession subsists is similarly within the charge to IHT unless such property qualifies as excluded property (see Chapter 13).

General comments

23.30 CGT does not apply to most non-UK resident persons (ie individuals, trusts and companies) except in limited circumstances (see paragraph 23.26).

23.31 UK income tax whilst leviable on UK source income is for many non-UK resident persons not chargeable where such income qualifies as disregarded income (see paragraphs 23.12 and 23.22) primarily consisting of dividend and interest income.

UK source rental (and trading) income is chargeable at marginal rates of income tax for individuals; 50% for non-UK resident discretionary trusts (effective 6 April 2010); and the basic rate (ie 20% for the tax year 2010–2011) for non-UK resident companies.

23.32 As indicated above, an income tax liability arises on all UK source income unless such income qualifies as disregarded income. For non-UK resident discretionary trusts disregarded income treatment is only available if all the beneficiaries are non-UK ordinarily resident. It may be preferable for any UK investments to be undertaken by an underlying non-UK resident and registered company. This not only increases the possibility of disregarded income treatment but the charge on non-disregarded income (eg rental income) is restricted to the basic rate (20% for the tax year 2010–2011) as compared to the trust rate of 50% (for the tax year 2010–2011).

Such a structure also insulates the property of the discretionary trust against charges to IHT as the property of the trust is non-UK situs property (ie shares in the non-UK resident and registered company) and not UK situs property (ie the UK situs property being held by the company); this assumes the trust is created by a non-UK domiciled settlor thus causing excluded property treatment (see Chapter 13).

23.33 Non-UK resident discretionary trusts created by non-UK domiciled settlors (who are also non-UK resident) owning non-UK situs assets and receiving no UK source income are outside all UK taxes. However, where any of the beneficiaries are UK resident, income or capital distributions to such individuals may create UK income and/or CGT liabilities for the beneficiaries (see Chapter 18).

23.34 *Non-UK resident taxation*

23.34 A non-UK resident trust may be used as a substitute will and probate is avoided (see paragraph 27.114).

23.35 Non-UK resident individuals who are UK domiciled are subject to IHT on worldwide property; similarly UK and non-UK situs property of non-UK resident trusts created by UK domiciled settlors is also within the charge to IHT.

Non-UK domiciled individuals are within the charge to IHT with respect to UK situs assets. Such exposure may be eliminated or reduced by, for example, transferring the situs of the property outside the UK (eg by transferring the property to a non-UK registered company); insuring against the liability; creating a borrowing against the property; or, in the event of death, leaving the property to the surviving spouse.

Double taxation agreements

23.36 The UK is a party to a number of double tax agreements whose provisions may affect the UK domestic tax law treatment of the non-UK resident set out above (see Chapter 26). There are two types of agreement, namely, those which address issues concerning income tax and CGT and those which address issues concerning IHT.

23.37 The provisions of such agreements override UK tax domestic law (see paragraph 26.9).

Income tax and capital gains tax

23.38 In general, with respect to income tax and CGT, such agreements offer no protection from a UK income tax charge on UK source rental income although many agreements preclude the UK from levying an income tax charge on UK source interest income.

Most agreements provide for reduced withholding taxes on dividend payments but as the UK levies no such withholding such terms are of little impact (subject to a possible reimbursement of a part of the attaching tax credit in some cases).

The UK typically levies no CGT on disposals of UK situs assets and thus the terms of the agreements offer no further protection.

23.39 Some individuals are resident in the UK (under UK domestic law) and resident in another country (under its domestic law) ie the individual is dual resident. Such individuals are subject to tax in both countries. The terms of most agreements resolve this problem by deeming the individual to be a resident of one of the countries only (see paragraph 26.15).

It is therefore possible for a non-UK resident to also be a UK resident and for any resolution to be in favour of the UK; the individual is then subject to income tax and CGT as a normal UK resident (in which case this chapter is of no application to such individuals).

Inheritance tax

23.40 Compared to the number of agreements to which the UK is a party which address income tax and CGT matters (in excess of one hundred) the number of IHT agreements is significantly less (see paragraph 26.24).

23.41 The agreements are not identical and there are significant differences between those agreements concluded in the days of UK estate duty and those of more recent origin (see paragraph 26.25).

23.42 Despite its importance under UK domestic law the concept of 'deemed UK domicile' (*IHTA 1984 s 267*) is not recognised under some of the agreements (see paragraph 26.27) and some of the agreements only address IHT issues with respect to death, not lifetime transfers (see paragraph 26.27).

However, protection from an IHT charge may be granted with respect to some UK situs property for the non-UK domiciled individual (see paragraph 26.29).

Summary

23.43 Non-UK residents are in principle liable to income tax on UK source income.

23.44 A category of income referred to as disregarded income is subject to income tax but subject to limit; in practice, such income is in fact exempt.

23.45 Non-UK residents are not subject to CGT on UK situs assets (with a few exceptions).

23.46 Exposure to IHT for an individual depends upon domicile and not residence status.

23.47 *Non-UK resident taxation*

23.47 Double tax agreements to which the UK is a party may offer protection to the non-UK resident individual from charges to income tax and CGT. Similarly, an IHT charge on UK situs property, may be precluded for the non-UK domiciled individual.

Chapter 24

The non-UK domiciled individual, foreign source income and foreign capital gains

Background

24.1 This chapter examines in detail the income tax and capital gains tax (CGT) issues of the non-UK domiciled but UK resident individual with respect to non-UK source income and non-UK source capital gains referred to in the legislation as 'foreign income and gains' (*ITA 2007 Part 14 Chapter A1*).

'Foreign income and gains' refer to an individual's 'relevant foreign income' (RFI); 'relevant foreign earnings' and 'foreign chargeable gains' (*ITA 2007 s 809Z7*).

'RFI' refers to income arising from a source outside the UK including interest; dividends and foreign rental income (*ITTOIA 2005 s 830*).

'Relevant foreign earnings' refers to the individual's 'chargeable overseas earnings' (*ITA 2007 s 809Z7* and *ITEPA 2003 s 22*).

'Foreign chargeable gains' refers to chargeable gains accruing from disposals of assets situated outside the UK (*TCGA 1992 s 12*).

In principle, such individuals are liable to income tax and CGT on foreign source income and gains on the remittance basis (*ITTOIA 2005 s 832, ITEPA 2003 s 22* and *TCGA 1992 s 12*; see paragraphs 2.6, 2.10 and 8.1).

24.2 A UK domiciled and UK resident individual who is *not* ordinarily resident in the UK is also able in principle to utilise the remittance basis although not in an identical manner to that applying to the non-UK domiciled individual (eg non-UK source capital gains are not subject to remittance basis treatment for the UK domiciled and resident but non-ordinarily resident individual).

24.3 *FA 2008* changed significantly the manner and extent to which the

24.4 *The non-UK domiciled individual, foreign source, etc*

non-UK domiciled individual is able to take advantage of remittance basis treatment whether for income tax and/or CGT purposes.

In this chapter the term 'non-UK individual' is used to refer to a 'non-UK domiciled but UK resident individual' unless otherwise specified.

24.4 The options available to the non-UK domiciled individual to 'enjoy' the fruits of non-UK source income and capital gains in the UK without tax charge, pre-*FA 2008*, have been severely curtailed following *FA 2008*; transitional provisions have, however, to some degree ameliorated the adverse impact for foreign income and gains arising pre-6 April 2008.

24.5 The basic thrust of the provisions introduced in *FA 2008* is, in principle, twofold:

- the introduction of the need for certain non-UK domiciled individuals to make a formal claim for remittance basis treatment for a particular tax year; and

- the levying of an annual additional amount of tax of £30,000 where the non-UK domiciled individual has been resident in the UK for at least seven of the nine tax years immediately preceding that tax year.

24.6 The original proposal was that an annual 'charge' of £30,000 would be levied on non-UK domiciled individuals who wanted to utilise the remittance basis of taxation for a particular tax year. Under this original proposal the £30,000 was an additional charge over and above any income tax and/or CGT charge which would have arisen on any remittance to the UK. Thus, even if the individual had remitted all his foreign income and gains to the UK arising in the tax year the £30,000 charge would have applied in addition to the normal tax charges.

The original proposal, however, was not implemented. The £30,000 figure is now an additional tax charge not a pure charge. Thus, if for example, the non-UK domiciled individual remits all foreign income and gains arising in the tax year 2008–2009 to the UK in, say, the tax year 2008–2009 the £30,000 payable for 2008–2009 would be deemed to have been paid on some part of the remitted income and/or capital gains. In this case the £30,000 will not be a charge over and above the tax liability arising on the remitted income and/or capital gains but a part of it; that part of any such remittance in respect of which the £30,000 tax will be deemed to have already been paid is referred to as the 'nominated amount' (see paragraph 24.19).

In essence, the £30,000 annual additional tax charge under *FA 2008* (not the original proposals) may thus, *de facto*, not represent literally an additional amount of tax to be paid although in practice due to the working of the rules introduced this may prove to be the case.

Remittance basis treatment: the claim

24.7 The general approach of *FA 2008* is to require that all non-UK domiciled individuals (subject to one or two exceptions) are required to lodge a formal claim for remittance basis treatment to apply for a particular tax year (*ITA 2007 s 809B*).

24.8 The claim is an annual claim and needs to be lodged within four years of the 31 January following the end of the tax year in respect of which the claim is lodged (*ITA 2007 s 809B* and *TMA 1970 s 43*); the limit of four years applies for tax years 2010–2011 and thereafter (*FA 2008 Sch 39* and *SI 2009/403*). Pre-the tax year 2010–2011 the limit was five years.

However, where HMRC have served notice on the individual requiring completion of a tax return (under *TMA 1970 s 8*) *TMA 1970 s 42* requires that any claims for relief (including a claim under *ITA 2007 s 809B*) must be included in the tax return itself (*TMA 1970 ss 42* and *43* apply for *ITA 2007 s 809B* purposes; *ITA 2007 s 809B*).

24.9 The claim for remittance basis treatment needs to be made in relation to the tax year in which the foreign income and gains arise, not the tax year in which any remittance actually occurs (*ITTOIA 2005 s 832*).

Example 1

Claus Berlin, a non-UK domiciled but UK resident individual, is in receipt of non-UK source income of £50,000 in the tax year 2008–2009.

He remits the £50,000 in the tax year 2010–2011.

In order to take advantage of remittance basis treatment with respect to the £50,000 Claus must file a claim in respect of the tax year 2008–2009 not 2010–2011.

Thus, remittance basis treatment applies to the £50,000 even if for the tax year 2010–2011 no such claim is made (the claim for 2010–2011 if made relates to the non-UK source income and capital gains arising in that tax year).

24.10 However, not all non-UK domiciled individuals are required to claim remittance basis treatment for a tax year (yet may still be taxed as if such a claim had in fact been made) (*ITA 2007 ss 809D* and *809E*).

24.11 *The non-UK domiciled individual, foreign source, etc*

24.11 A claim for remittance basis treatment must be lodged by all categories of non-UK domiciled individual except in the following circumstances:

(a) those individuals whose 'unremitted foreign income and gains' (basically foreign income and capital gains arising in the relevant tax year less the amount of such income and/or gains which are remitted to the UK in that tax year) for the relevant tax year is less than £2,000 (*ITA 2007 s 809D*); or

(b) those individuals who have no UK source income or gains other than taxed investment income (income or gains within *ITA 2007 s 946* which have been taxed at source) of less than £100 arising in the relevant tax year, who have been UK resident in not more than six out of the nine tax years immediately preceding the relevant tax year and who have remitted no income or gains to the UK in the relevant tax year (*ITA 2007 s 809E*); or

(c) those individuals who have no UK source income or gains other than taxed investment income of less than £100 arising in the relevant tax year, who are under 18 throughout the relevant tax year and who have remitted no income or gains to the UK in the relevant tax year (*ITA 2007 s 809E*).

However, if the following conditions are satisfied, (a) above (assuming that it does otherwise apply) does not apply and the individual is simply exempt from any liability to income tax. The conditions are that *ITA 2007 s 809B* does not apply for the relevant tax year (ie no claim is lodged) and the following conditions are also satisfied:

(i) he has employment income from duties performed wholly or partly in the UK;

(ii) if he has relevant foreign earnings they are £10,000 or less all of which is subject to foreign tax;

(iii) if he has relevant foreign income consisting of interest it is £100 or less all of which is subject to foreign tax;

(iv) he has no other foreign income or gains;

(v) he would not be liable to income tax at other than the basic rate of income tax or the starting rate for savings (if the remittance basis did not apply); and

(vi) he does not make a tax return under *TMA 1970 s 8*.

(*ITA 2007 ss 828A to 828D*)

24.12 Thus, for those individuals falling within (a), (b) or (c) of paragraph 24.11 remittance basis treatment applies automatically without the need for a formal claim to be made. However, it is possible for the individual under (a), (b) or (c) to disclaim such remittance basis treatment by giving notice in the tax return under *TMA 1970 s 8* that *ITA 2007 ss 809D* or *809E* (as the case may be) is not to apply in relation to the individual for that year (*ITA 2007 ss 809D* and *809E*).

24.13 For those non-UK domiciled individuals not falling within (a), (b), or (c) of paragraph 24.11, a formal claim for remittance basis treatment is required unless *ITA 2007 ss 828A* to *828D* apply (ie (i) to (vi) are satisfied). Such individuals include those whose unremitted foreign income and gains are £2,000 or more for the tax year and who are 18 or over in the tax year and have been UK resident for at least seven out of the immediately preceding nine tax years. Such individuals also inlcude those whose unremitted foreign income and gains are £2,000 or more for the tax year and who have been UK resident for less than seven out of of the immediately preceding nine tax years who have remitted foreign income or gains in the tax year.

Example 2

Bertram Munich is non-UK domiciled but UK resident and aged 50.

Bert has resided continuously in the UK for the last 15 tax years and his unremitted foreign income and gains for 2010–2011 are £2,000 or more.

For the tax year 2010–2011 Bert needs to lodge a claim for remittance basis treatment.

Example 3

Jose Madrid is non-UK domiciled but UK resident and aged 50.

Jose has resided continuously in the UK for the last four tax years prior to 2010–2011 and has remitted foreign income and gains from the tax year 2008–2009 in respect of which a claim for remittance treatment has been filed. The unremitted foreign income and gains for 2010–2011 are £3,500.

Example 4

Jose Estepona is non-UK domiciled but UK resident and aged 17.

Jose has resided continuously in the UK for the last five tax years prior to 2010–2011 and has remitted foreign income and gains which arose in 2010–2011 leaving unremitted foreign income and gains of £2,250.

For the tax year 2010–2011 Jose needs to lodge a claim for remittance basis treatment.

24.14 *The non-UK domiciled individual, foreign source, etc*

Examples 5 to 7 illustrate those non-UK domiciled individuals who do not need to lodge a formal claim for remittance basis to apply:

Example 5

Bertram Munich is non-UK domiciled but UK resident and aged 50.

Bert has resided continuously in the UK for the last 15 tax years.

For the tax year 2010–2011 Bert's non-UK source income amounts to £65,000 of which £64,000 is remitted to the UK in 2010–2011.

For the tax year 2010–2011 Bert falls into (a) in paragraph 24.11 and thus does not need to lodge a claim for remittance basis treatment.

Example 6

Jose Madrid is non-UK domiciled but UK resident and aged 17.

Jose has resided continuously in the UK for the last seven tax years prior to 2010–2011.

For the tax year 2010–2011 Jose's non-UK source income amounts to £65,000 of which £64,000 is remitted to the UK in 2010–2011.

For the tax year 2010–2011 Jose falls into (a) in paragraph 24.11 and thus does not need to lodge a claim for remittance basis treatment.

Example 7

Jose Estepona is non-UK domiciled but UK resident and aged 50.

Jose has resided continuously in the UK for the last five tax years prior to 2010–2011.

Jose has no UK source income or gains for 2010–2011 and has not remitted any of his non-UK source income or gains to the UK.

For the tax year 2010–2011 Jose falls into (b) in paragraph 24.11 and thus does not need to lodge a claim for remittance basis treatment.

24.14 The reference to 'less than £2,000' in *ITA 2007 s 809D* refers to the individual's 'unremitted foreign income and gains' for the relevant tax year.

The non-UK domiciled individual, foreign source, etc **24.16**

Thus, for example, if the individual's foreign income and gains for, say, the tax year 2010–2011 amount to £150,000 of which £149,000 is remitted to the UK no formal claim for remittance basis treatment is required; a remittance of £148,000 would however precipitate the need for a formal claim to be lodged.

Where the tax year is split into a period of residence and a period of non-residency (under ESC A11 and/or ESC D2) on the part of the individual (eg when a non-UK domiciled individual arrives in, or leaves, the UK) the 'less than £2,000' is ascertained for the complete tax year (ie the level of unremitted foreign income and gains is that for the complete tax year).

Consequences of the claim

Loss of allowances

24.15 Where it is necessary for the non-UK domiciled individual to claim remittance basis treatment such a claim is made as part of the individual's self-assessment tax return (see Supplementary Pages 'Residence, remittance basis etc SA 109'; see Chapter 5). However, the consequences of lodging such a claim are that the individual is not entitled for the tax year to which the claim relates to either a personal allowance or the annual exempt amount for CGT purposes (*ITA 2007 s 809G*).

For those non-UK domiciled individuals who are able to utilise remittance basis treatment without the need for a formal claim no loss of personal allowance or annual exempt amount occurs.

The £30,000 tax charge

24.16 For the non-UK domiciled individual who has been resident in the UK for at least seven tax years out of the immediately preceding nine tax years prior to the relevant tax year (and who is also aged 18 or over in that tax year), lodgement of the formal claim results in the need for a tax payment of £30,000 for the relevant tax year. This £30,000 is effectively attributed to the amount of foreign income and gains 'nominated' by the individual for the tax year (*ITA 2007 ss 809B and 809C*).

As part of the formal claim the individual is required to nominate an amount of foreign income and/or foreign capital gains (*ITA 2009 ss 809B and 809C*).

Example 8

Claire Texas is a non-UK domiciled but UK resident individual aged 22.

24.17 *The non-UK domiciled individual, foreign source, etc*

Claire has been resident in the UK for six tax years out of the preceding nine tax years prior to the tax year 2009–2010.

Claire is not required to pay the £30,000 if she claims remittance basis treatment for the tax year 2009–2010.

However, for the tax year 2010–2011 Claire has been UK resident for seven out of the immediately preceding nine tax years and thus if she claims remittance basis treatment for the tax year 2010–2011 she is required to pay the £30,000.

24.17 The £30,000 is to be paid through the normal self-assessment system but care is needed if the amount is paid out of foreign income and gains remitted to the UK for this purposes. Where the £30,000 is paid from foreign income and gains *directly* to HMRC by cheque or electronic transfer the £30,000 will itself not be treated as a remittance of the foreign income and gains (*ITA 2007 s 809V*). Thus, no tax liability arises thereon. In addition, if the £30,000 is not deemed to have been remitted this amount must be deemed to have remained outside the UK and thus continues to be available for matching whether under the ordering rules referred to in paragraphs 24.26 and 24.29 or the mixed fund rules referred to in paragraph 24.105.

Any cheque needs to be drawn on a non-UK bank account and any electronic transfer should not be made via a UK bank account.

Where the transfer of the foreign income and gains is via a UK bank account (eg of the individual), prior to onward transmission to HMRC, the £30,000 is treated as a remittance and potentially taxable depending upon the precise nature of the funds utilised to effect the payment.

The utilisation of nominated foreign income and gains to discharge the £30,000 does not cause the ordering rules of *ITA 2007 s 809J* to apply as the nominated income/gains are not treated as remitted (*ITA 2007 s 809V*; see paragraph 24.19).

24.18 The full amount of the £30,000 is required to be paid even if the non-UK domiciled individual is UK resident for only part of the tax year (ie there is no facility for an apportionment of the £30,000).

Nomination of foreign income and gains

24.19 As stated in paragraph 24.16 the individual is required to 'nominate' an amount of either foreign income and/or gains for the relevant tax year (*ITA 2007 ss 809B* and *809C*).

24.20 The nomination is designed to produce a 'relevant tax increase' (RTI) in the income tax payable of £30,000 exactly (ie the actual income tax and CGT payable of the individual for the relevant tax year is increased by exactly £30,000). The RTI is:

- the total amount of income tax and CGT payable by the individual for the relevant tax year (assuming remittance basis treatment) but also including the amount of tax levied on the nominated income/gains (which are to be subject to tax on the arising basis even though such income/gains have not de facto been remitted)

minus

- the total amount of income tax and CGT that would be payable by the individual for that tax year apart from the income tax and CGT charged on the nominated income and/or gains (assuming remittance basis treatment).

(ITA 2007 s 809C)

Note also that the RTI is based upon a comparison of UK tax 'payable' not a comparison of UK tax 'liability'; thus, *inter alia*, any foreign tax credits are deducted in ascertaining UK tax 'payable' (which means, other things being equal, a greater nomination of foreign income/gains will be required where foreign tax credits are available).

Example 9

Antonio Italy is a non-UK domiciled but UK resident individual.

In the tax year 2010–2011 he receives a UK salary of £40,000 (assume no income tax deducted at source) and RFI of £180,000 (not subject to any foreign tax).

No foreign income is remitted to the UK.

Antonio wishes to know how much of his foreign income he needs to nominate to produce a RTI of £30,000.

A

Non-savings income

20% on £37,400	£7,480
40% on [£40,000–£37,400]	£1,040

Savings income

40% on N (assume 'N' is the nominated income).

24.20 *The non-UK domiciled individual, foreign source, etc*

The income tax levied on N needs to produce an income tax charge of £30,000.

Thus:

N x 40% = £30,000

(ie N = £75,000).

Thus, of the RFI of £180,000 the nominated amount (N) is £75,000.

As a check:

A

Non-savings income

20% on £37,400	£7,480
40% on [£40,000–£37,400]	£1,040
Savings income	
40% on £75,000	£30,000
Total income tax payable	£38,520 X

B

Non-savings income

20% on £37,400	£7,480
40% on [£40,000–£37,400]	£1,040
Total income tax payable	£8,520 Y

RTI = X – Y = £30,000.

Example 10

Antonio Italy is a non-UK domiciled but UK resident individual.

In the tax year 2010–2011 he receives a UK salary of £40,000 (assume no income tax deducted at source) and RFI of £180,000 (after deduction of a 10% local withholding tax).

No foreign income is remitted to the UK.

The non-UK domiciled individual, foreign source, etc 24.20

Antonio wishes to know how much of his foreign income he needs to nominate to produce a RTI of £30,000.

A

Non-savings income

20% on £37,400	£7,480
40% on [£40,000–£37,400]	£1,040

Savings income

40% on N (assume 'N' is the nominated income).

The income tax levied on N needs to produce an income tax charge of £30,000 after credit for any foreign tax.

Thus:

$[N \times 40\%] - [[N/£200,000] \times £20,000] = £30,000$

(ie N = £100,000).

Thus, of the RFI of £180,000 the nominated amount (N) is £100,000.

As a check:

A

Non-savings income

20% on £37,400	£7,480
40% on [£40,000–£37,400]	£1,040
Savings income	
40% on £100,000	£40,000
Less: Foreign tax credit	(£10,000)
	£30,000
Total income tax payable	£38,520 X

597

24.21 *The non-UK domiciled individual, foreign source, etc*

B

Non-savings income

20% on £37,400	£7,480
40% on [£40,000–£37,400]	£1,040
Total income tax payable	£8,520 Y

RTI = X – Y = £30,000.

A comparison of the nominated amount in Examples 8 and 9 reveals that where foreign taxes are levied on foreign income which are creditable against any UK tax charge means N needs to be increased accordingly.

24.21 Examples 9 and 10 assume that no remittance of any foreign income has occurred. Where, however, foreign income is remitted the principles remain the same.

Example 11

Paulo Brasil is a non-UK domiciled but UK resident individual.

In the tax year 2010–2011 he receives a UK salary of £60,000 (assume no income tax deducted at source) and RFI of £180,000 of which £40,000 is remitted to the UK.

Paulo wishes to know how much of his foreign income he needs to nominate to produce a RTI of £30,000.

A

Non-savings income

20% on £37,400	£7,480
40% on [£60,000–£37,400]	£9,040

Savings income

40% on £40,000	£16,000

40% on N (assume 'N' is the nominated income).

The income tax levied on N needs to produce an income tax charge of £30,000.

Thus:

[40% x £50,000] + [50% x [N – £50,000]] = £30,000.

(Note that when N is added to the other taxable income it will fall into the 40% and 50% bands of income tax; 50% applies above £150,000.)

(ie N = £70,000).

Thus, of the RFI of £180,000 the nominated amount (N) is £70,000.

As a check:

A

Non-savings income

20% on £37,400	£7,480
40% on [£60,000–£37,400]	£9,040

Savings income

40% on £40,000	£16,000
40% on £50,000 (of N)	£20,000
50% on £20,000 (of N)	£10,000
Total income tax payable	£62,520 X

B

Non-savings income

20% on £37,400	£7,480
40% on [£60,000–£37,400]	£9,040

Savings income

40% on £40,000	£16,000
Total income tax payable	£32,520 Y

RTI = X – Y = £30,000.

24.22 There is no requirement for the individual to actually nominate an amount of foreign income and gains which produces an RTI of £30,000. However, where an actual nomination by the individual produces an RTI of less than £30,000 the individual is treated as if he had also nominated an additional amount such that the RTI on the actual amount nominated plus the additional amount treated as nominated equals £30,000 (*ITA 2007 s 809H*).

This distinction between actual amounts nominated and the amount treated as nominated is important.

24.23 *The non-UK domiciled individual, foreign source, etc*

24.23 First, any amount treated as nominated is treated as income (not capital gains) thus producing a charge to income tax (not CGT).

Second, the income which is treated as nominated is not subject to the ordering rules which are discussed below (ie where income and/or capital gains which have actually been nominated are in whole or in part remitted to the UK at a time when any non-UK source income/gains (non-nominated) have not been remitted, ordering rules apply to determine what income/gains are deemed to have been remitted) (*ITA 2007 ss 809I and 809J*).

Third, when the income which is actually nominated is remitted to the UK the £30,000 which has been paid in respect thereof is offsettable against any income tax or CGT charge thereon. However, where the income/gains treated as nominated is remitted to the UK an income tax charge arises thereon and no part of the £30,000 can be regarded as having already been paid in respect thereof. Double tax therefore appears to apply to the income treated as nominated should it ever be remitted to the UK.

24.24 Assuming the individual nominates the requisite amount so as to produce an RTI of £30,000 (ie there is no need for any income to be treated as nominated) the individual's personal tax position is relevant as this affects the quantum of foreign income and gains which need to be nominated.

Thus, for example, in the case of a 40% income tax payer the amount of foreign income to be nominated would be £75,000 (ie £30,000/0.4). An income tax rate of 40% on £75,000 produces £30,000.

If in the relevant tax year the individual is a basic rate (ie 20%) taxpayer the amount of foreign income to be nominated would be £150,000 (ie £30,000/0.2).

Where the nominated amount comprises exclusively foreign chargeable gains the nominated amount would be £166,667 (ie £30,000/0.18) assuming a rate of CGT of 18%; a rate of CGT of 28% would require a nomination of £107,143 (£30,000/0.28).

It is also possible for the nominated amount to comprise a mixture of foreign income and foreign chargeable gains.

24.25 Where it is necessary for HMRC to treat the individual as having nominated an amount of foreign income/gains (due to an actual under-nomination on the part of the individual) whether the individual has sufficient foreign income/gains to accommodate the nominated amount treated as having been made is irrelevant (*ITA 2007 s 809H*).

Example 12

Henri Nice is a non-UK domiciled but UK resident individual and has been resident in the UK for the last 15 tax years. He is 46.

Assume for simplicity that Henri has no UK source income/gains.

Prior to the tax year 2010–2011 Henri had never received any non-UK source income or gains. However, in the tax year 2010–2011 he anticipates generating one of the following amounts of foreign source income:

(a) £45,000.
(b) £93,700.
(c) £180,000.

Henri is proposing to claim remittance basis treatment for 2010–2011 as he does not wish to remit any of his foreign income to the UK.

(a) Henri decides to nominate the £45,000. This produces an income tax charge of [20% x £37,400 + 40% x £7,600] (ie £10,520).

HMRC therefore deem a further £48,700 to have been nominated so as to produce an RTI of £30,000.

It thus makes no sense for Henri to make a remittance basis claim as the cost to him is £30,000. Without the claim, a liability of only £10,520 arises (ignoring the personal allowance; recall that such an allowance is only available if the individual does not claim remittance basis treatment).

(b) It does not matter under this option whether a claim for remittance basis treatment is made or not. In either case the income tax charge is £30,000 (ignoring the personal allowance as above).

(c) By nominating £93,700 of income precipitates the £30,000 tax charge. By claiming remittance basis treatment an income tax charge of £67,520 is avoided; thus, producing a net tax saving of £37,520.

24.26 Given that £30,000 of tax has been paid on the nominated foreign income/gains it appears sensible that any remittance to be effected to the UK should be out of this nominated amount as the £30,000 is then offsettable against any tax charge on the remittance.

Unfortunately, where any part of the actual (not treated) nominated income/gains whether for the current tax year or any previous tax year (beginning with the tax year 2008–2009) is remitted to the UK and the individual has other non-UK source income and/or capital gains (not nominated) whether arising in the tax year or any previous tax year (beginning with the tax year 2008–2009) which have not in their entirety been remitted to the UK, the quantum of nominated amount remitted is treated as a remittance out of the latter (ie the non-nominated amount) and thus subject to tax (the £30,000 not being deemed to apply to this substituted amount).

24.27 *The non-UK domiciled individual, foreign source, etc*

The aggregate actual nominated amount thus remains intact (ie none of it is assumed to have been remitted to the UK) and an amount of the non-nominated income or gains is substituted thus precipitating a tax charge thereon.

The precise foreign income and gains which are regarded as so remitted in place of the nominated amount are determined under a set of 'ordering rules' (*ITA 2007 ss 809I* and *809J*; see paragraph 24.29) (any remittance of capital gains in the tax year 2010–2011 under these ordering rules are treated as remitted pre-23 June 2010 thus falling subject to capital gains tax at the 18%, not 28%, rate of CGT; *F (No 2) Act 2010 s 2* and *Sch 1*).

24.27 The implication of these ordering rules (according to HMRC) is that until the individual's entire foreign source income and gains (other than the actual nominated amounts) arising since 6 April 2008 have been remitted to the UK it is not possible for the individual to access the 'tax-free' actual nominated amounts for each tax year.

24.28 The substitution of non-nominated income/gains for remittances of actual nominated income/gains is carried out by applying a sequence of rules to the various categories of foreign source income/capital gains for the relevant tax year. Where insufficient non-nominated income/gains arise in the relevant tax year to substitute for the nominated income/gains remitted the whole process is repeated for the immediately preceding tax year and so on until a full matching has occurred; effectively a last in first out (LIFO) basis approach (*ITA 2007 s 809J*).

However, this matching process only matches remitted nominated income/gains with unremitted non-nominated income/gains which have arisen on or after 6 April 2008; pre-6 April 208 foreign income/gains are thus ignored for this matching purpose.

It should also be noted that the remitted nominated income/gains are matched to unremitted non-nominated foreign income/gains (as indicted above) on a tax year by tax year basis; such unremitted foreign income/gains includes such income/gains which have arisen in the tax year even though it may have been alienated by, for example, spending outside the UK. In other words any alienation of the unremitted non-nominated foreign income/gains is ignored and is treated as if it is still available for matching.

24.29 The categories utilised for matching and the order of the matching is as follows:

- relevant foreign earnings (other than those subject to foreign tax);
- foreign specific employment income (other than income subject to foreign tax);

The non-UK domiciled individual, foreign source, etc **24.34**

- RFI (other than income subject to foreign tax);
- foreign chargeable gains (other than gains subject to foreign tax);
- relevant foreign earnings subject to foreign tax;
- foreign specific employment income subject to foreign tax;
- RFI subject to foreign tax; and
- foreign chargeable gains subject to foreign tax.

(ITA 2007 s 809J)

24.30 According to HMRC, the ordering rules (of *ITA 2007 s 809J*) are invoked for the tax year when for the first time an amount of nominated income/gains is remitted to the UK. These rules then continue to apply until all the individual's foreign income and gains from that tax year and earlier tax years (back to the tax year 2008–2009) have been remitted to the UK.

Thus, once any nominated income/gains are remitted, even where remittances are then made from the non-nominated categories of foreign source income and gains the above ordering rules will also determine and then substitute the deemed remittances resulting from the application of these rules for any actual remittances (in other words, the actual remittances in a sense are deemed not to have occurred and in their place are substituted the remittances of the categories of income produced by the above rules).

24.31 However, it appears arguable that the ordering rules should only apply for the tax year in which any nominated income/gains are remitted; as stated in paragraph 24.27 HMRC disagree.

24.32 Where, however, the individual does not remit to the UK any part of the actual nominated amount in any tax year (ie does not remit any part of earlier tax years' nominated amounts or that amount for the tax year concerned) there is no requirement for the above ordering rules to be applied to determine which foreign source income and gains have been remitted to the UK. The amounts actually remitted will simply be identified with their specific source and subject to tax as normal (and/or subject to the 'mixed fund' rules; see paragraph 24.105).

24.33 The nominated amount is an amount which is to be nominated in each tax year (ie it is not a simple one-off nomination).

24.34 The nomination of foreign income and gains can be made in respect of any specific amount of such income/gains; thus, for example, the RFI (ie interest) arising from a specific foreign bank deposit may be nominated; a particular foreign chargeable gain may be nominated; etc. The important point

24.34 *The non-UK domiciled individual, foreign source, etc*

is that it must be possible to identify at any time any foreign income/gains so nominated in order that these amounts can be monitored and, in particular, any remittances out of such amounts be identified.

As a general rule, due to the penal ordering rules (see paragraph 24.29) remittances out of nominated income/gains should be avoided.

Example 13

Felix Stuttgart is a non-UK domiciled but UK resident individual who wishes to claim remittance basis treatment. Due to his period of residence in the UK he is required to pay the £30,000 tax charge and make an appropriate nomination.

In the tax year 2010–2011 Felix receives the following income and capital gains:

£100,000 of foreign bank interest (no foreign tax)

£200,000 of relevant foreign earnings (no foreign tax)

£300,000 of foreign capital gains (no foreign tax)

£150,000 of foreign capital gains (net of foreign tax at 20%; (ie £187,500 gross)).

Each of the above amounts has been credited to separate non-UK bank accounts (ie there are no 'mixed funds').

He nominates £75,000 of his 'relevant foreign earnings' but intends to remit none of this amount. As a consequence his income tax liability is based upon the actual categories of income/gains actually remitted.

The £30,000 tax charge has been satisfied out of the relevant foreign earnings; such an amount is, however, not regarded as remitted to the UK. This appears to mean that not only is the amount not subject to tax but this amount is still treated as existing in the foreign bank account (ie there is still £200,000 of relevant foreign earnings).

He wants to know his tax position should any of the following occur:

(a) a remittance of £50,000 of the bank interest; or

(b) a remittance of the £150,000 of the foreign capital gains subject to foreign tax; or

(c) a remittance of £50,000 of the foreign capital gains.

For simplicity assume Felix is a 40% taxpayer and pays CGT at 28%.

(a) The remittance gives rise to an income tax liability of £20,000 (ie 40% of £50,000). The aggregate tax liability is thus £50,000 (ie £20,000 plus the £30,000 tax charge).

(b) The remittance gives rise to CGT liability of £52,500 (ie 28% of £187,500) reduced by the foreign tax paid of £37,500 to £15,000. The aggregate tax liability is thus £82,500 (ie £52,500 plus the £30,000 tax charge).

(c) The remittance gives rise to a capital gains tax liability of £14,000 (ie 28% of £50,000). The aggregate tax liability is thus £64,000 (ie £14,000 plus the £30,000 tax charge).

Example 14

Felix Stuttgart is a non-UK domiciled but UK resident individual who wishes to claim remittance basis treatment. Due to his period of residence in the UK he is required to pay the £30,000 tax charge and make an appropriate nomination.

In the tax year 2010–2011 Felix receives the following income and capital gains:

£100,000 of foreign bank interest (no foreign tax)

£200,000 of relevant foreign earnings (no foreign tax)

£300,000 of foreign capital gains (no foreign tax)

£150,000 of foreign capital gains (net of foreign tax at 20%; (ie £187,500 gross)).

Each of the above amounts has been credited to separate non-UK bank accounts (ie there are no 'mixed funds').

Assume Felix transfers £75,000 of his relevant foreign earnings to a separate account and nominates the £75,000 of his 'relevant foreign earnings'. He remits £25,000 of his nominated income amount.

The £30,000 tax charge is satisfied out of the relevant foreign earnings.

He wants to know his tax position should any of the following occur, which are remittances in addition to the £25,000 remittance:

24.34 *The non-UK domiciled individual, foreign source, etc*

(a) a remittance of £50,000 of the bank interest; or

(b) a remittance of the £150,000 of the foreign capital gains subject to foreign tax; or

(c) a remittance of £50,000 of the foreign capital gains.

For simplicity assume Felix is a 40% taxpayer and pays CGT at 28%.

As Felix has remitted £25,000 of his £75,000 actual nominated amount and has not remitted all his non-nominated income/gains which have accrued since 6 April 2008 it is necessary to 'match' the remittances under (a), (b) and (c) in the order set out below (see paragraph 24.29):

- relevant foreign earnings;
- foreign-specific employment income;
- RFI;
- foreign chargeable gains;
- relevant foreign earnings subject to foreign tax;
- foreign-specific employment income subject to foreign tax;
- RFI subject to foreign tax;
- foreign chargeable gains subject to foreign tax.

(a) The remittance of £25,000 of relevant foreign earnings (ie the nominated amount) plus the remittance of £50,000 of bank interest amounts to £75,000. Under the ordering rules this £75,000 is deemed to have been remitted out of the £200,000 of relevant foreign earnings precipitating an income tax liability of £30,000 (ie 40% of £75,000). The aggregate income tax liability is thus £60,000 (ie including the £30,000 tax charge).

Although *de facto* only £170,000 of relevant foreign earnings actually exists outside the UK (as £30,000 has been used to discharge the £30,000 tax charge) as no remittance of the £30,000 is assumed the full £200,000 is deemed to continue to exist.

(b) The remittance of £150,000 of foreign capital gains subject to foreign tax plus the remittance of £25,000 of relevant foreign earnings gives rise to an aggregate remittance of £175,000. This £175,000 is deemed to have been remitted out of the £200,000 of relevant foreign earnings precipitating an income tax liability of £70,000 (ie 40% of £175,000) plus the £30,000 tax charge producing an aggregate tax liability of £100,000.

Although of the remittance of £175,000 some £150,000 is actually a remittance of foreign chargeable gains, under the ordering rules

The non-UK domiciled individual, foreign source, etc **24.35**

the £150,000 is deemed to be a remittance of relevant foreign earnings and thus any credit for the foreign capital gains tax is lost. In addition, although a capital gains tax charge at 28% would normally be levied as the remittance is deemed to be a remittance of income the 40% rate applies. Furthermore, a total remittance of £175,000 of relevant foreign earnings is deemed to occur even though de facto only £170,000 of relevant foreign earnings actually subsists (after the £30,000 tax charge payment).

(c) The remittance of £50,000 of foreign capital gains plus the remittance of £25,000 of relevant foreign earnings gives rise to a remittance of £75,000. This £75,000 is deemed to have been remitted out of the £200,000 of relevant foreign earnings precipitating an income tax liability of £30,000 (ie 40% of £75,000). The aggregate income tax liability is thus £60,000.

Although Felix remitted £50,000 of foreign capital gains (which should precipitate a capital gains tax liability based on 28%) the application of the 'matching' rules results in this amount being deemed to be a remittance out of 'relevant foreign earnings' on which the liability is to income tax at 40%.

Under each of options (a), (b) and (c) although Felix actually remits £25,000 from his nominated amount of £75,000 this is substituted as a remittance from 'relevant foreign earnings' which means that the £75,000 of nominated income is deemed to still exist outside the UK (ie the £25,000 of nominated income is not regarded as having been remitted to the UK).

Paying the £30,000 or not

24.35 Example 12 illustrates the benefit or otherwise of claiming remittance basis treatment given the need to discharge each tax year the £30,000 tax charge.

In taking the decision as to whether to claim remittance basis treatment or not account needs to be taken of the consequent effects of any anti-avoidance provisions.

For example, in the event that remittance basis treatment is not to be claimed, foreign income of non-UK resident trusts created by non-UK domiciled but UK resident settlors under which the settlor or his spouse may benefit is likely to be treated as the settlor's income on which an income tax charge arises (either under *ITTOIA 2005 s 624* and/or *ITA 2007 s 720*; see Chapter 18). Similarly, capital gains of non-UK resident companies are apportionable to non-UK domiciled but UK resident shareholders (*TCGA 1992 s 13*; see Chapter 18).

24.36 *The non-UK domiciled individual, foreign source, etc*

Thus, the application of the anti-avoidance provisions where remittance basis treatment is not claimed may significantly increase the individual's aggregate income tax and CGT liabilities. However, it also follows that the £30,000 tax charge does not need to be paid.

It is therefore a matter of 'trade-off' between each of the two options.

Example 15

Dominic Barcelona, a non-UK domiciled but UK resident individual, needs to pay the £30,000 tax charge for the tax year 2010–2011 should he decide to elect for remittance basis treatment.

Some years ago he set up a non-UK resident trust under which he may benefit. The annual income of the trust is usually around £200,000.

Under the anti-avoidance provisions this income is imputed to Dominic and thus subject to income tax on his part unless remittance basis treatment applies.

The 'trade-off' is thus claiming remittance basis treatment and incurring the £30,000 tax charge but avoiding the income tax charge on the £200,000 or, not claiming remittance basis treatment, avoiding the £30,000 tax charge but incurring an income tax charge at the 40% and 50% income tax rates (applicable for the tax year 2010–2011) on the £200,000.

Prima facie, claiming remittance basis treatment seems the better option.

Remittances to the UK

24.36 Pre-*FA 2008*, the provisions which determine whether a remittance to the UK occurs depend upon whether the remittance is one of employment income, RFI or capital gains (ie the provisions in each case are slightly different).

FA 2008 provides a new set of provisions which apply irrespective of whether the remittance is one of employment income, RFI or capital gains (ie the same rules apply).

In view of the changes, transitional provisions are provided designed to 'ease' the transition from the pre-*FA 2008* rules to the post-*FA 2008* rules (*FA 2008 Sch 7*; see paragraph 24.70).

24.37 *FA 2008* introduces broad ranging provisions designed to identify when remittances of foreign income and capital gains occur and the amount of such remittances. Provision is also made to exempt certain otherwise taxable

The non-UK domiciled individual, foreign source, etc **24.41**

remittances (see paragraph 24.92) and new rules are introduced to ascertain precisely which category of income/gains are remitted from so-called 'mixed funds' (*ITA 2007 s 809K*; see paragraph 24.105).

24.38 The new provisions apply specifically to:

- relevant foreign earnings charged on the remittance basis;
- RFI charged on the remittance basis;
- foreign chargeable gains charged on the remittance basis;
- offshore income gains (OIGs) (treated for remittance purposes as RFI); and
- various anti-avoidance provisions (eg *TCGA 1992 s 87*).

(ITA 2007 s 809K)

24.39 These new provisions are effective from 6 April 2008 although there is a degree of retrospection to them and thus it is not safe to assume that all pre-6 April 2008 foreign income and gains of the individual can be remitted and taxed according to the pre-*FA 2008* provisions.

24.40 In very broad terms, post-*FA 2008*, foreign income or gains of the non-UK domiciled individual may be regarded as having been remitted to the UK (and thus taxable) where the individual or a so-called 'relevant person' (see paragraph 24.50) effects the remittance to the UK, whether for the benefit in the UK of the individual or a relevant person, and whether or not the remittance takes the form of the actual foreign income or gains or some other form of property which represents that foreign income or gains.

Thus, under the new *FA 2008* provisions the following (by way of example) are taxable (assuming post-5 April 2008 generated foreign income and gains and post-5 April 2008 purchases):

- the bringing into the UK of a car purchased outside the UK by the individual out of the foreign income or gains;
- the bringing into the UK of a car purchased outside the UK by the individual out of the foreign income or gains but gifted to the individual's wife prior to bringing the car into the UK; and
- the gifting of the foreign income or gains to the individual's wife who then brings the monies into the UK.

24.41 Pre-*FA 2008*, where the individual utilised either foreign source

24.42 *The non-UK domiciled individual, foreign source, etc*

earnings and/or foreign source capital gains (ie not RFI) to purchase an asset outside the UK, which was then brought into the UK by the individual, a taxable remittance of the foreign source earnings/capital gains used to effect the purchase arose. However, the bringing into the UK of an asset by someone other than the individual following a gift from the latter outside the UK was not taxable.

Where RFI was used to purchase an asset outside the UK which was then brought into the UK (whether by the individual or some other individual to whom the asset had been gifted) no taxable remittance occurred; however, a subsequent sale of the asset, purchased out of RFI, whilst in the UK gave rise at that point to a remittance of the RFI used to effect the original purchase.

Thus, RFI could be used outside the UK highly effectively permitting purchases of foreign goods which could then be brought to the UK for enjoyment yet without precipitating any income tax charge.

Example 16

Chuck Toronto, a non-UK domiciled but UK resident individual, generates foreign source income and capital gains by 5 April 2006 as follows:

Foreign source employment income	£250,000
RFI	£150,000
Foreign capital gains	£125,000

Each of these three amounts has been credited to three separate non-UK bank accounts BC1, BC2 and BC3, respectively.

Chuck very much wants to purchase a very valuable vase (£125,000) he has seen in China while on holiday for display in his UK home. He accordingly purchases the vase in August 2007 and brings it into the UK the following month.

If he purchases the vase using monies from accounts BC1 or BC3 then a taxable remittance of the monies in BC1 or BC2 (as to £125,000) occurs in September 2007.

However, the utilisation of the monies in BC2 does not result in a taxable remittance (although a subsequent sale, while the vase is in the UK, constitutes a taxable remittance at that time).

24.42 *FA 2008* has now not only brought the rules applying to remittances of

RFI in line with those applicable to foreign employment income and foreign capital gains (pre-*FA 2008*) but has significantly broadened what actually constitutes a remittance.

24.43 However, *FA 2008* does provide some degree of transitional relief where pre-6 April 2008 foreign income and gains (and/or property representing such income/gains) is remitted to the UK.

Alienation of foreign income and gains and asset purchase

24.44 'Alienation' refers to the transfer (typically by gift) of the foreign income and gains (or an asset purchased therefrom) from the non-UK domiciled individual to another person (eg the spouse) who then brings the money (or asset) into the UK. The *FA 2008* provisions in principle treat such a remittance as a taxable remittance.

'Asset purchase' refers to the purchase of an asset (eg a painting) by the non-UK domiciled individual out of the UK utilising the foreign income and gains followed by the subsequent bringing into the UK of the asset either by the individual or a person to whom the asset has been gifted. The *FA 2008* provisions in principle treat such a remittance as a taxable remittance.

Remittance conditions

24.45 Under *FA 2008*, a non-UK domiciled individual's foreign income or gains are remitted to the UK if one of three sets of conditions is satisfied.

The first set of conditions is the 'catch all' category and seeks to treat as a remittance a broad range of activities ('Conditions A/B'); the second set of conditions is more specific and seeks to treat as a remittance property which has been given to one of a specified class of person ('Condition C'); and the third set of conditions seeks to treat as a remittance gifts to 'third parties' involving a 'connected operation' ('Condition D') (*ITA 2007 s 809L*).

Conditions A/B

24.46 The first set of conditions provides that a non-UK domiciled individual's foreign income and gains are remitted to the UK if:

> 'money or other property is brought to, or received or used in, the UK by or for the benefit of a relevant person, ... [and] the property *is* (wholly or in part) the income or chargeable gains ... [*or*] the

24.47 *The non-UK domiciled individual, foreign source, etc*

property ... derives (wholly or in part, directly or indirectly) from the income or gains and in the case of property ... is property of ... a relevant person'.

(ITA 2007 s 809L)

Condition C

24.47 The second set of conditions provides that a non-UK domiciled individual's foreign income and gains are remitted to the UK where:

'qualifying property of a gift recipient is brought to, or received or used in, the UK, and is enjoyed by a relevant person'.

(ITA 2007 s 809L)

Condition D

24.48 The third set of conditions provides that a non-UK domiciled individual's foreign income and gains are remitted to the UK where:

'property of a person other than a relevant person (excluding that referred to in Condition C ie qualifying property of a gift recipient) is brought to, or received or used in, the UK, and is enjoyed by a relevant person in circumstances where there is a connected operation'.

(ITA 2007 s 809L)

24.49 *ITA 2007 s 809L* also provides that remittances to the UK of foreign income and gains occurs:

(1) where the foreign income and gains are used outside the UK in respect of a relevant debt (broadly, a relevant debt is debt that relates to property brought to the UK); or

(2) where a service is provided in the UK to or for the benefit of a relevant person and the foreign income and gains are used as consideration for the provision of the services.

For simplicity of explanation the main consideration below is restricted to examining the implication of Conditions A/B, C and D above ignoring the extensions of the legislation to (1) and (2) referred to in paragraph 24.49; a brief look at the implications of (1) and (2) is taken at the end of this section (see paragraph 24.84).

Relevant person

24.50 For the purposes of Conditions A/B, C and D a 'relevant person' includes:

- the individual;
- the individual's spouse;
- the child or grandchild of the individual or spouse if the child is aged under 18;
- a close company (ie broadly a company under the 'control' of five or fewer shareholders) whether UK or non-UK resident, in which any of the other persons listed is a shareholder;
- the trustees of a trust where any of the other persons listed is a beneficiary;
- cohabitees living together as husband and wife; and
- bodies (eg a company, UK resident or not) in which the trustees are a shareholder.

(*ITA 2007 s 809M*)

Example 17

Albert and Claudia have been married for 20 years.

In examining whether Albert has made a remittance it is necessary to identify the relevant persons.

Albert and Claudia have a son, Tom, aged 27 and a daughter, Fiona, aged 31. Fiona is married to Brian aged 35.

Brian and Fiona have three children, Matthew (10), Karen (15) and Nicholas (19).

Under *FA 2008* relevant persons (in relation to Albert) are:

Albert; Claudia; Matthew and Karen.

24.51 This relevant person definition encompasses a wide range of individuals (including trustees) although it excludes, for example, children/grandchildren aged 18 or over, brothers, sisters, nephews, nieces, parents and grandparents irrespective of age.

24.52 *The non-UK domiciled individual, foreign source, etc*

The definition, extremely unusually, extends to cohabitees but only where the cohabitees are living together as husband and wife. Thus, two people (eg two friends) simply living under the same roof, but not as husband and wife, are not relevant persons.

24.52 The term relevant person somewhat strangely includes the individual concerned and is thus not, as might be expected, just a reference to persons related to the individual but excluding the individual. However, in ascertaining whether an individual has made a remittance of foreign income/gains, it is those persons who are relevant persons in relation to the individual who need to be identified. Thus, in Example 16, in ascertaining whether Albert has made any remittances it is necessary to identify those who are related persons in relation to him (ie Claudia, Matthew and Karen).

24.53 Non-UK or UK resident trustees, owning shares in UK or non-UK resident companies are relevant persons as are the beneficiaries of the trust.

24.54 However, trustees and the settlor are not necessarily relevant persons. Where, however, the settlor is a beneficiary of the trust then the trustees and settlor are relevant persons.

Where the settlor is not a beneficiary of the trust but his spouse is a beneficiary the trustees and settlor are relevant persons (as are the trustees and spouse).

Where neither the settlor nor his spouse is a beneficiary of the trust but his (or her) children or grandchildren are beneficiaries the trustees and settlor are relevant persons (assuming the children and grandchildren are under 18).

Conditions A/B

24.55 The amount of any remittance needs to be ascertained. A simple remittance of the foreign income and gains is an amount equal to the foreign income and gains remitted (*ITA 2007 s 809P*).

Where property other than the income/gains (but derived therefrom) is remitted the quantum of the remittance is the amount of income/gains used to effect the acquisition of the property (*ITA 2007 s 809P*). Thus, for example, where an asset (eg a painting) is purchased outside the UK and brought to the UK a remittance of the income/gains occurs equal to the cost of the asset at the time of purchase. Thus, the value of the asset at the date of its importation into the UK is irrelevant.

24.56 Thus, where the value of the asset purchased rises in value between purchase and importation the 'gain' is not subject to tax on importation. On the other hand, where the value of the asset has fallen over this time the 'loss' is still effectively taxed.

Exchange rates: income and capital gains

24.57 As UK tax liabilities are computed in sterling such liabilities are affected by exchange rate movements. It is therefore important to identify the date on which foreign income/gains need to be translated into sterling.

24.58 Unfortunately, the views of HMRC in this regard appear to have changed over time and are currently not in line with those adopted by practitioners (see 'Capital Gains Tax: Gains and Losses on Foreign Currency Bank Accounts held by Remittance Basis Users' 16 December 2009: *TCGA 1992 Sch 8A*). *Inter alia*, practitioners generally being of the view that it is the date foreign income arises which should be used to translate into sterling not (as per HMRC; see paragraph 24.58) the date of remittance.

24.59 HMRC's views are as follows:

- foreign income is translated into sterling at the date of remittance (not the date the income arises);
- foreign capital gains are computed by translating the disposal proceeds and the acquisition costs at the rates of exchange prevailing at the respective dates. This sterling capital gain remains fixed and is subject to CGT on remittance. However, an additional capital gain may arise if between the date of the disposal and the date of remittance of the foreign currency proceeds the rate of exchange has changed;
- in calculating whether the '£2,000 test' (see paragraph 24.11) is satisfied, the balance of any unremitted foreign income for the tax year is translated at the rate of exchange applicable on 5 April of the tax year concerned (but for the tax year 2008–2009 only, the translation into sterling is carried out at the date the unremitted foreign income arises or using average rates of exchange for that tax year). Unremitted foreign capital gains are the sterling amount computed as above; and
- 'nominated income/gains' (see paragraph 24.19) are effectively subject to income tax and CGT on the arising basis and thus the rate of exchange is that which applies on the date the income arises. Nominated capital gains are the sterling amount computed as above.

Example 18

Hubert China, a non-UK domiciled but UK resident individual, receives foreign interest income of $1,500 when the exchange rate is $2/£1 [ie £750].

He remits the $1,500 when the rate of exchange is $1.5/£1 [ie £1,000].

An income tax charge arises on £1,000 (not £750).

No CGT consequences arise.

24.60 *The non-UK domiciled individual, foreign source, etc*

Example 19

Torrence Spain, a non-UK domiciled but UK resident individual, purchases a villa in Spain for €100,000 when the exchange rate is €2/£1. He sells the villa for €150,000 when the rate of exchange is €1/£1.

He keeps the proceeds in Spain later remitting the whole amount when the rate of exchange is €1.25/£1.

The capital gain on sale of the villa is £150,000 less £50,000 (ie £100,000).

The Euros in the bank account on remittance precipitate a capital loss of £150,000 less £120,000 (ie £30,000).

Torrence is thus subject to CGT on the gain on the sale of the villa of £100,000 and has a capital loss of £30,000 available for utilisation against certain capital gains (see Chapter 9).

24.60 Reverting to the discussion in paragraph 24.55 if foreign income of $10,000 is used to purchase a car outside the UK when the exchange rate is $2/£1 and the car is imported at a time when the exchange rate is $1/£1 the remittance is of an amount of £5,000 (not £10,000) (ie the sterling equivalent of the foreign income used to purchase the car).

24.61 The remittance of the foreign income and gains does not necessarily need to be effected by the individual or indeed enjoyed by him in the UK for a tax liability to arise thereon.

Conditions A/B refers to the bringing, receiving or using foreign income and gains, or property derived therefrom, in the UK by, or for the benefit, of a relevant person.

Thus, the following give rise to a remittance of foreign income and gains by the individual:

- the individual purchases an asset outside the UK which is brought into the UK by the individual;
- the individual purchases an asset outside the UK which is brought into the UK by the individual who then gifts it to a relevant person;
- the individual gifts the foreign income/gains outside the UK to a relevant person who then brings the income/gains into the UK; or
- the individual purchases an asset outside the UK which is gifted to a relevant person outside the UK who brings the asset into the UK.

The non-UK domiciled individual, foreign source, etc **24.61**

In all these cases a remittance to the UK occurs on the part of the individual with respect to the foreign income or gains and a charge to tax is precipitated on the individual.

A situation may arise where the individual is unaware that a relevant person to whom a gift has been made outside the UK has in fact brought the gift to the UK (which gives rise to problems if the individual fails to declare the remittance on his tax return).

Example 20

Chiquita Sweden, a non-UK domiciled but UK resident individual, has foreign income (albeit in sterling) for the tax year 2010–2011 of £275,000. This money has been credited to a newly opened bank account in Bermuda. No interest has been credited to the account.

Chiquita uses the income in 2010–2011 as follows:

(a) she remits £75,000 directly to her UK bank account;

(b) she transfers £25,000 from the Bermuda account to her non-UK domiciled but UK resident husband's bank account in Stockholm of which he then remits £15,000 to his personal bank account in the UK;

(c) while Chiquita and her daughter are in New York she draws a cheque on the Bermuda account to pay for a pair of shoes she bought for her daughter as a birthday present; the cost of the shoes was £2,500. Her daughter (age 12) wears the shoes when she returns with her mum to the UK;

(d) while Chiquita and her daughter are in New York Chiquita purchases a set of golf clubs for £10,000 for her son (age 22) which she gives to him on her return to the UK; and

(e) she transfers £7,500 to her best friend's New York bank account who immediately transfers it to her personal bank account in the UK.

The tax effect of each of the above transactions on the part of Chiquita is as follows:

(a) £75,000 taxable. She has simply remitted foreign income to the UK.

(b) £15,000 taxable. The transfer to her husband's account of £25,000 gives rise at that point to no tax charge. However, the subsequent

24.62 *The non-UK domiciled individual, foreign source, etc*

> transfer by her husband of £15,000 to the UK is a transfer by (and in fact for the benefit of) a relevant person.
>
> (c) Not taxable. Property (ie the shoes) derives from the foreign income and has been brought to the UK by a relevant person. *Prima facie*, a taxable remittance has occurred. However, the shoes qualify as exempt property (see paragraph 24.92) and thus the income is treated as not having been remitted.
>
> (d) Taxable. Property (ie the golf clubs) derives from the foreign income and this property has been brought to the UK by a relevant person (ie Chiquita) albeit not for the benefit of a relevant person (ie the son). Nevertheless, the bringing to the UK by a relevant person precipitates a taxable remittance.
>
> (e) Not taxable. The transfer to her best friend's account of £7,500 gives rise at that point to no tax charge. The subsequent transfer by her friend of the £7,500 to the UK is not a transfer by or for the benefit of a relevant person.

Condition C

24.62 Condition C provides that a remittance to the UK also occurs where:

'qualifying property of a gift recipient is brought to, or received or used in, the UK, and is enjoyed by a relevant person'.

(*ITA 2007 s 809L*)

For Condition C therefore to apply there must be both 'qualifying property' and a 'gift recipient' with 'enjoyment' being that of a 'relevant person'. Effectively, this Condition is designed to prevent the individual gifting property or money to someone, subsequent to which, the property or money is brought into the UK but is then enjoyed by a relevant person (which includes the individual).

If, however, the relevant person provides full consideration for the enjoyment or, if the property or money is enjoyed to the virtual exclusion of all relevant persons, such enjoyment is to be disregarded (ie no remittance will have been deemed to have occurred in these circumstances).

24.63 For this purpose a gift recipient is a person other than a relevant person to whom the individual makes the gift (ie for no, or below market value, consideration) of money or property that is income/gains of the individual or derives from the income/gains of the individual. Thus, a gift to an individual who does not fall within the definition of relevant person constitutes a gift recipient.

The non-UK domiciled individual, foreign source, etc **24.66**

Whether the gift is to a relevant person or not is determined at the time of the gift (*ITA 2007 s 809N*). Thus, a gift may be made to a non-relevant person (ie a gift recipient) but subsequently the person may become a relevant person (eg the person becomes the spouse of the individual). However, as at the time of the gift the person is a non-relevant person, Condition C is in point.

24.64 Qualifying property refers, *inter alia*, to property that the individual gave to the gift recipient or anything that derives from that property. Qualifying property would thus, for example, include an asset which has been purchased by the gift recipient from a gift of income/gains by the individual (ie the asset would derive from the income/gains).

24.65 Condition C, unlike Conditions A/B, has no relevance to direct remittances to the UK by the individual. The individual is required, for Condition C to operate, to have made a gift to a non-relevant person of property or money.

Condition C is thus designed to 'catch' gifts to persons other than to relevant persons, for example gifts to brothers, sisters, etc. subsequent to which a relevant person enjoys in the UK the property or money gifted.

Example 21

Uruguay, a non-UK domiciled but UK resident individual, gifts £5,000 of his foreign income outside the UK to his sister, Paraguay.

Paraguay purchases a car which she brings to the UK. Paraguay allows Uruguay's spouse to use the car.

The car is qualifying property derived from Uruguay's foreign income and Paraguay is a gift recipient. A relevant person (ie Uruguay's spouse) enjoys the car in the UK.

Uruguay is thus treated as having made a remittance of his foreign income of an amount equivalent to that used by Paraguay to effect the car purchase.

Condition D

24.66 Condition D is an anti-avoidance provision which seeks to deal with transactions not falling under Conditions A/B or C and provides that a remittance to the UK occurs where:

'property of a person other than a relevant person (excluding that referred to in Condition C ie qualifying property of a gift recipient)

24.67 *The non-UK domiciled individual, foreign source, etc*

is brought to, or received or used in, the UK, and is enjoyed by a relevant person in circumstances where there is a connected operation'.

(ITA 2007 ss 809L and 809O)

24.67 Condition D is designed to stop the individual arranging his affairs so that foreign income and gains are not remitted due to an agreement with another person (who is neither a relevant person nor a gift recipient and thus neither Conditions A/B or C apply) that property of the other person is brought to the UK for the benefit of the individual or any other relevant person.

24.68 In essence, where the individual or a relevant person enjoys some form of benefit in the UK of income/gains or property derived therefrom belonging to a third person and the individual or a relevant person has transferred income/gains or property derived therefrom to the third party Condition D may apply.

24.69 If, however, the relevant person provides full consideration for the enjoyment or if the property or money is enjoyed to the virtual exclusion of all relevant persons such enjoyment is to be disregarded (ie no remittance will have been deemed to have occurred in these circumstances) *(ITA 2007 s 809O)*.

Transitional provisions of *FA 2008*

24.70 *FA 2008* provides for certain transitional reliefs to apply. These transitional provisions relate to foreign income and capital gains which arise pre-6 April 2008. However, it is necessary to consider the position separately for employment income, RFI and capital gains.

These transitional provisions apply to each of the above Conditions A/B, C and D.

Employment income

24.71 The remittance basis applies to the individual's chargeable overseas earnings which are earnings of a non-UK domiciled individual under a contract of employment with a non-UK resident employer where all the duties are performed outside the UK *(ITEPA 2003 s 22)*.

24.72 Such earnings, which arise on or after 6 April 2008, are treated as remitted in accordance with the new *FA 2008* provisions *(ITEPA 2003 s 22)*.

However, earnings arising pre-6 April 2008 but remitted on or after 6 April 2008 are not subject to income tax on the part of the individual where the remittance is

The non-UK domiciled individual, foreign source, etc **24.75**

by a relevant person (not the individual) and not for the benefit of the individual (*FA 2008 Sch 7*).

Thus, the individual is able to gift any pre-6 April 2008 arising chargeable overseas earnings to another person (relevant person or not) prior to remittance which does not give rise to a taxable remittance on the individual's part (assuming he enjoys no part of the remittance).

Remittances after termination of the employment continue to be subject to income tax (*ITEPA 2003 s 22*).

Relevant foreign income

24.73 The transitional provisions with respect to RFI (which includes mainly interest and dividends although extends to include non-UK source trading income and non-UK source property income) are more complex than those applying to employment income and capital gains. This is because the provisions which applied pre-*FA 2008* in determining when remittances of RFI occurred are different to those which applied to employment income and capital gains.

24.74 The transitional provisions in principle seek to retain the pre-*FA 2008* tax treatment for pre-6 April 2008 RFI.

24.75 With respect to RFI which arises pre-6 April 2008, *FA 2008* provides a general rule (see paragraph 24.80) to determine when a taxable remittance from such income arises. This general rule is subject to (ie overridden by) two specific situations either of which, if satisfied, result in no taxable remittance of such income.

The two specific situations are as follows:

(a) if, before 6 April 2008, property (including money) consisting of or deriving from an individual's RFI is brought to or received or used in the UK by or for the benefit of a relevant person treat the RFI as not remitted to the UK on or after that date (*if it otherwise would be regarded as so remitted*).

(b) if before 12 March 2008, property (other than money) consisting of or deriving from an individual's RFI was acquired by a relevant person, treat the RFI as not remitted to the UK on or after 6 April 2008 (*if it otherwise would be regarded as so remitted*).

The words in italics are important. The effect of the words is to preclude a taxable remittance arising with respect to the individual's RFI on or after 6 April

24.76 *The non-UK domiciled individual, foreign source, etc*

2008 where the RFI and property derived therefrom has been dealt with under (a) or (b).

Pre-12 March 2008 condition (ie (b) above)

24.76 For this exception to apply the property must have been acquired by a relevant person before 12 March 2008.

Where this is the case such assets can be brought to the UK at any point in time (eg on or after 6 April 2008) without precipitating a taxable remittance of the individual's RFI used to effect the purchase. It does not matter who remits the asset or for whose benefit.

Thus, any of the following if effected on or after 6 April 2008 will not give rise to a taxable remittance of the individual's RFI used to effect the asset purchase assuming the conditions of (b) are satisfied:

(i) remittance of the asset by the individual who owns the asset;

(ii) remittance of the asset by the relevant person (not the individual) who owns the asset;

(iii) remittance of the asset following a gift of the asset, at any time, by the person who then owns the asset; and

(iv) remittance of monies arising from sale of the asset outside the UK (or where the sale is effected in the UK).

There is no applicable time limit within which the asset must be brought to the UK and/or when it needs to be sold to avoid taxable remittance treatment.

Furthermore, it does not matter whether a relevant person (including the individual) or another person is involved in (i) to (iv) above.

Pre-6 April 2008 condition (ie (a) above)

24.77 For this exception to apply property (including money) consisting of or deriving from the individual's RFI must have been brought to, or used in, the UK before 6 April 2008 by or for the benefit of a relevant person.

As (b) in paragraph 24.75 above specifically refers to property (other than money) having been acquired by relevant persons pre-12 March 2008 then (a) has no application to such property.

Thus (a) refers to:

(i) property acquired by relevant persons on or after 12 March 2008 and brought to the UK pre-6 April 2008;

(ii) RFI which arose at any time pre-6 April 2008 if it was brought to the UK by a relevant person pre-6 April 2008.

Under (i) above no remittance of the RFI used to purchase the property occurs whether the relevant person is the individual or not.

Under (ii) above no remittance of the RFI occurs only if its remittance to the UK is not by (or for the benefit of) the individual; a remittance by or for the benefit of the individual constitutes a remittance. Thus, (ii) presupposes that the individual has gifted the RFI to the another relevant person prior to remittance.

24.78 Unlike (b) in paragraph 24.75, (a) refers to the RFI itself (ie money). In addition, however, for (a) to apply the property or RFI needs to have been brought to the UK on or before 6 April 2008 (ie a time limit is imposed). If, however, the property or RFI is not brought to the UK within this time limit, see paragraph 24.80.

24.79 Assuming the conditions in (a) in paragraph 24.75 are satisfied with respect to the property (including money) then any of the following if subsequently effected (with respect to the property including money) on or after 6 April 2008 whether within the UK or not will not give rise to a taxable remittance of the individual's RFI at that time:

(i) asset gifted by the relevant person to another person;

(ii) asset gifted by the relevant person to another person who then sells the asset;

(iii) asset sold by the relevant person;

(iv) RFI gifted by the relevant person to another person;

(v) RFI gifted by the relevant person to another person who purchases an asset; and

(vi) RFI used to purchase an asset.

There is no applicable time limit within which any of (i) to (vi) above need to be carried out (assuming the asset or RFI was brought to the UK pre-6 April 2008).

Furthermore, it does not matter whether the relevant person (including the individual) or another person is involved in (i) to (vi). For example, under (iv) above the gift of the RFI by the individual to another relevant person pre-6 April 2008 who then remits the RFI to the UK pre-6 April 2008 may, on or after

24.80 *The non-UK domiciled individual, foreign source, etc*

6 April 2008, gift the RFI 'back to' the individual (whose RFI it originally was) whether, within or outside the UK, without the individual then falling subject to tax on the RFI. This does presuppose that there was no collusion/agreement between the two individuals that this was to occur (ie there was no agreement pre-6 April 2008 by which the individual agreed to gift the RFI to the relevant person conditional on the latter then post-5 April 2008 re-gifting it back to the individual).

General transitional rule

24.80 The general transitional rule governs the position with respect to pre-6 April 2008 RFI which is not dealt with under either of the above specific conditions (a) and (b) in paragraph 24.75.

Thus, the general rule applies to:

- assets acquired on or after 6 April 2008;
- assets acquired on or after 12 March and pre-6 April 2008 but not brought to the UK on or before 6 April 2008;
- RFI not brought to the UK on or before 6 April 2008.

24.81 Under the general rule a taxable remittance of pre-6 April 2008 RFI only occurs on or after 6 April 2008 if the RFI and/or assets derived therefrom (falling within any of the categories listed in paragraph 24.86 to which the rule applies) are remitted to the UK for the benefit of the individual. If a relevant person (not including the individual) brings the RFI or assets to the UK no taxable remittance of the RFI occurs assuming that the individual does not enjoy the RFI or assets so remitted in the UK (*FA 2008 Sch 7*).

Thus, under the general rule, any of the following if effected on or after 6 April 2008 will not give rise to a taxable remittance of the RFI:

- assets acquired on or after 6 April 2008 by the individual but gifted to any person who brings the asset to the UK (not for the individual's benefit);
- assets acquired on or after 12 March and pre-6 April 2008 by the individual but not brought to the UK on or before 6 April 2008 which are then gifted by the individual to any person who brings the asset to the UK on or after 6 April 2008 (not for the individual's benefit);
- RFI not brought to the UK on or before 6 April 2008 but which is gifted by the individual to any person who brings the relevant foeign income to the UK on or after 6 April 2008 (not for the individual's benefit).

24.82 Some observations:

- the purchase by the individual of an asset outside the UK out of pre-6 April 2008 RFI on or after 12 March 2008 but not brought to the UK pre-6 April 2008 cannot now be brought to the UK by the individual without precipitating a taxable remittance for the individual; it could, however, be given to another person for them to remit assuming the individual doesn't then enjoy it; however, if the asset had been purchased outside the UK by the individual pre-12 March 2008 it could on or after be brought to the UK by the individual without precipitating a taxable remittance;

- pre-6 April 2008 RFI not brought to the UK pre-6 April 2008 can be remitted without precipitating a taxable remittance if gifted by the individual to any person prior to remittance (and the individual doesn't enjoy it);

- pre-6 April 2008 RFI not brought to the UK pre-6 April 2008 can be used to effect an asset purchase which is remitted to the UK without precipitating a taxable remittance if the asset is purchased by the individual and gifted by the individual to any person prior to remittance (and the individual doesn't enjoy it) or the RFI is given by the individual to any person who effects the purchase of the asset and brings it to the UK; and

- pre-6 April 2008 RFI brought to the UK pre-6 April 2008 by a relevant person (other than the individual), after the individual gifted the RFI to the relevant person, can then be used on or after 6 April 2008 for the benefit of the individual without precipitating a taxable remittance (in essence a gift can be made back to the individual).

Capital gains

24.83 Foreign chargeable gains which arise on or after 6 April 2008 are treated as remitted in accordance with the new *FA 2008* provisions (*TCGA 1992 s 12*).

However, capital gains arising pre-6 April 2008 but remitted on or after 6 April 2008 are not subject to CGT on the part of the individual where the remittance is by a relevant person (not the individual) and not for the benefit of the individual (*FA 2008 Sch 7*).

Thus, the individual is able to gift any pre-6 April 2008 arising chargeable gains earnings to another person (relevant person or not) prior to remittance which does not give rise to a taxable remittance on the individual's part (assuming he enjoys no part of the remittance).

24.84 *The non-UK domiciled individual, foreign source, etc*

Relevant debt and UK services

24.84 The discussion above concerning 'remittances' and 'alienation' concentrated on the position with respect to remittances of foreign income and gains and on property derived therefrom. However, Conditions A/B (and Conditions C and D) have a much wider application.

24.85 Conditions A/B also provide that a remittance to the UK occurs in two further situations, namely, where:

- a service is provided in the UK to or for the benefit of a relevant person and the consideration for the service *is* the foreign income or gains *or* the consideration derives from the income or gains; *or*
- a service is provided in the UK to or for the benefit of a relevant person and the foreign income or gains are used outside the UK in respect of a relevant debt or anything deriving from the income or gains is used outside the UK in respect of a relevant debt.

(ITA 2007 s 809L)

The term 'relevant person' is defined in paragraph 24.50.

The term 'relevant debt' means, *inter alia*, a debt (broadly, the obligation to pay a sum of money owed and includes a debt for interest on money lent) that relates to:

- money or other property which is brought to, received or used in, the UK by or for the benefit of a relevant person; or
- a service which is provided in the UK to or for the benefit of a relevant person.

(ITA 2007 s 809L)

24.86 Pre-*FA 2008* if the individual received a service which is supplied in the UK (eg advice from a firm of lawyers) and payment for which was made utilising foreign income or gains, no remittance arose. It was important, however, that the payment was made outside the UK (ie payment needed to be made into the non-UK bank account of the provider of the service, not their UK bank account which would have precipitated a taxable remittance).

This treatment continues post-*FA 2008* but only if the service provided relates wholly or mainly (see paragraph 24.88) to property situated outside the UK *and* the whole of the consideration is given by way of payment(s) to bank accounts held outside the UK by (or on behalf of) the person who provides the service *(ITA 2007 s 809W)*.

24.87 *ITA 2007 s 809W* appears to apply to, for example, a UK law firm acting with respect to the purchase/sale of overseas real estate or the acquisition/sale of shares in a foreign registered company; and investment advice provided by a UK investment firm with respect to an overseas investment portfolio of an individual or trust.

However, *prima facie*, accountancy advice provided in the UK with respect to the individual's UK salary and associated benefits does not qualify as the service relates to non-asset related income (ie the individual's employment income) and thus there is no property.

24.88 The 'wholly or mainly' reference (see paragraph 24.86) is a reference to the service provided, not the property. Accordingly HMRC suggest that this may be judged (albeit not solely) by reference to work done (ie normally time spent).

24.89 If a borrowing is incurred outside the UK to pay for a service provided to a relevant person in the UK the utilisation of foreign income or gains to repay the borrowing and/or any interest levied will precipitate a remittance of the income or gains (see paragraph 24.85) unless the exception (ie the service relates primarily to non-UK property) referred to in paragraph 24.86 applies.

It may be that payment for the service provided to a relevant person in the UK is by way of the use of an overseas issued credit card. It would seem that the individual whose credit card is used has created a 'relevant debt'. If the foreign income or gains of the individual are used to discharge the debt due to the credit card company, albeit outside the UK, a remittance of the income or gains will arise (see paragraph 24.85) unless the exception referred to above applies.

24.90 Whether property is situtated within or outside the UK for the purposes of the provision of services within the UK exception is determined by the rules applicable for CGT purposes (*ITA 2007 s 809W*).

24.91 The issue of 'relevant debt' has application not only in the case of the provision of a *service* in the UK to a relevant person but also to:

> 'money or *other property* brought to, or received or used in, the UK by or for the benefit of a "relevant person"'.

(ITA 2007 s 809)

Thus, the use of an overseas issued credit card or an overseas borrowing in connection with the purchase of goods outside the UK which are subsequently brought into the UK, by or for the benefit of a related person, gives rise to a related debt. The use of foreign income or gains outside the UK to discharge either of these two forms of indebtedness precipitates a remittance of the foreign income or gains.

24.92 *The non-UK domiciled individual, foreign source, etc*

Similarly, the use of an overseas issued credit card *or* an overseas borrowing in connection with the purchase of goods in the UK (ie not just *services*) by or for the benefit of a related person gives rise to a related debt. The use of foreign income or gains outside the UK to discharge either of these two forms of indebtedness precipitates a remittance of the income or gains.

Exempt property

24.92 *FA 2008* provides that certain types of property (ie exempt property) which are brought to, received or used in the UK by or for the benefit of a relevant person (including the individual) are not treated as remitted to the UK and thus precipitate no tax charge (*ITA 2007 s 809X*). As originally drafted, these provisions only applied where the property (except for the public access provisions; see paragraph 24.100) had been purchased out of RFI. *FA 2009*, however, removes this restriction and thus property whether purchased out of foreign employment income, foreign capital gains or RFI (on or after 6 April 2008) may qualify as exempt property (*FA 2009 Sch 27*).

Such property comprises:

- clothing, footwear, jewellery and watches if they meet the 'personal use rule';
- property of any description if the 'notional amount' remitted is below £1,000;
- property that meets either the 'temporary importation rule' or 'the repair rule'; or
- property that meets the 'public access rule'.

(*ITA 2007 ss 809X, 809Z, 809Z2, 809Z3* and *809Z4*)

'Property', however, does not include 'money' for exempt property purposes (*ITA 2007 s 809Z6*).

Clothing, etc and the 'personal use rule'

24.93 The personal use rule applies where the clothing, etc is the property of a relevant person and is for the personal use of the individual, the individual's spouse or children or grandchildren under age 18 (*ITA 2007 ss 809X* and *809Z*).

There are no monetary limits.

Example 22

Steven Alberta, a non-UK domiciled but UK resident individual, purchases a gold watch worth £300,000 for his wife, Henrietta, out of his foreign income which arises in the tax year 2010–2011.

The watch is purchased in Geneva and his wife imports the watch to the UK on her return.

No remittance of the £300,000 of foreign income occurs.

Similarly, if the foreign income had arisen in the tax year 2007–2008 and the purchase effected in 2010–2011 no remittance would be deemed to have occurred.

Under either option the watch qualifies as exempt property.

Example 23

Steven Alberta, a non-UK domiciled but UK resident individual, purchases an antique painting costing £300,000 for himself whilst in Geneva in 2010–2011 out of foreign income arising in 2010–2011.

Steven imports the painting into the UK on his return.

A remittance of the £300,000 of foreign income occurs as the painting is not exempt property and the transitional provisions of *FA 2008* do not apply.

Property below £1,000 rule

24.94 Any property involving a 'notional remitted amount' of below £1,000 constitutes exempt property (*ITA 2007 ss 809X* and *809Z5*).

The 'notional amount remitted' is the amount which would normally be regarded as having been remitted in relation to the property, which is the amount of foreign income and gains from which the property derives ie its cost (*ITA 2007 ss 809Z5* and *809P*).

24.95 The £1,000 limit applies to each item of property (unless the property forms part of a set).

24.96 *The non-UK domiciled individual, foreign source, etc*

Example 24

Jacobi Amsterdam, a non-UK domiciled but UK resident individual, whilst travelling abroad on work purchased for himself out of his foreign income a pen for £200; a jacket for £500 and a pair of shoes for £350.

No remittance of his foreign income used to effect the purchases arises.

Temporary importation rule

24.96 Property imported into the UK for 275 days or less in aggregate constitutes exempt property. The 275 days is not a limit applied per tax year but refers to the aggregate permitted days over the property's useful life (*ITA 2007 ss 809X* and *809Z4*).

Property imported for part of a day counts towards the day limit.

24.97 Where property imported meets any of the other three rules (ie personal use rule; repair rule and public access rule) the time during which it meets any of these rules will not be taken into account in ascertaining whether the temporary importation rule is met.

Example 25

Ronaldo Milan, a non-UK domiciled but UK resident individual, purchases a Ferrari in Italy out of his foreign income.

He imports the car into the UK in June 2008 where he uses it until the end of December 2008. He then exports the car back to Italy.

As the conditions of the temporary importation rule are satisfied the Ferrari qualifies as exempt property and no remittance of his foreign income arises.

Repair rule

24.98 Property brought to the UK for repair constitutes exempt property (*ITA 2007 ss 809X* and *809Z3*).

'Repair' extends to actual repair work and also storage both pre-and post-repair; it also extends to transit between a place outside the UK to the premises where the repairs are to be carried out and/or stored by the repairer pre-and post-repair.

24.99 *Prima facie*, however, the use of foreign income and gains to pay for the actual repairs gives rise to a remittance of the income/gains whether the payment is effected within or outside the UK.

Example 26

Zie China, a non-UK domiciled but UK resident individual, purchases an antique vase at an auction in New York out of his foreign income.

He brings the vase to the UK for repairs. After the repairs have been carried out the vase is transferred to his house in Italy.

The vase qualifies as exempt property as the temporary repair rule is satisfied.

Property and public access rule

24.100 Property utilised for public display/access broadly encompasses property which comprises works of art, collector's pieces and antiques which is available for public access at an approved establishment (eg museum, gallery) up to a period of two years from the time of importation (*ITA 2007 ss 809X and 809Z*).

24.101 Pre-*FA 2008* such property, if purchased outside the UK using foreign source earnings and/or foreign capital gains and if brought into the UK would constitute a taxable remittance. Where, however, the purchase had been effected using RFI no taxable remittance arose.

Post-*FA 2008*, however, whether such property is purchased out of any of the above categories of foreign income or gains it will now qualify as exempt property and as a consequence no taxable remittance occurs.

Exempt to non-exempt property

24.102 In the event that exempt property ceases to be exempt for whatever reason it is treated as remitted to the UK at that time (*ITA 2007 s 809Y*).

24.103 This occurs if the property (or part of it) is sold or otherwise converted into money (ie converted into money otherwise than from a direct sale for cash) whilst it is in the UK or if it fails to satisfy whilst in the UK (having previously

24.104 *The non-UK domiciled individual, foreign source, etc*

satisfied) any of the four exemptions (ie public access; personal use; repair, or temporary importation).

'Money' includes bills of exchange, traveller's cheques and debt instruments.

24.104 Whether the cessation for qualification as exempt property causes the foreign income and gains used to effect the original purchase to have been remitted depends upon the facts.

Thus, for example, no taxable remittance occurs where the foreign income and gains of the individual arose pre-6 April 2008 and the property is purchased after this date and was gifted to another person (relevant person or not) who brought the property into the UK (and the individual does not benefit therefrom).

Mixed funds

24.105 The term 'mixed fund' refers to:

> '... money or other property which, immediately before the transfer, contains or derives from–
>
> (a) more than one of the kinds of income and capital ... , *or*
>
> (b) income or capital for more than one tax year'.

(ITA 2007 s 809Q)

The income and capital referred to above is:

- employment income subject to UK income tax;
- relevant foreign earnings;
- foreign specific employment income;
- RFI;
- foreign chargeable gains;
- employment income subject to foreign tax;
- RFI subject to foreign tax;
- foreign chargeable gains subject to foreign tax; and
- income and capital not in any of the above.

The above categories represent the order in which remittances out of a mixed fund are deemed to occur when remittances are made to the UK (*ITA 2007 s 809Q*). Thus, the ordering is inapplicable where any transfers are not made to the UK (in which case the 'offshore transfer' provisions may apply; see paragraph 24.112).

Examples of the last category, 'income and capital not in any of the above', are gifts received; inheritances; gambling winnings; UK source income/gains (ie income/gains already taxed in the UK other than employment income).

Interestingly, the term 'mixed fund' refers to 'property' (although this term includes 'money') as well as 'money' and thus, for example, an asset purchased by the individual using a mixture of, say, RFI and foreign chargeable constitutes a mixed fund.

24.106 Mixed funds in practice are extremely common. It is by no means unusual for the individual to have one or more offshore bank accounts into which may flow various categories of income and gains. Thus, for example, the same bank account may be used by the individual to receive offshore dividend income; gains from the disposal of offshore assets; offshore employment income; self-employment income; capital gains; inheritances etc. Surplus UK source monies may also be remitted to one or more such accounts.

Inevitably, the monies in such accounts generate interest which is often credited directly to these accounts.

24.107 The precise nature of a remittance out of such funds needs to be clarified in order to determine any liability to income tax or CGT. Pre-*FA 2008*, there were no statutory tax provisions which governed the constituent elements of any remittance. Only be maintaining separate accounts for each source of income/gains was it possible to be able to identify the precise nature of any particular remittance and hence the tax consequences.

24.108 Inevitably some rules had to be laid down in order to be able to identify the nature of remittances from mixed accounts. Accordingly HMRC developed a set of 'unofficial' rules. These rules were as follows:

(i) Arising basis and remittance basis mixed income

Where an account contains income taxed on the arising basis and income taxed on the remittance basis any remittance is deemed to be out of the income subject to the arising basis first.

(ii) Income and capital gains taxable on remittance

Remittance is deemed to be out of income first.

24.109 *The non-UK domiciled individual, foreign source, etc*

(iii) Tax-free capital and remittance of taxable income

The remittance out of an account containing capital (ie not taxable if remitted, eg a gift) and income which if remitted is taxable is viewed as constituting a remittance of the taxable income first.

(iv) Tax-free capital and taxable capital gains

The remittance out of an account containing capital (ie not taxable if remitted) and capital part of which is a capital gain is a proportion of the capital and of the gain.

24.109 FA 2008 now provides statutory authority for determining the nature of a remittance from a mixed fund (*ITA 2007 s 809Q*).

Under the new rules a series of steps are employed which broadly involve attributing to the remitted amount foreign income and gains from each of the above nine categories in turn (see paragraph 24.105) commencing with UK employment income first, until the remittance has been matched in its entirety. The determination is made at the date of the remittance (ie the amounts in the various categories are determined immediately before the remittance). Thus, for subsequent remittances in the same tax year, the quantum of each (or some) of the categories will have been depleted by the matching to earlier remittances.

If, in the event, there is insufficient income or gains arising in the tax year of the remittance to match to the remittance it then becomes necessary to repeat the whole process matching the immediately prior tax year's foreign income and gains using the same procedure (in effect adopting a last in first out (LIFO) basis). This process is repeated until a full matching has occurred.

24.110 These new *FA 2008* provisions do not, however, apply to the individual's foreign income or gains for the tax year 2007–2008 or earlier tax years. In such cases the pre-*FA 2008* rules apply.

Example 27

The following RFI arises in each tax year and is credited to the same non-UK bank account:

	2008–2009	2009–2010	2010–2011
	£	£	£
RFI	1,000	1,250	1,100

On 5 April 2011 a remittance of £2,700 is made to the UK.

The account is a mixed account as it comprises foreign income from different tax years.

To determine the nature of the remittance the constituent elements are determined by matching the various categories of income/gains on a LIFO basis to the remittance. In this example there is only one category of income, namely, RFI.

The £2,700 is thus matched as follows:

2010–2011	RFI £1,100
2009–2010	RFI £1,250
2008–2009	RFI £350

The remittance of £2,700 is thus made up of RFI of £2,700 comprised of the relevant elements from each tax year; this leaves unmatched RFI in 2008–2009 of £650 for future matchings.

Example 28

The following RFI and gifts are credited to the same non-UK bank account:

	2008–2009	2009/10	2010–2011
	£	£	£
RFI 6.4.08	350		
Gift 5.4.09	500		
RFI 5.4.10		300	
RFI			nil

On 5 April 2011 a remittance of £750 is made to the UK.

The account is a mixed account as it comprises foreign income and capital from different tax years.

24.111 *The non-UK domiciled individual, foreign source, etc*

To determine the nature of the remittance the constituent elements are determined by matching the various categories of income/gains on a LIFO basis to the remittance.

The £750 is thus matched as follows:

2010–2011	nil
2009–2010	RFI £300 (5.4.10)
2008–2009	RFI £350 (6.4.08)
	Gift £100 (5.4.09)

The remittance of £750 is thus made up of aggregate RFI of £650 and capital (ie the gift) of £100.

Even though the gift of £500 in 2008–2009 is received later in that tax year than the RFI of £350, when matching the constituent elements in that (or any) tax year the matching of RFI precedes the matching of capital as confirmed by the ordering rules of paragraph 24.105.

24.111 The ability to convert foreign income and gains, otherwise taxable if remitted, into 'tax free' capital is unfortunately not possible. Thus, it is not possible, for example, to utilise foreign income to purchase say, shares, which are sold at a later date precipitating sales proceeds deemed to comprise a capital gain element and a capital element (the latter then capable of tax-free remittance).

This is not possible because the sale proceeds are treated as still comprising the initial elements of foreign income/gains used to effect the purchase.

Example 29

A mixed account consists of:

2008–2009 Gift of £100

2009–2010 RFI of £150.

In 2010–2011 the aggregate £250 is used to purchase an asset which is then sold for £330 making a capital gain of £80.

The mixed fund thus consists of:

	2008–2009 £	2009–2010 £	2010–2011 £
Gift	100		
RFI		150	
Capital gain			80

In 2010–2011 on 5 April 2011 a remittance of £240 is made.

The £240 is treated as a remittance of £80 (capital gain 2010–2011); RFI of £150 (2009–2010) and £10 Gift (2008–2009).

The above reveals that the asset purchased retains its constituent elements (ie £100 gift and £150 RFI) and on sale the sale proceeds are effectively broken back down into these constituent elements and reallocated to their respective tax years plus the new capital gain element (which is allocated to the tax year of sale 2010–2011).

Offshore transfers

24.112 Some transfers out of a mixed account may simply be made outside the UK into other non-UK accounts. Such transfers are referred to as 'offshore transfers' (*ITA 2007 s 809R*).

An offshore transfer takes place if an amount identified as forming part of a mixed fund is moved, spent or otherwise transferred in such a way that, at the end of the relevant tax year, it is not, or on the basis of the best estimate that can be made at the time will not be, remitted to the UK (under Conditions A/B of *ITA 2007 s 809L*) (*ITA 2007 s 809R*).

24.113 An offshore transfer may thus comprise not only transfers between offshore bank accounts but also where any monies in offshore accounts are simply withdrawn and spent outside the UK either discharging general expenses or purchasing assets.

24.114 Where an offshore transfer occurs the transfer is treated as comprising the appropriate proportion of each kind of income and capital in the mixed fund immediately before the transfer (*ITA 2007 s 809R*). This is different to the mixed fund rules described in paragraph 24.105.

The appropriate proportion is the market value/amount of the transfer divided by the market value of the mixed fund immediately before the transfer.

24.114 *The non-UK domiciled individual, foreign source, etc*

These rules are designed to prevent manipulation of the income/gains so as to reduce the quantum of taxable remittances; it precludes the siphoning off of one particular category of foreign income or capital gain.

Example 30

Descartes Paris is a non-UK domiciled but UK resident individual.

Her offshore account (OFC1) comprises £10,000 of RFI and a £10,000 inheritance from her father. No interest has been credited to the account.

Descartes would like to transfer the £10,000 of inheritance to her UK account which precipitates no income tax or CGT.

She therefore opens a second offshore account (OFC2) into which she transfers £10,000 (under the mixed fund rules believing that the £10,000 transfer comprises the RFI) leaving her £10,000 inheritance in OFC1.

She then transfers the £10,000 inheritance from OFC1 to the UK.

The transfer from OFC1 to OFC2 *prima facie* comprises an offshore transfer; the fact that the £10,000 transfer is then transferred to the UK soon thereafter means that the transfer from OFC1 to OFC2 is not in fact an offshore transfer. Indeed the mixed fund rules are also inapplicable as the transfer is not to the UK.

The result is that the transfer to OFC2 is treated as if it has not occurred and the £10,000 transfer to the UK is thus made out of the original mixed fund of OFC1; the transfer is thus a remittance of RFI (as the normal mixed fund rules apply).

Example 31

Safira Iran, a non-UK domiciled but UK resident individual, opened a new Swiss bank account (SB1) on 6 April 2010.

By 31 December 2010 the account contains:

£150,000 as a gift from her mother;

£60,000 dividend income on overseas shareholdings (ie RFI); and

£30,000 foreign capital gain (which arose following the sale of an investment of the £150,000 inheritance).

Safira decides to open a second bank account in Switzerland (SB2) and transfers £60,000 from SB1 to SB2.

As Safira does not intend to remit the £60,000 to the UK the transfer is an offshore transfer and the offshore transfer rules, not the mixed fund rules, apply to the £60,000 transfer.

Accordingly the transfer is not of the dividend income as is the case under the mixed fund rules, but a transfer of a proportion of each of SB1's constituent elements ie [£60,000/£240,000]ths of each element.

The transfer thus comprises £37,500 from the gift from her mother; £15,000 of RFI and £7,500 of capital gain. This leaves in SB1 £112,500 of the gift; £45,000 of RFI and £22,500 of capital gain.

24.115 As indicated in paragraph 24.113, an offshore transfer also arises where an asset outside the UK is purchased and it is not intended to bring the asset to the UK. The asset is deemed to comprise the appropriate proportion of the elements of the bank account used to fund the purchase.

The asset itself also then qualifies as a mixed fund.

Example 32

Stefan, is a non-UK domiciled but UK resident individual.

His offshore bank account contains £9,000 of non-UK source interest; £15,000 of non-UK source salary and £6,000 of foreign dividend income.

He purchases a desk for £3,000 outside the UK which is intended to remain outside the UK.

The purchase of the desk is an offshore transfer and is deemed to comprise [£3,000/£30,000]ths of each element of the account (ie £900 interest; £1,500 salary; and £600 dividends).

Assume that some three years later Stefan decides to bring the desk to the UK; this should not affect the original purchase constituting an offshore transfer. This precipitates a remittance from a mixed fund account (ie the desk itself) which is thus deemed to be a remittance of the £900 interest; £1,500 salary; and £600 dividends used to effect the original purchase (the value of the desk at the date of remittance is irrelevant).

24.116 *The non-UK domiciled individual, foreign source, etc*

Pre-and post-FA 2008

24.116 Where a remittance occurs out of a mixed fund which comprises both pre-and post-*FA 2008* foreign income/gains the post-*FA 2008* provisions apply to the post-*FA 2008* foreign income/gains. Once the post-*FA 2008* foreign income/gains are exhausted the pre-*FA 2008* provisions then apply to the pre-*FA 2008* foreign income/gains.

Thus, the post-*FA 2008* provisions do not apply to determine remittance issues out of pre-*FA 2008* foreign income/gains.

Segregation of 'income' and 'capital'

24.117 Mixed accounts, both pre-and post-*FA 2008*, are in general to be avoided as the mixed fund ordering rules are not particularly favourable. In practice, this may prove difficult if not impossible and perhaps inconvenient.

Thus, for example, a remittance from an account comprising RFI and foreign capital gains (see paragraph 24.105) is a remittance first, of RFI (subject to income tax at the marginal rate of 50% for 2010–2011) and, second, capital gains (subject to CGT at a rate of 18% for 2010–2011 depending on whether the remittance is before, on or after 23 June 2010; any remittance of capital gains in the tax year 2010–2011 are treated as remitted only where the nominated amount ordering rules apply (see paragraph 24.26); pre-23 June 2010 thus falling subject to CGT at the 18%, not 28%, rate of CGT; *F (No 2) Act 2010 s 2* and *Sch 1*).

However, if the income and gains are each credited to separate accounts, a direct remittance from the capital gains account is possible.

24.118 In view of the introduction of the statutory rules governing the order of remittances from mixed accounts, the introduction of the concept of the nominated amount and the possible need to avoid the remittance of this amount (whether in whole or in part) segregation of the various sources of foreign income/gains continues to be strongly advisable.

24.119 Ideally pre- and post-*FA 2008* foreign income/gains should be segregated. This then enables remittances to be effected in the most tax efficient manner.

Freezing all accounts as at 5 April 2008 was appropriate (ie no additions to be made to any of these accounts arising from post-5 April 2008 foreign income/gains). Where this has not been done and post-5 April 2008 foreign income/

The non-UK domiciled individual, foreign source, etc **24.120**

gains have been added to these accounts, it may still be appropriate to consider freezing the accounts.

24.120 Theoretically, the number of accounts should reflect those identified in paragraph 24.105 in respect of which the mixed fund rules apply although many may regard this as unwieldy and/or impractical. Nevertheless, this permits optimal planning from a tax perspective.

At the very least, separating out capital which if remitted precipitates no tax charge makes much sense (eg inheritances; gambling winnings; gifts from family and relatives).

Example 33

Ethelred Norway, a non-UK domiciled but UK resident individual, credits the following amounts of foreign income/gains, which arose in the period 6 April 2010 to 31 August 2010, to his sole bank account in the Bahamas:

Non-UK source employment income	£225,000
Non-UK source bank interest	£100,000
Non-UK source capital gains	£225,000
Gifts from his father	£225,000

The employment income is in respect of non-UK duties under a contract of employment with a Cayman Island company.

To pay for his daughter's lavish wedding in the UK on 1 October 2010 he remits £225,000 to the UK with a further remittance of £100,000 two weeks later.

Ethelred is a 50% taxpayer.

Ethelred precipitates an income tax liability of:

50% on £225,000 (on remittance of employment income).

50% of £100,000 (on remittance of bank interest).

Aggregate income tax charge	£162,500

Example 34

Egbert Norway, a friend of Ethelred of Example 33, a non-UK domiciled but UK resident individual, credited the following amounts of foreign income/gains, which arose in the period 6 April 2010 to 31 August 2010, to four separate bank accounts in the Bahamas:

24.121 *The non-UK domiciled individual, foreign source, etc*

B1. Non-UK source employment income	£225,000
B2. Non-UK source bank interest	£100,000
B3. Non-UK source capital gains	£225,000
B4. Gifts from his father	£225,000

The employment income is in respect of non-UK duties under a contract of employment with a Cayman Island company.

To pay for his son's lavish wedding in the UK on 1 October 2010 he remits £225,000 from B4 to the UK with a further remittance of £100,000 from B3 two weeks later.

Egbert is a 50% taxpayer.

Egbert precipitates an income tax liability of:

0% of £225,000 (of gifts from his father).

28% of £100,000 (of capital gains; under the new *FA 2008* rules the capital gains element of the sale proceeds is deemed to be remitted prior to the then capital element; 28% rate assumed).

Aggregate income tax charge	£18,000

Egbert, faced with the identical situation to Ethelred, of Example 33, has managed to save £134,500 in UK tax.

24.121 Example 34 graphically illustrates the potential tax savings possible where the application of the mixed fund rules is avoided by simply segregating the various categories of foreign income and gains into separate bank accounts.

In fact, an even greater tax saving for Egbert (Example 34) is possible.

If, for example, the non-UK source capital gains are actually comprised of capital gains of £375,000 and capital losses of £150,000 (producing the net capital gains of £225,000) Egbert could arrange for the disposal proceeds to be credited to two separate accounts; the disposals giving rise to capital gains to be credited to one account and those in relation to the capital losses to the other.

Egbert could then remit the £100,000 from the account containing the disposals proceeds from the capital loss transactions thus precipitating no capital gains tax charge. His aggregate tax liability is then reduced from £28,000 to nil.

24.122 Post-*FA 2008*, non-UK source capital losses for the non-UK domiciled individual are available for offset against non-UK (and UK) source capital gains albeit subject to strict rules (see paragraph 9.30). This in principle enables Egbert's non-UK source unremitted capital gains to be reduced by the capital losses thus precipitating a smaller CGT charge as and when any of the capital gains are remitted.

24.123 The remittance of any nominated amounts of foreign income and gains is generally undesirable (see paragraph 24.34). It is therefore advisable to segregate each tax year's nominated amounts to a separately identified account into which no other foreign source income and gains are credited.

This will then ensure that any movement of such amounts can be easily monitored.

Gifts of non-UK assets

24.124 A capital gain (or of course capital loss) may arise on the disposal of chargeable assets (ie assets which are not exempt) and with it a CGT charge. However, the disposal of a non-UK situs asset by the non-UK domiciled but UK resident individual is subject to a CGT charge only on remittance (assuming remittance basis treatment is claimed; see paragraphs 8.1 and 24.7).

24.125 Gifts constitute disposals and are assumed to have taken place at market value (*TCGA 1992 ss 17* and *18*; see paragraph 8.28). However, in such cases no monies are received by the individual, and if the asset is non-UK situs there is nothing which the individual can remit to the UK and thus no CGT charge arises. This was the position pre-*FA 2008*.

The recipient of the gift, however, is assumed for CGT purposes to have paid market value, which thus forms the base cost for CGT purposes when the recipient disposes of the asset in the future, thus reducing the quantum of any CGT charge at that time.

Examples of such gifts are a simple gift by the individual to another individual (eg brother, sister, son, daughter) or perhaps, much more likely, a gift into an offshore trust.

24.126 *FA 2008* now imposes a CGT charge in such circumstances and does so by treating the asset disposed of as deriving from the chargeable gain (*ITA 2007 s 809T*).

The effect of *ITA 2007 s 809T* is that should the asset (or property derived therefrom) subsequently be brought to the UK, by or for a relevant person, a CGT charge arises on the individual at that time with respect to the chargeable gain which arose on the original gift of the asset.

24.127 *The non-UK domiciled individual, foreign source, etc*

However, *ITA 2007 s 809T* is inapplicable where the individual gifted the asset before 6 April 2008 and any remittance of it occurs on or after this date. Thus, for example, a gift of an asset into trust pre-6 April 2008 and its appointment out to a beneficiary on or after 6 April 2008 does not cause the capital gain on the initial gift into trust to have been remitted. However, any capital gain which accrues to the trustees following their acquisition of the asset may, on appointment of the asset out to a beneficiary in the UK, cause a CGT charge to arise on the trust capital gain on the part of the settlor or beneficiary (*TCGA 1992 ss 86* and *87*).

Source cessation

24.127 Pre-*FA 2008*, a cardinal rule with respect to the taxation of income was that the source of the income had to exist in the tax year in which the income was remitted to the UK. If the source did not so exist then the income was not subject to income tax in the tax year of remittance.

Thus a common ploy was for the non-UK domiciled individual to close the source of the income in one tax year and then remit the income which had arisen from that source in the following (or a later) tax year without precipitating a charge to income tax. For example, a non-UK bank account ('Account 1') in which money had been credited would give rise to interest which would then be credited to Account 2. Account 1, when appropriate, would be closed down in a tax year and the interest would be remitted from Account 2 in the following tax year without precipitating a charge to income tax.

Another example might be the remittance of dividends credited to a non-UK bank account in a tax year following the tax year in which the shares which had given rise to the dividends had been sold or simply transferred to another person (eg the spouse).

24.128 The source cessation principle did not, however, apply to capital gains or employment income.

24.129 *FA 2008* introduced a specific provision designed to prevent this type of planning (*ITTOIA 2005 s 832*).

Accordingly, RFI which is remitted to the UK by the individual is subject to income tax in the tax year of remittance whether or not the source of the income exists in the tax year of remittance.

24.130 There are no transitional provisions and thus RFI remitted to the UK by the individual on or after 6 April 2008 is automatically subject to income tax in the tax year of remittance irrespective of the tax year in which the source of the income ceased.

The non-UK domiciled individual, foreign source, etc **24.134**

Thus, the last occasion where the principle of source cessation could be used tax effectively was where the source ceased in the tax year 2006–2007 (or earlier) and the income attributable thereto was remitted on or before 5 April 2008.

24.131 Where the source ceased pre-6 April 2007 (ie in the tax year 2006–2007 or earlier) but the RFI remained outside the UK as at 5 April 2008, the RFI can thus no longer be brought into the UK by the individual without an income tax charge arising on the individual.

However, the individual could gift the RFI to another person (whether a relevant person or not) who could then remit the income without tax charge (assuming the individual does not benefit therefrom).

24.132 Even though the source of income may have ceased the tax position may vary with respect to the utilisation of any income which has arisen from the source after the cessation depending upon whether the income was remitted to the UK on or after 6 April 2008 or before this date.

Assume RFI, following source cessation, has not been remitted to the UK pre-6 April 2008. The RFI is used to purchase an offshore bond (see Chapter 18) in 2008–2009 (or later tax years) and the permitted 5% withdrawals are remitted to the UK; such withdrawals will be regarded as remittances of the RFI used to effect the purchase of the bond and thus fall subject to income tax (as would the RFI had it simply been remitted).

Now assume RFI has been remitted to the UK pre-6 April 2008 after having successfully closed the appropriate source in an earlier tax year (ie no income tax charge on the RFI remittance as no source exists in the tax year of remittance). The remitted RFI is used to purchase an offshore bond and the 5% withdrawals are remitted to the UK. In this case, the 5% withdrawals do not constitute taxable remittances (due to the application of the transitional provisions of *FA 2008* under *Sch 7*; see paragraph 24.70).

24.133 Ironically, the tax position of the non-UK domiciled individual appears to be improved where (following source cessation) the relevant income which has arisen has been remitted to the UK prior to 6 April 2008 as opposed to where the income has been retained outside of the UK as at this date.

Offshore mortgages

24.134 Prior to *FA 2008* the non-UK domiciled individual was able to borrow monies outside the UK, import the monies into the UK and service the interest arising on the borrowing from RFI without precipitating any taxable remittance. The use of RFI to repay amounts of principal was treated as having been remitted and thus subject to income tax.

24.135 *The non-UK domiciled individual, foreign source, etc*

Typically, such borrowings were used to purchase UK real estate (eg a family home). The repayments of principal were generally speaking effected once the individual left the UK or out of monies which would not precipitate an income tax charge due to having been remitted; thus, for example, gifts from relatives, inheritances or UK source taxed monies would be used.

24.135 *FA 2008* has effectively stopped the above as such borrowings now rank as 'relevant debts' which means that the use of RFI to discharge interest payments thereon precipitate taxable remittances (Condition B *ITA 2007 s 809L*).

24.136 However, the transitional provisions provide for a degree of so-called 'grand-fathering' under which the pre-*FA 2008* rules continue to apply to existing loans and thus RFI may continue to be used to discharge interest payments on such loans without precipitating an income tax charge (*FA 2008 Sch 7*).

24.137 More specifically, the transitional provisions apply where:

- before 12 March 2008 money was lent to an individual outside the UK;
- the loan was made solely to enable the individual to acquire an interest in residential property in the UK; and
- before 6 April 2008 the money was received in the UK, used by the individual to acquire an interest in the property and repayment of the debt was secured on that interest.

(FA 2008 Sch 7)

24.138 The transitional provisions apply until 5 April 2028 (ie RFI may be used to pay interest on the debt up to this date).

However, where any of the following events occurs before 5 April 2028 and on or after 12 March 2008, RFI used thereafter constitutes a taxable remittance:

- any terms of the loan are waived or varied; or
- repayment of the debt ceases to be secured on the interest in the property; or
- repayment of any other debt is secured on the interest; or
- the interest in the property ceases to be owned by the individual.

24.139 The terms of the loan are treated as varied if for example the loan is for a fixed period and at the end of the period a new loan is agreed, even if the new loan is with the same party (eg the same offshore bank) and its terms are identical to the earlier loan. However, where the loan is for a fixed period (eg ten

The non-UK domiciled individual, foreign source, etc **24.144**

years) with the interest fixed for a period (eg two years) and thereafter the interest is then subject to the lender's variable rate for the balancing eight years this is not considered as a variation of the loan terms.

24.140 To fall foul of the last condition in paragraph 24.138 does not require a sale by the individual of his interest in the property. Thus, for example, a transfer of his interest in the property to his spouse (or a trust) would cause the transitional provisions to cease to apply.

24.141 Two final points to note with respect to the transitional provisions. First, the transitional provisions only apply to individuals, not money borrowed by trustees. Second, the provisions only apply where RFI is used to effect the interest payments; thus, if foreign employment income and foreign capital gains are used to effect interest payments taxable remittances occur.

24.142 The term 'residential property' is that used for stamp duty land tax (SDLT) purposes. It includes a building used or suitable for use as a dwelling and extends to a building that is in the process of being constructed or adapted as use as a dwelling together with the surrounding gardens.

Loans secured on property: inheritance tax impact

24.143 UK residential property is UK situs and thus falls within a potential IHT charge whether owned by the UK domiciled or non-UK domiciled individual.

Any such liability is mitigated by charging any borrowing against the property (eg a mortgage; see paragraph 20.102) because, in determining the value of an individual's estate for IHT purposes on death, any liabilities of the individual are taken into account (ie liabilities are deducted from assets to arrive at the net chargeable estate).

It is important, however, that a non-UK source loan is specifically charged against the particular UK property. Any such loan which is not secured against UK property is deductible from non-UK property which, for the non-UK domiciled individual, is in any event excluded property; the securing of any loan against non-UK property is thus totally IHT ineffective.

Often the loan to value of an offshore mortgage is lower than for an onshore mortgage and a charge may be sought over both the UK property and other non-UK property. This has the consequence of an apportionment of the amount of the borrowing and thus reduced IHT effectiveness.

Loans secured on property: capital gains tax impact

24.144 Where the borrowing is denominated in foreign currency any loss which may arise on repayments of principal (when measured in sterling terms)

24.145 *The non-UK domiciled individual, foreign source, etc*

is not an allowable capital loss (as it arises on a liability not an asset) and cannot thus be offset for CGT purposes; on the other hand, any gain due to favourable currency movements is not taxable.

Temporary non-UK residence

24.145 Pre-*FA 2008* it was possible for an individual to leave the UK, acquire non-residency, and whilst outside the UK remit previously generated RFI for enjoyment on return to the UK without an income tax charge arising. Similarly, it was also possible during this period to remit previously made non-UK source capital gains without precipitating a CGT charge.

24.146 However, this is no longer possible on or after 6 April 2008. *FA 2008* introduced a completely new provision designed to preclude the tax-free remittance of such RFI (*ITTOIA 1995 s 832A*) and broadened the scope of a pre-existing provision to also extend to the remittance of such capital gains (*TCGA 1992 s 10A*; see paragraphs 4.73 and 4.77).

Summary

24.147 *FA 2008* has dramatically changed the rules which apply to the taxation of foreign source income and capital gains of the non-UK domiciled but UK resident individual. In particular, the definition of 'remittance' has been significantly widened to encompass the newly created concept of 'relevant persons'.

24.148 A number of options available to the non-UK domiciled individual to enjoy tax effectively the fruits of their foreign income and capital gains in the UK pre-2008 are no longer feasible. In particular, tax-efficient alienation of income/gains is now much more difficult.

24.149 The new rules apply not only to the foreign income and capital gains of the individual but also to such income and gains of offshore trusts of which the individual (and/or family members) may be the settlor and/or beneficiary.

24.150 *FA 2008* has also introduced the requirement for certain non-UK domiciled individuals to lodge a formal claim for each tax year in respect of which remittance basis treatment is to apply. However, the need for a formal claim is not applicable to all non-UK domiciled individuals.

An annual £30,000 tax charge is now payable by certain non-UK domiciled individuals where remittance basis treatment is claimed.

24.151 New statutory rules (to replace the historic HMRC unofficial rules) have been introduced to identify the order in which monies are remitted from a mixed account. Accordingly, segregation of accounts continues to be paramount if UK tax is to be minimised on remittances to the UK.

24.152 The concept of source cessation has been abolished.

Chapter 25

The offshore dimension

Background

25.1 For the high net worth individual mitigation of tax is clearly a high priority. In practice this is often extremely difficult to achieve particularly where income arises in different jurisdictions and assets are similarly located in more than one jurisdiction. Mitigation of one jurisdiction's taxes may increase those of another and indeed the same problem may arise within one particular jurisdiction (eg mitigation of UK capital gains tax (CGT) may increase the charge to UK inheritance tax (IHT)).

25.2 Tax mitigation techniques vary in form and substance and it must be observed that what may be an acceptable tax mitigation practice in one jurisdiction may not be so in another. In the UK there is a very important distinction between tax 'avoidance' and tax 'evasion'; the former is perfectly legal whereas the latter is not.

25.3 Due to the increasingly sophisticated tax regimes of the so-called 'high tax' countries, the outright avoidance of tax in the individual's jurisdiction of residence may prove almost impossible. It is thus to tax deferral, rather than outright avoidance, that such individuals may be forced to turn. However, this is not necessarily problematic as it may be possible to defer tax for many years which arguably comes close to avoidance.

25.4 For the UK-domiciled and UK-resident individual the use of offshore (ie non-UK resident) trusts may well enable long-term tax deferral to be achieved (see Chapter 18).

25.5 The approach adopted to mitigate tax depends upon the particular tax under consideration. For example, for the UK domiciled and UK resident individual deferral of any income tax and/or CGT charge may be achieved by utilising an offshore trust from which the settlor and settlor's spouse (and minor children) are excluded (see Chapter 18). However, such trusts do not defer charges to IHT which are in fact brought forward (ie due to exit and ten-yearly charges on relevant trust property; see Chapter 16).

The offshore dimension **25.11**

25.6 It therefore behoves the individual to decide on his main objective(s). As a general rule, this objective amounts to a need to preserve aggregate wealth in the long term and to enable accretion to wealth to be made in the most tax efficient manner.

25.7 Optimal tax mitigation cannot invariably be achieved solely within the borders of the jurisdiction of residence of the individual; the use of both offshore locations and offshore vehicles is almost inevitable. Thus, cash deposits may be made with offshore banks in locations such as the Bahamas, Guernsey, the Isle of Man or Jersey; offshore fund investments in funds located in the Cayman Islands, Ireland or Luxembourg; equity investments on overseas stock exchanges such as Singapore; real estate investments in Italy, Spain or the USA and offshore bonds issued out of Gibraltar or the Isle of Man.

25.8 The offshore locations chosen and the offshore vehicles used are invariably located in what are now referred to as 'offshore financial centres' (OFC) (formerly referred to as 'tax havens'). There are various reasons for OFC use but a critical factor is usually the absence of any local taxes be it income tax, CGT or IHT equivalents. Thus, no additional layer of tax is imposed.

25.9 However, the role of double tax agreements cannot be overlooked. Such agreements in many cases reduce tax in the source country where income arises and/or on capital gains on disposals of local situs assets. As a consequence, in some cases it may be more tax efficient to use a vehicle in a moderately taxed jurisdiction as opposed to one in a tax-free OFC (as many OFCs are not parties to double tax agreements; see Chapter 26).

Offshore financial centres

25.10 There are almost as many definitions of the term 'offshore financial centre' as there are OFCs themselves. Typically, these definitions are not definitions as such but merely a list of attributes that appear to be common to such centres. The IMF in a working paper published in April 2007 defined the OFC as:

> 'a country or jurisdiction that provides financial services to non-residents on a scale that is incommensurate with the size and the financing of its domestic economy'.

25.11 The Organisation for Economic Cooperation and Development (the OECD) has described the term 'tax haven' (not in fact using the increasingly accepted term 'offshore financial centre') as a jurisdiction which has:

- no or very low tax on financial income;

25.12 *The offshore dimension*

- no effective exchange of information;
- a lack of transparency; and
- a lack of the need for any entity (eg company; trust) to have a local substantive presence.

25.12 Depending upon which definition of the term OFC is used there are probably, in any event, approaching 100 dotted around the world. These can be conveniently categorised, geographically, into those located in one of the following broad areas: the Caribbean; Europe; the Indian Ocean; and Australasia.

- *Caribbean*-located territories would include: Antigua, Aruba, Bahamas, Belize, Bermuda (although, of course, not technically in the Caribbean), British Virgin Islands, the Cayman Islands, Netherlands Antilles, Nevis and Turks and Caicos and Panama.

- *European*- located territories would include: Andorra, Cyprus, Gibraltar, Guernsey, the Isle of Man, Jersey, Liberia, Liechtenstein, Luxembourg, Madeira, Malta, Monaco, San Marino and Switzerland.

- *Indian Ocean*-located territories would include: Mauritius and the Seychelles.

- *Australasian*-located territories would include: Cook Islands, Hong Kong, Marshall Islands, Nauru, New Hebrides, Singapore and Vanuatu.

25.13 Many of these OFCs are British Crown Dependencies or former British colonies and, to a degree, their respective success has to a great extent arguably derived from this fact, although it may be counter-argued that this historic link militates against their use due to the continued direct and indirect influence the UK often has over their affairs.

25.14 Not surprisingly OFCs are viewed with extreme scepticism by the tax authorities of the high tax jurisdictions perhaps with some degree of justification given the fact that many OFCs have been used at one time or another for illegal purposes (eg money laundering; tax evasion).

In 2007–2008 HMRC obtained information from a number of British-based banks concerning deposits made by UK-resident individuals in the UK parent banks' offshore subsidiaries; of itself, this is not illegal, but apparently many of these individuals have failed to declare any interest income arising on the deposits. HMRC also received (and continues to receive) similar information through the European Savings Directive concerning interest payable to UK residents on deposits in the European Union (EU)(see Chapter 26).

The offshore dimension **25.17**

In a not dissimilar exercise a number of years ago it is alleged that the Internal Revenue Service (ie the US equivalent of the UK HMRC) forced 'Mastercard' to supply records of nearly two million transactions relating to accounts held by Americans in Antigua, the Bahamas and the Cayman Islands; similar account information was apparently sought from both Visa and American Express. In Germany it recently came to light that a significant number of German-resident individuals have allegedly been using Liechtenstein to 'hide' income and assets from the German tax authorities.

25.15 Fortunately, following receipt of the information from various UK banks concerning offshore deposits made by UK resident individuals, HMRC announced in April 2007 a so-called 'amnesty' (although technically was not an amnesty) for such individuals, the 'Offshore Disclosure Facility' (ODF). Broadly, under the amnesty HMRC agreed to charge a fixed penalty of 10% of any unpaid taxes (albeit covering a period going back 20 years) on the basis that individuals voluntarily disclosed their deposits and all income derived therefrom which had not been previously disclosed. A second, not dissimilar, facility was also launched by HMRC in early 2009.

A further and somewhat unique facility has recently (2009) been entered into between the UK and Liechtenstein, the 'Liechtenstein Disclosure Facility' (the LDF). The LDF is a bespoke service to support the reviews to be carried out by the financial intermediaries in Liechtenstein to identify those who may have liability to UK tax. It allows people with unpaid tax linked to investments or assets in Liechtenstein to settle their tax liability under this special arrangement. The LDF will run from 1 September 2009 until 31 March 2015. Considering Liechtenstein's historic posture on exchange of information and. in particular, bank secrecy, this is a startling change in attitude on the part of the Liechtenstein government.

Other countries including, for example, Australia, Ireland and Italy have adopted similar type amnesties with, it would seem, remarkable success in terms of tax collected and/or capital repatriated.

25.16 In addition to levying no or very low tax, OFCs are also notable for their secrecy laws and their unwillingness to supply or exchange information with the authorities of other jurisdictions. It is these three factors which have for many years caused consternation amongst the tax authorities of the high tax countries.

Times are, however, changing and the OFCs' secrecy laws and their unwillingness to exchange information have under recent years been under sustained 'attack' and, as a consequence, both have been significantly eroded.

25.17 In the UK two major initiatives in this area resulted in the production of two separate reports. The first, published in 1998, was headed 'Review of

25.18 *The offshore dimension*

Financial Regulation in the Crown Dependencies' (namely, Guernsey, the Isle of Man and Jersey) and the second, published two years later, headed 'Review of Financial Regulation in Anguilla, Bermuda, British Virgin Islands, Cayman Islands, Montserrat and Turks and Caicos'.

As recently as April 2008 the Treasury Committee announced yet another initiative which was designed to 'undertake an inquiry into Offshore Financial Centres, as part of its ongoing work into Financial Stability and Transparency'.

25.18 However, perhaps the initiative that really started serious international global cooperation to combat the use of OFCs for tax evasion, fraud, etc. was that launched in 1996 by the OECD into what was referred to as 'harmful tax practices' which led to the production of the report 'Harmful Tax Competition: An Emerging Global Issue' in 1998. Other reports from the OECD then followed, in essence providing updates on subsequent work being undertaken designed to tackle and eliminate 'harmful tax practices' (interestingly, 'harmful tax practices' were found to exist not only in OFCs but also in member countries of the OECD!). 'Harmful tax practices' are described as 'preferential tax regimes in the OECD member countries' and 'those occurring in the form of tax havens'. Thus, by definition, OFCs/tax havens are according to the OECD 'harmful'. The objectives of the 1998 report were as follows:

- to identify and eliminate harmful tax practices of preferential tax regimes in OECD countries;
- to identify 'tax havens' and seek their commitments to the principles of transparency and effective exchange of information; and
- to encourage other non-OECD economies to associate themselves with the harmful tax practices work.

25.19 The report produced a list of 35 tax havens referred to as 'uncooperative'. These included: the Bahamas, Barbados, the British Virgin Islands, Gibraltar, Guernsey, the Isle of Man, Montserrat, the Netherlands Antilles, Nevis, Panama, the Turks and Caicos Islands, and Vanuatu. To be removed from this list requires the OFC to enter into a commitment to eliminate its harmful tax practices (within a pre-defined time frame) which included a willingness to exchange information with, primarily, the high tax countries of the world (including access to banking information).

25.20 In 2007 the OECD released yet another report, 'Tax Co-operation towards a level playing field – 2007 Assessment by the Global Forum on Taxation', which indicated that a number of jurisdictions still fell short of the standards required by the OECD. The 2007 report stated that significant restrictions on access to bank information for tax purposes remained in three OECD countries (Austria, Luxembourg and Switzerland) and in a number of OFCs including Cyprus, Liechtenstein, Panama and Singapore. The 2007 report also stated that, despite commitments being entered into by tax havens to implement effective exchange of information arrangements, a number have failed to do so.

25.21 Nevertheless, significant progress has been made concerning exchange of information and many OFCs have now concluded agreements with various countries under which they have agreed to provide information to other, typically, high tax jurisdictions. These agreements are referred to as 'Tax Information Exchange Agreements' (TIEAs) and are based on a Model Agreement produced by the OECD in 2002. A number of such bilateral agreements have been signed by the UK and those currently in force are with Bermuda, the Isle of Man, Jersey, Guernsey and the British Virgin Islands (see Chapter 26).

In addition bilateral agreements have also been signed, but as yet are not in force, with Antigua, the Bahamas, Gibraltar and Liechtenstein.

TIEAs have also been signed with various OFCs relating to the EU Savings Directive either on a reciprocal or non-reciprocal basis. Those falling in the former category include the British Virgin Islands, Guernsey and Jersey and those falling in the latter include Anguilla, the Cayman Islands and the Turks and Caicos Islands (see Chapter 26).

Offshore financial centres: vehicles

25.22 The two classic vehicles typically set up in an OFC as part of a tax planning exercise are the trust and the company although partnerships may also be created.

Companies

25.23 OFCs have created basically two generic types of locally incorporated company, namely, the 'international business company' (IBC) and the 'exempt company'. In the Caribbean the former tends to have been adopted, whereas in Europe, the latter is more prevalent although they are basically the same.

The common characteristics of both types of company are that they are not permitted to do business within the location of incorporation (ie within the OFC itself) and non-local residents are precluded from owning any shares in such companies. The benefits typically include no local (or minimal) tax on profits; freedom of repatriation of profits; minimum (if any) local disclosure requirements (eg no need to file detailed or sometimes, any, accounts, etc.); flexibility with respect to the location of the 'books' of the company (ie possibility of

25.24 *The offshore dimension*

maintaining books in another location); and often no or minimal requirements with respect to the holding of company meetings (eg annual general meeting).

25.24 Historically, many OFCs permitted companies to issue bearer shares but as part of the OECD's drive for tax transparency bearer share companies are now unavailable in many OFCs (ie all shares issued are in registered form as applies in most high tax territories (eg the UK)). The logic in seeking to preclude bearer share company formations is that the identity of the shareholders may be more readily ascertained.

However, this assumption of shareholder identity is perhaps more illusory than real. First, not all OFCs require the true identity of the beneficial shareholders when the company is set up. Second, even where the OFC requires the identity of the true beneficial owners on set-up, the company is usually permitted the simple expedient of using local nominee arrangements (ie in the local register of shareholders the names shown are simply nominees who hold the shares for the ultimate beneficial owners whose identity to third parties (eg foreign tax authorities) remain hidden). While the authorities of the OFC may, as indicated above, demand to know the true beneficial shareholders invariably the local authorities will refuse to disclose such details to third party enquirers (eg the tax authorities of the high tax jurisdictions) subject to such requests for information falling with, for example, a TIEA or other form of agreement between the two jurisdictions

25.25 Where any form of local filing by the company is required with the local Registrar of Companies invariably the information filed is extremely limited. It may simply constitute, for example, the company's registered office address; the address and name of the locally registered agent (on whom 'service' may be served); and a register of shareholders. In some OFCs such information is available for public inspection; in other OFCs this is not possible; and in some OFCs the company's permission is needed in any event to inspect any documents so filed.

25.26 The permitted activities these types of company may undertake are virtually unlimited. Thus, for example, an IBC may be set up to hold real estate (including the matrimonial home); to hold portfolio investments; to trade; or to act as agent/broker in international transactions of whatever type. It is also possible for such companies to engage in activities which involve banking and/or insurance but, generally speaking, in many OFCs such companies are more tightly supervised and controlled although this is not true in all cases.

Thus, the IBC in principle offers the individual the opportunity to operate in a tax-free environment without restriction, with minimal supervision and no real disclosure with respect to either its activities or its shareholders.

Trusts

25.27 Trusts are very different from companies but are an inevitable part of any wealth planning structure. Trusts, while offering possible tax attractions, can also be used for other purposes.

25.28 Very few OFCs have any registration requirements with respect to trusts. The formation of a trust in an OFC can thus be carried out in complete secrecy (typically, using a local law firm). There is, generally speaking, no 'Registrar of Trusts' equivalent of the 'Registrar of Companies'. Trust deeds are thus not lodged with any local authority.

25.29 The trust is a creature of equity and over many years equitable doctrines have evolved into a bundle of rules which apply to trusts. Three such rules are the rule against perpetuities; the rule against accumulations; and the rule prohibiting purpose trusts other than those with charitable objectives. It is often perceived that such rules inhibit the flexibility of the trust and, as a consequence, a number of OFCs have modified them albeit in different ways.

For example, some OFCs have simply abolished the rule against perpetuities while other OFCs have simply increased the normal maximum period (eg the *Bahamas Perpetuities (Amendment) Act 2004* increased the period of a perpetuity from 80 to 150 years; in the British Virgin Islands the maximum perpetuity period is 100 years; the maximum perpetuity for Guernsey trusts until recently was 100 years, now unlimited for new trusts; and in Barbados, the rule against perpetuities does not apply).

25.30 With respect to the accumulation rule Barbados, for example, permits accumulation of income for up to 100 years whereas in Guernsey following the *Trusts (Guernsey) Law 2007* (which came into force on 17 March 2008) the accumulation period for new trusts is unlimited.

25.31 These amendments have greatly increased the attractiveness of setting up trusts in OFCs. Indeed in November 2009 the UK passed the *PAA 2009* designed to bring the UK trust into the twenty-first century (see paragraph 15.26).

25.32 With respect to the last rule namely, purpose trusts, the common law requires that the beneficiaries of a trust are identifiable and thus a trust set up for a specific purpose (other than charitable) is prohibited due to the lack of identifiable beneficiaries. Many OFCs have introduced specific legislation to recognise purpose trusts (not just those with charitable purposes).

For example, purpose trusts may be set up in the Bahamas, Belize, Bermuda and the Isle of Man under their respective legislation. However, in 1997 the Cayman Islands introduced its own legislation in this regard, namely, the *Special Trusts*

25.33 The offshore dimension

(Alternative Regime) Law 1997 which gave rise to the so-called STAR trust. The STAR trust may be set up for persons or purposes or both and the persons may be of any number and the purposes may be of any number whether charitable or non-charitable (enabling total flexibility).

However, the purpose of the trust must be lawful and not contrary to public policy.

25.33 Another innovation of the OFC in connection with trusts is the introduction of the role of 'protector'. A protector is in a sense an intermediary between the settlor and the trustees. Unlike the trust itself, the protector is not a creature of equity. The protector is a role created under the trust deed (ie the written instrument creating the trust and setting out the terms of the trust) and/or by legislation. The role of the protector may vary extending from a role which is primary reactive to a positive proactive role. The former role might be one where the protector is merely required to respond to trustee requests for help and/or guidance about trust matters. The latter role might be one where the consent of the protector is required before the trustees may carry out certain actions or take decisions in relation to trust property and one where the protector also has powers including the power to dismiss and appoint trustees and even to change the governing law of the trust.

25.34 The rationale behind the concept of protector is an attempt to offer the settlor some comfort about the manner and way in which the trust operates both during the lifetime of the settlor and, in particular, following the death of the settlor. A trust created in an OFC invariably requires the appointment of local trustees who are typically unknown to the settlor (and beneficiaries). Such trustees will thus not really understand the mentality of the settlor or what is in the settlor's mind about how in practice the trust should function. The protector is thus the person who is intended to bridge this gap and is normally in a position to do so because the protector is typically a 'family friend' who has detailed knowledge of the settlor, his family and the settlor's intentions.

25.35 Care is required to ensure that the trust is not in fact a sham due to, for example, the excessive degree of control exercised by the settlor through his protector. This would, or course, defeat the purposes for which the trust has been created as the trust, as a separate entity, would simply be ignored.

25.36 In fact the whole point of the protector role is to allow the settlor to be distanced from the trust so as not to be seen as controlling it, whether directly or indirectly, while at the same time offering the settlor some comfort that his views and/or wishes are not totally disregarded by the trustees. It is in this precise context that the 'letter of wishes' (sometimes also referred to as a 'memorandum of wishes') emerged.

The letter of wishes is literally a letter from the settlor to the trustees expressing the settlor's wishes with respect to certain aspects of the trust. It is not intended to be binding upon the trustees or be treated as part of the formal trust deed. The trustees can if they so choose ignore its content but not surprisingly, in practice, they will where possible take serious cognisance of its content.

25.37 By combining the appointment of a protector with the letter of wishes the settlor is typically well placed to convey to the trustees the factors the settlor would like the trustees to note and be aware of and, at the same time, not cause him to be seen as controlling the actions of the trustees.

Offshore financial centres: uses

25.38 The attributes of the typical OFC make them attractive jurisdictions in which to locate appropriate vehicles as part of a strategy involving, *inter alia*, tax planning, probate avoidance or asset protection.

Tax planning

25.39 The vehicle sited in an OFC is, as discussed above, normally a trust or company or a combination of the two. The vehicle's purpose may be to simply permit income and/or capital gains arising outside the jurisdiction of the residence of the individual concerned to accrue without tax charge. For example, a UK domiciled and UK-resident individual holding equities in a Hong Kong registered company is subject to UK income tax on dividend income thereon and UK CGT on any sale thereof. However, if a trust set up in the Cayman Islands was to hold the equities no tax charges arise (assuming the settlor and spouse are not able to benefit under the terms of the trust).

A non-UK domiciled individual is exposed to UK IHT on UK situs assets. However, by utilising a trust/underlying company structure set up in an OFC to own the UK situs assets, the exposure to IHT is removed.

25.40 It should be noted that there is, of course, no reason why both vehicles need to be within the same OFC. Thus, in the above scenarios, the trust could be governed by the laws of Jersey and the underlying company by the laws of the British Virgin Islands.

25.41 It may be that the simple use of an OFC bank deposit by a UK-domiciled and UK-resident individual allows interest thereon to be credited 'gross' (ie without tax at source first being deducted) permitting a greater roll-up over time than would apply if the deposit had been made in the UK (where income tax at source is deducted on crediting the interest) in effect producing a positive cash flow benefit.

25.42 *The offshore dimension*

25.42 An OFC corporate vehicle may be used in a nominee arrangement in order to enable the individual to remain anonymous. For example, the individual may wish to acquire a piece of land but at the same time does not wish the vendor to know of his identity. The OFC adds no additional layer of tax and can easily be administered with minimum administrative inconvenience.

Probate mitigation/substitute will

25.43 Not all countries operate the UK's system of probate following an individual's death. However, for those that do probate may be costly and time consuming. Direct ownership of assets by the individual in those jurisdictions operating a probate system may be circumnavigated by the interposition of an appropriate OFC vehicle. In addition, use of such a vehicle may enable local forced heirship rules to be avoided. In such cases the OFC vehicle owning the property is likely to be a company rather than a trust.

The death of the individual thus results in no transfer of ownership of the underlying property only the shares in the OFC company; as the company is registered in an OFC ownership transfer can be readily effected without local tax charges. Indeed if the shares are owned by an OFC trust no transfers of any nature are required as no property is owned by the individual on death.

25.44 The OFC trust may also act as a form of substitute will for the individual. While it is unlikely that the whole of the individual's worldwide assets will necessarily be placed in one or more OFC trusts a significant portion of such assets may be so settled. The use of the trust in this manner has a number of advantages including the fact that the terms of trust are confidential (the will becomes a public document following death); the trustees under a discretionary trust may take into account changes in legislation and the fortunes of the beneficiaries even after the settlor has died (whereas once the testator dies the will is 'set in stone'); and the trust assets may be located in a number of different jurisdictions yet simply administered by the same trustees.

Asset protection

25.45 All trusts offer some degree of 'asset protection'. The term 'asset protection trust' (APT), however, is a generic term and is commonly used to refer to trusts which are specifically set up to protect the assets of the settlor from third-party claims. Such third parties typically include creditors, those claiming under forced heirship rules and disgruntled ex-spouses. However, such third parties may also extend to governments seeking to expropriate the individual's assets following a coup for example.

25.46 Although the concept of asset protection from third parties underpins the APT the treatment of APTs in the OFCs often varies according to whether the trust is designed specifically to protect against creditors versus other third parties (eg forced heirship claims). In addition, OFCs vary in the extent to which foreign creditor judgements may be enforced locally in the OFC.

25.47 The effectiveness of the APT against creditors varies according to the particular circumstances of the individual. Many onshore jurisdictions (of which the UK is one) have specific legislation designed to prevent individuals from defrauding creditors and thus simply settling assets in an APT in an OFC may not fully protect the individual's assets as intended; although an APT offshore is, other things being equal, likely to offer in practice greater protection than an APT onshore.

25.48 Issues of forced heirship are increasingly common and many OFCs have introduced legislation designed to defeat such claims. Such legislation will typically ensure that despite the legal regime applying in the settlor's home jurisdiction trusts created in the OFC by the individual will be regarded as valid and foreign forced heirship judgements will not be recognised and/or enforced in the OFC.

25.49 APTs undoubtedly have a legitimate role to play in any form of financial planning. However, as indicated above, care is required to ensure that their use does not breach the rules in the jurisdiction of residence of the individual.

Offshore financial centres: the choice

25.50 Some OFCs are particularly appropriate for certain types of planning while not appropriate for others. The APT, for example, is not a vehicle available in all OFCs and, where it is available, the degree of protection offered by an APT in one OFC may differ markedly from an APT in another. Filing requirements for the IBC differ among the various OFCs offering this type of company.

25.51 However, there are certain minimum requirements for any OFC to meet if it is to be considered for use in any planning exercise.

These minimum requirements include political stability; financial stability; judicial stability; and a highly profficient and highly regarded professional infrastructure. For UK individuals, a preference for those OFCs whose legal system based on common law and English as the main 'professional' language would seem highly desirable attributes. The requirement for local legal and other documents to be constantly translated from, say, Portuguese (in the case of Madeira) to English, only adds to time, cost and the possibility of confusion.

25.52 A less stringent requirement but, again, possibly desirable are OFCs located in the same time zone as the individual, although with relatively instantaneous communication by phone, fax, email, etc. this, today, perhaps seems less necessary.

25.53 Once an OFC meets the above minimum requirements the choice may be then narrowed by investigating the reputation, laws and attitude of the OFC with respect to the particular planning purpose in mind. In addition, the strength of local bank secrecy laws should be examined and whether the OFC is a party to any agreements under which information may be exchanged (eg under TIEAs and/or exchange of information provisions contained within double tax agreements) with other countries should also be checked. Other things being equal an APT, for example, located in an OFC with strong bank secrecy laws and which is not a party to any exchange information agreements is likely to be more robust to external 'attack' than might otherwise be the case.

Similarly, the use of trusts to avoid 'forced heirship' rules is likely to be more robust from external 'attack' where the OFC is not a party to any information exchange agreements, where bank secrecy is strongest and where specific local legislation exists to deal with such issues.

25.54 As the trust is a vehicle of major importance in virtually all financial (and other) planning exercises a strong preference should be expressed for those OFCs whose legal system is based on that of English common law. Such jurisdictions are better equipped to understand the concept and whose courts are likely to follow UK court decisions. Civil law jurisdictions do not readily accommodate trusts and, other things being equal, should be avoided.

25.55 The company concept is generally understood in all OFCs. The choice is therefore less constrained and issues such as requirements as to company/shareholder meetings in terms of number per annum, location and whether meetings need to be held physically or whether they can be effected by telephone; minimum requirements as to the number of directors, nationality or residence requirements; the possibility of nominee arrangements; disclosure requirements relating to names and/or addresses of directors or the need for company accounts to be filed; and the position with respect to public access of filed information are all factors to consider.

Tax is less likely to be an issue as between OFCs as most levy no or very little.

UK tax and information disclosure requirements

25.56 Anti-avoidance provisions in the UK tax code may impose tax liabilities on UK domiciled and UK resident settlors on the income and/or capital gains of trusts and/or companies resident in OFCs (see Chapter 18). Thus, the settlor may be faced with a UK tax charge without having actually received any income/gains from the trust. Whilst the UK tax provisions provide for the settlor to be reimbursed from the trust with respect to any such liabilities complex issues arise.

25.57 The trustees' responsibility is to the beneficiaries, not the settlor; the trustees owe no fiduciary duty to the settlor. The issue arises as to whether reimbursement of taxes paid by the settlor (re trust income/gains) is a legitimate payment by the trustees. Even if the trust deed, somewhat unusually, provides explicitly for such payments to be made the matter is not that straightforward. For example, the beneficiaries may still choose to contest any such intended payment in the local courts and/or where payment has actually been made may choose to sue the trustees for breach of trust. The courts may hold under the principle of non-enforcement of foreign revenue laws that such a provision in the trust deed is to be curtailed and only in exceptional circumstances can foreign taxes owed by trustees be discharged. The reality is that, in general, reimbursement is unlikely unless it can be seen to be in the interests of the beneficiaries.

25.58 The onus to make returns to HMRC where any of the above anti-avoidance provisions apply is with the individual settlor/beneficiary not the offshore trustees. However, HMRC often dispatch Form 50(FS) 'Trust gains and capital payments' to offshore trustees requesting information as to the capital gains of the trust and any capital payments made by the trustees to trust beneficiaries. There is no requirement for the trustees to comply and complete the form although in many cases the forms are completed and lodged with HMRC (see paragraph 25.65 below re Form C41G (Trusts). The following statements appear on the form:

> 'Providing us with the information requested on this form may prevent checks being needed into these aspects of the settlor's and/or beneficiary's UK Self Assessment Tax Return. The information requested has nothing to do with any UK tax liability of the settlement and its provision is voluntary. You will not be charged a penalty if you do not complete the form or if any of the information you send in is incorrect. But if you do not provide this information we may need to ask for it from a UK beneficiary or settlor'.

25.59 The statement makes it clear that the trustees are under no obligation to complete the form although there appears to be the veiled threat contained therein suggesting that a failure to complete it will lead to 'hassle' for the settlor/beneficiaries. Where the form is completed by the trustees presumably HMRC simply cross-check the information provided with information disclosed by the individual (settlor/beneficiary) on his tax return; any discrepancies then no doubt leading to probing questions to the individual.

25.60 *The offshore dimension*

It would therefore seem sensible that the individual be made aware that the trustees are providing the information to HMRC and also of its precise nature (simply by providing a copy of the completed Form FS(50)).

25.60 Irrespective of any tax liabilities arising on the settlor the trustees may also have their own tax liabilities in respect of income received and capital gains made. Where the trust is resident in an OFC local tax liabilities are unlikely to arise; however, the trustees may have a liability in the countries in which the income arises or the capital gains are made.

Non-UK resident trustees of discretionary trusts are in principle liable to UK income tax on UK source income at the 50% trust rate (for the tax year 2010–2011; formerly 40%) and the dividend trust rate of 42.5% (for the tax year 2010–2011; formerly 32.5%). However, such trusts are not within the charge to CGT.

Non-UK resident trusts are also within the ambit of IHT. Post-22 March 2006, all lifetime trusts (except disabled trusts) constitute relevant property trusts and are thus in principle required to file Form IHT 100 where exit and ten-yearly charges occur. Non-UK situs property of such trusts created by non-UK domiciled individuals (irrespective of residence status) constitutes excluded property and thus no exit or ten-yearly charges arise thereon and hence no returns are required for the excluded property trust.

25.61 Inevitably HMRC may have enforcement problems should the trustees either fail to file an appropriate tax return and/or fail to discharge any tax liabilities. The trustees may, again, therefore be exposed to breaches of trust claims from the beneficiaries should they voluntarily pay such taxes.

25.62 In this regard it is interesting to note that under ESC the UK-resident beneficiaries of a non-UK resident discretionary trust are able to claim a tax credit for UK tax paid by the trustees on UK source income. *Inter alia*, for the beneficiaries to be able to so claim, the trustees must satisfy the conditions laid down in ESC B18 which are that the trustees must be fully up to date with their tax returns and must have paid any UK tax due.

Thus, if the trustees do not satisfy these conditions the UK resident beneficiary receiving income distributions from the trust out of UK source income will simply be subject to income tax on the amount received from the trustees (with no offsetting tax credits).

25.63 The existence of the trust should be known to HMRC as the settlor (assuming UK residency and UK domicile status at the date of set up of the trust) is under an obligation to notify HMRC of the trustees' details and the date on which the trust was set up. This information has to be provided within three months of the date the trust is set up (*TCGA 1992 Sch 5A*).

The creation of the trust may precipitate CGT liabilities which may require inclusion on the settlor's tax return and the transfer, if a chargeable lifetime transfer (as is, post-22 March 2006, highly likely) may also require notification on Form IHT 100.

25.64 *IHTA 1984 s 218* requires anyone concerned in the making of a non-UK resident trust in the course of a trade or profession to notify HMRC of the trust's existence assuming that the person believes the settlor is UK domiciled and the trustees are non-UK resident. The notification must be made within three months.

25.65 Form 41G (Trusts) is the form HMRC typically sends to non-UK resident trustees for completion. The form requires details of, *inter alia*, the names and address of all trustees; name and address of the settlor; whether the trust has been created by will or in lifetime; and details of all assets settled by the settlor.

In practice it appears that many trustees of non-UK resident trusts do complete this form despite the fact that HMRC cannot demand that it be completed. Presumably this occurs only after discussion between trustees and beneficiaries (and possibly the settlor).

25.66 It should not be forgotten that increasingly information is being exchanged between the UK and other countries under the UK's various double tax agreements; historically, such agreements have been primarily with high tax countries and not OFCs (although the UK has for many years had such agreements with some OFCs including Antigua, Barbados, Belize, Cyprus, Guernsey, the Isle of Man, Jersey, Malta and Mauritius). However, as discussed above, the number of TIEAs to which the UK is a party is growing and such agreements are specifically with the OFCs. Other things being equal, this increases the probability of HMRC becoming aware of the existence of a non-UK resident trust (in respect of which HMRC may not have been notified) set up by a UK-resident individual.

Relocation to an offshore financial centre

25.67 Perhaps the ultimate tax-efficient plan is for an individual to relocate to an OFC and become a resident thereof, effectively abandoning ties with the UK. Although local residents of an OFC may be subject to some, albeit minimal, local tax this is not usually the position.

25.68 Becoming a resident of an OFC, whilst automatically removing an individual from the ambit of UK income and CGT (except, of course, with respect to UK source income), does not automatically remove the individual

25.69 *The offshore dimension*

from the ambit of IHT. Removal outside the IHT regime requires a loss of any UK domicile and the acquisition of a domicile of choice in the chosen OFC.

25.69 Relocating, however, is, of course, a very serious option with all that it entails but is an option often pursued by the extremely wealthy. It is by no means uncommon for 'pop stars', tennis players, golfers and Formula 1 grand prix drivers to leave their original countries of residence (where taxes are relatively speaking 'high') and relocate to a country with a more favourable tax climate.

25.70 In many cases, however, the relocations in such cases are not to the conventional OFCs (eg Bermuda, the Bahamas, and the Turks and Caicos Islands) but to countries not normally categorised as OFCs, but which nevertheless offer favourable tax status to high net worth individuals; countries such as Monaco and Switzerland are two such notable destinations.

Guernsey, the Isle of Man and Jersey, whilst not 'tax-free' jurisdictions, are also popular options for UK residents, as have been Belize and the Seychelles.

25.71 The choice depends upon a multiplicity of factors. Once those jurisdictions with a favourable tax regime are identified, other relevant factors include language, geographical location, political stability, and accessibility.

25.72 The issue of so-called 'trailing taxes' needs to be considered. These primarily apply with respect to inheritance/death taxes. The term 'trailing taxes' refers to the imposition by a jurisdiction of its inheritance/death taxes on its ex-residents/ex-nationals for a period of time after the individual ceases to reside in the jurisdiction. The UK, for example, continues to levy IHT on its former UK domiciled individuals for a three-year period following the date of acquisition of a new domicile. Somewhat exceptionally, the USA continues to levy all its taxes on its citizens who have left the USA and acquired residency elsewhere.

25.73 Even following relocation to an OFC, many of the above issues continue to be of relevance, although of course mitigation of local tax is no longer an issue. However, issues such as family inheritance, probate and information disclosure all need to be addressed, as does the mitigation of foreign taxes on income/capital gains and inheritances.

Summary

25.74 Mitigation of UK taxes may be achieved by a variety of means. OFCs offer the individual one option to achieve such mitigation.

25.75 OFCs may also be utilised for non-tax reasons including the avoidance of forced heirship laws, creditor protection and general family planning.

25.76 OFCs offer vehicles tailored to achieving efficient family asset structuring. The two main vehicles are those available elsewhere, namely companies and trusts, but the attributes of both of these vehicles have been adapted under local legislation to make them more flexible than their on-shore counterparts.

25.77 The choice of a suitable OFC depends upon a number of factors. No one OFC is likely to be the 'best' for all purposes.

25.78 Relocation to an OFC may be the answer for some individuals.

Chapter 26

International taxation

Background

26.1 The affairs of taxpayers, in many cases, transcend international borders. This causes a taxpayer's income or gains to be subject to more than one jurisdiction's tax regime. Thus, for example a UK resident individual receiving dividend income on USA equities is subject thereon to both UK and US tax; similarly, a UK domiciled individual who dies owning French real estate is exposed to both UK and French death taxes.

26.2 Double tax (ie the levying of more than one jurisdiction's tax on the same income/gains of the taxpayer) thus arises and in the absence of some form of relief international activities would be severely curtailed. The double tax agreement is designed to provide such relief.

26.3 Double tax agreements also provide a mechanism designed to prevent tax evasion by provision for exchanges of information between the tax authorities of the jurisdictions party to the agreement.

26.4 The role of the double tax agreement has increased significantly over the years and the UK is currently party to well in excess of 100 such agreements which cover income tax, capital gains tax (CGT), corporation tax and inheritance tax (IHT); the agreements covering IHT are separate from those which address income and corporation tax and CGT.

26.5 Unlike the UK's tax legislation which is very specific in its wording the text of double tax agreements is, by comparison, much vaguer and less specific.

26.6 Common practice is to use terms such as 'agreements', 'conventions' and 'arrangements' when referring to treaties between jurisdictions which deal with tax. Technically, under international law, the correct term is 'treaty'. *VCLT 1969* defines a 'treaty' as follows:

> 'an international agreement concluded between states in written form and governed by international law'.

26.7 In order to have the force of law in the UK any double tax agreement concluded with another country requires incorporation into UK law (*McLaine Watson v Dpt of Trade* (1989)). This is usually carried out by a Statutory Order in Council (*ICTA 1988 s 788*).

26.8 As indicated in paragraph 26.2 one of the primary objectives of a double tax agreement is to prevent double tax (ie to provide for some form of relief). In this regard it is generally accepted that a double tax agreement cannot impose a liability to tax which is not already provided for under the domestic laws of the jurisdiction concerned (HMRC's International Manual, para 152060).

26.9 The general rule is that the provisions of a double tax agreement override UK domestic law; otherwise a breach of international law occurs. However, where the wording of a domestic statute (which post dates the date of the particular double tax agreement) is unambiguous it may override the terms of the double tax agreement despite the breach of international law which appears to occur (examples of such override are to be seen in *ICTA 1988 ss 808A* and *812*).

Nature of a double tax agreement

26.10 Most double tax agreements are bilateral in nature, (ie are agreements between two countries) although multilateral agreements do exist (eg *MCAA 1988*).

26.11 The UK is a party to two main categories of double tax agreement. The first are the so-called 'comprehensive' agreements which deal with income tax, CGT and corporation tax; the second category is those agreements which deal with IHT.

The UK is a party to in excess of 100 comprehensive agreements but a party to only ten agreements which address IHT.

Comprehensive double tax agreements

26.12 The structure of the typical comprehensive double tax agreement to which the UK is a party follows the OECD Model 1977 (as subsequently amended).

The OECD Model comprises some 31 'Articles' the majority of which deal with the tax treatment of a specific category of income (eg *Article 6* 'Income from Immovable Property'; *Article 11* 'Interest'; and *Article 13* 'Capital Gains').

26.13 *International taxation*

Other Articles address more general issues such as those involving 'dual' residence (*Article 4*); other income (*Article 21*); non-discrimination (*Article 24*); resolution of general disputes (*Article 25*); and exchange of information (*Article 26*).

26.13 The general approach of the OECD Model 1977 is to grant primary taxing rights to the jurisdiction of residence of the taxpayer albeit with the other contracting jurisdiction retaining rights to levy its own tax on certain categories of income/gains arising within their borders although often at reduced rates. Thus, for example, a UK resident individual may receive dividend income from the USA; the UK has the right to tax its own residents on such income but the USA retains its right to levy its domestic withholding tax on such income. The normal domestic withholding tax rate applicable to such income in the USA is 30%; however, under the double tax agreement between the UK and the USA this rate is reduced to 15% (*Article 10* UK/US double tax agreement).

26.14 The OECD Model also provides for relief from double taxation either by way of a tax credit or a tax expense (*Articles 23A* and *23B*). Thus, in paragraph 26.13, the UK is required to grant the UK resident taxpayer some form of relief with respect to the USA withholding tax of 15%. In the UK this relief primarily takes the form of a tax credit ie the 15% US tax is offset against the UK income tax on the income (*ICTA 1988 s 788*):

Example 1

Tim, a UK resident individual, is a 40% taxpayer. He receives £85 of dividend income after a 15% USA withholding tax levy.

Tim's UK income tax liability is:

Gross income (ie 85 + 15)	100
UK income tax liability @ 40%	40
Less: credit for US tax	(15)
Net UK income tax liability	25
Net cash (85 less 25)	60

26.15 The rules which determine an individual's residence status vary from one jurisdiction to another which in a number of cases inevitably leads to the individual being 'dual' resident (ie resident in more than one jurisdiction). *Article 4* of the OECD Model 1977 provides a resolution to this problem under its so-called 'tie-breaker clause'. The effect of this clause is to cause the individual to be regarded as resident in only one of the contracting jurisdictions for the purposes of the double tax agreement.

26.16 It is not really possible to address the taxation of every possible type of income which may arise and thus *Article 21* 'Other Income' provides that any item of income which is not specifically dealt with in a double tax agreement is to be subject to tax only in the jurisdiction of residence of the taxpayer. This Article thus extends to all categories of income which arise outside either jurisdiction.

26.17 *Article 21* may be particularly important where an individual is 'dual' resident in two jurisdictions which each levy their respective taxes on the worldwide income of residents. The 'tie-breaker' clause will usually (but not always) resolve the issue of dual residence and the Other Income Article will then be in point.

Example 2

Herbert is resident in Canada under its domestic law and in the UK under its domestic law. *Article 4* of the UK/Canada double tax agreement resolves Herbert's dual residence in favour of the UK (say).

Article 20A of the UK/Canada double tax agreement then precludes the Canadian tax authorities from levying Canadian tax on any income which arises to Herbert from outside of Canada.

26.18 Complications can arise for non-UK domiciled but UK resident individuals. Such individuals are subject to UK income and capital gains taxes if and when non-UK source income/gains are remitted to the UK (see paragraph 2.10) assuming that the remittance basis is claimed (*ITA 2007 s 809B*; see paragraph 24.7). Under many of the UK's double tax agreements income/gains arising in the overseas jurisdiction are only relieved from tax in the overseas jurisdiction if the income/gains are taxed in the UK; thus, if a remittance basis taxpayer does not remit the income/gains to the UK no UK tax arises and thus no relief in the overseas jurisdiction is available.

The UK's double tax agreements are not entirely consistent in this regard.

26.19 Whilst the structure of the OECD Model 1977 is in principle followed by the UK when negotiating and concluding double tax agreements with other jurisdictions inevitably the terms of all such agreements are not identical and recourse to the particular wording of the relevant agreement is always necessary. An area where there is often major differences is 'treaty shopping'.

26.20 *International taxation*

Treaty shopping typically arises in the following scenario. A resident of country X wishes to invest in country Y; however, the agreement between X and Y is not as favourable as that between Z and Y. X therefore creates a vehicle resident in Z which he then uses to invest in Y. The objective is to ensure that the overall tax position is mitigated. Historically, for example, UK resident companies invested in US real estate not directly from the UK but via the Netherlands Antilles (the Netherlands Antilles agreement with the USA being more tax favourable than that between the UK and the USA). Investments into India from the UK are often routed via Mauritius due to a favourable Mauritius/India agreement.

26.20 Perhaps not surprisingly many jurisdictions (including the OECD) found such practices to be unacceptable and a number of measures have been introduced to curb the practice. The most aggressive country in this regard has been the USA as is evident from *Article 23*, for example, of the UK/US agreement (*SI 2002/2848*). This Article effectively limits any benefits under the agreement to only 'qualified persons', very broadly UK resident individuals and companies listed on a recognised Stock Exchange owned by 'equivalent beneficiaries' (in principle residents of EU or EEA (this is a gross simplification of an extremely long and convoluted Article). In essence the approach adopted by the USA is a 'look through' approach – the ownership of, for example, a UK registered company is traced back through the relevant chain of ownership and if any person in the chain does not satisfy the conditions contained in *Article 10* the UK company cannot itself take advantage of any of the provisions of the agreement (in essence, the chain is only as strong as its weakest link) (see also *Article 22* of the UK/Japan agreement *SI 2006/1924*).

26.21 Other anti-treaty shopping measures include the prevention of so-called 'tax-favoured entities' from enjoying the provisions of an agreement. *Article 24A* of the UK/Cyprus agreement (*SI 1975/425*), for example, provides that tax-favoured Cypriot companies cannot take advantage of the Articles dealing with dividends, interest and royalties. The UK's agreements with Guernsey (*SI 1952/1215*), Jersey (*SI 1952/1216*) and the Isle of Man (*SI 1955/1205*) are similar, but in these agreements tax-favoured entities in these territories cannot enjoy any of the agreement's provisions (ie the restrictions are broader than those in the Cypriot agreement).

26.22 Treaty shopping is thus a practice which over the years has been severely curtailed but not yet entirely precluded.

Administration

26.23 For those UK resident taxpayers wishing to take advantage of the provisions of any of the UK's agreements it is usually necessary for certain specific forms to be completed (in particular where a claim for reduced foreign withholding tax is to be made); and formal claims may also need to be lodged as part of the normal self-assessment process within normal time limits (eg where a claim for a foreign tax credit is made under *ICTA 1988 s 806*).

Inheritance tax agreements

26.24 The UK is a party to ten double tax agreements which address IHT; significantly less than the number of such agreements dealing with income tax, CGT and corporation tax. The agreements are with:

- France (*SI 1963/1319*);
- India (*SI 1956/998*);
- Ireland (*SI 1978/1107*);
- Italy (*SI 1968/304*);
- Netherlands (*SI 1980/706*);
- South Africa (*SI 1979/576*);
- Sweden (*SI 1981/840*);
- Switzerland (*SI 1994/3214*);
- Pakistan (*SI 1957/1522*); and
- USA (*SI 1979/1454*).

26.25 These ten agreements can be conveniently divided into those agreements which were entered into *after* capital transfer tax (now IHT) was introduced, namely:

- Ireland;
- the Netherlands;
- South Africa;
- Sweden;
- Switzerland; and
- the USA.

and those agreements which were in existence previously which dealt with the then tax of estate duty (IHT ultimately replaced estate duty):

26.26 *International taxation*

- France;
- India;
- Italy; and
- Pakistan.

26.26 Of the above agreements the most recently concluded is that with the Netherlands in 1980 and the oldest is that concluded with India in 1956. Each of the six agreements listed above are similar in content and principle but are very different from the remaining four agreements.

Pre-1975 agreements

26.27 The four agreements which were concluded during the estate duty era (between 1945 and 1968) only apply on the death of an individual and not to lifetime gifts. Furthermore, these four agreements each disapply the UK's domestic rules for IHT purposes relating to the concept of 'deemed UK domiciled' (because under estate duty no similar rule existed) (see paragraphs 3.231 and 10.9). Thus, in considering the implications of these agreements deemed UK domicile status is effectively ignored.

26.28 Although concluded during the estate duty era the agreements now apply to IHT although their content remains unchanged. Despite the continued existence and current applicability of all four agreements, both India and Pakistan have in fact now abolished death duties (India in 1985 and Pakistan in 1979). Thus, today, the main effect of the agreements with India and Pakistan is to restrict the application on death of the deemed UK domicile rules; potentially of major significance in practice given the large number of Indian/Pakistani nationals who have resided in the UK for at least 17 tax years out of the last 20 tax years (and thus who, under UK domestic law, are regarded as having become deemed UK domiciled for IHT purposes; see paragraphs 3.231 and 10.9) but are not UK domiciled under UK common law (by way of a domicile of choice; see paragraph 3.74).

26.29 The basic (although not identical) approach of each of the four agreements is to deny the UK the right to levy UK IHT on death if the individual is domiciled in the other territory. The determination of the individual's domicile status, however, is under the respective domestic laws of each country. Thus, a determination as to whether, for example, an individual is domiciled in India is determined not under UK rules but those of India. The rules determining domicile under Indian law, or indeed the other three countries, may depend upon an individual's nationality or habitual residence and do not slavishly follow the approach adopted in the UK (see paragraph 26.36).

and in Switzerland under Swiss law (irrespective of the conclusion applying the tie-breaker tests) the country in which the property is situated (ie the UK or Switzerland) has sole taxing rights.

Third, the agreement contains a provision (*Article 10*) which specifically addresses inter-spouse transfers. In principle under this provision a better (ie more favourable) UK IHT position arises where the transfer is from a Swiss domiciled individual, who is deemed UK domiciled, to a non-UK domiciled individual on the death of the former ie the £55,000 limit (see paragraph 11.42) is effectively overridden (a not dissimilar provision (*Article 8*) is also contained in this UK/USA agreement).

26.40 The agreement between the UK and France does not extend to Northern Ireland and only applies on death. In line with the Model Agreement the country with primary taxing rights is the country in which the individual is domiciled (if necessary applying the tie-breaker tests). The other country is not then permitted to levy its tax on property situated outside its own country.

The agreement between the UK and the Republic of Ireland is quite different to the other post 1975 agreements. Inter alia, each country retains the right to levy its own tax as if the agreement had not come into effect (*Article 5*); this is likely to increase the probability of double taxation although *Article 8* provides for some relief in this regard.

26.41 Thus, despite the OECD Model Agreement 1982, there are material differences between the post 1975 agreements.

However, as it is generally accepted that double tax agreements (whether relating to income tax or IHT) cannot impose liabilities not otherwise imposed under UK domestic law it is probably fair to say that an individual's IHT position cannot be made worse under any of the above agreements as compared to the position under UK domestic law and may be much improved.

Tax Information Exchange Agreements

26.42 Recent years have seen new developments which are not really concerned with alleviating double tax but are solely designed to aid HMRC and other tax authorities in effectively combating tax avoidance/evasion. Thus, the concept of the TIEA has emerged (*FA 2000 s 146*) which provides purely for the exchange of information between the contracting jurisdictions in relation to those taxes covered in the agreement; like the comprehensive double tax agreement TIEAs are also bilateral in nature.

The purpose of such TIEAs is to promote international co-operation in tax matters through the exchange of information. The concept of the TIEA arose

26.43 *International taxation*

following the OECD HTC Report 1998 "Harmful Tax Competition: An Emerging Global Issue" (the '1998 Report'). This identified the lack of effective exchange of information as one of the key criteria in determining harmful tax practices (typically operated by the world's OFCs; see Chapter 25). The TIEA represents the minimal level of information exchange required by the OECD if a jurisdiction is not to be classified as one that effectively promoted harmful tax practices.

An increasing number of countries are entering into TIEAs with various OFCs including the UK. TIEAs entered into by the UK include those with, *inter alia*, Antigua, the Bahamas, Belize, Bermuda, the British Virgin Islands, Gibraltar, Grenada, Guernsey, the Isle of Man, Jersey, Liechtenstein, and San Marino.

The European Union

26.43 The EU was formally the EEC when it was founded in 1957. The UK became a party to the European Community on 1 January 1973. The primary organs of the EU are the Council, Commission, Parliament, the Court of Justice and the Court of Auditors.

EC law takes priority over national law and the main source of EC law is the EC Treaty. Legislation may take different forms including regulations, directives and opinions.

26.44 In 1998 the UK by way of the *HRA 1998* introduced the European Convention for the Protection of Human Rights into UK domestic law. The European Court of Human Rights (ECHR) was also created. It is not a creature of the EU/EC but of the Council of Europe in Strasbourg, an institution entirely separate from any organs of the EU/EC.

26.45 The legislation of the EC, the decisions of the Court of Justice and the decisions of the ECHR have each affected in varying degrees the UK's domestic tax laws. It is now very clear that where there is a conflict between UK domestic law and EU law the latter prevails (*R v Secretary of State for Transport, ex parte Factortame Ltd* (1991)).

26.46 One of the relatively recent initiatives of the EU in the tax field is the 'EU Savings Directive'.

The EU Savings Directive

Background

26.47 The EU Directive on taxation of savings income in the form of interest payments (*Council Directive 2003/48/EC*) has as its objective the prevention of tax evasion on savings income by providing for the automatic exchange of information between Member States of the EU on cross-border savings income payments made to beneficial owners who are EU resident individuals. However, three Member States are to apply a withholding tax on the cross-border savings income payments made by these States as opposed to supplying information to other Member States; they are Austria, Belgium and Luxembourg.

Thus, payments of interest by residents of one Member State to residents of another Member State fall within the Directive's provisions; payments of interest within the same Member State are not within the Directive.

26.48 The Directive applies not only to Member States of the EU. Before the Directive could enter into force it was necessary that similar arrangements were also in force with respect to certain identified third countries, namely: Switzerland, Liechtenstein, San Marino, Monaco and Andorra and also all relevant dependent or associated territories (ie the Channel Islands, the Isle of Man and dependent or associated territories in the Caribbean (note: this therefore excluded Bermuda and non-Caribbean dependent territories of the UK)).

26.49 Accordingly the UK and the other Member States entered into multilateral treaties with each of the above five mentioned territories (between October and December 2004) and bilateral treaties were entered into with the dependent or associated territories.

26.50 The Directive took effect on 1 July 2005 and relates to relevant payments on or thereafter.

Savings income

26.51 The term 'savings income' is perhaps misleading. The Directive only applies to payments of *interest* (thus, is inapplicable to dividends, rents, insurance benefits, pension benefits and any other form of savings income). Interest includes typically interest paid/credited to a bank account and interest relating to debt claims of every kind whether secured or not; any interest which is accrued or capitalised is also covered.

Income distributions of some collective investment vehicles (which invest in debt instruments) are also treated as falling within the definition of interest as is the income arising on redemption/sale of any interests in the vehicles.

26.52 As stated in paragraph 26.51 the Directive applies only to *interest* received *beneficially* by an *individual* who is a resident of the EU. The Directive thus applies irrespective of an individual's nationality; only EU residence is required for the Directive to be in point.

26.53 *International taxation*

Information exchange

26.53 Under the provisions of the Directive where a paying agent (broadly, the person responsible for making the actual payment of the interest to the recipient) makes a payment of interest to an individual resident in another Member State details of the individual are required to be automatically conveyed by the paying agent to the tax authority in which the paying agent is resident. The latter tax authority then passes this information to the tax authority in which the individual is resident.

The details collected and passed on include the identity of the individual (ie name and address) and their residence status; the account number giving rise to the interest or details of the debt claim giving rise to the interest if there is no account.

The provision of this exchange is automatic and is to be provided no less than once a year and within six months of the end of it.

Withholding tax

26.54 However, as indicated in paragraph 26.47 three Member States, Austria, Belgium and Luxembourg, are to levy a withholding tax rather than supplying information about the individual concerned.

This 'opt out' is to apply for a transitional period only. However, the transitional period ends only when Switzerland, Liechtenstein, San Marino, Monaco, Andorra and the USA agree to the provision of information exchange in accordance with the Directive (these territories, the USA excepted, currently agree only to levy the withholding tax). It may be some time before this occurs.

26.55 The amount of the withholding tax is set at 15% for the first three years (ie 1 July 2005 to 30 June 2008); 20% for the subsequent three years; and 35% thereafter. These withholding taxes are in addition to any other form of withholding tax that each of these countries already levies under their own domestic law on payments of interest to non-residents and thus, in aggregate, such withholding taxes could represent serious adverse cash flow to the recipient.

Where the withholding tax under the Directive is levied it is to be creditable against any tax liability (including CGT) arising on the part of the individual entitled to it and, to the extent it exceeds the individual's tax liability, is to be repaid to the individual by the tax authority of the country in which the individual is resident (*FA 2004 ss 107 to 115*). Any local withholding tax is to be credited before the withholding tax under the Directive (thus maximising the possibility of any refund re the Directive's withholding tax).

Non-Member States and Tax Information Exchange Agreements

26.56 The TIEAs entered into by the UK in connection with the Savings Directive are not all identical although they are very similar. They are divided into those agreements which are reciprocal and those which are not. The former comprises the agreements with Aruba, the British Virgin Islands, Gibraltar, Guernsey, the Isle of Man, Jersey, Montserrat and the Netherlands Antilles; the latter, those agreements with Anguilla, the Cayman Islands and the Turks and Caicos Islands.

26.57 Of these territories listed in paragraph 26.56 those which have opted for the levying of a withholding tax (as have Austria, Belgium and Luxembourg) are: the British Virgin Islands, Gibraltar, Guernsey, the Isle of Man, Jersey, the Netherlands Antilles, and the Turks and Caicos Islands.

26.58 In the case of Aruba, Anguilla, the Cayman Islands and Montserrat each of these territories have agreed to the supply of information, rather than adopting the withholding tax approach.

26.59 As yet no such agreements have been entered into by the UK with either Bermuda or the Bahamas.

26.60 It is possible for the individual to opt for no withholding tax to be applied where those countries have adopted this option. For a UK resident either the individual may simply instruct the paying agent to supply the required information as above to his home tax authority *or* the individual may obtain from HMRC (the local tax office who has the individual's details and to which a tax return is normally made) a certificate detailing, *inter alia*, the individual's name, address and tax identification number which can then be submitted by the individual to the paying agent requesting non-deduction of the withholding tax levied under the Directive (*FA 2004 ss 113* and *114*). Any such certificate issued is valid for up to three years and must be issued by HMRC within two months of the individual making the request (*FA 2004 s 113*).

26.61 It is, however, for the country which has opted for the withholding tax option to determine whether it will permit the individual to choose for information to be supplied rather than the levying of the withholding tax.

Implications of the Savings Directive

26.62 First and foremost the Directive only applies to *interest* payments made to *individual* beneficial owners who are *EU resident*.

26.63 The nationality of the individual is irrelevant; if the individual is EU

26.64 *International taxation*

resident the Directive applies. However, an EU national who is resident outside the EU receiving EU source interest will fall outside the Directive.

26.64 However, given the voluminous information which is being conveyed automatically under the Directive among the various Member States there is no guarantee that, by accident or otherwise, information will not be disclosed to the tax authorities of the individual's country of residence in circumstances where the Directive does not in fact apply. In such circumstances the 'damage" will be done irrespective of any remedy (if any).

26.65 For those individuals with monies deposited in Austria, Belgium or Luxembourg (and in those offshore territories levying the withholding tax) who, for whatever reason, may not wish the tax authority of their country of residence to know of the deposit suffer relatively penal rates of withholding tax, currently 20%, (increased from 15% post-30 June 2008). The next proposed increase to the extremely penal level of 35% is effective from 1 July 2011. Such withholding represents serious adverse cash flow.

26.66 In principle, the Directive applies to both the UK and non-UK domiciled but UK resident individual (ie there is no explicit reference in the Directive to individuals who are non-UK domiciled). Non-UK domiciled but UK resident individuals are subject to UK income tax only on remittances to the UK (see paragraph 2.10). HMRC have commented as follows:

> 'The Directive makes no mention of domicile or remittance. If you are resident in the UK and you receive savings income from a territory covered by the Directive (or a related agreement) then the details of the payment should be reported to the UK, or it should be subject to withholding tax. You may apply for a certificate from HMRC for the income to be paid gross. Alternatively, if tax is withheld, you may claim credit for the tax on your Self Assessment return.'

This seems relatively straightforward making the point that whether a remittance of the interest to the UK occurs or not (ie whether a UK income tax charge arises or not) is irrelevant and the Directive applies.

26.67 However, interestingly, the tax authorities of Guernsey, Jersey and the Isle of Man (each of which territories levy the withholding tax) took a slightly different approach. Their approach has been to apply no withholding tax (or supply information to HMRC) where the individual concerned is non-UK domiciled and is thus not subject to UK income tax on unremitted income (or is exempt from income tax). The evidential support required by the payor of the interest is left to the payor to decide; self certification by the individual may apparently prove acceptable to the payor (ie there appears to be no strict requirement for HMRC to have provided the certificate as would normally be necessary (see paragraph 26.60)).

26.68 This stance adopted by each of these three territories appears to operate in practice although as to its correctness under the terms of the Directive this may be open to challenge.

26.69 Following *FA 2008* presumably this approach may need to be reviewed. A non-UK domiciled but UK resident individual may be entitled to remittance basis treatment without a claim or may require a claim to be lodged (*ITA 2007 ss 809D* and *809E*; see paragraphs 24.7 and 24.11) or may be subject to tax on the arising basis. Where tax on the arising basis is applicable presumably each of these three territories would be required under the Directive to withhold tax (despite the non-UK domicile status of the individual). As, post-*FA 2008*, any claim for remittance basis treatment is on a tax year by tax year basis it would seem that the payors of interest will need to be informed of the non-UK domiciled's tax position each tax year.

26.70 The Directive is, however, inapplicable where the beneficial recipient of the interest is not an individual (eg a company). Thus, the simple expedient of setting up a company to receive the interest avoids the Directive's application.

26.71 However, the Directive applies to so-called 'residual entities'; broadly, non-legal persons (thus excluding companies) established in a Member State receiving interest for the benefit of an EU resident individual. In such cases the residual entity is treated as effecting payment of the interest and thus responsible for levying the withholding tax. This inevitably raises the issue as to whether trusts created in the EU qualify as residual entities.

26.72 It is probably arguable that trustees of discretionary trusts receiving interest are not within the ambit of the Directive (the individual beneficiaries are not entitled to the interest and indeed payments by the trustees to such beneficiaries are not payments of interest; see paragraph 17.25). However, the interest in possession beneficiary is entitled to the income of the trust, including interest income, and thus arguably the Directive applies in such cases (assuming the beneficiary is resident in the EU).

26.73 Perhaps the most obvious manner of mitigating the impact of the Directive is for monies to be no longer deposited in countries affected by the Directive. Such countries include financial centres such as Dubai, Hong Kong and Singapore. However, it is to be noted that in March 2008 the European Council reiterated its intention to broaden the network of savings tax agreements and the EU Council requested the Commission to start exploratory talks with Hong Kong, Macao and Singapore.

26.74 The fact that the Directive does not apply to interest beneficially belonging to companies and/or certain trusts hitherto will almost certainly be changed in the future thus closing down the use of such vehicles. In this regard the EU Commission is required to report to the EU Council on the operation of the Directive every three years and to propose any amendments to the Directive that may be required in order better to ensure effective taxation of savings income and to remove any undesirable distortions of competition. The Commission issued its first report on the subject on 15 September 2008.

26.75 On 13 November 2008 the Commission adopted an amending proposal to the Directive with a view to closing existing loopholes and better preventing tax evasion. The proposal is aimed at interest payments which are routed through intermediate tax-exempted structures (eg companies). It is also proposed to extend the scope of the Directive to income equivalent to interest obtained through investments in some innovative financial products as well as in certain life insurance products (presumably including, for example, offshore single premium bonds).

26.76 It seems inevitable that the current restriction of the Directive to 'interest' only payments to individuals will be broadened to encompass interest payments to other persons (eg trusts; companies; foundations) and/or other types of savings income (eg dividends). This seems a logical extension of the Directive's provisions. Within what time frame any such extensions will apply is difficult to predict.

26.77 Extension of the Directive's ambit to include other countries seems less likely in the short term.

The Savings Directive and Directive 77/799/EEC

26.78 *Directive 77/799/EEC of 19 December 1977* which concerns mutual assistance in the collection of direct and indirect (eg VAT) taxes of Member States also allows for information to be exchanged among Member States. Such information extends to interest payments. However, there are certain restrictions provided for in the 1977 Directive with respect to the supply of information. The Savings Directive thus specifically provides that such restrictions should not be allowed to preclude information provision under the Savings Directive. Despite the Directive being introduced some 30 years ago the UK only signed it in early 2007 becoming, at that time, the fifteenth country to do so.

Human rights

26.79 The *HRA 1998* basically provides for the incorporation into UK law of the ECPHR effective October 2000. *Prima facie*, the ECPHR would seem to be irrelevant with respect to the tax treatment of individuals.

26.80 However in *Holland (Exec) v IRC* (2003) the Special Commissioners held that the IHT inter-spouse exemption (*IHTA 1984 s 18*) refers to spouses who are legally married. It thus does not apply to an elderly couple (ie two sisters) even though they had lived together for 31 years. The Commissioners further held that this did not constitute discrimination against unmarried couples.

In late April 2008 the ECHR in deciding the appeal lodged by the two sisters in the above case held that to deny the inter-spouse exemption for IHT to the two sisters was not a breach of their human rights. No further appeals are possible.

26.81 It is highly likely that the European Courts (not just the ECHR) will increasingly be called upon to ascertain whether a number of the UK's domestic tax provisions are in some way discriminatory or are a breach of an individual's human rights.

Summary

26.82 Any tax advice needs to take into account the international, not just domestic, tax implications.

26.83 Double tax agreements, of which there are two types, generally speaking alleviate the tax burden. Unfortunately, the UK is a party to only ten such agreements that deal with IHT and, of those, four are from the era of estate duty and are inapplicable to lifetime gifts (only applying on death).

26.84 Double tax agreements dealing with income tax and CGT to which the UK is a party number in excess of 100 and may be extremely useful in mitigating non-UK taxes; in particular may significantly improve cash flow on non-UK source income (eg interest and dividends).

26.85 The EU is increasingly encroaching on UK tax domestic law and cannot be ignored. The EU Savings Directive is one example.

Part VI

Wills, probate and post-death issues

Chapter 27

Wills and probate

This chapter addresses the position where the governing law of the will is that of England/Wales. The position in Scotland or Northern Ireland may be different.

Background

27.1 The execution of a valid will permits the testator to direct how, on his death, his estate is to be divided amongst the various beneficiaries of his choosing. English law in principle places no restrictions on the testator's freedom as to the distribution of his estate (see paragraph 27.106). Some countries, however, including Scotland, France and many civil law jurisdictions operate a system commonly referred to as 'forced heirship' under which restrictions are placed on the testator. The essence of forced heirship requires certain proportions of the testator's estate to be left to specified persons, normally the surviving spouse and children (see paragraph 27.103).

The Annex to the *TA 2000 ('Glossary of Terms')* defines a will as:

> 'a document by which a person (called the testator) appoints executors to administer his estate after his death and directs the manner in which it is to be distributed to the beneficiaries he specifies'.

27.2 An individual may die intestate (ie without having made a will or where the will is invalid) or testate (ie having made a valid will). Not all wills made are necessarily valid; strict formalities need to be observed to ensure a will is valid (see paragraph 27.27).

A partial intestacy may also arise; this occurs where although the will is valid some part of the deceased's property have not been disposed of under the will (ie have been overlooked).

Under an intestacy the deceased's property is administered according to law (*AEA 1925*).

27.3 A will takes effect on death and thus has no effect until the testator dies. Prior to the testator's death the contents (and its existence; apart from the

27.4 *Wills and probate*

knowledge of the witnesses thereto and others to whom the testator may have confided) of a will remain entirely confidential. On death, after probate (see paragraph 27.114) is granted, the existence of the will and its contents become public knowledge. It is for this reason that an individual may make use of trusts as a form of will substitute the existence and contents of which remain confidential both in lifetime and following death.

27.4 As the will is ineffective until the testator's death the testator is free to deal with his property prior to his death in any manner whatsoever despite what his will states. For example, his will may provide for his house to be left on his death to his son; this, however, does not preclude the testator selling the house in his lifetime (in such cases the gift fails by 'ademption'; in other words, the son simply does not inherit the house; see paragraph 27.64).

27.5 It also naturally follows that prior to death a will may be revoked and a new will executed or simply revoked with no replacement will being executed.

27.6 On death there can only be one valid will. Where there appears to be more than one will it is necessary to ascertain which of them is to apply (in principle, often the later in time a document is executed the more likely it is to be treated as the will applicable on death). The testator's intentions as to the distribution of his property on death may be expressed in more than one document (eg in a will and one or more subsequent codicils) in which case all such documents are aggregated to from his will (a will is thus not necessarily one simple document).

27.7 Whilst the will primarily sets out the testator's wishes as to how his estate is to be distributed amongst the beneficiaries on his death, and by whom (ie through the appointment of executors; see paragraph 27.134), it may also contain other details. For example, it may express some emotional feelings felt by the testator (eg 'I hope that my children all live long and fruitful lives') or his wishes with respect to some of the gifts he makes in the will (eg 'I trust that my younger son's inheritance of the £10,000 is spent wisely and will not be gambled or spent on fast cars') which, as such, have no legal effect merely representing the testator's thoughts/wishes/sentiments. The will also invariably contains instructions with respect to the disposal of the testator's body and makes provision for an amount of money to be set aside for the funeral and modest refreshments thereafter.

Interestingly, however, the testator cannot give legally enforceable instructions as to the disposal of his body following his death; this is because, the law recognises no property in the dead body of a human being. It is thus for the executors (see paragraph 27.115), in whom possession of the body falls, to dispose of the body. However, in practice, subject to challenge by other family members (particularly the surviving spouse) the testator's wishes are normally respected.

Property not disposable by will

27.8 Not all the testator's estate is capable of being dealt with under the will and often lifetime gifts are made in preference to gift by will, some made literally almost on death (ie *donatio mortis causa*). Examples of property which cannot pass under the will are interests in property held as joint tenants (see Chapter 7); lump sum death benefits arising under certain pension schemes and (possibly) foreign situs property. Life insurance policies are usually placed in trust in lifetime rather than being gifted by will.

Joint tenancies

27.9 Perhaps one of the most significant assets not capable of disposal by will is property held beneficially in the form of a joint tenancy (see paragraph 7.8). Many homes owned by married couples are so held.

Where property (of whatever description) is held as a joint tenancy on the death of the joint tenant his interest in the property passes to the surviving joint tenant(s) automatically by survivorship (ie not by will). This may have unintended consequences.

For example a man, who is divorced from his first wife (with whom he had children), remarries and the new marital home is owned as joint tenants with his second wife. In the event of his death his interest in the home automatically passes to his second wife by survivorship; however, it may have been his intention that on his death his interest is to pass to his children from his first marriage.

27.10 Unfortunately, whilst a joint tenancy is severable in lifetime it is not severable by will (see paragraph 7.19). The solution to the problem referred to in paragraph 27.9 is, *ab initio*, to have structured ownership of the home as tenants in common rather than as joint tenants or to have severed the joint tenancy in lifetime. Ownership as tenants in common permits the interests in the property to pass by will (such interests not passing automatically by survivorship; see paragraph 7.9).

27.11 For inheritance tax (IHT) purposes the deceased's interest in the property, whether held in the form of joint tenants or tenants in common, forms part of the deceased's estate (see paragraph 10.64).

Pension scheme lump sum death benefits

27.12 Under certain types of pension scheme the death of an employee whilst in service may give rise to a lump sum death benefit. The conditions of the

27.13 *Wills and probate*

scheme may permit the employee to nominate someone (often, but not necessarily, the surviving spouse) to receive the benefit. The employee (or his estate) is not, as such, absolutely entitled to the benefit (and cannot thus be dealt with under the will); any nomination (which is made to the trustees of the scheme) is not one which binds the trustees (although in practice invariably the wishes expressed are followed).

27.13 The benefit does not form part of the estate of the individual on death as he is not beneficially entitled to it. However, any failure to make a nomination may result in the trustees paying the lump sum death benefit to the deceased's estate which has the undesirable effect of the lump sum forming part of the deceased's estate for IHT purposes (which is avoided where a nomination to someone else is executed in lifetime). In this case the proceeds are capable of being dealt with by the will.

Life insurance policies

27.14 The position with respect to life insurance policies is different from that just described with respect to lump sum death benefits under pension schemes.

27.15 The individual who takes out a life insurance policy on his own life is the beneficial owner of the policy and thus on his death his estate has the rights to the sum assured and may be dealt with by the will. However, it is often usual for the policy to be settled by the individual on trust when the policy is first taken out. The beneficiaries of the trust are often the surviving spouse (and/or the children).

27.16 The effect of settling the policy on trust is that on death the proceeds do not form part of the donor's estate for IHT purposes (such monies are often used to fund, by way of loan to the executors, any IHT arising on the estate thus expediting probate) (see paragraph 19.40).

Donatio mortis causa

27.17 Property may also pass under a '*donatio mortis causa*' which seems to fall somewhere between a lifetime gift and a gift on death by will; in a sense it is an incomplete gift. Such a gift is made in lifetime (ie possession of the property passes to the recipient in lifetime) but is conditional on death and must be made in contemplation of death in the near future (eg a gift by someone who has a terminal illness).

In the event that the donor does not in fact die the gift is revoked and the donor is entitled to regain possession; in the event the donor dies the recipient takes the gift absolutely.

A *donatio mortis causa* cannot thus by definition be left by will and such a gift cannot be revoked by a subsequent will (ie the gift cannot be revoked by the individual executing a will after having made the gift but before actual death).

27.18 For IHT purposes a *donatio mortis causa* is simply treated as part of the donor's estate on death (not a lifetime gift) and thus subject to IHT.

Foreign situs assets

27.19 A will drawn up in accordance with English law may not be acceptable to a foreign country. Thus, the disposition of foreign property (in particular real estate) under such a will may thus be effectively invalid. This is certainly likely to be the position with respect to foreign immovable property (ie real estate) where succession thereto follows the law of the country in which the immovable property is situated (local forced-heirship laws may also apply). A will drawn up under the relevant foreign law is likely to be necessary.

Types of will

27.20 The classic will is a single will executed by one individual which disposes of his property on death. However, other wills may take the form of mutual wills, joint wills or international wills.

Mutual wills

27.21 Mutual wills typically involve only two people, often a married couple, although they are not restricted in this manner. An agreement is made between the parties as to how their respective property (all or only some of it) is to be disposed of on death and they each then execute their respective wills accordingly (or they may simply execute a single joint will). The intention is that the survivor of the parties to the mutual wills is to be bound by the agreement. The agreement between the parties is critical; two wills executed in identical terms does not necessarily mean they are mutual wills.

As a general rule such wills are fraught with problems and should thus be avoided.

27.22 *Wills and probate*

Joint will

27.22   A joint will is where the same document is executed by each person; it is regarded as the separate will of each of them. Prior to death either may amend or even revoke the will in relation to those aspects of it which apply to them.

As with mutual wills, joint wills should as a general rule be avoided.

International will

27.23   An international will is one drawn up in accordance with the provisions of *CPUL 1973*. The concept underlying such a will is that it is to be regarded as valid and recognised in the various countries who have ratified *CPUL 1973* and who have also, where necessary, incorporated it into their own domestic law (as the UK has done; *AJA 1982 ss 27* and *28*). Whilst a number of countries have ratified the *CPUL 1973* as yet, not all have incorporated it into their domestic law.

Theoretically, where a testator owns assets in the various countries who are signatories to *CPUL 1973* it should in principle only be necessary to execute the one international will irrespective of where the will is actually made; the domicile nationality or residence of the testator; or the location of the assets.

27.24   Despite their potential attractiveness (at least in theory) such wills do not appear to be widespread.

Capacity to make a will

27.25   An individual must be of a sound and disposing mind and memory at the date of making the will (*MCA 2005*). A will executed at a time when the testator lacks sound mind/memory is invalid. In hindsight, ascertaining whether the testator was at such time of sound mind may be somewhat of a difficult task as those who have sought to challenge the validity of a will on such grounds have found.

27.26   Minors are unable to make wills (*WA 1837 s 7*). A minor is someone under 18 (if the will is made on or after 1 January 1970; *FLRA 1969 s 3*) or under 21 if made before this date. Apart from minors and persons of unsound mind most other persons may make a valid will.

Formalities of a will

27.27   The formalities necessary for the execution of a valid will in accordance with English internal law are laid down in the *WA 1837* (*WA 1837 s 9*). *WA*

1837 s 9 applies in respect of deaths on or after 1 January 1983 and provides as follows:

'No will shall be valid unless–

(a) it is in writing, and signed by the testator, ...; and

(b) it appears that the testator intended by his signature to give effect to the will;

(c) the signature is made or acknowledged by the testator in the presence of two or more witnesses present at the same time; and

(d) each witness either—

   (i) attests and signs the will; or

   (ii) acknowledges his signature,

in the presence of the testator (but not necessarily in the presence of any other witness),

but no form of attestation shall be necessary'.

27.28 Compliance with these formalities is extremely important. Failure to so comply is likely to result in the will being declared invalid (ie it will be rejected on application for probate; see paragraph 27.115). On balance, where possible, the courts attempt to validate wills rather than invalidate them (although this was not always so).

27.29 As is evident from *WA 1837 s 9* (see paragraph 27.27) a will must be in writing and signed by the testator in the presence of two witnesses who each sign and attest the will (or acknowledge his signature) in the presence of the testator. Normally, the signatures appear at the end or bottom of the will but this particular position of signatures is not a requirement.

There are few restrictions on who may act as a witness; the key criterion being that the witness understands the nature of his act. A minor may thus in principle act as a witness so long as he understands the nature of his act (however, a child age four for example, is unlikely to comprehend what is happening).

27.30 A will is made in writing if it is handwritten, typewritten or printed.

27.31 Any beneficiary under the will who signs as a witness in principle forfeits his (and his spouse's) inheritance (*WA 1837 s 15*). The will, however, remains valid.

27.32 *Wills and probate*

The determination as to validity is made at the time the will is executed; thus, where a beneficiary under a will subsequently marries one of the witnesses to the will the former's inheritance remains valid.

If, ignoring the attestation by the particular witness, the will remains valid (ie there are more than two witnesses to the will) gifts in the will to the beneficiary who witnesses the will (or gifts to the witness's spouse) remain valid and do not fail (the so-called 'superfluous attestation').

Revocation

27.32 Once made, a will may be subsequently revoked or amended. Revocation of the whole will is typically made consciously by the testator, either by executing a codicil or another complete will. Amendments, which are perhaps few or short in nature (where revocation is not required), are usually effected by executing a codicil.

A codicil is itself a testamentary instrument (as is a will) and is thus subject to the rigours of *WA 1837 s 9* (the witnesses of the original will and any subsequent codicil need not be the same). Any number of codicils may be executed subsequent to the execution of the will.

27.33 A will may also be revoked by its destruction (eg by burning) (*WA 1837 s 20*).

27.34 A lost will is not necessarily revoked although there is a presumption (albeit a rebuttable one) to this effect.

27.35 A will may also be revoked automatically in certain situations. Thus, marriage automatically revokes a will (*WA 1837 s 18*).

However, where a will is made in contemplation of marriage it will not be revoked on marriage; the will must be made in contemplation of a specific marriage not in contemplation of marriage in general.

27.36 Divorce does not revoke a will. On the other hand, in the case of the death of a testator on or after 1 January 1996 the former spouse is deemed to have pre-deceased the testator. This has two consequences, namely, that the former spouse is unable to inherit thereunder and, in addition, such former spouse is no longer able to act as an executor (*WA 1837 s 18A*).

27.37 The consequent lapse of any gifts made to the former spouse causes such gifts to fall into residue unless provisions exist in the will to cover this eventuality; where the former spouse was, for example, given an interest in possession in a trust created under the will the effect of lapse is that the remainder interest is accelerated.

27.38 Where a decree of judicial separation is in force the will of either spouse is not affected (*MCA 1973 s 18*) although either spouse cannot succeed to the other's property on an intestacy.

27.39 Good practice requires that following marriage or divorce any will/codicils in existence prior thereto should be urgently reviewed.

27.40 It is not uncommon for an individual who possesses overseas property (eg a property in Spain) to execute more than one will each will typically dealing with property located in a particular country; each will being executed under local law. It is important to recognise the possible implications of executing such multiple wills.

Thus, for example, the revocation of a will executed under English law may or may not necessarily result in the automatic revocation of a will executed overseas under local law. Similarly, the revocation of a will drawn up and executed under foreign local law may or may not necessarily result in the automatic revocation of the English will (see paragraph 27.102).

Types of gift

27.41 The correct terminology applicable to gifts made by will is that gifts of personalty are referred to as legacies whereas gifts of realty are referred to as devises (although in practice this is not always followed).

27.42 There are different categories of legacy/devise and the importance lies in their different characteristics. A determination as to the category into which a particular legacy/devise falls is made according to the construction of the will.

Legacies/devises

27.43 There are three types of legacy:

- specific;
- general; and
- demonstrative.

There are two types of devise:

- specific; and
- general.

Specific

27.44 A specific legacy is a gift of particular property within the deceased's estate on death; it is distinguishable from other property owned by the deceased. Such property may be a particular painting, a particular piece of jewellery, or a particular vintage car.

27.45 A gift of cash (eg a gift of £100) is not a specific gift unless it is, for example, a gift of 'all my cash in my brown wallet' which is readily identifiable in the deceased's estate.

27.46 A specific devise is similarly a gift of clearly and separately identifiable real estate. Thus, for example, 'I give my holiday home in Cornwall' is a specific devise.

General

27.47 A general legacy is a gift of property not identifiable in the deceased's estate; it is not a gift of a particular item of personalty (as is a specific gift). The gift is simply to be provided to the beneficiary out of the deceased's estate. Thus, for example, the gift may be of 100 shares in XYZ Plc; or a gift of £500 cash; or a gift of a gold watch of value £250.

27.48 In none of the above examples in paragraph 27.47 is a reference made to specific items of property owned by the deceased. It may be that the deceased does in fact own 100 shares in XYZ Plc; this does not, however, turn the general gift thereof into a specific gift. In this case the executors may then choose to allocate the shares to the beneficiary (the most likely scenario) or they may choose to purchase them in the market for delivery to the beneficiary. It may, on the other hand, be that the deceased does not own 100 shares in XYZ Plc; in which case the executors are required to purchase such out of the funds of the estate and deliver them to the beneficiary.

27.49 A gift of £500 cash is a general legacy becoming a specific gift only where it is, for example, expressed as 'I give £500 cash which is to be found in my black trunk under my bed'.

27.50 A gift of real estate is a general devise where, as in the case of a general legacy, the real estate is not specifically identifiable. Thus, 'I give 5 acres of pasture land' is a general devise.

Demonstrative

27.51 A demonstrative legacy is a gift which is to be made out of a particular part of the deceased's estate or a particular fund; to this extent it has the characteristics of a general legacy.

27.52 An example is 'I give £100 out of the balance in my Nat West account'.

Pecuniary

27.53 In a sense this is not a separate category of gift. A gift of money may be referred to as a pecuniary gift but it is in fact a gift which falls to be treated as a specific, general or demonstrative gift.

Failure of gifts

27.54 A gift made in a will may fail for a number of reasons including:

- death of the beneficiary prior to the testator's death;
- divorce of the testator;
- witnessing of the will by a beneficiary;
- subsequent revocation of the will by codicil;
- disclaimer of the gift by the beneficiary; or
- uncertainty as to the gift.

Lapse

27.55 The death of a beneficiary prior to the death of the testator causes any gift to the beneficiary to lapse. In the absence of any provision in the will to deal with this situation the gift falls into residue and the residuary beneficiaries benefit from the gift (which may not be what the testator would have wanted).

27.56 Accordingly, it is common for substitutional gifts to be provided for in the will. For example, the will may provide that if the beneficiary pre-deceases the testator the gift is to be made to another individual (eg the beneficiary's spouse) who is alive at the testator's death. Alternatively, the testator may provide for the gift to be given to the deceased beneficiary's executors (in which case the gift will fall within the deceased beneficiary's estate and pass under the latter's will).

There is one exception to the doctrine of lapse. Where the gift is to the testator's child or remoter issue and the beneficiary dies before the testator the issue of the deceased beneficiary (living at the date of death of the testator) take the gift (and if more than one in equal shares) (*WA 1837 s 33*); this statutory provision is subject to any contrary provision in the testator's will.

27.57 *Wills and probate*

27.57 The doctrine of lapse applies to all categories of gift.

27.58 It may be that in certain instances it is not possible to determine which of two individuals dies first; this determination is critical as it may cause the lapsing of a gift. Examples where this uncertainty may arise are typically where a catastrophic event has occurred and all lives are lost; this might include plane crashes; rail crashes; the sinking of a ship; or, closer to home, car crashes.

27.59 *LPA 1925 s 184* (which applies to deaths on or after 1 January 1926) provides that where it is uncertain which of two individuals dies first it is to be assumed that the elder shall have died first (ie the younger survives the elder). This means, for example, that a gift by the younger to the elder in the former's will lapses (but not vice versa) should both die in circumstances in which it is not possible to determine who died first.

27.60 *LPA 1925 s 184* does not, however, apply to the simultaneous deaths of spouses where the elder spouse dies intestate (*LPA 1925 s 46*).

27.61 It is important to note that this rule (ie *LPA 1925 s 184*) is applicable only with respect to ascertaining title to property but has no application for IHT purposes. The rule for IHT is that where a determination as to who died first cannot be made it is to be assumed that the individuals died at the same instant (*IHTA 1984 s 4;* see paragraph 27.71).

27.62 The implication of *IHTA 1984 s 4* is that IHT is payable on the estate of the elder on death; if the elder's estate is by will left to the younger of the two to die IHT is only then levied on the younger's estate (but ignoring the inheritance from the elder). This is due to the basic rule which is that IHT is chargeable on the death of an individual on the value of the deceased's estate immediately before his death (at which time the younger individual would not have inherited the elder's estate as the elder would not at that point have died).

The result for spouses is that the estate of the first spouse to die passes inter-spouse (and thus without IHT charge) to the surviving spouse and then to, say, the children under the will of the second spouse to die without IHT charge; only the estate of the younger spouse to die is subject to IHT on passing to the children (albeit subject to the availability of any nil rate band (NRB)) (see Examples 1 and 2).

The above IHT analysis assumes that no survivorship clause exists in either will (see paragraph 27.71).

27.63 Even where a gift does not lapse it is possible that the beneficiary who inherits dies shortly thereafter. It is, as a consequence, not unusual for a survivorship clause to be included in a will. Broadly, such a clause provides that unless a beneficiary survives for a minimum time period following the death of the testator the beneficiary does not inherit; a 28-day period is not unusual. The rationale for such a clause is based upon the hypothesis that had the testator known of the death of the beneficiary so soon after his own death he would probably have left the inheritance to another beneficiary so as to preclude the inheritance passing effectively under the former beneficiary's will rather than his own (see paragraph 27.71).

Ademption

27.64 Unlike the doctrine of lapse ademption is applicable only to specific legacies and devises (it has no application to general or demonstrative legacies or devises).

27.65 Ademption applies where the subject matter of the gift is no longer part of the testator's property at death. This may arise due to, for example, the disposal of the asset (eg by way of sale) or its destruction prior to death. It may also arise where there is a change in substance (but not form); this distinction, however, is not an easy one to apply in practice.

27.66 Examples of ademption include 'I leave my fountain pen purchased in Paris' and 'I leave my farm in Yorkshire'. In the event the testator, prior to his death, gives his pen or sells the farm to a person other than the beneficiary in his will causes the gift to fail (by ademption).

27.67 There is no specific solution to the issue of ademption. One, albeit not particularly satisfactory, solution is to leave some monetary amount as a substitutional gift. Alternatively, in the event of a disposal of the particular property the testator may execute a new codicil providing for another gift.

Disclaimer

27.68 A disclaimer is made where a beneficiary under a will simply does not wish to receive his inheritance. It is not possible for the beneficiary effecting the disclaimer to redirect the property to someone to whom he would like the inheritance to go; the gift falls into residue unless the will contains a substitutional gift in relation thereto.

A disclaimer cannot be made prior to the death of the testator. In other words, a beneficiary knowing about a prospective entitlement under a will cannot disclaim it during the testator's lifetime.

Uncertainty

27.69 The uncertainty principle applies if either the subject matter of the gift and/or the beneficiary cannot be identified with certainty. In this case the gift fails and falls into residue subject to a substitutional gift having been made. Examples of gifts which may be void for uncertainty include gifts which are to be applied in perpetuity for purposes which are not in law charitable gifts. Gifts for the maintenance of animals may or may not be regarded as charitable gifts; those not regarded as charitable must be subject to the perpetuity rule and thus restricted in time within the rule. A gift for the benefit of a particular animal (eg the family pet) is valid, but not a charitable gift, and thus subject to the perpetuity rule; on the other hand, a gift for the welfare of animals in general is likely to be charitable.

Capacity to inherit

27.70 Broadly speaking, any person has the capacity to inherit under a will. Incapacity is usually in relation to the inability to provide the executors with a satisfactory form of discharge. Thus, in the case of gifts to minors such gifts are valid but unmarried minors are, under general law, unable to give a valid receipt for capital or income until full age (ie 18). However, a married minor is able to give a valid receipt in respect of income only (*LPA 1925 s 21*).

Formerly, parents were able to give a valid receipt only if authorised by the will. However, the *CA 1989 s 3* confers on parents the power to provide a valid receipt for a legacy to which the minor child is entitled and they may require that the legacy be paid to him. *AEA 1925 s 42* also provides the executors power to appoint trustees (eg the minor's parents) to hold a legacy for a minor who is absolutely (but not contingently) entitled under the will.

Mental incapacity of a beneficiary does not preclude inheriting under a will. However, such an individual is not able to give a valid receipt. Normally, the attorney acting (or receiver) would give the valid receipt.

In general, a person who has unlawfully killed another is unable to profit in consequence of that killing as a matter of public policy (although there are exceptions).

Survivorship clauses

27.71 As indicated in paragraph 27.63 under a survivorship clause the beneficiary only inherits if he survives for the stated period after the testator's death. Failure to survive the requisite period causes the gift to pass as provided in the will. A common survivorship period often adopted is 28 days but may be as long as desired. However, where the survivorship period is in excess of six months the gift constitutes settled property to which the normal IHT rules apply (*IHTA 1984 ss 43* and *92*; (eg possible exit charges; see paragraph 16.18).

If such a survivorship period is required it may be preferable to utilise a 'two-year' discretionary trust (see paragraph 28.88).

27.72 Without the survivorship clause the beneficiary who inherits effectively controls the ultimate long-term destination of the gift, not the original testator.

Example 1

Jack leaves £5,000 cash to a close friend, Anita and £10,000 to his brother, Ted.

Anita dies seven days after Jack and under her will her sister, Susan, inherits everything (thus, Susan inherits the £5,000 left to Anita by Jack).

Had Jack known this he would have preferred to have left £15,000 to Ted. This could have been achieved by including a survivorship clause in his will.

27.73 It is, however, arguable that if the testator does have the above concern a survivorship period of only, say, 28 days does not really address the issue; it might be argued that a 28-day period survival condition in fact achieves nothing. Nevertheless, 28 days does tend to be the period adopted in many wills. This is probably because any longer period (eg six months) means that the intended beneficiary is unable to access the gift left in the will until the expiry of the survival period chosen which may, depending upon the circumstances, cause the beneficiary financial hardship.

27.74 The issue is particularly highlighted with respect to second marriages where there are children from the former marriage(s). If each spouse leaves their estate to each other it is the will of the surviving spouse which effectively determines the ultimate destination of their aggregate estates. This may mean that in the event of the father's death occurring first (who has children from the first marriage) his children do not inherit any of their father's estate unless the second wife provides for them to inherit under her will. In particular, in the absence of a survivorship condition where their deaths occur in circumstances where it is not possible to determine who dies first, the typically younger second wife will again inherit all (see paragraph 27.59).

27.75 The inclusion of a survivorship clause in the father's will prevents the above occurrence (see paragraph 27.74) at least in the event of simultaneous deaths (but not where, in other circumstances, the second wife survives the requisite period).

27.76 *Wills and probate*

In short, where one of the spouses is concerned to ensure that, for example, children from an earlier marriage(s) inherit certain property a survivorship clause is not the answer; in which case, the relevant property should be left directly to the children or in trust for the surviving spouse remainder to the children (see paragraph 27.79).

27.76 However, compounding the issue of simultaneous deaths are the IHT consequences. As stated in paragraph 27.61 above, where simultaneous deaths occur for IHT purposes (both are assumed to have died at the same time) favourable IHT treatment may arise if no survivorship clause exists in their wills.

27.77 Thus, for second marriages, the issue as to whether the wills of the spouses should contain a survivorship clause or not is not straightforward; in essence, the issue is whether the IHT advantage of excluding a survivorship clause is preferable to the risk of leaving the surviving spouse to effectively determine ultimate inheritance.

27.78 For those marriages not involving children from former marriages where the spouses are prepared to leave their respective entire estates to each other a survivorship clause is perhaps irrelevant.

27.79 The complication of second marriages involving children from earlier marriages is probably better dealt with by the use of will trusts which makes the survivorship clause concept (as between spouses) irrelevant.

For the spouse with children from a former marriage a will trust could be set up under which the second surviving spouse takes a life interest with the children taking the trust capital on the death of the spouse. This, in principle, provides financial security for the surviving spouse during lifetime but enables children from the former marriage to ultimately inherit.

Example 2

Jackie and her husband Michael have two children. Jackie and Michael work together and often, as a consequence, travel together on business. Neither has been married before.

They have each made a will leaving their respective estate to each other with substitution gifts to their children in equal shares. They have been advised that, for IHT purposes, given the likelihood of both dying in the same crash that no survivorship period in the wills should apply in such circumstances.

Their aggregate estate amounts to £2,025,000. Jackie's estate is £825,000 and Michael's £1.2 million.

Neither has made any lifetime gifts.

In May 2010 both Jackie and Michael are killed in a plane crash and it is not possible to determine which of the two died first. Michael is 52 and Jackie is 48.

As the elder of the two, under *LPA 1925* Michael is assumed to have died first and, as a consequence, his estate passes in its entirety to his wife Jackie (as she is in effect deemed to have survived him). Jackie's estate, which now includes that of Michael, passes to the children (as Michael, having been deemed to have died first, cannot benefit under Jackie's will).

However, for IHT purposes, both are assumed to have died at the same time. This means that although as a matter of the law of property Michael's estate passes to Jackie, for IHT purposes she cannot be treated as inheriting Michael's estate as she did not for this purpose survive him. Thus, Jackie's estate for IHT comprises only her own estate (ie £825,000).

Michael's estate (ie £1.2 million) is thus not included as part of Jackie's estate for IHT purposes but passes to the children under her will because under *LPA 1925* she does actually inherit Michael's estate.

Thus, a 40% charge (above the NRB) is levied on Jackie's £825,000 but no charge is levied on Michael's £1.2 million as it passes to Jackie as an inter-spouse transfer and then to the children. Total IHT charge on Jackie's estate is 40% of [£825,000 – £325,000] (ie £200,000).

If, however, a 28-day survivorship clause in the wills had applied, even on simultaneous death, Jackie does not inherit Michael's estate as she does not survive the, say, 28-day survivorship period. The children thus inherit from Michael (under substitutional gifts) and IHT is chargeable thereon (ie 40% × [£1.2 million – £325,000] namely £350,000).

Similarly, under Jackie's will, the children inherit and again IHT is chargeable thereon (ie 40% × [£825,000 – £325,000] namely £200,000).

Total IHT charge: £550,000.

An extra IHT amount of £350,000 is payable due to the inclusion of a survivorship clause which in this case is applicable even in the event of simultaneous deaths.

27.80 *Wills and probate*

Example 3

Jackie and her husband Michael have two children. Jackie and Michael work together and often, as a consequence, travel together on business. Neither has been married before.

They have each made a will leaving their respective estate to each other with substitution gifts to their children in equal shares. They have been advised to include a 28-day survivorship clause in their wills.

Their aggregate estate amounts to £2,025,000. Jackie's estate is £825,000 and Michael's £1.2 million.

Neither has made any lifetime gifts.

Michael is 52 and Jackie is 48.

Michael dies in July 2010 and ten days later Jackie dies (ie within the 28-day period).

On Michael's death the IHT payable is:

40% x [£1,200,000–£325,000] = £350,000.

On Jackie's death the IHT payable is:

40% x [£825,000–£325,000] = £200,000.

If no survivorship clause had been included in either will the IHT position is as follows:

on Michael's death no IHT is payable as his estate is inherited by Jackie.

on Jackie's death IHT is payable:

40% x [£2,025,000–£325,000] = £680,000.

In this case the failure to include a survivorship condition has increased the IHT payable considerably.

27.80 It should be noted that the impact of IHT on two deaths also varies with respect to the size of the respective spousal estates.

27.81 Where two deaths occur within a short period of each other (less than five years) quick succession relief (QSR) (*IHTA 1984 s 141*) is available to mitigate any double IHT charge which may arise on the same property (see paragraph 11.104).

Foreign issues

27.82 A will drawn up under English law by an English domiciled individual relating solely to English situs property involves no foreign issues; English law determines any area of conflict (eg the capacity of the individual to make the will; the validity of the will; the applicable succession law) and the English courts are competent to decide such issues.

27.83 However, the position is not so clear where one or more foreign dimensions are involved; in such cases it is necessary to not only ascertain which country's courts have jurisdiction to rule on any area of conflict but it is also necessary to ascertain which country's law should then be applied in making a determination.

Possible examples of such areas of conflict might occur where an English domiciled individual makes a will under English law but which purports also to deal with assets located outside the UK; or, a person with a foreign domicile (as determined under English law) leaves a will (or its equivalent) which deals with UK situs assets; or, an English domiciled individual makes a will under a foreign law governing property located in that country.

27.84 The resolution of such issues falls within the province of the conflict of laws (sometimes also known as private international law). The conflict of law rules differ from country to country; there is not a single universal set of conflict of law rules.

Succession

27.85 For present purposes perhaps the key issue relates to succession matters, namely, ascertaining the position under English law applicable to succession where foreign elements are involved. For example, if foreign property is left under a UK will whose law determines succession to the property

The broad discussion below is based on the English conflict of law rules.

27.86 Under English conflict of law rules it is the law of the country where the asset is situated (ie the *lex situs*) which determines whether the asset is to be considered *immovable* or *movable* (note under English *domestic* law the normal distinction is between personalty and realty). The distinction is not, it is to be noted, the same as a distinction between tangibles and intangibles; tangibles

27.87 *Wills and probate*

may be movable (eg a painting) or immovable (eg land) whereas intangibles (eg debts; shares; goodwill) cannot of course be touched and thus cannot be moved but are nevertheless treated for conflict of law purposes as movables.

27.87 The situs of an asset is determined as follows:

- *land* is situated where it lies;
- *choses in action* (eg debts; shares in companies; interests under trusts) are situated in the country where they are properly recoverable or can be enforced; and
- *chattels* (eg a painting; race horse; furniture) are situated in the country where the chattel is physically located at any given time.

27.88 With respect to succession, the general rule is that succession to immovables is governed by the *lex situs* (ie the country of location of the immoveable) whereas succession to movables is determined by the law of domicile of the testator's last domicile.

27.89 The High Court has jurisdiction to determine the succession to property of any person if there is a properly constituted representative of the estate before the court. In effect, such a person is someone who has obtained an English grant of probate (see paragraph 27.114).

The courts of a foreign country have jurisdiction to determine the succession to all movables wherever situated of a testator who dies domiciled (as determined under England's conflict of law rules) in that country and to all property which is situated in that country.

27.90 The following issues are relevant when considering succession matters involving foreign aspects:

- capacity;
- formal validity;
- material validity;
- construction; and
- revocation.

Capacity

27.91 The law of the country in which the deceased is domiciled at the time of making the will determines whether the testator has personal capacity to make the will dealing with movables. (eg a minor or a married woman).

Wills and probate **27.96**

This rule does not, however, govern the position as to the *material* validity of the will (see paragraph 27.94) which deals with issues such as whether a testator is permitted under the relevant law to leave his whole estate to whomever he pleases.

27.92 Although there appears to be no rule which specifies which law governs capacity to make a will of immovables it is generally felt that it is the *lex situs* (ie the law of the place where the property is situated) which governs the position.

Formal validity

27.93 Under English conflict of law rules the rule governing the validity of a will is widely drawn making it difficult for a will to be regarded as invalid. *Inter alia*, a will is treated as validly executed if its execution conforms to the internal law in force in the territory where it is executed *or* where the testator is domiciled either at the date of the will's execution or the testator's death (*or* had his habitual residence) *or* is a national thereof either at the date of execution of the will or the testator's death (*WA 1963 s 1*).

The broad range of *WA 1963 s 1* derives from *HCFVW 1961*.

Material validity

27.94 The material validity of a gift by will of *movables* is governed by the testator's domicile at the time of death (not the date of the making of the will as applied in determining capacity; see paragraph 27.91).

The material validity of a gift by will of *immovables* is governed by the *lex situs* (ie the law of the place where the property is situated).

27.95 Material validity refers to fundamental issues such as, for example, whether the testator has unrestricted freedom to distribute his estate by will or whether, for example, a proportion of his estate must be left to certain, typically family, beneficiaries (eg the children and/or surviving spouse).

27.96 As the determination of material validity in the case of real estate rests with the country in which the immovable is situated (see paragraph 27.94) this is an important point for those individuals of the UK who, for example, own holiday homes in France, Italy or Spain. Each of these countries' laws include 'forced-heirship' rules under which the owner of local immovables is not free to determine by will who should inherit on death (see paragraph 27.103). Thus, a will drawn up under English law by an English domiciled individual purporting

27.97 *Wills and probate*

to deal with, say, French immovables is overridden to the extent it is inconsistent with local French forced-heirship rules.

Construction

27.97 The interpretation of a will of movables is governed by the law intended by the testator which in turn is normally accepted as being the law of the testator's domicile at the date the will is made not the domicile at the date of death (this rule also probably applies to immovables although it may well be that the law of the *lex situs* applies) (*WA 1963 s 4*).

27.98 This issue is of particular importance where an individual's domicile changes between the date of execution of the will and death (eg an individual may be English domiciled on making a will but subsequent thereto may acquire a non-UK domicile of choice; any interpretation of terms in the will following death is made under English law which may or may not be what the testator intends).

Interpretation includes issues such as the meaning of words (eg 'child'; 'minor'; 'illegitimate child'; and 'next of kin').

Revocation

27.99 There appears to be no general rule which applies in all circumstances to determine whether a will has been revoked. This is particularly important given the not uncommon practice of executing more than one will under different countries' laws (each will typically dealing with property located within a particular country).

27.100 Marriage under English law automatically revokes an earlier will (see paragraph 27.35); this is not, however, common practice elsewhere (including Scotland). A determination as to whether a will is revoked on marriage is determined according to the domicile status of the testator at the date of marriage.

27.101 Under English law, for marriages pre-1 January 1974, a woman automatically acquires (as domicile of dependence) that of her husband (see paragraph 3.66). This therefore inevitably may impact on possible revocation of any will she may have made prior to the marriage. For example, if a Scottish lady makes a will before the above date and marries an Englishman before the above date she will on marriage have acquired an English domicile; thus, on marriage her previously executed will is revoked. On the other hand, if an English lady makes a will before the above date and marries a Scotsman before the above date her previously executed will is not revoked.

However, following the *DMPA 1973* (which abolished for married woman the domicile of dependence concept; see paragraph 3.67) the above issue should not arise.

27.102 Where wills under the laws of different countries are each executed at different times and where each will, for example, typically deals with assets in the country concerned, it may result in any earlier will (even if executed under the law of a different country) being revoked. To avoid such a possibility it may be advantageous to make any revocation clause in the will concerned explicit as to which earlier wills (and/or codicils and other testamentary dispositions) are intended to be revoked rather than simply including the standard English clause 'I hereby revoke all former wills, codicils and testamentary dispositions made by me'.

Forced heirship

27.103 This is the term frequently applied by common law jurisdictions (England being one) to the rules applicable in many civil law jurisdictions (eg typically countries on mainland Europe) under which a testator is not free to dispose of his estate in any manner he may choose (ie basically, the law lays down certain restrictions on the distribution of his estate on death).

27.104 Technically, the jurisdictions require that a 'legal reserve' or *'portio legitima'* or 'reserved share' apply to a proportion of the deceased's estate. Normally, this legal reserve is exercised in favour of children but also sometimes in favour of surviving spouses.

Such a legal reserve may apply in addition to any community property rules (see paragraph 27.110).

27.105 The concept of such rules is alien to English (albeit not Scottish) law and thus for those English domiciled individuals owning property in such countries it is important to ascertain to what extent they apply to 'foreigners'; such rules invariably do apply to foreigners owning immovable property therein.

27.106 Although as indicated in paragraph 27.1, English law permits a testator to distribute his estate in whatever manner is felt appropriate. This freedom was to some degree curtailed under *IPFDA 1938* now replaced by the *IPFDA 1975*.

27.107 *IPFDA 1975* provides for claims to be lodged against the testator's estate where the claimant believes that inadequate provision has been made for him/her under the will. The possible claimants are a spouse, former spouse, a child (not necessarily a minor) of the testator and any other person who

27.108 *Wills and probate*

immediately before the death of the testator was being maintained by the testator either wholly or partially.

With respect to deaths on or after 1 January 1996 the possible claimants are extended to include a cohabitee where such cohabitee lived with the testator as husband and wife for at least two years preceding the testator's death.

For a former spouse to be in a position to lodge a claim he/she must not have remarried (a claim cannot be lodged where a remarriage has occurred even if the marriage subsequently terminates eg through divorce).

27.108 An overriding requirement for the *IPFDA 1975* to apply is that the deceased dies domiciled within England/Wales; in addition, any claim needs to be lodged within six months of the date of the grant of probate (not date of death). Otherwise the claimant may have to resort to, *inter alia*, blocking the grant of probate or challenging the validity of the will.

27.109 Invariably those inheriting under the will in an attempt to 'fight off' any *IPFDA 1975* claimant typically seek to argue, in the first instance, that the testator did not die domiciled in England or Wales (see the case of *Cyganik v Agulian* (2006) *C/A*; see paragraph 3.162). It is for this reason that a number of court cases on domicile are not tax cases but arise due to claims made under *IPFDA 1975* (see paragraph 3.8).

Community property

27.110 Under English law property owned by a woman prior to marriage and property acquired by her after marriage belongs to her in her own right; the husband has no interest or rights therein. This, however, is not necessarily the position elsewhere, in particular in those countries with a civil law system.

27.111 The concept of 'community property', unknown under English law, is found in many other countries including Belgium, France, Germany and Spain in mainland Europe; South Africa; and many (eg California, Nevada, Texas and Washington) but not all states in the USA. The basic essence of the concept is that property within the marriage is jointly owned by both spouses.

27.112 There are, however, different degrees of community property.

Under some systems property owned at the time of marriage by the spouses and property acquired while married represent community property; under other systems only property acquired while married forms community property; and in others, only chattels owned at the time of marriage or acquired during the marriage form community property (land being excluded). Still, under other systems, property is not held jointly during marriage but in the event of death, for example, the surviving spouse is by law entitled to a percentage of the combined estates.

However, virtually all countries under which the concept of community property operates allow spouses to 'contract out' of the system.

27.113 In the absence of such a contract the requisite rights of either spouse in each other's movable property are determined by the law of the 'matrimonial domicile' which is the country where both parties are domiciled if they are domiciled in the same country. If not, then the applicable law is that of the country with which the parties to the marriage have the closest connection.

With respect to immovables, *prima facie*, it is the *lex situs* rules which would govern the position.

Probate

27.114 The death of an individual must be registered at the Registrar of Births, Deaths and Marriages (*BDRA 1953*). It must be registered within five days of the death with the registrar for the area in which the death occurred.

Following registration, the death certificate is issued, the original being retained by the registrar, with certified copies issued as appropriate. Registration of the death requires production of a certificate of death signed by a doctor.

27.115 Probate is the process which confirms both the authority of the personal representatives (PRs) of the deceased (ie in the case of a will the executors named in the will) and the validity of the will itself (where there is no will the term PRs is used to refer to the deceased's 'representatives' rather than the term 'executors').

27.116 The right to a grant of probate rests with the executors named in the will. It is under the will (not the grant of probate) that the executor is given authority to act and under which the executor's title to the deceased's assets derives; such title takes effect on the testator's death (whether probate has or has not been obtained). It is the grant of probate, however, which in practical terms provides the documentary evidence to third parties (eg banks) that the executor has the requisite authority to deal with the deceased's assets.

The executors' powers also derive from statute (eg *AEA 1925*).

27.117 As indicated in paragraph 27.116 the property of the deceased vests in the executors at death, the grant of probate providing proof that this has occurred.

27.118 *Wills and probate*

27.118 There is thus in principle no reason why an executor cannot deal with assets prior to the granting of probate but in practice third parties (in particular banks) are reluctant to release assets to executors in the absence of a grant of probate (some assets, however, do not require probate before they can be dealt with by the executors; see paragraph 27.125).

27.119 The application for probate may be made at any time after the testator's death but no such grant will be issued within seven days of the death; there is no time limit within which a grant of probate must be obtained.

27.120 The obtaining of probate requires the completion and lodgment of Form PA1 'Probate application form' and also any relevant IHT forms/accounts. Until any IHT is paid to HMRC probate cannot be granted (*SCA 1981 s 109*). It is necessary to determine whether the relevant forms should be submitted directly to the relevant probate registry or to HMRC; this in turn depends upon the IHT position of the deceased's estate (see paragraph 14.21).

27.121 The IHT forms requiring completion and lodgment depend upon the domicile status of the deceased at the time of death; the size of the deceased's estate; and whether the estate qualifies as an excepted estate (see paragraph 14.25). Thus, either Form IHT 205 'Return of estate information' or Form IHT 400 'Inheritance tax account' requires completion.

27.122 Where Form IHT 205 (eg the estate is an excepted estate or there is no IHT to pay) is the correct form to complete this form together with Form PA1, the will and death certificate are lodged directly with the relevant probate registry (not with HMRC).

On issue of the grant of probate the registry will then send the completed Form IHT 205 to HMRC who have 35 days (from the date of the grant) to request the executors to complete an IHT account (ie Form IHT 400). If no such request is received, the executors are deemed to have received a clearance from HMRC with respect to any IHT payable on the estate.

27.123 Where Form IHT 400 'Inheritance Tax Account' is the correct form to complete (eg IHT is payable or the estate does not qualify as an excepted estate). Form IHT 421 'Probate summary' also needs to be completed. This form (ie Form IHT 421) is then sent together with Form PA1, the will and death certificate to the relevant probate registry who will return the Form IHT 421 with their sections duly completed confirming the date and venue of an appointment with the registry.

Forms IHT 400, 421 etc then require lodgement with HMRC who, if all is in order, will send off Form IHT 421 directly to the probate registry duly stamped.

27.124 Once the IHT liability has been discharged (if appropriate) and a grant of probate is issued to the executors they are then in a position to administer the deceased's estate. This will involve, *inter alia*, collecting in all property of the deceased, discharging any liabilities thereof and finally making distributions to the various beneficiaries under the will (*AEA 1925 s 25*).

Assets not requiring probate

27.125 Probate is not necessarily required in respect of all the deceased's property and thus the executors may gain access to these assets before probate is granted. This is possible because such assets either do not form part of the deceased's estate for probate purposes or do form part of the estate for probate purposes but in respect of which the production of probate is not required for the assets to be realised.

It is to be appreciated, however, that even though assets may not require probate the deceased's interest in any such property still forms part of the deceased's estate for IHT purposes.

27.126 Assets where probate is not required include:

- assets held as beneficial joint tenants;
- death benefits paid under life policies written in trust;
- death benefits paid under pension schemes;
- chattels (ie tangible movable property); and
- bare trusts.

Jointly held assets

27.127 Assets held as beneficial joint tenants pass automatically on death by survivorship to the surviving joint owner(s) (see paragraph 27.9). In other words, the deceased's interest cannot, and does not, pass by will and probate is thus not necessary.

Typically, this form of ownership applies to the matrimonial home and joint bank accounts.

Production of the death certificate is sufficient evidence to ensure title passes to the surviving joint tenants (ie such evidence is sufficient to remove the deceased's name from the relevant documents (eg property registered at the Land Registry)).

27.128 If property (eg the matrimonial home) is held as beneficial tenants in

27.129 *Wills and probate*

common, however, the above does not apply. In this case the deceased's interest in the property passes by will (see paragraph 27.10).

Life policies

27.129 Any amount paid out on the death of the testator (ie the life assured) is, if the policy has been written in trust, payable to the trustees of the trust (not the executors qua their executor capacity) on production of the death certificate. Such proceeds do not in this case form part of the deceased's estate for IHT purposes and probate is not required.

Where the deceased (ie the life assured) retains title to the policy (ie has not settled it on trust) probate will be required and the proceeds form part of the deceased's estate for IHT purposes.

Pension death benefits

27.130 It is quite common under company pension schemes for death benefit payments to be made, as a matter of law, at the discretion of the pension trustees. The payment is usually paid to the individual nominated by the deceased whilst in employment (typically the surviving spouse). Production of the death certificate is sufficient to obtain payment from the trustees.

The proceeds do not form part of the deceased's estate for IHT purposes in such cases and probate is not required.

Personal pension schemes and retirement annuity contracts may be a little different and unless the benefits have been written in trust probate will invariably be required.

Chattels

27.131 Title to chattels (eg jewellery; paintings; pens; etc.) may pass by simple delivery and thus without the need for probate.

Bare trusts

27.132 A bare trust involves the holding of property by a trustee against whom the beneficiary has an immediate and absolute title to both the income and capital. As the legal title to the property resides with the trustee (and not the deceased) probate is not required.

The deceased's beneficial interest in the property is, however, part of the deceased's estate for IHT purposes.

Small payments

27.133 With respect to small sums of money (ie less than £5,000) it may be possible to access such monies without the need for probate depending upon the attitude of the holder of the asset (ie it is not possible to demand payment).

Usually banks/building societies will release small sums of money on deposit without the need for probate; an indemnity or release may be required by the bank/building society.

Executors

27.134 Executors are typically appointed by the testator under his will and may be given power under the will to appoint additional executors in certain circumstances (eg the death of an appointed executor). Generally the office of executor is not assignable and cannot be renounced once he has taken probate. The appointment of executor is for life.

27.135 Executors (unlike trustees) have joint and several authority (trustees must act jointly).

27.136 Executors are responsible for discharging any IHT payable on the deceased's estate (*IHTA 1984 s 200*).

27.137 Those who act as if they are executors, but are not, are referred to as executors de son tort (*AEA 1925 s 28*). Such persons who intermeddle with the deceased's assets are liable in respect thereof including any IHT liability in respect of property with which he has intermeddled (examples of intermeddling include selling the deceased's assets and receiving payment of debts due to the deceased).

Intestacy

27.138 Dying without a will is referred to as dying intestate. Under English law *AEA 1925 Part IV* provides the rules which apply in such circumstances.

27.139 The entitlement to any part of the deceased's estate depends upon the size of the estate and the extent to which a spouse, issue and other relatives survive the deceased.

27.140 *Wills and probate*

27.140 If the deceased dies leaving a surviving spouse and surviving issue (issue refers to lineal descendants (ie children, grandchildren and remoter descendants) *AEA 1925 ss 46* and *47*) and the deceased dies on or after 1 February 2009 the surviving spouse receives:

- the deceased's personal chattels absolutely (*AEA 1925 s 55*);
- a fixed net sum (often referred to as the 'statutory legacy') of £250,000 (*SI 2009/135*); from 1993 to 2009 the net sum was £125,000; and
- a life interest in one-half of the balance of the residuary estate (ie the estate remaining after provision for the personal chattels and the fixed net sum).

The fixed net sum refers to a sum net of IHT and costs but including interest payable thereon for the period from date of death to the date of payment.

27.141 In order to take the above the surviving spouse must survive the deceased by 28 days if the deceased dies on or after 1 January 1996 (*AEA s 46*).

27.142 Subject to the spouse's entitlements above, the other half of the residuary estate and the interest in remainder in the trust created for the spouse is held on statutory trusts for the issue (see paragraph 27.140 above) of the intestate (*AEA 1925 ss 46* and *47*).

27.143 The obvious disadvantage of dying intestate is that the distribution of the estate is governed solely by the law and views or wishes the deceased may have had in his lifetime are irrelevant; as a consequence, it is highly likely that not all those beneficiaries who the deceased would have liked to have benefitted will in fact do so.

Summary

27.144 A will allows an individual in principle to dispose of his estate as he wishes. Dying intestate (ie dying without a will) does not allow an individual to dispose of his estate as he wishes; the law dictates who should inherit.

27.145 A valid will requires strict compliance with statutory formalities (eg compliance with *WA 1837*).

27.146 A will once made may be revoked automatically (eg on marriage) or by intention (eg destroying or writing a later will).

27.147 It is important to try and ensure that any gifts made by will do not fail whether due to, *inter alia*, lapse (eg because the beneficiary dies before the testator) or ademption (ie where the subject matter of the gift no longer subsists on the death of the testator).

27.148 Survivorship clauses are often contained in wills but it may be that their inclusion leads to increased IHT on death; consideration to all factors (ie tax and non-tax) is necessary where such clauses are to be included.

27.149 Where property in more than one country is to be left by will it may be preferable for a will to be written under the law of each country where the property is located (in particular where the property concerned is immovable property).

27.150 Probate is necessary before the executors of the will can deal with the property of the deceased. However, not all property requires probate before it can be dealt with by the executors (eg jointly held property; bare trusts).

27.151 Where IHT is payable on an estate until it has been discharged by the executors probate cannot be obtained. The relevant form for lodgement in such cases with HMRC is Form IHT 400. Some estates qualify as excepted estates and some require no IHT to be paid; Form IHT 205 is the form which should be lodged in such cases.

Chapter 28

Wills and taxation

Background

28.1 Efficient tax planning involves not only planning for lifetime events but also for death. A carefully drafted will enables tax, in particular inheritance tax (IHT), to be mitigated on death thus profiting those who inherit under it.

28.2 As stated in paragraph 27.3 a will is of no consequence until death and thus in view of the not infrequent changes to tax law it is important to constantly review any will to ensure it remains tax efficient. Perhaps a classic example of the need for constant reviews arose when the transferable nil rate band was introduced in late 2007 for IHT purposes (see paragraph 11.44) and it became necessary to reconsider all earlier drafted wills to ascertain whether the then traditional approach of including NRB trusts in the wills of spouses was still good and efficient tax practice.

Another current example is the recent increase in the rates of income tax applicable to trust income from 40% to 50% (32.5% to 42.5% re dividend income) (effective 6 April 2010) pursuant to which the use of will trusts becomes potentially less income tax efficient.

28.3 In principle only two types of gift are possible by will, namely, absolute gifts or gifts into trust. Each gives rise to different tax consequences (both in the short and long term) and one type of gift may be preferable to the other depending upon the circumstances.

28.4 Unfortunately, there is an inherent clash between tax efficient lifetime planning and planning for death. The former, for IHT purposes, dictates the making of lifetime gifts (preferably potentially exempt transfers (PETs)) and dying with no more than a nil rate band (NRB) estate; on the other hand, for capital gains tax (CGT) purposes, gifting in lifetime precipitates CGT liabilities (albeit possibly subject to hold-over relief; see paragraph 8.45) whereas no such liabilities arise on assets owned on death thus favouring retaining asset ownership until death (when a CGT-free uplift occurs; see paragraph 8.40).

There is therefore the need to try and strike an appropriate balance.

28.5 Fortunately, it is possible even after the testator's death to carry out some degree of planning designed to either improve the IHT position on death and/or the fairness of the terms of the will as perceived by the beneficiaries.

One such planning option arises where the testator includes in his will a so-called 'two-year' discretionary trust which (under *IHTA 1984 s 144*) permits a degree of re-organisation/redistribution of the property left by will in the trust in the light of circumstances then prevailing (see paragraph 28.88).

In a not too dissimilar manner post-death disclaimers and/or instruments (normally deeds) of variation (*IHTA 1984 s 142*) also allow some post-death re-organisation/redistribution to be carried out (see paragraph 28.57).

Other post-death transactions if effected within strict time limits and by the executors prior to assent of property within the deceased's estate permit the impact of reductions in property values post death to be taken into account (*IHTA 1984 Part VI Chapters III and IV*; see paragraph 28.99).

28.6 The creation of more than one trust in a will requires consideration as to whether the trusts may constitute 'related settlements/trusts' (*IHTA 1984 s 62*). The consequence of trusts being related is that property in a related trust is taken into account in calculating the IHT charges on property in a relevant property trust (eg a discretionary trust) thus exacerbating the charges thereon (see paragraphs 16.23 and 16.28); it is therefore undesirable, for example, for the testator to create both a NRB discretionary trust and, say, an additional discretionary trust over residue as the two trusts would be related settlements.

However, a discretionary will trust combined with an immediate post-death interest in possession (IPDI) will trust under which the surviving spouse possesses the IPDI are not related trusts (an IPDI for any other person would, however, give rise to related trusts).

28.7 CGT liabilities do not arise on death and, as a consequence, CGT planning for death is not critical (*TCGA 1992 s 62*; see paragraph 8.40). However, post-death disposals by the executors prior to assent precipitate CGT charges (see paragraph 28.28).

28.8 Income tax should not be ignored although it is generally of less consequence than IHT. One issue which is pertinent to income tax relates to the need to identify the settlor where trusts are created under the will; this depends upon whether the trusts concerned are created by the testator or a beneficiary pursuant to the execution of a deed of variation (DoV) under *IHTA 1984 s 142* (see paragraph 28.84).

The importance of this need for settlor identification is that depending upon the nature of the trust any income thereof may be treated as that of the settlor not the trustees of the trust (see paragraph 17.66).

28.9 *Wills and taxation*

28.9 For a testator who wishes to leave a gift to someone who he does not wish, for various reasons, to name in the will (eg a mistress) provision is made to permit this to occur without additional IHT consequences (*IHTA 1984 s 143*). Thus, for example, a testator may wish to leave a gift to say, Y but proposes to leave it to X and in a separate letter to X asks X if he will simply pass the gift directly onto Y. Under *IHTA 1984 s 143* where X, within two years of the testator's death, passes the gift to Y, X is not regarded as having made a PET (which otherwise is the position) the gift to Y being treated as if it had been made by the testator under his will.

The 'letter of wishes' (to X in this example) is not legally binding and Y cannot sue X for the property should X renege on the arrangement; in essence the testator is relying on the goodwill and/or moral conscience of X.

28.10 Each of the three taxes are now considered.

Income tax

Pre-death

28.11 In the tax year of death it is necessary for the income tax liability of the deceased up to the date of his death (from the previous 6 April) to be determined and paid to HMRC. It is the executors of the will whose responsibility it is to ensure such compliance (*TMA 1970 s 74*).

28.12 Income arising from the date of death to the date of completion of the administration of the estate is that of the administration period (*ITTOIA 2005 s 653*) and the executors are responsible for filing appropriate returns and paying any income tax due.

28.13 It is important that income is correctly allocated as between that of the deceased and that of the executors (for the post-death administration period).

Income which is due prior to the testator's death is that of the deceased (even if it is actually paid after death). Thus, for example, dividends declared due and payable at a date prior to the death of the deceased but paid thereafter are the deceased's income; similarly with respect to rental income and bank interest.

Otherwise, income due and payable after the date of death forms income of the administration period.

28.14 Any income tax liabilities of the deceased outstanding at the date of death (whether for the tax year of death or any earlier tax years) are debts of his estate and thus deductible in calculating the value of the deceased's estate on death for IHT purposes (*IHTA 1984 s 5*).

28.15 The deceased is entitled to a full personal allowance in the tax year of death (ie it is not apportioned for the period 6 April to the date of death).

Administration period

28.16 The period of administration is the period from the date of the deceased's death to the end of the administration period which is generally taken to be the date when the residue is ascertained and ready for distribution (which may in practice be difficult to determine with precision).

28.17 Executors are not exposed to income tax on the estate income at the higher rates (ie 40%, 50% 32.5% and 42.5%) as they are not individuals and thus are liable on income during the administration period at 10% (with respect to dividends received (ie the dividend ordinary rate)) and 20% with respect to all other income (ie the basic rate); these rates apply effective 6 April 2008.

As executors are not individuals there is no entitlement to any personal allowances and any administration expenses of the personal representatives (PRs) are not deductible in computing their income tax liability.

28.18 Executors are UK resident where all of the executors are UK resident or non-UK resident where all the executors are non-UK resident. Where the residence status of the executors is mixed the residence, ordinary residence and domicile status of the deceased determines their residence status (*ITA 2007 s 834*).

28.19 Once the income tax liability is discharged on the income arising from the estate for a tax year and administration expenses have been deducted from the after tax income the net amount of income is available for distribution to the beneficiaries entitled thereto.

28.20 The income received by a beneficiary is included as part of his income for the relevant tax year and taxed accordingly. The income so included is the net amount received from the executors grossed-up at the rate of income tax already charged on that category of income on the part of the executors (eg 10% re income paid out of dividend income); such income tax is offsettable against the beneficiary's own liability thereon.

28.21 Not all beneficiaries are entitled to any income arising during the administration period to the executors; for example, a general legatee is not so entitled (although interest may be paid on the legacy if the will so provides). However, a specific legatee is entitled to the income which has arisen on the property to which he is entitled from the date of death (eg rental income generated on real estate to which he is entitled). The specific legatee is subject to income tax on the income for the tax year in which it arose, not the tax year of payment to him by the executors. The income received is grossed up for income tax paid thereon by the executors and thus in respect of which an appropriate tax credit subsists for offset; the beneficiary's income tax liability on the income arises only as and when the legacy is assented (ie vested) to him.

28.22 Residuary beneficiaries are entitled to an absolute interest in the residue (ie capital and income) or only income therefrom. Income payments made to either category of beneficiary are subject to income tax on the part of the beneficiary grossed-up at the rate applicable to that category of income for the tax year of receipt; the liability on the part of the beneficiary arises in the tax year of receipt by the beneficiary (ie there is no back-spreading of the income to earlier tax years as applies in the case of a specific legatee).

28.23 Any beneficiary receiving income payments from the executors receives a Form R185 'Estate Income' which shows the amount and category of income paid to the beneficiary and the income tax deducted (ie the income tax paid by the executors on the income) from those categories of income (the executors are obliged to supply this information; *ICTA 1988 s 700*).

Capital gains tax

Pre-death

28.24 As in the case of income tax the deceased is liable to CGT on disposals in the tax year of death up to the date of death. The executors are responsible for making the appropriate returns to HMRC on behalf of the deceased.

The full amount of the exempt annual amount (see paragraph 8.12) is available to the deceased (ie there is no reduction for death part way through a tax year).

28.25 Any surplus capital losses arising in the year of death (ie after offset against any capital gains arising in that tax year) and prior to death may be carried back for offset against capital gains made in the three tax years prior to death (*TCGA 1992 s 62*; see paragraphs 8.42 and 9.9). However, any remaining unrelieved capital losses of the deceased cannot be offset against capital gains made by the executors during the administration period.

Any refund of earlier CGT payments due to the carry back of capital losses forms part of the estate of the deceased for IHT purposes.

Administration period

28.26 On death there is no disposal (deemed or otherwise) of assets beneficially owned at death for CGT purposes (see paragraph 28.7); thus no

CGT liability arises on death. All assets owned beneficially by the deceased on death are deemed to have been acquired by the executors at their market value at the date of death (*TCGA 1992 ss 62* and *272*).

Where the value of an asset of the deceased has been 'ascertained' (ie determined and agreed by HMRC) for IHT purposes the ascertained value forms the base acquisition cost for the executors for CGT purposes (*TCGA 1992 s 274*). If all assets pass to a surviving spouse, and are thus exempt, the values of the assets have not been ascertained and non-ascertainment also applies to those assets comprised in an estate where the estate is below the IHT threshold (ie £325,000 for the tax year 2010–2011). HMRC do not accept that an asset's value has been ascertained where, for example, 100% business property relief (BPR) applies to the asset.

28.27 If the value of 'related property' (*IHTA 1984 s 16;* see paragraph 10.24) is ascertained for IHT purposes this may result in the base cost to the executors being higher than it would otherwise be (in the absence of the related party rules) which is beneficial for CGT purposes with respect to any future disposals of the property.

28.28 Capital gains precipitated on disposals (ie sales) effected by the executors during the administration period are subject to CGT at the 28% rate effective for disposals on or after 23 June 2010 (*TCGA 1992 s 4* substituted by *F (No 2) 2010 s 2* and *Sch 1*); 18% effective with respect to disposals on or after 6 April 2008 and pre-23 June 2010 (formerly, 34% until 6 April 2004; and 40% from 5 April 2004 to 5 April 2008). However, executors are only able to claim the annual exempt amount for the tax year of death (ie with respect to disposals in the period following death) and the two following tax years (*TCGA 1992 s 3*).

Any unrelieved capital losses arising in the administration period cannot be utilised either by the deceased or the beneficiaries entitled to the assets under the will; they are thus lost.

28.29 Where disposals of assets by the executors are made for values below the market values at the date of death it may be possible to substitute the lower values for the market values in computing the IHT liability on the deceased's estate (*IHTA 1984 Part VI Chapters III* and *IV*; see paragraph 28.99).

28.30 Capital gains tax liabilities arising during the administration period on asset disposals by the executors may be mitigated if, prior to sale, the assets are first assented to the beneficiaries thereto entitled who then effect the sales.

The assent (ie transfer) of an asset by the executors to a beneficiary is not a disposal for CGT purposes and thus no CGT liability arises to the executors (*IHTA 1984 s 62*); the recipient beneficiary is treated as acquiring the asset at the date of the deceased's death (ie not at the date of the actual transfer) at its then value.

28.31 *Wills and taxation*

28.31 By transferring the asset to the beneficiary prior to disposal any subsequent CGT liability (or capital loss) falls on the beneficiary. This may be advantageous where the beneficiary has an unused annual exempt amount for the tax year or unused capital losses for the tax year and/or brought forward.

It may also be advantageous where the beneficiary is non-UK resident (as such persons are not subject to CGT; see paragraph 23.23) or an exempt body (eg a charity).

An assent may be particularly attractive where the beneficial entitlement to the asset is divided (typically equally) amongst a number of beneficiaries. This has the advantage that the possible number of annual exempt amounts available exceeds the single annual exempt amount available to the executors (if any).

Example 1

Charlie Clause dies in 2009–2010 and leaves a holiday home to his four children equally.

At the date of his death the value of the property is £200,000 and at the time of a proposed sale (July 2010), £280,000.

By assenting the property prior to sale to the four children the aggregate capital gain of £80,000 produces a capital gain of £20,000 for each child less their respective annual exempt amount of £10,100 giving each child a CGT liability of 18% (or 28%) of £9,900 (ie £1,782 (or £2,772)) producing an aggregate charge of £7,128 (£11,088).

If the executors effect the sale the CGT liability is 28% of £69,900 (ie £19,752).

A saving of £12,624 (£8,664) is made by assenting the asset prior to sale.

28.32 An assent does not need to be in any particular form; it may thus be made orally (ie not in writing) or may in fact simply be inferred from the executors' conduct. It is important, however, that the position is clear as to whether such an assent has, or has not, occurred thus determining who is actually effecting the disposal (ie executors or beneficiary(ies)).

An assent may require some formality such as the need to be put in writing in order to pass *legal* (but not beneficial) title (eg in respect of land; *AEA 1925 s 36*). Pending the execution of such formalities (if any), the executors having assented to the transfer of the beneficial title, hold the asset as trustee for the beneficiary.

Inheritance tax

28.33 It is with respect to IHT that the major tax implications arise on death. Furthermore, the actions of the executors and/or beneficiaries after death may also impact upon the IHT levied on the deceased's estate.

28.34 The changes to trusts introduced in *FA 2006* (see Chapter 16) in principle makes the creation of lifetime trusts less IHT attractive. This has, other things being equal, caused the role of will trusts to increase in relative importance.

28.35 The basic principles of IHT as apply on death have been considered in Chapter 10. This section concentrates primarily on the period post-death after first reviewing the implications of the transferable NRB and the NRB discretionary trust on IHT liabilities arising on death (see paragraphs 11.44 and 16.24).

28.36 The issue of equalisation of estates as between spouses so as to mitigate overall tax liabilities, including on death, has been discussed elsewhere (see paragraph 11.45). The introduction of the transferable NRB (*IHTA 1984 s 8A*) has to some extent reduced the need for such equalisation because if the first spouse to die fails to utilise his/her NRB the surviving spouse is able to transfer it and use it on death which was not the position pre the introduction of the NRB's transferability (*IHTA 1984 s 8A*).

28.37 Nevertheless, transferability is just another option to consider in any IHT planning exercise and relying on it may not always be the best approach.

28.38 The following points are worth noting with respect to the transferable NRB:

- transferability of the NRB applies on death only. Thus, it does not help mitigate IHT in lifetime; a spouse owning little or no property is unable to take advantage of any lifetime exemptions and reliefs (eg the £3,000 annual exemption; BPR);

- transferability of the NRB is restricted to transfers between spouses (ie persons married albeit not necessarily living together). It thus does not apply to cohabitees (even if living as husband and wife); single individuals; or divorcees;

- there is no guarantee that the concept of the transferable NRB will remain available in the future; it may be repealed or changed in an unfavourable way;

- the NRB is linked to inflation (ie increased in line with inflation; *IHTA 1984 s 8*) subject to contrary provision; there is thus no guarantee that

28.39 *Wills and taxation*

this will necessarily continue in the future and indeed under *FA 2010 s 8* there is no increase in the NRB for the tax years 2010–2011, 2011–2012, 2012–2013 and 2014–2015 (the NRB of £325,000 fixed for the tax year 2009–2010 by *FA 2007 s 4* is thus the figure applicable for 2010–2011 *et seq.*); and

- utilisation by the first spouse to die of a NRB discretionary trust rather than relying on the transferable NRB may produce a lower overall IHT liability where the property placed in trust is likely to increase significantly in value. In such cases the IHT payable on the property in trust (and on any appointments out of trust) up to the time of the surviving spouse's death is likely to be much less than the IHT which would be levied on the same value (equivalent to the NRB) of property on the surviving spouse's death even allowing for the transferred NRB (the maximum rate of IHT applicable to relevant property trusts (eg a discretionary trust) at the ten-yearly anniversaries is 6% compared to the 40% payable by individuals on death; see Chapter 16).

28.39 It is also worth noting that the use of a NRB discretionary will trust may offer non-tax advantages; thus, for example, it permits the first spouse to die to provide for the surviving spouse (eg by way of a life interest) yet ensures that the underlying property settled is not squandered and thus is left intact for the children on the surviving spouse's death (this is particularly a valuable option where the marriage is a second (or later) marriage but safe provision for children from a first or earlier marriage is desired).

Married couples, cohabitees and single individuals

28.40 There is no one type of will which could be said to provide optimal tax mitigation in all circumstances. The type of will suitable for a married couple without children is unlikely to be the appropriate will for a married couple with children. Whilst will trusts are not suitable for all testators they do offer a high degree of flexibility and are adaptable to changes of circumstance and offer a viable alternative to gifting property absolutely.

Married couples

28.41 The creation of a will trust in which the surviving spouse is granted an interest in possession qualifies as an IPDI (where the trust is created on or after 22 March 2006). The settlement of property is an inter-spouse transfer (and thus exempt). No part of the deceased's NRB is thus used on the trust's creation (irrespective of the amount settled therein).

28.42 However, on the death of the surviving spouse his/her estate will include the trust property in which the IPDI subsists (as the IPDI is a qualifying interest in possession). If the trust property is thereafter held on discretionary trust the relevant property rules will then apply.

28.43 In the light of a change of circumstances the IPDI for the surviving spouse may, for example, be terminated and the trust property appointed to the spouse absolutely assuming the trustee possesses the appropriate power; no IHT charge arises (as the spouse is treated as owning the underlying trust assets in which the IPDI subsists).

If the estate has not been administered at the date of the above appointment and the property has not at that time been assented to the trustees no CGT charge arises on the appointment as the spouse is treated as receiving the property at the date of death (as if the testator had left the property to the spouse directly).

If, in the above scenario, the property has been assented to the trustees (or the administration of the estate had been completed (in which case the property would then have been assented)) prior to the date of appointment of property to the surviving spouse the trustees are deemed to have made a CGT disposal and reacquisition and a CGT charge arises (assuming of course that the property has increased in value between the date of death and the date of the appointment).

28.44 Where the IPDI for the surviving spouse is terminated (prior to her death) and the trust property in which her IPDI subsisted is appointed to the remaindermen (eg family members; a charity) absolutely the surviving spouse makes a transfer which qualifies as a PET, or is exempt, for IHT purposes.

For CGT purposes the analysis in paragraph 28.43 remains the same (ie the same CGT consequences arise whether the appointee is the surviving spouse or the remaindermen).

28.45 Where children are involved any of the above options are equally applicable with the children being included within the class of beneficiaries under the will trust for the surviving spouse. It may be that the will trust may take the form of a discretionary trust (rather than an IPDI trust) the beneficiaries consisting of the surviving spouse and children. In addition some of the deceased spouse's property may be given absolutely.

IHT arises on the deceased spouse's estate except in respect of absolute gifts to the surviving spouse (or the creation of an IPDI in his/her favour); to this extent the use of a discretionary trust may be a more expensive IHT option.

For CGT purposes no CGT liability arises on death (see paragraph 8.40).

Cohabitees

28.46 Cohabitees may comprise two people who live together as friends or two people who live together as husband and wife. Nevertheless they are treated as two separate individuals for all tax purposes; thus, none of the inter-spouse exemptions (whether for IHT or CGT) apply to transfers between the two of them whether on death or in lifetime.

Thus, transfers between the two of them effected on death, whether absolutely or on will trust, precipitate an IHT charge (subject to the NRB). However, for CGT no liability arises on death.

28.47 The simplest of options is for the first person to die to leave everything to the surviving person absolutely (perhaps having made some gifts to other family members and friends). It is therefore the surviving person who ultimately determines the destination of their combined property which may not necessarily be attractive to the first to die.

28.48 As an alternative the first person to die may leave the surviving person an IPDI with the remaindermen (be they charities; family and/or friends) inheriting absolutely on death of the surviving person; thus enabling a determination to be made by the first to die with respect to their own property as to who should ultimately inherit.

28.49 Another option is for the creation of a simple discretionary will trust the beneficiaries of which include the surviving person; this option perhaps providing the greatest flexibility.

Single person

28.50 Probably the most attractive option is the simple gifting of all property to family, friends, charities etc absolutely. Where there are reasons why an absolute gift to a particular beneficiary may be inappropriate/inadvisable a discretionary trust may provide the answer.

IHT arises but no charge to CGT arises.

Charitable gifts

28.51 Gifts to charities are exempt and thus if a testator leaves property to charity by will no IHT arises thereon.

28.52 However, the IHT position is particularly complex where the testator leaves his residuary estate for both exempt beneficiaries (eg charities) and non-exempt beneficiaries (eg gifts to family and friends). In such cases the IHT on the non-exempt part of the residue is borne exclusively by that part of the residue as the exempt part is not to bear the IHT on any other part of the residue

(*IHTA 1984 s 41*). The result is that the non-exempt residuary beneficiaries inherit less than the exempt residuary beneficiaries (after IHT).

28.53 It is therefore important that the testator appreciates this point as it may be that this is not his intention (ie he intended that each inherit the same amount). The testator thus needs to word his will according to that which he wants to happen; if the residue *after* IHT is to be split equally between exempt and non-exempt residuary beneficiaries it is then necessary that the non-exempt beneficiaries inherit a greater portion of the residuary estate (pre IHT) so as after bearing the IHT charge the amount left equals that of the exempt residuary beneficiaries.

Alternatively, if the testator simply wants to divide his residuary estate equally (pre IHT) the will should simply so provide.

28.54 Subject to contrary wording in the will specific gifts do not bear their own IHT, such IHT being borne by the residuary estate (as a testamentary expense). The IHT on such gifts is borne by the whole residuary estate (ie before any division of the residuary estate between the exempt and non-exempt residuary beneficiaries).

28.55 A testator needs to appreciate that leaving the whole or any part of his residuary estate to a charity (however well meaning) may result in legal challenges being made by the charity following his death. Such challenges may be made because, for example, the charity feels the executors are not implementing the terms of the will correctly (ie an interpretation unfavourable to the charity) or are incurring excessive or unwarranted expenses in administering the estate (which are payable out of the residuary estate thus reducing the amount of charity's inheritance).

Such challenges appear to be on the increase, whether valid or not. If the testator wishes to avoid such challenges to his will after his death but still benefit one or more of his favourite charities a better approach is to simply leave a specific sum of money rather than some ill-defined proportion of his residuary estate.

28.56 Prior to the changes introduced in *FA 2010 s 30*, gifts to non-UK based charities did not qualify for any form of UK tax relief (including IHT exemption); only gifts to UK based charities qualified for the various forms of tax relief.

However, for gifts made on or after 6 April 2010 UK charitable tax reliefs are extended to organisations equivalent to charities based in the EU and in the European Economic Area (EEA) countries of Norway and Iceland. This change follows a judgment in the European Court of Justice (ECJ) in January 2009.

Post-death events

Disclaimers, deeds of variation and discretionary will trusts

28.57 Following the testator's death a degree of re-organisation of his will may be carried out without precipitating either IHT or CGT charges. The re-organisation may take the effect of:

- a disclaimer (*IHTA 1984 s 142*);
- a deed of variation (*IHTA 1984 s 142*); and/or
- an appointment out of the two-year discretionary will trust (*IHTA 1984 s 144*).

Strictly speaking, the will is not in fact re-organised (ie the will still stands) but the effects of it are changed for IHT (and/or CGT) purposes; effectively, an IHT (and/or CGT) fiction is created.

Each of the above precipitates IHT and/or CGT consequences.

28.58 *IHTA 1984 s 142* provides for the IHT and/or CGT consequences which would normally follow where a disclaimer is effected or a DoV executed to be disregarded and for the tax consequences to be those which would have applied if the variation had been effected by the deceased or, in the case of a disclaimer, the disclaimed benefit had never been conferred.

Similarly, where *IHTA 1984 s 144* is in point (ie in relation to appointments out of a discretionary will trust) the normal IHT and CGT consequences are disregarded and the tax consequences are those which would have applied if the testator's will had provided for the property to be held as it is following the appointment.

Example 2

X leaves in his will equities worth £100 to Y; Y under a DoV redirects the gift to Z. Thus, Z takes the equities following a real world gift to him by Y.

The normal tax consequences are that Y has made a PET for IHT and a disposal for CGT.

The application of *IHTA 1984 s 142* is that the receipt by Z is 'deemed' to be a direct inheritance by Z as if X had left Z the equities directly in his will (ie for IHT (and CGT) the real world gift from Y to Z is ignored (hence there are no IHT PET issues or CGT disposal issues for Y)).

28.59 The above fictional tax treatment arises as a consequence of 'reading back' (ie the terms of the DoV are effectively treated as if they formed part of the terms of the will).

Not surprisingly various conditions need to be satisfied for this tax fictional treatment to apply. Depending upon all the circumstances it may be, however, that the 'normal' IHT and/or CGT consequences are preferred to the fictional tax treatment even where the conditions are satisfied. In other words even if a DoV or disclaimer is executed it is not necessary for *IHTA 1984 s 142* to apply in which case the normal IHT and CGT consequences follow (ie there is no 'reading back').

However, where the conditions of *IHTA 1984 s 144* are satisfied the section applies automatically (see paragraph 28.88).

28.60 It is often thought that a disclaimer or DoV rewrites the testator's will or changes the gifts made in it; this is incorrect. A disclaimer or DoV does not change the terms of the will but simply affects the effects of the will.

Disclaimers

28.61 A disclaimer is simply where a beneficiary under the will chooses not to accept the gift made to him by the testator. It is important that the beneficiary has not accepted the gift as it is not then possible to disclaim it. Theoretically, a gift by will is not required to be disclaimed within any particular time frame although in practice it would normally be disclaimed at the time when the beneficiary becomes aware of it

28.62 It is usually preferable for a disclaimer to be made in writing to the executors although it may be made orally.

28.63 A disclaimer will typically be made without consideration although the disclaiming beneficiary may seek some form of recompense from the person who then inherits. Unlike the situation in respect of a DoV the beneficiary disclaiming the gift is not able to re-direct it to a person of his choosing; the terms of the will apply (eg a substitutional clause may dictate who then inherits).

28.64 A beneficiary is unable to disclaim only part of a gift (ie accepts part of it).

28.65 The beneficiary who inherits following a disclaimer is treated as taking his interest from the date of death of the testator.

28.66 *Wills and taxation*

28.66 For IHT purposes the normal consequence of the execution of the disclaimer is that it is treated as a transfer of value (eg a PET) by the disclaiming beneficiary; for CGT purposes the normal consequences are that no CGT charge arises as no disposal occurs.

28.67 The IHT consequences of paragraph 28.66 are modified where the conditions of *IHTA 1984 s 142* are satisfied. The conditions are:

- the disclaimer must be executed by an instrument in writing (although a deed is not strictly necessary);
- the disclaimer must be executed within two years of the testator's death; and
- the disclaimer must not be made for any consideration in money or money's worth (other than consideration consisting of the execution of another disclaimer in respect of other property left in the testator's will).

Parallel provisions exist in *TCGA 1992 s 62* under which the normal CGT consequences (ie those in paragraph 28.66) are modified.

28.68 The instrument in writing does not have to be by way of deed, although this is common. (see paragraph 28.71).

28.69 Where the conditions set out in paragraph 28.67 are satisfied *IHTA 1984 s 142* provides that the disclaimed gift is regarded as having never been conferred on the beneficiary; thus, there is no transfer of value for IHT purposes. *TCGA 1992 s 62* similarly provides that for CGT purposes the gift is regarded as having never been conferred and that the disclaimer does not constitute a disposal on the part of the disclaiming beneficiary.

28.70 In practice, disclaimers are less popular than DoVs. The prime reason is that the disclaiming beneficiary has no control over the destination of the disclaimed gift which is often desired (which is not the case for a DoV). A disclaimer may thus be utilised where, for example, following a family feud a family member simply wants nothing further to do with the family including no wish to benefit under any will.

Deeds of variation

28.71 As indicated in paragraph 28.70 a DoV is far more common than a disclaimer. Although commonly referred to as a 'deed' of variation a more correct description would by an 'instrument' of variation (ie there is no requirement for a deed to be executed although this is invariably the method adopted).

The requirements for a deed to be valid are (for deeds executed on or after 31 July 1990) laid down in the *LP(MP)A 1989* and are as follows:

- the deed must be signed by the individual making it and it must make it clear on its face that it is intended to be a deed;
- a witness must sign the deed attesting the signature of the individual making the deed; and
- the deed must be delivered (ie the individual making the deed signifies that he adopts the deed irrevocably as his own).

Execution by way of deed means the variation is both binding and enforceable.

28.72 Under a DoV the beneficiary who inherits property under the testator's will varies the gift in favour of another person (eg individual or trust). Unlike the position with respect to the disclaimer the beneficiary effecting the DoV has accepted the gift but wishes it to be redirected to someone else.

The redirection under the DoV is not restricted to one of the other beneficiaries under the will; a redirection can be to anyone, beneficiary or not.

28.73 The normal tax consequences are simply that the beneficiary effecting the DoV is making a transfer of value for IHT purposes (eg a PET) and a disposal for CGT purposes.

28.74 As in the case of the disclaimer the normal tax consequences are modified where the conditions of *IHTA 1984 s 142* are satisfied. These conditions are the same as for a disclaimer but with an additional condition also requiring satisfaction:

- the DoV must be executed by an instrument in writing;
- the DoV must be so executed within two years of the testator's death;
- the DoV must not be made for any consideration in money or money's worth (other than consideration consisting of the execution of another disclaimer in respect of other property left in the testator's will); and
- the DoV must contain a statement to the effect that *IHTA 1984 s 142* is to apply to the DoV and/or that *TCGA 1992 s 62* is to apply to the DoV *(note this condition is not required for a disclaimer)*.

TCGA 1992 s 62 contains parallel provisions for CGT purposes.

In the discussion below it is assumed, unless otherwise stated, that the DoV contains the statement that IHTA 1984 s 142 and TCGA 1992 s 62 are to apply (ie the last of the above conditions is satisfied).

28.75 *Wills and taxation*

28.75 The DoV needs to be signed by all those whose interests under the DoV are being varied. The individual who chooses to redirect his gift obviously needs to sign the DoV but other beneficiaries under the will whose interests are affected also need to sign.

A failure of all relevant individuals to sign the DoV invalidates it.

28.76 Problems arise where the interests of a minor are affected because a minor cannot consent to a variation on his own behalf without the court giving its consent under the *VTA 1958* (a consent which will only be given where the court determines that the DoV is in the interests of the minor).

28.77 The executors are only required to sign the DoV where the IHT arising on the deceased's estate is increased due to the execution of the DoV (which might arise, for example, where a surviving spouse redirects her interest arising under the will to the children); in practice, the executors are often signatories due to the fact that the DoV does, of course, affect the administration of the estate.

28.78 Where the conditions of paragraph 28.74 are satisfied, for IHT purposes the variation is assumed to have been effected by the testator not the beneficiary. Thus, the beneficiary is regarded as not having made a transfer of value for IHT purposes. For CGT purposes the variation does not constitute a disposal and the variation is regarded as having been effected by the testator.

Example 3

The son (S) of the testator (T) is gifted £50,000 under T's will. Depending upon T's NRB at the date of his death IHT may be leviable on the £50,000.

S executes a DoV pursuant to which he redirects the £50,000 to his mother (M) (ie T's surviving spouse).

The gift to M is deemed to have been made by T under his will (and not by S) in which case no IHT is due thereon as it is a gift from H to W (ie an inter-spouse exempt gift).

On death there is no disposal by the testator for CGT purposes and thus the beneficiary benefitting under the DoV (ie M) takes the gift at its market value at the date of death qua legatee (in this case CGT being irrelevant as the property concerned is cash).

28.79 Although satisfaction of the conditions of *IHTA 1984 s 142* and *TCGA 1992 s 62* result in the above 'deemed' tax consequences it is possible for the

DoV to state that the provisions of one (or neither) of the Acts is to apply but not those of the other. For example, *IHTA 1984 s 142* is to apply but not *TCGA 1992 s 62* (or vice versa).

28.80 Generally, it is often preferable for both sets of provisions to apply but this is not always the case.

Example 4

Kent Car leaves an antique painting to his son, Tomas, worth £70,000 at the date of his death in October 2008.

In August 2010 Tomas executes a DoV in favour of his mother, Mary with respect to the painting; he states therein that *IHTA 1984 s 142* provisions are to apply but no such statement is made with respect to *TCGA 1992 s 62*. The painting is worth £80,000 at the date of then DoV.

For IHT, under *IHTA 1984 s 142*, Kent is treated as having left the painting to Mary which is an inter-spouse transfer. The IHT on the £70,000 paid on his death is thus reclaimable.

For CGT, the normal consequences follow (ie Tomas makes a CGT disposal for £80,000 making a capital gain of £10,000); however, no actual CGT liability arises assuming he has not used his annual exempt amount of £10,100). By not utilising the *TCGA 1992 s 62* provisions Mary acquires the painting with the higher £80,000 base cost.

Had Tomas stated in the DoV that *TCGA 1992 s 62* was also to apply no CGT liability would arise on his part (as Kent is then regarded as having left the painting to Mary) but Mary's base cost for CGT would be £70,000 (ie market value on Kent's death).

In short, whether both or indeed neither of the *IHTA 1984 s 142* and *TCGA 1992 s 62* provisions should be applied depends upon all the circumstances at the relevant times.

28.81 A DoV executed under *IHTA 1984 s 142* can only apply to property which forms part of the deceased's estate on death; this excludes property to which the deceased is treated as beneficially entitled due to the gift with reservation (GWR) provisions and also excludes any settled property in which the deceased is treated as beneficially entitled due to a qualifying interest in possession.

28.82 *Wills and taxation*

Interestingly, property jointly held on death is included as property to which a DoV may apply; this includes property which passes by survivorship under a joint tenancy as it is possible under *IHTA 1984 s 142* to retrospectively sever a joint tenancy thus enabling the interest that accrued by survivorship to pass under the deceased's will (and hence may be varied).

28.82 However, HMRC take the view that a qualifying interest in possession created by will cannot be subject to a DoV by the beneficiary thereof if the beneficiary has died (ie the executors of the estate of the beneficiary cannot execute a DoV redirecting the beneficiary's qualifying interest in possession). The logic, according to HMRC, is that the qualifying interest ceases on the beneficiary's death and thus the executors have no interest in any property which may then be varied (although HMRC accept that a disclaimer may be executed in respect thereof but only if the beneficiary has not taken any benefit from the interest).

28.83 It is not possible to effect multiple DoVs with respect to the same item of property (ie A cannot vary his interest in property 'X' in favour of B who then varies that interest in favour of C). However, multiple DoVs are possible where the same item of property is not involved (eg A varies his interest with respect to property 'X' in favour of B; C varies his interest in property 'Y' in favour of D).

28.84 A DoV is not restricted to redirecting property inherited by a beneficiary absolutely to another person absolutely; thus a DoV may redirect property to be held on trust. The trust may be set up in the DoV or the trust may already be in existance. As the redirection is treated as having been made by the deceased (if the deceased is the settlor for IHT purposes) the GWR provisions are inapplicable, even if the beneficiary actually effecting the DoV can benefit under the trust.

However, for CGT and income tax purposes, the beneficiary (and not the testator) effecting the DoV is treated as the settlor (*FA 2006 Sch 12*; and *ITA 2007 s 472* and *TCGA 1992 s 68c*).

The deceased is also the settlor for CGT and income tax purposes where the DoV does not create a trust but varies a trust set up by the testator in his will and transfers property out of the trust created by the testator in his will into another trust.

The execution of the DoV pursuant to which a trust is created and under which an interest in possession arises gives rise to an IPDI as it is the testator who is regarded as having created the trust for IHT purposes.

Example 5

Henrietta dies and under her will leaves her estate of £600,000 to her husband Dominic whose own estate is valued at £400,000.

Dominic feels that some provision should be made for their children.

He could transfer monies to them absolutely or settle the monies on trust. Either option may impact upon the IHT payable on his estate on death as some part of his NRB may be affected by such gifts.

By executing a DoV in an amount of the NRB in favour of a discretionary trust for the children ensures that his wife's NRB is utilised whilst not affecting his own NRB.

Example 6

Patrick inherits £500,000 absolutely under, Peter, his father's will in respect of which an IHT charge of £200,000 arises.

By DoV Patrick varies his inheritance in favour of a trust under which his mother, Martha, takes an interest in possession. Martha's interest is an IPDI as it is treated as if it had been set up by Peter (not Patrick). The transfer is thus an exempt inter-spouse transfer thus avoiding IHT of £200,000.

28.85 Whilst a DoV may redirect an inheritance into a trust created under the DoV there is no reason why the redirection under the variation cannot be to an existing trust (eg a trust set up by the deceased in his lifetime).

28.86 Whilst a DoV is often used to reduce the IHT arising on death (see Example 6) it may also be utilised for non-tax reasons. For example, a DoV can also be very useful where, for one reason or another, the beneficiaries under the will feel that perhaps a different distribution of the testator's assets would have been more appropriate. This may be the case where, for example, the testator disinherits one of his children but the surviving siblings and the surviving spouse do not agree with the disinheritance; the execution of one or more DoVs allow IHT (and CGT) efficient redirecting of some of the dispositions under the will.

It may be that between the date of drawing up the will and the date of death the circumstances of one or more of the beneficiaries changes and thus the original dispositions under the will may no longer be viewed by the beneficiaries as perhaps appropriate; the DoV again offers a tax efficient mechanism to permit a redirection of some of the gifts.

A DoV may be used where the beneficiaries of the will feel that the testator has not left sufficient of his estate (or indeed any of it) for charitable causes. One or more of the beneficiaries may then each execute an appropriate DoV in favour of the charity(ies) which are then deemed to be exempt gifts by the testator

28.87 *Wills and taxation*

under *IHTA 1984 s 142*; this has the effect of reducing the IHT charge on the testator's estate.

28.87 Where the effect of a DoV is to reduce the amount of IHT arising on the testator's estate it is preferable for the DoV to be executed prior to the obtaining of probate which then ensures that the IHT payable is based on the testator's estate taking into account the terms of the DoV (see also paragraph 28.92)

Discretionary will trusts

28.88 *IHTA 1984 s 144* is similar to *IHTA 1984 s 142* discussed above to the extent that if its conditions are satisfied it deems the IHT treatment to be different from that which would normally apply. However, there is no deeming with respect to any CGT treatment (unlike re *IHTA 1984 s 142*).

28.89 Under *IHTA 1984 s 144* where property which is comprised in a person's estate immediately before his death is settled by will and within two years of death an event occurs (ie an appointment out of trust property) which would normally be a chargeable event for IHT purposes (ie an exit charge) no IHT is charged on the event and it is to be assumed that the testator's will provided for the property to be held as after the event.

The appointment must be made more than three months after death because any appointment within three months does not normally give rise to an IHT exit charge (see paragraph 16.18) in which case *IHTA 1984 s 144* cannot apply (ie the appointment would not then be deemed to have been made by the testator in his will).

IHTA 1984 s 144 cannot apply if a qualifying interest in possession (ie an IPDI or a disabled person's interest) has arisen in the will trust property prior to the event.

28.90 Thus, *IHTA 1984 s 144* applies where an appointment is made out of a relevant property will trust (eg a discretionary trust) more than three months but not more than two years after the date of death of the testator (which normally precipitates an exit charge) in which case no exit charge arises; thus, *inter alia*, the trust may be terminated without any IHT charge arising.

The appointment may be made to a beneficiary absolutely or onto new trusts.

The appointment by the trustees of an interest in possession (whether for the surviving spouse or other beneficiaries) on or after 22 March 2006 does not give rise to an IHT charge (ie no exit charge as the interest in possession is not qualifying); thus *IHTA 1984 s 144* cannot apply. However, specific provision is

Wills and taxation **28.90**

made in *IHTA 1984 s 144* to permit the section to apply to such circumstances. The specific provisions apply to such appointments if made on or after 22 March 2006 irrespective of the date of death (ie whether pre- or on or after 22 March 2006).

Example 7

In his will Ben Good creates a discretionary will trust for his spouse and four children.

Twelve months after Ben's death the trustees appoint the trust property out to his spouse, Eileen, absolutely (ie the trust is terminated).

Such appointment would normally precipitate an IHT exit charge. However, as the terms of *IHTA 1984 s 144* are satisfied Ben's will is regarded as having made the gift to Eileen which qualifies as an exempt inter-spouse transfer.

Had the trustees appointed the trust property to Eileen within three months of Ben's death no exit charge would normally apply and hence *IHTA 1984 s 144* is inapplicable; which means that Ben's will is not treated as having made the gift to Eileen and thus no inter-spouse exemption is applicable.

Example 8

In his will Ben Good creates a discretionary will trust for his spouse and four children.

Twelve months after Ben's death the trustees appoint Eileen a life interest in the trust property (ie the property not vested is in Eileen as in Example 7). Such an appointment (if made on or after 22 March 2006) does not create an IHT charge; the interest appointed being a non-qualifying interest in possession.

However, (as indicated in paragraph 28.90) *IHTA 1984 s 144* provides that in such a case its terms apply (ie the testator is treated as having provided for the interest thus creating an IPDI).

Thus, in both Examples 7 and 8 inter-spouse IHT treatment is obtained whether the trustees appoint the surviving spouse (ie Eileen) the trust property absolutely or an interest therein.

28.91   *Wills and taxation*

28.91   Where the conditions of *IHTA 1984 s 144* are satisfied the section applies automatically (compare *IHTA 1984 s 142* which requires that a statement is included in the DoV for the section's back-dating to death to apply; see paragraph 28.74).

28.92   The effect of *IHTA 1984 s 144* (or *IHTA 1984 s 142*) may be to reduce the amount of IHT chargeable on the testator's estate (as may apply in Examples 7 or 8 where the inter-spouse exemption applies). This would lead to an IHT repayment to the executors. However, it would be preferable if in the first instance only the reduced amount of IHT was due and payable. This requires the appointment to be executed prior to the obtaining of probate (ie prior to the vesting of property in the trustees); HMRC accept that this is possible. It is therefore important that the terms of the trust permit the trustees to exercise the power of appointment prior to the obtaining of a grant of probate.

28.93   The typical use of *IHTA 1984 s 144* is where flexibility is required following the testator's death in order to take into account circumstances then existing. It may be that the will has been prepared some many years before the testator's death (without any subsequent modification) and when death occurs the situation may be very different from that applying when the will was executed.

IHTA 1984 s 144 provides a two-year 'window' during which some changes may be made IHT efficiently.

28.94   Although trusts are commonly referred to as 'two-year' will trusts it is not necessary that the trust should terminate within two years of death. However, where the trust continues in existence beyond this two-year period after death the normal IHT rules apply thereafter (which means exit and ten-yearly charges may apply).

28.95   The CGT implications arising from an appointment out of a relevant property will trust within two years are those which normally apply; there is no special CGT treatment as is possible under *IHTA 1984 s 142*. If following the appointment a person becomes absolutely entitled as against the trustees a deemed disposal at market value occurs precipitating a CGT liability on the part of the trustees (*TCGA 1992 s 71*) and the recipient beneficiary acquires the property at market value at the date the appointment is made (ie not at the date of death); this assumes that the property has vested in the trustees by the date of the appointment.

Where the property subject to the appointment has not vested in the trustees (ie remains with the executors) by the date of the appointment HMRC accept that the recipient beneficiary takes the property as if it had been left to him by the testator and thus the property is acquired at its market value at the date of death (ie its probate value); and no CGT liability arises on the part of the trustees as no disposal is deemed to have occurred.

28.96 Where a CGT liability arises on the part of the trustees on an appointment (under *TCGA 1992 s 71*) hold-over relief under *TCGA 1992 s 260* (see paragraph 8.45) is unavailable as one of the conditions for *TCGA 1992 s 260* to apply is that the appointment must precipitate an IHT charge (which is not the case because where *IHTA 1984 s 144* is in point the reading back treats the appointment as having been made by the testator not the trustees and so any IHT liability arises at the date of death not the date of the appointment).

28.97 Prior to the introduction of the transferable NRB, the discretionary will trust was often used by the first spouse to die to ensure full use of his/her NRB on death. The introduction of the transferable NRB to some extent has reduced the need for such trusts but it may still be sensible to utilise a discretionary will trust in appropriate circumstances (see paragraph 28.39).

However the use of such a trust does not preclude, if circumstances are appropriate, for the transferable NRB to be in effect reinstated following the death of the first spouse to die. This can be achieved by the trustees appointing a life interest to the surviving spouse before the expiry of the two-year period from the date of the testator's death; under *IHTA 1984 s 144* it is the testator who is deemed to have effected the creation of the life interest on his death and the life interest thus qualifies as an IPDI and the inter-spouse exemption applies and the testator's NRB is unused and available for subsequent transfer to the surviving spouse (*IHTA 1984 s 8A*).

28.98 One particular use of the discretionary will trust is where there may be some uncertainty as to whether, for example, BPR (see paragraph 11.61) is available with respect to some the testator's property. The use of the discretionary will trust provides the trustees with a 'window' of two years to ascertain the position in this regard. If, for example, it is found that no BPR applies (or the matter is still unresolved two years after the testator's death) the trustees could simply appoint the property to the surviving spouse (ie the inter-spouse exemption would apply and no IHT would arise with respect to the property).

If, on the other hand, it is found that BPR does apply at the date of the testator's death the trustees could appoint the property to, say, the children of the testator which would precipitate no IHT charge due to the BPR.

Executor sales

28.99 Capital gains arising on sales by executors during the administration period precipitate CGT liabilities on the part of the executors at 28% (on or after

28.100 *Wills and taxation*

23 June 2010; 18% prior thereto; *F (No 2) 2010 s 2 and Sch 1*) (see paragraph 28.28). The quantum of such gains is based on the difference between the asset values at probate and their value at the date of disposal.

However, it may be that the value of some assets after the deceased's death falls below their value at the date of death (ie their probate value). Any sale thereof thus precipitates a capital loss.

28.100 In such cases it is possible for the values of certain assets at the date of sale by the executors to be substituted for their probate values; this results in a decrease in any IHT liability originally arising on the deceased's estate. However, it also has the effect of substituting the lower values for those at probate for CGT purposes (in essence reducing any capital losses on sale to nil and thus precluding any claim to loss relief for CGT purposes on the part of the executors) (*IHTA 1984 s 187* and *TCGA 1992 s 274*).

28.101 The relevant provisions are contained in *IHTA 1984 ss 178* to *198* and relate to sales of qualifying investments and sales of land.

The relief provided by these sections must be claimed.

In addition, similar relief is also available under the 'related property' rules (*IHTA 1984 ss 161* and *176*; see paragraph 10.24).

Sale of quoted shares

28.102 Qualifying investments are defined as shares quoted at the date of death and holdings in authorised unit trusts.

The sale of such investments must be made within 12 months of the date of death and must be carried out by an 'appropriate person'. An appropriate person is defined as 'the person liable for [IHT] attributable to the value of those investments or, if there is more than one such person, and one of them is in fact paying the tax, that person' (*IHTA 1984 ss 178* and *179*).

28.103 Typically, the appropriate persons are the executors who are responsible for discharging any IHT liabilities arising on the deceased's estate. It is therefore crucial that the executors do not vest any of the assets in a beneficiary who then effects the sale (see paragraph 28.30).

28.104 If the executors sell a number of such investments within the 12-month period all capital gains and capital losses arising are aggregated.

Where a net capital loss arises the values on death may be reduced; where, however, a net capital gain arises no reduction in probate values is possible but equally no extra IHT arises.

Example 9

On his death Toby Cat had the following quoted shareholdings with probate values as follows:

£10,000 ABC Ltd

£20,000 DEF Ltd

£35,000 GHI Ltd.

The executors sold some of the shares in ABC Ltd, DEF Ltd and GHI Ltd:

ABC Ltd sale proceeds £6,000 (probate value £7,000).

DEF Ltd sale proceeds £9,000 (probate value £8,000).

GHI Ltd sale proceeds £20,000 (probate value £22,000).

Aggregate capital loss is £2,000.

The probate value of the shareholdings is reduced from £65,000 to £63,000.

IHT can therefore be reclaimed on the £2,000.

28.105 Where the executors sell investments but reinvest some or all of the sale proceeds in other qualifying investments any relief may be lost or reduced. This occurs if the reinvestment takes place within the period from the date of death to the date ending two months after the date of the last sale effected within the 12-month period (*IHTA 1984 s 180*).

28.106 The relief also extends to qualifying investments held in trust in which the deceased was a qualifying interest in possession beneficiary. The appropriate person in this case is the trustees.

Sale of land

28.107 Similar relief to that available for qualifying investments extends to land in which the deceased had an interest on his death (*IHTA 1984 ss 190* and *191*).

28.108 Thus, where such land is sold producing a capital loss the value on sale may be substituted for its probate value provided the sale takes place within four years of death; the operative date of sale is the date of the contract for sale (ie 'exchange' in common parlance).

Where the loss arising on an individual property sale is less than £1,000 or 5% of the property's probate value, whichever is the lower, it is ignored.

28.109 The sale must be effected by the appropriate person (see paragraph 28.103).

28.110 Any sale to a beneficiary under the deceased's will (or to persons closely connected) precludes relief being obtained (*TCGA 1992 s 191*).

28.111 Where more than one interest in land is sold within three years (sales in the fourth year after death producing capital gains are ignored) of death if relief is claimed in respect of any one such sale the other sales must also be taken into account. However, it may be that the overall aggregate position is that a net capital gain results. In this situation (unlike that applicable to sales of qualifying investments; see paragraph 28.104) the substituted values may result in an increase in the IHT paid on death.

28.112 Reinvestment of sale proceeds may also affect the quantum of any relief for losses on sales.

Example 10

Following Bob's death two pieces of land held at his death, valued at £75,000 and £100,000 are sold by the executors for £74,500 and £90,000.

Any claim is for £10,000 as the £500 loss on the other property is below the lesser of £1,000 and £3,750 (ie 5% of £75,000).

28.113 It is important for executors to examine the overall position of the deceased's estate before sales of assets followed by claims for reduction in probate values are made. For example, assume that sales (of neither land nor qualifying investments) are made by the executors precipitating substantial capital gains and, in addition, assume that sales of land and qualifying investments are also made giving rise to capital losses.

It may be in such circumstances preferable for no claim to be made to substitute lower values (for the land and qualifying investments) at the date of death which then enables the executors to reduce their capital gains by the capital losses. This may be particularly appropriate if the substituted lower values at the date of death (re the land and qualifying investments) do not in fact give rise to any IHT reduction on death.

Sale of related property

28.114 At the testator's death where property in his estate is valued as related property this value may be greater than the value of the property without such a valuation (*IHTA 1984 ss 161* and *176*). If the property is sold within three years of death by the executors (or a person in whom the property vested immediately after the testator's death) in an arm's-length sale the property's value at the date of death may be revalued.

If the revaluation of the property (which is now not a related property valuation) is lower than the original related property valuation the lower value may be used. Note that it is not the sales value which is substituted (as is the case with respect to sales of qualified investments and land) but the valuation at the date of death in the absence of the related property provisions.

Foreign aspects

28.115 Transfers, whether in lifetime or on death, from *UK* domiciled to *non-UK* domiciled spouses can be problematic for IHT purposes. Transfers from the UK to the non-UK domiciled spouse are not exempt without limit as applies to all other inter-spouse transfers whether UK or non-UK domiciled (*IHTA 1984 s 18*; see paragraph 11.42). On death (assuming no chargeable transfers have been made during the seven years prior to death) the UK domiciled spouse is able to leave the surviving non-UK domiciled spouse up to £380,000 (ie the NRB for the tax year 2010–2011 of £325,000 plus an exempt amount of £55,000 (*IHTA 1984 s 18*)); over and above this amount IHT at 40% is payable.

28.116 The UK domiciled spouse has basically two options on death, namely, to leave the non-UK domiciled spouse property absolutely or on trust. Under the former option the non-UK domiciled spouse is then free to arrange for the property to become excluded property thus falling outside the ambit of IHT.

For example, in the case of chattels these may simply be removed outside the UK thus then constituting non-UK situs assets (ie excluded property). In the case of UK registered shares these could be transferred to a non-UK registered and non-UK resident company whose shares are in turn owned by a non-UK resident trust (the transfer may precipitate CGT consequences although unlikely if effected soon after their inheritance as there is unlikely to be much price movement). UK real estate could similarly be transferred to such a company (possibly precipitating CGT and stamp duty land tax (SDLT)).

28.117 Under the latter option (ie UK domiciled on death leaves property on trust, whether UK resident or not) the property within the trust will not rank as

28.118 *Wills and taxation*

excluded property (as this requires a non-UK domiciled settlor) but perhaps greater future flexibility is obtained. Thus, for example, the trust could simply continue in existence or, within the two-year period following death appointments out of the trust could be made whether to the surviving non-UK domiciled spouse and/or other beneficiaries (eg the non-UK domiciled children) under *IHTA 1984 s 144*.

As the trust property (even if non-UK situs) can never rank as excluded property due to the testator spouse's UK domicile perhaps the discretionary will trust should be viewed as a vehicle which permits two years of reflection, following the death of the UK domiciled spouse, during which consideration can be given to taking appropriate decisions in the light of the then circumstances.

This option may be particularly useful where the surviving spouse's non-UK domicile status at the date of execution of the will by the UK domiciled spouse is reasonably clear, but which status may have become less clear at the date of the UK domiciled's death (eg the surviving spouse may have acquired a UK domicile of choice at this time or perhaps become deemed UK domiciled; see paragraphs 3.74 and 3.231).

28.118 For the non-UK domiciled spouse the choice of how to leave assets to the surviving UK domiciled spouse may be a little clearer. This is because non-UK situs property settled into trust (whether UK resident or not, but usually non-UK resident to mitigate CGT charges) by a non-UK domiciled testator is excluded property and remains so (ie it does not subsequently fall within the estate of the surviving UK domiciled spouse). The trust should preferably be discretionary in nature to offer maximum flexibility.

28.119 The above has addressed only the UK tax implications for the non-UK domiciled individual. Inevitably, however, overseas tax issues may be just as, if not more, important for such individual (particularly for the US citizen subject to all US taxes irrespective of residence status). It is therefore important to ascertain the domestic tax position in any other relevant country including whether any double tax agreements may be in point. In some cases such agreements may restrict the right of the UK to levy IHT only on certain UK situs assets (see Chapter 26).

28.120 The non-UK domiciled individual may also be exposed to issues alien to the UK (eg forced heirship rules; community property rules) and cannot be simply ignored.

28.121 It is therefore necessary for an holistic perspective to be adopted where the affairs of a non-UK domiciled individual are involved.

Summary

28.122 The will is an important part of any tax planning exercise in particular given the changes introduced in *FA 2006* which makes lifetime trusts less attractive for IHT purposes.

28.123 There is no one will which applies in all circumstances and IHT efficiency depends in part on the family structure and testamentary intentions.

28.124 The use of a discretionary will trust offers quite a high degree of flexibility and may be used in a variety of situations.

28.125 DoVs (and disclaimers) offer an IHT (and CGT) efficient manner of 'altering' the destination of dispositions under a testator's will.

28.126 Planning which involves a non-UK domiciled individual requires consideration to both UK and overseas tax issues, the latter possibly being in some cases the more important of the two.

Appendices

Appendix 1

Domicile

Categories of non-UK domiciled individual

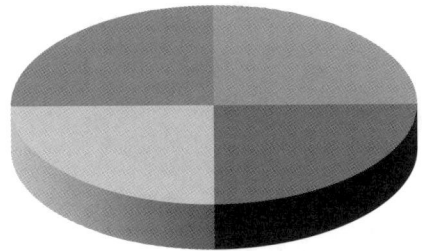

- Individuals aged 18 or over AND >= seven out of nine tax years
- Individuals under aged 18
- Individuals < seven out of nine tax years
- Individuals irrespective of age and length of time in UK with less than £2,000 unremitted income/gains

Appendix 1

Do I need to pay the £30,000 remittance basis charge?

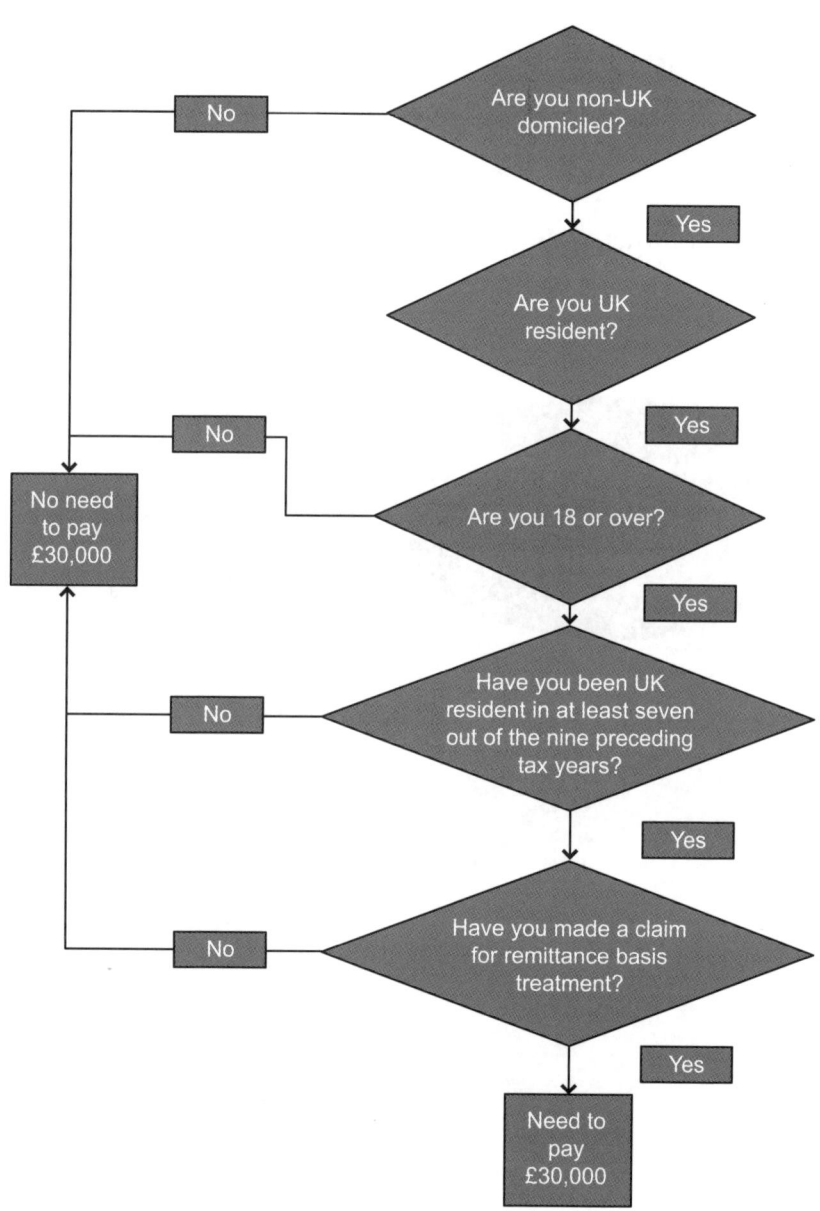

Appendix 1

Ascertaining when non-UK domiciled individual needs to make a claim for remittance basis treatment

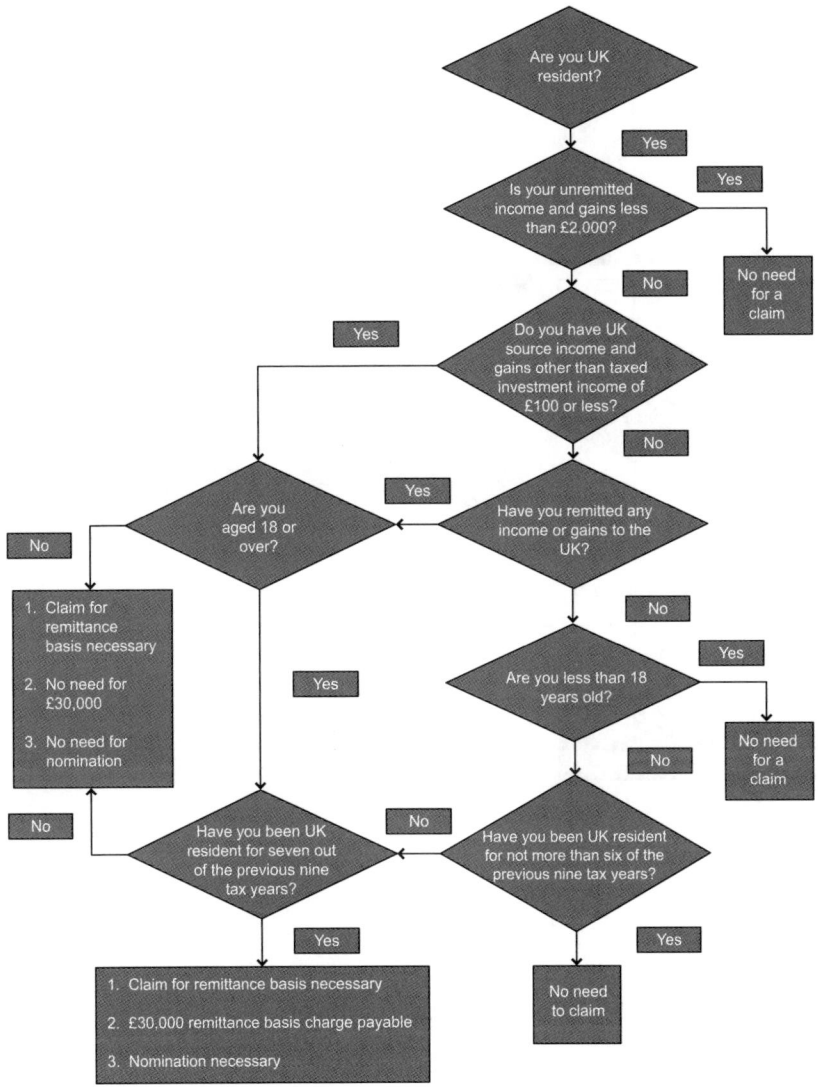

Appendix 1

Do I have an English domicile of origin?

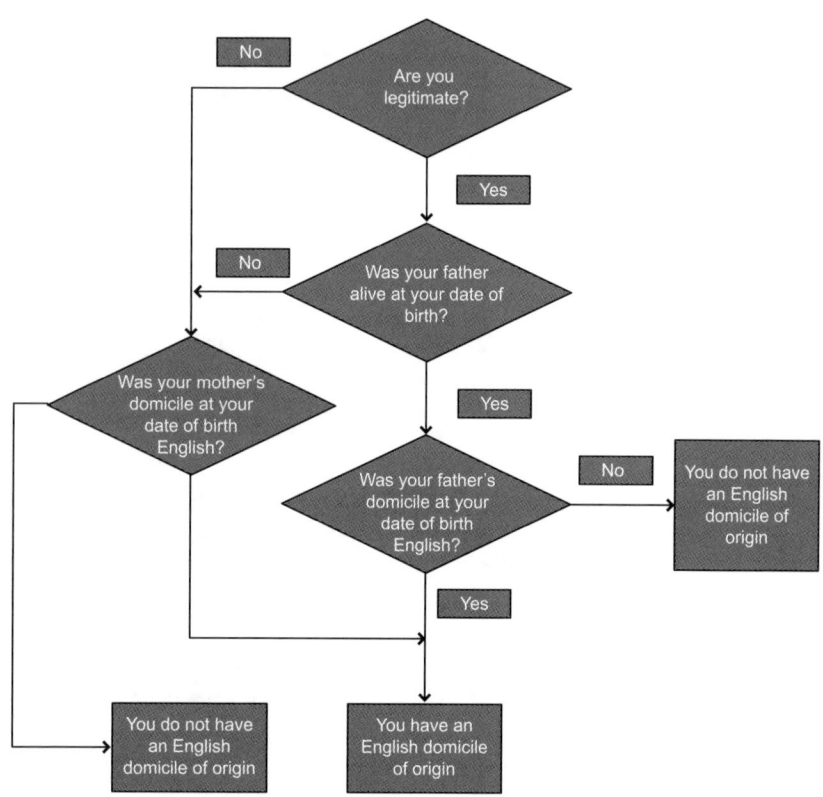

Appendix 1

Have I acquired a domicile of choice different from my English domicile of origin?

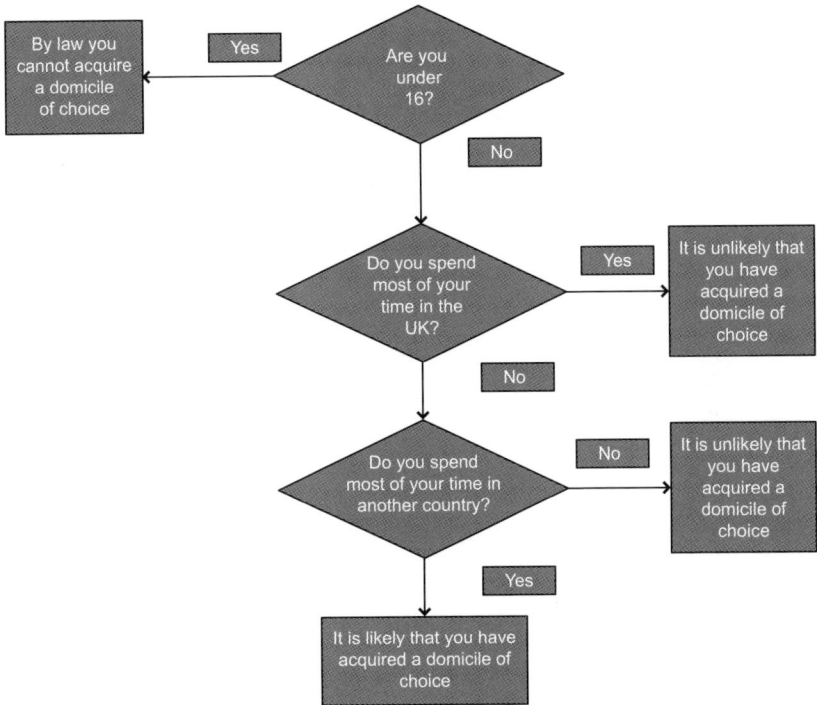

Appendix 2

Capital gains tax position on disposals pre-5 April 2008

Background

For completeness this Appendix is intended to provide a very brief overview of two major capital gains tax (CGT) reliefs, albeit now abolished.

Pre *FA 2008*, two major forms of relief were available to reduce the amount of capital gain subject to CGT namely:

- indexation allowance; and
- taper relief.

Neither of these reliefs applies to disposals on or after 6 April 2008.

Indexation allowance

An indexation allowance was an attempt to levy CGT only on the 'real' gain as opposed to the 'monetary' gain arising from an asset's disposal. In other words, it was an attempt to adjust any monetary capital gains due to the change in value of money over time; in effect attempting to take inflation into account.

The indexation allowance could reduce a capital gain, ultimately to nil. It could not, however, turn a gain into a loss nor increase the size of any loss.

An 'indexed gain' was thus the amount of the chargeable gain arising on an asset disposal after reduction by any indexation allowance.

The indexation allowance was, however, abolished for individuals (and trusts) on 5 April 1998. From 6 April 1998 taper relief replaced the indexation allowance (see below). Despite its abolition, any disposal of an asset on or after 6 April 1998 which was acquired before 6 April 1998 still qualified for an indexation allowance from the date of the acquisition of the asset to 5 April 1998 but not beyond.

Capital gains tax position on disposals pre-5 April 2008

The acquisition of an asset on or after 6 April 1998 (ie after the indexation allowance was abolished) meant that no indexation allowance was available on a future disposal (although taper relief would in principle apply).

The indexation allowance was arrived at by applying an 'indexation factor' to the relevant items of expenditure utilised in purchasing the asset. The indexation factor was equal to:

$$\frac{\text{RPI for month of disposal (or April 1998 if earlier)} - \text{RPI for month of purchase (or March 1982 if later)}}{\text{RPI for month of purchase (or March 1982 if later)}}$$

The 'index factor' was normally found as a decimal and rounded to three decimal places.

RPI refers to the Retail Price Index; a series of indices produced by HMRC.

Example 1

John Suez purchased an asset in June 1990 for £100,000.

He sold the asset in:

January 1996 for £150,000;

March 2006 for £200,000.

The RPIs for June 1990, January 1996 and April 1998 were, respectively, 126.70, 150.20 and 162.60.

Re (a), the indexation allowance is: [[150.20 − 126.70]/[126.70]] × £100,000 = £18,500

Re (b), the indexation allowance is: [[162.60 − £126.70]/[126.70]] × £100,000 = £28,300

Thus, under (a), the indexed gain will be: £150,000 − £100,000 − £18,500 = £31,500

Thus, under (b), the indexed gain will be: £200,000 − £100,000 − £31,500 = £68,500

If, however, John had purchased the asset in August 1998 (ie after 5 April 1998) no indexation allowance would have been applicable.

Example 2

Brian bought shares in March 1995 for £120,000 and sold them in July 1998 for £100,000.

Brian's gain will be £100,000 less £120,000, in fact a capital loss of £20,000.

Although in principle an indexation allowance was applicable it cannot be used to increase the size of any capital loss.

Thus, Brian's capital loss remains at £20,000.

Example 3

Brian bought shares in March 1995 for £120,000 and sold them in July 1998 for £125,000.

Brian's gain will be £125,000 less £120,000, (ie £5,000). However, an indexation allowance was applicable equal to: 0.102 × £120,000, (ie £12,240).

Brian's indexed gain thus, *prima facie*, equals £5,000 less £12,240, (ie a capital loss of £7,240).

The indexation allowance could not turn a capital gain into a capital loss.

Thus, the indexation allowance of £12,240 simply reduces the capital gain of £5,000 to nil.

Inter-spouse transfers are deemed to occur at no gain/no loss to the transferor spouse (see above). This has the effect that such transfers are assumed to have occurred for a consideration equal to original purchase cost plus the indexation allowance to the date of the transfer.

Example 4

Joan and Dick Garden are married.

Joan decided to transfer to Dick a factory she owned.

Joan had purchased the factory for £250,000 and at the date of transfer to Dick she was entitled to an indexation allowance of £14,000.

Capital gains tax position on disposals pre-5 April 2008

The transfer will be assumed to have occurred for a consideration of £264,000.

On a future sale by Dick the cost of the asset to Dick will be assumed to have been the £264,000.

Dick may himself also be entitled to an indexation allowance on a future disposal measured from the date he received the asset from Joan to the date of sale (or 5 April 1998 if earlier).

Following *FA 2008* no indexation allowance will apply to the disposal of an asset which occurs on or after 6 April 2008 irrespective of the date of purchase of the asset.

Thus, any asset purchased pre-6 April 1998 (and thus entitled to an indexation allowance up to 5 April 1998) and still held (ie not disposed of) on 6 April 2008 will on a future disposal lose any accrued indexation allowance. A disposal prior to 6 April 2008 to realise and thus utilise the indexation allowance might have been appropriate (see below 'Banking indexation allowance').

Taper relief

The indexation allowance was abolished for disposals of assets by individuals effective 6 April 1998 but was replaced by taper relief.

Taper relief applied to disposals on or after 6 April 1998.

Thus on the disposal of an asset, acquired pre-6 April 1998, on or after 6 April 1998 (but pre-6 April 2008; see above) both an indexation allowance and taper relief might apply. Taper relief reduced the indexed gain by a percentage determined by both the type of asset sold and the length of time for which the asset had been held.

The maximum taper relief percentage was 75% which applied on the disposal of a business asset held for at least two years.

The maximum taper relief percentage which applied on the disposal of a non-business asset was 40% which applied only when the asset had been held for at least ten years.

Example 5

Gertrude Smithers sold an asset making an indexed gain of £100,000.

Capital gains tax position on disposals pre-5 April 2008

If the asset qualified as a business asset which she had held for at least two years then the taper relief would be [75% of £100 000, (ie £75,000)]. The gain thus taxable would be £25,000.

If the asset qualified as a non-business asset which she had held for at least 10 years then the taper relief would be [40% of £100,000, (ie £40,000)]. The gain thus taxable would be £60,000.

The length of time an asset was held was measured in complete years (effectively being rounded down for part year ownership) and was measured from the later of the date of acquisition and 6 April 1998. The timing of an asset sale could thus dramatically affect the percentage of taper relief due. For example, a business asset held for one year and 11 months would be entitled to 50% taper relief; had the asset been held for one more month, (ie two years) 75% taper relief would have applied (see tables below).

Example 6

Bob Foot purchased a non-business asset in January 1996 and sold it in 13 November 2006.

Bob would be entitled to an indexation allowance measured from January 1996 to 5 April 1998 plus taper relief from 6 April 1998 (not from January 1996) to 13 November 2006.

Taper relief would thus be based upon a period of ownership of nine complete years (it will be noted that 6 April 1998 to 13 November 2006 amounts to eight complete years. However, a 'bonus' year is also available as the asset was owned on 17 March 1998 (see below) making nine years in total).

Where an asset is transferred inter-spouse, on a future disposal by the recipient spouse the transferor spouse's period of ownership is deemed to be a period of ownership by the recipient spouse for taper relief purposes. In effect, the recipient spouse is deemed to have held the asset from the date it was originally acquired (but only for taper relief purposes).

Example 7

Tom and Myrtle Bishop are married and in December 2005 Tom transferred to Myrtle a non-business asset he had acquired in September 1994.

Myrtle sold the asset in January 2008.

Capital gains tax position on disposals pre-5 April 2008

For taper relief purposes Myrtle is deemed to have owned the asset from September 1994 to January 2008. In terms of complete years this amounts to nine years plus one 'bonus' year making a total of 10 years (as taper relief only applies from 6 April 1998; indexation allowance applying before this date).

Inter-spouse transfers could, in certain circumstances, give rise to a loss of taper relief on a subsequent sale by the transferee spouse and thus caution needed to be exercised when such transfers were made (see below).

As indicated above the percentage of taper relief applicable on a disposal depended upon the type of asset and the time period for which the asset was held (post-6 April 1998). The tables below set out the various percentages applicable:

Non-business assets:

Qualifying period of ownership in complete years (after 5.4.98)	Percentage reduction	Percentage chargeable
1	Nil	Nil
2	Nil	Nil
3	5%	95%
4	10%	90%
5	15%	85%
6	20%	80%
7	25%	75%
8	30%	70%
9	35%	65%
10 or more	40%	60%
Business assets		
1	50%	50%
2 or more	75%	25%

In the case of a non-business asset only, which was held on 17 March 1998, one 'bonus' year of taper relief is normally granted on a disposal of the asset (this did not apply to business assets).

Business asset

A 'business' asset was defined (for periods post-6 April 2000) as:

- an asset owned by an individual, partnership, trustee or personal representative (PRs) and used in a trade carried on by the owner of the asset or by a qualifying company or by a third person; or
- an asset held by an individual for the purpose of an employment (full time or not) with a person (individual or company) carrying on a trade; or
- a shareholding held by an individual in a qualifying company (whether UK or foreign).

A qualifying company was a trading company where one or more of the following apply:

- the shares of the company were not listed (eg an AIM company) on a recognised stock exchange (NASDAQ is a recognised stock exchange); or
- an individual held at least 5% of the voting rights (if listed) in the company; or
- the individual was an employee or officer of the company; or
- a non-trading company if the individual was an employee/director of the company and held (together with connected persons): 10% of shares or voting rights (thus, an employee of an investment company may receive business asset treatment re the shares; effective for disposals on or after 6 April 2000). ('Shares' includes 'securities'.)

Trading company included, for example, the trade of furnished holiday lettings and property development but not share investment or property investment (eg activities of commercial or residential landlord).

It is important to note that the legislation applying to taper relief changed over time. For example, the definition of a business asset did not remain constant in particular in relation to shares. As a consequence, the nature of an asset held by the same individual might change through time for taper relief purposes (see below).

Taper relief and share sales

With respect to taper relief two important points are worth noting:

- the definition of 'business asset' changed materially on 6 April 2000; and
- the possible loss of taper relief on the sale of a business asset (eg (possibly shares) following a previous inter-spouse transfer).

Capital gains tax position on disposals pre-5 April 2008

Shares in trading companies pre-6 April 2000

For periods of ownership up to 5 April 2000 for a shareholding to qualify as a business asset required satisfaction of either of the two following conditions:

- ownership of ≥25% of the voting rights in the trading company; or
- ownership of ≥5% of the voting rights in the trading company exercisable by the taxpayer who was a full-time employee of the company (or full-time officer).

Pre-6 April 2000 (unlike the position post-5 April 2000) there was no distinction between listed or unlisted companies. However, with effect from 6 April 2000 these rules were changed and a distinction was introduced between listed and non-listed companies (see above).

One major impact of the changes was that many shareholdings pre-6 April 2000 qualified as non-business assets but qualified as business assets thereafter. For example, a pre-6 April 2000 shareholding of, say, 2% in a non-listed company would before this date qualify only as a non-business asset whereas from that date it would qualify as a business asset. The effect in such cases was that an apportionment of any gain arising on a disposal was required.

Example 8

George Smith owned 5% of an unlisted company. He was not an employee of the company.

He acquired the shares in February 1996 and sold them in October 2005.

Up to 6 April 2000 the shares qualified only as a non-business asset becoming a business asset thereafter.

For taper relief purposes the shares were held from 6 April 1998 through to October 2005, (ie seven complete years). However, from 6 April 1998 to 5 April 2000 the shares qualified for non-business asset treatment (ie two years).

From 6 April 2000 to October 2005 the shares qualified for business asset treatment (ie five complete years).

Thus, 2/7ths of the indexed gain would qualify for non-business asset taper relief and 5/7ths for business asset taper relief. (Indexation to 5 April 1998 would, of course, also apply.)

The taper relief percentages applied to each apportioned indexed gain would be based on eight years giving non-business taper of 30% (because of the 'bonus year' making eight not seven years; see above) and business taper of 75%.

(2) Inter-spouse share transfer and subsequent sale

An inter-spouse transfer of a shareholding followed by a disposal by the transferee spouse could lead to a loss of business asset treatment on the disposal.

On a disposal by the transferee spouse following an inter-spouse transfer, for taper relief purposes it was assumed that the transferee spouse owned the asset from the date it was acquired by the transferor spouse (see above). For business asset treatment on the disposal the shares must have qualified as a business asset in the ownership of the transferee spouse (ie from the date of acquisition by the transferor spouse). This may not always have been the case.

Example 9

Robert Swatch was an employee of XYZ Ltd, a listed company.

Robert acquired 1000 shares in XYZ Ltd in January 1992 which represented a shareholding interest in XYZ Ltd of <5%.

Robert gave these shares to his wife, Mary, on 1 April 2001.

She sold the shares on 10 April 2005 never having worked for XYZ Ltd.

For the period 1 April 2001 to 10 April 2005 the shares did not qualify as business assets on the part of Mary as she was not an employee of XYZ Ltd nor did she own at least 5%.

For the period 6 April 1998 to 1 April 2001 (a period of deemed ownership by Mary) the shares would not have qualified as business assets on her part.

As a consequence, for the whole period 6 April 1998 to 10 April 2005 the shares did not qualify as business assets on the part of Mary. Therefore non-business asset relief applied.

Mary is deemed to have owned the shares for the period 6.4.98 to 10.4.05 (seven complete tax years plus a bonus year, (ie eight years), (ie 30% taper relief based on eight years, ownership as a non-business asset).

Capital gains tax position on disposals pre-5 April 2008

It should be noted that had Robert retained ownership of the shares for the whole period and then sold them he would have been entitled to non-business asset treatment for the period 6 April 1998 to 5 April 2000 and business asset treatment from 6 April 2000 to 10 April 2005, (ie non-business asset taper of 30% (applied to 2/7ths of the indexed gain) and business taper of 75% (applied to 5/7ths of the indexed gain).

The above example demonstrates that transfer of shares inter-spouse may not always have been tax effective.

It was, and is, not unusual in tax planning for families for assets to be transferred inter-spouse. This may be effected in order to mitigate inheritance tax (IHT), for example. It is also quite common for such transfers to be effected to ensure each spouse can utilise their respective reliefs and exemptions including their CGT annual exemption (£9,600 for tax year 2008–2009).

The above Example 9 illustrates, however, that while such transfers may enable efficient utilisation of a spouse's annual exemption for CGT purposes the overall position may have been worsened due to a net loss of taper relief.

Following *FA 2008* no taper relief will apply to the disposal of an asset which occurs on or after 6 April 2008 irrespective of the date of purchase of the asset.

Thus, any asset whether purchased on or after or before 6 April 1998 (and thus entitled to taper relief) and still held (ie not disposed of) on 6 April 2008 will on a future disposal lose any accrued taper relief. A disposal prior to 6 April 2008 to realise and thus utilise the accrued taper relief might have been appropriate.

Index

A

AIM shares	19.30, 19.31
Asset situs	6.1–6.61
see also Income source	
capital gains tax	6.31–6.37
bearer shares	6.33
intangible property	6.34
land	6.37
nominees	6.36, 6.38–6.40
registered shares	6.32
tangible property	6.35
domestic law	6.7, 6.8
foreign currency	6.43–6.45
foreign currency bank accounts	6.41, 6.42, 6.46–6.57
foreign tax	6.5, 6.6
inheritance tax	6.25–6.30
bearer shares	6.26
intangible property	6.28
land	6.30
nominees	6.29
registered shares	6.25
tangible property	6.27
non-resident individual	6.4
non-UK domiciled indivual	6.3
UK domiciled individual	6.2

B

Bank accounts	
foreign currency location	6.41, 6.42, 6.46–6.57
Bearer shares	
location	6.26, 6.33

C

Capital v income distribution	1.8–1.11
Capital gains tax	2.43–2.51, 8.1–8.141
annual exempt amount	8.12–8.16

Capital gains tax – *contd*	
asset situs *see* Asset situs	
bargains not at arm's length	8.30
business assets	8.67–8.72
capital gain computation	8.26, 8.27
connected persons	8.29
departures and arrivals in UK	8.115–8.132
non-UK domiciled individuals	8.129–8.132
split tax years	8.119–8.128
disposal	8.3
double tax agreements *see* Double tax agreements	
Enterprise Investment Schemes *see* Enterprise Investment Schemes	
entrepreneur relief	8.79–8.97
amount of relief	8.89–8.94
claim for relief	8.89–8.94
disposal of assets at time at which business ceases to be carried on	8.84
disposal of assets consisting of shares or securities of company	8.85
disposal of whole or part of business	8.83
disposal qualifying as 'associated' disposal	8.86
relevant business assets	8.87, 8.88
trusts	8.95–8.97
exempt assets	8.4
FA 2008 (tax year 2008–2009 and 2009–2010)	2.46–2.49

Index

Capital gains tax – *contd*
  FA 2010 and FA (No 2) 2010
    (tax year 2010–2011)   2.50, 2.51
  foreign income and gains *see* Foreign income and gains
  gifts   8.28
  gifts (not inter-spouse)   8.43, 8.44
  holdover relief   8.45–8.54
  immediate charge to inheritance tax   8.55–8.60
  inter-spouse transfers   8.31–8.35
  joint ownership *see* Joint ownership
  key changes introduced by FA 2008   8.8
  main residence *see* Main residence
  non-qualifying interest in possession trust   8.66
  non-UK domiciled individual   8.78
    see also Non-UK domiciliaries
  non-UK resident taxation *see* Non-UK resident taxation
  non-UK resident trusts *see* Non-UK resident trusts
  non-UK situs assets   8.77
  offshore companies   8.98–8.108
    apportionment of capital gains   8.99–8.103
    capital losses   8.107
    de minimis limit   8.104
    non-UK resident trusts   8.108
    subsequent company distributions   8.105, 8.106
  offshore income gains   8.109–8.114
    non-UK domiciled but UK resident individuals   8.110–8.114
  payment of   8.36–8.39
  persons liable to   8.11
  termination due to death of beneficiary   8.61–8.63

Capital gains tax – *contd*
  position on disposals pre-5 April 2008 App2
  qualifying interest in possession trust
  termination due to death of beneficiary   8.61–8.63
  termination in lifetime of beneficiary   8.64, 8.65
  rates   8.17–8.25
    individuals   8.22–8.25
    personal representatives   8.20, 8.21
    trustees   8.17
  residence, and *see* Residence
  settlor–interested trusts   8.73–8.76
  split tax years *see* Split tax years
  tax returns *see* Tax returns
  timing of tax payments *see* Timing of tax payments
  UK resident trusts *see* UK resident trusts
  wills *see* Wills
  worldwide v territorial tax systems *see* Worldwide v territorial tax systems
  year of death   8.40–8.4
Capital losses   9.1–9.42
  connected person   9.11
  non-UK domiciled but UK resident individual   9.12–9.38
    formal claim for remittance treatment necessary, where   9.22–9.38
    no formal claim for remittance treatment necessary, where   9.20–9.21
    post-FA 2008   9.16–9.19
    pre-FA 2008 position   9.12–9.15
  UK domiciled and resident individual   9.6–9.10
Categories of non-UK domiciled individuals App1
Categories of tax   1.6, 1.7
Citizenship, acquisition of   3.140–3.144

Index

Collective investments	19.94, 19.95

D

Deemed domicile	3.231–3.250
17/20 rule	3.238–3.242
children	3.243
circumstances	3.235
dealing with	3.245–3.250
IHT conventions, and	3.244
three-year rule	3.235–3.237
Deposit-based investments	19.4–19.39
AIM shares	19.30, 19.31
individual savings accounts	19.32–19.39
money market accounts	19.16, 19.17
national savings income	19.18
offshore deposits	19.15
ordinary shares	19.21–19.29
SAYE interest	19.20
Dividends	
income source	6.12–6.14
Divorce	
main residence, and	20.83–20.100, 20.135–20.138
Domicile	2.5–2.15, 3.1–3.261
categories	3.25–3.31
common law concept	3.3–3.13
England and Wales	3.19–3.22
Form DOM	1 5.26
Form P85	5.28, 5.29
Form P86	5.27
importance for UK tax purposes	3.23, 3.24
inheritance tax	5.36–5.45, 10.5–10.12
importance of	5.42
information	5.39–5.41
international dimension	3.256–3.261
meaning	3.14–3.24
Northern Ireland	3.19–3.22
practice	5.1–5.49
current position	5.30–5.35
Scotland	3.19–3.22
split *see* Split domicile	
tax return	
Boxes 22 to 26	5.13–5.16

Domicile – *contd*	
tax return – *contd*	
remittance basis	5.17–5.22
supplementary pages	5.5–5.10
UK, deemed	3.231–3.250
see also Deemed domicile	
Domicile of choice	3.74–3.139
abandonment	3.218–3.227
acquisition	3.74–3.79
acquisition of citizenship	3.140–3.144
actual residence	3.89
age requirement	3.88
'choice'	3.80–3.84
conversion to	3.64
freely chosen	3.228–3.230
intention	3.89–3.92, 3.114–3.139
declaration	3.125–3.139
evidentiary issue	3.114–3.116
hearsay evidence	3.117–3.124
non-UK domiciled individuals spending significant time in UK	3.145–3.168
relevant factors	3.78
requirements	3.85
residence	3.93–3.113
see also Residence	
special categories of individual, and	3.228–3.230
UK-domiciled individuals failing to acquire	3.169–3.185
UK-domiciled individuals who have acquired non-UK domiciles of choice	8.186–3.217
Domicile of dependence	3.54–3.73
children	3.57–3.64
conversion to domicile of choice	3.64
illegitimate	3.60
legitimate	3.59
legitimation	3.61
parents live apart	3.62–3.63

Index

Domicile of dependence – *contd*
   married women   3.65–3.73
     exception to automatic
      domicile of
      dependence on
      marriage   3.71, 3.72
     post-31 December 1973
      marriage   3.73
     pre-1 January 1974
      marriage   3.65–3.70
Domicile of origin   3.32–3.54
   adoption, replacement by   3.49–3.53
   determination   3.35–3.42
   father dead   3.39
   legitimacy   3.36, 3.37
   legitimation   3.40–3.42
   loss of   3.43–3.45
   parents married but separated   3.38
   resurrection of   3.46–3.48
Domiciled individual   2.6–2.8
Donatio mortis causa   27.17, 27.18
Double tax agreements   23.36–23.42, 26.2–26.41
   administration   26.23
   capital gains tax   23.38, 23.39
   comprehensive   26.12, 26.22
   income tax   23.38, 23.39
   inheritance tax   23.40–23.42, 26.24–26.41
     post-1975 agreements   26.33–26.41
     pre-1975 agreements   26.27–26.32
   nature of   26.10, 26.11
Dual residence   3.102–3.113

E

Enterprise Investment Schemes   19.68, 19.69–19.77
   capital gains tax relief   19.76, 19.77
   chargeable gain deferment
     possibilities   19.87–19.93
   income tax relief   19.70–19.75
Equity
   trusts, and   15.9–15.12
EU Savings Directive   26.47–26.78
   background   26.47–26.50

EU Savings Directive – *contd*
   Directive 77/799/EEC   26.78
   implications   26.62–26.77
   information exchange   26.53
   non-member states
     TIEA, and   26.56–26.61
   savings income   26.51, 26.52
   withholding tax   26.54, 26.55
Executors *see* **Probate**

F

Foreign currency
   location   6.43–6.45
Foreign currency bank accounts
   location   6.41, 6.42, 6.46–6.57
Foreign income and gains   24.1–24.152
   £30,000 tax charge   24.16–24.18
   alienation   24.44
   annual charge   24.5
   asset purchase   24.44
   basic thrust of provisions   24.5
   capital gains   24.83
   consequences of claim   24.15–24.35
   exempt to non-exempt
     property   24.102–24.104
   exempt property   24.92
     clothing   24.93
     personal use rule   24.93
   gifts of non-UK assets   24.124–24.126
   loans secured on property
     inheritance tax impact   24.143
   loans secured on property:
     capital gains tax
     impact   24.144
   loss of allowances   24.15
   mixed funds   24.105–24.116
     arising basis   24.108
     income and capital gains
      taxable on remittance   24.108
     offshore transfers   24.112–24.115
     pre- and post-FA 2008   24.116
     remittance basis   24.108
     remittance of taxable
      income   24.108

Index

Foreign income and gains – *contd*
  mixed funds – *contd*
    tax-free capital   24.108
    tax-free capital and taxable
      capital gains   24.108–24.111
    nomination   24.19–24.34
    non-UK domiciled individual   24.1–24.152
    offshore mortgages   24.134–24.144
    paying £30,000 or not   24.35
    property and public access
      rule   24.100, 24.101
    property below £1000 rule   24.94, 24.95
    relevant debt and UK
      services   24.84–24.91
    remittance basis treatment:
      claim   24.7–24.14
    remittance conditions   24.45–24.49
      condition C   24.47, 24.62–24.65
      condition D   24.48, 24.49, 24.66–24.69
      conditions A/B   24.46, 24.55
      exchange rates   24.57–24.61
      relevant person   24.50–24.54
    remittances to UK   24.36–24.69
    repair rule   24.98, 24.99
    segregation of income and
      capital   24.117–24.123
    source cessation   24.127–24.133
    temporary importation rule   24.96, 24.97
    temporary non-UK
      residence   24.145, 24.146
    transitional reliefs   24.70–24.82
      employment income   24.71, 24.72
      general transitional rule   24.80–24.82
      relevant foreign income   24.73–24.79
Forced heirship   27.103–27.109
Foreign situs assets
  wills, and   27.19

G

Gifts
  capital gains tax   8.28

Gifts with reservation (GWR)   12.1–12.46
  aim of provision   12.2
  concept   12.5–12.8
  implications   12.5–12.8
  joint bank accounts   12.17
  land and chattels 'let-out'   12.13–12.15
  non-application   12.9–12.12
  pre-owned assets   12.22–12.42
    chattels   12.30–12.32
    de minimis let-out   12.42
    election   12.39–12.41
    exemptions   12.37, 12.38
    intangible assets   12.33–12.36
    land   12.27–12.29
    tracing   12.16
    trusts   12.18–12.21

H

Hearsay evidence
  domicile of choice, and   3.117–3.124
Home *see* **Main residence**
Human rights
  international taxation, and   26.79–26.81

I

Income source   6.1–6.61
  see also Asset situs
  dividends   6.12–6.14
  domestic law   6.7, 6.8
  foreign tax   6.5, 6.6
  interest   6.15, 6.16
  non-resident individual   6.4
  non-UK domiciled individual   6.3
  rental income   6.20
  trusts   6.17–6.19
  UK domiciled individual   6.2
Income tax   2.25–2.42
  double tax agreements *see*
    Double tax agreements
  Enterprise Investment
    Schemes *see* Enterprise
    Investment Schemes
  FA 2008 (tax year
    2008–2009)   2.27–23.4

Index

Income tax – *contd*
  FA 2009 (tax year 2009–2010
    and 2010–2011)   2.35–2.36
  FA 2010 and FA (No 2) 2010
    (tax year 2010–2011)   2.37–2.39
  foreign income and gains *see*
    Foreign income and
    gains
  joint ownership *see* Joint
    ownership
  main residence *see* Main
    residence
  non-UK domiciliaries *see*
    Non-UK domiciliaries
  non-UK resident taxation *see*
    Non-UK resident
    taxation
  non-UK resident trusts *see*
    Non-UK resident trusts
  personal allowances   2.40–2.42
  residence *see* Residence
  split tax years *see* Split tax
    years
  tax returns *see* Tax returns
  timing of payments *see*
    Timing of tax payments
  UK resident trusts *see* UK
    resident trusts
  wills *see* Wills
  worldwide v territorial tax
    systems *see* Worldwide v
    territorial tax systems

Individual savings accounts   19.32–19.39

Inheritance tax
  administration   14.1 *et seq.*
    clearance certificate   14.32
    death estate   14.19–14.32
    excepted estate   14.25, 14.27
    exempt estates   14.27
    foreign domiciliaries   14.28, 14.29
    inheritance tax payable   14.12
    lifetime transfers   14.5–14.18
    low value estates   14.26

Inheritance tax – *contd*
  administration – *contd*
    persons responsible for
      charge   14.13–14.18, 14.31
    tax payable   14.30
    trust property   14.5–14.18
  APR   11.61, 11.97–11.103
    BPR, and   11.100
    death within seven years of
      transfer   11.102, 11.103
    ownership requirements   11.101
  asset situs *see* Asset situs
  assessment   14.40
  basics   10.1–10.114
  bearing of charge on death   10.88–10.94
    beneficial asset
      entitlement   10.91–10.94
    gifts with reservation   10.89
    qualifying interests in
      possession   10.90
  BPR   11.61–11.96
    death within seven years of
      lifetime transfer   11.82–11.88
    excepted assets   11.70–11.72
    family transfers   11.77–11.81
    importance of   11.61
    inter-spouse transfers   11.77–11.81
    ownership condition   11.73–11.76
    ownership splitting
      problem   11.89–11.91
    qualifying interest in
      possession trusts   11.96
    relevant property trusts   11.94, 11.95
    settled business property   11.92, 11.93
  categories of lifetime
    transfer   10.20–10.34
    'additional' liability   10.27–10.29
    chargeable lifetime
      transfer   10.22–10.25
    chargeable lifetime transfer
      and chargeability   10.26
    exempt transfer   10.21
    reduction in value   10.30–10.34

Index

Inheritance tax – *contd*
  chargeable lifetime transfers
    and grossing–up 10.54–10.58
  claims 14.40
  comprehensive example 10.99
  death 10.60–10.76
    assets 10.61, 10.62
    assets beneficially owned 10.63–10.65
    domicile 10.5–10.12
    see also Domicile
    deemed UK domicile *see* Deemed domicile
    general power of appointment 10.66
    GWRs 10.67–10.69
    liabilities 10.74–10.76
    'qualifying' interests in possession 10.70–10.73
  double tax agreements *see* Double tax agreements
  Enterprise Investment Schemes *see* Enterprise Investment Schemes
  excluded property 13.1–13.59
    Channel Islands 13.36–13.39
    FA 2006, and 13.45–13.53
    gifts with reservation, and 13.43, 13.44
    Isle of Man 13.36–13.39
    minimum holding property 13.22
    mixing UK and non-UK situs settled assets 13.40–13.42
    non-settled property 13.4, 13.5
    non-UK domiciled individual 13.13–13.21
    deemed UK domicile risk 13.20, 13.21
    loss of excluded property status for settled property 13.13–13.19
    'qualifying' interest in possession trust 13.10–13.12
    relevant property trust 13.9
    settled property 13.6–13.12
    UK situs assets 13.23

Inheritance tax – *contd*
  AUTs 13.24, 13.32, 13.35
  foreign currency bank accounts 13.28–13.30, 13.34
  non-settled property 13.24–13.30
  OEICs 13.24, 13.32, 13.35
  settled property 13.31–13.35
  UK government securities 13.25–13.27, 13.33
  exempt transfers 11.6–11.59
    annual exemption 11.12–11.20
    death only 11.39
    dispositions for family maintenance 11.34–11.38
    gifts in contemplation of marriage 11.29–11.33
    inter-spouse 11.42–11.57
    lifetime only 11.11–11.38
    normal expenditure out of income 11.23–11.28
    ordering of 11.58–11.59
    small gifts 11.21, 11.22
    transfers exempt in lifetime and death 11.40–11.57
    exemptions 10.77–10.79, 11.1–11.116
  gifts with reservation *see* Gifts with reservation
  inter-spouse transferable NRB 11.44–11.47
  inter-spouse transfers 11.42–11.57
  post-8 October 2007 11.48–11.57
  main residence, and *see* Main residence
  nil rate band 10.80–10.84
  payment on death 10.85–10.87
  penalties 14.33–14.37
  planning consideration 10.101–10.106
  foreign income and gains *see* Foreign income and gains
  joint ownership *see* Joint ownership
  main residence *see* main residence

Index

Inheritance tax – *contd*
  non-UK domiciliaries *see*
    Non-UK domiciliaries
  non-UK resident taxation *see*
    Non-UK resident
    taxation
  non-UK resident trusts *see*
    Non-UK resident trusts
  potentially exempt transfers 10.35–10.44
    chargeability 10.40–10.44
    grossing up 10.59
  QSR 11.104–11.110, 11.116
    non-settled property 11.105–11.108
    settled property 11.109, 11.110
  rate on death 10.80
  rates 10.13–10.19
  reliefs 10.77–10.79, 11.1–11.116
  residence, and *see* Residence
  seven–year cumulation
    period 10.45–10.53
  specific gifts bearing own
    inheritance tax on
    death 10.95–10.98
  split tax years *see* Split tax
    years
  tax returns *see* Tax returns
  timing of tax payments *see*
    Timing of tax payments
  trusts 16.1–16.102
    accumulation and
      maintenance 16.85–16.89
    addition of property after
      trust commences 16.36, 16.37
    additions of property and
      exit charge 16.39
    additions of property and
      ten-year charge 16.38
    assignment 16.56–16.61
    assignment/revocation 16.54, 16.55
    charges after first ten
      years 16.34, 16.35
    computational principles of
      exit and ten-yearly
      charges 16.21, 16.22

Inheritance tax – *contd*
  trusts – *contd*
    continuing after termination
      of qualifying interest
      in possession 16.66–16.69
    creation 16.9–16.11
    ending after termination of
      qualifying interest in
      possession 16.70, 16.71
    excluded property 16.97
    exit charge arising between
      ten-year
      anniversaries 16.31–16.33
    exit charge before first
      ten-year charge 16.23
    first ten-year charge 16.26–16.29
    interest in possession 16.4, 16.45–16.71
    IPDI 16.80–16.84
    life and death rates versus
      relevant property
      rates 16.40–16.44
    lifetime termination of
      qualifying interest in
      possession 16.53
    nil rate band discretionary
      trust 16.24, 16.25, 16.30
    non-qualifying interest in
      possession 16.52
    principles underlying
      ten-yearly and exit
      charges 16.12–16.20
    qualifying interest in
      possession 16.4
    relevant 16.9–16.44
    relevant property versus
      qualifying interest in
      possession trusts 16.90–16.96
    surrender 16.62, 16.63
    surrender/revocation 16.64, 16.65
    TSI 16.72–16.79
  UK resident trusts *see* UK
    resident trusts
  unpaid, interest on 14.38, 14.39
  wills *see* Wills

Index

Inheritance tax – *contd*
  worldwide v territorial tax
    systems *see* Worldwide v
    territorial tax systems
Insurance-based investments 19.40–19.67
  husband and wife 19.45
  non-UK domiciled individual 19.59
  single premium bonds 19.46–19.67
    children, provision for 19.67
    new arrivals in UK 19.65
    partial surrenders 19.61–19.64
    temporary non UK
      residence 19.66
    trusts 19.60
  term assurance 19.41–19.43
  top slicing relief 19.57–19.58
  whole of life assurance 19.44
Intangible property
  location 6.28, 6.34
Interest
  income source 6.15, 6.16
International taxation 26.1–26.85
  double tax agreements *see*
    Double tax agreements
  European Union 26.43–26.78
  EU Savings Directive 26.47–26.78
    see also Savings Directive
  human rights 26.79–26.81
International wills 27.23, 27.24
Intestacy 27.2, 27.138–27.143
Investments 19.1–19.102
  collective *see* Collective
    investments
  deposit-based 19.4–19.39
    see also Deposit–based
    investments
  insurance-based *see*
    Insurance–based
    investments
  offshore funds 19.96
  tax-related factors 19.3
  tax treatment 19.2

J

Joint ownership
  capital gains tax 7.34–7.37
    non-spouse joint ownership 7.37

Joint ownership – *contd*
  capital gains tax – *contd*
    spouse joint ownership 7.34–7.36
  income tax 7.24–7.333
    non-spouse joint ownership 7.32, 7.33
    spouse joint ownership 7.24–7.31
  inheritance tax 7.38–7.41
  non-asset issues 7.42–7.44
  non-UK domiciled individual 7.45–7.50
  survivorship role 7.42
Joint tenancy 7.1–7.53
  see also Joint ownership
  beneficial 7.13, 7.14
  wills, and 27.9–27.11
Joint wills 27.22

L

Land
  beneficial ownership 7.17–7.23
  legal ownership 7.15, 7.16
  location 6.30, 6.37
Legacies 27.43–27.53
  demonstrative 27.51, 27.52
  general 27.47–27.50
  pecuniary 27.53
  specific 27.44–27.46
Life insurance policies
  wills, and 27.14–27.16

M

Main residence 20.1–20.142
  capital gains tax 20.8–20.19
    cohabitees 20.14, 20.15
    married couples 20.14, 20.15
    non-UK property 20.13
    overview 20.9, 20.10
    profit motive 20.18, 20.19
    total v partial capital 20.16, 20.17
    two or more residences of
      individual 20.11, 20.12
  death and sole or main
    residence relief 20.77–20.82

Index

Main residence – *contd*
  deemed period of residence 20.53–20.62
  divorce, and 20.83–20.100
  inheritance tax 20.101–20.138
    cash gift 20.115–20.118
    death, and 20.126–20.134
    divorce 20.135–20.138
    downsizing 20.106, 20.107
    gift plus rent payable 20.123, 20.124
    sale 20.119–20.122
    shared home arrangements 20.108–20.114
  lettings relief 20.63–20.68
  married couples 20.37–20.52
    inter-spouse transfers 20.42–20.52
  residence 20.20–20.25
  separation, and 20.83–20.110
  trusts
    sole or main residence relief 20.69–20.76
  two or more 20.26–20.36
    election 20.26–20.36
Money market accounts 19.16, 19.17
Mutual wills 27.21

N

National savings income 19.18
Nominees
  location of assets held by 6.29, 6.36, 6.38–6.40
Non-domiciled individual 2.9–2.15
Non-UK domiciled individuals
  spending significant time in UK 3.145–3.168
Non-UK domiciliaries and UK homes 21.1–21.51
  capital gains tax 21.6–21.7
  combination structure 21.30–21.38
    capital gains tax 21.31–21.34
    income tax 21.38
    individual ownership 21.5
    inheritance tax 21.8–21.14, 21.35–21.37

Non-UK domiciliaries and UK homes – *contd*
  company ownership 21.15–21.21
    capital gains tax 21.16–21.18
    income tax 21.19–21.21
    inheritance tax 21.15
  ownership structuring 21.4–21.14
  preliminary structure 21.44–21.46
  pre-owned asset provisions 21.42–21.43
  primary issues 21.3
  trust ownership 21.22–21.29
    capital gains tax 21.22–21.24
    inheritance tax 21.25–21.29
Non-UK resident taxation 23.1–23.47
  capital gains tax 23.26
  income tax 23.6–23.25
    companies 23.20–23.25
    disregarded income 23.11–23.17
    individuals 23.6–23.10
    trusts 23.18, 23.19
  inheritance tax 23.27–23.29
Non-UK resident trusts 18.1–18.199
  anti-avoidance provisions 18.57 *et seq.*
  income tax 18.60–18.88
    ITA 2007 s 727 capital gains 18.75–18.79
    non-transferor provisions 18.80–18.92
    non-UK domiciled individuals 18.93–18.98
    transfer of asset provisions 18.63–18.68
    transferor provisions 18.69–18.79
  capital gains tax 18.4, 18.6–18.14, 18.54–18.56, 18.99–18.138
    additional charge 18.132–18.138
    beneficiaries 18.55, 18.56, 18.108
    beneficiaries charge 18.108
    settler-interested rules 18.99–18.107
    trustees 18.54

Index

Non-UK resident trusts – *contd*
discretionary and
  accumulation and
    maintenance trusts   18.18–18.42
  accumulated income   18.37
  beneficiaries' position on
    income distribution   18.31–18.36
  non-UK domiciliary
    beneficiaries   18.41–18.42
  non-UK resident
    beneficiaries   18.40
  non-UK source income   18.38, 18.39
  trustees' liability to income
    tax   18.18–18.27
  trustees' position on
    income distributions to
    UK resident
    beneficiaries   18.28–18.30
income tax   18.5, 18.6–18.14, 18.15–18.53
  discretionary (and
    accumulation and
    maintenance) trusts   18.18–18.42
inheritance tax   17.116–17.121
interest in possession trusts   18.43–18.53
  beneficiaries' position   18.44–18.48
  non-UK domiciled
    beneficiaries   18.52, 18.53
  non-UK resident
    beneficiaries   18.50, 18.51
  non-UK source income   18.44
  trustees' position   18.44–18.48
non-UK domiciled but UK
  resident individuals   18.184–18.193
offshore income gains   18.139–18.167
  Irish offshore funds   18.165–18.167
  non-UK resident trusts   18.149–18.164
  UK resident trust   18.146–18.148

Non-UK resident trusts – *contd*
residency   18.4–18.14
taxation factors   18.3
trust income, offshore income
  gains and capital gains
  interaction   18.168–18.183

O

Offshore companies
capital gains tax *see* Capital
  gains tax
Offshore deposits   19.15
Offshore dimension   25.1–25.78
**Offshore financial centre
(OFC)**   25.10–25.73
amnesty   25.15
asset protection   25.45–25.49
Australia   25.12
Caribbean   25.12
choice   25.50–25.55
companies   25.33–25.26
definition   25.10, 25.11
Europe   25.12
exchange of information   25.21
Indian Ocean   25.12
Liechtenstein Disclosure
  Facility   25.15
OECD reports   25.18–25.20
probate mitigation   25.43, 25.44
relocation to   25.67–25.73
scepticism as to   25.14
secrecy laws   25.16
substitute will   25.43, 25.44
tax planning   25.39–25.42
trusts   25.27–25.37
UK tax and information
  disclosure
  requirements   25.56–25.66
uses   25.38–25.49
vehicles   25.22–25.37
Offshore funds   19.96
Ordinary residence   2.5–2.15, 4.1–4.83
see also Residence
183-day test   4.8–4.13
Anti-avoidance provisions   4.70–4.78
  capital gains tax   4.73–4.76

Index

Ordinary residence – *contd*
Anti-avoidance provisions – *contd*
  income tax 4.77–4.78
  Form P85 5.28, 5.29
  Form P86 5.27
  HMRC 6 4.7
  leaving UK
    permanently/indefinitely 4.19–4.24
  meaning 4.7
  new arrivals in UK 4.36–4.51
    long-term visitors 4.40, 4.41
    longer-term visitor 4.40, 4.41, 4.49–4.51
    permanent or more than three-year stays 4.38, 4.39
    short-term visitors 4.40, 4.41, 4.44–4.48
    true visitors 4.43
    working in UK 4.42
  non-temporary residence abroad 4.17, 4.18
  practice 5.1–5.49
    current position 5.30–5.35
    return visits to UK 4.25–4.28
    split tax years *see* Split tax years
    tax return 5.3–5.4
      remittance basis 5.17–5.22
      supplementary pages 5.5–5.10
    temporary residence abroad 4.14–4.16
  working abroad 4.29–4.35

P

Pension scheme lump sum death benefits wills, and 27.12, 27.13
Persons other than individuals 2.16, 2.17
Probate 27.1–27.151
  see also Wills
  assets not requiring 27.125, 27.126
  bare trusts 27.132
  chattels 27.131
  executors 27.134–27.137
  forms 27.120–27.124
  jointly held assets 27.127, 27.128

Probate – *contd*
  life policies 27.129
  nature of 27.115
  pension death benefits 27.130
  small payments 27.133
Property ownership 7.1–7.53
  beneficial ownership 7.8–7.12
  implications 7.1–7.53
  income tax 7.24–7.33
  legal 7.6, 7.7
  principles 7.1–7.53

R

Registered shares
  location 6.25, 6.32
Remittance basis charge
  need to pay App1
Remittance basis treatment
  need to claim App 1
Rental income
  source 6.20
Residence 2.5–2.15, 3.93–3.113, 4.1–4.83
  see also Ordinary residence
  183-day test 4.8–4.13
  Anti-avoidance provisions 4.70–4.78
    capital gains tax 4.73–4.76
    income tax 4.77–4.48
  domicile of choice, and 3.93–3.113
  dual 3.102–3.113
  duration 3.95–3.99
  Form P85 5.28, 5.29
  Form P86 5.27
  HMRC 6 4.7
  illegal 3.100–3.101
  leaving UK
    permanently/indefinitely 4.19–4.24
  meaning 3.93, 3.94, 4.7
  new arrivals in UK 4.36–4.51
    long-term visitors 4.40, 4.41
    longer-term visitors 4.49–4.51
    permanent or more than three-year stays 4.38, 4.39
    short-term visitors 4.40, 4.41
    true visitors 4.43
    working in UK 4.42

Residence – *contd*	
non-temporary residence aboard	4.17, 4.18
practice	5.1–5.49
current position	5.30–5.35
return visits to UK	4.25–4.28
split tax years	4.52–4.69
see also Split tax years	
tax return	5.3–5.4
remittance basis	5.17–5.22
residence status	5.11, 5.12
supplementary pages	5.5–5.10
temporary residence aboard	4.14–4.16
working abroad	4.29–4.35

S

SAYE interest	19.20
Separation	
main residence, and	20.83–20.100
Split domicile	3.251–3.255
Split tax years	4.52–4.69
capital gains tax	4.64–4.66
failure to satisfy ESC A11 or ESC D2	4.67–4.69
income tax	4.56
employment income	4.62
investment income	4.63
Stamp duty	22.1–22.41
Stamp duty land tax	22.1–22.41
arm's length provisions	22.33–22.35
bare trust	22.24
chargeable consideration	22.11
death, and	22.16–22.19
linked transactions	22.36, 22.37
matrimonial breakdown	22.31, 22.32
chattels	22.32
matrimonial home	22.26–22.30
non-UK resident trusts	22.25
rates	22.13–22.15
trusts	22.20–22.25
Stamp duty reserve tax	22.5–22.8

T

Tangible property	
location	6.27, 6.35
Tax Information Exchange Agreements (TIEA)	26.42
Tax returns	2.59–2.62
capital gains tax	2.59–2.61
income tax	2.59–2.61
inheritance tax	2.62
Tax systems	1.1–1.38
bases of taxation	1.1–1.38
examples	1.5
Tenancy in common	7.1–7.53
see also Joint ownership	
beneficial	7.13, 7.14
Timing of tax payments	2.63–2.66
capital gains tax	2.63–2.65
income tax	2.63–2.65
inheritance tax	2.66
Trusts	15.1–15.43
bankruptcy protection	15.23
bare	15.20
classification	15.16–15.20
concept	15.1, 15.2
constructive	15.19
creation	15.13–15.15
current use	15.21–15.25
definition	15.3–15.8
discretionary	15.34, 15.35
equity	15.9–15.12
express	15.17
Hague Convention	15.38
implied/resulting	15.18
income source	6.17–6.19
inheritance tax	16.1–16.102
see also Inheritance tax	
interest in possession	15.36, 15.37
non-UK resident *see* Non-UK resident trust	
Perpetuities and Accumulations Act 2009	15.26–15.30
protection of minors	15.22
tax aspects	15.31–15.37
UK resident *see* UK resident trusts	
will substitute	15.24, 15.25

Index

U

UK resident trusts 17.1–17.127
Anti-avoidance provisions 17.64–17.99
  bare trusts for unmarried minors 17.90
  capital gains tax 17.99
  capital sums paid to settlor 17.91–17.98
  discretionary trusts 17.73–17.77
  income paid to minor children 17.85–17.89
  income tax 17.66–17.98
  interest in possession trusts 17.78–17.80
  non-UK domiciled but UK resident settlors 17.82–17.84
  settler-interested 17.67–17.72
  underlying companies 17.81
capital gains 17.1–17.127
capital gains tax 17.52–17.65, 17.112–17.115
  annual exempt amount 17.58
  capital losses 17.59
  discretionary trusts 17.52
  hold-over relief 17.60–17.63
  interest in possession trusts 17.52
  rates 17.53–17.57
discretionary and accumulation and maintenance trusts 17.18–17.39
  accumulated income 17.32
  beneficiaries' position on income distributions to UK resident beneficiaries 17.29–17.31
  non-UK domiciled beneficiaries 17.38–17.39
  non-UK resident beneficairies 17.36, 17.37
  non-UK source income 17.35
  trustees: liability to income tax 17.18–17.24

UK resident trusts – *contd*
discretionary and accumulation and maintenance trusts – *contd*
  trustees' position on income distributions to UK resident beneficiaries 17.25–17.28
income tax 17.1–17.127
interest in possession trusts 17.40–17.51
  beneficiaries position 17.41–17.45
  non-UK domiciled beneficiaries 17.51
  non-UK resident beneficiaries 17.49–17.50
  non-UK source income 17.46–17.48
  trustees' position 17.41–17.41
residency 17.4–17.17
  capital gains tax 17.4
  income tax 17.5, 17.15–17.17
settler-interested trusts pre-FA 2008 17.101–17.104
taxation factors 17.3
UK taxation 2.1–2.71
capital v income 2.22–2.24
law, and 2.18
legislation 2.20
overview 2.1–2.71

V

Venture Capital Trusts 19.68, 19.78–19.86
capital gains tax relief 19.86
income tax relief 19.80–19.85

W

Wills 27.1–27.151
see also Probate
capacity to inherit 27.70
capacity to make 27.25–27.26
capital gains tax 28.24–28.32
  administration period 28.26–28.32
  pre-death 28.24, 28.25
community property 27.110–27.113

Index

Wills – *contd*
contents	27.7
death, effect on	27.3, 27.4
definition	27.1
devises	27.43–27.53
disposal of body	27.7
failure of gifts	27.54–27.69
ademption	27.64–27.67
disclaimer	27.68
lapse	27.55–27.63
uncertainty	27.69
forced heirship	27.103–27.109
foreign issues	27.82–27.102
capacity	27.91, 27.92
construction	27.97, 27.98
material validity	27.94–27.96
revocation	27.99–27.102
succession	27.85–27.90
foreign situs assets	27.19
formalities	27.27–27.31
income tax, and	28.11–28.23
inheritance tax	28.33–28.39
administration period	28.16–28.23
pre-death	28.11–28.15
international	27.23, 27.24
joint	27.22
joint tenancies, and	27.9, 27.11
legacies	27.43–27.53
see also Legacies	
life insurance policies	27.14–17.16
more than one	27.6
mutual	27.21
pension scheme lump sum death benefits	27.12, 27.13

Wills – *contd*
property not disposable by	27.8–27.19
revocation	27.5, 27.32–27.40
survivorship clauses	27.71–27.81
second marriages	27.74–27.79
taxation, and	28.1–28.126
charitable gifts	28.51–28.56
cohabitees	28.40–28.50
deeds of variation	28.71–28.87
disclaimers	28.61–28.70
discretionary will trusts	28.88–28.98
executor sales	28.99–28.114
foreign aspects	28.115–28.121
married couples	28.40–28.50
post-death events	28.57–28.114
sale of land	28.107–28.113
sale of quoted shares	28.102–28.106
sale of related property	28.114
single individuals	28.40–28.50
tax planning, and	28.1–28.10
types	27.20–27.24
types of gift	27.41–27.53

Worldwide v territorial tax systems
	1.12–1.34
capital gains tax	1.12
citizenship test	1.18–1.20
hybrid basis	1.15
income tax	1.12
inheritance tax	1.24–1.30
residency	1.17
source basis	1.21–1.23
territorial basis	1.14
trailing tax imposition	1.31–1.34
worldwide basis	1.13